The Odyssey of
an American Composer

The Odyssey of
an American Composer

The Autobiography of Otto Luening

Charles Scribner's Sons · New York

Grateful acknowledgment is made to quote from *Letters of James Joyce*, edited by Stuart Gilbert. Copyright © 1957 by the Viking Press, Inc. Reprinted by permission of Viking Penguin Inc.

Library of Congress Cataloging in Publication Data

Luening, Otto, 1900–
　Odyssey of an American composer.

　Includes index.
　1. Luening, Otto, 1900– 2. Composers—United States—Biography. I. Title.
ML410.L947A3   780'.92'4 [B]   80-11624
ISBN 0-684-16496-5

In memory of my parents, Eugene and Emma Luening,
who taught me to love and respect the traditions
and to explore and test the unknown

Acknowledgments

Because of space limitations it is impossible to give credit in these Acknowledgments to everyone who deserves it. But I know who they are and so do they. Some are mentioned in the text, but I want to call attention to and thank others—not there—who helped with this book, my projects, or my compositions.

First, my thanks to Norman Lloyd, the Rockefeller Foundation, and Columbia University for giving me ongoing support. Then, thanks to Alison Nowak, my assistant for many years, who typed the manuscript; Olga Gussow, who copied and catalogued my scores; Jill Bogard, research assistant; Jeannie Pool, who helped bring the project to its conclusion; and, at Scribners, Dwight Allen and Donn Teal for editing and copy-editing my manuscript.

For strong early support I am indebted to Professor Philipp Jarnach, Otto Strauss, and Dr. John Wilkinson and family. In the foundation world Edward D'Arms, James Mathias, Gordon Ray, Stephen Schlesinger, and J. Kellum Smith were my mentors. I would like to thank Charlotte and John Marshall, my gracious hosts at the Villa Serbelloni, in Bellagio, Italy—where I composed, began this book, and my wife, Catherine, and I played chamber music.

Ruth Ihrig at the Columbia Department of Music, Carol Truax and Rosalie Calabrese at the American Composers Alliance, Lois Carrollton at Composers Recordings, Inc., Theodora Zavin, Russell Sanjek, and James Roy at Broadcast Music, Inc., Katherine Teck, Marvin D. Levy, and John Corigliano cooperated with me on many projects.

Friends who were always on hand to help include Dr. Margaret Olds Strahl, Mr. and Mrs. Ernest S. Heller, the A. J. Michaud family, Chou Wen-chung, Evelyn and Henry Hinrichsen, the C. F. Peters family, Dr. Milton Smith, and Yancy Valentine.

To the following former students goes my appreciation: Joan Tower, Elliott Schwartz, Donald Keats, John Heiss, Dorothy Wilson, Henry Holder, and Gloria Coates (who directs the German–American exchange concerts in Munich).

And finally I want to sound a mingled chime of my favorite overtones for my wife, Catherine. She helped with everything and listened to me talk about my adventures right through the years with unflagging interest and encouragement.

Otto Luening
New York
February 1980

Contents

Preamble

WHEN I WAS FIFTY-TWO, LEOPOLD STOKOWSKI introduced my electronic music (or "tape music," as it was called then) at a concert for a distinguished audience at the Museum of Modern Art in New York. To my surprise this event immediately catapulted me into the rarefied atmosphere of the international avant-garde. I won many new friends. But they knew little about my early musical career and were not particularly interested in it.

Many of my old friends and associates looked on my venture into the world of electronic sound as a caper from which they hoped I would soon recover. When I tried to acquaint both new and old friends with those parts of my career they knew nothing about—even then, more than a quarter-century ago, I was "explaining" myself—I was asked repeatedly why I was not content to be either a traditionalist who moves slowly forward or an avant-gardist who never looks back. Why, I was asked, would I want to combine such drastically opposed points of view?

This question made me reflect, and I soon recognized that my entire family (all, themselves, great respecters of tradition) tended to use tradition as a launching pad for imaginative flights into unknown territory—sometimes on heroic and sometimes on quixotic missions and adventures.

In a pamphlet published on the occasion of my seventieth birthday, Oliver Daniel wrote: "The Luening lifetime contains enough action, even outside of composing, to fill more than one career." At that late date, when I talked about my career, my friends and students would say: "You ought to write that down." Or: "I never heard about that. Why don't you write an article?"

It was at about that time, too, that I began rediscovering my native state, Wisconsin. I began recalling my childhood, and as I looked into Wisconsin's history I gained new insights pertinent to my own life. In her *History of Wisconsin*, Alice E. Smith wrote: "The people of Wisconsin are something of an enigma. For nearly a century and a half they have sustained a remarkably cohesive society despite the unusual diversity of their cultural and economic interests. They have taken pride in the stability of their institutions, even as they have made Wisconsin a laboratory to test the new and untried. And their quite remarkable record of political and social innovation has far exceeded what the state's relative size and circumstances might reasonably have warranted."

Those early days in Wisconsin and the lives and traditions of my forefathers there and in Europe did have a strong influence on the course my life has run. I was twelve when I left Wisconsin with my parents to live in Munich, where I enjoyed—enormously—the two years before World War I. In 1917, I went to Zurich, a refugee from the war, where my contact with Dadaists and with great men like Philipp Jarnach, Ferruccio Busoni, and James Joyce brought me to a new dimension. My subsequent musical career in the United States—beginning with various pioneering activities in Chicago during the Roaring Twenties and at the Eastman School in Rochester, through the years of barnstorming as a composer, conductor, performer, and itinerant professor in New York City, the South, the Southwest, and the West, and through the no less active years at Bennington College and Columbia University—did not take me along a straight path of either traditional or unconventional artistic ascent or descent. And even though I found that an unbroken thread ran through it all, my experiences were so varied that when I discussed these with my friends I could not tie together even two or three of them in brief statements. The contrasts were too great.

One day, as I was talking with Norman Lloyd of the Rockefeller Foundation, he leaned back in his chair, looked at me thoughtfully, and said, "You ought to write a book." When I saw him a year later and he asked if I was writing my book, I realized that he had meant it. I gave way: I must write my story, I decided.

As I began, I realized that the only way to tell my story would be to begin at the very beginning—some four generations ago. I would try to recount all that had happened, and how it has brought me to where I am now. . . .

Chapter 1

From the Family Archives
1312-1904

MY MOTHER DIED IN 1950, AGED ninety. In the little white house on Lake Labelle in Oconomowoc, Wisconsin, where my parents had lived since 1922, I made, with the help of my Aunt Claire, the proper disposition of linens, china, and the Biedermeier furniture, pictures, and glassware—most of which had been brought here from Europe in the nineteenth century. We gave the Steinway grand to a school. Dr. Wilkinson, who had taken care of my parents and lived next door, bought the house. Mother had begged me to keep it in the family, but all of her sons were living in different parts of the country, far away from Oconomowoc, and it was impossible. Stacks of books and piles of magazines in the attic went to the libraries in Oconomowoc and Milwaukee.

In two trunks in the attic, in neat packages carefully labeled and dated, I found the story of my ancestors. A cursory examination showed me that many of the legends I heard about for years were here documented. A book, *This Book Belongs to the German People*, by Otto Lüning, made me realize I wasn't the only one. I sent the trunks to New York, locked the house, and that was the end for a while of direct contact with the state that my forefathers had pioneered.

In New York, I examined the contents of the trunks and found a seal with a coat of arms: a bird on a shield, holding a twig. There was also a genealogical chart, but no explanation of the bird. I went to the New York Public Library and in the genealogy department found that the bird was a sparrow and that the coat of arms on the seal belonged to the Hanover branch of the family; there were many other branches, and the family could be traced to 1312. I was positively staggered by the magnificent names I found in the family tree, but I remembered a saying I had learned in Chicago: "I looked into my family tree and found I was the sap." So I moved ahead cautiously.

The earliest ancestor was Machorius Dictus Lüninc (1312). The unbroken genealogical tree began with Manfried von Lüninck (1350), who was followed by Dietrick von Lünink zu Eiglestorp und Slebusch, married to Anna von Bellinghausen und Bernsquite, of a Catholic family. Next came the Lünings from an eastern province and Russian nobility, related to Manfried von Lünicke and the Teutonic knights' order in Cologne. This discovery shook me a bit because these knights do not have a good reputation, but one of them owned an estate in Wischlen in Kurland. Johann Lunick's signature appeared on documents; Henrick owned a house and Kort van Lonink a garden in 1503 in Riga. These splendid people had a magnificent silver seal, a black sparrow with two silver wings spread over a helmet. All this seemed farfetched, but I followed the flight of the sparrow. The principality of Waldeck seal and coat of arms showed a sparrow sitting on a beam; another seal was a green triangle, surrounded by decorative peacock feathers. There was supposedly a Baron Lüning in Waldeck who owned an estate, but it began to look pretty remote to me and I thought perhaps my search was strictly for the birds. But the family turned up in Westphalia and Hanover, the lower Rhine, and even in the Netherlands and England, where a Jacob Luning lived to be one hundred and three. He was, so it reads, a descendant of Martin Luther's sister.

Our letter seal belonged to the Hanover group, where my grandfather Dr. August Luening was born; and the author Otto Lüning came from the districts of Tecklenburg, Mühlheim, and Siegburg in Westphalia. In 1845 the entire family was allegedly knighted.

But in Hanover and Westphalia the men were mostly teachers, judges, doctors, and ministers, and there was a bishop of Münster. These radicals disavowed "von" and relied on their accomplishments for their distinction. As I proceeded through the genealogy it became clear to me that the conflicting character traits I found in myself had been inherited.

MY GREAT-UNCLE Dr. Otto Lüning, from Rheda, Westphalia, earned his M.D. at Breslau at the age of twenty-one. He was a radical socialist and editor of *Das Westphälisches Dampfboot*, a radical monthly review for socialist activities, which published early articles by Karl Marx and Friedrich Engels. Otto Lüning was also a poet, a humanist, and was sometimes called a "literary communist." He was a freedom fighter from the time he was in secondary school. Two of his brothers joined him in radical activity; they were sentenced to jail and had to flee to Switzerland, where they eventually settled. Otto, too, was frequently arrested, but in 1867 he was elected to the Diet in Berlin as a member of the Progressive party. He died the next year at the age of fifty. He was a true friend of workers and peasants, and some of these served as his pallbearers.

He was also an intimate friend of the philosopher Ludwig Feuerbach and was active in advancing neo-Hegelian philosophical thought, which seemed to anticipate the existentialism of Sartre, the socialism of Marx and Ferdinand Lassalle, and the philosophy of John Dewey. Otto Lüning was particularly influenced by Lassalle at the time the young Hegelians were seeking the unification of Germany, and he wanted reforms to take place within the framework of the state. He was foreign correspondent for a number of German-language newspapers published in the United States, and in letters to Feuerbach he expressed a strong interest in that country. In one he wrote: "I only breathe freely in an atmosphere that hasn't been poisoned by the pestilential breath of the European police. I am really interested in America, this alter ego of Europe. If I am to engage in journalistic activities it will be for an American newspaper." He wrote about social reform, political freedom, and freedom from the military. His sister Louisa married Joseph Weydemeyer, a friend of Karl Marx; Weydemeyer emigrated to the United States in 1851, became a colonel in the Union army, settled in St. Louis, and campaigned for Lincoln in Wisconsin in 1860.

MY GREAT-GRANDFATHER Justus Lüning was born, educated, and practiced law in Hanover. He became district judge in Polle, a small town in the grand duchy of Braunschweig. He was a tall, stately man who was popular and trusted in the district. A death sentence pronounced in 1805 at the high court of Bruchhausen, where he was a clerk, gives an idea of justice as practiced in good old Germany, the land of *Gemütlichkeit* and song:

> The trial of Gerdt Heinrich Victor Meyer von Wiehe will be public. . . . We demand repose, peace and quiet at this solemn trial. . . . The judgment will be read here word for word: "With a wheel [you] shall be punished. First [your] bones shall be cracked by being hit with heavy clubs from above downward, to bring [you] from life to death, then to braid [your] body onto the wheel by order of the Court of the Department of Justice at Wense. . . . It is a punishment you deserve and is given you to be a horrible disgusting warning for others. . . . You young children who will sing the burial service for the criminal, you will hear prayers of the dying sinner, witness his last prayer; let this protect you from the temptation of choosing the wrong path and stumbling at the cliff as this murderer did. . . . May God be merciful to thy soul."

MY GRANDFATHER Frederick August Luening was born in 1812. He matriculated as a medical student at the University of Bonn. He was a volunteer in the Polish army in the last uprising against Russia, 1830–1831. He was wounded, transferred to Göttingen, and graduated with honors; he practiced medicine in Harpsted, near Hanover, but was soon disenchanted with the German military and his bureaucratic heritage. Like most German emigrants he had a vision of America as "the land of liberty, freedom, and justice for all." He borrowed money from his father and emigrated in 1843. He settled near Milwaukee, built a log cabin called Cedarburg, was given a land grant in perpetuity from President Tyler, and built a mill to hull sunflower seeds and produce sunflower-seed oil. He moved to Milwaukee. There he was appointed health officer and became prominent as a gynecologist and a specialist in the treatment of cholera and smallpox. His son, my uncle Adolph, was a captain in the U.S. regular army during the Civil War and the Indian wars. He wrote this letter to his cousin Marie from the Army of the Potomac:

> I am writing to you on a very exciting day. Uncle Lincoln will be here in about an hour and our guns are already set up on the drill

grounds. Everything is in order. Any minute the bugle might call us to assemble. Surrounded by about five or six thousand noisy troopers I ought really not to write to you. . . . The review before the President is over; followed by General Hooker and thirty to forty other generals, the good man rode quietly past the troops. A free people had elected him as a leader for the freest country. . . . What a sad expression on that man, Abraham Lincoln's face. It seemed to me that in his pale face was an expression found in all of us. He was worn out by all the heavy burdens that he carries as the President of our beloved republic and he bowed his tired head before the people who had sworn to assist him in his hard task. . . . Please give my best greetings to Mr. Engelman. Beneath the uniform of a proud soldier and fighter for liberty beats a warm heart for his beloved teacher.

A telegram reached my grandmother: CAPTAIN ADOLPH LUENING HAS DISAPPEARED. WE FEAR FOUL PLAY. SIGNED SECRETARY OF WAR.

I never heard the whole story, but surmise he worked on the Southern Pacific Railroad, for there is a Luning, Nevada. He turned up in Hells Gate, Montana, in 1907. It is all still a mystery.

DOMINIK NEUKIRCH, a great-great-grandfather, was district forester at Roschweiler in Alsace on the Küh-Kopf. His wife was Henrietta Chapui, a Frenchwoman. It was rumored that on her side of the family we were related to Marshal François Christophe de Kellerman, Napoleon's cavalry general who later became the duke of Valmy. I am not sure the duke was married, but possibly a foraging expedition in the Alsace and a roll in the hay with a Mlle Chapui was sufficient to keep saps in the family trees.

Dominik Neukirch's sister, Tante Kranz, arrived in the United States in the early 1830s. After short stays in Pennsylvania and Buffalo, she settled in Milwaukee. In the early fifties she was active as a traveling pamphleteer for radical political parties. She was one of the first feminists in the West, and helped to establish the Democratic party in Milwaukee.

A letter from Dominik's eldest son, Wilhelm, was the oldest document that I found in the archives. It was addressed to his mother, May 29, 1814, from Paris.

I was privileged to be eyewitness to the most important happening of our time. . . . I saw all Europe gathered here at the foot of Montmartre to witness the dawning of peace. . . . Chaos came sooner than we expected in spite of the victory reports, which the cannons seemed to confirm. In the last days of March the general flight from the country to Paris began. . . . All streets in and outside of the city in all directions were crowded with people and vehicles of every description, mixed groups of cattle and soldiers returning or moving not knowing where to. . . . Preparations were made for defense, imagining that Napoleon would hurry on to bring help. Some hoped for his arrival, others feared it. . . . All day I was on the roof of our house with my telescope. I had a wonderful view. . . . I saw how the hills were conquered one by one and how the enemy closed in on three-quarters of this large city. I could hear the bullets plainly and a bomb soon struck the city. . . . In a very short time my courageous countrymen, especially the brave Prussians, had stormed the hills and driven away the National Guards who retreated into the city. . . . At half past four the streets were filled with French soldiers who had just asked for an armistice so they could leave the city quietly.

After Napoleon's departure we had one of our quietest evenings. . . . The thirty-first of March was the happiest and most unforgettable day. . . . A German friend of mine and I ran through the streets. . . . Early in the morning one saw strange officers accompanied by Cossacks. This gave the Royalists courage and they took the white *cocarde* and put white bands around their left arms, gradually following the white flags of the Royalists and shouting, "Long live the King!" . . . I was so excited I ran through the crowds and pushed ahead until I reached the king. I wished him and General Schwarzenberg good luck and pressed their hands. . . . The next day the happiest of all revolutions was fought, without unrest or bloodshed. Bonaparte, having lost his throne, ordered his statue to be taken down and all signs of his reign removed. A new government was installed. . . .

NEUKIRCH'S YOUNGER SON, my great-grandfather Franz Neukirch, was born in 1796 and lived for sixty-nine years. He was a forest ranger in German Alsace for twenty-four years, a very good conservationist, and quite popular there in spite of his anticlerical and antibureaucratic tendencies. Eventually the bureaucracy and militarism in the Rhenish province disgusted him so that he took his small savings and immigrated to Wisconsin in 1839. He arrived with a German group of about eight hundred, one of the many groups that left around that time because of religious and political oppression and to improve their economic condition.

After sailing forty-five days from Le Havre to New York, he continued via the Hudson River, the Erie Canal, and the Great Lakes to Oakwood, Wisconsin Territory. There he became a citizen and bought eighty acres of land for one hundred dollars. He built his own log house and then wrote to his wife, five daughters, and son to join him. He instructed his wife to bring from Europe a piano, a new flute, a dictionary, a prayer book, a hymn book, schoolbooks, household supplies, and a doctor's book. The family arrived by covered wagon and found the log cabin when they heard from a distance Neukirch playing his flute.

Neukirch was not only a pioneer immigrant but a colonizer. At the time he arrived, Milwaukee had a total population of about four thousand. Neukirch's letters to Germany describing pioneer life in America were so vivid and impressive that they were printed in German magazines and books, and he was credited with bringing many of the early immigrants from Germany to Wisconsin.

He made the first barley beer in Milwaukee and was active in all civic affairs and in the German Democratic Association that taught German emigrants the principles on which the state and federal governments of the United States were built.

His son Karl was postmaster in Milwaukee and became captain in the 26th Wisconsin Volunteer Regiment. He died from wounds received at Chancellorsville.

Neukirch's daughter Elizabeth was my father's mother. She married Dr. Frederick August Luening, my paternal grandfather. Like Franz Neukirch, he was very active in political matters and all civic activities. He worked to bring about cooperation between Anglo- and German-Americans, and toward the founding of schools and the public library. His collection of minerals became the basis of a small museum that eventually became the present natural history museum in Milwaukee.

MY MOTHER's father, Colonel William H. Jacobs, came to the United States in 1850, from Holzen, near Braunschweig, when he was twenty. His career led him into four professions: banking, politics, colonel of the 26th Wisconsin Volunteer Regiment in the Civil War, and music. He opened a toyshop and an exhibition center, and founded the Second Ward Savings Bank (which later was known as the Brewers Bank and is now the First National Bank of Milwaukee). In 1857 he was made railroad commissioner, then Democratic mayoral candidate, and was elected state senator. As colonel of the 26th Wisconsin Regiment, which he recruited in two weeks in 1862, he fought in the campaigns in the South and at Chancellorsville, where he was wounded. He resigned his commission in 1864 because of the illness of my grandmother.

From 1854 until his death in 1882, with the exception of the war years, he was the leading tenor soloist with the Milwaukee Musical Society and an administrator and patron of the society. The society performed important choral, symphonic, and chamber music works for the Milwaukee music lovers, including the modernists of that period: Bruckner, Grieg, Dudley Buck, Humperdinck, Liszt, and many others. The first opera on an Indian subject, *Mohega,* by Sobolewski (a student of Weber and Liszt), was premiered, enthusiastically received, and dropped after one performance. Excerpts or complete operas by Berlioz, Wagner, Weber, Goldmark, Verdi, Schumann, and many others were programmed. Colonel Jacobs sang the leading tenor roles in nine operas by Lortzing, Bellini, Flotow, Auber, Weber, Sobolewski, and Mozart. Critics considered him one of the finest singing actors in the Midwest at a time when Milwaukee, Boston, and New York were allegedly the music centers of the United States.

Colonel Jacobs's mansion, called the House of Music, was the center of musical activities in Milwaukee. Famous musicians in the years 1864–1882 were entertained at his home after their concerts. These included members of the Strakosch and Meyendorf opera companies; the singers Anna Louise Cary, Clara Louise Kellogg, and Adelina Patti; the violinists Wieniawski, Vieuxtemps, and Ole Bull; and the pianist Anton Rubinstein. The colonel's five daughters were all well trained musically, took part in performances of the Musical Society, often in leading roles, and were prominent patrons of Milwaukee's cultural life until the mid-twentieth century.

MY GRANDFATHER Dr. F. A. Luening was one of the organizers of the bilingual German-English Academy who engaged Peter Engelman, a humanist, scientist, and excellent pedagogue, as director. Influenced by neo-Hegelian ideas and those of Pestalozzi, Engelman's educational philosophy was somewhat similar to that of John Dewey as it was later practiced at Bennington College, Black Mountain College, Columbia University Teachers College, Bard College, and secondary schools such as the Lincoln School and the Horace Mann School in New York. The Engelman school went through several transformations. The University of Wisconsin (Milwaukee campus) now occupies the original site. Both of my parents and my uncles and aunts were educated at the old German-English Academy.

≫≪

MY MOTHER, Emma Jacobs, was born on February 19, 1861. When she was nineteen, a carriage in which she was riding with a sister and a friend was hit by a freight train. She was the only survivor. She told me she was thrown into the center of the tracks and seventeen railroad cars rolled over her as the train backed up. She fully expected the engine to run over her, which meant certain death, but the locomotive stopped two cars from her. The experience had a lasting effect on her disposition and character. She was a gentle, kind person but could be very firm when necessary. She was completely fearless in any and all situations and cheerful even under the most difficult conditions.

Emma Jacobs married my father on July 26, 1883. They had five sons and two daughters. My father told me he never heard her complain—and neither did I.

MY FATHER, Eugene Luening, was born in 1852. He studied piano privately, but his daily practice was supervised by his grandfather, Franz Neukirch. In many ways he was self-taught, but he was accomplished enough to be accepted by the Leipzig

Conservatory in 1869 when he auditioned for Ignaz Moscheles (a friend of Beethoven), performing a Beethoven sonata.

After studying briefly with Moscheles, he worked with Carl Reinecke, studied counterpoint with Salomon Jadassohn (a Liszt pupil), and harmony with Richter. He sang in the chorus in the Gewandhaus symphony concerts, was piano soloist at the conservatory concerts, and in 1872 performed his own compositions at the conservatory. In the same year he was elected delegate from the conservatory for the cornerstone-laying of the Bayreuth Festspielhaus. There he met Richard Wagner and spent time with him and Cosima Wagner, both at public meetings and at Wagner's home. He sang under Wagner's direction in the performance of Beethoven's Ninth Symphony at the dedication of the Festspielhaus. Arthur Nikisch and Anton Seidl were fellow students. They later conducted the Boston Symphony and New York Philharmonic, respectively, for many years.

He returned to Milwaukee in 1873, made his debut with the Milwaukee Musical Society as soloist in Beethoven's C Minor Concerto, and was recognized as a first-rate pianist. At the same concert he played a Chopin scherzo and conducted several choruses by Richard Wagner. Soon he was conducting and performing works by Wagner, Rubinstein, and Liszt, Haydn symphonies, and his own compositions. For the centennial celebration he set Bayard Taylor's *Centennial Ode* to music for a Fourth of July performance.

In 1877 he returned to Leipzig for further study. He was delegate of the Richard Wagner Society and saw the composer at Bayreuth, where Father enrolled in the School for Conductors that Wagner tried unsuccessfully to launch. The composer read the entire libretto of *Parsifal* for the delegates, at Wahnfried.

A collection of four-hand piano pieces of Father's were published by Schott that same year.

Father returned to Milwaukee in 1879 and was made director of the Musical Society, remaining in that post until 1904. In addition to his previous activities, he attempted to organize orchestral and chamber music groups, lectured on Wagner's works, and introduced many important oratorios and his own compositions to the Milwaukee public. A song of his was reviewed as being "a true pearl of the musical song literature." After his performance of Niels Gade's cantata *Korsfarerne* (*The Crusaders*) the press stated: "Eugene Luening did Gade's work so beautifully that it probably never had a better performance."

In 1883, Theodore Thomas premiered Eugene Luening's *Comedy Overture*. The press called it "an independent musical work; the creation of a musically felt and thoughtful tone poem, not the compilation of a learned musician, and not conductor's music. It doesn't consist of musical phrases but of musical thoughts and their development, bringing about a beautiful musical form."

In the same year, the *Herald* said of *In Memoriam*, a cantata dedicated to Garfield: "Luening's composition is a powerfully effective, deeply moving, and musically significant work."

Besides conducting Liszt's symphonic poems and his *Heilige Elisabeth*, Haydn, Mozart, and Beethoven symphonies, Mendelssohn's *Midsummer Night's Dream*, and Wagner excerpts—including the introduction to *Parsifal* for the first time in America—my father gave a performance of Gluck's *Orfeo und Euridice* in which my two aunts sang the leading roles, and in the 1890s he and Theodore Thomas arranged an American composers concert. In that decade he also conducted Beethoven's Ninth Symphony with a chorus of one thousand and an orchestra of one hundred and ten at the Saengerfest in Milwaukee. He gave a series of historical concerts at his conservatory. Soon thereafter he and his family moved to a farm in Wauwatosa.

Chapter 2

On the Farm:
Wauwatosa, Wisconsin
1903-1909

JUNE 15, 1903, WAS MY THIRD birthday. I remember that day
because it was the first time I was able to respond consciously and
in a lively fashion to the world of sight, touch, taste, and sound.
There had been previous musical experiences that stayed with me
all my life, but they were more like dreams remembered. Father,
who was now teaching music, was the protagonist who in the evenings played Beethoven on the Steinway, behind the closed door
of the mysterious music room. These first impressions of our
magical world of sounds I can conjure up to this day.

A shiny, silvery toy trumpet with a red tassel was on the
breakfast table for my birthday, and I produced a few sounds as I
blew on it. This was my first direct experience with an instrumental sound other than hearing the piano.

My mysterious father ate breakfast with me and seemed to
have changed into a loving and friendly human being. He sat at
the sunlit table and drank chocolate out of a blue mustache cup.

Father seemed to be both impressive and a warm and jovial
person as he joked with me. His brown hair was brushed back
neatly in a pompadour and his luxuriant mustache gave dignity to
his appearance without in any way seeming outlandish, formidable, or funny.

But I was puzzled that he alone drank chocolate. I asked
Mother why, and she explained that it made him sleep better.
Her answer made the mustache cup seem very special, and I ex-

amined it. I saw a fine porcelain piece with a plain flowery
design, with two handles that were gracefully curved. Father
used it with assurance, making slight sipping noises that were not
at all disagreeable and sounded as though he were carrying out
this particular job with dispatch and precision.

The cup with its blue-and-white design blended with the russet color of the dining room set. The enormous dining table had a
large chair at each end, Father's with arms, and a smaller one
without arms for Mother. Twelve straight-backed ordinary chairs
completed the set. The backs and seats of the chairs were of dark-
brown leather. A scroll design on the wood back of each one led
up to a wooden medallionlike figure that was just above my head
when I sat on a pillow. The medallion was slightly larger than a
silver dollar. Six circles diminishing in size were carved into the
wood leading to the center of the medallion, a raised wooden button about the size of a dime and approximately a quarter of an
inch thick.

The windows were framed with yellow curtains, and the dining room was flooded with sunlight. The glow seemed to mix the
silver of the trumpet with the red of the tassel, the design of the
mustache cup, the brown of Father's hair, the blue of his eyes,
the russet of the furniture, and the white of the tablecloth. The
scene was like a large painting that was hung in the music room,
and I felt happy, lighthearted, and warm inside. I was excited by
the occasion and sensed that the day was special.

After I had blown the trumpet, Mother brought in oatmeal
porridge and cream, and the sight of it made me feel slightly
nauseated. I was much more interested in Father's breakfast: two
oranges, halved, the juice of which Father extracted with a spoon;
two soft-boiled eggs that were broken into an ordinary cup and
eaten with a spoon slightly larger than the one he had used for his
oranges; and two white rolls carefully divested of their doughy insides, spread with sweet butter and eaten with the eggs and chocolate. I was fascinated when I saw the napkin that was tucked into
Father's collar begin slipping to one side. Father noticed it just
before it was about to drop and tucked it in with a slightly disor-
ganized gesture. Mother urged me to eat my oatmeal, and I
forced some down. Eventually, the rich cream was too much for
me, so Mother brought up a nice, cool glass of milk from the

cellar. Father finished his chocolate in a hurry, wiped his mustache with his napkin—which he then pulled unrolled through his napkin ring—and, with a friendly pat on my head, picked up his hat on the way out of the front vestibule to begin his brisk fifteen-minute walk to catch the eight o'clock streetcar to the city.

Even though the colors still danced in a lively fashion, and the trumpet when I played it blared as brightly as before, I suddenly felt lonesome. Mother had gone to the kitchen and I had become keenly aware of the cold, unappetizing remains of my porridge. It had a crust that I nibbled at but still could not eat.

I straddled my chair horseback fashion. Holding myself with my left hand, I noticed the medallion on the chair right in front of my face. I put my hand on it and found it fascinating to handle the button and to trace the six mysterious circles with my fingers. The feel of it gave me back a sense of security which had left me when Father departed.

Finally I examined the breakfast table to see if I could find food I liked. The remains of the oranges were on my father's blue-and-white breakfast plate. The shade of orange further brightened the room.

I slid off my chair and took Father's place at the head of the table. His chair was too high for me, so I had to stand as I picked up the remains of each half-orange and squeezed a few drops of juice into my father's spoon. As I swallowed the juice I knew I had never tasted anything quite as good. I squeezed the orange rinds with my hands and sucked them, gradually eating most of the pulp.

After I had finished this ritual, I walked through the kitchen and out the screen door onto the porch. I sat down on the top step of the stairs, and soon I heard the sound of a dragonfly. I watched as it stayed suspended a few feet above my head, quivered for a moment, and then landed on a porch post, where it continued quivering. It suddenly darted up, then stopped flying but continued quivering. Its wings moved so swiftly that they were almost invisible. From a distance I heard the drone of summer insects carried on the gentle June breeze. The dragonfly darted away and then came back. After a few seconds that seemed like an eternity, it gently glided into the warm June breeze.

For a moment I was still, then walked to the screen door. I

hesitated before I opened it and turned back to look into the trees and bushes in the backyard. After a while I opened the screen door and ran into the kitchen. Mother took me in her arms, kissed me, and then sent me on my round of simple daily chores.

I went to the porch to fetch some kindling wood, and the magic of the breakfast room seemed to have been transformed into the hum of the heat, the sounds of insects, the songs of the birds and the breeze, and the sound of gently rustling leaves.

Under a lilac bush I lay down on the grass and slept for a long, long time. The barking of a dog in the distance awakened me; clouds were covering the sun and I was anxious to return to the kitchen and finish my chores. Mother said I was just in time for my birthday surprise, and she took from the oven a gorgeous meringue torte, filled it with whipped cream and strawberries, and cut a piece that I lapped up greedily as she said, "Happy birthday, my boy," and the screen door, blown by the rising wind, closed with a bang.

※※

AFTER THIS impressionistic experience stemming from my birthday, I seemed to become conscious of my surroundings. I began discovering the house I was in and the objects and life around me.

House rules were simple. Papa left at 8:00 A.M. to go to Milwaukee, where he taught music and conducted the Musical Society. He returned around five; when where were evening rehearsals, he returned at eleven. Mama managed everything on the farm with the help of my sister, my four brothers, and the hired girl, Katy Nortman.

My brothers and sister were often away at school or doing odd jobs. I was alone much of the time, so I turned for company to our beloved, unusual, and beautiful housecat named Mama Kitty. She was a big, strong white cat with black ears and a thick black tail. She was the mother of all the cats on the farm and in the neighborhood and was much respected. She liked me to be with her when she rested on her stomach with her paws folded in under her chin. She let me fondle her and blow into her ears, which she would flick. When I put my fingers into her paws, she would extend her toes and push out her claws, but she would never use them on me. When I scratched her back where her spine turned into a tail, she enjoyed it for a time, but eventually she retired with dignified steps behind the sofa to rest and to meditate.

Mama Kitty kept in condition by sharpening her claws on the wallpaper. She was occasionally chased for this but was far too highly honored a member of the household to be punished. In several rooms the wallpaper was scratched to shreds a foot and a half above the floor. As tribute to her habit, the paper was never replaced.

Soon after my third birthday, I was given small boxing gloves. I taught Mama Kitty to sit on her haunches and box with me like a small white kangaroo. This she enjoyed enormously. When I boxed with bare hands she always kept her claws hidden, but when I was too rough she fought back and sometimes scratched me. I carried these battle scars with pride. Once she disappeared. Mama found her in a closet where she had deposited a litter of kittens in Mother's new hat. Kitty's prestige was so high that Mama just laughed and laughed, let her keep the hat for her brood—and made a new one for herself.

Mama Kitty was responsible for my first sex instruction. One of her litters reached a certain age, and as I investigated the kittens I found that some had little pouches under their tails; others did not. I asked Mother about this. She said those with little pouches were boys and the others, girls. I asked why. She said it was so we could easily tell them apart. This experience changed my relationship with my sister. Until then, she sometimes had me in the bathroom while she sat on the toilet. After the kitten episode, I must have looked at her too closely for her comfort, for from then on she carefully latched the bathroom door.

I WAS always sent to bed early, so I didn't see very much of the family. I was lonely, but Mother's solution was to have me tag along with her while she attended to her endless tasks. When she was finished with her cleaning in the playroom, the room was mine to explore.

On my first visit there, I found a magnificent collection of red-and-blue brick building blocks from Germany. A booklet with slightly modified architectural drawings showed how to build German-style churches, houses, farmyards, and shops. Mama selected one for me to work from, chose a few blocks for me to work with, set two together, and told me to finish the job. I asked her many questions, and she answered every one of them. I tried to follow her directions, and then and there the foundation of my education was laid. It was to raise questions and get answers and directions for doing jobs from people and books and to put these into practice.

Mama stimulated my curiosity by patiently answering all my questions.

"Are all building blocks red and blue?"

"No, some are made of other colors."

"Could they be green and yellow?"

"That might be very pretty."

"Will they always be pretty?"

"Not if one of the colors is too bright."

"How can you tell if they are too bright?"

"Sometimes the sun is so bright that it makes things glare. That's brightness. When a cloud comes along, things darken."

"What happens at night?"

"It can be very dark, but then the moon shines and the stars sparkle, and that makes a different kind of brightness."

Mama would often illustrate points by using her lovely voice and teaching me a song to fit the occasion. She illustrated brightness by singing:

> *"Good morning, Mary Sunshine.*
> *Why did you wake so soon?*
> *To chase the little stars away*
> *And frighten off the moon."*

She sang "Twinkle, Twinkle, Little Star" to illustrate night. My ear and memory were excellent, and Mother told me later that when I was three and a half, I had a repertory of fifty songs. After I could sing "Twinkle, Twinkle," she played Mozart's piano variations based on this theme, so that I could hear how it sounded on the piano. All the songs were in fine books with cartoonlike illustrations and texts, many of them in German. The moon was made familiar to me through one of these, "Guter Mond Du gehst so stille." The favorites with family and friends were "She Hit Him with a Shingle, It Made His Trousers Tingle," "Muss i' denn, muss i' denn," and "Oh, Where, Oh, Where Has My Little Dog Gone?" My brothers taught me college and other popular songs.

In the hot summer, I discovered the virtues of the front porch. Rocking chairs sat on it and, in the place of honor, hung a hammock. On very hot days I would lie in the hammock while the two dogs lay underneath panting and puffing. I became conscious of the great feeling of well-being that came with the summer. The sounds of insects vibrated like telephone wires in the wind. We called some of them "darning needles" and some dragonflies. The sound of bees buzzing was an in-and-out drone. I heard hens in the chicken coop and a dog's barks from the valley below the house, with the gentle rustle of wind through leaves as a background. Sometimes a cow's moo floated up from the barn. Mourning doves mourned.

On the hottest days the dogs stopped panting and lay on the porch sleeping or retired to the packed cool ground under the porch. At that point I went to sleep. My dreams about friendly and beautiful people and places were all pleasant. A princess might float through them, but eventually I would dream of nothing but the silvery gray curtain, beyond which I couldn't see. I saw mysterious and meaningful marks on it, but then a nice, deep, warm sleep would envelop me—unless I had moved and rolled out of the hammock.

None of this has changed much in seventy years, except that there are no dogs, and instead of a hammock I sit in the same rocking chair that rocked on the porch I just described. My dreams are meditations now, and there are fewer floating princesses. The silvery gray curtain is still impenetrable. The mysterious marks are more elaborate and resemble hieroglyphics; sometimes they become abstract designs with or without color, of the kind Picasso, Mondrian, Klee, and other painters have captured. Eventually, the silver curtain disappears and deep sleep wins out.

My love of nature has not diminished and the sounds of birds, insects, animals, trees, and the colors of the leaves I now hear and see are on the banks of the Hudson River. Fortunately the childhood habit of filtering out irrelevant sounds and sights that so easily destroy the direct contact with nature belongs to my earliest memories and is still alive.

THE KITCHEN was immensely important the year round. Mama spent much of her time there, and as her helper I became conscious of its independent life. It contained the modern appliances of that day. There was an enormous range, which had six holes for heat with heavy iron removable lids, each about the circumference of a large pot, a water tank that provided all the hot water for bathing and washing, and an enormous oven, because all breads, cakes, and pies were homemade. The stove was fired with wood; coke was used for a continuous fire, with walnut coal to bank it and keep it going through the night. Mama supplied me with a small coal scuttle and shovel and showed me how to bring up coal from the big bin in the cellar and to keep the fire going. The iron lids for the holes had a special handle. When the lids were lifted and partially opened they worked like a draft, along with a regulator on the flue. When halfway open, more heat reached the pots resting on them. When they were opened too wide the coal would sometimes kick up a roaring flame that could scorch us and the food. The oven temperature was controlled by leaving the door open when it needed cooling. There was no thermostat.

Drinking water was pumped by hand into the sink from a well. When the well went dry much priming and vigorous pumping went on to make it stop coughing. To make it deliver water was great fun.

Mama ran things in the kitchen like the captain of a ship. The party-line telephone was cranked every morning to give the butcher explicit directions about the meat: "Good morning, Mr. Schmidt, how are you this morning? Have you any nice rack lamb chops? I want the third, fourth, and sixth. Are they nice and lean? About two inches thick, please, but remove all of the fat and crack the bones at two inches. Save the scraps for the animals. Send along enough pluck [heart, liver, and lungs] for the dogs."

The specific information for her highly professional butcher conversations was contained in a two-volume German cookbook that had been in her family for two generations. The directions called for incredible amounts of herbs, butter, condiments, spices, vinegars, and cooking wines from which—with hours of work and infinite pains—sauces, gravies, and relishes were concocted.

Every three weeks, provisions came from Steinmeyer's Grocery and Fancy Delicatessen in Milwaukee; they were delivered in a big wagon pulled by a team of magnificent Percherons with plumes, straw hats against heat stroke, feed bags, and jingling harnesses. The driver cracked his whip in our driveway and hollered, "Giddup," as the team negotiated the small rise, welcomed by the two dogs barking their heads off, while the rest of the family waited at the kitchen door.

The storeroom in the cellar was built on a wooden platform, which kept it dry, and yet it was far enough away from the furnace to be quite cool. Part of the cellar floor was cement. There were large earthenware jugs for cider, milk, and for cooling water, and a room for vegetables and preserves. The cellar was roomy and had a good Miller Brothers furnace, a large coal bin, and a large wood bin.

Except for the phone, there was no electricity. Refrigeration was supplied by a rather small, old-fashioned icebox that stood on the back porch. The iceman came once a week with a wagon, pulled by a team of even more beautiful and powerful Percherons, with a more rugged harness that didn't jingle. He was welcomed with cheers, and Mama would order either twenty-five or fifty pounds of ice. He would fish out the ice with ice tongs from the sawdust in the wagon, wash it, chop it into the right size, and drop it into the upper part of the box. (Ice chips were for me to suck.) A drain led to a dish in the floor. The most delicate and perishable foods were kept in the box from week to week, so if he missed us it was a tragedy.

I had duties in the kitchen when Mama did baking. I soon learned how to knead bread, an operation that had to be continued until the dough was absolutely smooth. Mama gave me a very small bread pan so that I could learn to make tiny loaves for myself. I was also delegated to pick straws from the broom and wash them so they could be used to test the bread for doneness.

Pies were Mama's specialty and needed her full attention, so I was allowed only to butter the pie plates. As she nursed her pies and cakes to perfection the expression on her face resembled that of a doctor giving his patient an examination—testing heart, lungs, and stomach carefully, with that particularly concentrated look and critical but objective comments all first-rate doctors and first-rate cooks make when at work.

Mama entrusted the baking of tortes and special cakes to no one else. This became a family tradition that was a ritual for all birthdays and holidays. Pumping water, washing vegetables and fruits, and burning the smaller and lighter amounts of garbage in the stove and the heavy waste in the furnace were my kitchen duties. I was soon promoted to dusting and polishing the piano and chairlegs in the music room with an oiled cloth or chamois, but as the summer wore on this bored me and slowly I discovered the out-of-doors.

I LIKED watching flies and darning needles when they flew about on top of each other. I asked Mother what they were doing.

"They're playing," she answered.

"When a rooster gets on a hen are they playing?"

"Yes."

One afternoon while the beer truck was unloading, I noticed one of the Percheron stallions take a heroic position and then, from what seemed like a thick hose, let go an endless cascade that formed itself into the largest pool I had ever seen on our driveway, even on a rainy day. I asked Mother about the hose.

"It's the same as the *Zeppel* you pee with."

"Will mine be that big when I grow up?"

"I hope not."

From then on I became slowly conscious of the great variety of activity in the animal world, and its rules. I was helped by our two dogs—Laddie, a purebred Scotch Collie, and Sport, a cross between a Newfoundland and a St. Bernard. I believe they adopted me because they thought I was a retarded dog—an underprivileged puppy who had only two legs to run with, could not bark, and whose fur grew only on the top of his head. I must have had other noticeable deficiencies, but to put me at my ease the dogs made the first overtures. One afternoon on the porch, with tails wagging, they sniffed me. After tasting my perspiration they licked the back of my hands and slobbered over my arms and face with great gusto. Mother took me into the kitchen to wash, but seemed to approve. "Now go back and play with the dogs. They are your best friends and will always protect you." From then on the dogs and I spent long hours together daily for almost six years.

Many dogs are trained to retrieve, but Sport taught *me* the retrieving game. One day he brought a stick to me. I didn't react so he picked it up and literally pushed it into my hands. Then he began a gentle tug-of-war, using just enough force to balance my feeble tugs. Then Laddie joined the game until I threw the stick. The dogs chased it and the winner brought it back, and they waited tense and poised for the next round. I soon caught on and made the false starts and difficult throws they expected.

⤞⤝

BETWEEN THE out-of-door dog interludes, Mama had me follow her around the house. The music room and library had rows of bookcases and shelves of books and music that had to be dusted. I became vitally interested in the music room as soon as I could make the piano sound, and in the playroom when I discovered more games and books. There were six bedrooms and a bathroom on the second floor and two rooms in the attic. The mahogany double bed in Papa's and Mama's room came from Polle in Germany along with mattresses and pillows. Two beds for the older children had rosewood frames, and the others were brass. Pillows were filled with home-grown goose feathers. The bathroom upstairs was modern, with good plumbing unless the well went dry. One hot bath on Saturday night was our ration. To take care of nocturnal emergencies fancy chamber pots were kept under each bed. One of my sister's jobs was to empty them into a slop jar each morning. The bedrooms were papered in solid colors—blue, yellow, rose. The house was painted yellow with white borders.

In the attic there were shelves of English and German books under the rafters, yearly files of German and English magazine subscriptions, piles of German-English newspaper clippings, and stacks of letters, some of them tattered and fragile. A broken spinning wheel, pictures with broken glass or split frames, boxes full of photographs, old suitcases filled with ribbons, Mother's wedding dress, Grandfather's stovepipe hat, hand-painted china, discarded games, stuffed birds, black and brown shoes, tennis shoes that might come in handy on a rainy day, and a trunk full of goose feathers to stuff pillows with made it a mysterious haven. It was later much cherished by me and my brothers as a quiet place for reading and writing.

While we were doing chores, Mama taught me to read. Her instruction was based on the do-it-yourself philosophy that dominated our home. She let me choose from a pile of my brothers' discarded first readers (McGuffey's was among them), then partly filled a copybook to serve as a model for my exercises. She taught me the alphabet and explained how letters formed words. The books were nicely illustrated and planned, so that they were a literary supplement to the kind of life I understood. It had a picture of a boy. Then "BOY," printed. A Spencerian sample of handwriting, *boy*, came next—an art I never mastered, alas. But soon I was reading and writing: "cat," "dog," "Mama," "chair". . .

I explored every book I could get my hands on even when I couldn't understand what was in it. I was so anxious to write that before I had any real foundation in spelling I invented my own alphabet and wrote long letters in this unknown language.

MAMA WOULD sing Schubert's song *Die Taubenpost*—about a carrier pigeon that delivered letters. We had some homing pigeons, so I put used stamps on my letters and placed them on the roof of the porch for the carrier pigeons to pick up. Mama saw to it that the letters were collected, but one day she explained that using canceled stamps was a federal offense, and I could be put in jail. The thought of a jail term was a great blow to me as I had just begun to discover the house, the out-of-doors, and the animals. I didn't like the idea of being captured and put in jail. I settled the problem by inventing my own stamps.

Mama taught me many English and German songs as she tended to her duties. "Peeping Through the Knot Hole in Father's Wooden Leg" was one of my favorites. "Hiawatha" had an exotic sound. "After the Ball Is Over" was a fine waltz. The uncle of the young composer Charles K. Harris brought him to Papa and told him that the boy was always composing music. Papa asked to see a score and was told that the boy whistled his compositions. Papa suggested learning to notate them. Harris whistled "After the Ball" and his uncle offered Papa ten dollars to notate it. Papa was insulted, so the uncle found someone in Chicago. The piece was a hit and Harris made a fortune.

"Mr. Dooley," "Under the Bamboo Tree," "I'm Afraid to Go Home in the Dark," "Oh, Didn't He Ramble . . ." "Rufus Rastus Johnson Brown, Whatcha Gonna Do When the Rent Comes Roun'?" "In the Good Ole Summertime," "In the Shade of the Old Apple Tree," "The Animal Fair," and "By the Light of the Silvery Moon" rounded out my English repertory.

The German songs ranged from "Dr. Eisenbart," about a legendary physician in the Neckar valley who cured his patients by poisoning them, to "Schneider Meck-Meck die Hosen voll Dreck," describing a tailor who was lousy, filthy, and itchy. The colorful text of "Dr. Eisenbart" included the line *Ich bin der Doctor Eisenbart/Vidi, vidi, vit, boom, boom."*

I used to sing a drinking song . . .

> *"So leben wir, so leben wir*
> *So leben wir alle Tage*
> *In dir allerlustigsten*
> *Suff Kummpanie."*

("We live it up, we live it up/ We live it up each day, boys/In the most congenial and/Drunken company.") "Fuchs Du hast die Gans gestohlen" told how the fox stole the goose, and "Kommt ein Vogel geflogen" was about a bird that sat on the singer's foot. This one I sang on the porch, hoping that a bird would join me.

One day, as I was dusting the piano bench, Mama said, "It's time for you to learn how to play piano."

I had loved hearing Papa play behind closed doors, and because of my duties as piano duster I had great affection and respect for the instrument—although it seemed more like a strange animal in a stall than anything I would ever care to touch.

Mama sat me on the bench, adjusted it, and put R. Damm's *Piano Method* on the stand. She then placed my hand on middle C and told me that there was a musical alphabet just like the one for words, except that the musical alphabet spelled sounds that did not have an exact meaning. "For instance," she said, "C, A, T spells cat, and C, E, G spells a chord that sounds like this. The chord has many meanings." She then played the different intervals and showed in the book how the clefs, the staff, whole notes, and half-notes were drawn, explaining about counting the beats.

She produced a music notebook. "While you're learning to read music, you must always put everything you've learned down in the music notebook—the clefs and the notes you've learned today are in the first lesson in the book. Write them down and then play on the piano what you've written. After you practice, if you feel like it, just play anything on the piano, explore it, and see how it sounds."

My first attempt at writing down notes was like my letters. I invented what I didn't know. I was not yet four when I gradually learned that notation meant something. After reviewing the lessons in the *Piano Method*, music began to be very interesting for me.

FOR ENTERTAINMENT I was pretty much left to my own resources until I was eight or nine. Only then did I see my first plays and hear band and other concerts and see Burton Holmes's travelogue lectures with slides. A magnificent collection of games had been saved for twenty years, and they were now mine. I played games both solo and with partners. We enjoyed a stereopticon with a fine collection of exotic scenes, and produced Japanese shadow shows with sheets, finger motions, and cardboard cutouts. There were Indian games, such as Spearing the Fish. Here we tossed a piece of leather, with holes and ten rings tied to a thong, into the air and tried to spear them with a small stick tied to the other end of the thong. A question-and-answer game used an electric battery. By moving a wire into the proper question and answer slots the machine would be made to buzz, and we were being educated. Our Magic Lantern repertory included not only exotic slides and travelogues but comic series like "The Katzenjammer Kids" with Hans and Fritz and the Captain and his wife in the leads. A punching bag for the boys who were engaged in the manly art of self-defense, a rowing machine, Indian clubs, and dumbbells for building muscles were in the attic. We played with darts that had rather heavy and dangerous steel tips. Nobody tried to stop us, but we were warned to keep out of the way of the darts or we'd be killed.

I got to know more animals when Mama gave me outdoor

chores to do. Our menagerie included about five hundred chickens, ten Bantams, two goats, two geese, ten ducks, and three cows, one golden pheasant, one silver pheasant, and a covey of ringling pheasants. Mother thought it would be very practical to breed pheasants because the feathers were useful for ladies' hats. She did save enough feathers to make a beautiful plume for her own hat, but didn't get further than that.

The two goats were named Hamlet and Julius Caesar. When brother Eugene was around he liked to declaim, "Come forth, Hamlet," with Shakespearean accents, and the goat would appear.

But Father discovered that goats smell. "Phooey, phooey," he exclaimed, "those animals stink. Get rid of them at once."

And that was the end of the goats. Too bad; they used to pull me around in a little wagon.

The chickens did quite well for some time, and my job was to feed them. They laid enough eggs for the family plus several dozen to sell to neighbors. One night an unusual bustle and noise in the house brought me out of my bedroom.

The rest of the family was staring out the window watching the chicken coop go up in flames. Father sounded sad as he said, "It's all gone up in smoke."

Mama had been so busy that she had forgotten to put water into a brooder to cool it. The stove blew up—and that ended our chicken farming. The volunteer fire department from Wauwatosa arrived after the coop had burned to the ground.

I did make a new friend because of the disaster. A tiny bantam hen, not the most intelligent bird I have ever seen, had roosted on the hot stovepipe until her toes were burned off. I felt sad and took care of her. Recognizing an equal, she adopted me and became my personal pet. I could walk around the yard and the house with her on my shoulder or head and she seemed quite content. Eventually, when things got back to normal, she even laid eggs for me. She would join the dogs and Mama Kitty, and we would have very peaceful social gatherings.

Evenings, when Papa came home from his conservatory, the two geese ran toward him for almost half a block and greeted him with enormous honks and wing flappings.

I became interested in the cows, Desdemona, Laura, and

Lady. They grazed in the grove on the hill above the barn. It was near the house, so I had a chance to get acquainted with them. They were more formidable than my other animal friends, and I think they liked my brothers best. Once our neighbor, Frank Rogers, brought a bull for breeding purposes. I watched the proceedings from the top of the hill and asked questions.

Mother said, "They are playing."

It advanced my knowledge of sex by several steps. "What's the difference between a bull and a cow?"

"A bull is a gentleman," Mama said, "and a cow is a lady."

The bull was led away, but the cows were lively, and Desdemona jumped on Lady. I asked Mama, "Do the lady cows play with each other too?"

"Sometimes, when there's no bull around or they are tired of him."

This satisfied my curiosity. A few more observations of the dogs' antics and later careful examination of an illustrated veterinarian's encyclopedia and the dictionary told me all I needed to know about sex until I went to school at age seven. There I discussed fine points with some new friends. I believe when I was eight I knew just about everything that one could pick up about sex without being a participant. I had also developed a very colorful vocabulary, including a set of cuss words that would have made Mark Twain blush.

After the first summers on the farm, my brothers, who were home on vacation and present during the day, took me in tow. Eugene—nicknamed Dix—took me through the farm to a path in the woods that led past Dewey's Insane Asylum to the village drugstore. It was a long, hot walk, but I was rewarded by having my first ice-cream soda with fresh pineapple. The drugstore with its large globes filled with red and green fluids, medicines marked with skulls and crossbones, and mysterious medicine cabinets, fascinated me. The soda fountain too seemed efficient and flashy. Two sodas cost twenty cents and Dix threw down two dimes with a flourish.

Dix was a sophomore at MIT and an inventor. He showed Hans and Bob how to string up a telegraph wire between our house and that of our neighbors, the Goulds. The boys learned Morse code and spent many an evening telegraphing from our attic to Dan Gould half a mile away. Dix also worked on a flying machine. I was to be the first passenger because I was light. His boxlike contraption had a wheel on the side that I was supposed to turn steadily to flap the wings that would carry me off the hill. The trouble was that fellows of my size didn't have enough strength to make the wings flap and carry them, while heavier passengers had the strength but were too heavy to be carried, so Dix had to wait for the Wright brothers to straighten things out.

⊰⊱

My FIRST excursions into the woods were magical. Mother was fearless, and by the time I was four she let me go into the woods with the dogs as protectors and stay as long as I liked. I would sit on a mossy bank and listen to sounds as they floated on the air on a still summer day. Birdcalls, sometimes interrupted by the cawing of crows, sharpened my ear so that I became aware of different kinds of sounds—rustling leaves; the sound of water in the creek; the sound of a rock that I threw onto the ground, into water, or against a tree. The dogs would run around for a while, return panting, lie down, cool off, and go to sleep. Gradually all kinds of insect sounds—the very high, drawn-out vibrations of the darning needles, the hum of bees, and perhaps even the buzz of one stray fly—would join in a natural symphony. At the proper time on the proper day if the light was just right, the croaks of frogs and toads could be heard. A cow might moo in the distance and from the Menominee valley that loneliest of all lonely sounds, a passing train whistle tuned in minor, would blend with the melancholy sound of a mourning dove, a stranger symphony than I heard from the porch.

I sometimes think that these lone sessions in the woods with the dogs made me aware of the infinite varieties in nature and did more to awaken me to music and the other arts than anything I was later taught about them.

The consciousness of sounds was accompanied by a growing awareness of colors and shapes. My interest in leaves, plants, rocks, grass, hay, and flowers was not that of a botanist, but from childhood that of an artist. I found them all so fascinatingly beautiful that I studied each one just to drink in its beauty. A blade of grass was interesting not only because of its shape but because of its texture; the roughness and smoothness I would try with my tongue. The shades of green were never quite the same, I discovered, and I saw that light could change green hues to purple or black, depending on just how it fell.

These magic hours ended only when a storm or hunger and fatigue made the house seem like some desirable fairy castle the dogs and I could escape to, and we would run home.

ONE DAY, Hans took me to the creek. By clearing out all the stones and making a beautiful sandy bottom, he showed me how to build a swimming hole. Then, from around the shore and from other parts of the creek, we hauled larger stones and built a dam that contained the water until it was deep enough to swim. A stone border held the water on the sides. The pool was about fifteen feet long. At the upstream end we built a miniature dike that allowed fresh water to trickle into the pool slowly so that it could not wash away our walls. The creek was fed by springs. The discovery of these in its bed and then on the bank was a revelation for me. The water bubbled out, pushing the sand up in a miniature mound. Hans carved a little willow branch with his knife and made a spigot for springwater. That springwater bubbling right out of the ground looked like spilled mercury and tasted like nectar.

We then made a fishing hole. There were minnows and perch in the creek. The water was just strong enough to wash them over, and the rocks were high enough to hold them in until the pool was filled to overflowing. When I waded in the pool the minnows brushed and tickled my legs. They were so friendly that we caught them with our hands, inspected them, and then let them go. Later, Hans taught me how to fish with a pole from a willow tree with ordinary butcher string, a bent pin at the end, and an angle worm. We caught a fish or two, but the pins were not hooked properly so the fish weren't really injured. After inspecting them carefully—their colors, shape, feel, smell, size, and expression (we decided that fish always looked either slightly surprised or unhappy)—we tossed them back into the pool. They were part of our woodland family. I don't remember that we ever ate one of our catches while we were on the farm.

Another day, on high ground above the bank, we discovered a cave. The dogs sniffed through it and assured us it was uninhabited, so we cleared it out, pounded down the ground until it was hard, and then covered it with dry leaves. On subsequent visits we made some crude latticework from willow branches and covered it with burlap sacks we had gotten from the barn. We camouflaged the entrance so that no one could tell that there was anyone inside. It was an absolutely dry refuge during the many violent summer thunderstorms that came up in a hurry. We were afraid of tramps who sometimes came to town by riding the rods on freight trains and who foraged for food in woods and on farms. When one of the boys would warn in a subdued voice, "Cheese it. A tramp," the dogs were corralled before they could bark and we retired into the cave. The entrance was covered until the danger was past. Once a drunken Civil War veteran from the Soldiers' Home lurched around the swimming hole in his Union uniform, stumping with a wooden leg and cursing as he tried to keep his balance. The dogs went after him, and we had a hard time calling them off. We all retired to the cave to escape what we thought would be dire revenge on the part of the old soldier, and possibly a visit from the sheriff.

With our shelter established in the woods, we had to find a way of feeding ourselves so that we could stay out all day. We discovered fine crops of wild blackberries, raspberries, chokecherries, sour cherries, strawberries, thorn apples, crabapples, and wild grapes. All of these were delicious, and there was an element of danger in picking the thorn apples with their inch-long, heavy thorns, which made them taste all the better. There were various kinds of grasses, the sprouts of which we found very tasty when the outer blades were removed. We brought cornstalks and split the stalk and ate the sweet inside. We were also fond of honeysuckle. A few wild sour cherry trees in the woods and a few maple trees brought variety. In the appropriate season we would drive nails into the maple trees and insert pieces of straw in the holes we'd made to suck the syrup. When there was no suitable straw we would suck the tree. Green apple trees bore small, hard fruit that had to be eaten in moderation for fear of bellyache. The woods were full of hazelnut bushes, and we generally dried these nuts for future use, but sometimes we ate the succulent fresh ones, which we cracked with a couple of rocks. The few black-walnut trees yielded rich harvests when there was a storm with much wind. We gathered the nuts, removed the outer skin and, staining our fingers brown in the process, went to work with rocks; after much toil we extracted the delicious meat. Dandelion greens were bitter but good. If we were hungry between foragings, we pulled resin from a tree and chewed it into a wad that tasted better than chewing gum. We discovered that the branch of a willow tree could be cut and hollowed to make either a whistle or something very nice to chew on. Of course, the bark had to be removed. We thought it was poison.

᠀

BESIDES MAMA, Papa, my brothers Fred, Dix, Hans, and Bob, and my sister Helene, there were living with us the hired girl, Katy; and later Emma Felix, a poor student of Papa's who helped in the house; Shorty, the hired man, who slept in the barn; and an occasional washwoman.

Even before the Depression of 1907 money seemed to be in short supply, and Mama mended all our clothes and made dresses and shirts. She supervised the pressing and cleaning of our suits when we visited town. Seven to eleven people in the household were fed by Mama every day, with Katy's help. If the washwoman didn't arrive, Mama did the washing herself and superintended the ironing. Helene and Emma were Father's secretaries at the conservatory.

Fred and Dix took care of the cows with Shorty's help. When Dix was away at MIT, Hans and Bob were apprentice helpers. Mama became ambitious and bought a horse and a milk and egg wagon with LUENING'S FARM painted in beautiful letters on the side. Fred drove the milk route, but he couldn't sell enough milk to feed the horse.

When I was old enough, I delivered milk by hand to some neighbors, a walk of about two miles. On hot days I would take a sip of milk to cool off.

The sun must have been mighty hot one day, because Mrs. Moss called up Mama and reported that I had brought a quart of milk with the cream missing. Mama was rather shocked at the idea and defended me until I told her that I had taken a very small sip. "Then," I said, "I took another sip."

"Any more?"

"I guess so."

She called Mrs. Moss to explain, and to me she said, "Now you have to take a full quart over to Mrs. Moss and see that she gets it. That's your job. She has paid for it. You will keep on delivering until she gets what she has paid for."

The episode made a lasting impression on me.

MAMA HAD a vegetable garden, which she taught me how to weed with a set of miniature tools. She was a good gardener and insisted that the soil around every plant be properly loosened, raked, and spread. I was a conscientious gardener and was delighted when carrots and radishes began to grow. I eagerly pulled these from the ground and ate them, complete with dirt. Later, regular tomatoes and muskmelons ripened; plum tomatoes were the delicacy.

A half-acre was set aside for fruit trees and a flower garden. We grew rose bushes, chrysanthemums, lots of dahlias, nasturtiums, and asters. Although I pruned the flowers, we didn't know how to take care of any of them. They bloomed irregularly and died before their time. But the fruit trees were rewarding. The wild sour cherry trees produced a lot of fruit magnificent for pies and preserves. Plum, pear, and apple trees, when mosquito netting kept the birds away, bore good fruit. In the berry patch grew raspberries, gooseberries, blackberries, and currants. Our rhubarb and Swiss chard were exotic plants in those days. Wax beans were a specialty. Otherwise, we grew standard garden-variety vegetables, all very good.

When I was about four I ate a piece of lettuce with a worm. I didn't like the taste, and I have had difficulty eating certain kinds of lettuce ever since. Mother recited a poem:

> "Nobody loves me,
> Everybody hates me,
> I'm going to go eat worms!
> Big fat juicy ones,
> Little thin squirmy ones,
> I'm going to go and eat worms!"

Hans and Bob, when not in school, had supervision over the garden and fruit trees, and ran the gasoline engine in the pump house to supply the house with water. There was one bathroom. Hot water came from the kitchen water-heater attached to the coal stove.

Because of the heavy bathroom traffic, Mother decided that the outhouse that had been on the farm for many years should be left standing behind the chicken coop in case of emergencies. It was a classic two-holer, with vines growing up the sides and flowers around the entrance. Hans and Bob were superintendents of the outhouse as well as of a beautiful compost heap and a manure pile. This was entrusted to their care when Fred and Dix had a date in town.

MY BIG brothers Fred and Dix introduced me to life around the barn. I had developed a taste for natural grains, so I was nicknamed Oats. The barn, at the bottom of the hill about half a mile from the house, had its own well, which supplied water for the animals with enough left over for a duck pond. The cows—Desdemona, Laura, and Lady—were all good milkers. After getting me used to the barn, Dix, who was very inventive in such matters, urged me to stand against the wall with my mouth open. He took careful aim and delivered warm cow milk directly from teat to boy. Dix also made studies of the effect of music on cows that were being milked. Lady, for instance, gave several quarts less when Dix sang the song "Louisa Schmidt." The other two cows were less sensitive, but all produced more milk when he sang "In the Shade of the Old Apple Tree."

As I gradually got to know the farm and my brothers, I also grew aware of two close neighbors. The Rogerses had a farm across the road that was appropriately named Otto Avenue, one of the few landmarks that still exist. Frank Rogers, Jr., took care of their farm's daily work and helped Fred when there were disasters. In the winter, Sis Rogers, Frank's sister, would sit at the kitchen window for hours looking out and combing her hair. She was only about twenty-five but she would start gazing early in the morning and often be in the same spot when the sun went down. She made a deep impression on me. Nobody ever did anything about it, nor was anybody worried. Neuroses and psychoses were attended to privately until the victims became unmanageable.

Then they went to Dewey's Insane Asylum or to the county insane asylum, a grim-looking fortress that we didn't enjoy seeing
when we passed it on walks.

In SPITE OF Mama's and the animals' magnificent sex instruction,
the women in the house (Mama, Helene, and Katy) were clothed
in mystery for me. Under light summer dresses layers of petticoats peeked out, and there were some miscellaneous heaving
noises to be heard when the ladies laced up their corsets. The
secrets of women's attire hung on the wash line. There one could
see protective boardlike corsets flapping in the air, or a pair of
enormously wide-cut lacy pants billowing in the breeze, and
various kinds of petticoats ranging from flannel to silk and linen.
For swimming, the ladies wore two-piece, loose-fitting bathing
suits complete with shoes and stockings and loose, flapping rubber caps. So much dead weight tended to pull them down, unless
with their suits filled with air pockets they then floated like balloons. Only very good swimmers could venture out.

Both men and women often wore high-laced and high-but-
toned shoes. The women, on semidress occasions, wore shirt-
waists with whalebone collars, muffs and fur pieces, and sometimes even sealskin coats. Bearskins were reserved for carpets
and for sleighing.

There were two great moments when styles seemed to
change. The first was Helene's coming-out party. She was seventeen when she appeared in a low-cut evening dress. This dropped
as close to her nipples as decency allowed and showed to great
advantage her very lovely neck and hair and some outlines of her
figure. I thought her beautiful and seductive. The best photog-
rapher in town took some lovely shots of her for the family
archives.

The other great moments came when Mama and Papa were
invited to a dinner party or a reception after a concert. On these
occasions Mama would disappear for several hours and come out
in some kind of low-necked gown, generally with beautiful imported lace on it, long white gloves, and a hand-painted fan that
she handled very gracefully. A hat with ostrich plumes, a veil,
and a muff completed the outfit. The low-necked dress was so
daring that it definitely showed the cleavage between her breasts,

something that Papa noted with satisfaction and the rest of us gaped at because of its absolutely astonishing audacity and novelty. She generally wore a very attractive new hairdo and rubbed behind her ears just a bit of Roger et Gallet perfume imported from Paris. After the ball was over Mama Cinderella would unlace and unbuckle, and at 5:00 A.M. she would be on the job making oatmeal on the kitchen stove.

⊱⊰

I RAPIDLY developed my reading and writing of music and English, mostly because my native curiosity compelled me always to look ahead to the next page. This somewhat lonesome but rich and gradual testing of life went on until I was sent to school at age seven. In the intervening years, Mama tried to teach me German with the help of illustrated German morality books. "Hans Gazing at the Sky" (from *Struwel Peter—Snarled-Up Peter*) taught me the dangers of not watching my step, for instance. I learned a little German, but my brothers didn't believe in the family bilingual tradition. In those days anyone who spoke German was a Dutchman. Nobody wanted to be a Dutchman, so we didn't speak much German.

Papa began to take a hand in my general education. His method was rooted in the Greek saying "Never too much." No matter what I would do, Papa would say after a while, "Now, don't overdo that. You'd better do something else now." After twenty minutes of piano practice, he would announce, "I think you should stop now and go out and play in the garden." Soon he would come out into the garden with a cautionary "You're overdoing that, my boy. You'd better come in and read awhile." Then in twenty minutes he would remark, "I think you're reading too much. It's bad for your eyes. You had better go out and play with the dogs." But in fifteen minutes he would boom at me, "Now come in and help your mother." His method accomplished two things for me. It got me interested in taking on new jobs and provided me with a great variety of experience.

From the outset, I learned how to read music well enough to try out new pieces without any help. I was much interested in the content of the compositions I explored, and I avoided just pecking away at them mechanically and then limping through them like a dog with a thorn in his paw.

Papa did approve of my life with nature and the animals and of my love of books. I learned not to get in his way when he was at home. When he was reading, playing the piano, or just thinking, everybody had to be absolutely quiet, except in the playroom or in the attic, where we were given some freedom.

Papa did discover that I had a very good memory, not only for songs but for other things. So he drilled me in facts about the great. For instance: "Who wrote *Faust*?"

"Goethe."

"Who wrote the opera *Faust*?"

"Gounod."

"How many symphonies did Beethoven write?"

"Nine."

"Who wrote *Hamlet*?"

"Shakespeare."

This was so that he could show off his youngest on Sundays and holidays to the aunts and other company. My brothers got wind of the new plan and took a hand in it. Before company arrived they conducted a rehearsal. After I had given all of the right answers they told me I was wrong, then scrambled things a bit more, and when the big moment arrived it went about like this: "Otto, come here. We want to see if you've learned anything, my boy. Now, how many symphonies did Beethoven write?"

"Three."

"Well, he's a little nervous. . . . Who wrote *Hamlet*?"

"Goethe."

By this time the boys were laughing their heads off behind the bushes, but Papa went right on. "We'll try again. What did Shakespeare do?"

"He wrote *Goethe*."

By this time the company was very much amused, and finally Papa, in order to save face, started laughing too, and I realized I was holding the bag. So I beat a hasty retreat to the dogs, and we ran into the woods where things seemed to be much more logical.

I am afraid this experience had a rather bad and lasting effect on me, for although by nature I had an excellent memory that has stayed with me, I still overreact when I am questioned about anything and go to considerable lengths to check and doublecheck my opinions. But I have learned to turn this initial indecision into something quite strong. I eventually muster the necessary facts for a discussion and then talk.

Chapter 3

Piano Lessons—
and a "Very Modern" Waltz
1904-1909

WHEN I WAS FOUR, MAMA AND Aunt Claire, who taught piano in Milwaukee, decided that Papa really must teach me. He listened to me play and looked at my notebooks. Then Mother announced, "Now Papa will play for you."

Preparations for his performance were impressive. He first removed his coat, then loosened his collar, opened his vest, and loosened his gold watch chain. He snapped his gold watch open and shut to tell the time. He then adjusted the piano stool to precisely the right height. Mama helped. The stool sagged a little on one side and he wanted it exactly one inch higher. Then, in his suspenders, he tackled the piano, much like the heavyweight champion John L. Sullivan would defend his title. He played for two hours and I was overwhelmed. He said he would give me a lesson the next day.

After my audition he said, "Now, my boy, we will have a review." And be began at the very beginning. He showed me the difference between sound and silence and explained that the white was the paper and the black lines were the staff. Then he took the Damm *Piano Method* and went through the first ten lessons very carefully, explaining everything as though discussing the fine points with a man of thirty-five. He said, "Now, my boy, you know these first ten lessons. Study the next ten lessons by yourself and practice everything. When you have mastered them, we will have another conference. Practice slowly. If you make a mistake you are playing too fast. Slow up until you don't make any mistakes and then play faster." He continued his own piano practice behind closed doors.

I learned later that Papa played Beethoven a great deal of the time, as well as Chopin, Liszt, Schubert, and some Mozart. Works by American composers—MacDowell, Arthur Whiting, Arthur Foote, George Chadwick, and Edgar Stillman-Kelley (who was born in Sparta, Wisconsin, and made a career in Europe)—all became familiar to me as I gleaned details of their lives and heard Papa play their music. He steered me to *Grove's Dictionary of Music and Musicians* for other information.

I spent much of my time at the piano. I loved the sound and the feel, and nobody had to drive me to it. When I had worked out the second ten lessons and asked Papa to give me another session, he was always busy and kept stalling. Finally Mama cornered him, and six months later he heard me play some Haydn, Mozart's Serenade from *Don Giovanni,* and a movement from an easy Beethoven sonata.

He was pleased, even astounded. "My boy, you have done very well. Of course, no one knows if you will keep it up. Many people start well but don't finish the race. But if you give a concert at the same age that Mozart gave his first concert, I will give you a pony. Now practice the next fifteen lessons, and then we will have another conference."

The thought of the pony really got me going, and I perfected Beethoven's G Major Sonata and played some Schubert variations. I was almost five and had only a year left to catch up with Mozart. I needed another lesson, but Papa was hard to catch— busy, preoccupied, disinterested, immersed in Schopenhauer or Tolstoy. He forgot about the pony and forgot about me. Mama scolded him, but it didn't do much good. Eventually, about six months before my sixth birthday, Mama cornered him and he suddenly began to whip me into shape for the proposed concert, but it was too late to make up for lost time. After I had passed my sixth birthday, he looked at me with an expression that often crossed his handsome face, which said: *I am telling you this because it is my duty. I know that it will hurt you more than it will hurt me, but it's necessary, and will make a man out of you.* Then he spoke. "My boy, you realize you haven't prepared the concert in time, so I can't give you the pony."

For some reason or other, the news didn't damage me as much as it might have. True, I spent the fall and winter trotting around the neighborhood with the dogs trying to get subscriptions for *Farm and Fireside*. The prize was a pony and I didn't win. I also took a dislike to horses in general, but many years later became somewhat addicted to the trotting races, perhaps because of some subconscious wish that I would pick the right pony.

My revenge on Papa was simple. I caught him the next week. "I have a present for you, Papa," I announced, and I presented him with my first two compositions for piano.

As I look at them now, they were good—the first, a waltz in A major that ended with a C-sharp minor chord, very modern; the second with simple but nice chromatic harmonies. Papa was astonished and patted me on the head. But later I heard his booming voice from the next room telling Mama, "No, no. I do not want any of my children to be a musician. It should be discouraged. An artist's life is much too difficult in the United States."

He continued to discourage my musical activities for another six years. It was Mama who kept me going and eventually brought him around.

But there was always much music in our house. Fred learned piano and violin, but soon moved into the pop field and concentrated on mandolin, banjo, Jew's harp, ocarina, and the singing of popular songs with his reedy, somewhat quavery but not inexpressive tenor. Dix played the piano and cello. He was noted for his brilliant performance of the piano solo "Hiawatha." For nine years he got stuck in the same place. Helene played piano but didn't get very far, because she had the bad habit of curling up her little finger like a snail, and this interfered with her technical fluency. She became a very good professional singer. She began her studies with Papa. She didn't respond to his gospel about tone production, so he called her a silly goose. This wrenched her psyche, and unfortunately she and Papa confined their conversation to "Good morning," "Good day," "Good night," and "Goodbye" for the next fifty years.

Hans played cello and piano. He did some remarkably wild improvising on the piano, but Papa didn't encourage him, so

Hans gradually transferred to Hohner's mouth organ, which he learned to play with great skill. He had absolute pitch, and later as an engineer he could test gas pressure in pipes by ear. Bob played piano but soon became a virtuoso on mouth organ, ocarina, Jew's harp, accordion, and guitar. Mama, of course, played the piano and sang. My aunts—Claire, Gretchen, and Tillie—all played piano and had sung in the big oratorio performances that Papa had conducted in the nineties.

The younger generation made their music when Papa wasn't around. My own musical life was secret. I was aided and abetted by Mama, Helene, and my Aunt Claire. Somehow I was so fascinated and loved the art so much that Papa's indifference did not stop my explorations, and I believe I played the role of Mozart better than Papa played the role of Mozart's father. But these early experiences did have the effect of making me somewhat secretive about some of my musical life. In front of audiences and students I had to fight nervousness, and I sometimes lacked confidence when I performed.

EVEN WITH all the work, study, diversion, and music on the farm, Mama made great meals for festive occasions. Including Grandma's and my aunts', there were sixteen birthdays to celebrate. For the Fourth of July, Thanksgiving, Christmas, and New Year's we sometimes made huge batches of fudge and nougats with walnuts; we also popped corn in an old-fashioned wire popper over the kitchen range, and then drenched it with butter and served it in washtubs.

Easter was a particularly beautiful celebration because it usually meant our first long foray into the woods for the express purpose of picking May flowers. Even when the dates didn't coincide exactly with Easter Sunday, Hans, Bob, and I would gather up baskets of these wildflowers, which were put in vases and placed all over the house. For us cowslips, blood lilies, pussywillows, violets, and lilies-of-the-valley were exceptional and exotic flowers.

On the afternoon of the Fourth of July, the Milwaukee Musical Society that Papa directed for thirty years gave its annual picnic. The society, sometimes over one hundred strong, seated on planks in huge wagons and surrounded by cartons of food and kegs of beer, announced their arrival with bursts of German songs. In Wellauer's Woods behind our farm a campsite consisting of planks on sawbucks or sawhorses was set up. The festivities began with eating and beer drinking. Then Papa conducted the society in song. At the head of his troops he was impressive. He was a very precise and effective conductor, and everybody loved to sing with him. He knew a lot about the voice and brought the best out of any chorus. But he also knew the great tradition of the *Liedertafel*, the same *Tafel* that Goethe's friend and Mendelssohn's teacher, Zelter, had established in the nineteenth century. This male-chorus tradition was exported to the Midwest, notably Wisconsin, in the first half of the nineteenth century. Many of the songs were in praise of Germany and the German spirit, such as "Lied vom Rhein" and "Freut euch des Lebens" ("Rejoice in Life"), and Kücken's "Ach, wie ists möglich dann" ("Oh, How Is It Possible?") and "Lisette." These sentimental songs, when backed by sufficient quantities of beer, caused nostalgia to well up in the chorus, which led to singing more songs and drinking more beer. The picnics sometimes ended with everybody crying in their beer. Occasionally, somebody would rise and recite a poem, *"Erlkönig"* perhaps, or Schumann's *"Die beiden Grenadiere."* Impersonations were in order. Occasionally, a small scene from an opera was enacted, something from *Zar und Zimmerman* by Lortzing or even from Leo Blech's *Alpenkönig.* Some of the singers stayed for the evening fireworks.

In the evening, all the adults in the neighborhood would gather on their front porches while the kids would send up their individual collections of skyrockets, red fire, and other spectaculars. Every farm and every house had its own celebration, and each celebration was different. One would have skyrockets, another bursts of stars; some would have red fire or pinwheels, making an impressive showing on the hill and in the Menominee Valley.

FRED WENT away for a while, and I learned why years later. He took a job on Howie's farm, which was five miles from ours, to earn some spending money. Our yearly incomes consisted of twenty dollars in birthday and Christmas gifts from Aunt Gretchen and Grandmother plus what we earned by cutting lawns, weeding gardens, and picking strawberries. Papa didn't believe in giving us allowances. Fred needed ready cash to go out on the town, so he became the all-round assistant of Farmer Howie.

Fred's problems began when he sang the popular hits of the day on Howie's porch in the evening after work, accompanying himself on mandolin or banjo. Mrs. Howie was his appreciative audience. Mr. Howie slept. When Fred's quavery tenor voice bleated out "By the Light of the Silvery Moon," while the silvery moon was shining on the porch, Mrs. Howie was thrilled. The final arrow in her heart came when he sang "In the Shade of the Old Apple Tree" while lying under the tree. Mrs. Howie broke the sad news to her husband. She was madly in love with Fred and wanted a divorce and to leave Wauwatosa!

Mr. Howie was a wise man and figured out all by himself that as she was twenty-five years older than Fred, things might not work out . . . so he paid a call on Papa and told him about the sordid romance.

"Mr. Howie," Papa said, "my son has disgraced his family and himself, broken the hearts of you two good people, and brought into your home unbearable sadness. I can only apologize in the name of my family. I will take care of Fred personally."

When Fred came home Papa took him into the parlor and then declaimed, "Fred, you have disgraced your family. Here is twenty-five dollars. Go upstairs, pack your suitcase, and get out. I suggest that you go West, and when you have made a man of yourself, you will always be welcome here at your home—but not before."

Two weeks later, Fred wrote that he was a Jefferson guard at the St. Louis World's Fair, where he saved a Japanese lady's life when the Japanese pavilion burned. Out of gratitude, she wanted to marry him, so he took off for Oklahoma. Infrequent letters indicated that he worked as a section hand on the railroad, as chief cook and bottle washer on the Triple X Ranch, and finally as hired hand on a farm where he had to handle a team of four horses. He finally headed for Colorado. He wrote Mama a vividly descriptive letter of life on the ranch and followed it with one to me describing everything in even greater detail. Mama sent my letter to a farm magazine, *Green's Fruit Grower*, and they bought it for five dollars. When Fred got the news and the five bucks he immediately quit his job and borrowed enough money to start home.

One morning I saw a romantic-looking figure with a suitcase coming up the drive. It was Fred, his hair parted in the middle, looking lean and hungry in a new red turtleneck sweater. In the kitchen Mama fixed him an enormous plate of fried eggs and bacon, and as he did away with them he announced that he was going to be a writer.

He fixed up a studio for himself in the attic. A cot and washbasin, *Webster's Unabridged Dictionary* on an iron stand, a bookshelf full of O. Henry, Kipling, and Jack London, a typewriter on his big desk, the hide of a cow used as a carpet on the floor, an imitation human skull that served as a tobacco holder, a rubber tobacco pouch, and a Turkish hookah that purified smoke—all made a cozy den.

When Fred wasn't busy helping on the farm, he pounded out short stories on the typewriter. After a pile of rejections, he was published in *Black Cat* magazine and the *Saturday Evening Post*. Although he published a number of short stories, his problem was that he lived out his romances in real life and avoided any mention of love in his stories. This finally narrowed his work down to animal stories. A beautiful one about an elephant in India was published by the *Saturday Evening Post*. Then Papa moved in. He was proud of Fred, but felt it his duty to point out that Fred would ruin his career as a writer if he didn't include some love interest in his stories. He suggested beginning with animal mating habits and working up from there, because Fred knew so much about this from his farm life. Fred didn't take fire. Instead, he got a job as a reporter on the *Milwaukee Sentinel*.

Forty years later Carl Sandburg, who since his Wisconsin days knew Fred and the rest of the family, told me that Fred was then considered the best rewrite man on the paper. His fellow reporters thought his stories were just as good as the best by O. Henry (who was all the rage in those years). "Whatever became of him?" asked Sandburg.

I explained that he was an editorial writer on the *Milwaukee Journal*.

Sandburg took a deep draft of bourbon and asked with a kind of neigh, "And what was the woman's name?"

He was close to the target. Fred's wife Harriet told him to stop the short-story-writing nonsense and develop his newspaper career, so he burned all his manuscripts, including an autobiographical novel called *Zimmerman* that brother Bob said was marvelous. He worked his way up to editorial writer and, long before it was popular, became a leader in conservationist circles. His books on this subject were read widely and were used in schools. He did much to keep the natural beauties of fields, streams, and woods alive and unpolluted in Wisconsin with the same veneration and love of nature that was a dominating part of our life on the farm. His artistry was tied to nature, and his good works live on in the Wisconsin woods.

VICTOR SAUDECK, a member of Father's orchestra, was interested in Papa's student, Emma Felix, and came to see her at the farm one weekend. He brought his flute. When I saw the beautiful black wooden flute with silver keys, I knew I must someday have one and learn to master it. So it was to be, for although it was a mysterious instrument, and the keys seemed almost unmanageable, Mr. Saudeck taught me how to produce a few notes on it when I was seven, and I thank him here for showing the way to countless hours of pure enjoyment that still continues.

ᴙᴋ

IN ADDITION to his other talents, Papa was an omnivorous reader. The philosophers were his friends, particularly Schopenhauer and Hegel, and Spinoza, the last of whom he admired above all. Father was a nature worshipper and saw God in the workings of nature. His almost mystic identification with nature was transmitted to some of us. Sometimes he would stand on the hill for an hour to watch a storm come up. He enjoyed thunder and didn't seem to be much worried about lightning, even after it struck one of the trees in our yard and flashed through a screen door. He observed his own rule, "Never too much," for a healthy mind in a healthy body. He sat in a cold tub bath every morning for forty minutes while sponging his head and making walrus noises. He walked one or two hours daily to take care of his legs. He caught his first cold in decades when he was eighty-seven. He died at the age of ninety-three, so his rules certainly worked for him, but the bath treatment almost killed me when I tried it.

The table in the library was covered with the best magazines of the time: *Scribners, Atlantic Monthly, McClure's, Century, Redbook, Harper's, Ladies' Home Journal, Youth's Companion, St. Nicholas, American Boy, Dial, The Nation, Review of Reviews, Saturday Evening Post, Black Cat, Elbert Hubbard's Life's Little Journeys, Scientific American,* and *Green's Fruit Grower* were all there, along with morning and evening newspapers from Milwaukee in English and German.

The following excerpt from an article in the July 1906 *McClure's* was received with enormous interest by the family and was for a while thoroughly discussed:

New Music for an Old World
Dr. Thaddeus Cahill's Dynamophone
An Extraordinary Electrical Invention
For Producing Scientifically Perfect Music
by Ray Stannard Baker

Largest Music Instrument Ever Built. . . . Instead of bringing the people to the music, the new method sends the new music to the people . . . by opening a switch we may "turn on" the music. . . . Democracy of Music. . . . Dr. Cahill's instrument, without in any way overestimating its capabilities, or suggesting that it will displace the present forms of musical art, gives us a hint of what the music of the future may be like. . . . The best music may be delivered at towns, villages, and even farmhouses up to a hundred miles or more from the central station. Small country churches, town halls, schools, at present holding up no ideals of really good music, may be provided with the same high class selections that are daily produced by the most skillful players in the cities. . . . A HUNDRED INSTRUMENTS IN ONE. . . . Lord Kelvin encourages the Dynamophone. . . . Learning to play the instrument has been like some new wonderful discovery in an unknown musical world. Here were limitless musical possibilities waiting to be utilized. The musician uses his keys and stops to build up the voices of flute or clarinet, as the artist uses his brushes for mixing color to obtain a certain hue. . . . The workmen in the shop speak of "electric music." In the end the public will probably choose its own name. . . . WE SHALL KEEP THE OLD WITH THE NEW, but it would be absurd to say that the new instrument will ever seriously interfere with the presentation of great music of any sort. It will rather add to the public interest in music and the appreciation of musical art. . . . We welcome the new with eagerness; it has a great place to fill; it may revolutionize our musical art; but, in accepting the new, we will not give up the old.

The family had also been immensely interested when the Victor Talking Machine appeared on the market around 1902. A few years later we had Victor and Columbia machines in the house, complete with horns shaped like gladioli and a repertory that perhaps did not reach today's technical standards, but that provided music education, amusement, and entertainment. I recall Alma Gluck singing "Ave Maria" by Bach-Gounod and "My Heart Ever Faithful" by Bach; John McCormick singing Irish songs; the pop songs "Oh, Didn't He Ramble . . . ," "By the Light of the Silvery Moon," "Rufus Rastus Johnson Brown, Whatcha Gonna Do When the Rent Comes Roun'?"; the "Ave Maria" by Schubert; Brahms's Hungarian Dance in G Minor; Joachim Raff's *Cavatina for Violin and Piano;* and the popular melody *Carnival of Venice* for cornet.

Dix, who was on vacation from MIT, read the article about Cahill and immediately tried the phonograph, first without horn, then with a pillow stuffed into the horn. He cranked the machine slowly by hand and created speed variations that sounded screamingly funny, and led us to speculate about the future of music. We put pillows in the piano, made it into a harpsichord by weaving toilet paper through the strings, and tried other experiments, but the novelty wore off after a while and soon we were all back singing and playing as usual.

Slowly I began to be interested in and to follow the debates that Papa and the big boys had about what they read in the magazines. These were loud, and many centered around the Socialist Victor Berger. Berger was elected to Congress in 1911, and Papa backed him. Papa went on tirades against the trusts, the robber barons, the railroad kings, and other capitalistic adventurers, but also against anarchists who were throwing bombs—all of this in the great old political tradition that made our family leave Europe. My brothers were more conservative. I liked the rumpus and Papa's predictions of impending doom, which, unfortunately, had already hit us with the Depression of 1907.

YEARS LATER, I learned how Father bought the farm and how sadly it turned out. A number of his cronies in Milwaukee got involved in the back-to-the-land movement, Tolstoy's belief in nonviolence and the simple life, and almost Rousseauesque ideals. Uncle Edgar, an eye, ear, nose, and throat doctor, bought an apple orchard. Papa bought our farm. Everything went reasonably well until around 1906 when things began heading into the 1907 depression.

From then on, we could hardly afford food or produce that we didn't raise. When Papa was appointed professor by the University of Wisconsin, he had to borrow money to make the move to Madison. The collapse of the farm explained his pessimistic moods.

He had ended a distinguished career in Milwaukee. The Musical Society no longer gave the fine concerts that had gone on for seventy-five years. When I was four, I watched him conduct an enormous mixed chorus including a children's chorus. That ended his Milwaukee conducting activities for sixteen years. He seemed to sparkle with electricity as he led the chorus with great assurance and ran the rehearsal with a discipline that impressed me greatly. But the transition from local music director, composer, and conservatory director to academia was very hard on him, and eventually took its toll.

IN SPITE OF the impending depression we put up a good front. Occasionally we went to Milwaukee to visit Grandma and Aunt Gretchen. The city, with some monumental architecture like the Public Library–Museum, some colorful churches and homes, the Pabst Theatre, and the beautiful Lake Park, seemed grand and stylish to farm boys.

Grandma Jacobs, a typical German grandmother who sat in her rocking chair knitting, in a satin dress, her hair in a bun, spoke little English. She was kind, friendly, and loving. She didn't talk much but liked us to be around. She lived with Aunt Gretchen, a widow, at 422 Terrace Avenue. This very well built late nineteenth-century town house, on a bluff overlooking Lake Michigan, had a fine wild garden. At the bottom of the bluff a cultivated garden, livery stables, and a beautiful beach brought us right to the icy-cold waters of Lake Michigan. Uncle Frank Falk's early death was a great blow to Aunt Gretchen. For many years she retired to her room every day at four o'clock to mourn an hour and a half for her husband. Her social life dried up. She was only fairly well off and spent her entire income on helping out family members who were temporarily in trouble. She helped Mother when she became ill and used little of her relatively modest income for herself. I suppose she bailed every one of us out at least once.

On Thanksgiving and Christmas the entire family would come to her house to celebrate. There were many bedrooms and the younger generation would overrun the place. Her dinners were in the great family tradition because everyone brought special foods and helped, and Aunt Gretchen had a cook, a gardener, and a coachman. The dinners were served complete with cut glass, china the aunts had painted, silver napkin rings, old linen napkins and tablecloths, and silver that had been in the family for several generations. Aunt Gretchen was one of the first ladies in Milwaukee to drive an electric automobile—a slow contraption that did not have a horn but a bell that sounded like an alarm clock. Elegant it was, but not as good as a horse for either speed or endurance. After Uncle's death she lived, mostly at home, to the ripe age of ninety-four.

ANOTHER GREAT event was the circus parade.

Ringling Brothers circus headquarters was in Baraboo, Wisconsin. Their main publicity stunt was the circus parade. This elaborate spectacle passed through the main streets. It consisted of hand-carved and carefully painted circus wagons, some of which depicted events in the circus and others exotic scenes from foreign lands. There were some beautiful Greek, Roman, and mythological floats; a number of them were used as cages for the usual array of circus animals. All were accompanied by calliope music.

At the state fair in Milwaukee, I heard political candidates make their great speeches. With no other amplification but a good pair of lungs, they would bellow forth their messages. Robert La Follette, Sr., made his first bid for the Senate at the state fair. Both William Howard Taft and William Jennings Bryan spoke. Papa would get into a high state of excitement while these giants of the lecture platform stamped, snorted, and yelled their denunciations of the evildoers of the other party and hollered forth their promises for a better world to come—if and when they were elected. I can still hear Papa saying "What a splendid delivery," or "Mama, don't you think he looks very manly?" or "It's high time that we threw the scoundrels out!" Of course I hadn't the slightest idea what these giants of the platform were talking about, but Bob La Follette with his red face and white hair and William Jennings Bryan with his sanctimonious, postage-stamp diplomat's face made an indelible impression on me.

⊁⊀

THIS INNOCENT and beautiful life changed when I was enrolled in the Wauwatosa public school at the age of seven, and my brief formal education began affecting me. My reading, writing, and arithmetic as taught by Mother was sufficiently fluent to get me into third grade. The principal, Thomas Lloyd Jones, allegedly an uncle of Frank Lloyd Wright, said it was a crime to put me into such advanced company. Mother insisted and won. Intellectually I think she was right, but physically I had to match my muscles against those of boys and girls who were at least two years my senior, and it was difficult at times.

My lonely and self-centered life came to an abrupt end when I met the Winship twins, and it was a good thing because the depression began to nibble away at the life we had enjoyed on the farm. The twins and I became inseparable companions, and they were accepted not only by my entire family but also by the dogs.

My reports for third grade showed a yearly average of "Excellent" in reading, spelling, language, and arithmetic; "Poor" in penmanship; "Poor" in drawing. I was excused from singing. Too advanced! I was absent for forty half-days and tardy eleven times due to excessively cold weather or deep snow. We walked a mile and a half to school. In good weather we came home for lunch, which meant walking six miles daily. In fourth grade I averaged "Excellent" in reading, spelling, language, arithmetic, geography, and singing, every quarter.

Our music instruction was based on two books published by Silver Burdett, *Songs of America and Homeland* and *Rudiments of Musical Notation.* (It took a long time for me to get back to the Silver Burdett books, but when in 1965 I was appointed special consultant for basic music concepts for its series "Making Music Your Own" for elementary school students, I recalled my experiences in the Wauwatosa School and with early phonograph records, and how enormously they had helped me. I made twelve recordings with illustrations to be used for instruction in public schools. I used the same approach I had learned in Wauwatosa, considerably expanded. Most of the musical examples I used in the series I played myself.)

The Wauwatosa Public Library, one of the chain of libraries founded by Andrew Carnegie, was another source of enlightenment. Mother and Father had opened up their library to me on the farm and I had read *Huckleberry Finn, Tom Sawyer, Arabian Nights,* Jules Verne's *From the Earth to the Moon,* a collection of English fairy tales, and Jack London's *Call of the Wild.* Father told me that the village library had a much wider selection of books than our own and a whole section for children, so he got me a library card and turned me loose. I discovered series called "A Child's History of Greece" and "A Child's History of Rome." I read all thirty volumes before I was nine.

FATHER TOOK me to see some shows in Milwaukee. One of them, *The Red Feather,* was about American Indians. The leading lady, Cherida Simpson, a former student of Father's who had wowed New York, fascinated me. After we had waited for three long acts, a red feather dropped from her headdress. It was immediately spotted by both the spotlight and the leading man. He was wearing armor, but he bent over and with some difficulty picked it up, to the astonishment of himself and the audience—and with that won the fair maiden.

The famous Italian bandleader Creatore made a great impression on me. He was a "profile conductor" and liked audience participation. At climaxes he would swing around completely and conduct the audience so that they could watch his unique facial expressions. Although his mimicry was superb (fierce frowns and ecstatic smiles strengthened the music), he didn't have the martial dignity of Captain John Philip Sousa conducting "Stars and Stripes Forever." Captain Sousa, as the transitional passages began leading the way into the Trio of that gorgeous march, stepped aside without losing a beat, while an ensemble of eight trombones marched in strict time to the front of the stage followed by four piccolo players, also in step, who landed on a slightly elevated platform. On signal the trombonists raised the bells of their horns and blared out the main theme of the Trio, accompanied by the most magnificent piccolo obbligato in the literature of music. Just before their cue Sousa would turn around and face the audience with impeccable military bearing. Then, swinging his long baton down to his knees in perfect rhythm, he led the audience to the march's climax. Amid salvos of applause piccolos, trombones, and Captain Sousa would retire from the stage. His impressive performance contained within it all the elements of motherhood, the Marine Corps, pumpkin pie, and the Fourth of July.

Father also sent us to vaudeville shows. Seats in the gallery were twenty-five cents. The shows included jujitsu artists, tumblers, jugglers, and a magnificent acrobat who walked on all fours upside down with his back facing the ground and his stomach in the air. There was also a magician.

Inspired by such a display of art, we bought a box of magic tricks for entertainment on the farm. Bob limbered up until he could do upside-down walking. I became the foil for jujitsu and the farm became the training grounds for a circus. We tried to get the dogs to sit up and jump through hoops but they laughed at us and ran away with the hoop. We made this into a clown act.

The homegrown circus in the pasture cost one cent for admission and two pins for lemonade. Our audience consisted of the family, friends, and a few neighbors. I opened, dressed as a fat clown. My stomach fell down. The audience cheered. Bob stood on his head and the dogs knocked him down. Dix led the cows around the pasture, joined the parade, and knocked over our lemonade stand. The dogs chased the cows and Hans and I chased the dogs. Everybody thought it was part of the show, laughed themselves sick, and told us how clever we all were. It was then and there that I learned never to refuse a compliment, even when it isn't deserved. We admitted only that the cows were supposed to do other tricks but that they had forgotten them. Father said, "You must perfect this. You could make a fortune on the road."

THE WINSHIP twins and a few other school friends brought out certain suppressed sides of my nature with startling results. We did things on a dare. My initiation took place when they dared me to hitch freight trains for the half-mile ride to school. I was good at it, but occasionally a slow freight at the crossing became a fast freight before I jumped off. Sometimes I rolled into a cinder bank, bruised and scratched. These adventures came to an abrupt end when another boy fell under a train and lost both his legs.

Our daring soon changed into real rural juvenile delinquency. A village gang confronted me when I was crossing the Menominee Bridge and commanded me to throw a sack into the river. I feared that next they would throw me into the river, so I pushed the bag in and then simply stared the gang down and went my way to the post office. Having overcome my fright with dignity, I felt like a big shot and a tough and began to act like one, aided and abetted by my friends. I began a new career as a big spender. On the way home from school I invited all my old and new friends into the country store for a jelly-bean-and-cookie treat. I bought in large quantities and charged to my mother's account. My reputation as a sport was soon secure. A large group of admirers followed me on my way home from school, and Mother had a large grocery bill. She had a financial conference with me and the grocer at the end of the month that put an end to both my spending spree and my popularity.

One day, Glen Winship pulled a package from his pocket. "Have some?"

It was chewing tobacco. I took a small wad and soon learned how to chew and spit. For several months the twins and I were not happy unless we had our chewing tobacco, either Nigger Hair or Navy Plug. I kicked the habit when I accidentally swallowed a plug and became violently ill.

Then we tried our hand at smoking—first, with leaves, and

then with corn silk in cigarettes and corncob pipes. We discovered Cubebs, widely prescribed as relief for asthma. Finally we began picking up cigarette butts. One day, I found a nice one and lighted up. My father came sailing around the bend. He sized up the situation and said, "So you pick up filthy cigarette butts from the road. You've been around animals so long that you're beginning to act like a pig." Whereupon, with his eyes flashing, he slapped me on the mouth, rather gently. It was the only time he ever touched me in anger, and it made an impression.

Now THAT we had reached maturity our minds turned to sex. My background in this area was good, but the twins and their friends added information that was not only juicy but accurate. By the time we were eight or nine we not only had a theoretical knowledge of the whole business but a magnificent collection of pornographic expressions, plus an imaginary world of exploits that would have shamed Doctor Alex Comfort.

Women remained a mystery for me because their clothes at that time made them look like mummies. Even the girls at school were all buttoned up. Helene, Mama, Katy, and every other woman that ever appeared on the farm belonged to this strange tribe. My curiosity about what I might possibly find underneath all these adult swaddling clothes was insatiable. But romance and sentimentality were not openly encouraged on the farm. Love was considered a bit silly. Sentimental gestures, except on official holidays and birthdays, were ridiculed. Nonetheless, you can't stop a boy from dreaming, and I had wonderful fantasies about practically every woman I sighted. They seemed to notice this and were always very nice to me. Nights, before sleeping, my private life turned into a kind of imaginative harem. For the next twenty years, hardly any woman I met was safe from such speculations.

THESE EARLY experiences showed me that it was possible to have a secret life that was quite satisfying when the overt life was restricted. Papa didn't pay much attention to my musical instruction; both my piano practice and initial composing efforts became increasingly secret activities because I thought he wasn't interested in me. I learned later that we were already heading for disaster in the Depression of 1907 and that the poor man was having grave financial troubles. Mother told me that he earned about five hundred dollars that year. By 1908 he knew that the farm would have to be sold. Gradually the food began getting skimpier, there wasn't much money for meat, and some of the cows had to be sold, but Mother put up a good front. She invented glamorous dishes like red oatmeal. This was farina with raspberry juice, chilled in a fish mold. With a little milk it was handed out as a great and special treat. Goose fat on rye bread with a little salt was a special delicacy of the house. (The same kind of fat was rubbed on chests to cure colds and coughs.) A special recipe, potato pancakes with applesauce, became a main meal. I once gorged myself on twenty-one of them. Potato soup, farina soup, and lentil soup were other fillers. Burnt-flour soup, a sure cure for digestive ailments, was much in demand when Father thought he was about to die.

IN SEVEN YEARS on the farm, there was fortunately not much illness. Robert broke his arm about once every year. Helene had what would now be considered a neurosis—whenever it thundered she went to her room and locked the door. Mother had occasional severe migraine headaches. She took Bromo Seltzer and stood with her head against the wall, sometimes for an hour, until the headache went away. Dix and Fred were never really ill, and I don't remember Father being really sick until he was eighty-seven. I went to the doctor twice. Once I had eczema. He prescribed vegetable-silk underwear instead of wool, and told Mother my heart was too small for my body. Mother didn't pay much attention to this, but in very cold weather my fingers would turn waxy white, and this scared me. Mother got the circulation in shape by slipping my hands under her wool armor and warming them on her breasts. When Bob fell out of a tree and his heel landed on my left hand and splintered it, the doctor looked dubious but finally pronounced it a green-twig break. I had visions of a shattered left hand, but Mother made me rest and it healed.

Of course there were minor upsets but Mother, with the help of the German Dr. Bock's medical encyclopedia, *About Sick and Well People,* nursed us through. This masterwork was published in the 1880s and kept us going for years. Temporary lack of energy was cured by a whiff of ammonia. For severe croup, hot lemonade and camomile tea did the trick, plus a special hot bath before Saturday night. For severe cases Mother had an ample supply of other herb teas—peppermint, sassafras, linseed, and green tea. These were often served with rock candy. Linseed was also used as a poultice. Beef bouillon, for regaining strength, was made with a kind of beef paste. Farina soup, good for almost any ailment, was served plain with a few herbs and a touch of butter added for the sick.

From time to time, patients from Dewey's Insane Asylum escaped and visited us. Mother responded to their fantasies in a calm and interested manner. One of us would phone for a keeper, who would arrive saying, "Now, Your Highness, it's time to get back to the castle. Thank the countess for her hospitality."

⋊⋉

THE COMING mechanization of the world helped to keep the Winship twins and myself out of reform school. Aunt Gretchen's electric buggy and a Buick owned by a friend of Fred's were the only automobiles that ever drove to the farm. They were spectacular enough to transform our former destructive activities into caddying at the golf club for fifty cents an afternoon so that we could buy pop and indulge in spectator sports. Car watching was a fascinating one. Enough autos drove along Blue Mound Road to keep us busy for an afternoon. We learned to recognize most of them. There were Ramblers, Stanley Steamers, Buicks, Fords, Stutzes, Pierce-Arrows, and Rolls Royces; electric buggies, Cadillacs, Studebakers, Benzes, Daimlers, Oldsmobiles, Maxwells, Franklins, and Chalmerses. They were open, lumbering, noisy, puffy, shaky vehicles. All of them except the steamers had to be cranked—a dangerous job because the kickback could and often did break a man's arm.

Life on the farm slowly disintegrated during the depression. Dix left MIT after his sophomore year to get a job in a factory and marry. Fred made a weekly salary of seven dollars as a reporter on the *Milwaukee Sentinel*. Aunt Gretchen arranged to finance Helene's vocal studies in England. Hans and Bob had paper and magazine routes and caddied to earn money for new suits. Shorty and Katy offered to work for room and board only, out of loyalty and love for us all. Soon their own families felt the squeeze so they left, but Shorty came back. Mother's migraine headaches took longer to control and she moved more slowly as she tried daily to patch things up. She was often depressed and it affected us. I continued to sing and compose, and I learned the Mozart Fantasia in D Minor by myself.

There were long parental discussions behind closed doors. We overheard Father time and again: "But how can we pay this eighteen-dollar grocery bill?" or "Can't you make shorts for the boys out of their old overalls?" At the dinner table he would announce to Fred, "The miserable robber barons and the trusts are ruining us all." On one occasion Sandburg was there and a socialist state was developed in theory. "Money is the root of all evil. When speculators control it they control us. The state must step in."

Mother began selling things to make a few dollars. The decline of the farm was slow and depressing. The immediate effect this had on Bob, Hans, and myself was that we saw the world as a tough place and embraced the manly art of self-defense as a protection. We slowly became rather proficient boxers. We graduated from barefisted brawling to boxing gloves and could handle ourselves for a few rounds with considerable skill.

IN SPITE OF the misery of the depression, Mother and Father decided to have one more big festival for family and friends on July 26, 1908—their silver wedding anniversary. Aunt Gretchen contributed rather heavily to the festivities and they came off with unforgettable style. Twenty-one family members and fifteen students and friends of Father's conducting triumphs came. Tables were set in the dining room and on our large porch. All the family tablecloths and napkins, homespun in Holzen, Germany, by previous generations, were laid out. The best family china, hand-painted and carefully saved for several generations, and the old family silver were brought by the aunts. Gorgeous wine goblets, long-stemmed, many-colored, and with a marvelous sound as they were clinked, were taken out of closets and baskets by Uncles Edgar and Franz.

The celebration began with a quartet of Father's ex-students singing romantic German songs including the bridal hymn from *Der Freischütz*, "Wir winden Dir den Jungfernkranz" ("We Weave for You the Bridal Wreath"), a tribute Mother accepted with dignity as she stood next to Father, surrounded by her six children. A group of men sang some *"juch-he, juch-he"* choral songs that echoed through the woods.

All the aunts and cousins pitched in so Mother could bask in her glory. My brothers and cousins were waiters. Gasoline stoves and chafing dishes that were warmed with candles or wicks kept everything steaming. Preparations for the feast had gone on for ten days and the aunts brought in various dishes by horse and buggy well ahead of time.

The menu was patterned after one that was used for the duke of Braunschweig's wedding in Grandmother's native German province. It began with mulligatawney soup prepared from leg of veal, marinated herbs, whole white peppers and salt, cooked and then drained; a calf's head and a capon were added. Butter, onions, and garlic were cooked slowly for an hour; this, combined with curry powder, cayenne pepper, roasted flour, and lemon juice, made a dough which was added to the soup. Served with rice this magnificent recipe from the old German cookbook was an unforgettable overture for the meal.

Truffles in Burgundy was a second course. The main dish of roast beef (served with roasted potatoes, patties filled with small peas, puréed snails, young roasted pullets, and toast with ox marrow) was followed by Victoria pudding, homemade vanilla ice cream, and small cakes. The Victoria pudding, a meal in itself, consisted of beef kidneys mixed with bread crumbs, flour, apples, apricot marmalade, candied citron, dried cherries, sugar, salt, eggs, cream, and two teaspoons of cognac. This memorable meal was washed down with Rüdesheimer and Rhine wines, champagne, and then red French wine. After the feast everyone joined in a few more songs like "Still wie die Nacht" and "So leben wir" ("This Is Our Life," a drinking song).

The excitement gave me a hot head. I noticed how beautifully Mother was dressed in a low-cut gown that was such a contrast to the mummifying costumes she usually wore in the house. Father was magnetic and electric in turn, and cut up in great style with anyone within earshot. Before the banquet he outdid himself as he played Beethoven's Sonata in E Minor, Opus 90, as a musical farewell.

I learned much later what a magnificent front he was putting up. Three months before the silver wedding anniversary he and my Uncle August sold the old homestead, the Lüningsburg in Polle, Germany, for $2,500. Within the year the farm went to a relative for $500. The sale of cows, some tools, and chickens brought another hundred dollars. Father's Milwaukee empire and his dream of a quiet life on the farm faded away. We had a year to wind up our affairs, for Father had been appointed director of the School of Music at the University of Wisconsin, with the rank of associate professor. His despair lifted and soon he began looking forward to the new life with high expectations. Dix, who was now married, and Fred agreed to stay on the rather dismantled farm, watch it for the new owner, and take care of the dogs and cats.

Our last winter on the farm was heavy with snow. We used snowshoes, made a ski run down the hill to the barn, and sculpted enormous snowmen and snow castles. These we doused with water inside and out to create ice palaces that served as caves. But Hans, Bob, Helene, and I were becoming more interested in our new life.

WHILE WE were wondering how it would be in Madison, Mother, who was both a great collector and a great packer, saw to it that all of our important books, favorite toys, and tools went with us. Father's annual salary was to be all of $3,500, a staggering sum. A moving van with two teams of horses transported our furniture to the Chicago, Milwaukee & St. Paul station, where it was loaded in crates onto a boxcar on a slow freight train for Madison. It was the kind of train I had once jumped to go to school. Mother supervised in both Wauwatosa and Madison and not one thing was broken.

Trunks were hauled to the baggage room at the Wauwatosa station by a team and finally Father and Mother, Hans, Bob, Helene, and I got onto a large farm wagon supplied by a neighbor and were driven to the station.

Father, who knew what to do to cheer us up, bought parlor-car seats. We trooped in and sat at windows to have a last look at the farm and Wauwatosa and then to look toward the new land that would be our territory for the next years.

As he settled down, Father began playing with the gold watch chain that stretched across his vest. Then he declaimed, "Well, this is a new adventure, children; you will have an opportunity to go to the University of Wisconsin later and learn all of the things you don't know. You, Otto, will just go to school and help Mama, and Helene will be in Europe."

"And what will you do, Father?" the boys asked.

"I have planned to recruit an orchestra of eighty-five and a chorus of three hundred from the splendid young students who are at the University of Wisconsin. I think the first work I want to produce is Mendelssohn's *Midsummer Night's Dream*. We'll do it on the lake—the soloists in canoes, the chorus on rafts. The orchestra will be on a barge and for the fairy scene I'm sure that we could arrange some very amusing things by having the actors fall out of the canoes into the water. Tiny magic lanterns and sticks of punk offshore will simulate fireflies. I am looking forward to a beautiful new life, where I can serve art and humanity in a humble way following in the footsteps of such giants as Wagner and Beethoven, but we must eat now, it's late," and he led us to the dining car.

After a sumptuous meal of tenderloin steaks with trimmings, Father lit a cigar, blew smoke rings that his eyes followed dreamily, and in his rich baritone softly intoned, *"Nur wer die Sehnsucht kennt, weiss was ich leide"* ("Only he who has felt longing knows how I suffer").

Mama dabbed at her eyes. "Papa, that's so beautiful."

Chapter 4

In Town: Madison, Wisconsin
1909-1912

THE TRIP TO MADISON was my first train ride and it was exciting
to see the various lakes on our way. In Madison we carried our
bags from the station to a stuffy hotel. The next morning we all
piled onto a streetcar that landed us within two blocks of our new
home.

The house was painted like the one in Wauwatosa, light
yellow with white borders, but it was a great disappointment for
it had nothing else in common with the farmhouse. Madison Avenue was a dirt street, tarred occasionally to settle the dust. Side-
walks were of wood. The houses and lots were all about the same
size. Architectural designs varied little and the decorative element was the paint job on each. There was a medium-sized front
porch facing the front yard, which was twenty-five feet square.
The back yard, about twenty-five by a hundred and fifty feet, had
a small vegetable garden where we later grew salad greens, radishes, and excellent wax beans and Swiss chard. A small back
porch and a toolshed completed the estate. Mother had furnished
the house a month before. The entrance hall was tiny. In a small
library-study on the left were a sofa and a modest collection of
German and English books. The music-sitting room on the right
housed the Steinway and a few chairs. A dining room with our
leaf table had only enough room to seat six people. The kitchen
was too small to do any of the preserving we were used to. The
basement had a dark game room. Electricity consisted of a few
dim bulbs and we preferred our old oil lamps from the farm. The
sleeping quarters on the second floor were modest: a room for
Mother and Father that held two small armchairs, a dresser, and

a double bed; a room for Bob and Hans; one for Helene; and a small one for me. The attic was used for permanent storage. After Wauwatosa the house seemed crowded and cramped, but when Father was out of the house there was more time for piano practice, composing, improvising, and reading than in Wauwatosa.

Neighboring houses crowded us, but there was an empty lot behind the garden and there we played horseshoes, batted and played One Old Cat, and even kicked a football around. All the children who lived on the block came out to play on the street and in the lot in the evenings. The games were tag, hide-and-go-seek, marbles, stickball, and penny tossing. Curfew was at eight o'clock, when mothers appeared on the back porches and let out yells for their offspring to come home. Walking around the immediate neighborhood brought us no further than the butcher and the grocery store, and although some streets were shaded by rather nice trees and the lawns were well kept, there were few flower gardens and I found the whole neighborhood quite uninteresting.

Dean Sellery, Professors Wagner, Turnure, Buell, Ross, and Prokosch, and their families, were our university neighbors. Most of them lived on University Heights, and I thought them a bit snooty. But Professor Prokosch became our hero when we heard that he had learned twenty-two languages as he pumped water from his well on the farm where he grew up. The Randall School, five blocks from our house, became the center of some of my activities for the next three years. I entered fifth grade.

SCHOOL WAS a bit more difficult than it had been in Wauwatosa because a number of faculty children attended and some professors were on the Randall School Board. I took to geography and history in a big way. I read much outside of class. In class I did a lot of reciting from "classics" such as *The Lady of the Lake, Hiawatha,* and *The Courtship of Miles Standish*—mostly from memory. We read aloud from *Walden, Thanatopsis* by W. C. Bryant, and from other American authors. The drama of literature soon began to impress me, and my recitation of *The Charge of the Light Brigade* was cheered and became a model for elocutionists. In music the instruction was in group singing. We used the Silver Burdett Bronze books with folk songs from all nations in good translations, arranged in unison or two parts, unaccompanied, and in four or five easy keys and different rhythms. Twice weekly the music teacher came with her pitch pipe. She had a way of throwing out her enormous bosom and relaying to us in a large soprano voice the pitches she heard on the pipe. She had a large tremolo that gave us leeway of at least a quarter and sometimes a half tone above or below the pitch. She conducted with enthusiasm and everybody had a good time and learned new keys, new rhythms, and new songs. The solid foundation laid in Wauwatosa was continued in Madison and became one of the cornerstones of my musical life. The only other school music was a four-hand piano march to exit by and for fire drills. I resented deeply that in my three years at the Randall School I was never asked to play that march. This is undoubtedly the reason that sixty-eight years later I demand occasionally that my wife, Catherine, play a four-hand march with me.

We did much drawing and painting but my work was considered too arty; teachers preferred the work of Emil Schmidt, who knew how to copy illustrations in magazines, and they predicted a brilliant career for him. I thought he was too slick. He later sold greeting cards.

The Indian tradition in handicrafts was kept alive in many Wisconsin schools, and manual training was an important extension of skills needed on the farms. My efforts in the latter were limited for I was afraid of cutting my hands and slowing up my piano practice, but I did produce a very nice breadboard and a wooden bowl. When it came to mat weaving, necklaces, and moccasins, the Indian in me came to the fore and I produced several attractive and serviceable table mats, one of which is still being used in my household.

In Madison, arithmetic problems were more concrete than the magic with numbers I had learned in Wauwatosa. I have kept some problems since 1911. One was about a farmer who raised thirty-eight acres of oats averaging forty-eight bushels an acre, and how much his profit would be if the oats were sold at 48⅛¢ per bushel. On the finer calculations in this problem, I not only worked out the cost of the oats but the cost of a horse needed to market the oats including fourteen dollars for bedding and fodder for seven months. We were being geared to think big, and my interest in arithmetic diminished from week to week as the transactions grew more and more colossal. I took my brothers' high school algebra book and tried to learn it by myself but failed.

In geography, history, and research generally, we used the textbooks approved by the school board. I was assigned to do a paper on one of the Civil War battles. In our home library I found textbooks my brothers had used that seemed much more detailed than the schoolbooks. I used the references as footnotes on my paper. My teacher told me to stop including extraneous material and to stick to what I found in the regular textbook. This constructive experience taught me the limitations of classroom learning. In silent protest I began exploring our home library and read what I could find there about the Civil War, the American Revolution, and the Black Hawk Indian War fought near Madison. I was given the two wonderful William H. Prescott works, *The Conquest of Peru* and *The Conquest of Mexico,* and my interest in them and in many of the other books I discovered at that time continued for years. Arthur Conan Doyle's Sherlock Holmes books were among these. Robert Louis Stevenson and Jack London were two of my other favorite authors. The books and poems we read in English class became dramatic events in my imagination, but *Walden* was so close to my own experience in Wauwatosa that I relied on it to help me find some connection with nature in the new and strange surroundings in Madison.

To GET OUT of the house my brother Hans and I explored the county on ten- or fifteen-mile weekend hikes. We found Lakeview and Pheasant Branch and discovered the beauties of Eagle Heights and Blue Mound. Near Lake Wingra we saw our first automobile accident, in which eleven men were seriously hurt—a rare event in those days. On the Saturdays when we did not hike, Mother arranged for me to help the mailman, so I delivered mail on one side of the street and he on the other. This lasted for several months and I thought of it as a career more glamorous than streetcar conductor or motorman. Occasionally a lady would invite us in for coffee or milk, but someone reported that the United States mail was being delivered by a ten-year-old boy, and a postal inspector arrived and suggested that I resign. From then on my interest in the postal service was limited to stamp collecting.

I made heroic attempts to make life as interesting as it was on the farm. In winter there was often a foot of snow, and cutters and other sleighs were the means of transportation. I hitched to school on the runners of sleighs. It was fun, but some drivers whipped their horses just before we arrived at school, and we were either thrown off or had to jump before the ride became too dangerous. School sports were loosely organized or nonexistent, so we arranged snowball fights between classes, complete with forts, tunnels, commanders-in-chief, and soldiers. There were sometimes regular army infantry maneuvers at Camp Randall near our house. We kids would gather there and get a postgraduate course from the soldiers in sex instruction, pornography, and dirty stories. Father stuck to his premise that we were to have no money unless we earned it, so we were quite busy. In summers, Bob got jobs as farm helper. Hans drove an ice wagon. I mowed lawns, delivered groceries, picked strawberries for two cents a box, and weeded gardens. There wasn't too much energy left for us to get into real mischief.

CHILDREN AND parents were immensely relieved when the second Boy Scout troop in Madison was organized in our neighborhood with a twenty-year-old scoutmaster and all the paraphernalia. Our uniforms, like those of the U.S. Infantry, included campaign hats, leggings, and gun-metal buttons. The Scout handbook told us marvelous things about camping, hiking, swimming, outdoor cooking, tying knots, and handling canoes and rowboats, as well as first aid and public health. I was elected assistant patrol leader and treasurer. Dues were two cents a week, but parents pitched in to purchase uniforms and a hunting knife, a knapsack, a flashlight, and a walking staff for each of us. We often hiked thirty miles in a day. Our outdoor cooking was primitive: corn, baked potatoes, and occasionally a fresh-caught trout. The meals were topped off with fresh-picked wild berries.

≫≪

THE FIRST months in Madison were very unsettling for me. Helene was with us for a short time, but she and Father were not speaking so Aunt Gretchen sent her to London to study voice with Blanche Marchesi. This Father considered a further insult.

Bob and Hans attended high school. When Father was at home none of us talked much or did anything but study because the house was so small. Father and Mother had great discussions about his plans and we heard everything. He said none of his children were to be musicians, myself included, because a musician's life in the United States is too hard. This hurt me. The house was too cramped for me to have my friends visit so I turned to music when Father was gone and reading when he was in.

Father became more and more moody, and when he wasn't preparing a concert the atmosphere was pretty unbearable. His temper improved only when he played Beethoven sonatas. Hans almost stopped talking, but then blew off steam by doing very interesting, wild improvisations at the piano. Father heard him once and said it was all nonsense, so Hans quit playing. Bob had been criticized so much that he left the house whenever he could and only spoke to Father in bad German. I concentrated on piano practice and stamp collecting. I discovered some modern compositions by Max Reger, Philipp and Xaver Scharwenka, and Debussy, and taught myself some of them and read the rest, an exciting adventure because the sound was so new. I played movements from the easier Beethoven and Mozart sonatas; and as Father would not give me lessons I taught myself, out of boredom, to transpose them into many different keys. Mother bought an eight-keyed French piccolo and an instruction book, so I began teaching myself that stirring but sometimes painful instrument—when Father was out of the house.

As time rolled on I discovered James Fenimore Cooper's *Pathfinder* and *Deerslayer*, which made me look at Wisconsin's Indian background and local Indian history. Our neighbor Charles Brown was head of the Wisconsin State Historical Society and showed me and his son Odie a great collection of Indian relics. He arranged for the three of us to measure and mark Indian mounds in the neighborhood, to explore and measure Indian burial grounds, and to hunt for arrowheads. This was a mysterious adventure, particularly when he explained the symbolism of the mounds, which were in the shape of birds and other animals. Sometimes we did find arrowheads, a few beads, a thong, or a piece of a bow. Mr. Brown was a professional and our surveys were so good that I discovered in 1965 that some of the measurements we made in 1911 were still on file at the State Historical Society in Madison.

Mother and Father showed their usual disapproval of the Madison school system when, with some neighbors, they organized experimental classes in God-knows-what, under the direction of a nice English gentleman named Lloyd George. Naturally I was immediately enrolled, but I couldn't at the time figure out what the gentleman was trying to do or say. Now I believe that he was trying to help us find certain ethical insights, and I suspect that the whole business was an early exercise in progressive education. My particular genius was in giving wrong answers unintentionally, but to the great amusement of the parents—who "observed."

Mr. George told us about Napoleon, his conquests, and his dictatorship, probably to make us recoil. When he asked, "Now, why don't I like Napoleon?" I jumped forward with "Because you're an Englishman"—to the astonishment and guffaws of the gallery.

Our good teacher took it in his stride, but went into a long-winded story about a bee that had been flying around making honey and in general leading an active life. Then he asked (I imagine to illustrate the possibilities of conflict and confrontation) what he would do if he walked into the bee and was stung.

The class didn't seem to react. But to save the honor of the group, I raised my hand and announced, "You'd say 'Ouch!' "

Now this good Englishman did not know what "ouch" meant, so much time was spent explaining why and when in America we say "ouch." He found this very interesting, but he and the bee got off the track and nobody remembered what the story had been about.

Then, with the professional poise of an enlightened teacher he volunteered, "You mean you would cry out?"

I considered the whole business hopeless and nodded my head as he fumbled ahead to other deep topics.

CHRISTMAS WAS uneventful and depressing. Father's secretary at the university had tipped him off that the president was searching for a man to replace him. We overheard Father's discussions with Mother and pieced together his story, although it wasn't until some time later that I really understood it. To keep my sanity I played more piano, improvised, and read the original edition of *Grove's Dictionary of Music and Musicians,* almost from cover to cover.

Father's appointment at the University of Wisconsin had been initiated by Aunt Gretchen's brother-in-law Otto Falk, a wealthy businessman and a general in the Wisconsin militia. The trustees Thwaites and Vilas nominated him, while President Van Hise was searching unsuccessfully in the East for a director for the School of Music. Father was appointed acting director for one year at a salary of $3,500. From some of Father's letters it appears that President Van Hise told him the permanent director would need a Ph.D. and a music degree in addition to other qualifications. At the beginning of his appointment Father had high hopes and didn't seem to get the message that the president wanted him out before he had even arrived.

Father's first budget letter to the dean was unique in the annals of American universities. He philosophized about the American fear of poverty and mothlike habits of flying into dazzling light and splendor; just why, he didn't explain. He stated that his own qualifications were second to none. Then he unloaded his rather heavy humor, saying that he didn't plan to embezzle any of the funds that would be entrusted to him. He asked for $5,000 to give brilliant concerts with star soloists, a large chorus, and a good orchestra. He explained that only big things musically would bring big returns. He recommended that his secretary's annual salary be raised to $500. The band leader had asked for a raise to $150 a year. In a jovial tone Father asked for a Steinway piano and announced that the typewriter had shown some signs of rheumatism.

President Van Hise worked in the fields of geology, microscopic petrology, and the conservation of natural resources, and he apparently neither knew nor cared anything about the arts. He turned down most of Father's requests. Within a month, Father again wrote to the president with complaints, and sent copies to the dean and to Mr. Thwaites. Then, in January, the president announced that Louis B. Coerne, a Harvard Ph.D., had been appointed director but that Father could stay on with permanent tenure. Father reacted by suggesting that he give a performance of Bruch's *Lied von der Glocke*, and that the regents guarantee to meet the deficit. Dr. Van Hise was startled and suggested a regular budget. Father settled for a performance of Haydn's *Creation* with piano accompaniment and tried to line up support for his ventures in other schools and departments, starting with the German department. President Van Hise counterattacked by calling Father to task for not having a counterpoint class. Father said the students were not ready for counterpoint and needed elementary musicianship. Dr. Van Hise paled. "Harvard offers counterpoint; Yale offers counterpoint; the University of Wisconsin must offer counterpoint." Father saluted but prepared an ambush.

When his semester grades were turned in, he received an irate call to see Dr. Van Hise immediately. As Father told the story, the president opened up with, "Professor Luening, I have your grades for strict counterpoint. On the scale of one hundred the highest mark you have given is forty-eight, and there are four zeros. Why, if this were done in every department we would have to close the university. Can you explain yourself?"

I wasn't there but in my mind's eye I can see Father leaning back looking innocent and sincere as he said, "I was being generous. Bach gets one hundred. I myself don't get more than seventy-five."

Dr. Van Hise sputtered and muttered, "We will have to change these grades. Good day," and opened the door.

Father carried on his losing battle courageously but he made other plans at the same time.

I DECIDED to cheer up Father by playing a piccolo solo for him on his birthday. I settled on "The Marseillaise." While Father was having breakfast I posted myself in the library and played. I knew nothing about attacking tones and my embouchure was breathy and rather wavery. This I confused with feeling. When I finished, there was no sign from Father. I coughed and played again. There was still no reaction so I went to the dining room where Father was wiping his mustache, which had trapped a bit of egg yolk.

"Good morning," he growled.

"Good morning, Father."

"What was that noise I heard coming from the library?"

I coughed, "Um . . . uh, I was playing a piece for your birthday."

"You were playing a piece? I can't believe that was playing. I thought it was a squeaky water tap."

On this cheerful and encouraging note I sneaked out of the room and resolved to continue my piccolo activities in private.

Father tried to heal his wounds by reading Schopenhauer. This great man's writings convinced Father that all human beings are bastards and not to be trusted, a conclusion that Father had just about reached by himself. I learned that Schopenhauer played the flute, which was nice, but in spite of his profound insights he once lost his temper and threw his housekeeper down the stairs. I asked Father, if Schopenhauer was such a great philosopher why did he toss his housekeeper down the stairs? Father lost his temper and told me to get the hell out of the house and play ball. Later he read Schopenhauer's "Essay on Women" and told me that the Master had proved conclusively that women weren't any good.

"Does that go for Mother?" I asked.

"Well . . . Mother may not be an intellectual giant, but she's good-hearted."

I asked Mother about this.

"I know when to shut up," she said.

Whenever Father had an uncalled-for outburst of temper, Mother would apologize for having caused it. This made him doubtful and he would read Goethe to calm himself. Once this resulted in the profound saying "It takes a lot of people to make the world go round." When I remarked that I thought it turned around without human help, I triggered another black mood and he grumbled, "You know what I mean; don't ask such stupid questions."

FATHER HAD built up an active musical life without much help. He conducted the Madison Male Chorus, arranged chamber music recitals at the university where he often played, introduced some good singers whom he accompanied, and coached in programs mostly from the German repertory with a few semipopular songs to hold the audience; occasionally he played a Beethoven sonata in recital. This impressed his two teaching fellows, Le-land B. Hall, who later had a good career in the Midwest, and Arthur Locke, who eventually became head of the music department at Smith College. They asked Father to coach them in the Beethoven sonatas. He also engaged visiting artists: the brilliant Steindel Trio—Alvin, violin; Ferdinand, piano; and Bruno, cello—all of whom, like myself, landed in the Stratford Theatre movie orchestra in Chicago ten years later. Apparently chamber music didn't pay well. The Kneisel Quartet played Beethoven and Schubert in Madison, German-style, without much vibrato, but precise rhythmically and nicely in tune. The few concerts I was taken to were a great stimulus to me.

The music event of the Madison years was a concert by the New York Symphony Orchestra with Walter Damrosch conducting. It was the first time I had seen or heard a full symphony orchestra. The beautiful shapes of the string instruments, varnished with shades of brown and sometimes yellow; the woodwind instruments, in those days made of wood with a beautiful array of silver keys, mysterious and complicated; the shiny brass instruments and the forbidding timpani and bass drum made me want to have something to do with an orchestra. And the artists in full dress with white ties looked magnificent. Walter Damrosch had the airs and manners of the ambassador to the Court of St. James. When he conducted he projected the dignity of Metternich presiding at the Congress of Vienna. His conducting was restrained but the program was dashing. Isadora Duncan danced Beethoven's Seventh Symphony. She pranced about on the stage trailing a pink veil, sometimes winding herself up in it and sometimes daringly showing some bare shoulder. Her impression on me was that of a woman with great vitality, athletic and fun to watch as she created gestures supposedly to make Beethoven's symphony more palatable. Mother thought she was pretty risqué, trotting around in public in bare feet, but Father found the whole business a definitely needed shocker for President Van Hise and his stuffy university faculty. I believe the orchestra played the Overture to *Tannhäuser* also, but nobody noticed it. Isadora was the star.

Father was nurturing new plans. His former contempt for capitalists, robber barons, and trusts was now transferred to the University of Wisconsin president who had insulted him, and to the faculty. After attending one or two University Club meetings, he described his fellow professors as being hypocritical, deceptive, cowardly, rude, and probably dishonest. So he built up a following off campus. In the male chorus he discovered that Carl Fischer, the bookkeeper for the ice company, had an extraordinary voice. Father coached him without pay and Fischer began singing beautifully. When he sang Francesco Paolo Tosti's "Goodbye Forever" at concerts, and on "goodbye forever" let his voice slide from a high B-flat down to croon in his middle range, the audience sighed with satisfaction.

✄

FATHER SUDDENLY called a family conference one evening and looked very important. Hans, Bob, Mother, and I waited anxiously for his message.

"I have something to discuss with you that you must not divulge to anyone or it won't work. I think Fischer has the makings of a first-rate German opera singer. I will teach him an hour every day free of charge. He knows nothing about singing or music. He should be ready in about a year. Then I will take him to Germany for auditions and prepare him for the German stage. I shall take a leave of absence without pay."

Mother looked shocked. "But how will we live?"

"Fischer and I will give recitals in Europe; this will attract students, and I will establish myself as a vocal coach second to none, in one of the great music centers in Germany."

Hans asked, "What will we do? Come along?"

"No, that would not be advisable or practical. Of course, Mama will come and we will have to take Otto, he's so young," he said rather disapprovingly. "No, you boys must go on in school. I will get you a small apartment. You can take what furniture you need from the house. I will give you thirty dollars a month for three or four months. You will find jobs and have a fine time living your own lives. Perhaps you can even work your way through the university. This will make men of you," he said ominously to the boys who were just eighteen and twenty.

They looked startled, and I was cowed, but Mother said, "Father, that's the best idea you have had since you decided to perform Beethoven's Ninth Symphony in 1899. We can go to

Braunschweig, visit Polle and Holzen, where our parents came from, and enjoy the wonderful prinzregenten torte that they just don't know how to make over here. After twenty-five years, how wonderful it will be to return to Europe!"

Helene returned from England in the winter of 1911 with an English accent and ideas about singing that made Father livid. She continued her silent treatment and said only good morning and good night to him, in German. He heard her sing and decided it was all wrong. Scenes developed between Helene and Father—and Helene and Mother, who tried to mediate. We boys just kept out of the way.

FATHER HAD been notified that his salary had been cut to $1250 for the first semester and that his leave of absence without pay had been granted, so he decided to leave in March of 1912. His plan was to build a private class in Munich, to earn enough money in six months to have Mother and me join him, the boys having by then presumably recovered from having been kicked out of the house into their own apartment.

Mother filled some trunks with his finest clothes (including a dress suit and patent leather shoes), the best books in the library, and the choice scores from the music collection. Proceeds from the sale of the farm and what he had saved from conducting and private lessons gave him just about enough to make it, but it was pretty risky business. Still, he had perked up considerably and looked bristly, electric, and confident when he kissed us goodbye to leave on his journey. He was sixty but he looked fifteen years younger.

THE HOUSE was dead and empty without Father and his moods. I played piano a lot and learned a Schubert impromptu, which I loved because the melody and the rhythms were so clear. A piece by Max Reger—quite modern, difficult and almost atonal—and some composing satisfied my artistic nature. I graduated from seventh grade in June and this ended my formal education. In July I entered a track meet and lost all the events except the wheelbarrow race. Hot and tired after the meet, some of us walked a couple of miles to Picnic Point, swam, and walked back. I felt strange. Mother sent me to bed.

I had nightmares and my head seemed about to burst. In the

middle of the night I had fantasies about Ellen, who used to sit in front of me in school and with whom I had been secretly in love. She was beautiful and sweet but had died two months before, at age thirteen. In my dream I thought she was in heaven and that I spoke to her, for in my nightmarish visions I thought I had died and was with her. All through the night I thought I was dead but when the cool morning breeze came through the window I felt pain in my feet and legs and that brought me back to consciousness. I told Mother I ached all over and couldn't move my legs very well. She diagnosed growing pains, made me stay in bed, and got a doctor, who diagnosed muscular rheumatism and prescribed several months of bed rest. He gave me medicine and put me on a diet of vegetables and gruel.

The pain and muscular stiffness worked their way up from my ankles to my calves and crept a little higher each day. I couldn't move at all and figured out that if this stiffness kept advancing it would reach my hips and I wouldn't be able to walk; and then it would reach my heart, and I would die. Day and night I seemed to be fighting this mysterious enemy, trying to keep it from doing fatal damage.

Bob developed facial neuralgia and lay in great pain in the room next to mine. Helene wound up in her room with nervous prostration. The family doctor was a busy man. There were no therapists or psychiatrists available to help with emotional problems, so Mother became the nursing angel and faith healer. The atmosphere that she and I were trying to dispel was the gloom, the sense of loss, and the fear of weakness and destruction that had begun to infiltrate our lives six years before on the farm in Wauwatosa. Since then we had had to give up the good and natural things little by little, move about, change, adjust, and learn new habits in a crazy-quiltlike pattern.

For myself, the lonesomeness of having to do all the creative things I liked most—music, drawing, reading—by myself and practically without direction was exhausting psychically. The mysterious muscular rheumatism began improving in about six weeks. By September, I was up and walking a little.

Father had written a letter from Munich saying that Fischer was a great success and that he, Father, had six students at from five to thirty dollars a week, plenty to start a new life. So Mother closed up the house, sold the piano, put things in storage, settled the boys in their apartment, and took trunksful of things to furnish an apartment in Germany. Most of the familiar objects and furniture now disappeared from my life like the animals on the farm, and the Wauwatosa woods had disappeared when we moved to the city. Mother withdrew the last of the money from the bank and bought two tickets to Munich. In two weeks I learned how to use my muscles and passage was booked for October. The doctor thought the sea voyage would be beneficial.

In Chicago we saw brother Dix and his wife, Marge. They had had a baby, making me a twelve-year-old uncle, which made me feel better. We took the 20th Century Limited to New York. After a bus ride that showed us Riverside Drive, Fifth Avenue, and the Flatiron Building, we sailed on the S.S. *Pennsylvania* of the Hamburg-America Line, and crossed in two weeks. Sea air, sea baths, deck games, walking around the promenade, and eating much fish seemed to restore my strength. But in Hamburg my left leg was still weak because of previous injuries and the illness. It was shorter than the right one, and I walked with a slight limp.

Since then, doctors have been unable to pinpoint what that illness really was, but I think I know how it happened. Being overheated, then chilled, swimming in possibly polluted water, and overexertion certainly contributed to my breakdown. But I believe also that I had so strongly identified with the farm that when I was left to my own resources in music, art, and reading, and when Father finally took off with a stranger, I felt that our whole establishment had crumbled into nothingness; I was tired of fighting, so I crumbled with it. I'm inclined to think that some of the boys' and Helene's problems had similar causes. It was Mother who taught us all to be patient and to have faith.

Chapter 5

An Unconventional German Education
1912 - 1917

WHEN WE ARRIVED IN HAMBURG it was cold and damp, and I was still sick. We were met by Aunt Josephine, a very high-strung lady who was married to a bandbox-correct, heel-clicking, charming German naval officer. Anxious to make a good impression on my mother, he took us to the Alster Pavilon, a fancy café-restaurant where we clinked glasses through a magnificent dinner. While we had dessert and he sniffed brandy the orchestra tore into a potpourri from one of Puccini's operas. My two girl cousins, aged thirteen and eleven, began sniffling and then burst into tears. I inquired what the trouble was and Sabine whispered, "We always cry when we hear music in a café." For a Wisconsin boy it was all very strange and I was glad that we left for Munich the next day.

Father was earning thirty dollars a week, a generous income for the three of us to start a new life in Munich, and we looked forward to such luxury. The train trip was exciting because the little village and town houses looked like those I used to put up with my building blocks in Wauwatosa. At every stop I noticed the station name, "Abort." I yelled to Mother that we were in Abort again. Everybody laughed. Mother told me to pipe down and explained that *Abort* meant toilet, and told me not use words until I knew what they meant. I blushed.

We arrived in the great station in Munich that evening and Father embraced us fondly. Bristly, commanding but friendly, he hailed a taxicab with an imperious gesture. This, my first taxi ride, was to the Pension Romana at Akademiestrasse 7. Father paid with a twenty-mark gold piece, tipped generously, and told the cabby to help the house porter haul the bags to the pension so that Mother and I would arrive in proper style.

The owner, Fräulein Riesenhuber, curtsied, smiled, and to my astonishment welcomed us as Frau Professor and Herr Otto. Our pleasant rooms had high ceilings, all the amenities, and large feather beds that seemed to billow halfway to the ceiling. In an hour the dinner gong sounded. Father ushered us into the large dining room where a dozen people were sitting at table. Frau Professor Luening and Herr Otto were introduced to Herr and Frau Doktor Hübner, Baronesse von Haxthausen, Gräfin Bothmer, Herr Diplom Ingenieur Schmidt, a Herr Oberverwaltungsrat ausser Dienst Rindfleisch, and others. After each introduction, Father would give me a slight bump in the rear with his knee to remind me to click my heels and bow. I caught on fast.

FATHER INSISTED that we become acquainted with the art world. He had arranged that his friend Carl Marr from Milwaukee, now professor at the Academy of Visual Art, invite us to visit his studio the day after we arrived. In the wing of the enormous academy building there was a vast room where, behind huge hangings and high ladders, there was a colossal painting by the recently ennobled Professor Carl von Marr. Professor Marr told us that *The Raising of Lazarus* was commissioned by a South American multimillionaire who wanted it for his vast hacienda in Rio de Janeiro.

Mother and I were speechless because of the mural's size.

Father was impressed but soon cooled down. Pointing to the hand of the main figure, he asked, "Marr, is the nail on the little finger intentionally so square or did you perhaps miscalculate?"

Marr stroked his Vandyke beard thoughtfully, took a good look at the nail, backed off several feet, sized up the hand from another angle, and finally brought out a very fine brush, putting in a black edge about one-sixty-fourth of an inch thick and one one-hundred-and-twentieth of an inch long. He backed up to where Father was standing. "Has it improved?"

"Much better, Marr, much better."

Father's classes grew rapidly and we soon moved to more

spacious quarters, an elevator apartment at Tengstrasse 33. The furnished apartment had a silent piano keyboard so I did silent finger exercises while Father was teaching. Father told me that to learn the scores Richard Wagner had copied all of Beethoven's symphonies, so I began copying music. Father didn't believe in schools so I wasn't attending. Officially I was a truant, but the authorities didn't catch up with me for four years. My parents did nothing about music lessons but I practiced piano and piccolo and copied music for an hour and a half a day. Eventually I worked five or more hours a day on music.

To earn spending money I ran errands and was elevator operator for Father's students. My income was a dollar a week. While bringing students up in the elevator, I got to know them. They had daily lessons. Carl Fischer of the Madison ice house was making a fine reputation. Frau Ackerman and Fräulein Ackerman (later Fischer's wife) were also frequent callers. They taught me to play chess and other games with them and Fischer in their apartment while having tea and rum. Mr. and Mrs. Rieder from Madison were attending the university and lived at the Pension Führman in Schwabing where the sisters of the famous World War I ace Baron von Richthofen were fellow boarders. By keeping my ears open I learned about the many avant-garde artistic and "free love" events taking place at this pension. For the business world, Father told me, I must become more independent and fearless and learn how to handle money; so he also made me his rent agent. Every month I took ninety-five marks in cash and walked eight blocks to pay our landlady, Mrs. Hammond.

Father's most glamorous student was Frau Doktor Hübner, a very beautiful contralto who was married to a nonproductive Ph.D. The good doctor seemed to be honored that his wife was being pursued by Prince Georg of Saxe-Meiningen and Baron Leist. My other elevator pals included our neighbors Count Bopp von Oberstadt and General von Nagel zu Aichberg, who was chief of staff of the Bavarian army. The Bavarian Princess Gisella once rode with me, adding more royalty to my clients. Lothar Hoffmann, a student who drank until three or four every night, sounded like a foghorn when he had his morning lesson. He was so frightful that General von Nagel zu Aichberg sent his orderly one day to ask if the lesson would soon be over.

I was accepted as an adult by my new friends because I never patronized adults. The Germans soon learned their lesson and didn't patronize me either, probably because I was so different from German boys. My new friends were interested in my musical studies and philosophical observations, and I in turn was interested in their work and ambitions. They rewarded me by introducing me to café life, taking me along to the Hofbräuhaus, and, with the help of Mother and Father, teaching me to play solitaire, euchre, poker, and a German game called Sechs und Sechzig (Sixty-Six). When I was not at the opera, we often played cards until late at night.

Frau Hübner, Prince Georg, and Baron Leist were my closest friends. The prince called for his "flame" after her daily lesson and while waiting he told me all about himself and his brother, who was a composer. Prince Georg was twenty-six, six-foot-four, and nearsighted. He constantly pushed a monocle into his left eye, which made him look very aristocratic. Baron Leist had perfect vision but he too liked to push a monocle into his eye for the same reason. Frau Hübner invited me to visit her and told me all about the life and times of her two boyfriends. I could see that both of them had to get on the right side of me and her boxer dog Putz if they wanted to make any headway with her. She told me that Prince Georg was an important and busy man. He often went to balls, came home at 6 A.M. dog-tired, bathed, had his breakfast at seven and was at the university at eight. For a while he was accompanied by three adjutants, but she finally convinced him that her boxer and I were sufficient protection, so the prince dismissed the adjutants.

When the prince first came to the apartment, he left two visiting cards, one for Mother and one for Father. He was handsome, likable, and very courteous to my parents. From the beginning he asked my opinions about everything under the sun and seemed to like my unself-conscious responses. One morning he showed up in a morning coat and a silk hat that made him look about seven feet tall. He was to have lunch with Prince Regent Luitpold of Bavaria.

A small entry in my diary said: "He always looks at the stuff I copy and talks a lot with me. . . . He is just like a brother to me."

Frau Hübner reported that at the luncheon with the prince regent the court guests remarked that Papa was the best singing teacher in Munich. I think they remembered that Lüning was an old German name.

≫≪

MY RECOVERY from illness was slow. Mother and Father's theories of convalescence—doctors were not consulted—gave them an excellent excuse for just letting me roam around to pick up information where I could find it. There was a certain method in their madness. Father prescribed a daily walk of about an hour or an hour and a half. With a map and a Baedecker guidebook I worked out a schedule for museum, gallery, castle, and park exploration. Nobody told me where to go. I learned by what modern educators call the "discovery" method. Mother believed in at least ten hours of sleep to get ready for these tours. It took all of four years, but I got to know the town like a book.

I walked the broad streets, went into Bavarian baroque churches, and saw the castles built under the shadow of King Ludwig I. It was so impressive and at the same time so pleasant that I made the transition to European life and culture rather painlessly. The Englischer Garten was great for walks and one could stop at a café and have ice cream and tea. The park went through the middle of town. It was perfectly safe for a boy to go everywhere alone and almost every street was interesting.

The Deutsches Museum was a treasure trove not only entertaining to a boy but an educational resource. There were beautifully constructed experiments in aeronautics, electricity, and radiology for the visitor to do.

A harmonium in third tones fascinated me. Primitive flying machines varied from imitation birds and gliders to one that the inventor thought he could pedal through the air. It reminded me of my experiments with brother Dix in Wauwatosa. As I discovered the museum's resources they became one of the most important forces in my education.

The astronomy exhibit, with all kinds of telescopes and photographs, opened up new vistas. The chemistry experiments I could do by following directions, seeing how things worked, and observing the results. My diary read: "I have found out that one must really study the things in a museum and not just glance over them. I saw how an automatic telephone works. I also looked through telescopes." There was a beautifully constructed model coal mine, a "rocket" model steam engine, and an original engine called Puffing Billy. I took X-rays of my hand, and saw just how the X-ray machine and my hands functioned.

I did further study of early flying machines including the original Wright biplane and the Blériot and Rumpler monoplanes. The latter had made history with a flight from Munich to Berlin. Benjamin Franklin's printing press was in a room with early writing machines that were precursors of the typewriter and the teletype. I saw the departments of optics, geology, electricity, spinning and weaving, and acoustics, a study that I followed for the rest of my life. The Deutsches Museum introduced me to the world of the future and prepared me to meet it.

IN DECEMBER 1913, Mother took me to my first moving picture. The admission price was fifty pfennig. The program included two bad features, two cartoons, and one short showing Annette Kellerman swimming. Another moving picture show had very good American films that didn't jerk. Three out of five were entertaining (funny) and admission was minimal. Later, Mother and I saw Edison's latest invention, the Kinetophone. It was probably one of the earliest demonstrations of "talking pictures."

The newspapers were printing ominous items about an artistic revolution called Futurism. King Humbert of Italy had been assassinated in 1900. King Emmanuel liberalized the government. By 1907 the Futurists in Italy were active. Manifestos about the world of the future came from Marinetti in 1907, then from Pratella and Russolo about music and Boccioni about sculpture in 1912. All of these disturbing proclamations reached Germany.

The Glass Palast held painting exhibits of the Secessionist and Blaue Reiter groups in 1911 and 1912. News came from America that a wild man named Ornstein had played a piece called *A la Chinoise* and actually composed a "Wild Man's Dance" that shook up the concert-going public. Even at the Pension Führman a cavalry officer, Major Netto, recited futuristic poems and gave pornographic lectures. He was definitely ahead of the army.

The new world of art and my discovery of and reaction to

painting had a telling effect on me. The new art was pretty shocking at first and seemed "crazy." But soon these exhibits of modern art and poetry readings began to have a liberating influence. I liked the drawings of George Grosz, published in the satirical magazines *Simplicissimus* and *Jugend,* which tackled royalty, the clergy, and the military. Kandinsky and Macke excited me because they used such fanciful, lively colors and forms. Their work seemed much closer to me than many of the classical paintings I had seen. Paul Klee appealed because he saw things very much the way I did as a child in Wauwatosa.

MY SISTER Helene liked to visit the Pinakotheken with me to see classical and nineteenth-century paintings. I was indifferent to the Rubenses, Van Dycks, and Rembrandts. On a second visit their beautiful sketches impressed me and made them seem more human, and helped me to understand their major paintings. I discovered the angularity and colors of fifteenth-century art. All I could afford were Munich scenes under glass for between five and thirty pfennig. I felt that the higher art was out of my reach. Among the nineteenth-century painters I did like was Goya. He seemed to have an imagination similar to Edgar Allan Poe's and Hawthorne's. Böcklin's *Toteninsel,* with its morbid tone, appealed to me. I was trying to read Lenau, Eichendorff, and Hölderlin poems and was open to this romanticism. Lenbach seemed a modern extension of the Rembrandt tradition and Von Stuck influenced many of the up-and-coming avant-garde. I found his pictures a bit like the imaginative world of MacDowell's music and some of Poe's stories.

I was sightreading works by Max Reger and read that he had composed music based on pictures by Böcklin. I went to the Schack Gallerie where I saw a larger collection of German romantics: Feuerbach, Schwindt, Lenbach, Böcklin, and Spitzweg. This introduced me to a new type of German romanticism.

I READ that Arnold Schoenberg had won the Liszt Prize on the recommendation of Richard Strauss.

Father sent me to get some of Schoenberg's music. I found his *Harmonielehre;* the piano pieces, Opus 11; the Five Orchestral Pieces, Opus 16; the *Gurrelieder;* Two Songs for Baritone and

Piano, Opus 1; his string sextet *Verklärte Nacht;* the F-sharp
Minor String Quartet, Opus 10; and the Chamber Symphony No.
1, Opus 9. Father read the scores and announced, "This man is a
great master. It's not my type of music, but he's a great master.
Now, my boy, we'll start studying his *Harmonielehre.*"

He went through the first few lessons with me and I did a
few pages of exercises. I was astounded that Schoenberg could
start with the same materials I had learned in Wisconsin and expand them step by step into a new world of sound. I worked over
every example, on paper and at the keyboard. I was further impressed when a painter who had seen Schoenberg's *Self Portrait
from the Rear* decided that the man was completely mad. I began
devouring his scores and was elated when I found "Ach, du lieber
Augustine," one of my Wisconsin German songs, in his Second
String Quartet. It was a contrast to the cosmic illuminations he so
beautifully expressed by setting the Stefan George poems for the
last two movements. The latter's "Litanei" seemed to me melodious but mysterious and esoteric, and his "Entrückung"—"I
breathe the air from other planets"—transported me. I played the
slow piece from Opus 11 on the piano, and found the free sounds
refreshing.

Schoenberg's philosophical and aesthetic comments also
made an enormous impact on me. I gained technique from his
musical examples and courage from his philosophy. I explored
new territory and my compositions became much more free and
inventive. I felt quite secure even though I was breaking away
from the traditional music I knew.

THE AMERICAN Library at Salvatorplatz 1 was another source of
education. It was a simple reading room with an Episcopal chapel
at the far end. The collection of English and American books, en-
cyclopedias, and reference sources was good. I discovered Oscar
Wilde's *Picture of Dorian Gray,* which fascinated me although I
didn't really understand it, and much Edgar Allan Poe and Mark
Twain I hadn't known.

Tea and toast were served in the afternoon at the library for
fifty pfennig (twelve and a half cents). The American colony consisted of students, exchange professors, well-to-do American
women who had married German officers, and a few mysterious

male and female characters who generally came at five for an hour of gossip.

I FIRST SAW the full spectacle and dazzling power that royalty and the military machine exercised over the German people at the funeral of Prince Regent Luitpold on December 12, 1912. Kaiser Wilhelm II, the heads of the other royal houses in Germany, and dukes and princes of smaller states were followed by foreign royalty and diplomatic representatives. All were in full-dress uniform with jangling sabers and chests covered with medals. The procession was preceded by a long parade of crack Bavarian troops in field uniform. Hundreds of thousands of people lined the streets, applauding and cheering the royal parade, proudly affirming their allegiance. It seemed as though more than half of the townspeople were in the lines.

By reading German magazines I learned about contemporary life and the German point of view. Sometimes Father would show us around the city and comment on everything. One Sunday he took us to Dachau by cab. This was a real German idyll with a lovely old castle and garden. We had a fine meal in an old restaurant, paid for in gold, of course. As we walked around the village, everything looked beautiful and Christmassy. The trees glistened with frost. A blackbird sang.

I saw Dachau again in 1936. The idyllic village was gone. It had become a jail, a barracks settlement, and later a human incinerator. Carl Jung once wrote that only a nation as sentimental as the Germans could be so brutal. It made me wonder.

✄

IN 1913, MOTHER arranged tutoring for me with Dr. Carl Loewe and his wife. I was to study German, French, Latin, arithmetic, and geography. I finally talked them into ancient and modern European history instead of French and Latin. I was tutored every morning for an hour and then did homework. They drilled me in German grammar, the articles and genders, and how to write in the old German script. Their instruction was so solid that I never forgot how to speak or write German and in the 1970s I was still writing articles for German books.

After mastering grammar I was introduced to German lyric poetry by reading, reciting, and singing Goethe, Heine, Bodenstedt, and Hölderlin. Then I read longer poems like Goethe's tragedy *Götz von Berlichingen,* and also northern mythology. I constantly carried a German dictionary. After less than seven months I wrote a long essay in German script comparing America and Germany in every way I could imagine.

Dr. Loewe called me for a conference when I was not yet sixteen. He addressed me over a cup of tea. "Otto, about your education. You speak two languages, know how to use a dictionary and an encyclopedia, and you respond to symphony concerts and the opera. You have learned how to use a museum to gather information and you know your way around the American Library and the Bavarian State Library. You have been to Munich's great art galleries and have reacted to the paintings. You play piano and piccolo, know harmony, and can read music. You can deal with adults and have even done some tutoring yourself. You are an educated man. How you use your knowledge is up to you. Stand on your own feet now and decide what is important in your life and use the learning tools you have to pursue your ideals by yourself. You need no more lessons, my boy. Good luck to you and keep in touch."

This was a continuation of the parental philosophy of do-it-yourself, but Dr. Loewe made me feel strong. All I had to do was stand on my own two feet!

IN APRIL 1913, I discovered and began to study the Berlioz orchestration book in the edition of Richard Strauss, a wonderful book that described the functions of the individual orchestral instruments as well as their expressive and poetic qualities. I loved Berlioz's text. I copied sections from Haydn's *Symphony in B-flat Major,* Gluck's *Orfeo und Euridice,* the Good Friday Music from *Parsifal,* and Beethoven's Fourth Symphony. This taught me about the clarity of Haydn, the poetry of Gluck, and that *Parsifal* came right out of Beethoven's slow movements.

FATHER HAD SAVED some money and as usual had to figure out how to spend it. A vacation in the mountains was the answer. Mother found a house in Rottach-Egern am Tegernsee. Father convinced all of his students, including Frau Hübner, her boy-friends, and her dog, that they needed some Tegernsee mountain air to reconstruct their health.

We took the top floor of a typical Bavarian peasant house that had one extra downstairs room with a wood-burning stove. The barn and manure pile were at the rear of the house; a primitive bathroom over the barn had a galvanized iron tub for bathing and a two-hole toilet. The furniture included puffy feather beds. We had breakfast on the lovely balcony with fresh-baked country rolls, fresh butter, honey, and café au lait. When Father found a beaten-up old grand piano he was in business.

I celebrated my thirteenth birthday in Rottach-Egern. Father made me his assistant and I taught his students the elements of music.

Maria Stadler, the daughter of the primary school principal in Egern, was the musical spark plug for the entire region. She was an accomplished violinist, a good pianist, an attractive singer, and a good conductor. She studied voice with Father and I took violin lessons from her. She introduced me to many new friends, including the Slezak family. Leo Slezak was a famous tenor at the Vienna Opera House and at the Metropolitan Opera in New York. He was an international star. Gretel, his thirteen-year-old daughter, was my first love. She became a famous operetta singer in Vienna. His son, Walter, age eleven, later became a movie actor in the United States. The Slezak establishment consisted of Leo and his wife, mother-in-law, sister, cousin, and two children, as well as the French teacher, German tutor, governess, cook, janitor and wife, second maid, gardener, and music coach. Their garden was two acres square and they all had coffee and torte every afternoon.

Fräulein Stadler taught all the children in the neighborhood. She was a devout Catholic and for the Sunday Mass rounded up the professionals, amateurs, and students in the vicinity to rehearse and perform simple German masses by Johann Aiblinger and Max Filke under the direction of her father. This was my first encounter with what I call, now, "music for use"—moderately difficult but artistic music composed for a specific purpose and also intended for practical use by amateurs. It was my first experience in an orchestra. I played violin and flute. When I heard horns behind me and the chorus in front, clarinets on one side and the organ on the other, it was scary. After a few Sundays I felt quite at home.

Fräulein Stadler's forces included Carl Müller, a medical student who was an accomplished pianist and a fine sight reader; Herr Schuster, the concertmaster of the Mannheim Opera; and Frau Generalarzt Zollitch, the wife of a general in the medical corps. This lady was in her seventies. She was covered with warpaint and various paddings but was a tireless and good pianist who loved to play flute sonatas with me. Baron Schallach was in the audience. Countess Bothmer was a Munich operetta singer who studied with Father. Many others came and went but I was always taken along, the only boy in this company of adults. At first, I was official page turner and handyman, but I had taught myself to play the piccolo and I brought along some potpourris of Verdi operas for piccolo and piano. These Frau Generalarzt Zollitch sandwiched between a Beethoven sonata and Mendelssohn's Violin Concerto in E Minor. I also was drafted to play Haydn and Beethoven symphonies transcribed for four hands.

I had learned the flute by the summer of 1915 and played Kuhlau sonatas. Kuhlau seemed to me to be the Beethoven of the flute. I then tried three Handel and Bach sonatas with Frau Generalarzt. It all culminated in 1916 with a benefit concert for the Red Cross in Egern that included trios by Kummer, Handel, and Hummel, played by Fräulein Stadler, Herr Müller, and myself, and we raised quite a bit of money. The concert was repeated two weeks later, again for the Red Cross, and I felt very professional.

FATHER'S IDEAS about physical therapy were simple: his cold tub every morning and a walk daily. His motto was "Never too much," and he couldn't be cornered in this. I once asked him if there were such a thing as too much wisdom and he answered, "Certainly, and it's very bad." When I asked him whether one could be *too* virtuous, he advocated kicking over the traces every now and then.

Father perfected his therapy for me when we went to the Tegernsee for Easter. We took a long walk along the lake. After a while he faced me. "You are in Bavaria now, my boy. Become a Bavarian. Make friends with the peasants. Now we will climb that mountain." He pointed to one about three thousand feet high.

We changed direction and made the ascent. I felt like a hero. Later at an inn, while we were having refreshments, he sounded off. "You must build up your strength, my boy." I was still catching my breath after the ascent. "Don't be so lazy, my boy. Move! Move! You must strengthen and harden yourself if you want to accomplish anything in life. You should take a cold bath every morning. It's good for the nerves."

OUR PEASANT neighbors had a get-acquainted Easter-egg hunt. They asked me to join them and help them feed the chickens. My Wisconsin experience came in handy. They hid eggs in the fields, in barns, haylofts, pigsties, and between rocks in the river. It took hours to find them. I had doubts about the whole peasant business but when we came back in the summer I went right on with my ethnic studies.

Rottach-Egern seemed to remind Father of his "back to the land" days in Wauwatosa. He began reading Tolstoy again and urged me to latch onto all the peasants in the neighborhood, promising it would be a new experience. He suggested that I make myself useful to the peasant population.

At first, this population seemed strange because there were some retarded children around, dwarfs, hunchbacks, idiots, and tottering old folks; but there were also some very nice-looking peasant girls with dirndl outfits that showed their charms to great advantage. When one of them looked at me invitingly and sang "Uff der Alm doa gibts koa Suend" ("On the Alp There Is No Sin") it got me thinking. To integrate me with the peasants Mother went the whole way and bought me leather shorts embroidered with a ribbon on the side, woolen calf-warmers, hobnailed boots, linen shirts, green and red ties held in a ring made from a deer's antlers, a green-trimmed gray loden coat, a blue linen jacket for warm weather, a knapsack large enough for a day's supplies, and a big loden coat that covered everything in case of rain. I got along fine with the peasants and became friendly with some enormous bearded woodsmen and hunters and their kids. I saw that these families took care of their mentally retarded, crippled, sick people, and even the alcoholics who got frightfully drunk every night and made a horrible racket when they came home from the inn. All peasants had great manure piles behind their houses and pigsties pretty close by. This was less refined than the farm in Wisconsin, and Father's vision of idyllic peasant life wasn't quite true to life.

The peasant theater performed peasant plays by Ludwig Thoma. The music was played by zither and violin. The Bavarian dialect was so thick that I could not easily understand it. A peasant band played Suppé overtures, including *Poet and Peasant—Dichter und Bauer*—and polkas. The players were so bad that they had to be floated to a raft a mile offshore to make their intonation tolerable. One Saturday the peasants and all of Father's students, including the prince, the countess, the baroness, and Frau Hübner, danced a *Schuhplattler* at the inn. This is a jig where a stein of beer must be downed between each round. In about an hour and a half everyone was dead drunk and the party and dancing became very funny as everyone rocked to an unsteady close.

By now, Father's physical training and ethnological education began to blend. I hauled and piled firewood with my peasant friends, worked in the fields, pitched hay, did broadjumping, threw the javelin, and played ball.

I was in pretty good physical shape, so Father thought he ought to do something about it. "My boy, you see these mountains around here." With a sweeping gesture: "You must climb every one of them. They are not high and it will give you a view of the world that you don't get in the valley. And take a daily swim in the lake." I remarked that, fed as it was by mountain springs, it was cold as ice. "That will toughen you," he pointed out. Then he rented a two-man boat ("I will teach you how to row"). He took me on the lake and showed me how to handle the boat and suggested quite a bit of rowing ("It is good for the chest").

My parents were absolutely fearless, so I tried everything and soon I was in very good physical and mental shape. I swam halfway across the lake and back without a boat and once rowed for four hours to the end of the lake and back in a rough storm. Occasionally I packed my knapsack and climbed a mountain. The climbs, some five thousand feet high, were easy, and at the inns on the slopes I could get lemonade and a sandwich and admire the alpine panorama. I took my piccolo and played tunes when I had reached the peak. On the climbs I picked alpine flowers for Mother.

≫≪

IN THE FALL of 1913, Father had a large class in Munich, so we moved to Georgenstrasse 40, a beautifully furnished garden apartment. He bought a Bechstein grand piano and engaged a butler by the name of Lorenz for sixteen marks a month plus room, board, and a uniform. Father paid all bills with twenty-mark gold pieces.

We were close to the big military parade ground, so I watched soldiers drill and the primitive attempts at military flying. The soldiers were mostly peasants or men from the "lower classes." Noncommissioned officers worked them to death. Bayonet drill was brutal. Commissioned officers showed up only for maneuvers. The gossip was that war was inevitable and the army had to be made strong in order to defend Germany from encirclement by France, England, and Russia.

The Munich garrison was expanding in 1913. I sensed how important the army was in the lives of the Germans. Although flying was in its infancy, there was a pre-Zeppelin balloon called *Parsifal II* that soldiers held on a rope. A monoplane flew around it low enough for me to see the pilot leaning out of the cockpit to orient himself. Planes reached altitudes of about a thousand feet. The balloon descended while planes flew around it. Thousands of people watched this very daring business. A few biplanes flew around at altitudes of about two hundred and fifty feet. A few officers stayed aloft for all of two hours, a record.

Joseph Brucker, an explorer and balloonist who knew Father in Milwaukee, came to visit and told us about his proposed balloon flight over Germany to test wind currents. He was a very romantic figure and explained the dangers of ballooning and the difficulty of raising money for balloon flights. He thought of balloons as a new and important means of travel. In February 1913, his own balloon, *Suchard II,* was scheduled to ascend from the parade ground. The grounds were fenced in but I found a knot-hole and saw that the bright yellow balloon, including basket and netting, was about sixty-five feet high. Two companies of soldiers kept it steady with ropes. *"Abfahrt,"* coughed the captain and in two minutes the balloon was lost in the clouds.

The press reported next day that the "round and free balloon *Suchard"* had floated off in the wrong direction and landed in a peasant's field in Luxembourg. Brucker had not told us his real destination, and he didn't return. His flight preceded those of the many Zeppelins that began floating around the place a year later. Flying machines, as the airplanes were called, flew in increasing numbers, and in a few months the famous French stunt flyer Pégoud did fantastic flying in a light monoplane—single and double loops, upside-down somersaults, and other swoops.

I wrote in my diary: "It was just like watching a bird. I was speechless. Papa thinks that I will live to see the day when there is an airship."

Later in 1913 came maneuvers on the military parade ground. A batallion from the noncommissioned officers' school was followed by half a dozen regiments of crack infantry, several of sappers, artillery, heavy and light cavalry, lancers, the King's Guard, and air corps officers, with five flying machines hovering overhead. The troops were reviewed by Bavarian and visiting royalty, medals sparkling in the sun, on prancing white and black mounts. Prince Regent Ludwig of the long white beard was in charge, followed by Crown Prince Rupprecht, Prince Franz, Prince Konrad, and the fourteen-year-old Prince Luitpold, who looked marvelous in his lieutenant's uniform. Then, to my great astonishment, I saw my friend Prince Georg of Saxe-Meiningen in the uniform of a first lieutenant, with a monocle in his eye. I waved to him; he saluted, his horse snorted, and everybody noticed.

FATHER WAS remarkably generous about letting me select concerts or operas to attend. Admission was one mark for standing room and I was soon going out three or four times a week. Father gave me yearly tram, museum, and gallery tickets so life was active and interesting.

From the winter of 1912–1913 until I left Munich in 1917, I

attended the Sunday-morning concerts of Bruno Walter and the Munich Court Orchestra. I first heard Walter conduct when he performed the *Mass of Life* by Delius, a fellow student with Father at Leipzig. Delius lived in Florida in his youth and was self-taught. This was the first contemporary oratorio I had heard and I liked its exotic quality.

Until the beginning of World War I, the military bands played in halls and parks all over the city. Grieg, Johann Strauss, Bizet, selections from *Rienzi, Rheingold, Siegfried, Tosca,* and *Feuersnot,* marches by Richard Strauss, and selections from Chabrier's *Gwendoline* were heard. The Germans were really fond of music and thousands attended these concerts.

Generalmusikdirektor Walter ran not only the symphony concerts but the Royal Munich Opera and the Oratorio Society. His second program included Beethoven's Fourth Symphony and Wagner's *Faust Overture.* Both of them made indelible impressions on me, the Fourth because of its lyricism and *Faust* because of its drama. The *Symphonie fantastique* of Berlioz seemed noisy but very descriptive.

Richard Strauss was the great German modernist in symphony halls and opera houses, and famous as a song composer throughout the world. I first heard his *Macbeth* and was not impressed, though I thought two baritone songs with orchestra were first-rate. I noted in my diary that *Don Quixote* and *Don Juan* were too noisy for me. I knew Lenau's poem *Don Juan* and thought that Strauss's tone poem was rather crude. A week later, I heard *Death and Transfiguration* (in Germany announced, of course, as *Tod und Verklärung*), and was sufficiently conditioned to his style to find it especially fine. Under these musical conditions I began developing likes and dislikes.

Ferdinand Loewe was the regular conductor of the Tonhalle Orchestra. He was a student of Bruckner and a fanatical advocate of the Bruckner symphonies. He was an excitable but very good conductor. I heard a half dozen Bruckner symphonies in Munich. The slow movements always impressed me with their wonderful singing quality. The outer movements seemed like some of the mosaic ceilings I had seen in art galleries, rather out of control. Loewe projected the symphonies beautifully, but I got an early overdose from which I have never quite recovered. Bruckner struck me as being an overblown bore except in his slow movements. Loewe also played Pfitzner, who at first made a stronger impression on me than most of Strauss. Brahms's Third Symphony also had a great impact. Later, when I discovered Haydn, Mozart, and Beethoven, I turned away from the Brahms symphonies.

The famous Meininger Hoforchester gave a concert under the equally famous Max Reger. Germans considered him in the tradition of the three Bs, and he was the most popular concert composer in Germany. Alcoholism ruined him and he died at age forty-four. I had already heard him play piano beautifully in concert, but he had to be helped on and off the stage. Under his leadership the Meiningen Orchestra gave a very smooth, silky performance; I thought the brass was more refined than Munich's, and the strings played with uniform bowings. Reger performed his own four tone poems of Böcklin's pictures: *Der geigender Eremit, Spiel der Wellen, Die Toteninsel,* and *Bachanal.* I knew the pictures and found his pieces new and colorful, and his performances of Brahms's Second Symphony and *Serenade* and Beethoven's Egmont Overture overwhelmed me. Reger was enormously fat and conducted while sitting in an armchair, but the music was clear and elegant.

Bruno Walter performed a number of Mahler's symphonies. I thought they were melodious. However, they did not seem to make an impression on the younger generation. I liked Mahler's orchestration but did not get to know the symphonies well until several years later. Walter regularly performed the classics such as Haydn's *Creation* and *Four Seasons* with the best soloists from the Munich Opera. His reading of Mozart's Requiem made an indelible impression on me although I was only fourteen. I felt the tragedy and the sadness. Beethoven's Missa Solemnis was equally convincing. So was the brilliant Verdi Requiem. Bach's St. Matthew Passion and St. John Passion seemed dull and long, and the recitatives were a real bore. It took quite a few years for me to repent.

Walter played all the Beethoven symphonies. The Second, Fourth, Sixth, Seventh, and Ninth were performed with transcendent clarity and great expressive power. The Mozart E-flat, G Minor, and *Jupiter* symphonies were performed with an incredible elasticity and a rubato that was somehow related to the tone quality and the typical sound of the Munich orchestra. With the *Rhenish* Symphony of Schumann Walter seemed to project visual images of the Rhine. Schubert's *Unfinished* Symphony and *Rosamunde* Overture, Mendelssohn's *Midsummer Night's Dream* music and Violin Concerto in E were rapidly paced but with a beautiful, limpid tone quality that was never sentimental.

The first opera I heard Walter conduct was Strauss's *Der Rosenkavalier*, on April 9, 1913. The staging was beautiful and the singing fine, and the orchestra played with élan and rhythmical flexibility. The second beats of the waltzes were a little ahead of time to give them a lift. The Munich Orchestra's tradition went back to Richard Wagner and had been continued by von Bülow, Anton Seidl, Felix Mottl, and Strauss. As an ensemble the players were unbeatable and the overall tone was remarkable. Details were not always sharply etched and performances were not as brilliant as they are today. Since then, pitch has risen more than a half tone and the tendency is to push dynamics to extremes. Walter was a lyric, romantic, gestalt artist. He paced *Die Meistersinger* so beautifully that it didn't seem a minute too long and the Finale startled me with its strong vocal counterpoint. *Das Rheingold* was my favorite because it was short. *Götterdämmerung* and *Siegfried*, in spite of fine performances, seemed much too long. I gave a detailed critique to my father: "Bearded men in Nordic costumes with horns on their helmets and heavy women on their arms stood still and sang for twenty minutes in ununderstandable German and it seems to me to be theatrically dull and funny." I was deeply impressed by the drama and music of *Der Fliegende Holländer*, and I liked *Lohengrin*. I did not yet know that the perfect Wagnerite knows the libretto, the leitmotivs, the philosophy, and the piano score. Today, a recording of the entire work helps, but then there were no records.

Hermina Bosetti and Maria Ivogün were my favorite sopranos. The former could sing a beautiful Eva in *Meistersinger* and was a rather opulent coloratura. She was elegant in *Die Lustigen Weiber von Windsor*. I heard Ivogün do the Doll in *Hoffmanns Erzählungen* and fell madly in love with her. She was only twenty-two when she came to the opera. This remarkable coloratura sang virtuoso passages with great security but with limpid tone quality. After singing Sophie in *Der Rosenkavalier,* many Mozart roles, and *La Traviata,* she won the reputation that she could sing anything, brilliantly and beautifully.

Richard Strauss regularly conducted his *Elektra, Salome,* and *Der Rosenkavalier,* and a series of Mozart operas. Strauss was a dramatic maestro. Walter conducted with large movements and used any gesture to make the orchestra play; Strauss used a long baton and conducted from the wrist. Strauss's beat was small and very, very clear. His pacing was on the fast side, but he knew the form of the operas so well that proportions were never lost and everything held together whether he chose a fast or a slow tempo. When conducting Mozart at fast tempo, Strauss never pushed the voices beyond what they could sing convincingly. Each scene was a complete picture in itself but was related to the preceding and the following sections so that the pacing always seemed right. I heard him do *Die Zauberflöte, Die Hochzeit des Figaro, Don Giovanni,* and *Così fan tutte*—all, as by custom, in German. He made the orchestra into an instrument that responded to his vision of dramatic values. It was a lyric-dramatic sound, but not mellow.

Superficially, his conducting seemed matter-of-fact, but he coaxed and carried away his singers and orchestra until they became part of the big musical picture or musical poem he wanted to project. There was no time for meditation or personal interpretation. This was most noticeable in *Elektra* and *Salome.* He was a composer-conductor for whom the composition was supreme. *Don Giovanni* did not sound like the psychotic ravings of a sick man, but rather was strong, mature, and straightforward in its presentation of a dynamic life that led to ruin. Strauss built a dramatic climax that started with the overture and ended with the last note. The famous minuet was played at a very slow tempo. The lyric coloratura and humorous passages moved forward rapidly with no trace of sentimentality and Mozart's clear, clean, and dramatic vision came through. *Die Zauberflöte, Così fan tutte,* and *Figaro* followed somewhat the same interpretive lines but naturally with greater or lesser intensity depending on the stylistic differences in the scores and libretti. In *Figaro* he moved the work in an ascending curve from the overture through the finale of the second act. The rest of the opera he took in a curving, lyric, dramatic line that culminated in the lovely finale of the fourth act. He projected a large picture within which all of the small sections were related. Singers and stage action had to fit into his symphonic ensemble. I can say that I think his Mozart performances were the healthiest I ever heard.

Strauss appeared quite often as an accompanist for famous singers like Claire Dux, Lotte Lehmann, Hermine Bosetti, and Maria Ivogün in programs of his songs. He had a fine piano touch. Performances of his own songs were nonsentimental. The structure and the poetic message were projected without exaggerated humor or coyness. His stage manners were those of a successful banker. He came on with a no-nonsense stride, made a quick, businesslike bow to the audience, sat down at the piano, and went to work. He did his job quietly and received even the ovations of the audience in a laconic spirit and with no fuss.

SOLO RECITALS were all sponsored by the artists themselves. Box-office receipts paid expenses. The Munich debut of Edwin Fischer at the Bayerischer Hof took place before a half-empty house. Still in his twenties, he played the *Hammerklavier* Sonata of Beethoven with enormous verve, but missed the first chord by a quarter of an inch. The small audience was rapturous in its enthusiasm, and Father said he played like Anton Rubinstein. Joseph Szigeti also played to a half-empty house. He performed a transcription of the Handel A Minor Flute Sonata, no. 7. His tone was penetrating and he had a strong sense of rhythm. He was then an elegant performer. In his later career he was more interested in the musical contours of a piece than in violinistic niceties. The famous Eugene Ysaye played a Mozart sonata, Beethoven's Violin Sonata in C Minor, and the Bruch Concerto in G Minor. He played the Beethoven sonata with great firmness, rhythmic life, and a beautiful, strong tone. Every phrase in this work impressed itself on my memory. Claudio Arrau, about age twelve, made a solo debut at the Bayerischer Hof concert hall. In knee pants and lace collar he played a formidable program that was received with great enthusiasm. Beethoven's *Pathétique* was for me the high spot because of Arrau's technical accuracy.

≫≪

IN ADDITION to having taught myself piccolo, orchestration, and harmony, I had kept up my piano practice. Mother tried to get Father to give me piano lessons but he stalled. Finally she insisted, and the lesson was a disaster.

He strode into the room and boomed, "Now, my boy, what are you going to play?"

"I don't know. My hands are cold," I faltered.

"Play all of the scales in octaves; that will warm them up."

I played them all but with the C-major fingering. He was disgusted. "What are you doing there?"

"I am playing the scales."

"What is that fingering you're using?"

"The same one for all of them."

He let loose a disagreeable laugh. "That's ridiculous. Don't you know the fingerings for these scales?"

"How can I know them? Nobody told me and I don't have a piano method or a teacher," I said, and I began to cry.

"You mustn't be so sensitive, my boy. You'll never get anywhere that way. Now sit down and play these."

He taught me the scale fingerings and all sorts of other things. But that evening over his beer he went on, "Of course you know, my boy, you are too old to be a piano soloist. You can become a good accompanist, but never a soloist."

He remembered that I had missed my debut when I was six, but not that he had not helped me to prepare. But he decided to use me as a guinea pig and sailed in from time to time with theories to try out. His main theory was that if you made a mistake you were playing too fast. He assigned Beethoven's C Minor Sonata, Opus 10, the Chopin "Black Keys" Etude, and Beethoven's Piano Concerto in C Minor—with instructions that I was to practice all so slowly that I could make no mistakes and then gradually accelerate the tempo. His recipe was very good. Eventually I played the works with quite a bit of brilliance, particularly the sonata, and also played the Grieg *Piano Sonata* with a lot of snap. Father's instruction was sporadic but authentic, because he had himself studied with the great nineteenth-century pianists Moscheles and Reinecke.

One evening, I heard my mother say in the bedroom, "I'm going to have the boy take proper music lessons if it's the last thing I do. It's a shame to let the poor fellow beat his brains out indefinitely. Get him a teacher if you're too lazy or too tired to do the job yourself."

There was further talk, and when Father came out of the bedroom he looked ashamed of himself and said I could study with his pupil Zimmerman, a rough-and-ready pianist and a fair musician.

Mother took me to audition for Direktor Bussmeyer at the Royal Academy of Music. After the proper introductions and knowing that I had my piccolo in my pocket, Mother boldly suggested I play something. How could Professor Dr. Bussmeyer refuse to listen? I played a few of my favorite tunes and passages. He waved me off with a pained look and suggested that I take private flute lessons with Professor Schellhorn, the principal flutist of the opera and symphony orchestras in Munich. On October 17, 1913, I had my first flute lesson. Professor Schellhorn switched me to a regular cylindrical Boehm flute built from specifications of Richard Wagner and Theobald Boehm and handmade by Bürger in Strasbourg. This was the beginning of a love affair with the flute, an affair that still continues. This flute was lost fifty years later, but I found another one in Munich in 1965 and played it often in New York concerts. One of Powell's flutemakers became interested in this instrument, studied its measurements, and decided to use it as a model for building contemporary wooden flutes for playing baroque and nineteenth-century flute music. A number of these new instruments are now carrying on in this country the Munich flute tradition, that of producing a beautiful, mellow, and expressive tone.

MY COMPOSING had become quite secretive and I didn't want Father involved. I always carried small notebooks and notated my ideas immediately, sometimes in bed. I also composed in the Hofbibliothek—the Court Library—where it was quiet and there were no interruptions. A young American tourist, Newton Wagner, introduced me to ragtime and I worked out some syncopations that seemed "American."

FATHER'S UNIQUE educational experiment had landed me in a regular peasant school in Egern on the Tegernsee when we moved there for vacation in April 1914. He said it was the only way to get to know these rugged Bavarians. I was registered and found myself in a schoolroom under the tutelage of a Herr Lehrer Angerer, a redhead with a Vandyke beard. The benches were hard, open admissions seemed to be the practice, and the teacher's job more one of discipline than of education. It is nice to know that in these matters we have made little progress in the last sixty-five years. We did a little reading and writing in German but used Latin script that presented no problems. Physical culture was good and rugged. The boys would be turned loose at recess and would start fighting like goats in the schoolyard. Herr Lehrer Angerer said it would toughen them up for the army.

※※

AFTER CLOCKWORK precision in international accusations, defenses, and counteraccusations, war was declared on August 4, 1914, when we were in Rottach-Egern. We all continued to believe that the war would be over in two months and we kept on working from day to day. But the external picture changed dramatically. All roads around the Tegernsee were barricaded; there was a rumor that some Russians and the Serbian Countess Woynewich, who studied with Father, were trying to smuggle two million marks of gold bullion over the Austrian border in a car. The peasant militia, mostly hunters and woodsmen armed with rifles and shotguns, looked quite frightening as they searched passing cars. Mark Twain's daughter, Sarah Clemens, who had made her debut as a soprano in Munich, was picked up with her husband, Ossip Gabrilowitsch, on suspicion of spying and jailed for several days in Rottach-Egern am Tegernsee. My piano teacher, Willie Zimmerman, was an admirer and friend of the countess. He had an excited talk with Father behind closed doors, then went to the countess's boarding house. He came back after a few hours saying she had escaped. He was a rabid socialist and I believe he helped her outwit the police by providing her with a peasant costume and taking one of her trunks to the railroad station. She left everything else in her boarding house and the authorities found nothing damaging. Zimmerman said she had taken papers and gold with her and told me later she had been a spy.

It is hard to believe now, but we came to Germany without passports and lived that way until the war. With the war, the era of passports, visas, thumbprints, identification with number and passport picture, and the registration of all foreigners at police precincts began. Father's habit of paying with twenty-mark gold pieces stopped because gold was confiscated. The tempo and lifestyles slowed down in some ways and changed completely in others. Father's aristocratic students and friends, Prince Georg, Count von der Schulenburg, Baron Leist, and others went into the army as officers. His women students engaged in charity work and nursing, but his class was still large enough to support us.

We always moved when the income expanded or shrank, and in 1914 we found on the Kaulbachstrasse a darker, smaller apartment with a straggly little garden. Father's studio was in the apartment. Music remained the beacon light, not only in my life but in the life of the city. The opera and concerts went on full blast even though the city soon began running down. Helene was with us during the war, but unfortunately her feud with Father persisted and they never spoke. It helped me develop a sense of humor for I would make cracks and tell jokes until they laughed, but then they would drift back into silence.

The streets were filled with soldiers and soon the first wounded reached Munich. I tried to keep up practicing and took lessons, but I was swept up into the war when the Episcopal Church and private philanthropy established an American Red Cross Hospital in Munich.

Helene became a nurse and, at the end of August 1914, I volunteered to be an orderly in the hospital and was accepted. I served for nine months. I began as entertainment director and librarian. The wounded were from Bavarian regiments and many were peasants. I spoke Bavarian dialect well and I knew the types from my Tegernsee days. Some soldiers were by profession small tradesmen, craftsmen, and teachers. There were some students. A few were socialists. All were permanently disabled, and I felt sad as they tried to rebuild their lives. Some were bitter about this war and all wars and predicted a political change after it was over.

I tried to guide their reading and combine useful literature with the romances and trashy novels that most of them liked best. Our book collection was small, but I got along famously with the soldiers. They all called me Herr Otto. I arranged programs for the soldiers, played piano and flute for them, and conducted them in both American and German songs. I decided that what these Bavarian wounded needed was to celebrate an American Thanksgiving, so I explained to them what this day was all about. They listened attentively. Then I tried to tell them what ragtime was and made a German translation of Irving Berlin's "I Want to Be in Dixie":

> *"Ich möchte sein, ich möchte sein,*
> *Ich möchte sein in Dixie,*
> *Wo die Hühner Hund gegangen frohe sind,*
> *Rühreier zu legen in dem neugemachten Heu.*
>
> *"Ich möchte sein, ich möchte sein*
> *D-I-X, ich weiss nicht wie mann's buchstabiert,*
> *Ich möchte sein, Ich möchte sein,*
> *Ich möchte sein in Dixie."*

The soldiers wondered how in the hell chickens could lay scrambled eggs among new-mown hay. I insisted that it was quite common in the United States. By so doing I contributed to the confusion of the Bavarian army and probably helped win the war for America.

Dr. Franz Jung and his wife, Dr. Sophie Jung, ran the hospital and gave me all kinds of assignments. I was given a Red Cross armband and insignia which brought me salutes from soldiers on the street and a "present-arms" from most sentries. Dr. Jung finally had me take out columns of twenty-four soldiers for an evening's entertainment. I felt pretty chesty walking at the head of these outfits, at my side a bearded sergeant major old enough to be my grandfather. I steered them to movie palaces and other places without incident until one night when the soldiers begged me to take them to a beer hall for a couple of steins. Fearing mutiny I relaxed military discipline. My job was to get them away from the beer hall and back to the hospital, but they were happy and on their way home and in the hospital sang all the songs I had taught them. I was promptly demoted to the library.

But the nurses needed me to do chores. The head nurse had me help with bandaging. She gave me a detailed history of every wound in the ward. She assigned me to help ambulatory cases and do physical therapy. One fine-looking young fellow had been shot through the temples and the nerves of his eyes were destroyed. She asked me to help him adjust by training his very fine singing voice. I chose Schubert's *Frühlingsglaube*. He visualized the poem so clearly and projected the song with such poignancy that I have never forgotten how he sounded. He expressed a real longing for spring by a man who could never see it again.

I did so well with my paramedical work that the assistant doctor—who looked about twenty-two but was probably a bit older—decided that I would make a good doctor. He graduated me from bandaging to the operating room to assist him. He performed a number of minor operations and had to remove many bone splinters. My job was to catch these as he extracted each one and preserve them for further study. He showed me how to cauterize wounds and taught me the value of soap and water as disinfectants. I also prepared injections. This tour in the operating room was a wonderful experience for me, but Dr. Jung walked in while I was fixing some bandages and raised the roof with his shouts, yelling to the assistant surgeon that you can't run hospitals with children on the staff. That hurt!

AFTER MY SUCCESSES in the hospital, I was promoted to messenger for official documents and also took over the guest book of the hospital. I brought the book to guests who had forgotten to sign when they visited.

Dr. Jung called me into his office and gave me the guest book and a letter addressed to "Prinz Ludwig Ferdinand, Nymphenburger Palast." He told me that the prince was an accomplished violinist who played second violin in several local orchestras. He was also a practicing ophthalmologist, a good-natured, heavyset chap who wandered about the streets of Munich like any citizen and was much beloved by the Müncheners. If the prince was busy, I was to leave the book with the princess.

At Nymphenburger Palast I walked through the beautiful gardens to a sentry who saluted when I asked to see the prince. Another sentry came over but neither was sure where the prince lived; these soldiers were enormous fellows from Bavarian villages and they were sly and tough but not very intelligent. When they didn't know directions, the Germans would send you to some other place or to somebody else who was also lost. After I had wandered around the palace grounds for some time, a sergeant ushered me to the suite of Countess de Carmandie, a lady-in-waiting of the princess. She greeted me in German and explained with a very heavy American accent that the prince was on hospital duty. I answered in English and she was enraptured.

This charming lady of about sixty was lonesome, and she told me her life history. Born in Philadelphia, she had married a Spanish count. He was attached to the Bavarian court as aide-de-camp to the king and master of the stables. This meant that he had to keep an eye on the horse apples. The countess remarked that I looked thin. I told her Mother wouldn't hoard food, and rations at home were often in short supply. She ordered the maid to bring in a large pot of hot chocolate, a torte, and cognac. I drank all of the chocolate and gobbled two enormous slices of torte with cognac. The countess confessed that Ethelbert Nevin's *Narcissus* was her favorite piece. I gave her a lecture on good music. The countess invited me to come back.

I got home at quarter past nine and Father was waiting.

He had a stormy look. "Where have you been in the middle of the night, ruining your health and morals?"

I told him to relax if he would like to hear an interesting story.

Father was very inquisitive, so while waiting for me to finish supper he recovered his poise and told me to hurry up. I told him about the entire Nymphenburger Palast adventure. When I came to the hot chocolate and torte he was enormously impressed and asked for all kinds of details, including the number of buttons on the soldiers' uniforms. He finally smiled, figuring that his educational theories were eminently valid or I couldn't have had such an experience.

I went to the palace the next morning to get the guest book but the countess was busy. One of her rather acidy ladies-in-waiting handed it to me, frowning while I checked to see if the prince had indeed signed.

After this successful foray, Dr. Jung ordered me to take the guest book to King Ludwig III of Bavaria. I dusted the dandruff off my blue suit, polished my shoes, and washed my neck and ears with special care. At the entrance to the Wittelsbacher Palast the sentries did their usual foot-stamping and presented arms when they saw my Red Cross sign. I was escorted by an adjutant through long halls to a major who in turn ushered me right to the door of the king's study. I saw His Majesty sitting at his desk signing documents.

The major took the guest book and delivered it to the king. I recall thinking that he was a big bum because he wouldn't let me go in to shake hands with the king. The king was a very friendly chap with a white beard and he looked like Santa Claus in a Bavarian general's uniform. As he handed the book back to the major he looked my way and raised his hand in sort of a slightly fatigued but still regal farewell gesture. King Ludwig was such a good-natured monarch that when he walked the streets he waved and winked at everybody and petted stray dogs. He wore a field marshal's uniform, but his pants were never pressed and they were too long, so they crinkled and bunched up at his heels. This made it difficult for him to handle his sword and he had to walk slowly for fear of tripping. His subjects interpreted this as being the mark of a very democratic and loving king. They showed their appreciation by deposing him in the 1918 revolution.

IN THE FIRST year of the war, at victory celebrations thousands of people gathered at the Odeonplatz and sang German patriotic songs with enormous fervor. "Altniederländisches Dankgebet," or "Old Netherlands Prayer" ("We Gather Together"), was one of the favorites. "Ich hatt' einen Kameraden" was another.

The war soon began to be felt by the civilian population. Crowds were smaller, the singing less fervent, until the celebrations stopped altogether. Two days a week, people went without meat. Clothes were rationed. Some staple foods became impossible to get. Tile stoves had little coal and peat, so apartments and restaurants were cold. We adjusted because the war was supposed to be over in two months. In the meantime concerts, operas, and plays continued to take place and saved us from complete demoralization. I was ready to audition for Munich's Royal Academy of Music, so after nine months of service at the American Red Cross Hospital I resigned. A book signed by the patients and a letter of commendation from Dr. Jung were my material rewards. This experience in the real world had a profound influence on me.

⊁⊀

MY FLUTE TEACHER, Professor Schellhorn, suggested registering at the Royal Academy of Music. Mother took me to see Direktor Bussmeyer, who asked what plans my parents had for my career.

"We want him to be a composer and conductor," she replied.

Bussmeyer looked disgusted. "Fifteen-year-old boys should not be thinking about such things. He can take flute as his main instrument, piano as a secondary instrument, and the usual theory courses. We will accept him."

At fifteen I was the youngest student at the academy.

My piano teacher, Professor Becht, always wore a brown derby hat at lessons, chewed a cold cigar, and from the studio window watched the pigeons on the roof. He was dumpy and wore ill-fitting baggy clothes and shoes that showed his corns and bunions. His fingernails were dirty and his wispy hair was noticeable when he removed his derby to wipe his brow after he had been excited by the pigeons. Director of sacred music, organist and choirmaster at the Munich Frauenkirche, and a famous Lassus scholar, Becht always began his lessons exactly fifteen minutes late. He knew the classical and romantic piano literature from memory and had graded everything. We never heard him play.

Each week he assigned to us one étude and one piece for "expression," or to learn how to project. The right hand of each piece was practiced slowly, then the left hand. At the lesson he checked each hand on the side of the score. Then both hands were played together slowly and double-checked, then the right hand alone faster, double-check; the left hand alone faster, double check; both together faster, triple-check. He gave us a week to memorize and then a review lesson. "Play," sighed Becht as he sighted a pair of pigeons cooing on the roof. While the student played Becht watched the pigeons. But oh, how he listened! At the slightest slip he bellowed, "F sharp!" or, "Too loud!" But he booted us through all of the standard Czerny études, Cramer études, Clementi *Gradus ad Parnassum*, Haydn sonatas and rondos, Mozart sonatas, moderately difficult Beethoven sonatas, and classical variations. Then, for dessert, good little students who had had all of their checks checked would be rewarded with something daring—"I want you to play the Grieg Sonata." He also tossed in some Schumann and Schubert. His special musical health diet was all composed by J. S. Bach. He explained that this music was organic. The Two- and Three-Part Inventions, the French Suites and English Suites, and *The Well-Tempered Clavier* were obligatory even for students with piano as a secondary instrument. The advantages of his method were that we all knew the same works and could play and discuss every note. The disadvantage was that we learned nothing new. Professors didn't care one bit whether we liked what we were studying or liked how they taught us. The repertory was what we needed to know and that was all.

Professor Schellhorn, the flutist, also had a prescribed course of study but he was less rigid than others. He taught us to produce a beautiful tone and introduced us to flute étude composers like Tillmetz, Briccialdi, Anderson, Demersseman, and Theobald Boehm. These workouts gave us mechanical security on the instrument. We then studied standard flute works by Haydn, Mozart, and Bach, and learned romantic pieces like the *Undine* Sonata by Reinecke, Heinrich Hofmann's *Konzertstück*, and shorter pieces by Max Reger. Then we mastered the difficult solo passages from the classical and romantic opera and symphonic repertory, solo passages from Wagner's operas, and the works of Richard Strauss. Together with my Berlioz and Strauss instrumentation studies, Schellhorn's approach gave me a real introduction to the orchestra before I had ever played in one.

The theory teacher, Professor Anton Beer-Walbrunn, had a reputation as a modernist. The professor had a lopsided face. His expression was especially sardonic when he corrected our exercises. Carl Orff had just finished studying with him and impressed me because he was conducting in a theater, knew Arnold Schoenberg, and had been influenced by him, though he later switched directions. Professor Beer-Walbrunn showed his modernism by including Bavarian folk and salon music in his own compositions. His works were pretty weak and didn't sound, but he had an influence on Orff. I think he gave me the courage to include occasional vulgar passages in my own music.

In theory class all examples were corrected at the table or on the blackboard. Nothing but the professor's voice ever sounded in his studio. Examples were right or wrong; a correction meant you hadn't obeyed his orders. We never asked him to explain why he did anything because we knew he'd sneer at us with his lopsided face. I was ambitious, impatient, and quite good and the class was too slow for me. I arranged to take private lessons with him.

My progress was so fast that I decided to show him a song I had composed.

He listened attentively as I played and sang. "Yes, yes. . . . Are you melancholy?"

"I have never thought about it. I don't think so."

"Hmm . . . I would have thought you were melancholy. Now let's go on to the dominant seventh chord. The leading tone must go up unless it goes down."

He took me through the harmony routine with great style. I never mentioned my compositions again and I finished his three-year course in six months.

Professor Becht suggested that I study organ with him. His method was like his piano instruction except that I had to do the right foot alone, the left foot alone, the right hand alone, the left hand alone, and then put them all together. His pedal studies seemed quite pedestrian to me but I lumbered my way right up to and through a Mendelssohn sonata.

As usual, I was doing secret composing. I had notated material that I used in my First String Quartet, later performed in Berlin and Chicago, and I desperately wanted someone to hear something. I decided on Professor Becht. While he was enjoying his smoke I played my *Trio for Women's Voices* on the organ. After repeating it several times, I fantasized that he would come in soon with, "Oh, by the way, what was that interesting music you were playing?"

"Which music?" I would ask.

"That last piece."

"Oh, that? A little piece of my own that I thought . . ."

"Oh, you don't say! I didn't know you composed. It sounded very interesting. It has a classical touch but it is also modern. Register with our main composition teacher and study with him."

But that wasn't exactly what he said.

"Now, pedal studies; right foot slow, left foot slow."

Etc., etc., etc.

After I had finished the études, a Bach fugue, and the Mendelssohn, he relented. "By the way, what were you doing in here while I was having my cigar?"

"I wasn't doing anything in particular."

"Well, I heard something going on here."

"I was playing a little trio I composed for women's voices."

"Oh, I thought somebody had let a cat loose in the organ pipes. Now let's get on with this little fugue by Bach. Not too fast."

I got even with Becht later. I was a good organist but stopped taking lessons. He summoned me.

"Why are you stopping your lessons?"

I told him I wanted to compose and conduct and that an orchestral instrument like the flute was more practical than the organ.

"Well, if you really want to spend your life blowing air into a tube rather than playing the queen of instruments, I can't help you. Oh, look at that big black pigeon out there. I think he's chasing the white one. I wonder what he wants?"

I never saw nor heard of Becht again, but what he taught me was solid.

A LAW in Germany read that students at professional schools must attend a continuation or trade school two afternoons a week until age seventeen. The authorities caught up with me and raked me in.

The teachers all seemed to have red beards and nasty tempers. The teacher of a hygiene and biology course told us to always wear our underwear when we slept in a strange bed. This was to keep off germs, fleas, lice, and other visitors. In the second week a red-bearded teacher collected an orchestra and read through Beethoven's Piano Concerto in C Minor. I played first flute. But when Mother heard about the hygiene class she said I was to stay at home. For a year and a half, she had a great time outfoxing truant officers. They finally sent a bailiff with a red beard and a warrant to escort me either to continuation school or to reform school, but Mother did not reveal my whereabouts.

MY STUDIES at the academy pleased Father. I could practice at home in the evening while he had beer and at half-past seven in the morning while he took his cold bath. He pretended not to listen but like Professor Becht his response was fast if I made a mistake or rushed the tempo. I was a very good sight reader and read opera scores by D'Albert and Puccini, and new music by Schoenberg, Strauss, Reger, and others. Father liked this diversion. Sometimes I switched to the flute. He really enjoyed this because Schopenhauer had played the flute and Papa admired Schopenhauer.

In the winter of 1916, I wrote a set of piano pieces. Paul Boepple and Walter Lang, two excellent young Swiss musicians who were students at the academy, heard the pieces and liked them so much that they shared with me their monthly food packages from Switzerland of chocolate, cheese, and cookies—a rare treat that really cheered me up in the wartime gloom. I was encouraged by my friends to play the pieces at home.

After I played the last one a few times, Father came in. "What was that piece you were playing, that intermezzo?"

My experiences with professors Beer-Walbrunn and Becht had made me cagey. "You mean the Chopin?"

"No, no, it was some modern piece."

"Oh yes . . . this one?" And then: *ta, tata, tee; ta, tata, tee.*

"That's it. What was that?"

"That's a piece by Max Reger."

Then he sounded off. "My boy, Max Reger has all the fine traditions of the romantics but he has classical training. A piece like the one you just played is both significant and beautiful."

"Yes, Father. Tell me more."

He described this lovely piece, the colorful harmonies, the curve of the melodic line, and the ingratiating rhythm. He finished with a big salvo of praise for Max Reger.

I had waited a long time for this. "Okay, Father, I've got you in a corner. *I* wrote the piece. What have you to say about *that?*"

He almost collapsed. He was quite respectful for a few minutes, having suddenly realized that he had a genius on his hands. He began working on this. "I had no idea, my boy . . . that anything like this was going on in this apartment. This is marvelous and we must do something about it. When the war ends or something else happens we will get you fixed up. You know, I want you to rise to great heights. This is simply stupendous."

He rumbled on to Mother in the bedroom way into the night. The next morning it was obvious that he had not rested well, for his mood had changed slightly.

"I hope you understand that any remarks I made last night were only meant to encourage you. Of course, writing a piano piece like yours, nice as it may seem, still does not mean that you know anything about composing. Possibly you don't know anything about music. I suggest that you continue your studies with good teachers and go forward as far as you can with whatever talent you have, even if it is limited."

MY PROFESSIONAL LIFE began when I played a Grave from a concerto for flute and harpsichord by Frederick the Great at an academy concert. I was nervous and my hands were cold and clammy and shaking so that it interfered with my tone production, but Direktor Bussmeyer came backstage and said I had a beautiful tone. This recommendation helped me get an engagement as flutist in the orchestra for Handel's *Judas Maccabaeus*, and I was launched on a professional career that still continues.

A young violinist offered me a job as piano accompanist in a café, five marks for two hours. The café seemed elegant but very private. The violinist played only soft music with mute and all accompaniments were soft-pedaled. Nobody ever came in through the street entrance, but several couples left by that door. Nobody ordered food or drink and there was only one waiter. It all seemed rather strange.

I told my mother about it and she flashed me a rather quizzical, diagnostic look. "What? No food? No drink? You played soft music? Men and women came out together from little alcoves with curtains in front? You must resign immediately."

I checked with my friends and they told me I had been playing in a fashionable bordello. They thought I was silly to quit. I would have gotten generous tips later and perhaps even picked up free services. I wasn't impressed.

My next engagement was to play a flute obbligato in *Abendlied* by August Reuss, a fine local composer, for a fee of eight marks. The concert was in the great Bayerischer Hof Konzertsaal. The big-bosomed Kammersängerin Johanna Dietz from the Munich opera was soloist; the program with my name in big letters was posted on all the billboards in Munich. I steered girls from the American Library in front of these until they discovered my name. When they squealed with joy I remarked, "Oh, I hadn't noticed that."

At the concert, Reuss decided to make the song realistic. The poem described a distant flute so he hid me behind some potted palms. The applause was so enthusiastic that Dietz called me out from behind the bushes for a bow. My Cherubino-like appearance juxtaposed with her Hofbräuhaus stance stimulated the audience to shout bravo. There were even good press notices and I was instantly famous around town and at the conservatory. The main critic said I played with taste. We had to repeat the program five months later for the benefit of the academy and the reviewer said that we played with expression and devotion. There was another review of a concert for the Society of Munich Artists. The Andante from Mozart's Concerto for Harp, Flute and Orchestra was played, it was said, "most convincingly," with piano accompaniment.

FERDINAND WAGNER was one of my best friends at the academy. He was seventeen and a brilliant clarinetist who wanted to be a composer and conductor. These were also my ambitions and as we were not eligible for any pertinent courses at the academy we invented one. Wagner would line up a quartet of singers from the regular opera department for a rehearsal. I learned the operas by accompanying the singers at the piano, Wagner learned by conducting me and the singers, and the singers learned by studying at home and by private coaching with Wagner and me. Everybody was happy, the singers learned their roles, I learned to play the scores, and Wagner got experience conducting. He imagined an orchestra and pit and used the piano as a soundbox. It was smashing to see him pull a great climax out of the nonexistent brass section. The story was soon leaked (possibly by us) that we were both budding opera conductors.

Bruno Walter was conducting *Parsifal* at the Prinzregenten Theater festival, and sent a message to Ferdinand Wagner that the "Highest Angel Chorus" couldn't hear the orchestra. From the highest part of the theater Wagner, as assistant conductor, was to sound their pitch on his clarinet. He couldn't see the conductor from that altitude so I was engaged as assistant-assistant conductor to follow the score, hear the orchestral sound float up from the far-distant pit, conduct in the proper tempo a few measures in advance, and cue in Wagner when it was time for him to give the correct pitch to the chorus; at this point the regular assistant conductor would pick up the beat and get the chorus to sing. The word soon traveled that I had been appointed Walter's assistant conductor at the Prinzregenten. This set me way up in the musical world and I did not explain the details of this triumph.

Wagner's subsequent career was brilliant. He was conductor and assistant to Felix Weingartner at Darmstadt when he was eighteen. He then became Generalmusikdirektor in Nuremberg and at the Vienna Staatsoper. He died of leukemia at the age of twenty-six. Many German musicians told me that he was considered the greatest conducting talent in Germany at the time. Wagner offered me a job as deputy first flute and assistant conductor at the Darmstadt Opera when I was sixteen, but the war interfered.

MANY AMERICAN painters stayed on in Munich with the hope that the war would be over soon. The American Artists' Club arranged trips to mountains, skiing, café jaunts, boxing matches, beer parties at the club, and visits to nightclubs in Schwabing. I was sometimes taken along. Huge logs were made into rafts and floated down the Isar River from Wolfratshausen to Munich. With a couple of sawhorses and planks, three kegs of beer, cheese, sausage, pumpernickel, a peasant violinist and accordionist, and two raftsmen, the true Bohemian atmosphere reigned. This was about the last group festivity before the city slowly began blacking out because of the war.

Father's students had introduced me to the best Munich café life and "five o'clock tea." Café food consisted of chocolate, tea with rum, coffee, and mounds of whipped cream in puffs, in chocolate éclairs, on tortes, in hot chocolate, and in coffee. Café orchestras played potpourris of old operettas and novelties and operatic selections from Weber to Puccini. The musicians were excellent though they played with an excess of schmaltz. I'm afraid I developed a certain taste for the rather cheap but very pleasant type of life represented by Munich café culture. Everybody watched everybody else. Handsome officers in sky-blue dress uniforms, civilian sportsmen, elderly roués in Prince Alberts and spats, gray vest and gray gloves, stylishly dressed ladies sometimes from high society, and local and international prostitutes sized each other up and expressed mild approval or disapproval in stage whispers. I made it my job to observe them all without prejudice. The musicians played soulfully, always soulfully. As the war continued café life began tapering off and the blue-clad officers were replaced by wounded comrades in field uniforms. The dress, food, and music gradually became less glamorous. Eventually the menu consisted only of imitation coffee and tea sweetened with saccharin.

✑✐

EVERYTHING BEGAN slowly to grind to a complete halt in the terrible winter of 1916–1917. We moved to a tiny fourth-floor walkup. All foods and clothes were gradually rationed. It was a nasty winter but we could neither afford nor could I find an overcoat. I wore my suit jacket and in the pockets had two small charcoal stoves to warm my hands. Later a friend gave me an overcoat, too long and too large, but much needed. Mother refused to hoard food so soon practically everything we ate was made from turnips. We had turnip bread, turnip coffee, turnip cakes sweetened with saccharin, turnips boiled and turnips baked. Mother flavored them with herbs so they were palatable. Nourishing they were not. I developed a stomach sensitivity that stayed with me for years. It was never diagnosed but was probably malnutrition. I was five feet eleven and a half inches tall and weighed one hundred pounds. Even that was better than what most people had to endure.

Dr. Vollmer, the husband of a student of Father's, sent us a chicken from the Russian front for Christmas. This terrain had been crossed a number of times by the Austrian, German, and Russian armies. All of them had foraged for food. Our Christmas chicken was so thin and emaciated that not one soldier in those hungry armies thought it was worth catching. But Father was delighted when it arrived: "It is the smallest chicken in the world," he declared. Mother looked businesslike; she knew how to flavor the turnips, and with a lemon she found someplace, a cupful of rice and some herbs, some turnips, turnip coffee, and turnip cake sweetened with saccharin, she assembled a magnificent Christmas dinner.

Father was pretty thin, and as the breadwinner he had first choice. There wasn't much meat on that chicken and he ate it all. My sister Helene then got what remained of the gravy and rice. Mother was not easily defeated so she fished around and came up with some neck bones for me. She said these were delicious when sucked and I was to have them all. She explained that she had tasted so much of the meal while cooking it that she had lost her appetite and didn't care for any dinner.

I had to go three miles to get a bag full of coal or peat for the tile stove. On one trip a boy of about nine or ten didn't move ahead in the lineup and when people investigated they found he had died from malnutrition and cold.

This affected me deeply; I saw the impersonal brutality of war at first hand, and this boy became a symbol of the innocent people who suffer in wars. Psychically I never recovered from this experience.

The great victory demonstrations of the early war years had now deteriorated into food riots. I saw a mob of irate and hungry women take a Prussian major who was giving a patriotic speech and throw him into the fountain at the Rathaus. The soldiers there to keep order consisted of some rather shabby reservists of sixty-five as well as recruits of fifteen. But they refused to move against their wives, mothers, and sisters who were rioting because there was a bread shortage. The mob and soldiers finally went home, and as we walked down Ludwigstrasse at around eight o'clock we could see how it had deteriorated.

On February 3, 1917, the United States broke off diplomatic relations with Germany. Benevolent Professor Schwickerath at the academy, complete with his Vandyke beard and Prince Albert coat, told the assembled student body that when a government does foolish things individuals have to suffer and that I was herewith expelled. He explained that the Bavarian government had nothing against me personally. He shook my hand and wished me luck and the class gave me some subdued, enemy-alien applause and that chapter of my life was over.

I WAS ALMOST seventeen—of military age, and ripe for internment. The Spanish consulate represented the United States, and Father arranged exit visas for Helene and me for Zurich, Switzerland.

While preparing to leave, I thought about my positive accomplishments. I was fairly proficient on the flute and piano, spoke and wrote fluent English and German, had a good knowledge of musical literature, a museum and library knowledge of the arts and sciences, and the ability to get along with adults and to act like an adult and a young professional. I owned my own flute and had composed piano pieces, songs, choruses, and sketches for a string quartet. On the negative side, I was rundown and bloated from eating turnips for six months. Malnutrition had affected my circulation, and my fingers, when cold or damp, became dead white and bloodless. I was always hungry. For six weeks, while waiting for our visas, Helene and I dreamed about the filet mignon with an egg we would have when we crossed the Swiss border.

We left on a cold, snowy, slushy, and dark day. Mother gave us a cup of chocolate and two biscuits she had hoarded for just such an occasion. The goodbyes were fast and sad as my parents saw their youngest child and only daughter take off for a strange country. I was scared but also excited.

Chapter 6

Refugees and Dadaists in Zurich
1917-1920

WHEN WE LEFT MUNICH, Father gave us, in a magnanimous gesture, a one-thousand-mark bill plus travel money. "This will be enough for several months," he said, "but should you be temporarily embarrassed, cable Aunt Gretchen. She is a good woman and will know what to do." Unfortunately, Father had forgotten that the German mark had been devalued. We had only enough money to support ourselves for two weeks.

We cabled Aunt Gretchen immediately and she sent us five hundred dollars. After several weeks, she wrote us that she would be glad to help Helene with her studies, but that she and my oldest brother Fred thought that I should come home and get a job to help win the war. Now that I was sixteen I should be doing my bit. Fred stated his position very clearly in a letter to me.

Dear Skeezicks,

Glad to hear that you outwitted those Huns [and] escaped to Zurich. Now that you are a full grown little weasel you must begin acting like a man. You know I never thought much of your wasting time with music. Nobody should be a musician unless he can be either an Irving Berlin or a Paderooski. You, fella, are neither and never will be, so forget about it and keep on playing the ocarina if you like until you are a doddering old man, but give up that silly idea of wanting to be an "artist," a composer, or a conductor. Oh, yah, if you could get ahold of a good band like John Philip Sousa, o.k., but I think you are still too young to go to the Army where they have bands.

No, we can't send any money to help continue your musical

studies. We can't support you while you're wasting your life. On the other hand, in Oconomowoc, I have lined up a nice job for you in a pea cannery. You will be a separator, classifying the peas tiny, medium-sized, and large. This is done by rolling them on a board with different sized holes in it. You will probably be especially good at this because of your experience with half notes, quarter notes, and eighth notes. In any case, it's a job. When you arrive, I will be glad to introduce you to the foreman personally. Good luck, fella—and cut out your childish foolishness.

Fred

I thought it all over and I decided that if I were needed for war service the consulate would inform me. I didn't like the idea of sorting peas. My professional appearances as a flutist were behind me and I thought of myself as being pretty special as a composer, so I answered:

Dear Fred,

Your letter came yesterday and I assume that because you can still write you must be well. I hope you are reasonably happy. That Oconomowoc deal doesn't sound right to me. It's too much like a pearade [joke]. Besides, I have other plans here that are most interesting. There is some talk about grooming me for chief conductor at the opera, but the famous Zurich Symphony Orchestra is also bidding for my services as General Music Director, so let's put the Oconomowoc job on ice for later. If you think it's really so fine and important to roll peas, why in hell don't you go there and roll them yourself?

Your loving brother,
Skeezicks

After that declaration of independence I used some of my few remaining francs to register at the Zurich Conservatory of Music. I was sure that Dr. Andreae, the director, would recognize my genius. After further studies I would undoubtedly land a conducting job. I went to the conservatory for an appointment. Dr. Andreae, a major in the Swiss militia, was in military service. I went ahead and registered anyway for a semester for fifty francs, or $12.50.

Zurich, in addition to being a center of espionage and the home of many questionable characters, was also the international cultural center of the world during World War I. Besides welcoming artists from all of the warring countries, the city gave asylum to countless others, many of whom later became world-famous. The city had a population of approximately two hundred thousand. Many diverse cultural activities took place simultaneously and often conflicted in their artistic aims. At times, and in a rather tenuous fashion, cultural dividing lines were crossed and people from the Swiss establishment rubbed elbows with the avant-garde artists. Far-out literary people met with painters and musicians from the establishment, if only briefly, and sometimes even exchanged views with members of the developing psychoanalytic group around Dr. Jung and Dr. Riklin.

I was roaming through the corridor of the conservatory one day when a fellow bumped into me.

"I beg your pardon, I'm so sorry; I hope I didn't do any damage," he said. This was followed by a kind of fast laugh that then modulated into solicitous phrases such as "very stupid of me" and "I didn't see you."

I looked at my apologetic bumping partner. I saw a rather fat young chap of about twenty with a moonlike face, slightly curly hair, twinkling black eyes, and volatile hands and arms, who used fairly fast footwork while he talked. His sentences came out in a sputter and a torrent. At times it was hard to know what he was saying, but his intent could easily be deduced from the expression on his face and his dance movements. I put him at his ease. Then he introduced himself.

"I'm Otto Strauss. Are you a stranger here?"

"Yes, I'm an American and I'm going to study here."

"An American. How wonderful! Have you just arrived and will you stay for a while? . . . I hear that business is fine in America and everybody is getting rich. . . . Are you rich too? Wonderful to be rich, isn't it?"

I answered, "My name is Otto Luening. . . . Not everybody in America is rich. . . . No, I'm not rich, I'm poor. . . . It's wonderful to be poor."

Strauss looked astonished. "Why wonderful to be poor?"

I explained that there are not so many responsibilities when one is poor. One has only to scramble around and make a living, and I thought scrambling was fun.

Strauss sputtered a bit and I heard him mutter, "Nonsense. . . . What an asinine point of view." He then asked me to accompany him to the Pfauen Café, a famous artists' hangout, for coffee and kirsch.

While walking across the Pfauenplatz, he said he had heard that Americans drink only whiskey and gin and that all Americans were armed. He himself believed that only people on Indian reservations carried weapons. He laughed. "I'm exaggerating, you know. . . . No hard feelings. . . . But they are armed in the West, no? . . . Will you have a cigar?"

In the café, he ordered coffee, insisted on lacing it with kirsch, and looked at the international papers for a few moments. Then we began exchanging further information. He told me that his grandmother was African and his grandfather German Swiss. His father was a physician in the Italian canton of Ticino. His very beautiful mother became incurably manic-depressive when she was thirty-five and had been confined in an institution for many years. Strauss wanted to be a concert pianist and had already been coached by Ferruccio Busoni.

I then gave him a brief account of my adventures. Strauss looked thoughtful and his face reflected various degrees of elation and depression as my story became inflated or deflated, and my own emotional thermometer rose or fell.

Finally he said, "You seem to be in terrible shape financially. You must do something about it immediately. I believe I have an idea that will improve your financial condition considerably. Yes? I think so. Do you think so? I think you should, I think you should."

"I should what?"

"Tivoli, Tivoli. It's a restaurant near the university. All the students eat there, also famous refugees. . . . Tivoli extends credit up to three months, but"—and his face took on a searching, solemn, detectivelike expression—"you have to pay your bill by the promised date; otherwise they not only throw you out but never extend credit again, and"—he leaned over and whispered in my ear—"one time they had a fellow jailed."

He lowered his whisper. "But I think that he not only ran up

a bill but fooled around with the proprietor's minor daughter.
. . . You know . . . pregnant." He got up and with an expressive hand motion simulated a pregnant woman in her eighth month, as he signaled with the other hand for the check.

Next day, Strauss introduced me to the Tivoli owner and my credit was established with a handshake. The restaurant was soon jammed with students and a few older, impressive-looking guests who sat at reserved tables. The food was excellent and plentiful: soup, meat, potatoes, vegetables, salad, and dessert were included in the regular dinner—cost: thirty-five cents.

☙❧

STRAUSS STEERED me around town between meals, and I soon felt quite at home in what appeared to be the peaceful atmosphere of Zurich. At table three days later, he suddenly leaned over to me and hissed apprehensively, "Sshh, sshh. Revolutionaries . . . over there," and pointed to three men who were making their way to a reserved table in the rear of the hall. When they were out of earshot Strauss continued: "Ulyanov, a Russian revolutionary, also known as Lenin. . . . Don't look now." Strauss went on: "They come here almost every day for the midday meal. They just sit in the corner and eat and talk a little, and then leave."

"Do you know anything about them? Who are they?"

"Lower your voice . . . we don't want anyone to hear us."

Ulyanov, who used the cover name Lenin, had been living in Zurich for about a year. The Lenins rented a room in Spiegelgasse 14 near what is now the Jacob's Fountain in the old part of Zurich. The little street was rather dark and narrow and only a block and a half from the Restaurant Meierei where the Cabaret Voltaire, the famous Dada nightclub, held its programs.

Strauss, as a Swiss from the Ticino, had learned Swiss German and had a direct pipeline to the Swiss Social Democratic party through his friend Büttner, the kettledrum player of the opera and symphony orchestra, a radical socialist who attended every meeting of the Party. Büttner told Strauss that Lenin paid twenty-four francs for his room, that Lenin's wife sometimes made simple meals on a kerosene stove, that Lenin produced all his political manifestos in the tiny double bedroom, and that he occasionally ate a meal in the Restaurant Meierei, carefully avoiding the Dadaists. Although they were a quiet and unobtrusive couple, Lenin was a well-known figure in the central library, in the museum, and in the Central Archive for Social Literature. He was in close contact with Otto Lang and Fritz Platten, two prominent members of the Swiss Social Democratic party, and other radicals. In addition to the Tivoli restaurant, Lenin liked Zur Eintracht, a simple restaurant that had a private room where he could hold meetings of Russian émigrés, the Café Adler with its small lecture room, and the Odeon, which was headquarters for most of the intellectuals and artists in Zurich. Lenin, too, could spend an undisturbed afternoon reading international magazines and papers while enjoying a cup of coffee in the Odeon.

Lenin came to the Tivoli fairly regularly. It was whispered that he was broke and needed the credit. His entrance was always unobtrusive. He was generally accompanied by two or three other men and they passed fairly close to our table. Strauss, who was very well versed in Swiss restaurant manners, got in a *"Guten Tag!"* whenever he could catch the eye of one of them, who, in turn, might quite correctly return his greeting. I'm afraid that my own attempts on these occasions were rather furtive. Europeans had a style about their restaurant behavior that is not natural to Americans and it took me awhile to catch on and fit in.

As Lenin sat at his table, it was possible for us to observe him without being noticed. His clean, clearly sculptured features and his well-barbered Vandyke and mustache gave a certain decisiveness to his facial expression, unlike the straggly and somewhat Santa Clauslike appearances of some of the other bearded radicals in Zurich. I think it was his pale face that made him look to me like a workingman's Cardinal Richelieu. But the main impression was that of his almost marblelike forehead and his eyes, which transmitted a sense of great concentration and power. There was something statuesque about him, not a classical statuesqueness, but more that of certain Renaissance men. His appearance was neither particularly benevolent nor malevolent. He simply gave out the vibrations of a completely coordinated human being, charged with electricity, in total command of the moment, even in the relaxed and public atmosphere of a restaurant. I can't help thinking of him now as being what the yogi Patanjali called "one-pointed."

Toward the end of March, Strauss was more and more mysterious when he spoke about Lenin. But eventually I wormed out of him that Büttner the kettledrummer had heard from Swiss socialists that they in turn had heard from Russian friends, who had the message from a Polish émigré, that Lenin was planning to leave Switzerland. Strauss, who had many connections in town, was a railroad buff who generally landed at the main depot at least once a day and had friends among the train personnel and the station administration. They told him that the German embassy in Bern was trying to make a deal for Lenin to travel through Germany to Finland and then to Russia. The Germans hoped that Russia would be thrown into turmoil and revolution and that the country would collapse and be easy to control. Lenin had lined up ten people to accompany him to Russia, and the party kept growing in size. Most of the Swiss dropped out, but some Poles joined. Strauss even whispered that Romain Rolland was supposed to go along, a completely unfounded rumor.

ON APRIL 7, Strauss said he had heard that the Russian party was actually leaving from the main railway station around noon on Easter Monday, April 9.

We arrived at the Hauptbahnhof at ten-thirty on Monday morning. It was a typical Zurich spring day—drizzly, cold, foggy, and rather dark. There was an air of great expectancy among the station personnel and the onlookers. A few of these were more conspicuous than they might have wished, but on the whole it was not an impressive group.

Lenin and his party arrived. Lenin had a knapsack on his back, crammed with books and papers. With a companion he walked briskly to the stationmaster and made the last arrangements for boarding the train. He was quite self-possessed and in passing greeted acquaintances in the group of onlookers with a smile as though nothing unusual was happening. He talked to the station master in a businesslike manner and without visible signs of emotion. What looked like about thirty, mostly Russian émigrés followed him. They were shabbily dressed and carried knapsacks, small trunks, baskets, pillows, and blankets. They looked decrepit and rather pitiful. But they were obviously moved by the thought of this new adventure and showed it, if only furtively, in their expressions and actions.

After Lenin had arranged matters with the stationmaster, the émigrés moved slowly toward the train. From behind the rope that cut us off from the train itself, we observed some last-minute shoving and hauling. Lenin grabbed one fellow by the collar and threw him out of the group; Strauss identified him as a Swiss socialist by the name of Blum who tried to force his way into the Party after Lenin had forbidden him to join because he was accused of being an agent of the Russian secret police.

The small group of onlookers behind the rope shouted insults at the émigrés, bellowing at random "Rascals!" . . . "Pigs!" . . . "Spies!" . . . "German agents!"

The émigrés shouted back half-heartedly and finally sang the "Internationale." The stationmaster herded them onto the train. The Swiss railroad personnel sealed the baggage cars and we watched the train slowly pulling out through the smoke and fog until it disappeared from sight. We heard the coughing of the engine gradually fade away. For a moment, there was complete silence in the station.

The little group that had come to watch straggled away. Strauss and I, at first only curious, were now excited and disturbed. We returned to the Café Odeon for an espresso.

≥≤

STRAUSS KNEW everyone in Zurich and was tireless in introducing me to his favorites. One day in the Café Odeon he called over a sad-looking man.

"*Salut!* This is David Rubinstein, a great cellist, the nephew of Anton Rubinstein. . . . Otto Luening, a great American composer—rich, too, but financially embarrassed, temporarily."

After a couple of cognacs, Rubinstein asked me to compose some cello pieces for him. Strauss remarked that Rubinstein performed often and was a member of the Zurich Symphony Orchestra and a fine soloist, so I accepted his invitation.

As our conversation waned, Strauss pointed excitedly to a weird fellow who was looking for a table. "Shh, shh, quiet. He's completely crazy. Dada. Do you want to meet him?"

The wild man joined us. His name was Hans Heusser. He

was a student at the Zurich Conservatory of Music, but also the professional music director for the Dada group. I mentioned Busoni and Richard Strauss.

Heusser looked pained and said, "Very old-fashioned; we play only Schoenberg, African music with percussion, and sometimes improvisations."

Strauss told Heusser that I had composed many cello pieces for Rubinstein, so Heusser invited us to play them at the Meierei, the headquarters of the Dada movement. I was very anxious to hear more about this group for they sounded like some of the wild, pre–First World War artists in Munich. Heusser talked at length about Dada in the Odeon and over our daily coffee and kirsch in the Meierei.

Heusser said that Tristan Tzara, a Rumanian poet, was the real founder of Dada. Tzara surrounded himself with an international collection of artists, anti-artists, pacifists, draft dodgers, deserters, junkies, real and phony physicians, and other camp followers. Heusser explained that Tzara, a conscientious objector, had learned to simulate schizophrenia so convincingly that the military attaché and physicians at the Rumanian embassy in Bern classified him as unfit for military service because of mental illness.

The Dadaists did much of their philosophizing in the Café de la Terrasse. The coffee was good; cocaine fixes could be arranged and were popular, for had not even the great Dr. Sigmund Freud praised the virtues of this drug and himself used it for a while? There were lengthy discussions of its effect on creative artists. Some of them, of course, alleged that they had been freed. Not so one musician, a brilliant violinist who became habituated and cured himself only by spending a summer high in the mountains practicing Bach solo sonatas six hours a day, playing in a hotel for room and board, and climbing mountains to exhaust himself the rest of the time. He regained his health and had a distinguished career without a recurrence, but two of our young artist addicts suffered complete mental breakdowns, and there was also a suicide. But these events were blamed on improper dosages. Eventually most of the group agreed that at least a minimum of self-discipline was needed even to create and sustain Dadaistic chaos.

The collage of Dada activities became part of my life for a

period. I was already a "radical" composer, and I now found the
uninhibited atmosphere of Dada exciting. I listened and looked
carefully as I attended the various events and met the people involved.

I learned that Marinetti, in his "Futurist Manifesto" of 1909,
and Russolo's noise music had anticipated many Dada twists.
Some of Marinetti's ideas turned into proclamations such as "War
is an eruption of possibility, a simultaneous poem, a symphony of
screams, shouts and commands by which one tries to solve the
problems of life." This now has a fine Fascist ring about it, but
then it influenced the Dadaists enormously, along with thoughts
like: "Music is an harmonic art—an action of common sense" . . .
"Bruitismus shows life as it is" . . . "Wagner was a pathological
liar" . . . "The noises of a brake can at least stop a toothache"
. . . "Death is vomiting, screaming, and choking." Everything
new to the Dadaist seemed important, artistic, and true.

Busoni, Stravinsky, and Varèse were all claimed as blood
brothers by the Dadaists, but I never saw or heard of them being
present, although Busoni had written his radical book *Sketch of a
New Esthetic of Music* in 1907 and looked tolerantly upon Marinetti and the Futurists. When Stravinsky visited Zurich he did
not attend Dada events. During Busoni's stay in Zurich I never
heard him or his followers mention the Dada events or people.
Years later, Varèse too disavowed any connection.

Heusser, Rubinstein, and I played at the Meierei one night
at 1:30 A.M. The program included one of my compositions for
cello and piano, known as the "Wet Dream Gavotte"! We also
played an aria and a one-step. Why Rubinstein and I also played
Saint-Saens' "The Swan," I don't know, but Heusser found it
suitable for his interesting programs. These included his own
works for piano, voice, and harmonium, which were much hated
by the Establishment. African dancers with masks were accompanied by Arabian tunes and tambourines. One-steps, ragtimes,
noise music, balalaika concerts, music with magic lantern slides,
piano improvisations, folk songs, brothel songs, and bass drum
solos rounded out his programs. There was a huge crowd, an
unearthly din, and blue smoke clouds, and everybody talked. Nobody listened except Heer, the Swiss poet. When we finished he
banged a beer mug on the floor and bellowed, "Silence! A con-

cert! Encore!" We repeated the program. Again nobody listened, but there was much applause, and we were offered drinks and were cheered. One fellow kept hollering, *"Eff-a, eff-a."* I finally understood he wanted me to play the notes F and A on the piano. I did. There were shouts of *"Encore!"* "F, A" went on for ten minutes. At half-past two the police closed the place. A few years later Heusser became music director in St. Gallen and made a reputation as a composer of marches for band—Swiss marches with a Dada twist!

I met Tzara and saw him in action once or twice, but he was too mad for me and I too square for him. He declaimed poetry and sometimes sang. He used bells, drums, whistles, and cowbells, beating the table to punctuate his declamations and to incite the audience to participate in his performance. He would curse, sigh, yodel, and shriek when the spirit moved him. His famous prescription for a poem—cut out words from a newspaper article, shake them in a hat, and spill them on a table, using their random order to reveal the poet's mind—smacked of the I Ching. His constant mobility was tiresome. Most of the Zurich artists thought him a poseur. They said of him, *"Er spinnt"*—"He spins" (or "is spinning")—and I agreed.

Far more interesting to me were Dr. Walter Serner and Hugo Ball and his mistress, Emmy Hennings. Serner was an adventurer, professional nihilist, and anarchist. Ball and Hennings, who were later married, were cabaret artists of some distinction. Hennings sang chansons and folk, brothel, and satirical songs. She had a thin voice and was like a rather anemic Yvette Guilbert or Edith Piaf. Ball was a poet and pianist of sorts. Together they were somewhat pale precursors of Kurt Weill and Lotte Lenya.

I had to face many conflicting interests in Zurich. Dr. Andreae and Philipp Jarnach introduced me to the larger professional world of music. My meeting with Ferruccio Busoni, a world figure, soon showed me that Bach and Milton, Mozart and Beaumarchais, Berlioz and Delacroix, Liszt and Cervantes, were all paths leading to the twentieth century. Busoni's prophetic genius pointed out possibilities for the future but demanded continuing self-education and self-discipline.

MY CONTACT with many of the other branches of the Dada movement was less immediate. The awakening dance movement in

Zurich was led by Alexander Sakharoff and Clotilde von Derp of the Pfauen Theater. They gave numerous interesting and, for that period, daring recitals in the municipal theaters and concert halls. Mary Wigman and Rudolph von Laban were allied with the Dadaists. Wigman's dances with percussive and exotic musical accompaniments attracted much attention because of their angular and nonsentimental type of movement. When performers were available, exotic art forms were presented, including African and Kabuki dances. Von Laban's studio was the center where Wigman and a group of other young dancers could develop new dance ideas, in movement, in choreography, and in notation. Wigman used masks and abstract stage settings.

Von Laban, after perfecting his notational system, made a spectacular career in Germany, where, in 1936, he became involved with the Nazi Ministry of Propaganda. Over his signature he invited Martha Graham to appear at the Olympic Games in Germany, an invitation she turned down because of its political, nonartistic coloring. Von Laban had come full circle from the chaotic, creative efforts and contributions of the Dadaists in 1917 to the state-controlled art of the Nazis in 1936.

The painters were unusually active; many of them later became internationally famous. They held exhibits all around town. When I arrived in Zurich they were moving to the Gallerie Corray on the Bahnhofstrasse, just across from my lodgings at Bahnhofstrasse 24, so I saw most of those exhibits. They also showed in the "Zurwaag" hall and in the Kaufleuten (the same hall that was host to James Joyce's English Players and to a Viennese operetta company that later engaged me as a flutist and conductor). These exhibits were distinguished by their high artistic quality and included works by Picabia, Picasso, Duchamp, Franz Marc, and Kandinsky. Further exhibits of paintings by Paul Klee, Giacometti, Kokoschka, and many other outstanding artists made a powerful impact on the artists, connoisseurs, and art dealers in Zurich. The Dada group also arranged exhibits of Chinese, African, Japanese, and other exotic art.

The tireless activities of the Dadaists included the printing of a number of flyers, pamphlets, magazines, and proclamations that appeared sporadically, depending on available funds. The periodical *Dada*, with contributions by Apollinaire, Picasso, Modigliani, Arp, Tzara, Kandinsky, and Marinetti, was more permanent. Café conversations concerning these manifestos were endless and ranged from discussions about the destruction of art, the resurrection of art, and the discovery of new art, to the inclusion of African and other exotic arts in Western civilization. Discussions of new materials and how to pull down the Establishment and its traditions were frequent. Hugo Ball summed it up when he wrote that Dada considered art an adventure of liberated humanity. He stated that the Dadaists "painted" with scissors, plaster, paper, stockings, adhesives, and other new tools and materials; he described how they made collages and montages and how exciting it was to find in the corner of one's own room a pretty leg, a train ticket, a stone, an insect, a clock movement—anything that inspired direct and pure feeling. He considered Dada an alarm signal against routine and speculation and all declining values: not a school of artists, but a desperate appeal for a creative basis on which all forms of art could find a new and universal consciousness. He pointed out Dada's influence in poetry, architecture, films, typography, music, and articles for everyday use. Sixty years later, there is no doubt in my mind that the effect of the movement can be seen in much commercial art, certain literary and musical trends, and in many of the other areas that Ball mentioned.

HEUSSER INTRODUCED me to a French medical student named Albert. During one of our debates in the Café Odeon, Albert spoke glowingly of Dr. Paul Eugen Bleuler's course in abnormal psychology at the university. Dr. Bleuler was director of the Burghölzli Sanatorium, an institution that became internationally known when James Joyce brought his daughter Lucia there for observation and diagnosis in the twenties. Albert explained that in Bleuler's monumental work *Dementia Praecox, or the Group of Schizophrenias,* published in 1911, Bleuler had written that schizophrenia was not a dementia but rather a disharmonious state of mind in which contradictory tendencies coexist. He was the first to believe that it could be helped and often cured by psychoanalysis and he pointed out that there were often spontaneous recoveries. Albert invited me to attend Bleuler's course in abnormal psychology in the Aula, or assembly hall, of the university.

Patients that Bleuler borrowed from Burghölzli were used as

examples and living stage props in his memorable lectures on diagnosis. Professor Bleuler walked to his lectern in a relaxed manner and talked to the class in a low key. He looked and dressed like a country family doctor, and there was a touch of country pastor about him. He exuded good will, kindness, and understanding, both in his facial expression and through his gestures as he escorted the patients to the platform. Bleuler began his first lecture by introducing a woman, a religious fanatic. He explained to the students that no matter what he would say to her, she would eventually relate his statement to Jesus. Bleuler was a skillful and kind interviewer, and he led her to prove his point that she was a religious maniac. He told us that this type of fixation would be hard to cure.

At another lecture, Bleuler brought in a very pretty young woman patient who looked like a zombie. He steered her to a corner of the platform and moved her arm up into a Statue of Liberty pose. She held it for fifteen minutes, until he posed her in another position, which she rigidly held for the rest of the session. During this interminable episode Dr. Bleuler explained that her rigidity came from a psychic fear, that it was a deep fixation on something that probably frightened her into immobility. Hot baths could bring her out of it sometimes, but he could never predict how long the relief would last.

Professor Bleuler admitted that he could neither predict nor explain spontaneous cures and remissions. Patients would sometimes almost walk out of their symptoms (so he expressed it), ask for their clothes and transportation home, and perhaps never return. He explained that often only a small adjustment in their everyday life was necessary to keep them functioning. He also explained that through psychoanalysis it was difficult but no longer impossible to help many patients and so restore them to society. None of this seemed in the least depressing, for Dr. Bleuler was renowned for being the first psychiatrist who was confident and optimistic about possible relief for schizophrenics. What I learned in his lectures and remembered for more than half a century was that almost no psychic illness is really hopeless.

Albert was delighted that I had been impressed by Dr. Bleuler. As a senior medical student Albert seemed to me a very sophisticated older man (he was about twenty-five) who knew all the answers, so I asked him about some of the fine points of psychiatry.

One day, one of Bleuler's patients insisted that there was an angel sitting in the front row of the lecture hall. I told Albert that such fantasies often inspired artists, and mentioned William Blake.

He looked rather bored as he said, "Oh yes, we know that; you should read the articles by Dr. Carl Jung."

Jung had been Bleuler's student and his assistant at Burghölzli at the beginning of the century. He had a large private practice. His dissertation was entitled *On the Psychology and Pathology of So-Called Occult Phenomena.* He analyzed mediums, went to seances, studied autism, hallucinatory visions, sensations, inner voices, and automatic writing. I asked Albert whether I could meet people who were involved in these analytic studies. Albert suggested that I attend a party given by one of Jung's patients.

The party began around 9:00 P.M. and lasted until 4:00 A.M. The guests included musicians, painters, writers, and many university students, some of them in the faculty of medicine. I was the only composer. I met a Dr. Franz Riklin and felt attracted to him. His friendly blue eyes, pleasant face, and soft-spoken manner had the effect of making me want to talk. He was soon questioning me about composing and in particular how I composed and what it meant to me. I told him I had discovered the Dadaists. This interested him and he asked how I reacted to this whole business and what I thought of painters like Picasso and composers like Schoenberg. Although we had had a glass or two of wine and everybody was rather lively, it was Dr. Riklin's conversation that animated me and seemed to open new facets of my nature. I went on at length about how I composed from inner aural images. He told me that he had been Jung's assistant for a time and how they had collaborated in conducting a laboratory for experimental psychopathology at Burghölzli. He had made many studies in free association, and, like Jung, was very much interested in the arts.

The host, a young literature student, had on his piano a rather nicely sculpted head of an African woman. He was being analyzed and told me he had made the head as part of his therapy. He explained that thinking about the head, dreaming about it, and then using his hands to shape it had helped to restore his emotional health. His remarks made me consider the possibility of therapeutic benefits from artistic activities.

ONE DAY, Dr. Andreae, the conservatory's director, arranged an outing for his students in the foothills near Zurich. Before we began our excursion, a few of his friends joined us. One of them was a striking-looking man with very sensitive features but otherwise seemingly rather energetic and rugged.

"Students," said Dr. Andreae, "this is Hermann Hesse. Hesse, these are the students."

I asked Otto Strauss, who had joined the group at the last minute, "Who is Hesse?"

"The greatest German poet since Goethe," he responded.

On our outing and afterwards, I learned that Hesse had been in Switzerland off and on for many years but now was a permanent resident, totally opposed to the war and to the mentality that had helped bring it on. In 1916, because of family problems and overwork, he had had a severe emotional crisis and was unable to function normally. Dr. Joseph Bernhard Lang, a student of Jung, became his friend and introduced him to the writings of both Freud and Jung; he had between sixty and seventy psychiatric interviews with Dr. Lang. This treatment and his study of Nietzsche turned him away from "art for art's sake." He immortalized Othmar Schoeck and Dr. Andreae, both Swiss composers, in his *Journey to the East*—in which "Othmar played Mozart in the lofty hall of the castle," and Andreae was transformed into Leo.

Although Hesse seemed not to have a direct contact with the Dada group, he could hardly have escaped some of their exhibits and performances. Later when he, Hugo Ball, and Emma Hennings moved to Italian Switzerland, they became close friends. Hesse's understanding of the underlying motives of the Dadaists without doubt had a strong influence in helping to release his creative powers.

Chapter 7

Edith Rockefeller McCormick
and the Zurich Conservatory
1917-1920

I WENT TO THE CONSERVATORY for my entrance examination. A tough-looking little German, Mr. Paul Moeckel, gave me dictation: I was to notate themes from Richard Strauss's *Ein Heldenleben* after two hearings.

"I am surprised that you didn't get it the first time. You'd better take dictation," he said in a discouragingly nasal tone of voice.

Karl Vogler, the acting director, who had a long black beard, watery eyes, and wavy hair, didn't bother to hear me play. He showed his administrative genius by filling out my schedule without any conversation at all. He assigned me to what I soon found were secondary teachers, and I suffered for six weeks until Dr. Andreae, the director, returned from military service.

I immediately made an appointment with him. I took my flute and my own *Improvisation for Violin and Piano*, Bach's *Well-Tempered Clavier*, my new song with text by Oscar Wilde with an accompaniment figure that was repeated for three pages under a nice melody, and a collection of Palestrina, Obrecht, and Lassus choral works in four clefs.

Andreae was most cordial. "American, are you. What are you doing here?"

I explained things. As I spoke, I could observe him as he paced around the room, a middle-sized, stocky figure, with close-cropped hair and a mustache, not in any way arty. He looked more like a Swiss banker and a colonel in the militia than like the conductor of the great Zurich Tonhalle Orchester.

He accompanied me as I played the Bach C Major Flute Sonata.

"Very good. How is your piano playing?"

"I'm a composer," I said, "but I can get around."

"Let's try this one," he said, and he opened up *The Well-Tempered Clavier* to the C-sharp Minor Fugue.

Although I wasn't practicing much piano, I had developed into a fluent sight reader.

After I was about halfway through, he patted me on the shoulder. "Very musical. Have you any compositions?"

I showed him my *Improvisation*. The harmonies in this piece moved with independent voice leading and there was a good sense of melodic momentum. It was an unpretentious but decently written linear piece.

"Very interesting, and what else do you have?"

I showed him the Wilde song with the *ostinato* accompaniment—*ostinato* meaning obstinate, and that is what the accompaniment was. Andreae played it.

"A very nice poem. . . . Your music . . . well, the sins of one's youth must be forgiven and hopefully eventually forgotten. Can you read scores?"

I played something rather easy by Obrecht that I had to transpose.

"Very good. What classes were you assigned to?" I told him. "Excuse me a minute," he said, and walked into Direktor Vogler's office.

I heard rumbling voices, and through the thick Swiss German dialect I heard Dr. Andreae say, "Composition, conducting, canon and fugue, change to Nada." He rejoined me.

I said, "Dr. Andreae, the real object of my visit was to apply for a position in the orchestra. I am running out of money and must have a job."

He looked thoughtful. "I could engage you as fourth flutist, but that would be too bad. You really should study. Direktor Vogler will change your schedule. Incidentally, do you know Mrs. Edith Rockefeller McCormick?"

"No."

"She's the daughter of John D. Rockefeller."

"I know who *he* is."

"She's the richest woman in the world."

"She is?"

He was silent for a few moments. "I will write you a letter of introduction. I think you should meet her." I said I just wanted a job and not an introduction to anyone, but he went to his desk and penned a letter. "Send it to Mrs. McCormick with a note. You should meet her and talk with her." I pocketed the letter, thanked Dr. Andreae warmly and left.

Vogler was standing in front of the door, probably eavesdropping. "Oh, Mr. Luening. I have decided to change your schedule. You will take composition, orchestration, score playing, and conducting with Dr. Andreae. You are promoted from harmony to my canon and fugue class. You will drop dictation, and Mr. Baldegger, your new piano teacher, will see you tomorrow. He was formerly a monk. Mr. Jean Nada was not a monk. He is the first flutist of the Tonhalle Orchestra, and will teach you flute."

This, with slight alterations and some additions, was the schedule I followed for three years.

I WROTE TO Mrs. McCormick, enclosing Dr. Andreae's letter of introduction. I explained that I did not know what he had in mind. A few days later, I had a cordial invitation to have tea with her at five o'clock the next day at the Hotel Baur au Lac. I arranged to do that, having absolutely nothing else to arrange.

My clothes were in terrible condition. I wore a castoff overcoat, a half-foot too long, shoes that were loose at the toes and needed resewing, and a suit with a green coat, blue trousers, and a weird, baggy brown sweater-vest. To put it briefly, I looked down-and-out.

The Baur au Lac was the most fashionable hotel in Zurich, and I was received with a strange stare from the doorman. Doubtfully, he let me approach the concierge, who passed me along to the bellcap, who ushered me to the desk. The staff indulged in much hemming, hawing, and talking back and forth—a very embarrassing experience. Guests in the lobby were by then wondering what this bum was doing. But the man at the desk had sent a bellboy to Mrs. McCormick's suite. He returned, bowing and scraping, and said I was to follow him to her suite. At that, everybody who had watched and listened bowed and scraped, figuratively speaking, for I had passed the test. I was obviously some sort of a great young refugee sexpot, a cocaine pusher, or a spy, who had an "in" with the richest woman in the world. I was to be treated with respect. Two ladies smiled at me as I passed them.

I reached the suite after being guided through a labyrinth of corridors. The bellboy knocked. I handed him one of my few remaining francs, and entered.

At one end of the large room a very impressive-looking lady was seated in a chair. Her ankles were crossed, which made her feet look crossed—the style European ladies found proper in those days. She looked like her father, John D. Rockefeller, Sr. Her face was plain and oval, with remarkable pale-blue eyes. Her glance was sympathetic, warm, and understanding, and she seemed to observe everything that was going on about her. Her skin was like old parchment, only creamy. She seemed either to be skillfully made up or not to use any makeup at all. Her hair was tied in a very plain German style. When I entered, she rose from her chair and waved me to a sofa.

Not knowing why I was there, I was a little nervous. She put me at my ease with some remarks about the weather and then said, "I have this letter from Dr. Andreae," and held it up. "He suggested that I see you."

I said, "He did say I should write to you and send you his letter, but he didn't tell me why."

"Well, first, tell me how you happen to be here. You are an American, aren't you?"

I told her the story of my life. She then asked, "What are you planning to do?"

"I am enrolled in the conservatory and I told Dr. Andreae I must have a job because I can't go on like this. My family would like me to go home and work in a pea cannery, and I don't see why. I'm just as much under American military rule here as I would be at home, and I can retain my citizenship by reporting to the consulate. But I want to go on with my music studies. I think it's silly to stop them now. It wouldn't help anyone. I hope Dr. Andreae is going to get a job for me."

"What are you interested in?"

"I'm interested primarily in composing and conducting."

She looked pleased. "Yes, that's very good . . . fine. How do you plan to develop these interests?"

I thought for a moment or two. "I have already composed quite a bit. I can't tell at this point how the conducting is going to work, but I do play the flute, the piano, and the organ, and I plan to learn other instruments."

"How did you get along at the Munich academy?" she asked.

"I had very good marks and I played professionally when I was fifteen."

"How old are you?"

"I'll be seventeen in June."

She seemed rather serious as she said, "You know, of course, that we do need composers very badly in America. We don't need conductors as much, because we have many. Do you know Campanini?"

"I know his name but I have not heard him. I do know Strauss, Walter, and Reger from Munich."

She rang for the waiter. He arrived with tea and a plate full of cakes. As I was still half-starved from the German experience, it was hard to keep from jumping on the plate of French pastry. I finished off about six or seven tarts.

She watched me with a mixture of wonder and sympathy and eventually asked, "How much do you think you will need each month to live? What will you have to earn?"

"I don't know. Probably if I could skimp along I could make it on very little."

"You need a vacation. When does your school start?"

"I think in August."

She smiled. "I want you to have a two-month vacation. What will that cost?"

"I haven't the slightest idea. It might be about three hundred francs a month."

She got up and went to a wall safe. She took out a roll of Swiss bills, put them into an envelope, and handed it to me, saying, "I would like you to take this and have a rest for two months. Come back and see me after your vacation."

I almost fell off the sofa as I stuttered, "This wasn't really why I came here."

"I know that," she said, "but I think this should be yours right now. We will have another talk in the fall, when you return and school starts."

I literally stumbled out of the hotel. Once outside I counted the money—six hundred francs! As I had only about ten francs left in my pocket, this seemed like a gold mine. It meant that I could have some good food. The idea of a vacation, after the debilitating German experience, was almost too good to be real.

⋊⋉

I SPENT THE summer at an expensive spa recommended by a distant cousin. I so enjoyed my newfound riches that I returned to Zurich almost broke—and the conservatory was opening in two weeks. I had just enough money to pay for my room, but not enough for food. Every day, I got bread, marmalade, and a jug of milk, and that was my menu three times a day. The rest of the time I practiced and composed, the one way I knew to fight bad luck—and because there wasn't anything else I could do. I secretly believed then, as I do now, that music gives me strength.

Dr. Andreae was not in town, I heard nothing from Mrs. McCormick, and Helene had just enough money for herself. An old friend of our family from Milwaukee named Ackerman arrived. A cellist from Munich named Grupp arrived, also broke. We met occasionally to talk, walk, and wait for money. Ackerman noticed that I never went out for breakfast and wouldn't meet him for lunch or dinner. He asked when I took meals, and I told him I had been in training and I didn't think it was good for me to overeat at this time because of the very bad rations we had had in Germany.

A few days later, Ackerman came to my room and found me with the milk jug, bread, and marmalade.

"Is that what you're having for lunch?"

"Yes."

"Well, what do you have for dinner?"

"I'm not going out."

"How do you expect to live this way?"

I finally confessed that I had been eating like this for two weeks.

"This is going to stop," Ackerman said. "You come along. You, Grupp, and I will go out and have some food."

We went to a good restaurant, where for fifty cents we had a splendid meal. I was hungry and it tasted wonderful.

I was soon down to twenty francs. I took a deep breath, and decided that I couldn't wait for Dr. Andreae to give me a job. I would have to go to the various movie houses, cafés, and nightclubs where they had music and offer my services, if only for board and room. Ackerman was beginning to pay bills and I didn't like it. So, on a September morning, I took my flute under my arm and went to look for work.

A letter was in the mailbox, a typewritten letter, addressed to me. I thought it was an advertisement and ignored it, but on second thought came back to pick it up. It was a notice from the Eidgenössische Bank stating that the sum of 1,800 francs had been deposited in my name. I also found a letter from Mrs. McCormick that said she hoped I had enjoyed a nice vacation and that I must have a chance to study and not work immediately, so she had sent me a stipend for the semester. In six months I should write her.

I was in a state of shock as I went to the bank—across the street from my room—opened my account, and swaggered out, feeling like a big shot for once. Grupp and Ackerman dropped by, and were delighted.

I felt so grateful to Ackerman for his warmhearted help and to Grupp for his company that I invited them for a real party at the Locanda Ticinese, the best restaurant in town. We had a marvelous Italian meal with chianti. The bill was twelve dollars, an enormous sum in those days. We ended up with cognac and then went to a nightclub, where I had my first champagne cocktail. Grupp tasted whiskey and soda for the first time. We were ejected at one o'clock.

In great shape and full of good cheer, we sailed down the Bahnhofstrasse in the direction of my room. We were raising cain, singing, and having a good old European kickoff when we saw coming from the opposite direction a chap arm-in-arm with two girls, a woman's hat slanting on his head. He was having a hot time with the girls. As he approached, I recognized a man from the Baur au Lac.

As I sailed by I was not happy. *My God*, I thought. *Now, after this enormous windfall, this chap will probably report to Mrs. McCormick that the boy she is helping at the conservatory has taken off on a great big terrible binge with two other bums.*

But nothing ever happened. I did have a rough time in my room and on my balcony, balancing all the food and champagne and trying to balance myself while keeping the bed from floating out of the window, but it had a happy ending. Next day, I had a beautiful hangover, but we three sinners met for a fifty-cent lunch that straightened us out. Then I composed a good song, *In Weinachtszeiten (At Christmastime)*, to a poem by Hermann Hesse— an example of a postsickness composing habit that continued through my life. The song was later performed in Switzerland and in the United States.

A few days later, I reported this happy story to Andreae, and he was mightily pleased. Proud of initiating my good fortune, he spread the story around town as benevolent gossip. He told his choral society that the right people always meet the right people, which I thought was moving; I wished it would continue all my life. Alas, it did not, but Dr. Andreae personally wished me good luck as I started on my studies.

WHEN THE six-month stipend ended, I was invited to visit Mrs. McCormick.

She came right to the point. "How are your studies going?"

I told her they were going well, what I was doing, and that I was seriously studying to be a conductor and a composer. She asked me what my future plans were.

"I want to continue studying," I said, "and get a job in the orchestra as soon as possible, as I originally planned."

She was very friendly. "That's very sensible. You just go along, and we'll keep in touch." She didn't mention my financial future.

In my mind I wrote it all off as the whim of a rich woman and started looking for a job again. There was only one opportunity, in a shabby café. Several days later, I looked into my mailbox and discovered a letter from the familiar Eidgenossische Bank, notifying me that there had been deposited to my account the sum of 5,400 francs. I also found a nice letter from Mrs. McCormick, saying she was very much pleased with the way I had progressed. She did hope that this stipend would help me get through a year of study. She suggested that I devote most of my energies to composing. She set one other semicondition for her patronage: that I eventually return to America and settle in Chicago.

Mrs. McCormick never interfered with my studies in any way. She seemed to enjoy my visits. She listened to my adventures with obvious interest and was often quite complimentary about my development as a human being. She liked the way I tackled my problems and managed my studies. I did not, as she put it in German, have much *Wahn* (madness) about me. Later, as life rolled over me, I sometimes wondered if she was right about that. At eighteen I was very sure of myself—at least I thought I was—and this self-assurance was a kind of youthful arrogance that pleased her. From the vantage point of many years, I have reached the conclusion that I appeared more mature than I actually was.

Mrs. McCormick was, incidentally, a patroness on a grand scale. Among her other prominent protégés were James Joyce and Philipp Jarnach.

Mrs. McCormick had come to Zurich to be psychoanalyzed by Dr. Jung. After her analysis, she became a lay analyst herself. I heard from others—and I agree—that in her relations with many of us she functioned partly as therapist. She let us talk without trying to direct us, but she gave us some guidance, assurance, and reassurance in our work. For me, this was very helpful. She was definitely not a patroness of the ordinary kind. One felt from her a strong understanding and an empathy that were often unspoken. Later, she was appreciative of anything I did that was in any way substantial, and when I had a performance she was pleased and supportive. My relationship with her has had a lasting influence on my life, and I honor her memory.

≫≮

WHEN I registered in the conservatory, I was assigned to Herr Koehler, the deputy first flutist of the opera and symphony orchestras, a charming gentleman of about sixty-five years, a little on the fat side with a bouncy walk that made his entrances cheerful. At my first lesson he produced the weirdest flute I have ever seen, a Meyer Reformflöte. All the fine points of Rube Goldberg's inventions were included, as were designs of early-nineteenth-century plumbing and gas pipes. How Koehler played the thing was more than I could figure out. My own flute was a wooden Boehm and a nice one. At the first lesson, I discovered that poor Koehler's best days were behind him. He attempted an Anderson étude. All I could hear was the rushing wheeze of the wind from his asthmatic lungs and the rattling of the flute. As for the music, it remained strictly on the printed page. I soon discovered that I could play better than Koehler. When Dr. Andreae heard me play, he transferred me to Jean Nada.

This *maître* from Nice had studied in Paris. He spoke little German and I thought him elegant and romantic. When he heard me play, he shook his head sadly, indicating I had had the wrong schooling, but that perhaps he could straighten things out. He disapproved of my German wooden flute. Before I had finished my first lesson, he sold me two volumes of the Altes flute method and a silver Bonneville flute at bargain rates. I paid $150 for the flute in 1918; after using it for fifteen years I sold it for a hundred dollars, and it was still good. Nada started me on page one of Altes and practically every time I played a note he'd *tsk, tsk, tsk* and play it for me the way it should be. Finally he was reasonably satisfied. He had absolute control over the instrument and played with Paris Conservatoire accuracy. His way was the only way to play, but he did allow me to experiment with vibrato. Soon I had a real swinging flute tone. Fired by his approval, I practiced more, and soon was playing engagements around town.

The real upswing in my playing came when I joined the Tonhalle and opera orchestras as third flute, piccolo, and deputy first flute, sitting next to Nada most of the time. He coached me on every single passage, so I was in fact getting music lessons right in the orchestra. The greatest fun was when Nada and the clarinettist, Edmund Allegra (later with the Boston Symphony Orchestra), took me in hand and showed me the traditional French way to play *Carmen*. In performances we would take the bit in our teeth and tear into all the exposed woodwind passages with brilliance and fine tonal sense. When the conductor saw us warming up for our attacks, he had the good sense to follow us, because he knew that the woodwinds were going to have it *their* way. One other flute triumph came when, in the Tonhalle, I played the piccolo solo in Mahler's G Major Symphony and was congratulated by the first horn player—a fleabitten roughneck most of the time, but on this occasion a welcome friend. He said he had never heard the solo played so beautifully by anybody. I felt so encouraged that I was soon playing chamber music around town, at church concerts, and in the summer in a marionette theater. I was engaged as a soloist for the Bach concerts with the harpsichordist Wanda Landowska and the soprano Madame Noordewier. Bach arias with two and three flutes were pretty high class, and the two great ladies were happy after the first runthrough.

I soon won the reputation of being the second-best flutist in Zurich and was engaged as first and one-and-only flutist in the operetta orchestra that played in the Kaufleuten. One of the operettas was called *Der Frechling (The Impertinent One)*. By then, I had a following among the girls at the conservatory.

Two sisters became quite interested in Otto Strauss and myself and came around to see the shows more than was necessary to learn the tunes. Strauss and I followed them around on the Bahnhofstrasse. One thing led to another and a café, and there they dropped the news that their parents would be away on a certain day.

It was a cold and snowy Swiss evening, but Strauss and I trotted all the way up the Ütliberg. I had taken my flute and proceeded to serenade the two girls with excerpts from *Der Frechling*. Some of the sounds finally penetrated, and they looked out.

When they saw the two of us in the snowstorm—me playing the flute and Strauss just freezing—they were charmed, and had us in for a cup of tea with cognac. All of this was, of course, a most risky business in Switzerland, and I imagine that if their papa had caught us he probably would have had us arrested and put the girls in a convent.

Our visit was brief and an artistic success only, for the girls were expecting their parents soon and tearfully asked us to exit fast and come back in a week.

I found the episode very interesting, because it showed me that the flute was good for other things than simply playing in an orchestra.

NADA WAS elegant-looking, with wavy hair and a well-trimmed black mustache in a style that made him look like a barber. When he began playing he resembled a faun. He had an unusually mellow tone for a French flutist, but he could also produce very sharp and brilliant staccati with single, double, and triple tonguing. He phrased with mechanical precision and played with an external brilliance that was refreshing. I sometimes had the feeling that he didn't understand the expressive content of the German music, but he played all of the French repertory beautifully.

Nada really took pains to explain everything to me. In adjusting my embouchure, he looked at me, shook his head, and moved the flute along my lip about a thirty-second of an inch.

When the tone wasn't to his satisfaction, he stood back and deliberated for a few minutes, moved forward, raised the flute one one-hundred-and-sixty-fourth of an inch and said, "Try it again." Going to the other side of the room, he listened, shook his head, came back, took my flute away, looked at my mouth, and asked me to stick my tongue out. Inspecting the tip of my tongue, he again shook his head and worried, and finally worried me.

I imagined that he had found some horrible thing, perhaps a cancer.

Then he said, "I think your tongue is a little too pointed to get the proper flute tone, but let's try again."

I played and he listened in a very concentrated fashion and, with a surgical look, said, "You know, I think it's the formation of your mouth that's causing the trouble."

This was said with such professional conviction that I had a mental image of a mule's mouth with the pointed tongue of a snake. I felt that Nada secretly thought that only an operation would be able to make that unpliable part of my anatomy suitable for flute playing.

Nada coached me in Bach sonatas and the Mozart concerto with harp. As a final triumph, for my exit from the conservatory he taught me the *Concertino* by Cécile Chaminade, a Paris Conservatoire examination piece. This I played with the Tonhalle

Orchestra. Nada conducted. It was a great success for all. I was never, however, very enthusiastic about that funny little piece. It did have a great many flute tricks in it, but it was salon music and not exactly my cup of tea. Too sentimental!

MY PIANO teacher was Herr Baldegger. Rumor had it that he was an unfrocked priest or a retired monk, and this intrigued me.

Baldegger's studio door opened exactly at the appointed hour. A minute's tardiness brought a reprimand. His greeting never varied: "Good morning. Let's get to work." And then he laid it all out. He gave the same pieces to all his students. First came the usual Czerny graded scale studies, then the Kramer études; Clementi's *Gradus ad Parnassum* followed. He checked first the left hand and then the right. His ideas about how to use arm muscles seemed to be a bit like shifting gears in a car. I never got it right. Eventually, I would just sit down and play the pieces musically, and he would say, "Exactly what I mean." On his off-days he would go to the piano and beat out an étude fast and mechanically. Showing his teeth, he would leer at me from the piano bench, meaning "That's how you *should* be playing, but of course *you* can't play that way." Sometimes the look was accompanied by a soft chuckle.

I was quite busy with the opera and symphony orchestras, causing me to neglect piano practice, but I was a fluent piano sight reader too. I eventually read new lessons at sight.

Baldegger had me play the Preludes and Fugues from the first volume of *The Well-Tempered Clavier*, and I got so that I could play some of these with considerable style and accuracy. He also gave me some Beethoven sonatas, not for their musical values but solely as technical exercises. He did me no harm, and probably not much good.

At one point, he got fired up and decided that I must play in public. He chose Rachmaninoff's C-sharp Minor Prelude. I enjoyed the piece because it sounded very difficult but wasn't, and I liked the grim mood. I practiced the thing like a fool, and I banged it out with an amount of busto-crusto that astonished all of the conservatory girls and made the pianists say I could be a very good player if I wanted to be. I don't think I played piano in public again until I returned to the States.

CHAMBER MUSIC classes were run by Josef Ebner, a violist who knew the repertory although he was not a great performer. His method was to pick out a nice piece and get his players interested in it so that they would practice at home. With that approach things improved. I played the Handel Trio in C Minor for flute, violin, and piano, the Bach G Major Trio, and Bach's *Musical Offering* for the same combination.

Ebner had the advantage of being cross-eyed, so that he seemed to be watching everybody at the same time. While the music was being played, his face had a peculiar expression from which one could not read whether he was highly pleased or highly displeased. This spurred us on to our greatest efforts— which he rewarded by saying, "So . . . now the next movement." He taught me the pleasures of playing baroque music, a lively and expressive but not terribly difficult repertory.

MY AIM at the conservatory was to learn everything I possibly could, in breadth if not in depth. I signed up with Herr Luz, the best organist in town. He was a sallow, sad-looking, stooped gentleman who reminded me of Abraham Lincoln. The entire organ staff seemed even more Lincolnian when it turned out that the man who pumped the practice organ by hand was a fine-looking Swiss gentleman of eighty-five who alleged that he had been General Grant's coachman.

Although Luz looked sad he played with considerable gusto. I knew he was a great teacher because he immediately recognized my talent by giving me some fairly difficult Bach chorale preludes to play and also some Mendelssohn sonatas.

The practice organ was an overblown harmonium with pedals. General Grant's coachman pumped in rhythm. If I pulled out too many stops, using up too much air for the pace he liked, the organ simply stopped sounding until the bellows was filled. He didn't notice these lapses because he was deaf. Besides that, he could pump while sleeping, and there was nothing I could do about it. I practiced from 7:00 to 8:00 A.M., and when I think of the late hours I kept, I suspect I took a short nap myself once in a while. But these practice hours were enough fun to straighten everything out.

Luz gave me my lessons in the beautiful Fraumünster. In

the church he looked less like Lincoln and more like one of the sadder saints in a seventeenth-century religious painting. He would turn me loose on the magnificent organ. As I looked over the bank of stops, I would always pick out something special like a Quintflöte (a flute with fifth doublings) or a snarly Krummhorn or perhaps a Vox Humana, of course without tremolo. After warming up, I tore into the Mendelssohn sonatas like a maniac, and with the swell pedal worked in crescendos that almost smashed the windows. I really thought I was damned good.

I soon substituted in a French church. In the rehearsal the pastor viewed me with considerable suspicion—on general principles. I thought he looked much too worried for a minister. He was always nagging me about the tempi of the hymns, crying *"Plus vite! Plus vite!"* When I jazzed up the organ to a *presto* tempo, he still hissed, *"Plus vite!"* At one point, I ventured to tell him if he tried to get the congregation to sing at that clip, they would be *"plus mort."* He didn't appreciate my humor, and gave me an unusually sour and jaundiced look as though he were, without much success, working on a too-large dumpling he had eaten for lunch.

I THOUGHT I didn't know enough about orchestral instruments, so I signed up for lessons on the double bass. Fricke, the bass teacher, spent much time teaching me how to hold the bow according to the German method. It reminded me very strongly of the way we used a saw back on the farm in Wisconsin. Exercises on the strings were fine as long as I played on open strings, but when I began fingering the monstrous cables on this colossal instrument (I am referring, of course, to its size only) I decided it was not for me, and that I had better get out of this engagement as fast as possible.

ERNST ISLER lectured about music history. He was the leading music critic of the *Neue Züricher Zeitung*, and an organist. His reviews were excellent and his reputation as a lecturer was good, so I decided I would give him a try, even though I had been exposed to some pretty windy musicology by Professor Kellermann and Professor Sandberger in Munich and should have known better.

Isler began his course with a lecture on the beginnings of music. His lecture went something like this:

"There are natural beginnings of music on our earth. We can of course imagine the first grunts and roars from our coinhabitants, the animals, with perhaps a hiss now and then to warn of an attack or to indicate an injury. For the origin of music we must look further and elsewhere. We owe a real debt to our feathered friends. Imagine the little female bird sitting near her nest, lonesome, and longingly waiting for her mate. Imagine her mate sitting on another tree in the vicinity or perhaps flying hither and yon, bursting with ardor and longing, suffering those same tensions that exist between any species that has two sexes.

"As the tension in the little male gets to be so strong that it is practically unbearable," Isler would say, "he quivers on his bough in his tree, and then, no longer able to stand this glorious, rapturous agony, what does he do?"

Isler would look around at the class expectantly, and I think he would have enjoyed having someone raise his hand to say, "I know, he . . ."

But after a short pause Isler continued, "What does he do? He bursts into song and with this anguished but joyous cry of the male to his little mate we have the beginning of music, a beginning which has led to innumerable such calls. I need only mention *Tristan und Isolde, Fidelio,* Beethoven sonatas, or *Ein Heldenleben,* by our contemporary, Richard Strauss. Sometimes the mate is near, sometimes far. Sometimes alive, sometimes dead. Sometimes the male calls to another male to warn him that he is on forbidden territory and that if he does not leave he will be treated accordingly."

Isler went on and on about this bird psychology. When he began to talk about the birdcalls in Haydn's *Seasons* and Beethoven's *Pastorale* and tried to connect the birdcall in *Siegfried* with the mythology of *Der Ring des Nibelungen,* some of us decided to absent ourselves from this sexy course in music history.

Today I must revise this opinion. Messiaen, one of our leading composers, claims that only birdsong is authentic and uncontaminated musical material.

Was Isler right, after all?

≽≼

I WENT TO Dr. Andreae in 1918 to again inquire about a job in the symphony orchestra. He told me there were certain conditions. "I can use you as fourth flute later, but for now . . . do you play percussion?"

"I do not," I answered.

"Then you must study with Herr Büttner, for there will be an opening in the orchestra in three months."

I met Büttner, a stocky, rugged little Saxon with a goatee (a tiny goat's goatee), flashing blue eyes, and a hale and hearty drive about him that made him one of the best kettledrummers I have ever heard. At my first lesson, he introduced me to the triangle. Usually this was attached to one of the drum stands, but Büttner showed me how to hold it on a string. This, he claimed, was essential for a real artist, because sometimes he needs to raise the instrument or lower it or even swish it around a bit for effect.

Next, he showed me how to hold the metal rod that was used to strike the instrument. No clumsy way of holding the instrument or the rod would do. One held it the way Nikisch held his baton, elegantly but efficiently. "Strike the triangle for single notes!"

My first try sounded tinny. Büttner looked disgusted.

"You're off-center, and you're not holding your rod firmly. Again."

Things went better.

"Now play several notes in succession."

Büttner looked very unhappy when I finished. "Give me the rod." He stepped up to the triangle, and, gazing up at the ceiling with an expression that was a combination of an angel about to fly and a horse about to whinny, he played a series of single notes, so beautiful and bell-like that I hated to hear him stop.

I have never forgotten that sound.

I applauded. He bowed. When I tried to imitate him, I just couldn't make the triangle come through with that celestial quality.

"You can also hit the sides, you know, but for special effects only. This goes rather well in Tchaikovsky," he said, producing a tinkly sound on the left side of the triangle. "This one I like for

Liszt's famous solo in the E-flat Piano Concerto," and he produced a ping from the other side. "When you get through mastering these strokes, I want you to try a tremolo, like this," and showing his teeth, he tore into the triangle like a dog after a bone, and began shaking the rod from side to side so fast that the little instrument sounded like a gong. "Try it."

I did, and I produced an uneven, sick sound.

"I think I'd better try you on an easier instrument. Have you ever heard or seen a bass drum?"

I said yes.

"This is the drumstick. That's the drum. You're supposed to hit the drum with the stick. Can you do that?"

I said I would try.

"Regular, steady beats, *forte*."

I began.

"*Forte, forte*."

I played a little louder. Silence for several moments.

"I told you to play *forte*!" he yelled.

I beat the tar out of the drum. He stopped me.

"Three times I have begged for *forte*. You've been playing *fortissimo*. Give me the stick."

He then proceeded to play a series of repeated notes, starting with a triple *piano* and working up to a triple *fortissimo*. When he hit the ultimate note, he relaxed for a moment, looking very much like a victorious cavalry general after a successful charge. "Practice that. And this."

Pulling out a two-headed drumstick, he beat a tattoo on that poor bass drum the like of which I have never heard since.

"Now let's try the ratchet. . . ." he said.

This fine instrument sounded like pulling a cane over a picket fence. Büttner did not think it was capable of much expressivity. He played, I thought, rather indifferently. When it came my turn on the ratchet, I set up a little pattern—*piano, mezzo forte*, and *forte*—and made a little composition out of it then and there, improvised of course.

When I finished my one-minute piece, Büttner was positively moved, and smiling at me like some friendly mongrel dog, he said, "I've never heard the ratchet played so beautifully; you have great talent for this instrument."

A few weeks later, we had tried most of the usual percussion instruments, and I was tagged for glockenspiel, celesta, and easy xylophone parts, along with ratchet, triangle, bass drum, and cymbals. I was practicing studies on the kettledrum one day when Büttner put the sticks up on the stand and said, "I think you're ready to have lessons in the opera house. Meet me there at three P.M. tomorrow."

I arrived promptly and was ushered through darkened halls and other mysterious byways into the percussion section of the orchestra pit. The opera house itself was completely dark. There was nobody on stage or in the auditorium. Only the orchestra light over the kettledrum stand showed that someone was nearby.

Büttner uncovered the kettledrums and polished the copper, then tapped the heads and tuned them, tried a few soft beats, and said, "You know, Richard Wagner conducted in this pit." This set me back just a little. Then he pulled out a book, *Kettledrum Passages from the Works of Richard Wagner*, and put it on the stand.

Büttner tested the drums by playing an enormous crescendo, which in the empty theater sounded like an earthquake in a cavern. "Play this passage from *Götterdämmerung*."

I looked it over, loosened up my wrists, and played: *Boom.* Pause. *Boom.* Pause. Short *boom.* Long *boom.* Pause.

Büttner looked quizzical. "Technically, not bad," he said, "but you don't put any expression into it. You know this is supposed to represent the downfall of the gods, and it sounds too happy the way you play it. Try again."

The second time I gave it a little more English and Büttner announced, "It's better, but it's not right. You see, Wagner was a great philosopher, and in this story about the rise and fall of the gods, he was in a sense also including the rise and fall that is in every one of us. Haven't you ever felt a sinking sensation when things aren't going well?" After reflecting for a moment, I had to admit that I had experienced such spells. "Play it like that, but in the middle of the drum."

This time the booms had a hollow, somewhat unpleasant sound, which reminded me of certain days when I couldn't readily digest the schweinshaxen I had had for lunch. By this time Büttner was getting irritable.

"No, no, you are expressing a superficial unhappiness, as

though you had a stomachache. Wagner's unhappiness was above these things, it was tragic. Give me the sticks."

Büttner braced himself, loosened his wrists, raised his eyes heavenward, and then played *boom . . . boom . . . boom boom. . . .* But he didn't pound the drums—he slid into them, gently and firmly, and after each stroke his hand bounced gently into the air, as though he were pulling out the vibrations after the drum had been struck. The result was a most beautiful performance of that passage. Every *boom* had an umlaut over it, but beneath the umlaut one could hear that the firm hand of a master had guided the drumstick on its initial attack.

We went through all of Wagner's operas, *boom* by *boom.* When we got to *Tristan,* he taught me how to make love on a timpani, or rather to suggest passionate lovemaking through proper playing of the instrument. He held out great hopes for me as a kettledrum player. He said I had the poetic temperament to play the instrument properly, and he enjoyed it when I used a different attack for each composer. His only direct word of warning about playing percussion was, "Don't drop cymbals during the performance or you will probably be fired"—a piece of wisdom that I needed then and still follow on many occasions, some of them having nothing to do with music.

Büttner was a great pedagogue, and I joined the Tonhalle Orchestra as third percussion player after only four months of instruction. At not yet eighteen, I was the youngest member of both the symphony orchestra and the opera orchestra and the first American to be engaged.

PHILIPP JARNACH was a magnificent teacher. He was twenty-five years old when I studied with him. He had been trained in Paris at the conservatory and spoke respectfully of his teachers Lavignac and Risler. When he was eighteen he was a professional accompanist in Paris, accompanied premieres of Debussy songs, and had some music published. He married a Bavarian woman who was related to Richard Strauss. Because of World War I he immigrated to Zurich and became Busoni's musical secretary. He made piano scores of Busoni's operas and played second piano when Busoni rehearsed concerti. Jarnach was not satisfied with his contrapuntal training, so he retired to the Swiss Alps for two months to master all of the standard contrapuntal procedures. He emerged from this tour of self-teaching as the foremost teacher of counterpoint in Europe and as a formidable and original composer, whom Busoni called "that little warlock, Jarnach."

Jarnach was a superior pianist, a magnificent sight reader, and a score player of the first rank. He knew a great deal about the voice and could himself sing most expressively. He was also a solid conductor, though somewhat tied to the score. In his counterpoint classes he demanded a fugue or several canons every week. If we procrastinated, or if he wished to demonstrate something, he went to the blackboard and then and there wrote a few intricate and at the same time very lovely canons or fugal expositions. He taught us that if we could write expositions and master canons, our counterpoint would be fluent and the rest of fugue writing would be possible.

When I was nineteen, I took the examinations for the state diploma as a teacher of theory. Besides composing a triple fugue (a fugue with three subjects) for string quartet (a radical work), I was locked in a room for four hours and asked to write half a dozen canons of different kinds and a vocal fugue, the subject of which was given by none other than Karl Vogler. This was folowed by a tough three-hour oral examination in which one had to demonstrate a general knowledge of theory, to do figured bass settings at sight at the keyboard, to harmonize melodies at sight, and to notate Bach excerpts after one hearing.

Jarnach had done a fine job in preparing me for this ordeal. As an analysis teacher, he restricted himself to a note-by-note, rhythm-by-rhythm study of the preludes and fugues of the first volume of *The Well-Tempered Clavier*. The harmonic and contrapuntal movement was studied in detail until the overall form became clear. The net result of this workout was that I really learned how to read and analyze a composition carefully and to study every note in any composition. It helped me immensely in my conducting and teaching then and later.

Jarnach's course in score playing was also exemplary. He started us reading four-part choral works at the piano in the old clefs and we progressed until we were playing eight parts. Then we played, progressively, easy Haydn string quartets, moderately difficult ones, and difficult ones. He used this same approach for

Mozart and Beethoven quartets, and symphonies by all three composers. We ended with a good knowledge of the standard repertory and I played Liszt's *Faust Symphony* and some Mahler to the
satisfaction of Jarnach.

As a private teacher, Jarnach had a great and lasting influence on me. Every day, I went to his apartment after lunch for
black coffee. Either I would present my own work-in-progress or
he would show and analyze some works that he had composed or
was working on. We went over every detail of my First Sonata for
Violin and Piano; my *Sextet,* for violin, viola, cello, flute, clarinet,
and horn; my First String Quartet with clarinet obbligato; the
orchestration of a Loewe ballad that Jarnach began and I finished;
several songs; a quartet for four horns and *Chorale Prelude for
Organ;* some shorter piano pieces; pieces for cello and piano; the
Sonatina for Flute and Piano; settings of Swiss folk songs for
chorus and orchestrations of songs by other composers; and many
fugues, canons, and other contrapuntal works.

Both Jarnach and Busoni professed that nothing should ever
be notated unless one has heard it mentally—and they really
meant what they said. This was in direct contradiction to Stravinsky's statement, made later, that every musical idea should be
tested at the piano to get an objective impression. It always
seemed to me that the objective impression of a symphony orchestra was impossible, because one could not get the men in to
try out one's pieces—too expensive!

The aura around Jarnach was one of high craftsmanship and
dedication to the highest artistic ideals, and his own works were
progressive and original. He set a fast pace and never wavered in
pursuing the highest artistic aim.

Chapter 8

Strauss, Nikisch, Busoni, Joyce
1917-1920

I WAS SIGNED UP FOR THE TONHALLE and opera orchestras by Herr Boller, who always wore a black derby and smoked a Brissago—a Swiss cigar aged in alcohol. This gave him, while doing orchestra business, an advantage over all the players. My monthly salary was 360 francs (seventy-five dollars). I was on call seven days a week for any and all performances of the standard repertory, both operatic and symphonic, as well as for performances of any contemporary works. Stage duty in the opera house paid two dollars extra per performance. There was a tacit understanding that rehearsals were to end at an agreed-upon time but enthusiastic conductors were able to con the orchestra beyond the limits—without overtime pay, of course.

Volkmar Andreae, the boss of musical life in Zurich, was director of the Tonhalle Orchestra and of practically all other important organizations that needed conducting, with the exception of the opera orchestras. He was a solid musician, trained in the German tradition, but also sympathetic to French and Italian music. Technically, he was stumpy and a bit rough, but he made a strong impression with his interpretations of Beethoven symphonies, Berlioz's works, and Mahler symphonies. He handled a large part of the standard classic and romantic repertory with more than acceptable results. He was a fine but loud Strauss conductor and later, in the fifties and sixties, was noted for his Bruckner performances. He had a habit of huffing and puffing while he conducted, which he did with more vigor than was necessary and with something less than elegance, but his readings were compelling. To have him as mentor for my own conducting and composing efforts was ideal. He carried out this duty with patience and enthusiasm and he saved my orchestral career a number of times when my inexperience and brashness might have brought me into conflict with the other conductors.

The personnel of the orchestra included superannuated functionaries who should have been but never were pensioned, as well as brilliant virtuosi like the flutist Jean Nada and the clarinetist Allegra. (The latter played in the first concert performance of Stravinsky's *Histoire du soldat* and eventually with the Boston Symphony Orchestra.) Most of the musicians were Germans of varying abilities.

There were really three ensembles. The first orchestra, under a first-rate conductor, was astonishingly good. The veterans lent solidity, the virtuosi gave brilliance. Zimmerli, a violinist who was one year my senior, and I, by giving our genius to the performances, added a certain quality that we couldn't produce otherwise, never having played the works before. Under a mediocre conductor, the second and third opera orchestras could sag pretty badly. I soon realized that there were some players in the viola section who produced such a cutting tone that they would have been of more value in a surgical ward than in any orchestra.

The standard repertory was rarely rehearsed, so I often found myself sight-reading before the audience. I stopped sight-reading and began practicing after a disastrous experience playing piccolo in Gounod's *Faust;* the parts were so faded that players like myself, who didn't know the operas from memory, were at a disadvantage. On that evening, one of the singers was indisposed and we had to transpose numerous arias down three half-steps. To do this at sight, on a piccolo, in front of an audience, was a harrowing experience and I messed things up, as the conductor pointed out. I am sure the event left some permanent scars on my psyche.

I soon realized that this kind of on-the-job training for a budding conductor and composer was unique and I thanked my lucky stars for being paid for the privilege. I learned all the then-current works in the repertory by performing in them. I also remembered the techniques, approaches, and results that the good, bad, indifferent, or great conductors achieved under the varying conditions of actual performance.

The orchestra was exposed to a long parade of conductors during any season. Fortunately, I had weekly lessons in conducting and score reading with Jarnach and Andreae. There I was able to discuss the high points, low points, techniques, and end results of all the performances in which I took part.

Most of the guest conductors were experienced but dull. Ermanno Wolf-Ferrari, the composer of *Il segreto di Susanna,* was an exception. After two hours of tearfully rehearsing the second orchestra, he got them to play his work *Le donne curiose—* in German, *Die neugierigen Frauen*—softly and in the style of Mozart. Wolf-Ferrari had a limited stick technique, but a handsome face and a fine head of hair. When things went wrong he would cry. This made the orchestra feel bad, so they improved, but he would continue to whimper, saying, "Softer, gentlemen, softer." When the viola section stopped playing altogether, he wiped away his tears and said, "That was better, gentlemen, but tonight, the violas, *please,* still softer."

THE MOST famous guest conductors were Richard Strauss and Arthur Nikisch. Strauss was internationally known as a composer, conductor, and accompanist, and his imprint on music history is very much apparent today and will probably last. The mere knowledge that Strauss would conduct in the Tonhalle immediately improved the orchestra, for the players practiced and took home the parts of the Strauss works. This gave a lift to all our intervening performances.

Strauss was tall and slender and seemed more like a bank president than a composer. But his dreamy eyes and modern hairdo gave him away. He was admired for being an astute businessman and we had heard that he had been paid an advance of 100,000 marks for his *Alpine Symphony.* He used a fairly long baton, and got an expressive movement from it with a flick of the wrist. The tip of the stick had a click to it, so that the rhythm was quite precise. He often used very small motions and sometimes hardly conducted at all. He called himself "an expressive musician." As a composer he put expressivity into the music; as a conductor he called the orchestra's attention to it—but never, under any conditions, would he go into physical gyrations or dance steps to make his point. He used his left hand sparingly, and once remarked that a conductor's left hand should be kept in his pocket. Occasionally at climaxes he would rise to his full height and look around at the players in a commanding fashion in order to get a big effect.

He used a score and had a very fine conducting trick. He would glance at the score, which he probably knew from memory, and then look up and nod to a particular player or section of the orchestra when he wanted some special effect. His dreamy blue eyes, unlike Nikisch's, were not hypnotic but magnetic, and very expressive. His comments to the orchestra were rather frequent. They were generally about basic musical matters and were given in a matter-of-fact way that put the burden for an actual musical performance on his players. He did not always like music to be "beautiful." Sometimes he would call for a blunt performance of a section in order to make the overall musical experience more vivid. Sometimes he would call for greater vulgarity in playing. Once he said, "Gentlemen, this passage was perfect and very smooth . . . much too perfect and too smooth. There has to be a certain vitality and boniness in music to make it really expressive."

His ear was so sensitive that he could detect any kind of imbalance immediately and would correct it without stopping the orchestra. Because he expected the players to respond as mature musicians, he could generally achieve a balanced sound in twenty minutes of rehearsal time. When he conducted us it was astonishing to feel the orchestra change into the equivalent of the Berlin Philharmonic. He was patient up to a point, then it was a kind of "three strikes and you're out" technique. He would stop and say, "At letter B, the horns were dragging. Again, please." He would stop a second time. "The horns are still dragging." If, on a third try, they did not correct the error, he would go on without stopping, hoping that things would correct themselves. Sometimes he gave up, turning to the concertmaster as he proceeded, with an expression that said, "What kind of oxen do you have in the horn section?"

He liked fast tempi, and I don't believe it was—as his detractors alleged—because he had to make a train or get to a restaurant or a card game, but rather because of his musical conceptions. These were that the right speed was necessary to make the ties and relationships between the various musical phrases musically expressive. This was a matter of individual taste and experience and could not be precisely defined. *Allegro* to him meant lively, but not necessarily a fixed and mechanical beat.

He had a great pictorial sense about music, developed both from his opera composing and his symphonic poems. He claimed that a sensitive listener could determine by the sound of the music alone whether in his symphonic poem *Don Juan* the libertine's ladies he described were blond, redhaired, or brunette; also that one could describe a knife and fork in music. All of the larger pictures and musical descriptions that were in his scores and that he detected when conducting other works were carefully paced and held together.

Strauss had a rather earthy Bavarian way when he wanted results and he spoke an expressive Bavarian dialect. The *Symphonia Domestica* was a symphonic poem about the home life of Herr and Frau Strauss and their son, Franz. The directions in the first forty score pages indicate what went on; they read: Dreamy, Fiery, Fresh, Graciously, With Feeling, Angrily, Very Tender, Tired, Tearful, Stubbornly, A Slumber Song, Singing, and Swinging. In the rehearsal, he had an extended private conversation with the concertmaster, who had a long and difficult solo that illustrated the character and temperament of Frau Strauss. We couldn't hear what Strauss said, but on a second try the concertmaster's solo was much more capricious, cajoling, seductive, angry, and tranquil in turn. Schreep, the oboist, played an oboe d'amore solo with a prosaic tone. Strauss tried to indicate the proper degree of expressivity by asking for more *piano*, but this didn't work. He then told the player about his son, Franz Strauss, and what a darling baby he had been. He was unusually sentimental in his descriptions, and the verbal picture he painted of the little pink baby in his crib was vivid enough to make everybody play softly, so as not to wake the little dear. On the next try, Strauss got exactly what he wanted. In the fugue theme at the end of the work the strings sounded rather limp; this Strauss corrected by calling for a downbow on every beat, something he mentions in his Berlioz book on orchestration. He liked the horns to range from a mellow, warm tone to a brilliant, brassy sound. For the latter he would ask them to put their bells up into the air and blow hard!

We also performed his *Alpine Symphony*, a musical description of life in the Bavarian Alps. The subheadings convey the general idea. They read: Night, Sunrise, The Ascent, Entrance into the Forest, Wandering Beside the Brook, At the Waterfall, Apparition, On Flowery Meadows, On the Alm, Lost in the Thicket and Brush, On the Glacier, Dangerous Moments, On the Summit, Vision, Mists Rise, The Sun Is Gradually Hidden, Elegy, Calm Before the Storm, Thunderstorm, The Descent, Sunset, Night. This seemed naive to the critics, who didn't like the work. Only conductors and audiences liked it, and under Strauss's direction it was really effective.

The symphony has a part for wind machine, and Max Hengartner and I were assigned to take care of it. It was an old-fashioned contraption, consisting of a wooden frame with a wooden wheel on the principle of a mill wheel, over which was stretched a piece of heavy canvas weighted down at both ends. When turned it gave out a whishing sound that was much like the white noise we now produce electronically. The loudness and softness of the wind sound varied with the speed of the turning.

Hengartner was six feet three inches tall, and heavy, so he did the manual work of turning the wheel and keeping the stand in shape. Being the young genius of the conducting and composition class, I was assigned to the artistic work. The machine was offstage, and my job was to relay Strauss's beat to Hengartner. I had a stand and a score and the wind machine part was underlined in blue. I watched Strauss through a crack in the door, picked up his beat from there, and passed it on to Hengartner.

As an experienced orchestra player, it was no problem for me to bring Hengartner in right on the dot. We came out even with the rest of the orchestra, but Strauss stopped, nevertheless, and asked, "Who is operating the wind machine?" Hengartner and I were both pleased and surprised at this recognition of our precision and stepped forward proudly to accept Strauss's compliments. He said "Gentlemen, at two measures before one-oh-eight the wind machine is *piano*. There is a *crescendo* in the next measure and at one-oh-eight it is *piano* again. One measure after one-oh-nine there is a *crescendo*, a *diminuendo*, and then a *forte*. It doesn't reach *fortissimo* until number one-twenty-four. You know, gentlemen, the wind blows musically, sometimes loud and sometimes soft; and you can even be good musicians on a wind machine." He repeated the passage. This time he didn't stop.

I never forgot the episode, and I've always referred to myself as a pupil of Richard Strauss. I took his statement as a motto, and in recent years decided that one can even be a good musician when producing electronic music.

≫≪

WHEN ARTHUR NIKISCH conducted the Tonhalle Orchestra in two concerts as guest conductor the program consisted of a Handel concerto for strings, Beethoven's *Eroica* Symphony and Strauss's *Death and Transfiguration*. Nikisch's reputation as a conductor was formidable. He had been the regular conductor of the Leipzig Gewandhaus, conductor of the Boston Symphony, director of the Budapest Opera, and guest conductor in Berlin, Hamburg, and St. Petersburg. He took the Berlin Philharmonic on long tours and was for a while director of the Leipzig Opera. He appeared as guest conductor of practically all the internationally known orchestras.

The Nikisch legend of infallibility was well known to the Tonhalle players. When he arrived for his first rehearsal, the entire orchestra rose and remained standing until he had reached the podium and had taken his baton, bowed to their applause, and signaled them to be seated. He was a middle-sized man, extremely elegant in appearance and movement, with just a slight hint of a stomach, which gave him the necessary weight for the big climaxes. Pale, he wore an elegantly trimmed beard, and had wavy hair on the longish side, but so beautifully barbered that at certain spots in certain works a curl would fall over the right half of his right eye, giving him a most romantic appearance. Some of his enemies claimed that he practiced this stunt in front of a mirror before every concert. Below this fine head of longish hair one soon became aware of two of the most remarkable musically hypnotic eyes that one could imagine. They can best be described as a kind of smoky gray, engulfing rather than piercing. After he looked at me for a while I felt that he owned me musically. There was nothing oppressive about this relationship because once under his spell we felt freer and played better.

His baton technique was unique. He used a rather long baton that seemed to be light and flexible. He held it almost like a violin bow. With his right hand he gave very clear beats, but he did not use a preparatory beat. It was a little difficult to get used to this, but once we made the adjustment he seemed to be indicating the musical events with the stick about one beat before they were played. This gave the players a feeling of great security and freedom.

His left hand was used mostly to indicate the dynamics of the compositions. Often he rested it on his hip or placed a few fingers in his pocket, giving him a most elegant stance that drove the ladies wild but in no way interfered with the quality of his interpretations. His way of signaling for the famous Nikisch *crescendo* was to hold his left hand above his head, making a circle with his thumb and third finger for *pianissimo*. He would then gradually lower his left hand, the orchestra in the meantime building up very gradually until his hand was about on a level with his chest. At this point he would open the thumb and third finger, keep on lowering his hand while extending his fingers, and when it was a little below his waist but was still visible to the orchestra, he would slowly ball it into a fist, which he would then raise slowly upward until he could bring in the brass on their final, colossal snort, or urge the rest of the orchestra on to an even greater climax.

At times, Nikisch wore a diamond ring on the little finger of his left hand. In properly lit halls it would glitter as he signaled for the famous *crescendo* and it was said that he synchronized it with a cymbal crash in Tchaikovsky's *Pathétique*. The overall results of the Nikisch performance were that he drew a silky tone from the orchestra, which was completely under his quiet control, with sonorities ranging from a whispered *pianissimo* to a thundering *fortissimo*. The thunder was never ill-mannered. The interpretations were sensuous, the orchestra rich in timbre contrast, the tempi very elastic, sometimes with a rubato that was somewhat Slavic in its effect and at times even gypsylike.

He was a superior psychologist when it came to handling

orchestra players. He arrived ten minutes late for all rehearsals. On this occasion, after unhurriedly removing his elegant cloth coat with a fur collar, he chatted a moment with Andreae, and then as he walked past the standing orchestra to the conductor's chair he singled out one or two of the men whom he knew, saying, "Why, my dear DeBoer, how nice to see you again. I believe the last time was when you played the solo in *Heldenleben* so beautifully in Leipzig. And how is your charming wife?" And then, still on his way to the conductor's stand, he waved to the first horn, saying, "Ah, Mr. Franck, and how has your embouchure been since you played the Siegfried-call with me in Munich?" Eventually arriving at the conductor's stand, he bowed to the orchestra, saying, "Gentlemen, *please* be seated." Then, removing his gloves, he reached into a container and selected a baton suitable for the occasion. He tested several of them as to length and flexibility, finally settling on one that was quite long but thin. It seemed almost like a braided silk whip. After testing it a few times more as to its give, and dropping a few downbeats strictly from the wrist, he started us going on Strauss's *Death and Transfiguration*. After giving us a few tries without any comment, to get used to his unprepared downbeat, he took us through the first half-dozen pages of the score.

His appearance at the stand was that of a man in deep concentration, but watching at every moment. Soon the playing became very easy, indeed quite free. Nikisch stopped the orchestra. "Gentlemen, that was excellent, but do you mind if I make a few minor suggestions?" Then, turning to the first oboe (who had a rather raucous tone), he said, "Mr. Schreep, you played your part beautifully, but I believe you put more drama into it than it needs. Would you mind giving it a more lyric interpretation?" Schreep sat back in his chair and proudly sucked his reed to soften it, while Nikisch turned to the brass section: "What a warm and voluptuous sound you have produced, gentlemen. Do you mind if I suggest saving that for the end of the piece? We have a long way to go, and, by the way, listen to the strings. If you can't hear them, you are playing too loud." Then to the strings: "Your *legato* is impressive, gentlemen. Sing! Sing! Sing! And in the woodwinds, gentlemen, listen to everybody and blend with them, if you please. Now once more from the beginning." And to everyone's astonishment, the Zurich Tonhalle Orchestra suddenly became the Berlin Philharmonic, the Boston Symphony, and the Gewandhaus Orchestra, all rolled into one. We played the piece happily right through to the end. It was easy; it was stimulating, and it was wonderful to hear even the weak players in the orchestra come to life.

At the end, Nikisch put down his baton and looked at us incredulously, saying, "I am astonished, gentlemen. Astonished! I have never had a better first rehearsal of this work, or even one as good, with any of the great orchestras I have conducted. But one final suggestion. The big theme of Transformation comes three times. The first time"—and here he crouched low over the stand—"not too intense, perhaps *mezzoforte*. The second time the theme appears"—now he was sitting up in his chair and speaking with a more resonant and somewhat more agitated voice—"play it *forte*, gentlemen, *forte*." Rising to his full height and pointing his baton heavenward, he thundered, "The last time, everything you have—*fortississimo!*" After a suitable pause to let the drama sink in, he pulled out his gold watch on a gold chain, looked at it, and then announced, "I just remember that I have an important engagement at my hotel. I wonder if you would excuse me, if all goes well, fifteen minutes before the end of the rehearsal? Let's play the piece through once more before intermission."

At this point, he had the orchestra eating out of the palm of his hand. They knew that Nikisch himself never made a mistake. They knew, further, that he had now asked them please not to waste his time; he had to attend to other business. The other business was generally a poker game or perhaps a rendezvous with one of the many glamorous opera singers he had been involved with—who had, maybe, traveled to the city especially to see whether beautiful Arthur, as they called him, was still as magnetic, as willowy, as romantic, as fascinating as he had been the last time.

With this in the back of their minds, the orchestra now launched into the piece for a complete runthrough and played it magnificently, without a slip. And Nikisch called for an intermission, for time for a smoke.

As guest conductor, Nikisch did not feel it necessary to retire to the green room, but thought it more diplomatic to stay with the orchestra men and engage in enlightened conversation about the relative merits of various wines and cognacs and some recommendations for dining out at restaurants that served small and tender blue trout and properly chilled champagne or perhaps specially prepared venison (this he recommended as an excellent snack after the concert). With some cultured comments about the relative merits of cigarettes with Persian versus Turkish tobacco, the intermission ended and we went back to work.

He now moved right into the *Eroica* Symphony. The orchestra played about eight measures. He stopped. "Crisp, gentlemen, more precision, more accent," and then, looking heroic and ominous, he said, "Remember, gentlemen, *Beethoven—Napoleon*. Once more, gentlemen"—this last in a commanding, military tone of voice.

When we came to the funeral march, he stopped. "It's too cheerful, gentlemen. Think of all the things that you have lost in your life and that have gone wrong—your buried hopes. And now sing about them, gentlemen, sing!" The orchestra tried again, this time producing a dignified, doleful, dirgelike sound.

In the Scherzo, he told us what to do in advance. "Now"—he smiled a little, as though at some secret joke—"humor, gentlemen, abandon yourselves. Let go. This is the enjoyment of happy moments, but, of course, don't forget to play the proper notes." His smile widened a little bit and the orchestra responded with a symphonic group laugh. Before the last movement, he simply said, "This is man again, taking on heroically, cheerfully, and with energy, the daily battle of life, hence the title *Eroica*. But one thing, gentlemen. In the slow section where the oboe solo comes, that is a yearning, a yearning for peace, a resignation, those things we hope for—and, perhaps, who knows? Someday they may be ours. Now, gentlemen!" And using his baton more like a rapier, he fenced the orchestra into an impressive statement of the first subject.

After the symphony he said nothing, took out a silk handkerchief from his inside coat pocket, and wiped away what might have been two drops of perspiration, or perhaps two tears, one couldn't quite tell which. After a short pause he said, "I don't think it's necessary to keep the winds, brass, and percussion any longer. Handel's Concerto Grosso for Strings, next."

Nikisch once held a theory about conducting which was that all conductors should be violinists, and that the bow technique was the best preparation for a communicative baton technique. In his rehearsal of the Handel concerto, one saw what he meant. He had a way of drawing the baton through the air with complete control, and in the slow movements very slowly without subdividing beats, making it almost impossible for the orchestra to play *staccato*. The other phrasing indications such as accents and *staccati* he would get either through a flick of the wrist or at times with discreet signals with his left hand. He was also able to indicate quite clearly with the baton the more detailed phrasings and bowings that he wished to underline. The net result of all this was that the string body of the Tonhalle Orchestra achieved a richness and a mellowness within which one could hear the punctuation and outlines of the various phrases quite clearly, but with an elasticity that was, in fact, a very subtle, almost unnoticeable *rubato*.

Nikisch's effect on the audience was electrifying. The orchestra men liked him because he was really quite kind and thoughtful. Other professionals thought he was the greatest conductor in the world. Some criticized him because of his "beautiful" orchestral tone and said that his performances were not "classical." My experience with him was unforgettable.

⋈⋉

THE *Neue Züricher Zeitung* announced the first performances of Ferruccio Busoni's *Arlecchino* (in one act) and *Turandot* (in two acts), both with his own libretti in German. *Turandot* was specially adapted for the Zurich Opera from incidental music for Gozzi's play. Busoni was conducting the performances, and I got a ticket and read the libretti. They had unique qualities —unrealistic, but with a theatrically effective tone. Their witty comments and brevity reminded me of Commedia dell'Arte and at times of Mozart's *Zauberflöte* and *Entführung aus dem Serail*.

At the performances dialogue, recitative, and set pieces alternated with lively contrast and projected Busoni's thought. The orchestration was clear, the vocal lines expressive, and the stage sets alluring. I came under Busoni's spell. Even though the acting, singing, and dancing were somewhat heavy and the performance lacked virtuosity, I was amazed, after having heard heavy German music for almost five years, to discover an art lucid and transparent, melodious and rhythmically clear, yet not superficial; dramatically effective but brief in time, never turgid, and often profound.

Busoni's ability to compose in various styles without losing his identity was impressive. The Mozartian ending of *Arlecchino*, the minuet in *Turandot*, taken from one of his sonatinas, and his parody of an Italian operatic quartet all showed me a musical and dramatic mastery I had not yet experienced, but one that made a lasting impression on me.

Busoni conducted in an unobtrusive manner, bringing out the expressive contents of the score without military precision— due possibly to his lack of experience as a theater conductor.

A DESCRIPTION of Busoni's piano playing must begin with the statement that technically he could play anything at any speed. His control of dynamics was complete and ranged from a whispering and haunting *pianissimo* to a *fortissimo* that rivaled the power of an orchestra. His pedaling was unique and set him apart from any other pianist I have ever heard. He sometimes used two or three pedals at the same time, setting sonority patterns that were somewhat veiled but within which he played with great, bell-like clarity. At times, he would raise or lower a pedal with great rapidity, even on a single note or chord, creating myriad tone colors and strange vibrations. His touch and attacks were always related to the pedaling he was using so that he could transform the piano sounds at will from a vaguely harpsichordlike resonance to a modern resonating box on which he could simulate singing and orchestral instruments. His method of performance and his programs would today put him at the peak of contemporary piano wizards.

His finger technique, too, was impeccable; his fast octaves and thirds sounded like single-note passages and he never missed even the greatest leaps. With all its virtuosity, his playing often seemed to be based on a memory of song and dance. The songlike approach led him to passages that sounded like folk songs or simulated operatic arias and recitatives. His dance world included rhythmic projections of gavottes, sarabandes, minuets, waltzes, and freer and ever more imaginative dances. The mazurkas, tarantellas and other dance-oriented pieces were at times unmetrical, but so rhythmic in their phrasing that they projected a floating, unearthly quality. The songs became disembodied, like the memory of a song.

Busoni avoided strict metrical playing in all performances; he was interested in projecting the form of each piece so that it could be remembered. This concept resulted in *rubato* playing based on the phrase relationships within each piece. Because these varied in each work, his style of interpretation also varied from work to work and in different performances of the same piece. His sense of phrase affected his tempi, so he never played a piece fast just to dazzle listeners with his virtuosity. His technical equipment was so secure that he was not afraid to play a really slow tempo when he thought it was called for.

He fascinated me with his strong projection of particular ideas in each work he played. He was sometimes called a romantic because he often found new relationships in familiar works that others had missed. He proclaimed that this same freedom of expression was known to Beethoven, Mozart, and Haydn; that neither Bach nor Handel avoided free interpretations of their own works or those by others; that an improvisational approach to music-making was practiced by the baroque composers; and that C. P. E. Bach's *Versuch über die wahre Art das Klavier zu spielen*, or *Essay on the True Art of Playing Keyboard Instruments*, was the standard work in Bach's time that formulated this stylistic practice.

His performance of the Chopin Ballades, which I heard in 1917, went beyond brilliant piano playing. Sometimes he made the instrument sound like an Aeolian harp as described by the poets, or like sound floating from a box of electric resonators with apparently no relationship to a hammered-string sound. Under his hands the piano became both a picture projector and a storyteller, and in the Ballades Busoni became a bard. (When I heard him play these, I knew nothing about the influence of Heine and Mickiewicz on Chopin, but from Busoni's performances I received distinct poetic impressions as moving as those evoked by the original poems, which I read many years later.) Busoni's Chopin playing was unsentimental. It projected the musical forms with a firmness and balance that I have never heard other pianists achieve with the same clarity. In the performance of his own transcription for modern concert piano of J. S. Bach's *Goldberg* Variations, he stressed the melodic lines and individualized the contrapuntal voice leadings while still bringing to the harmonies their individual colors. He brought to life the deep spirit of this music in such a way that it awoke in many listeners at one and the same time a vision of the past and of music of the future. This he accomplished with what seemed to be great ease.

His Liszt performances, too, were unique. In works such as *Années de pèlerinage* the pictorial images animated Busoni, as did the poetic images in other Liszt works, like the *Dante Fantasia Quasi Sonata*, other Transcendental Etudes, and the drama in the *Don Juan* Fantasy. When playing Liszt, Busoni used a pianistic palette so delicate in its tone colors that the shimmering relationships became unique sound forms. Schoenberg's term *"klangfarben Melodie"* is a fitting description in an interpretative sense.

Within the framework that Liszt had established for works like the *Mazeppa* Etude and the *Don Juan* Fantasy, Busoni made the piano take on the quality of a symphony orchestra. Difficult passages in octaves, double sixths, double thirds, and chromatic runs were part of the overall form. He gave to Liszt a prophetic quality that transcended the virtuoso brilliance the works always contained. Liszt wrote about his *Vision from Venice* to Lambert Massart: "Don't try to know. Your lot is not to know. Don't try to do. Your lot is not to do. Don't try to enjoy. Your lot is renunciation." Busoni's performances were in that vein.

On stage Busoni looked tall, elegant, and relaxed. He had a noble profile, a full head of hair, and a graceful stride. As he walked onto the stage in deep concentration, the audience gave him an enthusiastic welcome. When he heard the applause he seemed rather surprised to see them all there. He bowed first to the house in general, then greeted his friends with a personal and most elegant wave of the hand—a greeting that was sometimes directed to beautiful ladies who had attracted his attention.

When he played he was completely absorbed and seemed in

a trance. At the end of each group he responded to the enormous applause graciously and with hand waves to his friends. The enthusiasm was often so great that the audience would not quiet down until he was again at the keyboard. He gave generous encores, even after long and difficult programs. The final applause continued until the lights were turned out.

To prepare himself for these concerts, Busoni played the pieces through once at a moderate tempo, *mezzo forte*. This was all he needed to refresh his memory, for he had total recall.

In 1919, when I played flute and percussion in the Zurich Tonhalle Orchestra, Busoni gave a series of five popular concerts entitled "The Development of the Pianoforte Concerto." He played one concerto each of J. S. Bach, Johann Nepomuk Hummel, Schumann, Mendelssohn, Weber, Brahms, Anton Rubinstein, and Saint-Saëns, as well as two each by Mozart, Beethoven, and Liszt, and Busoni's *Concerto for Piano, Orchestra and Male Chorus*. It was a wonderful opportunity to see and hear what he and Andreae emphasized in the various works as we rehearsed them.

Busoni spent quite a bit of time in the tuning room where he conversed with my brilliant French flute teacher, Jean Nada. I was quite happy to listen while my teacher and other colleagues discussed music and other subjects with him. During the concerto series, it was my special duty to bring Busoni a half-bottle of champagne before he played. He always received me in great style, drank a glass to my health, and asked me how I was getting on with my composing. The champagne helped Busoni to work himself to a high tension before concerts; Andreae claimed that Busoni's pulse rate was sometimes as high as one hundred and fifty when he played.

In the concerti he treated the piano solo as an integral part of a musical event that needed to be molded differently from either a solo performance or a straight orchestral performance. He knew the orchestra both as a pianist and as a conductor of contemporary and classical works. He completely integrated his piano sound with the orchestral sound and made the piano into a new section of the orchestra. At moments it was indeed the concertizing section of the orchestra; at other moments it blended with the different sections of the orchestra to carry forward the main musical ideas. Busoni envisioned the orchestra and the piano soloist separated into sound sections or ranges independent of one another, but used in an infinite variety of combinations and timbre variations.

In the concerti, the timbre of Busoni's solo playing combined with the orchestra sound so that the players established new balances. Dr. Andreae and the orchestra had to adjust to Busoni's elastic and at times almost improvisational style. The fifteen concerti were stylistic challenges for any conductor and orchestra. Many of them were not often played and five were completely new to the Tonhalle Orchestra.

We were not a virtuoso group, but the players were very good—a few were brilliant—and led by Andreae, the orchestra was impressive. As the title of the series suggested, Busoni had arranged the programs so that the stylistic transformations and changes in the concerto form itself were made clear.

Dr. Andreae began rehearsals with the orchestra alone. If we knew a work, Busoni would immediately begin playing and we would shape the work together as we progressed. When works were new to us, Andreae spoke about them briefly and Busoni played passages to illustrate. When Andreae mentioned that Hummel had studied with Mozart, Busoni explained that Hummel's highly decorated and harmonically colorful piano writing had influenced Chopin and even Liszt, and was different from that of Mozart and Beethoven. When we had difficulty matching Busoni's *rubati*, he would repeat passages with infinite patience until we felt completely free.

Mozart's D Minor Concerto became an inspired performance as Busoni made it into a drama in the concert hall—an opera without scenery, singers, or libretto, but with all the psychological tensions present in *Don Giovanni*. The performance had *Geist, élan vital*—the inner life, positive and idealized, needed to project Mozart's real message. In Beethoven's E-flat Major Concerto (*Emperor*) we sensed in the first movement a hero striding into areas of conflict; in the second movement, a transcendent contemplative, imaginative world, a spiritual bridge to the exuberant, dancelike, vigorous, joyous, almost muscular activity that the last movement expresses. Busoni gave to the Liszt E-flat Major Concerto a vigor, a triumphant forward movement, and a playful imaginative quality that pushed it far beyond the tinsel of its triangle solo. In the A Major Concerto he emphasized a lyric quality, so that in spite of the work's brilliance it made a far more human communication than when played with machinelike glitter and brilliance by many of Busoni's contemporaries.

He played the Brahms D Minor Concerto with great firmness and a splendid sense of its symphonic qualities. He performed with a sense of structure that deviated from the current Brahms style, which included a number of exaggerated soft spots in every interpretation.

The final work in the series was Busoni's *Concerto for Piano, Orchestra and Male Chorus.* This work, lasting an hour, is neither a symphony with an obbligato piano part nor a piano solo with orchestral accompaniment. It represents Busoni's belief that the solo instrument in a concerto should be part of the symphony orchestra. The composer's performance was a completely new musical experience for me, for the work, combining elements from the nineteenth-century symphony and concerto, was a new musical form. The work seemed to end the nineteenth-century era and suggested a twentieth-century aesthetic. In it German expressivity and complexity contrasted with Italian clarity and brilliance—style contrasts that demanded monumental dimensions. The fifth movement is a setting of a poem by Øehlenschlaeger, an affirmation of the eternal power of Allah, that Busoni had translated from the Danish.

BUSONI'S COMPOSITIONS were known only to a small group of admirers. Many of his later works in particular were puzzling to the usual audiences, and he rarely played them. I remember Busoni playing his powerful *Fantasia Contrapuntistica;* and I thought the *Carmen Fantasy* was contrapuntally more sophisticated and tighter in form than Liszt's opera paraphrases.

Since I knew relatively few of his works, and those had showed me new musical possibilities, I turned to his *Sketch of a New Esthetic of Music,* published in 1916 in German. (It was first published in English in 1907.) In the book Busoni wrote that music was born free and was being choked by routine. He wrote of new scale structures, harmonies, notation, microtones, and even about electronic music, which he said could be made "plastic" through ear training and experimentation. Reading his book in 1917, I saw Busoni as a daring pioneer who had opened new doors for a new generation of musicians. When I read an open letter in the *Frankfurter Zeitung* called "Futurist Danger," in which Busoni was attacked by the German composer Hans Pfitzner, Busoni became even more of a hero to me.

Although Busoni had taught in Helsinki, Moscow, Vienna, at the New England Conservatory of Music, and at the conservatory in Bologna, he was not a pedagogue in the usual sense of the word. His reactions and suggestions to students were those of a practioner and a philosopher of the arts; he was an animator and a mentor, but never a drillmaster.

Busoni spoke Italian and German fluently and wrote eloquent prose and poetry in both languages. He had a good knowledge of French, English, and Spanish. He had published essays, articles, and opera libretti. He was sensitive to the other arts. He sometimes spoke of the spiritual values of the arts and the priestlike function of the true artist. Most people who knew him considered him the greatest genius of the time and a true Renaissance man. His enemies called him everything bad: a nineteenth-century-hangover artist, too intellectual to be good as a musician; a fantasist, a futurist, and an antitraditionalist who spoiled music by his arrangements and editions.

BUSONI'S RELATIONSHIP to people he was coaching was mostly respectful, but he was demanding and acted as though they understood everything he was talking about. If they didn't, they would be quiet, disappear, practice, read, or study until they felt more or less at ease with him. He expected students to know the important areas of old music and the standard repertory, but wanted them to be alert to contemporary trends. He expected composers to master the theory of music through self-study. This centered for him around contrapuntal techniques. He did contrapuntal exercises every day and greatly influenced all the younger composers because he was an exemplary model of the great artist at work. Every morning he worked on his opera, *Doktor Faust* (his major opus in Zurich), yet he had energy left to lead other lives as performer, teacher, and social being.

He assigned major works to his piano students and expected them to be perfected and memorized before he heard them. Then he made interpretative suggestions and spoke of technical problems in detail. He used aphorisms and slogans to get his points across; these were passed around town and literally became commandments among his followers. One was, "When you have solved a problem you have established the basis for the next one"; a difficult slogan to understand was "Never look back," for he was very well aware of the past and on another occasion said, "The old and the new are the same." He was demanding; when Otto Strauss explained his absence from a lesson by pleading illness, Busoni remarked: "Illness is a sign of a lack of talent." His student Ticciati once played a Liszt étude for him, and Busoni went to the piano and said, "I think, Ticciati, this would be better"—and played the passage in a spectacular way. Ticciati responded, "Oh, Maestro, how did you do that?" Busoni shrugged his shoulders. "One must practice." The most devastating crack was delivered, along with a pat on the back, to a student who had just finished playing his own composition: "One knows what one means, doesn't one?"

When Richard Strauss conducted at the Tonhalle, Busoni and Strauss and friends met at the Bahnhof Enge restaurant after the concert for the usual refreshments, which meant champagne and pheasant. I was one of the younger generation allowed to listen to the great men talk. In this period there was a great "back to Mozart" movement led by composers as diverse as Strauss, Weingartner, Busoni, and Wolf-Ferrari.

On one evening, Strauss asserted that opera had moved as far as it could along the lines of post-Wagnerian orchestral sizes and libretto lengths. We needed to reduce the means, he said, to get back to the Mozartian orchestra, to use only moderately large casts. Instead of overdeveloped, pseudosymphonic passages, we should restore the set pieces—arias, duets, trios, ensembles—and the recitatives to their rightful places in opera in order to bring clarity to the musical and dramatic ideas. He spoke of Mozartian melodic writing and finished by saying, "Yes, we must go back to Mozart."

His remarks were followed by a resounding silence.

Eventually Busoni said drily, "It took you a long time to discover this, Dr. Strauss."

The two men were not on speaking terms for five years.

※※

AFTER I had worked with Jarnach for about a year, he said to me, "I think it is time for you to meet Busoni. He has heard about you and is interested in you, and would like to meet you in his home."

I was astonished by this invitation. I told Jarnach I was doubtful about some of the time-wasting hangers-on around Busoni.

Jarnach explained that Busoni called such people "Hamlet types" and didn't have the heart to turn them away, so he sometimes spent much time and took great pains to help them. I was afraid Busoni's personality would be to me like a flame to a moth, but Jarnach reassured me: "If he likes you he will invite you for black coffee, and if you bring scores, he might look at them and even give you some tips and suggestions—although these can be on quite a grand scale."

It all sounded glamorous to me.

A few weeks later, we walked to Busoni's apartment at eight-thirty in the evening. Frau Busoni, a very beautiful woman, was extremely friendly and warm-hearted in her greeting as she answered the doorbell. In the music room Busoni was sitting behind his desk, smoking a cigar and drinking brandy.

He rose as Jarnach brought me forward, and bowed, saying, "I've heard about you; I've heard a great many things about you; and I have heard a great many fine things [viel schönes] about you. Will you have a cigar?" He handed me the box. "Some cognac?" he asked, leading me to a comfortable chair.

It was a princely reception. His manner was dignified, respectful, and warm. I settled down with the brandy and the cigar while Jarnach and Busoni proceeded to converse about recent musical events.

They discussed our orchestra concerts and Busoni asked me, "What are you doing in music besides composing?"

I explained that I played in the orchestra because I thought this was a good way to get an introduction to music.

"Oh, yes," he said, "one gets to know music from the inside. Do you play the piano?"

I replied that I played badly, but Jarnach piped up, "No, he plays quite well."

Busoni remarked that piano was a very practical instrument and to keep it up. We talked about other instruments, and I mentioned that I had learned percussion because I wanted to know something about rhythm instruments. He discussed these in detail and suggested using percussion sparingly.

I told him I was studying flute with Nada. We had some exchanges about French and German schools of flute playing. Busoni had reservations about both. The French was too superficial; the German was too rough technically, but he did admire Nada's impeccable style. After telling me again that he had heard quite a lot about my compositions from Andreae and others (my First Violin Sonata and two songs had been performed publicly and received good reviews), he said that he was most anxious to become acquainted with some of my music and asked if I would be kind enough to bring him some scores.

After the strange life as a student in Munich, it was a thrilling experience to have men like Andreae, Jarnach, and now the legendary Ferruccio Busoni treat me like a man, a professional, a fellow artist. This was what I wanted to be and what I felt I had accomplished at the age of eighteen, but to have it recognized on such an intimate social occasion surprised and gratified me.

After further conversation, we tried to leave, but Busoni wanted to know about my American background and about America in general. He said he had been in the United States several times and hadn't liked it. He hinted that at the New England Conservatory of Music he was put on a twenty-minute-lesson schedule and that it seemed like a factory. He also told, with much relish and, finally, raucous laughter, of a rehearsal of Beethoven's *Emperor* Concerto with Mahler and the New York Philharmonic. The orchestra had stopped and he and Mahler were discussing some matters of balance and tempo. A lady board member watched the discussion and, noting that the orchestra was not playing, got up angrily, saying, "This will never do," and left to report this work stoppage to the management and the board of directors. This led to Mahler's dispute with the Philharmonic and his subsequent resignation.

Busoni also complained that while he was giving a concert on a tour out West, a slide projector flashed on a screen the various sections of the sonata he was playing—introduction, bridge, first subject, transition, second subject, in the dominant or related key, etc. He insisted that the following Texas story was true: While playing, he happened to glance up and see a sign hanging high on the stage behind the piano. It said, "Don't shoot the pianist; he's doing his best."

In Chicago he had met and admired Bernard Ziehn, the theorist, whose ideas completely changed Busoni's concept of composing techniques; Wilhelm Middelschulte, the organist, a great contrapuntist; and the conductor Frederick Stock, who also won his admiration. One of his Boston students, Natalie Curtis, was among the first to collect Native American music. Busoni was interested in this music and in Indian culture in general. He had used material she had collected for his *Indian Fantasy* for piano and orchestra and his *Indian Diary* for piano solo. But for Busoni, as for most European artists, the United States was the place to find money, efficiency, and bad taste. (I have never known any of them to refuse the money.)

It was time to leave.

At the door he said, "I shall expect to receive some scores from you, and perhaps you will have a cup of coffee with me some afternoon."

I was now on my best and most elegant behavior, said it would be an honor, thanked him for his hopsitality, bowed in an artistic (not military) manner, and left with Jarnach.

On my way home I thought about Busoni's aesthetic, which he had related indirectly by talking of other composers. He had been enthusastic about the transparent and transcendental or floating quality in Mozart's music and commented that Andreae's interpretation of the *Haffner* Symphony was too heavy-handed and too Beethovenian. He then proceeded, again indirectly, to point out that Beethoven had held back the progress of musical composition by overemphasizing the heroic and the forceful. He admitted the greatness of the last sonatas, particularly the *Hammerklavier* Sonata, the G Major and *Emperor* concerti, and the *Eroica* Symphony. But he stated that Beethoven's followers had taken over the turgidity and heaviness of his works and that in doing so they had completely forgotten the superior musical virtues of lightness, transparency, and what I can only translate as a floating kind of transcendentalism that brought one into touch with a supernatural dimension, expressed fully in such works as Mozart's *Zauberflöte, Don Giovanni,* and his G- and C-minor piano concerti. Jarnach defended the very power of Beethoven that Busoni was trying to decry. As the conversation went on they made allusions to Wagner, who served as a horrible example of nineteenth-century composing; to Berlioz, the real pathbreaker; and to Strauss, admired by Busoni for his intelligence but criticized for his overcomposing and his bombast.

Inspired by my visit with Busoni, I put my First Sonata for Violin and Piano and my *Sextet* into what I thought was good shape. Jarnach and Andreae had no further comments about the two pieces. I had even attracted a group of young students and disciples who called me Maestro and worked as my copyists. I was so busy playing in the opera and symphony orchestra that I decided to attend black-coffee sessions at Busoni's only when I had scores and could hope for direct or indirect comment. I took him the violin sonata and sextet a few weeks later. Frau Busoni received me. I heard some mumbling and grumbling from inside the apartment, and after about five minutes she returned to tell me that her husband was unfortunately busy, but would I care to leave the scores so he could study them at his leisure? After the regal reception of the first evening, I found this chilling, but dutifully left the scores and went on my way.

When examining new works, Jarnach told me, Busoni preferred to read scores and not play them on the piano. He was a magnificent score player, but he felt that the piano detracted from a proper study of works that were for voice or other instruments. He had an uncanny way of sizing up works by paging through them and seemingly absorbing the musical content at a glance. He kept my two works for three weeks. Jarnach told me Busoni spent two full working days studying them. Busoni always sent handwritten letters or notes to people by messenger. He had no phone and said that he had probably not used a telephone more than twice in his lifetime.

A letter arrived by messenger, saying that he would be very happy to have my *Sextet* read through in his apartment, if he and I could find the musicians.

Jarnach reported to me that Busoni felt the editing was imprecise and that Busoni had some doubts about me if I thought so little of my ideas as to present them in such a casual way. This made quite an impact. Here I was, the great young genius and professional man-about-town, being told by a very great artist that my casual attitude about my own work raised some doubts in his mind about my dedication to music and my talent as a composer!

I refrained from advertising this experience, and Jarnach was discreet, but I began working with great care and cleaned up both the violin sonata and the sextet. (There is an ending to the *Sextet* story, which I learned only in 1965 or 1966. Edward Weiss, a piano student of Busoni's in Zurich from 1917 to 1920, told me that Busoni was constantly talking about my Sextet and had remarked on several occasions that it was one of the finest works by a member of the younger generation of composers.) I did not try to arrange a reading at Busoni's apartment, but after I left Zurich one of my students, Hans Zimmerman, later director of the Zurich Opera, conducted the *Sextet* in a concert. Busoni and Jarnach attended and were pleased with the work.

Busoni was constantly working on various kinds of contrapuntal studies. He believed that within our twelve-tone system any harmony could be explained logically. But he also believed that the individuality of the composer and his real personality were expressed through the melodic-rhythmic line and, of course, in combinations of two or more of these lines that brought the contrapuntal principle into play. Jarnach showed me a three-part contrapuntal exercise to which Busoni had said a fourth voice could not be added. We worked at the example for some hours but it was not possible to get another satisfactory voice to fit into the style he had established.

Busoni insisted that everything must be imagined so strongly that testing at the instrument would be quite unnecessary. This presupposed, of course, knowing the possibilities and characteristics of the instruments very thoroughly. He also believed that one should invent original musical materials for each particular instrument, although this did not really match his theories about musical transcription. He professed that every composition was merely a transcription or a rearrangement of known sounds. His many transcriptions included rearrangements for piano of other composers' symphonic, operatic, and organ works.

He expected us to be familiar with different styles of music, and in his larger works like *Doktor Faust,* the early piano concerto with male chorus, the Second Violin Sonata, and even *Arlecchino,* he used various styles as a part of his overall form. This multistylistic composing caused consternation and aroused comment from the purists. He was a very individualistic composer who wanted this same kind of search for the "real self" to be lived by his students. He did not try to organize us into a school. Although accused by conservative German composers of being a futurist, he was actually trying to bridge the gap between the old and the new by accepting traditions but transforming them into music for the future. He also tried to blend the cultural characteristics of the Germans and the Italians—"the north and the south," as he expressed it.

I played in the first performance of his *Concertino for Clarinet and Small Orchestra,* which Edmund Allegra played in 1919 under Andreae's direction. It was graceful and witty, with a melodious slow movement. In this work, as in his *Arlecchino* and *Turandot,* Busoni demonstrated what he called the "young classical" movement. This was the term he used whenever anybody turned out a good piece. Young classical movement meant "conclusion as perfection and conclusion after the organic development of the original idea." The *Concertino* had a decidedly Mozartian lift about it without being imitative. It influenced me to write clearly heard music. With all of the Mahler-Bruckner repertory we were playing in the Tonhalle, there was a purity about Busoni's work that made a deep impression on me.

Another event that had strong impact and considerable influence on my attitude about composing was the first performance of his *Sarabande* and *Cortège,* "reduced models" for his opera *Doktor Faust.* I played celesta, other percussion, and third flute and piccolo in these pieces and was impressed by the great nobility of the *Sarabande,* a quality hard to find in most of the contemporary

music of those years. The *Cortège* was a fantastic processional that
projected images from a dreamlike world. Busoni's music often
had this power to transport one into a strangely beautiful but
sometimes very fantastic world, a world of visions and transcendental experiences. Busoni conducted a rehearsal of these two
pieces, and although his baton technique was in no way routine in
the orchestra players' sense of the word, he animated the orchestra—mostly by eye contact—to do some extremely imaginative and expressive playing with intellectual force behind it.

The first performance of the *Sarabande* and the *Cortège* was
on Busoni's birthday, April 1, 1919, and after the performance
friends were invited to Dr. Andreae's villa for supper and music.
Andreae invited a few of the younger musicians, including me.
After supper Andreae suggested to Busoni and the concertmaster,
Willem de Boer, that they play the maestro's Second Violin Sonata. This curious but beautiful work showed Busoni's mixture of
styles to its best advantage and was given a magnificent performance. The work conveyed a moving kind of spirituality because
of the selectivity Busoni had shown in forming the basic materials.

Busoni followed this piece with the Liszt-Busoni *Mephisto
Waltz*. I sat on a small platform right next to the keyboard, so I
had a chance to observe him as well as to listen. The spirit of the
piece was one of real Mephistophelian abandon, but it was a kind
of enjoyable abandon that evoked beautiful pictures of wine,
women, and the sounds of dance music on some hell-raising occasion. It was the epitome of all the wild parties that had ever existed.

One sensed an enormous tension between Busoni's consciousness and his subconscious drives and insights in this music.
I was again astounded by Busoni's technical security. He played
octaves so fast that his hands were a blur.

THE EFFECT of Busoni's musical personality on my own composing was strong. I worked for nine months on my next work, my
First String Quartet with clarinet obbligato in the last movement.
I composed much more slowly and carefully than I had in the
past. My writing became much more contrapuntal and was tonal

and polytonal at different times. Each of the string parts had a melodic life that was quite independent of the others, but I had also worked out a type of motivated development that gave to the harmonies a contrapuntal touch, even when the harmonies were only accompanying chords. I was much more preoccupied with what the work was expressing, with the musical style and idea and the expressive content, than in earlier works. I let this ripen as I myself became more introspective and found wider horizons than I had imagined existed. Above all, the overall form or gestalt of the entire quartet concerned me and was slowly revealed to me. The work was in three movements and was forty-five minutes long.

I showed the work in progress to Jarnach, who was most encouraging. When I finished the quartet, Jarnach suggested that I take it to Busoni for examination and criticism. I didn't like the idea of hanging around at Busoni's door with my quartet in hand, but I was anxious for him to read it so I left it with him.

A few weeks later, I heard from Jarnach that Busoni was extremely interested in my work and had spent a week studying it. He told Jarnach he was quite surprised at the amount of inventiveness it revealed and the care with which it had been worked out. The second movement contained a passage which I had composed when I was fourteen years old, a free use of a primitive type of twelve-tone writing. In the last movement there were several clearly defined polytonal and fugal passages. Busoni was delighted with the solution of the formal problems, and he made a speech to Jarnach, saying that he had to confess that he recognized qualities in this work that he had not fully recognized in my other two compositions. He thought the clarinet solo at the end was inspired. Busoni made these comments on various occasions around town and they were of enormous help in establishing me further in the artistic circles of Zurich. I became again the fair-haired young composing genius.

My contact with Busoni continued rather casually in cafés and restaurants. Before I left for the United States in 1920, I made a farewell call on him, which went something like this:

"I have come, Maestro, to say goodbye."

"What are your plans for the future?"

"I am going back to America."

Busoni looked positively shocked and unbelieving. "America?" he said in a questioning tone of voice.

I said, "Yes, to the United States."

He asked, after a pause, "Aren't you afraid?" And then relighting his cigar, he mumbled, "Too bad. You have real talent."

I said I thought I should return to my native country.

Busoni settled back and gathered his thoughts as he poured out brandy. "One city is quite musical, and that is Chicago. Frederick Stock and Wilhelm Middelschulte, the organist, and many former pupils of Bernhard Ziehn live there, and you may use my name in introducing yourself."

He continued to point out the folly of my decision to go to the United States and spoke quite favorably about my musical career possibilities in Europe. I countered by pointing out that for an American to make a career in Switzerland or Europe might prove to be difficult. But he wouldn't accept my argument. He just shook his head and said that it made him sad to see such a promising young fellow leaving Europe to walk into a torture chamber. (In Chicago I soon learned what he meant.)

NEITHER BUSONI nor Jarnach forgot my First String Quartet. When they moved to Berlin in 1921, it was recommended for a performance by the Roth Quartet at the Melos Society, which in 1924 gave four concerts with the International Society for Contemporary Music. The four concerts included songs by Anton Webern; the *String Trio* by Zoltán Kodály; the String Quartet, Opus 7, by Arnold Schoenberg; and *Three Pieces for String Quartet* by Igor Stravinsky. The series received international press coverage; this did me a great deal of good in Chicago, where I was then playing flute in a movie orchestra.

The reviews in Europe were quite good, and some critics pointed out that I was trying to combine modern dissonant music with a more simple and straightforward kind of writing. This was true enough and it still holds in my recent compositions. I always saw the simpler and more direct statements as a foil or contrast for the more complicated musical communications, and I considered these stylistic extremes as great contrasts but not incompatible. Five months after the premiere of my work, Busoni died, on July 27, 1924.

One of the reasons for his own phenomenal accomplishments was that he had perfect recall. He once said that his heaviest burden was that he could never forget anything. If he were active today he would still be, as he was then, the towering virtuoso and fantastic musician of the contemporary scene. As a composer, he is only now coming into his own. Much of the composing by process, which has become so fashionable today, was anathema to him. Many of our contemporary improvements on older civilizations would not have appealed to him. He hated war, brutality, and violence, and seemed to reach a realm of pure spirit at times, far removed from his raucous and sometimes sharp and bitter comments about human pretentiousness. All in all, he was one of the rare geniuses that humankind produces.

≫≪

I FIRST HEARD the name James Joyce from Philipp Jarnach, whose family had shared a duplex house with the Joyce family. Jarnach admired him. Apropos of nothing in particular, Jarnach said in a music composition class, "And then, of course, there are real artists, like James Joyce. He never writes one single word that does not stem from the inner world of his subconscious self. Like a sculptor, he shapes his words into sentences and makes his imagined world become alive and vivid to his readers. Like all great artists he works slowly."

I was curious to learn more about Joyce. I bought *Exiles* in a German translation and found it extremely interesting.

In the spring of 1918, in the Pfauen Café, I met a young Englishman named Charles Fleming. He was about twenty and was the perfect model of an English barrister out on the town. He wore striped trousers, a cutaway coat, and a gray fedora. He was extremely dignified at our first meeting and remained that way during the two years of our friendship. Fleming invited me to visit a rehearsal by a theatrical group called the English Players. Before accepting his invitation I asked him to tell me something about them, and it took him all afternoon to do so.

Apparently, a typical Zurich World War I adventurer named Jules Joe Martin tried to get James Joyce to write a movie scenario in the spring of 1917. Joyce was struggling to support his family by teaching English and coaching voice. He saw the project as a way out of his financial difficulties, so he agreed to do the job. Claud W. Sykes, a former actor in the company of Sir Herbert Beerbohm Tree, was his assistant. This speculative adventure collapsed, but Sykes suggested to Joyce that the two of them found a resident company to present English plays in Zurich with Sykes as producer and director and Joyce as business manager. The company was named the English Players.

Their first production, Oscar Wilde's *The Importance of Being Earnest*, took place on April 29, 1918, in the Kaufleuten hall before a sold-out house. The play was enthusiastically received and the company made a small profit. Fleming explained that unfortunately Joyce had gotten into a real row with an actor in the English Players named Carr who worked for the British Consulate. Carr had left in a huff. The company now needed a replacement and some actors as understudies. Fleming, who was their stage manager, thought that I could fill the bill even though I had had no experience, so he suggested that I meet Joyce, Sykes, and the rest of the company after their next rehearsal.

At the time, the company was preparing *The Twelve Pound Look* by J. M. Barrie, *Riders to the Sea* by J. M. Synge, and, lastly, *The Dark Lady of the Sonnets* by G. B. Shaw for a performance on June 17, 1918. I attended the first dress rehearsal.

Having been conditioned to the German style of tragedy and comedy in Munich, my reactions to the three plays were immediate: the Barrie and the Shaw were extremely convincing in their brevity, but I had a hard time following the message of the Synge play with its Irish undertones.

It didn't take long to observe (and to hear from Fleming) that the company consisted of amateur, semiprofessional, and professional actors. Sykes appeared to be an efficient, if somewhat prosaic director. Joyce coached the actors in diction and then ruled the production from the prompt box. Sykes and Tristan Rawson, a singer at the Zurich Opera, were the most experienced actors. Joyce's wife Nora was remarkably convincing in the Synge play, but the others needed much coaching. Proofs of the program notes written by Joyce were handed around for comment.

In the break I met Sykes, who sized me up with apparent favor and then steered me to Joyce, who made an elegant impression on me with his black jacket, gray flannel trousers, and little round black hat. His pale blue eyes, a small tuft of hair under his lower lip, and a smart mustache gave him a slightly rakish appearance. His handshake was relaxed and he moved with a willowy gait. He seemed more like a friendly, very competent man of the theater than an intellectual or literary figure of the kind we had come to know in Zurich. After the rehearsal, Sykes and Joyce took me to the Pfauen.

Over cognac, Sykes asked me to join the company and to be second understudy for a part in the next production, *Hindle Wakes*, by William Stanley Houghton. Joyce, in his role as business manager, told me that members of the company were offered the opportunity to purchase shares for fifty francs. In addition to sharing the profits, they were paid a nominal fee and expenses. I agreed to join, and bought shares.

After Sykes and Joyce left, I questioned Fleming about Joyce, and he explained, "He's an Irishman and he's sitting out the war here. Berlitz sends him students because they reneged on a job for him. He's written a couple of books that you might find here. We may produce his play, *Exiles*. You might like to read his *Portrait of the Artist as a Young Man*. He also has written some poems, entitled *Chamber Music*. He's very good." No one, even in Joyce's circle of friends, thought of him as a possible international celebrity, but he was definitely recognized as a contributor to the cultural life of Zurich.

AFTER PRELIMINARY rehearsals for *Hindle Wakes*, the revolution that had spread through Russia and Germany caught up with Zurich in the form of a general strike that shut down all services in the town including streetcars, the post office, and most shops. Cavalry regiments of the Swiss militia from mountain districts, which had little sympathy for urban troublemakers, moved in to keep order. Soon streetcars were run by soldiers with fixed bayonets. Horror was added to horror when the flu epidemic struck the city, paralyzing everything that had not been knocked out by the strike.

The epidemic hit close to home. Otto Strauss and David Rubinstein landed in temporary hospitals with pneumonia. My roommate, Oser, and I were nursed for three weeks in our apartment. Theaters and concert halls, including the Tonhalle, and many restaurants closed because of the epidemic. The Tonhalle was transformed into a hospital, but the orchestra kept on rehearsing in the opera house. All schools were closed and many of them were made into hospitals.

The Swiss Socialist Party was very active in spearheading the agitation. The strike was allegedly led by some of Lenin's Swiss disciples who had been indoctrinated by him while he lived in Zurich. Eventually, the Socialist paper *Volksrecht* announced a protest meeting in the square adjoining the Zurich Fraumünster. Bulletins were posted all over town and Strauss and I, by then barely recovered from the flu, went to the meeting at one o'clock to see the action.

The square was occupied by about three thousand people, ringed by cavalry. With our backs against the walls of the church, we were close to the dramatic events that took place. After we listened to inflammatory speeches and protests about various abuses inflicted on the proletariat, a militia captain came forward, silenced the crowd, and ordered it to disperse and leave the square within fifteen minutes. He was greeted by jeers, boos, and catcalls; nobody moved. At the deadline, he gave an order to the cavalry. The troopers trotted around the square to disperse the crowd with sabers, without success. The captain next climbed a platform and announced that if the square were not cleared in fifteen minutes, his troops would fire. After a few jeers and boos, the crowd stood still, sullenly. When the deadline arrived, the captain ordered the troops to set up machine guns. Within five minutes, he barked out a command that was followed by a rat-tat-tat from the guns.

Strauss and I were hit by chunks of bricks falling from the wall of the church. We looked up and saw that machine gun bullets had hit the church about two feet above our heads. We got out of the square in a hurry, frightened by the continuous rattle of machine-gun fire that lasted for about fifteen minutes.

After an hour, we returned to see what had happened and found the square occupied by soldiers. The remnants of the angry mob were moving in small groups to various parts of the city. As we spoke with a number of people, we pieced together the story. Forty-four people had been killed and seventy wounded. It was the closest that the Swiss Federation had come to a complete breakdown of civil authority.

Against these odds, Joyce and Sykes decided to go on with the play and the cast rehearsed almost every evening in the apartment of Mrs. Turner, one of the actresses. She lived about two miles distant from the rest of us. Sometimes we walked to her place in a group through streets that were patrolled by soldiers with fixed bayonets. Often we were caught up in mobs that were waiting to get bread. One of the actors, Bernard Glenning, died of influenza shortly before the opening. Fleming took his place and I became the understudy. Because of my sometimes conflicting duties as a member of the opera and symphony orchestras, I used the stage name James P. Cleveland.

Joyce's row with Carr had developed into a lawsuit that was scheduled for trial on October 15, 1919. Occasionally, Carr or some of his friends would come to rehearsals when they were sure that Joyce had left, to argue with Sykes and the cast about the merits of the case. Sometimes they attacked Joyce in a most insulting way, but most of the cast defended him enthusiastically. Whenever Joyce's literary reputation was attacked, Sykes would fight back. Joyce had been writing *Ulysses* and Sykes had typed the entire manuscript for him. Some sections had been published in Harriet Shaw Weaver's *Little Review* in Chicago. He had read some of these for members of the company. One evening, a detractor pointed out vehemently that Joyce's writings were extremely questionable and obscene. Sykes defended his friend so firmly that his opponent blushed in anger and barked, "Well, I don't care what you say, but 'asshole' is a dirty word." Everyone was shocked and didn't know quite how to react, because in Zurich's artistic circles this was not really the way most people talked or acted! The emotional temperature was high and the morale and concentration of the company were at a low ebb; however, most of the actors were loyal to Joyce, and Sykes pulled them together in time for the *Hindle Wakes* performance on December 3, 1918, at the Kaufleuten. (Fortunately for me, I had not been cast. I was having a bit of trouble with Houghton's Lancaster dialect.) The performance was a disaster. Because of the flu epidemic, the attendance was small, and the company lost money. There were no reviews.

The company had recovered by December 11, when it performed before a polylingual audience Cavallotti's *Il cantico dei cantici*, acted by Italian amateurs recruited and coached by Joyce; de Banville's *Le Baiser*, played by actors from the Théâtre-Français; and Robert Browning's poetical play, *In a Balcony*, performed by the English Players. It was at a rehearsal of the Browning that I first heard Joyce, accompanied by a guitar, sing the canzona "Amante tradito" by Giovanni Stefani from offstage after the curtain had gone up. Jarnach had told me that Joyce had a disagreeable and rather loud voice, a composer's reaction when he is being disturbed by a singer. I found it was a light voice, a cross between an Irish tenor and an Italian lyric tenor. His diction was impeccable and his interpretation expressive. He was applauded during the opening scene at the premiere.

After this performance, Joyce announced that the publicity about his lawsuit with Carr was damaging the players and he withdrew as manager of the company. Actually his interest and participation continued as long as he was in Zurich. He attended most rehearsals, helped with the planning, generally acted as prompter, coached diction, inflections, and movement, sometimes helped Sykes with the overall production, and at the end raised money for the company.

My real chance as an actor came when I was cast for the juvenile lead in G. K. Chesterton's *Magic*, opening February 1, 1919, in the Kaufleuten. I was a natural for the part: a young half-American who was skeptical about immortality and anything pertaining to the spiritual or supernatural realms watches a conjurer do some tricks, all of which the lad can explain rationally. When the young man finally sees a trick that he cannot explain and it brings him to the threshold of madness, he collapses. The memory of the Bleuler lectures in abnormal psychology helped me to do a convincing job for I knew just how delicately the lines between fantasy, reality, and madness are drawn. Joyce was in the prompt box and was largely responsible for the smoothness of the performance, for he had a marvelous way with nervous actors who had forgotten their lines. He mimicked and mouthed cues over and over again until the actor had recovered himself and could carry on.

The audience was large and enthusiastic. The reviewer in the *Züricher Zeitung* said that without exception the performers were very good. After the show I was in the heady position of being a full-fledged partner in the company, destined to do juvenile leads and character parts and eventually to be the stage manager of the company at the ripe age of eighteen!

After rehearsals some of the actors enjoyed meeting in the Pfauen Café for food, drink, and conversation. Contrary to the expectations of many people who came to the Pfauen to chat with Joyce, he was most of the time more of a listener and observer than a lecturer or propagandist for his favorite ideas. Although he enjoyed the relaxed atmosphere on these occasions, he made many notes and wrote comments on envelopes, menus, and odd bits of paper to keep the ideas and images that came to him from being forgotten or blurred by our indulgence in good food and heady wine.

Joyce was a remarkable mimic. Sometimes after a few glasses of wine he would rise and do a kind of pantomimic dance— willowy, graceful, and with great suppleness. He danced as if he had trained at Mary Wigman's studio. Sometimes he would lead a number of us in a group charade, or, on our way home from a café, in a snake dance—to the astonishment of any Zurich burghers still on the street.

From my first conversation with Joyce in the Pfauen, we established a very easy, interesting relationship. It began, of course, when we discussed the plays in the company's repertory. These he explained in detail, discussing particularly the relationship of the characters to each other and their underlying personality traits. On such occasions he seemed to be curious about my reactions to what he said, probably because I was sufficiently active as a musician and an actor to be very sure of my opinions and feelings; after my initial shyness, I displayed all the arrogance of an eighteen-year-old who fancied himself a junior celebrity.

I told him that in the previous year my *Piano Variations* had attracted attention at the conservatory and that my First Sonata for Violin and Piano had been given an excellent public performance that was followed by a fine review in the *Züricher Zeitung*.

Both pieces had definitely put me on the map in musical circles. The Sonata had enough youthful verve in it to be performed a few years later in Chicago. Fifty-five years later it was revived in New York and published. My *Sextet*, which was partially a salute to the "Back to Mozart" movement then in vogue, had also attracted much attention.

Joyce's own distressing financial problems were, like mine, solved for a time by a stipend from Mrs. Edith Rockefeller McCormick, who supported him and his family for a year—an arrangement that terminated only when she tried to persuade Joyce to be psychoanalyzed by Dr. Jung. In the interim she enabled Joyce to devote his entire energies to his creative work. Many years later he paid tribute to her generosity.

The English Players were going ahead with ambitious plans. Sykes and Joyce cast me in the part of an Irish doctor, aged forty, for the March 10, 1919, production of *The Heather Field* by Edward Martyn. Sykes went to some lengths to costume me. He found a greenish coat, an embroidered green vest with a gold watch chain dangling across it, baggy knickers, and gaiters. Joyce spent much time helping with the final touches.

Since October 1918, I believe Joyce had been working on "Lestrygonians," "Scylla and Charybdis," "Wandering Rocks," "Sirens," and possibly "Cyclops" from *Ulysses*. In the Pfauen, he began questioning me more and more about music. His tastes were unconventional. He thought that the Swiss song composer Othmar Schoeck, who was also greatly admired by Hermann Hesse, was one of the greatest composers in the world—an opinion that may yet prove to be valid, since Dietrich Fischer-Dieskau in 1970 recorded Schoeck's songs. Joyce also mentioned a number of seventeenth-century Italian composers whose arias or canzone he had sung and liked. He told Charlotte Sauermann, a soprano with the Zurich Opera, that he had once auditioned for opera and was not impressed. She promptly arranged a tryout for him for chorus and small parts in the Zurich Opera, but he refused to go through with it.

Joyce was not well known to the young musicians connected with the conservatory in Zurich, but he was a familiar figure at opera and concert performances. Donizetti, Bellini, and Puccini were composers that he really enjoyed, and Verdi was his favorite. He liked to talk about him and often sang phrases from his operas. Sometimes he would speak with nostalgia of old light operas like *The Bohemian Girl*.

With the exception of *Die Meistersinger*, he disliked Wagner and he enjoyed ridiculing at great length both Wagner's *Tannhäuser* and the *Ring*. Once, after a performance of *Die Walküre*, he devastated that work and *Tannhäuser* verbally and with mimicry. As I had had my fill of both these works (we had given about a dozen performances that year) this pleased me greatly, and I joined in the fun by giving an impersonation of the Ride of the Valkyries as rehearsed in the Zurich Opera. With a bit of coaching from Joyce this became a performance that remained in my impersonation repertory for many years.

Joyce had a strong interest in Italian and Irish folk music. He sometimes hummed Thomas Moore's Irish melodies, particularly "O Ye Dead," and he remembered from his youth Irish, French, and Elizabethan sentimental and humorous songs. Sometimes he accompanied himself on the guitar, which he played indifferently. He was particularly convincing when he sang snatches of Gregorian chant, *a cappella*, of course.

Joyce seemed rather dapper and used a cane with grace. His tapered hands were quite beautiful, particularly when he used them to emphasize points. The shape of his face reminded me of Pan. Sometimes he looked a bit like a Mephisto who had reached a certain level of success and maturity in other than his usual occupation.

As I CAME to know Joyce better, he had a great influence on me. I sensed that he put up with my brashness, my vigor, and sometimes my impertinences because he knew that these habits were not ends in themselves, nor were they merely assumed. He understood that they existed because I had the excessive energy and drive of a young professional trying to function in the real world without giving up his ideals. He seemed to respect this. It was not his manner ever to be condescending, nor was there anything patronizing about him. He was always extremely stimulating.

Once, while we were having wine and cheese, he paused for a moment and then asked out of the blue, "Who do you think are the greatest composers?"

I was embarrassed as I answered, "That is difficult for me to say; I've played so many works and I myself compose. I haven't really settled on any favorite."

With an expression that sometimes came over him when anticipating the shocked reaction he would get as he said something outrageous, he continued, "For me there are only two composers. One is Palestrina and the other is Schoenberg."

It took me a moment to get my bearings, because I couldn't remember that Schoenberg had been played in Zurich in those years, except by Hans Heusser at the Dada gatherings. Joyce had never mentioned these so I had to assume that he had heard about Schoenberg from Philipp Jarnach, who was a great admirer of the Austrian composer. On this occasion and on others I was never quite sure whether a Joyce statement came from a profound and primal conviction he was confessing or whether his statements were made solely to draw me out and to make me talk more about the things he was interested in. He was remarkably successful in the latter, because on the surface I was at first rather shy with people I didn't know well. From the outset I was more open with him than with others, and I could sense his interest in my responses.

One afternoon, he opened a long discussion about religion. He spoke of the Catholic Church and its rituals—something I could follow because I had played in orchestras and sung in Catholic choirs in Bavaria, including the Munich Frauenkirche (the cathedral in that city). I had studied Catholic music rather carefully at the Munich academy, particularly the works of Orlandus Lassus. My family was not Catholic but I was encouraged to explore the Church in my own way. From my twelfth to my seventeenth year, the Catholic Church fascinated me: the incense, the music, and the ritual the church provided lifted my spirits and worked on my subconscious. As soon as Joyce learned that I had lived in this atmosphere, he created an unforgettably vivid verbal picture of what this all meant. On that day he seemed to be rather positive about the Church. He only occasionally voiced doubts and raised questions that unfortunately seemed so profound that I didn't feel equipped or secure enough to respond. After some silence, he said, rather aggressively, "And what is your religion?"

This took me by surprise because, with the exception of an

Episcopal archdeacon in Munich who, when I was thirteen, suggested that I was going to Hell because I attended religious concerts instead of church services, no one had been interested in my beliefs. My father had always called himself a Monist or a Free Thinker and that had influenced me, but after listening to Joyce speak about the Catholic Church I felt strangely embarrassed and guilty. Eventually I answered, "I don't really have any religion."

"Everybody believes in something," he said. "What do you believe in and call yourself?"

After further hesitation, I parodied my father and replied, "I am a Free Thinker."

He looked at me doubtfully. "Oh, come, come. None of us is free and few of us can think."

This relieved a certain tension and he suggested that we go for a walk.

The café was almost empty, and as we left he did a beautiful improvised dance that was spectacular because of his sophisticated movements. The café staff watched approvingly and applauded enthusiastically. This was one of the many ways he showed the spontaneous side of his nature to his friends, a side that belied his reputation as a forbidding intellectual, an opinion that was already held by some people.

He was often preoccupied with thoughts and memories of Dublin, and he began telling me about that city. He was completely absorbed in *Ulysses* during that year and I think this informal verbalization helped him to let off steam and relax or to concentrate completely on the things he was describing. No matter what his motivation, listening to him that day was a spectacular experience for me. He created a word painting of Dublin. He described it in such detail and with such precise use of language that his inner image came alive and it seemed that I myself had been in Dublin. Even today I sometimes wonder if I haven't lived there.

As Joyce described a street, he began with the kinds of cobblestones . . . the shape of a stone and its relationship to the others that made up a stretch in the road . . . how they connected . . . and whether there was anything growing between them. He described stalks of dried grass still standing and growing green shoots that enlivened one or another spot. He made vivid the sound of horses' hooves and the sound of footsteps on the cobblestones and their different echoes, and then the smells—musty sometimes, sometimes of dirt and sometimes of the fresh or dried horse manure that he called horse apples. He illuminated this street of the mind by describing how it looked at different times of the day in different kinds of light.

He talked about the shops with their particular stoops, entrances, and colors, and why some looked like poor and some like rich shops. He described their interiors—how they were sometimes light, but then dark and gloomy as the sky clouded, and how they were filled with inside smells and sometimes outside smells that had wafted in through the door. He told how it felt to touch the objects in the shops and how they often made him come alive inside and respond with a purchase. His mural-like yet detailed portrait was done with such color, simplicity, and clarity that it taught me something new about art. No one else has ever shared with me an even remotely similar experience. I learned then of the great warmth that his sharp intellect could radiate and that his mind was not remote and distant, but at once precise and alive with a warm, human understanding.

Sometimes his wife, Nora, would join us and the conversation would be somewhat more relaxed. She was a friendly, warmhearted Irish woman. When their son, Giorgio, was there both parents were very attentive and kind to him and gave him the run of the restaurant. Like most European boys, Giorgio was well behaved, but Joyce encouraged him to roam around while we drank our wine and modulated our conversation into small talk. At other times I noticed what a remarkable observer of people Joyce was—sometimes sarcastic, sometimes scurrilous, but always extremely sensitive with a capacity for deep friendship and a sublimated love for many of the people he knew.

During the period of these meetings in the Pfauen, I was composing my First String Quartet. I had also looked into the works of what my fellow composers called "the old Netherlands school." I was fascinated with these studies and practiced and applied the fanciest kinds of inversions, symmetrical and otherwise, transpositions, and passages in augmentation and diminution, both separately and combined. I used the most intricate kinds of canonical passages, in retrograde or in retrograde inversions, combined with anything else I could possibly dream up or discover. Of course, there was nothing new about these techniques. They had been practiced for centuries, but they had been carried to a new plateau by Schoenberg, Busoni, and Jarnach. Joyce had had ample opportunity to discuss these musical materials with Jarnach, but he seemed fascinated as he heard about their application in my quartet. Because I was young and unknown, he could ask me about details that might not interest Jarnach. These I explained at length. At that time I was just beginning to be interested in acoustic relationships, the relationship of a fundamental tone to its other partials. This too interested Joyce a great deal, particularly when I pointed out that the third partial of the note C was G and the fifth partial was E and that I saw no reason why polytonal passages in which the music was played in C major, G major, and E major at the same time were not only logical but were rooted in natural relationships in the harmonic series.

Joyce's actual experience with music was so different from his intellectualizing about counterpoint that he seemed to be two people. He had heard Hans Zimmerman, a student of mine and later director of the Zurich Opera, conduct a chamber orchestra for which I had arranged and performed a suite of Gluck's music, including the famous flute solo "Dance of the Departed Spirits" from Gluck's *Orfeo ed Euridice*. Afterwards, Joyce said that he considered this solo to be the greatest piece of music ever written. He began going through the piece, note by note and phrase by phrase, literally transposing it first into word inflections and then into verbal images. At the end of this evening with Joyce I had learned more about the relationship of language to music than ever before or since.

Joyce enjoyed giving literary interpretations of the contrapuntal techniques in music. This turned into a kind of intellectual exercise in which he professed to use the devices for his own purposes in his own medium.

On June 18, 1919, he walked with George Borach around the Zurich See justifying his writing of "Sirens." He said, "I finished the 'Sirens' chapter during the last three days—a big job. I wrote this chapter with the technical resources of music. It is a fugue with all musical notations: *piano, forte, rallentando,* and so on. A

quintet occurs in it too as in the *Meistersinger*, my favorite Wagnerian opera. Since exploring the resources and artifices of music
and employing them in this chapter, I haven't cared for music any
more. I, the great friend of music, can no longer listen to it. I see
through all the tricks and can't enjoy it any more."

In a letter to Harriet Weaver on August 6, 1919, he wrote:

> Perhaps I ought not to say anymore on the subject of the Sirens
> but the passages you allude to were not intended by me as recita-
> tive. There is, in the episode, only one example of recitative, on
> page 12 in preface to the song. They are all the eight regular parts
> of a fuga per canonem: and I did not know in what other way to
> describe the seductions of music beyond which Ulysses traveled. I
> understand that you may begin to regard the various styles of the
> episode with dismay and prefer the initial style much as the wan-
> derer did who longed for the rock of Ithaca, but in the compass of
> one day to compress all these wanderings and clothe them in the
> form of this day is for me only possible by such variation which, I
> beg you to believe, is not capricious. . . .

Later, when Joyce lived in Paris, his musical interests were
reawakened, mostly because of his contact with George Antheil,
the American avant-gardist, Darius Milhaud, and Erik Satie.
Antheil told me he had planned an "electric" opera that used the
"Cyclops" episode of *Ulysses* as a libretto. He wanted to use thirteen electric pianos and recorded drums, xylophones, and noise
instruments. The singers were to be invisible and their voices
amplified. The action was to be in pantomime. Joyce was fascinated but Antheil abandoned the project. By a strange coinci-
dence, when Joyce's *Ulysses in Nighttown* was produced in New
York in 1958, the director used electronic music by Luening-
Ussachevsky; he probably used it in the production in London
also.

THE MAY 7 production by the English Players had been well
received by the press, so we were finally able to go ahead with
the production of Oliver Goldsmith's *She Stoops to Conquer*. The
play had been chosen by Joyce, Sykes, Frank Budgen, and myself
a short while before, sitting over cognac in the Café de la Terrasse.

For the production of *She Stoops to Conquer* on May 26,

1919, Budgen was cast as Stingo the Publican and for want of any-one better, Sykes gave me the part of Tony Lumpkin.

Joyce was, as always, animated and extremely helpful from the prompt box in rehearsals. My part included some singing and the recitation of an epilogue by J. Kraddock, so Joyce coached me carefully in diction and I colored my midwest accent so that I spoke with a slight Irish inflection. This was an incredible experi-ence, for he made me so aware of the particular musical and expressive qualities of our language that I wrote to my parents, in describing the rehearsals: "I am learning to speak English."

The performance of *She Stoops to Conquer* in the Pfauen Theater was an outstanding success. There were repeat perfor-mances and the company was engaged to appear in the Stadt-theater in Basel. Unfortunately, these triumphs possibly induced the treasurer to abscond with the company's funds. It was a most inopportune time for there were many outstanding bills. On June 23 the company was scheduled to do *The Twelve Pound Look* by Barrie, *The Dear Departed* by Houghton, and *Overruled* by Shaw.

Sykes was desperate. But at a rehearsal on June 12 Nora Joyce burst into the theater and announced that her husband had just received $700 from Padraic and Mary Colum's millionaire friend, Schofield Thayer, and $300 from J. S. Watson, Jr. Of this money Joyce gave $200 to the English Players to bail them out. Through the good offices of Colum and Harriet Weaver he again received substantial funds from the United States. In July Joyce gave the English Players 10,000 francs so that they were able to plan future productions of *That Brute Simmons* by H. C. Sargeant and Arthur Morrison and a revival of *The Importance of Being Ear-nest*. The former was performed on September 10, 1919, and was very well received by the audience and the critics, who hailed the company for providing a part of Zurich's artistic life. I received my first "name review" in the *Züricher Zeitung:* "Mr. Cleveland [my stage name], as John Culver, was the young son of the house, a handsome, dear boy just as he is in the play." I could find no mention of the superior quality of my acting, but after the perfor-mance Sykes suggested that I leave the musical profession and join the company on a permanent basis. He assured me that we soon would be touring Europe, a somewhat optimistic prediction.

Joyce was connected with the English Players from April 1918 until he left Zurich in October 1919. He was entrepreneur, then founder, and later business manager and treasurer. He was active in one way or another in every production during his stay in Zurich, even after he had severed his official connection with the company. He assisted Sykes in directing and costuming the plays, gave suggestions about the sets and the actors' movements, served as prompter in every production and as an incomparable diction coach for what was a heterogeneous group, and personally sold tickets. He exerted a great influence on Sykes in choosing the plays. In addition to the English authors Houghton, Chesterton, Barrie, Browning, and Arnold Bennett, Joyce saw to it that Ireland was well represented—Wilde, Shaw, Synge, Goldsmith, and Martyn. He wrote program notes for *Riders to the Sea, The Twelve Pound Look,* and *The Dark Lady of the Sonnets,* and coached an Italian company in Cavallotti's *Il cantico dei cantici.*

His devotion to the English Players was obviously rooted in his love of the theater, for it took much energy to sustain the company. Joyce's relationship to most of the actors was less that of the famous literary figure he later became than that of a brilliant Irish writer and English teacher who sang, was dedicated to the English theater, and wanted it to be properly represented in the international artistic circles of Zurich.

Chapter 9

Züricher Cadenza: Mountain Climbing
1919

WHEN THE SYMPHONY AND OPERA SEASON ended in 1919, I loafed around Zurich, bored, and with little cash. Each afternoon, I went to the Café Odeon for coffee and cognac and to meditate.

One hot afternoon my friend Hans Oser, a pianist, joined me. "By the way," he said, "are you tied up this summer? I'm looking for a flutist for a rather interesting engagement."

I said I might possibly rearrange my schedule.

Oser explained that an international exhibition was to include a "marionette theater." Gustave Doret, a famous French-Swiss composer, friend of Scriabin and Stravinsky, was having several of his marionette operas performed (including one about Dr. Faustus). They were based on old marionette plays but with his own music. He needed an "orchestra" consisting of flute, violin, and piano; we would double on percussion. Oser had signed up as pianist and Karl Zimmerli as violinist. The fee was eight francs per show but there were at least three or four shows a day and we would play three days each week. That meant ninety-six francs in a good week. As the cost of living was low—two francs for a first-rate meal with wine and a hundred francs a month for a snazzy apartment—the engagement seemed tops.

At rehearsal in the marionette theater Doret thought that he had the Paris Opera orchestra before him, and he gave his three-man band so many cues, signals, and signs for deep expression that we had a deuce of a time just keeping together. He always became particularly excited when Mephisto appeared on stage.

Here he demanded the sound of a hundred-man orchestra. I whispered to Oser to beat the hell out of the cymbals and that did it. Doret was very pleased, and eventually left us alone.

Under Oser's direction we got the score into very nice shape, and after a couple of performances everything was completely routine.

On our free days we swam across the lake and back, rowed along the shore, and drank cognac in the Odeon, but there wasn't enough action to keep us occupied.

One day, Oser proclaimed, "We're all getting soft. We need some real workouts in the Alps. You, Luening, as an American, really ought to see what our mountains are like."

Oser said he knew of two budding mountaineers: Plotti, a very personable young fellow, handsome as a gigolo, who was studying engineering at the Technische Hochschule and at the same time working for a concert diploma in piano at the conservatory; and Frederick Schlorr, a deserter from the Austrian army. Plotti lived in a nice bourgeois home with his mother, but Schlorr was a colorful character.

In the First World War, distinctions among men were clear. There were no conscientious objectors, draft-card burners, or men who were AWOL. There were simply soldiers, deserters, and those who had not been called up. Switzerland was a haven for deserters and also for escaped political prisoners and international spies. In Swiss cafés, too, was an interesting collection of international prostitutes. Schlorr played piano from nine in the evening until two in the morning at the Terrasse, allegedly a center for the cocaine traffic. He knew every call girl in town. He was an unmarried "family man," who supported his father and sister. His father was an Austrian man-about-town who set up small gambling games of various kinds and introduced his son's friends to the girls who hung around the café. Schlorr's sister was a very steady girl. She generally had a gentleman friend who would set her up in an apartment for six months or a year. But she was warmhearted and was not averse to an occasional one-night stand with close friends.

Fritz Schlorr had musical ambitions and was working for a concert diploma in piano at the conservatory. Every morning he would play the most difficult Beethoven sonatas, Liszt études, and classical and romantic concerti for anyone who would listen. With iron tenacity he finally got his concert diploma, played one concert, and continued his unique programs at the Terrasse. When I saw him half a century later, he had moved down the lake to a smaller town where he still played in a nightclub and did little dramatic sketches.

Oser was a man of action, and arranged that Plotti, Schlorr, and he leave the next morning for Lucerne and climb the Rigi for training. Because I was rehearsing for a special program I had agreed to play for the Swiss Society for the Hard of Hearing, I had to follow later.

I ate on the train, Swiss-mountain-fashion. The vendors sold very hard sausages that were impossible to chew but possible to gnaw and suck like lollipops. (These, with good rye bread, hot tea, and Swiss milk chocolate, sufficed for many of our smaller meals during the summer. We topped these off with nasty little cigars called *Stumpfen*. It was alleged that these cigars had been cured in alcohol, and when I tried my first one this sounded reasonable, for I had to throw the cigar out the window to keep from being sick.)

In Lucerne, it was already getting dark, so I decided to climb up the front of the mountain instead of taking the regular road. Within a short distance from the top I tripped over a log in the half-dark and rolled downhill about twelve feet. My knapsack opened and my baggage spilled. I picked up what I could find and retraced my steps to the road and took the easy path to the top.

Rather sheepishly, I arrived at eleven o'clock, but was received with cheers by my mountaineer friends. The hostel had almost run out of food, but they made me a kaiserschmarren, a very light, four-egg omelette covered with powdered sugar, and a large dish of preiselbeeren, a kind of mountain cranberry. A bottle of sour Swiss wine gave everything added flavor, and while we had our cognac and coffee, Oser announced that we three foreigners had the makings of real Swiss mountaineers.

Oser and I returned to the marionette theater the next afternoon. Schlorr and Plotti had left messages saying they wanted to do more mountain climbing. Oser then suggested we climb the

Glärnisch—a high but easy mountain—for training purposes. The rest of us didn't know a damn thing about the Swiss Alps, but we cheered and planned to take off the following week.

IN GLARUS, Oser led the way with a slow but incredibly steady mountaineer's lope. We plowed along for about seven hours before we reached the alpine hut. In addition to the sausage and milk chocolate, our provisions consisted of a flask of cold tea, brandy, and the inevitable cigars. Nobody ate much. The bunks in the hut were adequate but I was so tired, so nervous, and so full of anticipation that I scarcely slept at all.

Up at sunrise, we headed for the mountain peak. After a two-hour walk over a frozen snowfield, we reached a rock wall. Oser grabbed hold of the rocks like a squirrel and began edging his way up, and we followed. We were not roped together because the climb was not considered dangerous, but it was plenty scary for novices. We got to the top in an hour and a half of pretty strenuous climbing.

I had seen mountain vistas before, but there is a difference between the Bavarian hills and the Swiss Alps, and the view was overpowering. Breathing in the light air and looking over the glaciers and spotting higher peaks in the distance was very stimulating. There was a strange satisfaction in having reached the peak through my own efforts: although this was an easy climb, there was an element of danger and it took great endurance to make it. We stayed on the peak only briefly because the sun was melting the snowfields and glaciers, and this could make them quite dangerous. We had to cross the last icefield by 11:30 A.M.

As we approached the alpine hut, the snow got softer and softer and we sank in over our ankles, making the trek tiresome. At the hut, we flopped down for a good sleep.

The rest of our descent was much faster. Oser, in the lead, took every shortcut and went straight down the side of the mountain. I came in last because I had a weak left knee—injured when I was a boy—and it gave out, so I had to use my *Alpenstock*. After danger is over, Swiss mountain companions have a tendency to gallop ahead, leaving you to your own speed and devices. There is no impulse to be charitable and help you on your thorny path downward.

In the village of Glarus we headed for the nearest inn, where
we ordered the most stupendous meal the house had to offer:
soup with dumplings, venison with magnificent brown gravy,
enormous quantities of knödel on the side, a green salad with absolutely genuine, first-rate Swiss cheese, butter, and rye bread.
Some excellent Italian wine came with it and we drank quite a lot
of it. For dessert, there was plum cake, coffee with whipped
cream, and a dish of preserved blackberries, topped off with one
or maybe six cognacs.

Fully restored, we took the train to Zurich—tired but triumphant mountaineers back from a great conquest. We slept for
twelve hours and went to the marionette theater the next day to
recover.

That evening in the Café Odeon, Oser spread out several
maps of the Swiss Alps, saying, "You men are no longer novices.
Now we must climb a big one."

We decided on the Sustenhorn and studied the trails and
weather reports.

The day before we were leaving, Oser was called home for a
family conference. He was upset because he felt that we needed
him as a guide. We weren't so sure. We considered ourselves old-
timers and quite able to take care of ourselves, and decided to go
without him. However, we did want a fourth member for the
party.

Schlorr suggested another Austrian deserter whom I had
met. The man was about six feet two and broad in proportion,
with dark hair and eyes that were, I thought, too dark, too watery, and too innocent to be trusted. Besides, his ass was fat and
his name was Alois. His Danubian temperament seemed to me to
be soft and not too reliable. This was all hunch, but I did know
him as a composer and despised him professionally. He was
always talking about writing strict Viennese waltzes with an introduction and six parts. He never played a note of these and we
couldn't see what he was trying to prove, when so many good
Viennese waltzes were floating around in the cafés. But Schlorr
insisted, so Alois came along. We wore rather sloppy mountaineer clothes but he showed up with shoes without any hobnails
and an *Alpenstock* that looked more like a cane that he might
have used on the Prater. Besides, he wore one of those damn fool

hats with a feather on the back, and I felt that after we had pains-takingly roughed up our appearance he was deliberately spoiling our group image.

We arrived at Amsteg-Silenen and hiked for a long time through the beautiful, carless Maderaner valley. We took the trail to the Sustenhorn and found a very nice inn, where we took rooms for a few days.

Our new partner decided he wouldn't climb, but would rather sit on the veranda, enjoy the view, drink tea with rum, and eat torte and chocolate drops, in the hope of luring some unsuspecting but hungry Swiss girl to his side. The worst thing about this was that he talked Plotti into joining him.

Schlorr was disgusted. He called me over to the restaurant and announced that he would do a solo climb if no one would join him; in a spirit of good comradeship, I said I would go with him.

He pointed to a small peak about a mile from the hotel and said, "Let's climb that; it is the Maderaner Schwartzstöckli."

Off we went. About five hundred feet up, we found only rock on the side we were ascending.

Schlorr said, "I think we'll have to make a jump to the left here. I see a flue that goes right to the top."

I hung on while Schlorr took a great stride to the left and disappeared. I yelled, "How is it?"

He yelled back, "I'm on a ledge, but it's a broad stretch. Wait until I get started going up and then follow me."

I waited awhile and asked how he was getting along.

He called, "Fine. You can come now. I'll wait for you."

I peeked around the corner, saw the ledge, hugged the rocks, took a long stride, and just made it. Unfortunately, I looked down and saw the five-hundred-foot drop. This did not help my stomach any, but there was no way of either going down or turning back, and Schlorr was already well on his way up the flue. Each time he reached a higher ledge, part of the ledge he had been on would crumble, leaving me little to hang on to. Then, when I left the ledge I was on, the rest of it would break off, leaving me with no possible way of either standing still or going back. As the flue was about forty feet high, I realized that I had better forget everything and keep my mind on worming myself out of the mess, or I would fall.

We inched our way toward the top of this little peak, and

after an hour and a quarter Schlorr disappeared. He shouted that he was okay and had hold of a tree. I was scared, because the last two steps on the ledge below the top had broken off as he edged his way up. But Schlorr was resourceful. He hung on to the trunk of the tree with both arms, put his leg over the top of the flue for me to grab, told me to hang on, and pulled me up and over.

When I hit the grassy knoll, I had a severe attack of mountain sickness. I vomited, got the shakes, and was very frightened.

After lying around awhile, I found, however, that I had not completely lost my nerve; but I hadn't found it, either. I told Schlorr I'd be damned if I would climb down that murderous little peak and that we would have to find somewhere where the descent would be reasonably easy.

Eventually we discovered a mountain brook. By sitting in it and sliding from rock to rock, we made the descent via a safe but chilly sitz bath. We arrived at the hotel drenched, tired, sick, hungry, and cold, with some doubts about whether we were going to go on with this quixotic program of mountain climbing.

As we staggered through the lobby, we saw Alois, the Austrian waltz king, and Plotti with two Swiss girls in tow, dancing around a table filled with pots of chocolate, whipped cream, torte with rich frosting, and an enormous dish of chocolate drops. Several other girls were hanging around, waiting for their turns.

Schlorr and I—completely disgusted—went to our room, hung up our damp clothes, and fell into a deep sleep. The next thing I heard was a knock on the door and a voice shouting, "It's late; time to get up."

I looked at my watch. It was only 5:30 A.M. It was the damned waltz composer, who kept on shouting, "We have mountains to climb!"

We shook ourselves. Our togs had dried and we went out for breakfast. Plotti and Alois, looking somewhat the worse for wear, were urging us to tackle the Sustenhorn. We said okay and took off.

We reached the midway hut at about seven o'clock. The waltz composer stood on the ledge in front of the hut and, scanning the horizon like an Austrian field marshal, said, "A storm is coming up. I think it would be foolhardy to attempt to climb this morning. I don't think I'll go."

Plotti, under his spell, echoed him, and the two of them

decided to back out, perhaps remembering the Swiss girls. Schlorr and I were really angry. After a short conference, we agreed to climb the mountain in tandem.

Schlorr's actions on the day before had been so courageous and steady that I had great confidence in him, but it occurred to me that he did not look the part. He wore an ordinary gray fedora hat, a pince-nez that was constantly slipping off his nose, an ordinary blue serge jacket over a flannel shirt tied with a stringy necktie, and old gray pants wrapped up in army leggings borrowed from the Austrian army. Shoes that looked definitely too thin for a safe ascent completed his outfit. We had a rope and our picks, of course.

After the usual tedious climb, we crossed the first snowfield and soon walked onto the first glacier we had to cross. We were roped together.

It was a beautiful day. Schlorr stood on the edge of the crevice, removed his hat, cleaned his pince-nez with a silk handkerchief, and then commented on the beautiful view. At this very moment, his right foot slipped and he began sliding down the crevice. As he braced his left foot the rope tightened around his waist, and now it was up to me to brace myself to keep him from falling into the crevice. My hobnailed boots held. When he had straightened his pince-nez and the rest of himself I asked him, for God's sake, to be more careful. But then his left foot slipped, and I held him as he scrambled to hard snow. This sobered him up.

We had an enormous snowfield to traverse before we could reach the peak. We climbed sedately until we were about two hundred yards from the top. The sun had not hit this spot and the ice was very hard and slippery, so we had to chip steps up to the peak. We did this with a surprising amount of skill for greenhorns and made the climb with no further trouble. The view from the peak, where there was a small weather shelter, was magnificent. The air was clear, the sun was shining, and we could see an entire chain of the Swiss Alps spread out before us, with the snow blanket and glaciers sparkling in a dance of lights. There was no other motion. The only sound was that of the wind as it whistled and moaned around the weather house. Here beauty and nature were wedded. This was sublime, grander than anything I had ever experienced. For a moment, my psyche seemed cleansed of even my musical and artistic experiences and to be communing with the natural beauties I saw and felt outside myself. Music was remote. Only the mountain sights and sounds were real. Schlorr's expression showed that he felt the same. The ascent had been reckless but made with the courageous bravado of youth, for we had made it alone. Even now, more than half a century later, I see the scene in my mind's eye and feel animated.

In the weather house there was a book that mountaineers signed. I was surprised and nonplussed to see entered: *"Professor Doktor Otto Lüning, Cantonschule Schaffhausen, 1898."*

Much later, when I had a chance to make inquiries, I found that this gentleman was a musicologist and a distant relative of mine. (His articles on Wagner, Liszt, and Chopin were still read in the 1960s. This discovery also made me look for other relatives in Switzerland, and I found some in Zurich and elsewhere.) Finding a lead to my family tree on the top of a mountain was a sobering experience, and there was nothing to do but descend. We slowly went down the ice steps and crossed the snowfields with fast leaps, because the snow was soft but not yet dangerous.

Galloping down was a lot of fun, so when we came within sight of the hut, Schlorr, with his usual sense of adventure and nerve that never failed him, said, "Let's ski."

He picked the steepest incline, braced his feet and, using his *Alpenstock* as a ski pole, began sliding down the side of the mountain toward the hut at an ever-increasing speed. I followed his lead, but he was faster. I tried to catch up by sitting and sliding down the snowfield. It was dangerously steep. I slid so fast that I was afraid I would crash into the rocks at the bottom and get hurt or killed. Digging in my heels and steering very carefully slowed me up a bit and when I hit the rocks in front of the hut I only bruised my side and cut my hands.

After dusting off the snow and gravel and blood that had accumulated, I was greeted by the waltz composer, Alois.

"Tsk, tsk. I watched you through binoculars and I could see you are very inexperienced. One should never sit down and slide down a mountainside. I remember well when I climbed the Matterhorn."

At this point I couldn't take it any longer. I lost my cool and made myself feel better by saying, "Listen, you fat slob, the only thing that you've ever climbed has been a chocolate drop, and I don't like your busy waltzes either."

Schlorr joined us and, seeing that I was pretty mad, stepped between us and said, "Come on, Luening. All Austrians aren't like this fellow. Remember Johann Strauss, Sigmund Freud, and Nikolaus Lenau."

So I said, "Okay, okay. Let's go back to Zurich, Schlorr. These fellows probably have some more whipped cream to eat before they can leave."

After the usual enormous meal, we headed for the nearest railroad station. The waltz king brought up the rear. Our trip to Zurich was silent; we parted company with the two sissies, and then Schlorr and I went to the Odeon, where we met Oser.

He wanted to know all about our trip, and listened with great approval. Then he announced, "You fellows are really routined now, and as a final climb this season, we must tackle one of the big ones. I have guidebooks here for *all* the Alps! Let's take a look."

We examined the whole map and read descriptions of certain of the climbs. We finally concentrated on the Tödi and read that it was extremely difficult to climb from the west wall, an ascent made only about once every three years because of the hazards.

After further discussion, Oser said, "I don't like the way Plotti behaved on your last trip. If we are going to climb a mountain, everyone in the party has to agree to see it through. No one can turn back, and I don't want to be dragging Plotti home on a rope or have him leaving the three of us high and dry. The climb is too dangerous, so he is out."

We decided that to do a really professional job we would hire a Swiss guide who would know every step of the way. We broke up at two o'clock and went to our rooms to dream about the trip.

Next day, Oser and I were back in the marionette theater. Maestro Gustave Doret had called a special rehearsal for twelve noon.

He made a little speech. "I heard two of the recent shows and gentlemen, you are losing the true intensity of my music. The trouble is that you young men stay in the city all the time around the café table drinking cognac and, of course, overeating, and there are the ladies. Ah yes, I understand these things, but they sap your energies. In the interest of the performances here and for your own welfare, on your free days you should take trips to the mountains. There, surrounded by the magnificent glaciers, breathing the pure air and enjoying the scenery, you will renew your spirits and be able to play my music as it should be played. Now let us rehearse." He raised his hands for attention.

While he prepared to launch his score, I whispered to Oser, "Get going on your own and beat the tar out of the cymbals."

Oser nodded with a diabolical grin and we started playing before Doret could give us the downbeat. He capitulated as conductor and we played his score through to the end without him.

He looked surprised and rather pleased. "Ah, gentlemen, even just hearing me speak about the Swiss Alps has improved your playing one hundred percent. Now may I invite you to some chocolate with whipped cream and torte and chocolate drops. And do visit our mountains."

≫≪

WE LEFT FOR Graubünden the next week and stopped at an inn in Truns. Oser had found a Swiss guide named Zgraggen. He was the youngest of a long line of mountaineers and made a fine impression. He was about six feet two inches tall, straight as a ramrod but flexible, and he seemed strong as a mule. He sized us up and I thought he looked a bit doubtful when he noticed Schlorr's pince-nez and more doubtful when I asked him whether all four of us would be roped together.

He snorted. "Did you think we would rope three together and let the other fellow slide into a crevice? Ugh."

Under his watchful eye, we put in special provisions this time. Besides the soup cubes, cold tea and hard sausages, we brought a kind of hardtack much like dog biscuits and a larger quantity of cognac than we usually carried.

When I asked about the latter Zgraggen said, "We must be prepared to climb for about thirty-six hours with only two to four hours sleep. We must cross glaciers that will thaw out in the morning, beginning at about nine, and if we don't get across we'll never make it except into the bottom of a crevice. We'll need that cognac."

We also took dried apples, apricots, and prunes, and a new brand of chocolate bar filled with nuts that he said was very nourishing. The guide tested our rope, threw it away, and got one of his own, which he had seasoned. He approved of our *Alpenstocks* and marched us off to the trail.

We left at about three in the afternoon, and it took us about six hours of monotonously steady climbing to get to the shack. We made a fire and rested in the bunks from 9:00 P.M. until 1:00 A.M. As always, I was so tired and excited that I couldn't sleep; but I dozed and in my mind climbed that mountain half a dozen times.

After warming up with tea and cognac, we left the hut shortly after one in the morning for the real climb. We hadn't gone very far when we had to descend a steep snowbank. It was a difficult takeoff and Schlorr was the first man. Because of the darkness, he lost his footing and skidded, but Zgraggen was braced, pulled him up short on the rope, and put him on his feet with one hand. He snorted in disgust, and Schlorr looked sheepish but went right on. No other incidents befell us until we reached the foot of an extremely high rock wall.

The kind of climbing we were about to encounter was completely new to the three of us. Zgraggen, who knew the terrain, went first, to pick out footholds that would enable us to climb slowly to the top. The entire wall was covered with a sheet of ice. We had to chip it away to make steps. But merely chipping and plodding upward did not solve the problem. We had to duck falling rocks and stones that came loose either because some of the ice had softened or because Zgraggen had loosened them. He was an incredibly fine guide, and as number two man on the wall, I really felt that he was lifting me up that icy surface not only physically, but through his knowledge of climbing and of the dangers in those trails.

After edging along for some time, we reached a little semi-cave with a ledge where we sat drinking tea and cognac and eating biscuits. In the dark and foggy early morning, it was surprising to me how little nourishment we needed to restore our strength and spirits. In all, we had five glaciers to traverse and so far had only crossed one of them. Zgraggen got up after ten minutes and told us we must concentrate completely on the difficult ascent before us.

After three hours, we were over the wall and beginning to get into the last, long but easy stretch before reaching the peak. Finally, about two hundred and fifty yards below the peak, we again had tough rock climbing to manage, and when we reached the top we hardly knew it because we were in the middle of clouds and saw nothing but the rocks under our feet. There was a little weather house and we signed the register. Very few people had made the climb, so even without any view we felt triumphant. Zgraggen didn't give us much chance to rest and urged us to get going, otherwise we would not cross the glaciers in time. Our descent on the other side of the mountain was easier but long.

We relaxed somewhat and kidded around as we took the descent, but Zgraggen pulled us up short with some first-rate Swiss profanity, saying that if we didn't move our asses we would be crossing the glacier down below at just about the time the sun would melt the snow over the crevices. We would probably all slide into one of them. We pushed ahead for a few hours and then hit the glacier that still had snow covering it. As it softened, walking became more and more difficult. We were knee-deep in snow, but by strenuous efforts we managed to keep up a pretty good pace. Soon we were over our knees and had to work to move forward. Some crevices opened. By now, frightened, Zgraggen had roped us up tightly and dragged us along, as if he were the lead dog on a dogsled team. We were happy to have him pace us.

When we saw some rocks ahead, we heaved sighs of relief and slogged along for another half-hour, finally reaching the rocks exhausted but no longer anxious. We found the trail that led down the side of the Tödi, and after plodding on for what seemed like hours we landed in Truns and headed for the nearest inn. We each ordered two complete meals. We were too tired to have alcohol so we washed our food down with a strange Swiss pop that Zgraggen recommended for mountain climbers. After finishing dinner, we lit our cheroots and had coffee and brandy.

Zgraggen relaxed and said, "Congratulations, gentlemen. You have climbed the Tödi from the west side. It's very rarely done. When I first saw you, I thought you would never even make it to the trail. Many times on the mountain I wondered how I could carry three corpses to Truns. When you were dawdling toward that dangerous glacier, I thought we would all disappear in a crevice, but I must say, gentlemen, that what you lack in skill and experience you make up in luck. I hope next year you will engage me to tackle the Finsteraarhorn, and after we've conquered that, we'll try the Matterhorn."

We paid Zgraggen and thanked him first solemnly and then profusely. After sleeping sixteen hours, we walked stiffly to Disentis to get a train. We reached Zurich in the afternoon and had another gargantuan dinner at one of our favorite restaurants.

At the marionette theater, Maestro Doret looked pleased as we played his score, and after the show he said, "You played with much spirit, gentlemen. I hope you will have time between our next shows to take a nice tour in the mountains. It's good for body and soul and it will improve your playing even more."

We smirked and bowed to him and didn't let on that he was now talking to veteran mountaineers.

IT SLOWLY dawned on me that I had been a reckless, damn fool to go on these tours, and I only realized how ridiculous it was many years later. But at that time I didn't realize that I would never forget the enormous sense of satisfaction I had felt when we reached the peaks on these excursions or when we had escaped some dangerous situation or come upon the breathtaking views of the Swiss Alps. The fascination with climbing seems to be that you can never turn back and that you have much more strength than you think. Father had trained me pretty well to control my muscular rheumatism, heart murmurs, and other minor physical problems, including managing one leg that was a half-inch shorter than the other. By facing icy lakes and mountains, conquering them, and using my legs for walking when I wasn't using my lungs playing the flute at the opera house, I became tougher in every way. It taught me how to survive. I am sure the experience helped me to get through many difficult times later in life. Neither the peaks nor the valleys of academic life frightened me. A critic even wrote about me: "[He] travels his chilly path, alone."

I now swim only in a pool, and walk three miles a day. But I learned things in the mountains that have influenced my life and are alive in my memory.

Chapter 10

Chicago in the Twenties
1920-1925

IN 1920, I WAS OFFERED A JOB as third conductor of the Lucerne Opera, a post that Mengelberg had held many years before, an opportunity for beginning an apprenticeship in the European opera houses. I was also offered a job as harmony teacher at the Zurich Conservatory. But Dr. Andreae said that in most European countries native musicians would be preferred for any desirable post. I had promised Mrs. McCormick I would return to Chicago. Andreae and Jarnach thought that in Chicago I would be offered the conductorship of the Chicago Symphony or a job conducting at the Opera. The farewell at the railroad station was rousing. Thirty-five colleagues and fellow students arrived with a small band and played marches and serenades as the train pulled out. Otto Strauss and Karl Zimmerli accompanied me to Basel.

I stayed in Paris for two weeks. I heard *La Légende de Saint Christophe* by Vincent d'Indy at the Opéra and found the performance bad and the work dull, but at the Opéra-Comique I heard *La Bohème* and *Louise,* and the singers were lively and the orchestra alert. I was housed in a cheap hotel room next to a prostitute who was quite busy. She liked my looks and offered me a free ride as a bon voyage present but I didn't like *her* looks: I was afraid I might catch something.

The sea voyage home was relaxing and uneventful, excepting for a series of romantic episodes with a middle-aged Serbian chemist, a deaf lady, and two young twins from Alabama. They all had conflicting plans and they all wanted to come to my cabin to hear me practice flute. The chemist won, and explained body chemistry as it was used in Serbia. Everybody got seasick and romance was put to sleep. When we reached dry land, business took over.

In New York my brother Hans met me at the dock, took me out for dinner, and looked shocked when I told him I had only fifty dollars. He gave me twenty-five dollars to help me back to Wisconsin. I put up in a flea bag back in Chicago and phoned my brother Eugene. No answer. I located his neighbor and found that Eugene had left for a vacation. I took the train to Milwaukee and started calling relatives there. Brother Fred's office reported that he and his wife were on a camping trip. I tried two aunts but they had left for a vacation in Switzerland. Two cousins were in northern Wisconsin.

I headed west to Oconomowoc. There I found Mother and Father nicely established in a duplex apartment house on Lake LaBelle. Our reunion after an absence of more than four years was heartfelt. Mother fixed sweetbreads, macaroni with hollandaise sauce, potato puffs, and strawberry shortcake. Father opened a bottle of champagne and clinked glasses, his favorite way of celebrating. He followed this routine until his death at age ninety-three.

THE NEXT DAY, he began hinting about my compositions. I played my First Sonata for Violin and Piano. He looked astonished and was rather short of breath. Then he boomed, "That's the greatest slow movement since Beethoven." There wasn't much I could do but agree silently. He then elaborated on the fine points of my work and what I had in store as a composer. Obviously I was going to be one of the greats, perhaps even top Mozart, Haydn, and the three Bs. After I retired I could hear him wondering to Mother how they had ever been able to produce such a colossal genius without even trying. I realized that he was talking about me and there was nothing to do but fall asleep dreaming of beautiful women and unwritten symphonies.

At 7:30 A.M. I heard a bellow from the bottom of the stairs. "Get up, my boy! Don't waste your life in idle dreaming. Action is better than sleeping. Remember Goethe's 'All theory is gray, but life's golden tree is green.'"

At breakfast, Father recapitulated the last evening's events. "My boy, I may have been overenthusiastic in my response to your sonata. The excitement of seeing you after so many years, and your mother's obvious pleasure at hearing your piece, carried me away. It isn't enough to write just one piece, no matter how good it is. A man isn't a composer until he has written many works of significance. That takes years and it takes many more years before audiences decide whether you have any talent at all. Just keep on. I suggest that you now go swimming and then to the village. Get me four ten-cent cigars and take my shoes to the shoemaker. They squeeze my corns. Ask your mother if she needs any groceries. Take the dog to the lake and give him a bath. He is beginning to stink."

Father disappeared into the living room, where he continued for the third time in his life to read Goethe's complete works. I think he had come to Volume 25. I did my chores, rowed for an hour, thought it all over, and decided to set two poems by William S. Sharpe for soprano and piano. A week later, Father asked to hear the songs.

The first one I played was subdued. I noticed his face fall and his expression become quite tragic. He said nothing. I caught his eye. He looked angry.

"Is it necessary to creep around on the keyboard like that?"

I was flabbergasted and asked what he meant.

"You crawl around and slide along on the keyboard like a lizard. It is all so dreamy and subdued."

I pointed out that it was a subdued text, but asked him what he suggested. He thumped his chest. "Write something heroic."

"Heroic? Heroic like what?"

"Like Beethoven. Beethoven strides and you crawl."

When he relaxed I said, "Last week you said that my slow movement was like Beethoven."

"Ah, yes. That was last week. I was under a sentimental strain."

I finished the choral works but didn't show them to Father. Years later, they were published; in 1976 a choral group in the great state of Texas discovered one of them and it was sung widely.

≫≪

AFTER TWO MONTHS in Oconomowoc, I left for Chicago. My brother Eugene and his wife, Marge, gave me a room on the back porch with breakfast, laundry, and Sunday dinner—all for four dollars a week. Armed with introductions from Mrs. McCormick and Busoni, I presented myself to the music leaders of Chicago. Frederick Stock, conductor of the Chicago Symphony, had played in my father's orchestra.

He looked at my First String Quartet, admitted that I knew my business, and suggested that I look for jobs in Cincinnati or Cleveland. I asked what was open in Chicago. He offered me without pay the post of third flute in his student training orchestra. I attended one rehearsal, where I played the piccolo part in Strauss's "Blue Danube Waltz" under the baton of a run-of-the-mill assistant conductor. Having played with Nikisch, Strauss, and Busoni, I quit and auditioned for the opera.

Assistant conductor Isaac Van Grove was in charge. He gave me the most difficult piccolo parts from *Aida* to play while he conducted. His technique was of the pump-handle variety. His beat was always behind the tempo. He was overweight and gasped and sputtered with the exertion, hitting me in the eye with some spray during the more exciting passages. He thanked me very deeply and I never heard a word from the opera company.

I presented my credentials to Felix Borowski, director of the Chicago Musical College. Borowski had a Vandyke that twitched excitedly as he paged through my string quartet, I wasn't sure whether in approval or disapproval of my genius. He looked thoughtful, cleaned his glasses with his handerchief, and suggested that I visit Mr. Bradley, director of the Bush Conservatory. I tried to tell Mr. Borowski about my vast experience, but he wouldn't listen. I disliked him immediately and intensely. (I'm ashamed to admit my great satisfaction when I read a few years later that one of his jilted graduate students had shot him in the arm.) The Bush Conservatory was not much interested in enlarging their theory and composition department. I asked Mr. Bradley for other leads and he suggested that I see Frederick Stock. I had completed the circle and had no more money.

Dix told me that he had met a violinist, Edmund Zygman, who could perhaps give me practical suggestions abut musical life in Chicago. I went to Zygman's studio. A Polish Jew, he looked like a count who was temporarily unemployed. He examined my violin sonata and quartet and commented that I was obviously the greatest composing genius in Chicago if not the United States, possibly the best in the world since Beethoven. He then settled back in his armchair, chomped on a cigar, and looked dreamy. I believe he was thinking. "Unfortunately," he told me, "one has to take care of the practical sides of life, my dear master, unless you are independently wealthy or your brother wishes to finance your career." I assured him that I expected no such luck. He offered to introduce me to the contractor and conductor of the Stratford Movie Theatre and explained how to join the musicians' union. My cash reserve was down to two dollars, so I immediately arranged for an audition at the union.

I went to Local 10, American Federation of Musicians, James Caesar Petrillo, president. The latter was rising in labor circles. In the smoke-filled hall where the auditions took place a big cigar-smoking fellow emerged from a corner.

"Whad'ye want?" he growled.

"An audition," I said.

He waddled to a bookcase, took out two sheets of music and kicked over a music stand. "Put it together and play this part." (He was too big to bend over.)

I fixed the stand and prepared to play. The music on the stand was Sousa's "Semper Fidelis." The big fellow sat down.

I played three measures and he hollered, "That's enough. Come over here." I filled out a form and gave it to him with ten dollars I had borrowed from my brother. "You're in," he told me, "but you can play only substitute jobs for two months."

I asked him how I could find them.

"Just wait," he said.

I felt that I had now really conquered the higher regions of the art.

In two days the phone rang. "This is Local Ten. Are you free tonight at eight o'clock?"

"Yes."

"Okay," the speaker said and hung up.

An hour later the phone rang again. "This is Jimmy Haynes,

Armin Hand's contractor. He has a job at Grant Park this evening. I understand you are free. We need a second flute and
piccolo. Union scale. Rehearsal at seven."

I arrived at quarter of seven.

The contractor said, "Your uniform is over there," pointing
to a portable rack. It was an ill-fitting American Federation of
Musicians band uniform coat with a cap like a train conductor's.
"Button up," the contractor said.

"I can't. I'll choke. Okay?"

"Okay."

During the rehearsal we didn't play a note but arranged the
music, the routines, and the repeats. The great moment was
when Armin Hand walked in: a tall, slender, blond, godlike figure
who resembled an animated and electrified Gary Cooper. There
were at least eight thousand people in the audience, and they
roared their approval as he prepared to drop his downbeat. He
launched us in a thrilling reading of the *William Tell* Overture. I
had trouble catching his beat and learned only later that never,
under any circumstances, should musicians watch and follow
Armin Hand's beat. Cues in his band were picked up from the
first trumpet player and in his orchestra from the concertmaster.
Fortunately, precisely at the storm scene it began to rain. The audience put on raincoats and put up umbrellas.

As *Tell* came to a rousing finish, there was much applause
and in the following number, Tchaikovsky's *Marche slave* I was
able to lean into the piccolo and play with considerable fervor.

By quarter to nine we had reached the *Poet and Peasant*
Overture—affectionately known to the musicians as Poet and
Peanuts—by Franz von Suppé. The wind blew music from our
stands, it was beginning to pour, the audience was running out of
the park to the elevated, and Armin Hand gave his baton to his
assistant and joined the retreating throng. Union rules said that
when wind blew music from stands or rain ruined strings and
pads, and the audience left followed by the conductor, the concert was officially over. You got paid just the same. We hung up
our drenched uniforms and headed for home, richer by eight
dollars.

A week later there came another phone call.

"I'm the contractor for Roy Bargy. I understand you are an

experienced player of popular music, ragtime, and jazz. Bargy is playing for the Loeb wedding." I told him I could play anything if the notes were on my instrument; if not, I would whistle my way through. He liked my attitude. "Do you have a piccolo? That will pay five dollars over scale." I reassured him. "Are you free tomorrow from nine P.M. until we stop? You'll be paid overtime." The deal was on.

The wedding was a colossal affair at the Near North Side Loeb mansion. It was a lovely evening and the lawn was covered with a tent that Barnum and Bailey would have envied. There were hundreds of tables, dozens of waiters, and tons of the most delectable food. The wine waiters hauled in buckets full of champagne bottles and the cork-popping gave a certain aleatoric accompaniment to Bargy's band.

Roy Bargy was one of the very popular jazz and recording artists of that time, a successful commercial artist who played at fashionable weddings. Straight from the Zurich Symphony and Opera, I was surprised to find that I really loved the songs "Whispering" and "Avalon," and I felt the bump and grind of "He's Got Hot Lips When He Plays Jazz." Bargy was a fine pianist and a good arranger. He gave us jazz breaks so we could improvise. Inspired by the moonlight and champagne I did hot work on the piccolo, and the boys in the band predicted a great future for me when I was a little more routined.

(A few years later Richard, the young son of this immensely wealthy Loeb family, was involved together with Nathan Leopold in the thrill-killing of Bobby Frank and in spite of a sensational defense by Clarence Darrow was given a life term. He was killed by a fellow inmate in Joliet Penitentiary in the sixties.)

≽≼

ZYGMAN NOTIFIED me that there was an opening at the Stratford Theatre and referred me to the contractor, Walter Blaufuss. Remembering Aunt Tillie's advice that the early bird catches the worm, I rang the doorbell of Blaufuss's apartment at half-past eight the next morning. There was an ominous silence.

After several rings a bedraggled gent in a nightgown opened the door. "What the hell do you want?" he mumbled.

"My name is Otto Luening and I am a composer, conductor, and flutist with worlds of experience in all fields. Here is my state diploma from Zurich, Switzerland."

"You damn fool. What the shit would I want with that? Haven't you more sense than to get a man out in the middle of the night and try to arrange an audition? I'll be at the Stratford at midnight. Goodbye, and don't show your face around here again." He slammed the door.

I arrived at the Stratford stage door at five minutes to midnight. In the tuning room I was greeted by a very suave gentleman with brilliantined hair who looked a little like a cross between Rudolph Valentino and Ronald Reagan. An expensive green suit with white pinstripes, tan oxfords, a stiff turnover collar, and a carnation in his lapel completed his outfit.

Zygman was there, and did the honors. "This is Mr. Blaufuss, our contractor."

Blaufuss bowed and said in an oily voice, "I didn't want to be short with you this morning, but I had another engagement and it wasn't the place or time to talk business. What can I do for you?"

I brought him up to date, telling him about Strauss, Nikisch, and Busoni. He looked bored until I said I had played with Roy Bargy.

"Oh, you're one of Bargy's boys. He's going to record an arrangement of mine, 'Your Eyes Have Told Me So.' Do you know my tune?"

I said I hadn't been in town long enough to enjoy any of the special arrangements.

A tall, fine-looking blond man who resembled the humorist Robert Benchley joined us.

"Meet Rudy Mangold, our music director," Blaufuss said.

Mangold grinned. "Does he want to sing, play, or dance, Walter?"

"He plays the flute and piccolo with Bargy. I think we can use him here."

Mangold looked puzzled. "Have you ever played any straight music?"

"Yes," I said, "I have played opera and symphony with Richard Strauss, Arthur Nikisch, and Volkmar Andreae."

Mangold looked at me with an expression that indicated he

thought I was a most accomplished and brazen liar. "Okay. Show up tomorrow. We play one a day from seven to eleven every evening, matinees on Saturday two to four and on Sunday rehearsal at eleven o'clock and you play right straight through to eleven at night, time off for meals of course. We can pay you scale, fifty-six fifty a week. Bring your piccolo."

Zygman was waiting at the door and congratulated me for having landed this fine job in the same orchestra he played in. We celebrated with a shot of Prohibition liquor that seemed to consist of a mixture of witch hazel, furniture polish, and axle grease.

The Stratford Theatre was one of the great movie emporiums like the Balaban and Katz chain, the Tivoli Theatre, the Chicago Theatre, and the Pantheon. All the theaters had orchestras ranging from twenty-five to sixty players, put on elaborate hour-long "stage presentations"—or "leg shows" as they were called in the vernacular—and served as neighborhood social centers. The Stratford was at 63rd and Halsted. This was a very tough part of town. Many gangsters either lived or had shady businesses in the neighborhood, or made forays to fight with rival gangs, so there were many shootings. I recall the names of Al Capone, O'Banion, "Yellow Kid" Weil, Bugs Moran, Johnny Torio, and Big Jim Colosimo. Some of them were great lovers of Italian opera and others liked flowers. They all liked power, shooting, money, and women. They and their families were strongly represented at all Stratford shows.

My first evening on the job started when the librarian handed me a buff-colored uniform coat. As the tuning room filled up, I saw about twenty-five musicians. We were ready to play at exactly five minutes to seven.

Rudy Mangold, the conductor, stepped on the podium precisely at seven o'clock. He was dressed in custom-made tails. His violin hung on the conductor's stand. He was followed by a pink spotlight that gave him an otherworldly appearance—but a healthy one, for he was rather corpulent. Other pink spotlights bathed the orchestra in a fine theatrical haze.

We began the evening's program with Tchaikovsky's *1812 Overture*. To my astonishment, the orchestra was first-rate and I really exerted myself to make the grade artistically. Mangold was a fine conductor. He knew the works from memory and gave every cue. The audience was enthusiastic. Mangold bowed once and tapped for attention, the lights went out, and the screen flickered. The fun began with a newsreel.

Each segment—and this applied to all movies, whether comedies, features, or news—was underlined by some kind of musical segment. There were snippets from masterpieces of the past, from pop music, from symphonic movements by Strauss and Mahler, and interludes in which the percussionist improvised and made a collage of background music to fit the events of each picture.

Besides this vast repertory we used albums of ready-made music for all purposes by such masters of the cinematographic musical art as Gaston Borch, Dr. William Axt, and Erno Rappé. There were also anonymous masterpieces that were listed under such titles as "Hurries, Nos. 1–10." These were used for all kinds of chases on the screen, whether by automobiles, animals, boy chasing girl or vice versa, or cowboys chasing each other. The latter finally became a special category under "Music for Westerns," an anthology of both actions and feelings that emerged in the great open spaces out West. There were albums entitled "Dramatic Scenes," "Love Themes," "Water Music," and finally a special category, "Chase Music," that dealt with fox and rabbit hunting. This comprehensive library was administered by a full-time librarian of background music who also occasionally made collages inspired by and made to fit the moving picture like a glove. The music for one short reel might jump from fifteen seconds of the slow movement of Beethoven's Fifth Symphony to twenty seconds from "Hurry No. 12" to ten seconds from the "Love Death" from *Tristan und Isolde,* to one minute of David Popper's *Gavotte* because it was danced on the screen, followed by the ring from an alarm clock played by the drummer for exactly seven seconds, to the "Méditation" from *Thaïs,* played for twenty-one seconds, and the Finale from the *William Tell* Overture, which lasted eighteen seconds.

My debut was inauspicious because I was not used to the interruptions and I tried to finish the phrase I might be playing.

Mangold caught me in the intermission. "Jeez. Don't you know enough to be ready with the next piece?"

"I thought you would like to have the phrases finished."

"To hell with that. Be ready to hit the next piece and fast. You have to get on your toes if you want to stay on this job."

I told him I composed a bit and asked if I could show him my violin sonata and string quartet.

MANGOLD SOMETIMES conducted with his violin or violin bow. He had an enormous tone and a very secure technique. His beat was very precise and supple. Like many of the conductors of that time he was first a musician and then a showman. He used his left hand sparingly. He was rather imposing—six feet tall, blond, blue-eyed, with a pompadour—and he kept in fine physical condition by swimming and boxing. He expressed his pleasure for a well-played passage with a wide smile of approval. If things weren't going well a slight frown could turn into an angry scowl. We were supposed to play everything smoothly but with brilliance.

Mangold educated the audience by playing longer and longer sequences with the pictures and eventually entire movements from symphonies or chamber music. He featured the orchestra in the overtures. These included *Tannhäuser; Masaniello* and *Fra Diavolo* by Auber; and von Suppé's *Beautiful Galatea, Poet and Peasant, Light Cavalry,* and *Boccaccio.* The *1812 Overture* and *Marche slave* by Tchaikovsky were other staples.

The expanded repertory of background music eventually included sections of Mozart operas, movements of Beethoven symphonies, overtures and sections of Wagner's operas, Brahms chamber music and some symphonic movements, Strauss songs and chamber music, the Adagio from Mahler's Fourth Symphony, and even some Bruckner. Rudy's performances and repertory became so famous that music critics came to the Stratford to review us.

This was the period when arrangers were virtuosi in making crosscueing so that most of these pieces could be played with varying instrumental combinations. *Poet and Peasant,* for instance, could be played in fifty-nine combinations. Selections from operettas by Victor Herbert were very popular. Some of the men who had played with Herbert told us that on tours Herbert retired to the baggage car where, on a trunk, he composed a number of his works, notably *Babes in Toyland.* Herbert was a fine cellist and had conducted the Pittsburgh Symphony. He perfected a kind of *rubato* that became a tradition in light opera performance. One held slightly or slowed up the first few notes of a melody and then played it in a regular but slow tempo or, with a very good orchestra, moved immediately into a fast but regular tempo. We used this hesitation at the opening of the tunes with stunning effect that was sometimes quite electrifying. Mangold conducted and coached Viennese waltzes in a true style with the after-beats played *rubato,* the first one being always a little ahead of time.

LOCAL 10 prescribed our intermissions. During these, a fellow named Eddie played the Wurlitzer organ. Eddie could scarcely read music but he was one of the greatest improvisers I have ever heard. He watched the picture and made up the music as he went along. He rarely repeated himself and could imitate any style of music that was played by the orchestra. During the shift between 11:00 P.M. and midnight, I heard him improvise background music with one hand and the pedals and saw him sleeping on his other hand while he was drunk with gin. Eddie's solos, medleys of pop music on which he improvised while bathed in spotlights, shook me up but fascinated me. I had never heard an organ outside of a cathedral or concert hall, nor quite so much tremolo anywhere.

One night, the cops picked up Eddie and accused him of being at the head of a ring of auto thieves. Police worked him over in one of the precincts. His arm was swollen up like a pillow, and the story reached the papers. He returned to the theater accompanied by a bodyguard. Gangsters met him in the tuning room. He was never convicted, and it was whispered that he had connections with both police and gangsters, and that he was untouchable.

Eddie gave up drinking and became a Christian Scientist for a while. He and I had long spiritual discussions because I was studying yoga, but one night in the pit I stumbled over what felt like a sack of potatoes. It was Eddie. "I'm a lousy Christian Scientist," he said, reeking of gin and crawling toward the organ bench.

A few years later he died an uneventful death. What an improviser!

FOR EVERY show we did an elaborate stage presentation. Comedians, dancers, special events, and special settings changed weekly. My sister Helene did the doll scene from *The Tales of Hoffmann* with scenery and action. Another showstopper was soprano Charlotte van Winkle in scenes from Herbert's operettas, ending with "Kiss Me Again." When she sang "Kiss me . . . kiss me . . . AGAIN," the members of the audience had an irresistible impulse to reach for their neighbors and follow the music with a salute of appreciation.

It is impossible to recount all the masterpieces of stage presentation. When Bob Hope joined us as master of ceremonies at the beginning of his career, we thought he was marvelously suave and elegant. I still do. And there was Frisco, whose idea of Deep Throat was to make a lighted cigar disappear in his mouth to the cheers of the audience; glamorous Gloria Swanson, who did a turn; Jack Norworth, who sang society jazz; Eddie Cantor of the Popeyes, not yet so very well known but greatly appreciated by the boys in the band; and Ed Wynn, who did tricks with a fire hydrant. Sometimes there were animal acts.

Once, the management decided to mount a scene from Dame Ethel Smyth's opera *The Wreckers*. The set was a lighthouse and a ship that was supposed to sink. It got stuck and a stagehand slid out on his stomach to unravel the snag; he hit a rise in the ocean and his rear end came into view. The audience shouted, "Sink it." He gradually retreated, the lights went down, and we continued the show.

I, too, was once a soloist. I played František Drdla's *Serenade in A* with orchestra in my buff uniform coat; bathed in a pink spotlight. This triumph was followed by Anton Emil Titl's *Serenade for Flute and Horn*, a magnificent piece that was played in every kind of arrangement in every movie theater here and abroad and at English seaside resorts. Nobody believed me when I said I had never heard this piece. It was cosmic schmaltz.

An unwritten law forbade that we watch the picture or stage while playing. We all saw a vast repertory of fragments from the current movies in the twenty-minute orchestra "intermissions." I waited half a century to see some of the pictures in their entirety, some only on television. Also, we played throughout the year without any vacation. Anyone who sent a substitute was fired promptly. The theater paid us and they owned us—holidays, Sundays, Christmas, and New Year's.

MOST OF THE younger orchestra members at the Stratford had personal fan clubs whose members were known as orchestra watchers.

The girls would sit through all shows, from two to eleven o'clock or from seven to eleven, watching pictures over and over and their favorite orchestra player in action. They might date after the last show. They were a curious lot, some very charming but a bit dangerous for various reasons. May was a friend of mine and of the gifted pianist Heinz Roemheld. We used to take her out together. One night as we sat on her front porch her father arrived and told us quite politely that this was a tough neighborhood and that he kept a shotgun in his kitchen. He explained that if anyone fooled around with May he wouldn't hesitate to use it. Our passion cooled.

Aggie, a beauty-shop owner, was charming. She lived in Evanston, a fifteen-dollar taxi trip from the theater. One night after the show I went to her store carrying my flute. She couldn't turn the lights on because the store was supposed to be closed. After a few romantic passes, a box of hairnets and other beautifiers fell down, and I got all tangled up. My ardor had diminished and it was about quarter to four, so I left. A detective squad on the prowl found my flute case very suspicious and came at me with flashlights and drawn guns. They were looking for a holdup man.

※※

IN SPITE OF the variety of action in Chicago, there was a melancholy undertone that was hard to define. Everybody was money-mad. Everyone speculated. Everybody was overactive and often not pleased with his work. There wasn't much space for radical young composers and playwrights. Architects, painters, sculptors, and writers were more active. The artists' section was the Near

North Side. At clubs like Cliff Dwellers and a place called The Little Room, Hamlin Garland, Floyd Dell, and even Isadora Duncan held forth, but they were still out of reach for young Turks. Lorado Taft seemed to be interesting, but he belonged to high society. The real wild ones in sculpting were the Pole Stanley Szukalski and Sherwood Anderson's wife, Tennessee. Frank Lloyd Wright and Taliesin were an influence on me and my friends. Ivan Meštrović's exhibit of sculpture at the Chicago Art Institute made a deep impression on me. His sculpture seemed to grow out of the ground and was gravitational in effect. After the museums in Europe, though, the Art Institute seemed pallid.

It was the literary people in Chicago who affected my career. I knew nothing about contemporary American writers, many of whom had a strong effect on the young of various persuasions. Harriet Monroe, whom Joyce had mentioned in Zurich, established *Poetry*, a magazine that introduced us to Rabindranath Tagore, Vachel Lindsay, Ezra Pound, William Butler Yeats, and Amy Lowell. Good writing was published in the newspapers. Ben Hecht wrote a column for the *Daily News* titled "1001 Afternoons in Chicago." These were attractive vignettes or sometimes essays on life in Chicago, the people, the scenes, and the problems, and we all loved them, though some readers considered them the product of an antisocial radical. Carl Sandburg wrote wonderful movie reviews for the same paper. Theodore Dreiser was frequently seen around town. Sherwood Anderson's *Winesburg, Ohio*, Hecht's *Eric Dorn*, and Sinclair Lewis's *Babbitt* were the last word in "sophistication." Sophistication meant that one had to keep out of bourgeois traps like marriage, too much money, an unsatisfactory job, or not enough real adventure. This meant the hero would escape in time with a sex partner who would generally leave in the last chapter, for the wrong reasons. Edna St. Vincent Millay, Edwin Arlington Robinson, and Ring Lardner were other important influences. Occasionally Dr. Ben Reitman, the anarchist, sounded off.

Goethe's dictum "Praise of another is depreciation of oneself" impressed the young: With Maxwell Bodenheim, Hecht founded a left-wing paper, the *Chicago Literary Times*. "The cognoscenti pull the fly paper out of their ears. Sandburg's tom-tom sounds through the new tar-smelling subdivisions. Szukalski thrusts his walking stick into the eye sockets of LaSalle Street. Hecht explodes an epithet under the Old Ladies Home. Beating his bosom, Anderson sinks to his baggy knees gurgling mystically to God. The cubistical Bodenheim ululates on the horizon. Ehu! Ehu! The Pleiocene fogs are lifting." Hecht's comments about books, magazines, and papers cheered us up. Of critics he wrote: "They depress us. They have long ears. They have long noses. They seem to be suffering from the lack of a good drink or a good physic. They are continually talking about Art as if it were their dead grandmother." George Grosz, whose cartoons I remembered from *Simplicissimus,* was doing drawings for the *Literary Times!*

MY OTHER ESCAPES into literature were the discovery of Walt Whitman, William Blake, Tagore, and of Havelock Ellis's *Dance of Life.* What struck me about these writers was their feeling that no matter what you did life was too restricted. These literary experiences were quite different from what I had learned in Europe, and they opened up a new view of America and the world. The effect was strange. Blake and Tagore moved me in a new direction. After reading Blake's poem "Auguries of Innocence" I had a spiritual awakening that led me first to some books about yoga by Yogi Ramacharaka. His real name was Atkinson but nevertheless he was the one who led me to Vedanta philosophy. I became deeply involved in Hindu philosophy of all kinds. I visited the Theosophical Society headquarters in Chicago. There I discovered that the most prominent Vedantist, Vivekenanda, had come to the World Parliament of Religions in 1893 in Chicago to expound his doctrine. He had a profound effect on such groups as New Thought and other spiritual offshoots. Ralph Waldo Emerson, Mary Baker Eddy, and Thoreau were influenced by Hindu thought and philosophy. I found at the Theosophical Society the writings of Ledbetter, Annie Besant, Colonel Osgood, and the journals of the Theosophical Society.

THE CHICAGO SYMPHONY was Theodore Thomas's orchestra in the nineteenth century. It set standards for orchestral playing in the United States that still hold and was thought by many to be the greatest orchestra in the world. Since then it has maintained an enviable reputation and now under the leadership of Sir Georg Solti it is again widely considered the best orchestra in the United States, if not the world. In the early twenties Frederick Stock, a violinist of Thomas's orchestra, took command. The musicians had great pride in their orchestra and considered their membership in it the ultimate position to hold. Stock and the orchestra were very routined. Sometimes movements would be played without conductor. Works from the standard repertory were performed with either no rehearsal or only a run-through. Busoni had told me Stock was one of the best musicians in the United States.

My first impression was mixed. In a symphony by Miaskovsky and Beethoven's Third the orchestra was powerful and massive but sounded more like an organ than an orchestra. I liked a more transparent sound, a more soloistic use of the instruments. I was most impressed by Stock's readings of Brahms's symphonies, Beethoven's Third—particularly the last movement—Strauss's symphonic poems, Tchaikovsky's symphonies, and particularly his exemplary readings of Schumann. The A Minor Piano Concerto with Arthur Schnabel as the soloist was magnificent. I didn't like Stock's Mozart, Schubert, or Haydn much, nor his Debussy or even his Rimsky-Korsakov. He seemed to prefer heavy works; he did a brilliant performance of Stravinsky's *Rite of Spring*, and did works by Honegger, Milhaud, Glazunov, and Casella with style.

He also played more American works than any other conductor in the country. I heard some by Charles Tomlinson Griffes, Charles Martin Loeffler, Henry F. Gilbert, Henry Hadley, Leo Sowerby, and William Grant Still as well as some by the local composers John Alden Carpenter, Adolph Weidig, Edward Collins, Henry Eichheim, Stock, Stillman-Kelley, Edward Burlingame Hill, Arthur Farwell, Karl Goldmark, Frederick Converse, and Ernest Bloch. Griffes, Loeffler, and Hill seemed solid composers influenced by the French school. Hadley, Goldmark, Stillman-Kelley, Weidig, and Stock were conservative. Sowerby was a jaunty "original." Gilbert, Still, and Bloch were also originals, Arthur Farwell and Eichheim "ethnic," Carpenter modern and jazzy. Most of these composers seemed to lack orchestral technique and craftsmanship, but the ideas were for the most part non-European. Neither these composers nor the concert and opera life in Chicago influenced me much. Jazz did.

THERE WAS great musical activity on the South Side near the Stratford Theatre. Not too long before, there had been a real jazz center at the Fountain Inn at 63rd and Halsted, and all kinds of bands appeared in the early twenties. After shows, we went to the Midnight Frolics and to the Friars Inn at Wabash and Van Buren streets.

Much of this took place in what was known as the Black Belt, and a favorite haunt was the Sunset Café (or Inn), known as a "black and tan joint." Other favorite spots were the Plantation, the Dreamland, and the Lincoln Gardens. I remember Louis Armstrong, Eddie Condon, "Fatha" Hines, Benny Goodman and the Blue Friars, and Fats Waller. The young Chicago players came out of the public schools and the high school band music programs. Austin High School was a particularly good one and from it emerged many of the best young players. Gene Krupa was a product of Fenger High and Benny Goodman of the Lewis Institute. In addition, Eddie Condon and Bix Beiderbecke came to Chicago from the Midwest at an early age. I learned enough from listening to these players to improvise in jazz numbers when we played them at the theater. But universities too were moving into the act, and when Paul Whiteman played Gershwin's *Rhapsody in Blue* at Northwestern University, it made a strong impression on everyone. I wrote a piece called *Coal Scuttle Blues*, which attracted little attention then. But I was later asked to play my *Blues* a lot, and for many years, in the East. The great influence of the jazz sessions was in my realization that music was interpreted quite differently by these players than by my friends in Europe. It freed me.

☆☆

I WAS SPIRITUALLY and artistically isolated in Chicago. I took a room near the theater—small, unattractive, with no piano, but with a desk. The restaurants were terrible. I ate a little fruit for breakfast, a little lunch about every second day, and two doughnuts and a cup of coffee for supper. I weighed one hundred and twenty-five pounds. The family I lived with was a run-down Irish clan; the father was heavyset and helpless, the mother heavyset and toothless, the daughter heavyset and sexy. Brothers and sisters-in-law addressed envelopes in the basement, in what was possibly a shady business. We had nothing in common, but I was a big shot because I played at the Stratford.

In June 1921, I had news from Zurich that my *Sextet* had been premiered on April 30 with great success, conducted by Hans Zimmerman, later director of the Zurich Opera. The press praised the progressive tendencies of the sponsors and said that the *Sextet* combination was strange but experimentally interesting and sometimes humorous. The audience response was apparently enthusiastic, and I had a number of letters from performers and composers. I wrote Mrs. McCormick about the performance and told her that I was playing in a silent-movie orchestra. A cable-gram came: "See my daughter at 1000 Lakeshore Drive." There I visited Muriel McCormick, whom I had met in Zurich. She was a very beautiful, very sympathetic, and sensitive young lady, and she asked how she could help my career. I explained I wanted to start a chamber music group for the sole purpose of presenting contemporary chamber music in Chicago. She was interested and said I would hear from her. I wrote to Lake Forest outlining my proposal in detail. A letter explained that she was much inter-ested but could be of no help because she was going South for the winter.

Mrs. McCormick returned to Chicago in October 1921. She invited me to the beautiful Harold McCormick mansion and was not pleased that I hadn't had better luck getting established in Chicago. She asked me to arrange performances of my First Sonata for Violin and Piano and my *Sextet* for a musicale on December 9 at her home. She was pleased that I had done some composing and offered me $400 monthly to quit my job and de-vote my time to composing music and arranging concerts at her house. The news caused a sensation at the Stratford.

Mangold had eventually read my compositions. I heard him telling some of the orchestra members that he thought I was a faker. No one as young as I could write works as mature as my vi-olin sonata and my string quartet. Older members who had played with my father explained that I came from a musical family and that I might well be a good composer. He accepted this and then told me he thought I was the strongest talent of any American composer he had performed or met.

For Mrs. McCormick's musicale I engaged Mangold to play the violin sonata with me. Members of the Chicago Symphony prepared my *Sextet*. We had six rehearsals for a fee of fifty dollars. We played the Sonata at the Melodist Club, which was run by Mrs. Archibald Freer, a student of Godard, Massenet, and Bemberg. The performance was a great success, the ladies enthusiastic, and I was given a $1,000 fellowship for the MacDowell Colony. I suggested instead that I use the money to open a music studio so that I could support myself away from the orchestra pit. They agreed to this and I founded the Chicago Musical Arts Studio, located at 829 Kimball Hall, in May 1922. Patronesses were Mrs. McCormick and a list of Chicago socialites. The staff included Madame Stavenhagen, piano; Mangold, violin; Theodore Stearns, opera and operetta; Margarite LaMar, voice and diction; myself, theory, composition, and music appreciation; and orchestral instruments by members of the Chicago Symphony Orchestra.

THE MACDOWELL scholarship, plus Mrs. McCormick's stipend, gave me freedom and time. I felt the desire to compose, and subsequently wrote a lot of music.

A *Trio for Violin, Cello and Piano* included well-defined bitonality based on the harmonic series. A First Sonata for Cello Solo was first performed ten years later and since then in Munich, New York, and elsewhere. The last movement is very difficult technically. My *Symphonic Poem*, retitled First Symphonic Fantasia, was premiered in Rochester by Howard Hanson five years later, played eight times in New York by Toscanini's associate Franko Autori in 1938, then recorded by the Vienna Symphony with Charles Adler in 1956. To my surprise, this early orchestral piece of mine was still being broadcast over a number of radio stations in 1979. A *Concertino for Flute and Chamber Orchestra*, a very nice piece, was too fancy in the orchestration to be popular. For strings, celesta, and harp there are only a few plunks, so no one has played it—except myself, with great success, in

Philadelphia. (I am planning to condense harp and celesta for piano in a new edition.) Then there was my Second String Quartet, highly praised by Philipp Jarnach. It was examined with interest by most of the leading quartets for more than forty years and rejected as being unplayable. In 1965 it was premiered by the Group for Contemporary Music at Columbia University. It presented no great problems and the performers and audience at that time responded very well to the aesthetic content. It was then performed several times in Munich, recorded by Composers Recordings, Inc., and was well received by the press here and abroad. The recording has been broadcast widely in the United States.

The general indifference in the twenties to American works led me to say in an interview in *Musical America* in late July 1921 that "limited ensembles sponsored by different states should give creative musicians opportunities of hearing their works. . . . They would provide an incentive for a composer to write if he could be reasonably assured that his work would be produced under satisfactory conditions." It took some time for this idea to be realized. About fifty years.

CHICAGO HAD little experimental or even advanced music, but a very distinguished school of contrapuntal composers had developed around Bernard Ziehn. His theoretical findings and system of symmetrical inversion and canonical techniques revolutionized Busoni's ideas about composing. John Alden Carpenter and the virtuoso organist, austere contrapuntist, and foremost Bach authority of his time, Wilhelm Middelschulte, had reached a wider public. Busoni had suggested that I visit Middelschulte, and when I did I showed him my works. He studied them for an hour. "A recommendation from Busoni means you are a fine artist. Your scores show that you have a fine technique, so what can I do for you?" I explained that I knew of his profound contrapuntal knowledge, his compositions for organ, and his Bach editions, and I wanted to study Ziehn's approach to composing. We arranged a weekly eight-dollar lesson.

Middelschulte was an imposing man. He was about six feet two inches tall with a mane of white hair, a flowing mustache, pink cheeks, flashing blue eyes, and a fluent way of expressing himself that ranged from raucous jokes to bitter comments about people who had wronged him and snide remarks about the quality of music in Chicago. He had been organist for the Chicago Symphony, and was a bit pro-German during the war; because he wouldn't stop speaking German, he was fired. He gave concerts and taught privately. In our lessons he plowed through stacks of literature I had never heard of and J. S. Bach works I didn't know. He himself worked out my weekly assignments in fifteen different ways to show me *the* way. It annoyed me that he was a better student than I was. I thought I had matched him when I arrived at 126 solutions to a harmonic progression that interested him. He was pleased, but he said, "I'm sure if we searched a little further we would find other possibilities."

So far, my performances consisted of only two, my violin sonata at the Melodist Club and my *Sextet* at the Madrigal Society in Milwaukee. The latter created little attention and I was referred to as a boy composer, so I was greatly encouraged when Middelschulte invited me to write a piece for an organ series he was giving at Notre Dame University where John J. Becker, a very active radical composer, was director of music. Middelschulte performed my *Organ Introitus* in July 1921. This introduction to a larger audience in America resulted in repeat performances and a request from Middelschulte to compose a *Chorale Fantasy for Organ* for his 1922 program. He played my *Chorale Fantasy* again at the American Guild of Organists at St. James Church in 1923 in Chicago. His registration was masterly and his performance spectacular. I told him he played the piece so magnificently that I really had no idea how good it was until I heard him. All of the attending organists were enthusiastic but the piece lay dormant for many years. Almost fifty years later, the brilliant California organist Fred Tulan found it and began playing it in the big cathedrals in San Francisco and Washington, D.C., in Notre Dame in Paris, and in Westminster Abbey in London. I wrote a *Fugue* for Tulan recently, and both works were published in 1972. The World Library brought out another version called *Variations on "Fugue and Chorale Fantasy" for Organ with Electronic Doubles,* in which I use the original material but then transform it into the contemporary world by making electronic variations. These works were recorded and quite well received by the press.

RAINBOW RECORD Company made discs for Homer Rodeheaver, the trombone-playing evangelist who was Billy Sunday's only rival. These were gospel hymns for export and missionary work in Japan. Homer the evangelist was ingratiating, smooth-talking, and sanctimonious. He looked like a cross between a baseball player, an off-duty cop, and a country sheriff. He had a rather pleasant voice. His playing was groovy even when out of tune.

I arranged a batch of hymns for eight instruments for him. I was contracted for eight dollars a hymn; there was no conductor, so I wrote directly into the parts. All my arrangements were beautiful; they were promptly recorded and I was urged to do more.

Rodeheaver's steely-eyed brother was business manager, and when I tried to collect for my first dozen hymns he remarked, "Oh, we've put you down for seventy-five dollars' worth of recordings when they come out."

"What the hell am I going to do with recordings of hymns with Homer and his trombone?"

Brother looked stern. "Watch your language. We don't use profanity here."

My check didn't arrive. Homer and his trombone disappeared into the clouds with the angels. I think his steely-eyed brother started drilling a dry oil well. I never collected, but I won the reputation of being an experienced orchestrator.

Harry F. Alford was the most prominent arranger in Chicago, had too much to do and needed help. Somebody dragged me up to see him. Alford may have been the first assembly-line arranger in the business, certainly the first in Chicago. Our introduction took a minute and a half, then he asked me about my specialty. I told him I was an all-around orchestrator. I noticed the room was filled with fellows feverishly scratching notes.

Alford explained, "We don't work general, we work special here. Joe here does only after-beats for the second violins and violas. Hank works the bass and cello. Bill does brass breaks and Hartzel writes in the melodies. Schmidt looks over the chords on the piano and I give it a final inspection to see if everything is in shape. When do you want to start? It's eight hours a day and we pay three dollars an hour, six days a week, twenty minutes off for lunch."

I told him I had a great many previous commitments, but I would let him know when I would be free. I didn't go back. I do think his philosophy has prevailed right into the computer age. Today, in the field of pop music, the manager—who may not even be a musician—often puts together the fragments produced by specialists because "he knows what the audience likes."

REHEARSALS FOR the musicale at Mrs. McCormick's mansion went well. Mangold did a first-rate job with my violin sonata and the *Sextet* sounded fine. The rest of the program included songs by Mrs. Freer and by John Alden Carpenter with the latter at the piano. The concert took place after a dinner party to which I was not invited, just like Haydn at Esterhazy's estate, only I ate supper at a fast-food counter and not in the McCormick kitchen.

About twenty-five prosperous-looking ladies with gentlemen in full dress listened. I recognized some of the music leaders who had turned me down when I was looking for a job. They looked uncomfortable and nobody said anything.

After Mangold and I played my sonata, we heard an astonished buzzing, no applause, just lively and continuous verbal comments for five minutes. My *Sextet* was then beautifully played, but there was just a shocked silence and then relatively strong applause and positive remarks by the audience. John Alden Carpenter shook my hand solemnly and commented that the orchestration was most beautiful. Carpenter was not only a fine composer and a good theorist but was socially prominent, a successful vice-president of an awning company and a millionaire. Nobody else spoke to me; I must have looked out of place in tails and a white tie—maybe I scratched a little. But Mrs. McCormick kept me until the guests had left. Then, beaming, she held my hand and said it was all a great success and that we would have another evening very soon.

She wrote me within a week, setting February 14 for the next concert, featuring my First String Quartet. I was to have ten rehearsals.

I BECAME quite involved with a society with the improbable name The Opera in Our Language Foundation. Its aim was to establish opera in English in the United States, and American opera in particular. Mrs. Freer was president. She was wealthy and had social standing in Chicago. She had composed one hundred and fifty songs that were widely sung. She had won the Shakespeare prize of $1,500, wrote her own libretti, and had her operas performed in Chicago, Boston, Brooklyn, and California.

Theodore Stearns, the musical director, was a handsome man-about-town in his forties who knew how to handle spats, gloves, and a cane. He bragged of having a touch of Indian blood and looked the part. He was musically very experienced and very literate and had written the texts to two of his operas.

The foundation was assembling a repertory of American operas to be performed in English at the Studebaker Theatre. I was surprised to find that there *were* any American operas. I was made associate music director.

The libretti were being rewritten, edited, and in some cases written by Charles Henry Meltzer, who seemed scholarly because he wore a pince-nez. He showed me the libretto and some score pages of Carl Ruggles's opera in English, *The Sunken Bell*, based on Gerhart Hauptmann's play. Ruggles had been in Winona, Minnesota, from 1907 to 1917. Not until he moved to New York did he win his reputation as a composer. The foundation was much interested in producing his opera.

Most of the works I studied had poor libretti, but a number were new and sometimes interesting. Our favorite was *Shanewis*, by Charles Wakefield Cadman, a prolific and successful song composer who came from a musical family. He was mostly self-taught but had studied for a short while with Emil Paur, conductor of the Pittsburgh Symphony Orchestra. A number of his comic operas had been performed in the early part of the century. He collected American Indian songs, was himself part Indian, used Indian motives, had composed more than two hundred songs and many choruses, and had published more than three hundred and fifty works. His librettist was Nellie Richmond Eberhart, who had also studied Indian cultures on the reservations in Nebraska. *Shanewis* had been performed five times by the Metropolitan Opera in 1918 and toured many times after that. Cadman's music was melodious and vocal, and the Indian motives gave a certain distinctive quality to the work.

Most of the works that we studied had orchestral scores that could only be rented. Duplication processes were not yet available. We had to imagine the orchestration until the production was actually under way, for we could only afford to rent the score for performances. But we found and recommended works that later made their way. The best talents were Hamilton Forrest, a Chicago composer who used innovative jazz in his opera *Camille*, in which Mary Garden sang the lead. Another jazz opera, *Deep River*, by W. Frank Harling, was given thirty performances in New York. His other operas were produced in Boston, Chicago, elsewhere in the United States, and in Paris. Besides jazz, he used Creole folk tunes and New Orleans street cries. We also examined Henry F. Gilbert's *Fantasy in Delft*, a delicate, poetic, and humorous work, but we lacked the resources for production. Ralph Lyford's *Castle Agrazant* and Parker's *Mona* were the post-Wagnerian heavyweights.

Stearns's opera *Snowbird* was accepted by the Chicago Opera. He resigned from the foundation and recommended me as music director. I was only twenty-one and felt it. The responsibility of helping to build a company to do opera in English seemed fine and I asked Stearns if I could handle the job. "There's nothing to worry about," he reassured me. "Just teach everybody—the singers, the patrons, and later the orchestra— everything you know about music and you can't go wrong."

I continued building the Chicago Musical Arts Studio at this time, but the more active I became the more I became absorbed with Vedanta philosophy. The sudden new activities were energy-consuming and I needed to replenish myself.

≫≪

I READ EVERYTHING I could find at the Theosophical Society. I realized that any serious student of yoga would have to accept the disciplines, so I became a vegetarian, took no stimulants or alcohol, had no sex, did breathing exercises, and in general tried to get control of my somewhat overactive imagination. The results were strange but rewarding. I began leading a double life; one part of it included complete concentration on composing, which took on new meaning for me. My *Trio for Violin, Cello and Piano* had considerable activity and agitation in two movements. In the third movement the material was resolved and transfigured. It was somewhat the same style that I used in my First Symphonic Fantasia.

The strongest effect of the theosophical and Indian studies was apparent in *The Soundless Song*, for string quartet, flute, clarinet, piano, and soprano, and for which I wrote my own text:

I

Sometimes alone, at eve
I sit with you my friend
And watch you play.
I see colours, undreamed of,
Formless form I see
And the scheme that cannot be found.

II

In the silent voices
Of Angels,
I hear the Soundless Song
Of things to be;
Of beauties, here, but unrevealed;
And of the sunlight,
Which, thru its warmth,
Is singing, the Soundless Song.

III

In the distant voices
Of children,
I hear the Soundless Song
Of all that is;
Of the timeless years, long dead;
And of the future,
Which, even now,
Is singing, the Soundless Song.

This work has yet to be performed.

I bought the Upanishads, translated by F. Max Mueller, *The*

Secret Doctrine and *The Voice of the Silence* by Madame Bla-
vatsky, and the Bhagavad Gita. I read a number of shorter theosophical books about various aspects of occultism. I began to have
a new reaction to language. Because the content in these works
was so poetic, suggestive, and symbolic, I was soon reading the
books as I would read an orchestra score, looking less for literal
meanings than letting the real content of the texts filter through
my subconscious. This was so particularly with the Upanishads
and *The Secret Doctrine*. My studies and the disciplines had a
strange effect on me. I felt more clearheaded and sometimes in a
state that I can only describe as weightless.

I learned to use my imagination in ways I had never tried
before. One of the books suggested that in viewing an object one
should see it from many points of view in the imagination—the
back, the side, the inside, and all possible relationships. I practiced this and I got to be pretty well sensitized. It is something
that I have developed since then. Now I find it quite easy to sit in
a room and be quite conscious of not only the objects in the room
and their functions but of the hundreds or even thousands of people who invented them or developed them and made them available to me. I began sizing up people in the same way. One book
went into the matter of color impressions or auras from people
and I noticed that with different people I would get different
color impressions, sometimes dark green, red, light blue, or other
shades, and this had something to do with the temperament of
the person. This developed into an empathy for other people that
made it easier to communicate with them.

At that time, much was written about thought transference
and extrasensory perception.

I experimented first by sitting in a room or on the elevated
train and trying by concentration to get someone to scratch his
head or put a hand to his face. It often worked, and of course I
had seen this used by great conductors like Nikisch and Strauss. I
had felt such influence, very subtle, very indirect, but still very
strong, from people like Busoni and Jarnach. When I meditated I
was able to go from the immediate in space and time and expand
this until I began to identify with other parts of the world and
even other periods in history, and then with outer space and the
universe in its immensity and its infinity—which I did not think

of as being only infinitely large, but also infinitely small. I had learned this from William Blake. Contemplation of the universe made the senses play a different role. I had read somewhere that on other planes of existence and other planets our senses had no function and there were other means of communication. All of this brought me to the point in my meditation where I could pretty well blot out everything that had a sensory or terrestrial connection and for a moment feel an identity with the cosmos, or God, or my subconscious, or whatever it might be called.

As CHICAGO GREW wilder and wilder in every way, I withdrew more and more into these subjective planes, except in my music. I became so involved that several Freemasons I knew began telling me about some of their beliefs and suggesting that I was on the right road. My mind turned to India, seduced by the poems of Tagore and somewhat romantic notions about that country. At one point, I was about to leave the United States and go to Madras, the headquarters of the Theosophical Society, to refine my knowledge of the occult and to continue my spiritual growth.

In one of the books I was reading I found that there were two types of people in India on the path to enlightenment: the bhodis and the bhodisattvas. The first achieved complete spiritual release and renounced the world and reached nirvana; the second were also intent on enlightenment but had not achieved it and decided out of compassion and empathy to continue to work to alleviate suffering and to develop in every way in this world until everyone was saved. This put me on a new plane of thought. I saw that karma was destiny that had to be lived through, and that the path for spiritual insight and development was exactly the same in Chicago in 1922 as in New Dehli or Tibet or even Jerusalem at the time of Christ. I began to understand what was meant when the Upanishads spoke about "the Creator, the Preserver, and the Destroyer." In my simple-minded way I realized that beings nourish themselves, that they discard what they no longer need, and that the waste itself becomes a compost heap or a fertilizer that is needed for new growth, the transformation continues, and the cycle repeats itself. I remembered Busoni's axiom that the old and the new are the same. Gradually I decided that my job was to accept my background, the mixed and wonderful but sometimes painful experiences in Europe and America, and to work to gain further insights, doing my duty and living my life where it was, instead of trying to escape from it.

I TACKLED everything with renewed energy, including the ten long rehearsals for the February 14 quartet performance at Mrs. McCormick's. Three players were from the symphony, with Mangold as first violinist. They gave my First String Quartet a fine reading. The program opened with a concerto for violin, cello, and piano by Clarence Loomis, followed by a group of his songs.

My quartet lasted forty-five minutes. I watched the audience and saw that in the second movement they were beginning to wilt. During the last movement—a quadruple fugue at times atonal, at other times polytonal, and always completely uncompromising—jowls quivered and there were visible signs of displeasure. When the piece was over there was no applause at all. Nasty looks in the direction of the quartet made them slink out of the room, leaving me to hold the fort all alone. Frederick Stock looked disgusted and angry and left without saying goodnight. Nobody spoke to me except Mrs. McCormick, who was very charming and gracious. Two days later, I had a letter from her thanking me for the quartet and explaining that new works are not readily accepted, but that she thought my music was fine and would develop in the direction of the last movement, which had a linear drive to it. Within a week everybody in town knew about this terrible young American protégé of Mrs. McCormick who wrote such ghastly music and was now engaged in organizing an opera company.

≫≪

WHILE LAUNCHING the Chicago Musical Arts Studio, I kept up my professional performing connections. A pupil of mine, Frank Votava, played in a vaudeville theater. He told me that the management was looking for a piano leader and he wondered if I was interested. I was, and went to the theater to do the Saturday matinee and evening show. The pit was small and grubby. The piano was a battered upright with no pedals, for vaudevillians like the sound dry and rhythmic. The felts were worn down. I had to pound to be heard. My folder consisted of ten cue sheets for the various acts. There were lead sheets—smeared, illegible, and cut. From these I made up the accompaniments.

The first act was a tightrope job with a waltz. It went pretty well, except I couldn't read the sheet and watch the act at the same time, so Votava put in the punctuation with percussion and ended each section with a cymbal crash. The second number was a trained-dog act—difficult to follow because I was supposed to play fast when the dogs ran and play a tremolo hold when they sat up. I couldn't see them so Votava would give me frantic signals, along with a *sotto voce* dog bark. Next came a juggling act. This artist liked a nice, smooth, slow dance like *Valse triste* by Sibelius. I was supposed to stop whenever the audience applauded and he bowed, but my eyes and ears were fully occupied trying to improvise those accompaniments in front of a big and responsive audience. Votava rolled the drums for the bows. A tap dancer liked "He's Got Hot Lips." I knew this from the Stratford and played it magnificently. When he finished he pointed to me in appreciation. Three girls sang a medley of pop songs. Not having the harmonies in front of me and never having heard them, I found it difficult to improvise a suitable accompaniment. I escaped by keeping out of their range and making a free setting in the upper ranges of the piano with percussive sounds in the bass. This may have been the beginning of aleatoric music and I got away with it. I kept up this farce for two hours and came out shaking.

The manager wanted me to stay on at $150 a week, but I declined with thanks. It was without doubt the most difficult musical job I have ever undertaken. I learned to admire these weird geniuses, vaudeville piano leaders and organ improvisers like Eddie.

THE CHICAGO Musical Arts Studio patron list of nine ladies from the Social Register was headed by Mrs. McCormick. Our circular stated: "Those whose ambition in life is to be telling and practical as well as absolutely artistic will find in the Chicago Musical Arts Studio and its internationally-known faculty of teachers an undivided aim and contentment for the pupil—not disappointment later on in life—the goal." My main faculty supporter, Madame Stavenhagen, had been a Busoni pupil and was the widow of Bernard Stavenhagen, one of Franz Liszt's favorite students. She was a brilliant concert pianist and was being psychoanalyzed by Mrs. McCormick, who had by now become a lay analyst.

The studio opened on June 1, 1922. I arrived at nine every morning to welcome an expected rush of students. A couple of boys from the Stratford showed up for theory lessons, ten lessons for thirty dollars. I covered the whole field verbally. But I had not time to include ear training. The lessons were fine for people with good ears; the others should have asked for their money back. New students were scarce.

The studio was supposed to be a cooperative. I had signed the lease and had ordered a piano on the installment plan, but of the faculty members, only Mangold paid his share. But my class grew, and soon I was just about breaking even. I decided to put the studio on the map by giving a concert of unknown old and new music in Kimball Hall—just what Chicago was waiting for.

I engaged Mangold, the great cellist Bruno Steindel, Middelschulte, and Ella Spravka, a fine accompanist. I played flute. The program was a Handel sonata for violin and piano; *Sonatina for Flute and Piano* by Philipp Jarnach; my own *Trio for Violin, Cello and Piano* with the motto "and from the depths of despair we shall ascend until we see the light"; *Chromatic Fantasy and Fugue* by Middelschulte (a contrapuntal masterpiece); and the Sonata from Bach's *Musical Offering* in a new and completely authentic realization done by Middelschulte. Everyone was paid fifty dollars.

The date of the concert was October 26, 1922. It was a stupendous success but few people attended. There were fifty paid admissions, and the press coverage was comprehensive. There were a few snide remarks about a lack of melody in my trio, and the leading critic wrote that he was engaged as music critic and not unmusical critic and "as the *Trio* is not music, I will retire." But another review described me as a musical thinker, though hard to grasp at first hearing. Another said my trio was modern in intention and strictly formal in fact and praised my developmental skill. Jarnach's sonatina was very well received and our excellent performance and my "mellow tone" were highly

praised. Middelschulte's magnificent Bach realization went unnoticed by the press. Deficit: $400.

❦

IN OCTOBER 1922 the Opera in Our Language Foundation organized the Chicago Chamber Opera Company under the patronage of the same ladies who backed the Chicago Musical Arts Studio. We announced two subscription series of six performances at the Playhouse of five American operas, which would be selected from a list of fifty-seven. We planned for simple but adequate scenery and costumes and an orchestra of eighteen. It was my job to reorchestrate the scores for this combination. Subscriptions were slow coming in, and we were soon in financial difficulties. To balance the operating budget, Mrs. Freer suggested that we mount the operas with minimum scenery and costumes—"à la Shakespeare and the Elizabethan theater," as she put it. She suggested cutting the orchestra to seven players: piano, harmonium, string quartet, and harp. Gilbert Wilson and I believed that to introduce American operas under these conditions would do much more harm than good. To do the operas with eighteen musicians, we needed only an additional $5,000, a modest request for six new operas. I made a decision then and there that I have followed ever since: to agree with my patrons against my best artistic judgment would badly damage my relations with the professional musical community, an impossible condition. Mrs. Freer's suggestions were amateurish and Wilson and I stood for minimal professional conditions. After many discussions we presented Mrs. Freer with the "suggestion" that either the modest underwriting we needed be granted or we would find new patrons.

The *Chicago Examiner* had a front-page story, "Chamber Opera Torn by Quarrel; Artists Insist Seven Musicians Are Inadequate; Mrs. Freer Stands Firm."

Peace or war is expected to be the outcome of a conference tomorrow between Mrs. Archibald Freer and the members of the Chamber Opera Company of which she is chief patroness.

Mrs. Freer plans to present operas by American composers at the Playhouse. The present difficulty stems from the conviction of

the artists that seven instruments may be enough for a jazz band but the number is entirely inadequate for opera.

Mrs. Freer thinks otherwise and by way of emphasizing her conviction she may resign.

"It all depends on this conference tomorrow," says Mrs. Freer. "I don't wish to give out any statements which may have to be corrected. You know how artists are—always squabbling. Well, there are two people who have been especially disagreeable. If they could be persuaded to go on their way peaceably, why well and good." Mrs. Freer did not say who these "especially disagreeable" persons were.

They were, of course, Wilson and myself. The conference was unproductive, and the two of us organized the American Grand Opera Company and rented the Studebaker Theatre, which was across the hall from the Playhouse. We raised enough money to announce Cadman's *Shanewis* for a Chicago premiere on November 9, 1922.

The cast worked without fee. The chorus was recruited from the American College of Physical Education. I engaged the Stratford Theatre Orchestra. Wilson drummed up an Indian ballet from the Hagedorn Conservatory and there were incidental dance numbers, "Fantasy of Ancient Java," "A Dream," "Ave Maria," and "Oriental." An Indian ballet, "At Dawning," served as an introduction to the opera. People gave us free rehearsal space in their homes or in special studios and of course we used my own studio. Wilson rented scenery and costumes. He was a member of the American Legion, and he talked the national commander and the commander of the Theodore Roosevelt Post into sponsoring the event because it was announced as the first all-American opera performance in the history of the country, meaning that composer, librettist, director and cast, orchestra, and stagehands were all Americans. This was news in the opera world at that time and a daring move toward Home Rule in the world of opera.

I had one three-hour dress rehearsal with the orchestra, and that was it. There was no orchestra score, so I conducted from the piano/vocal score. The theater had not cleared the pit for the rehearsal, so the orchestra put their music up on seats in the auditorium. The tenor lost his cool and began yelling and beating time. I established my authority in the wrong way by saying that if I

heard one more peep out of him the orchestra and I would walk out of the theater and he would never see us again. There were no more problems.

The opening was quite well attended. Since the American Legion had put up some money, Wilson arranged to have a flag-raising ceremony. We also had a benefit performance for them a week later. I had invested seventy-five dollars in striped pants and a cutaway. When I made my entrance there was a gasp of astonishment from the audience because of my tender years and sleek appearance. There were cheers led by my sister-in-law Marge and some of her friends. The ballets and opera proceeded without casualties, and at the end the audience was very enthusiastic. The reviews of the performance were excellent. The *Chicago Evening American* wrote that we were a "valiant band of pioneers [who] succeeded in laying the foundation stone of what may be a lasting edifice of art—American opera by American artists." We gave a second performance that was also well received. The press suggested that we keep going for a long run, but we went broke and disbanded.

After our second performance Mrs. McCormick wrote that she was sure I would understand that although she had the highest regard for my talents, she could no longer be a patroness for my ventures. She was an old friend of Mrs. Freer's, and because of their social connections it would be embarrassing were she to take my part in this dispute. She wished me the best of luck and knew I would succeed. I was distressed because I was very fond of Mrs. McCormick.

A few days later, Madame Stavenhagen called, looking quite disturbed by this turn of events. I explained that, as a professional musician herself, she must realize I had no other course if I was to preserve my standing as a professional and an artist.

"I know, I know, but it's really most unfortunate," she said.

"Why?" I asked.

"Mrs. McCormick was very fond of you, and she thought you were a man of outstanding gifts. She told me that if the originally planned series went reasonably well she would build a theater for American opera for a quarter of a million dollars and you would be the director."

Chapter 11

Chicago Coda:
Ethnological Conducting
1924 - 1925

THE OPERA BILLS WERE ARRIVING and the total sum was disastrous. Mangold resigned from the studio because he didn't need it. Other people were renting for short periods only. I was liable for the concert expenses, the piano payments, and, as contractor for Local 10, for the cost of the orchestra. The opera company was broke.

My debts were now $1,500. I called Mangold to say I needed a job right away. "You can have your old job back in two weeks— eighty-six fifty a week for two shows," he suggested.

When I played my first show, the boys were all very friendly because the orchestra had been mentioned in the opera reviews. About half the orchestra signed up with me to take harmony lessons.

Among the orchestra watchers I noticed a girl from the opera named Nicky. She attended matinee and evening performances, so it seemed only right to ask her out for a meal. She wanted to see my studio and arrived at noon. We lost no time getting acquainted. I asked Nicky how old she was. She looked about fifteen and in Chicago in the twenties that was "jail bait." She insisted that she was twenty, lived with the sophisticated Ben Hecht and his wife, and had dated actors and other sports. She then began talking fast. "Let's quit fooling around. You need some physical culture." I learned the exercises rapidly. "Now down on the floor." She showed me a few new holds.

We wound up with no holds barred. Nicky thought this

should be the prelude to a profound liaison or even marriage, everything so far having been so pleasant.

Until then I had been protected by yoga. Now I felt that I needed all the spiritual purification I could get to help me settle my bills. I told Nicky I would think it all over and meet her after the evening performance. I told her that I was trying to get on my feet as a composer and conductor and was having a hard time. I thought it would be disastrous for us to get tied up.

She told me she felt the same about physical culture. She cried a little. "Well, we wouldn't want to hold each other back. I'd like to work together with you but if that isn't in the cards, I agree that we had better call it off before we get in too deep."

So we did call it off. A very understanding girl, Nicky. I have never forgotten her—and still do one of her deep-breathing exercises.

MANGOLD WAS a friendly fellow, and I had found out why through gossip in the tuning room. He had had a first-rate musical training, was a first-class concert violinist, an accomplished pianist, and a singer good enough to audition as a soloist at the Chicago Opera. I had observed that he was quite a stylish conductor. In the Chicago Symphony he rose under Frederick Stock from the second violin section to be assistant concertmaster, but when the first chair became vacant Stock hired someone from the East, so Mangold resigned and became concertmaster of the Chicago Opera for eight seasons. But in the twenties in Chicago everybody wanted money. If they were making it they wanted more, so Rudy worked as concertmaster in a downtown movie palace for $150 a week, which was a fortune in those days, but then he was discovered by the Stratford Theatre and offered $1,000 a month. He decided to make money until he had saved enough to retire and then to play chamber music.

Mangold lived frugally and invested his savings in one-hundred-percent-safe bond houses until the early thirties, when he was fired because of the Depression. The bond houses failed; he lost his savings and became concertmaster on a radio station. He was then pushed back to assistant concertmaster and, some years later, to the last stand of the second violins. He retired on social security. A mutual friend told me that Rudy had become a do-it-yourself man in the suburbs. In 1963, when a heavy Midwest blizzard damaged the roof of his house, he tried to fix it, although he was seventy-three. He lost his glasses, slipped, fell off the roof, and broke both legs. In the hospital he asked for his violin, tried to play but couldn't, and died in his sleep. At the Stratford he was my very good friend and was very helpful.

MANGOLD AND my landlady decided that I was run down. Mangold invited me to enjoy his mother's cooking and she stuffed me with food and homemade beer. In the summer we worked it off at the beach by boxing. My landlady used to leave after-theater snacks in my room.

One night, I found an apple, which I enjoyed. The next night she brought me two apples, then on successive nights a banana, a bunch of grapes, and a layer cake with rich filling. I ate the fruit and half the layer cake and threw the other half away. Then I found a plate of plums, a mince pie, and some doughnuts. She was kind-hearted, so I kept the plums and put the doughnuts and pie in the garbage can. I found a note—"I'm glad you liked the pie"—and with it she left a whole chocolate layer cake, some spareribs, and soggy wheat bread. I took the whole mess and threw it into a trashcan. The next day she remarked, "I see you don't like fruit much, but want something more solid." That evening I found a couple of greasy and tough cold pork chops, cold potatoes, and half an angel-food cake. I took a nibble of pork chop and couldn't manage to swallow it, so another load went out the next day. This went on for three more days. I had to give her notice.

This was during the period when it was usual to fatten thin people for their health, and had I succumbed to the cure, disaster would have hit. My slow return to yoga saved me for a time.

I MOVED IN with the family of Carl Bohnen, the painter, old friends from Munich who were ideal people to room with. My roommate Arthur was up at five getting ready to work on architectural construction jobs. He retired about nine o'clock. I got in at about one or two and slept until ten or eleven. We rarely conversed. Roman Bohnen (who later won fame as an actor in Hollywood and in the Group Theatre in New York) sat up until four or five o'clock learning new roles, painting, or reading. I often composed for a few hours after the theater.

I applied for the Rome Prize. We had to copy out our material by hand. I couldn't afford photographing. Arthur was a draftsman. He couldn't understand how I could compose without a piano. I asked for some graph paper and then notated part of one of my piano compositions. The melodic part I traced horizontally on the graph paper, the chords vertically, explaining the relationship of this notation to the keyboard and to musical notation. My studies in linear counterpoint in Switzerland helped me with this demonstration. It was graph notation!

In my 1924 *Trio for Flute, Violin and Soprano*, composed at this time, I had indicated in the last movement pitches only, with no rhythms, no dynamics, no phrasing, and no entrances, giving the performers leeway to supply these themselves. Henry Cowell later wrote in *Musical Quarterly* that this and a work of Ives's were the first contemporary examples of aleatoric music.

But the American Academy in Rome turned my application down. I was too radical. *Music for Orchestra*, my first orchestra piece, was linear and used melodic lines that were constantly being transformed. It was alternatively tonal, atonal, and bitonal, and held together by repetition. Everyone thought it difficult, if not impossible, to play. On May 26, 1978, Gunther Schuller premiered it at an American Composers Orchestra concert in New York.

≽≼

IN THE 1920s, Chicago was called "the second largest Polish city in the world." Milwaukee, South Bend, Gary, and other cities nearby also had large Polish populations, somewhat hidden to be sure, but recognizable to those who took the trouble to look. Polish churches, schools, newspapers, social clubs, and musical societies kept alive, like those of other ethnic groups, the particular traditions of their mother country. In an unguarded moment, I told my friend Edmund Zygman, the Polish violinist, that my grandfather, Dr. Frederick William Luening, had been a volunteer from Germany in the Polish insurrection (the November Revolution) against Russia in 1830–1831, and that soon after the

Poles were defeated, the doctor emigrated to the United States to seek the freedom he could not find in Europe. Zygman was delighted with this background, and he decided I was qualified and should be drafted to help with the Polish renaissance in Chicago. For an introduction to the Polish community, he invited me to participate in a concert for the Kosciusko Society.

The program and program notes were printed in Polish. It included three songs of mine (poems by William Sharpe), a song by Ignazy Lilien sung by my sister Helene (with myself at the piano), a sonata by Handel, and my own 1919 *Sonatina for Flute and Piano* played by myself with Mme Zygman at the piano. Chamber music by Grieg, Gannego, Dvořák, Karlowicza, and Arensky rounded out the original if somewhat strange program. The concert took place in a Polish social club and it was such a success that after the stamping and bravos had died down I was approached by a retired Polish colonel who wished to discuss privately possible guest appearances for me as conductor of General Haller's Polish Veterans' Band.

The colonel, who was rather corpulent and red-faced, slowly steered me to a private room. He ordered slivovitz and vodka, dark rye bread, and Polish sausage. He drank a toast to my grandfather, to Chopin, Kosciusko, and innumerable other Polish patriots. Between drinks his expression was melancholy but with each toast his eyes would light up, and they flashed when our glasses clinked.

I asked about General Haller and was informed that the general had recruited a Polish brigade in Chicago and in neighboring towns and had led them bravely in France. General Haller's Polish Veterans' Band was the main cultural and recreational arm of his brigade. "And now, my dear Major," mumbled the colonel, "we must discuss business."

I pointed out that I held no military rank.

"Impossible. The Veterans' Band must have a permanent drum major and you will be it if we come to terms. It is a simulated rank, of course. Our last major's pay was seven dollars and fifty cents for a three-hour rehearsal. Is that satisfactory?"

I held out for $8.50. We compromised on eight dollars plus unlimited food and drink on rehearsal nights. To seal the agreement the colonel stood and started to click heels and salute, but he lost his balance and knocked over a salt cellar. He gave up the idea of a salute. Instead, we walked out of the hall arm in arm, humming fragments from Chopin's "Revolutionary" Etude.

Two days later, the band assembled in the hall of the social club. The huge room was ringed with benches and long tables and chairs for banquets, and was cleared in the center to accommodate the band. The men, ranging in age from twenty to fifty, wore their rather tattered uniforms with a certain dash, and this helped them to look at least a bit like the tough, fleabitten soldiers they once had been. The colonel introduced me in Polish and they applauded long and loud. I bowed from the waist and made a short speech in English, telling them about my grandfather. They looked puzzled and I saw that I was not communicating.

The colonel handed me a pile of music. Every piece was the clarinet part of some Polish march I had neither heard nor seen, ever. I asked for scores. "You have the scores," said the colonel, so I put the parts on my stand and sized up my forces.

I counted sixteen clarinets, ten trombones, nine piccolos, eleven cornets, five baritones, three tubas, six flugelhorns, three euphoniums, and six percussion players with plenty of cymbals, bells, glockenspiels, and bass drums. A total of about seventy players. With my baton I repeatedly tapped for attention, with no results. I then yelled and finally bellowed for attention. The band looked at me.

"Please tune to the B-flat of the first cornet."

There was a second of silence and then every player began groping for the pitch. I tried to control them and coax them toward a B-flat, but when they were only a half-tone away from the pitch their facial expressions reflected such a sense of supreme achievement that I didn't have the heart to disappoint them, so I gave up on pitch for that day.

Then we read one of the Polish marches. The din was terrific, and I believe it exceeded the rock 'n' roll levels of the sixties.

I stopped the band and said, "Too loud."

The bandsmen nodded in agreement, but when I repeated the march they played louder than before. I cut down my beat to almost nothing but it didn't help. Finally I turned my back on the band and walked off of the podium and out into the corridor, but they had their noses buried in their music and I don't think they even noticed that I was gone.

When the rehearsal was over the colonel took me to a table and plied me with slivovitz. He had a sad but firm look in his eye that signaled, "This is going to hurt you more than it is me." He had nothing at all to say about the rehearsal, and I was exhausted.

The next week we went through the same routine, and there was absolutely no change. After the rehearsal I told the colonel that the band was always too loud. Following a couple of slivovitzes and vodka, he looked at me sadly and began recounting the various battles in which General Haller's brigade had been engaged.

I was quite impressed with his description of the military exploits of this group but rather shaken when he wound up his battle lecture by saying, "We didn't win those victories by having the band play softly. They always played just as loud as they could and I'm afraid that that's how they're going to continue. . . . We need a loud conductor."

I told him I understood and considered my guest appearances to be terminated. This time he saluted and clicked his heels. I bowed from the waist as he paid me sixteen dollars. He ushered me to the door.

"Goodnight, Mr. Luening," he said, reducing my rank and ending my career as a bandleader with a wave of his hand.

AFTER THE Polish concert, a gentlemen named Chrzanowski came to see me in my studio. He was about five feet two inches and rotund, with large feet. I had trouble seeing his legs and he seemed not to walk but to roll.

"I am baritone," he said and then hummed and later boomed some phrases from *Boris Godunov* with a remarkably sonorous voice.

He related that he had been a member of the Russian Opera Company from Moscow touring the United States and had jumped ship in Chicago—"like Flying Dutchman," he chortled. "Politics make me do only roles of character and the Debil. . . . Diction problem," he said, "so I leabe." He rolled to the end of the studio. "I want to sing Godunob." He intoned the climax from Boris's monologue with passionate resonance.

I applauded. He beamed.

"You understand because you hab soul of slob."

"Slob?" I queried.

"Yes, soul of slob like Rahshahn, Czech and Poles."

"You mean Slav!"

"Berry true; Sobiet hab soul like hyena."

"Really?"

"No, but dog."

"English bull, perhaps?"

"Ho, ho, ho, ho. . . . Now we talk business." He then said that he had recommended me as director of the Zvonimir Croatian Choral Society, with a rehearsal the next night at eight.

Business had been slow, so I accepted with thanks.

The next evening, following his directions, I rode by tram to 22nd Street and Wentworth Avenue, a notorious gangster section of Chicago popular with Al Capone's boys. The address I had been given was that of a poolroom and saloon. A door led from the poolroom to a rehearsal hall and social club where the music library and a good, well-tuned Steinway upright piano were housed.

I was greeted inside by a tough-looking fellow, stocky and athletic, with what proved to be a permanent black shadow on a slightly purplish, alcoholically flushed complexion. He wore a straw hat with the crown cut out.

He introduced himself. "Pete Milosh. I own joint—bar and pool palace. . . . Also manager Zvonimir." He handed me a beaker of Prohibition red wine and took a pint for himself. We clinked glasses. "How much pay you like?" he asked. "Last director five dollars. No good."

"I'm good, so my fee's eight dollars per rehearsal."

"Okay, and all you can drink."

Clink!

After twenty minutes, six men showed up—and a motley crew they were. They seemed to be laborers, truck drivers, and porters. They went into the saloon and came back, each with a pint of red wine. Nobody spoke English very well except Pete. I had them sing some Croatian songs they knew and soon could see (and hear) that no one could read music. But they had remarkably fine voices and loved to sing.

When the rehearsal ended and Pete and I were enjoying some marvelous dark bread, cheese, and red wine, I told him that the situation was impossible and I didn't think I could continue. Taking on the expression of an ex-pugilist, he said, "You come back . . . I'll fix."

The next week, I arrived for the rehearsal and found twelve singers present but only one tenor. When I complained, Pete merely said, "You wait, I'll fix." He disappeared into the poolroom and returned in five minutes with two big bruisers whom he escorted to the tenor section. This procedure was repeated weekly until I had a nicely balanced male chorus of about twenty-four voices.

The men were often so tired that after their wine they would fall asleep in the rehearsal. Pete would boot them awake and prop them up. When I complained that attendance and deportment were not what they should be, the answer was, as always, "You wait, I'll fix," and he did. For some occult reason he always wore his crownless straw hat indoors while he was managing and removed it when he sang.

I quickly realized that if I wanted to conduct this outfit I would have to get a Croatian–English dictionary and learn to phoneticize the texts. Having done this, I sang along in Croatian with what must have been pretty good inflections, for the singers had the mistaken impression that I was fluent in their language. They would enter into long conversations during intermission, and when I would say I couldn't understand them they would just laugh and answer, "But you sing Croatian better than we do."

I finally gave up, and conversed by using the song texts. "Good evening, pretty princess, won't you favor me with a glance?" is a good example of my style. Undoubtedly, I owed this triumph to my elocution lessons with James Joyce in Zurich.

After the singers had learned about a dozen choruses by memory, Milosh announced, "Now we give concert." I protested that we did not have a concert manager, but Milosh, looking pugilistically efficient, said, again, "You wait. I fix concert."

From then on, there was an enormous amount of hustle and

bustle after each rehearsal. Men and women ran in and out, passing around tickets and programs, and finally Pete told me, "I fix concert for next Sunday evening. Croatian Hall. Eight o'clock. We have drinks and food." I told him the chorus must promise not to have drinks before the concert, or I wouldn't conduct. Pete told them this emphatically and with a clenched fist. They promised to control themselves, and they did.

The concert was a great success. The hall was packed and my singers were all scrubbed and sober and looked snappy in their dark suits. I wore a cutaway and a red carnation and mingled afterwards with the Croatian audience backstage, who, like the singers, very much enjoyed conversing with me. For my part I kept on reciting parts of the choral texts. I soon won a reputation as an erudite and very poetic director.

After the concert, everybody adjourned to the social hall and the chorus got rip-snorting drunk and insisted on singing the entire program over and over again. This they did badly, but with enthusiasm.

At the next rehearsal, I was surprised to see a number of women in the hall. When I asked about this Pete said, "Women liked concert. We now have mixed chorus." There were twenty-four men and four women, so I told Pete that wouldn't do at all. He squinted at me and said, "You know me. I fix."

The following week a dozen women attended, and some of them had fine, strong voices. In another week the chorus had grown to about fifty, and they sang a number of songs with real spirit.

Pete held a conference with them and came to me to announce, "We give concert with mixed chorus." I told him I thought the sopranos were too weak. He pushed his straw hat to the back of his head and said, "I fix up."

At the next rehearsal, twenty children were sitting in the corner—boy and girl sopranos and altos. Now, with about seventy singers, I really had a workable unit.

From then on, the rehearsals resembled great family parties. When the children were not singing, they played tag. If they made too much noise, mothers would leave the chorus and smack them. If they cried they were smacked again. Pete planned an elaborate concert.

The concert was a great Croatian social event. Parents, children, the priest, teachers, dogs, and other dignitaries showed up in force and the chorus sang beautifully. Afterwards, the chorus and audience adjourned to the Dalmatian Fish and Game Club, where we were served a dinner consisting of every kind of fish that swam in the Midwest lakes, as well as venison, partridge, grouse, pheasant, and other goodies. I was expected to taste everything, and did. I washed it down with home-brewed sour red wine. One of my tenors, a Checker cab driver, took me home, slightly the worse for wear, around three-thirty. It took me a full day to recover, and I declined all subsequent invitations to that club.

At the next rehearsal, Milosh called for attention. "Now we tour," he announced.

I was shocked. "Where?"

"North Chicago."

And so it was. A couple of weeks from that time we gave a concert in Croatian Hall in North Chicago. During the intermission, Pete made a fiery speech—in Croatian, of course—and presented me with a gold fountain pen and pencil. There was the usual social get-together and we went back to Chicago triumphantly in a cavalcade of Checker cabs that Pete had commandeered someplace.

A week later Pete proclaimed, "Now we go other state. We have concert in Milwaukee."

What could I do but agree? But I warned him that Milwaukee's Croatians were very musical, that it was my hometown, and that we must have some extra rehearsals. He soon arranged four rehearsals each week. The singing was quite spectacular.

When the great day came, Pete informed me that the society had rented a private car on the North Shore Railroad, and that we were going to go to the station via Checker cab. On the morning of our departure there were twenty-five cabs in front of the poolroom, all driven by Croatians. On the first one there was a huge blue-and-white flag with ZVONIMIR emblazoned on it. In the first cab the priest, the editor of the Croatian paper, the principal of the parochial school, and I rode in state. Following us, and divided up into groupings and rankings that I didn't understand, came the rest of the gang. Our lead taxi driver put his hand on the horn, all the other drivers followed suit, and so, making an enormous racket, our cavalcade drove through the streets of Chicago, taking the longest way around to reach the train station.

The train was packed but comfortable, and we arrived in Milwaukee about two hours before the concert. The Milwaukee Croatian Society had arranged a "little reception" for us. The refreshments turned out to be enormous quantities of sausages with sauerkraut, Croatian rye bread, and kegs of rather sour Prohibition wine.

As the chorus met Milwaukee friends and relatives, I had no way of controlling anybody, and by the time the concert began, the entire chorus, women included, was in a state of very happy hoopla which they called a *schwipps.* They began the first number by singing loudly and off pitch, but as the audience was also *beschwippst*, it was a great success. From then on singing and applause increased in volume. All cares were forgotten. Nothing made any difference. Everything we sang was cheered thunderously.

To the shouts and stamping of the audience and chorus, Pete presented me with a billfold at intermission, and at the end of the concert and after an enormous fracas ending in some fights, we made our way back to the special train car and Chicago as best we could.

I knew that I could never top this performance, and somewhat later I told Pete that I was soon leaving for the Eastman School in Rochester, and that I had better resign while I was ahead.

Pete looked at me almost tearfully and finally muttered, "Can't I fix?"

I had to tell him that even he couldn't arrange it this time. Life had to go on, and I had to go along with it.

There was a long pause, and he said, "You best choral leader Zvonimir ever had. You always can have job with Zvonimir. Send telegram Pete Milosh, Poolroom, Twenty-second and Wentworth, anytime, and we fire director and put you back in."

Then, after a man-to-man handshake and, I must admit, with a rather heavy heart, I left an organization that had without doubt the greatest manager I have ever known . . . Pete Milosh.

IN MID-MARCH 1924 my First String Quartet was performed by the Roth Quartet in a series given by the Melos Society and the International Society for Contemporary Music (ISCM) in Berlin. I believe my quartet was the first American chamber music to be performed professionally in Berlin after World War I. Word of this got around Chicago and my stock went up.

In the summer of 1924, E. Robert Schmitz, president of the Pro Musica in Paris, was conducting a master class in Madison, Wisconsin, so I packed up my scores and visited him. I showed him half a dozen works. He took my *Sextet* to New York to study. Later, the press reported that *Sextet*, on the recommendation of Edgar Varèse and Carlos Salzedo, had been presented to the newly formed music committee of the United States section of the International Society for Contemporary Music. The committee consisted of John Alden Carpenter, Howard Hanson, Salzedo, Schmitz, Frederick Jacobi, Lazare Saminsky, and Emerson Whithorne. They recommended the *Sextet* for the international jury in Zurich to be considered for the Prague and Venice festivals in 1925. The other American works recommended included Charles Griffes' *Pleasure Dome of Kubla Khan*, Henry Eichheim's *Oriental Impressions*, Carl Ruggles's *Angels*, Louis Greenberg's *Daniel Jazz*, George Antheil's *Jazz Sonata*, and Leo Ornstein's *Piano Sonata*. This news hit all the leading papers in the country, and there were interviews, with reproductions of a beautiful drawing of me by Carl Bohnen. The work was not played in Venice but the publicity definitely put me on the map here. I made up my mind to move to the East as soon as possible.

Ernst Bacon, with whom I had become friends, went to New York and Boston in the fall to look for a job. He wrote that he had found one at the new Eastman School, the finest conservatory in the country, if not the world. Howard Hanson, the director, was twenty-nine years old and was looking for young faculty. Bacon recommended me and arranged an interview at his parents' home in Chicago during the Christmas vacation.

HANSON AND Vladimir Rosing, the director of the opera department at Eastman, gave me a searching interview and immediately offered me the job of coach and assistant conductor in the opera department at a salary of $3,000 a year. My contract read that I was to coach individual singers, rehearse ensembles, train the chorus when necessary, and be on call to conduct any opera in the standard repertory or any contemporary opera selected by the director.

I closed the Chicago Musical Arts Studio and went home for a week's visit. Brother Fred was there. After listening to the story of my triumphs he leaned back and, drawing slowly and philosophically on his pipe, proclaimed, "You know, young fellow, it's silly to go into music unless you're a Paderooski or an Irving Berlin. You are neither one and never will be. But you've been hired by George Eastman. He's a fine American businessman. Maybe if you follow in his footsteps you can make something of yourself."

Via the beautiful Hiawatha deluxe train, I left Oconomowoc for Chicago and then took the New York Central Twentieth Century Limited to Grand Central Station in New York. I took a bus ride around the city, bought a ticket for the Hudson River night boat to Albany, and from there went on to Rochester. This was almost the same trip, in reverse, that my great-grandparents had made by boat and covered wagon when they went to Wisconsin in 1839. When I arrived in Rochester in September 1925, I felt a bit like a pioneer.

I couldn't help remembering my grandfather Colonel Jacob's interest in opera as I walked into the Eastman School opera department. I thought I heard someone say *"Achtung!"* but there was no one around. It must have been my imagination.

Chapter 12

The Eastman School of Music
1925 - 1928

HOWARD HANSON TOOK ME TO THE Department of Opera to
introduce me to the staff. The entrance to the department was
made by ascending a beautiful marble staircase to the promenade
balcony. The studios were effectively soundproofed and had fine
Steinway pianos. The large rehearsal room was quite adequate for
choral groups and full-cast rehearsals. Singers arrived on the
scene looking important and disappeared into the studios, leaving
the doors open for brief periods so that their beautiful voices
might be noticed. I had never heard of or seen such luxury in a
conservatory and had barely recovered my poise when the introductions began.

Among others, I met Herman and Cecile Genhart—fellow
students of mine in Zurich. Herman was now the infallible choral
conductor of the opera department. Cecile had premiered my
First Sonata for Violin and Piano in Zurich. She was a mouselike
woman when off the piano bench but a lioness at the keyboard,
and was scheduled to play with the Rochester Symphony Orchestra. Ernst Bacon arrived and took me to his studio, where he
showed me some of his remarkably original and beautiful songs.
He had acquired the posture of a Viennese baron, elegant but
with plenty of backbone. While we were discussing Beethoven's
Mass in C he told me that he was related to the Esterhazy family,
which explains why, whenever we discussed the tempi of Haydn
symphonies, I found his opinions rather rigid. He took me to
Emmanuel Balaban, the assistant music director of the opera department, a brilliant sight reader who had been Heifetz's accompanist for many years. Young Paul Horgan was the liaison man
with the Eastman Theatre. Although only twenty-two, he had

written a volume of poems, painted in oils, and drawn beautiful cartoons. He sang well enough to have publicly performed the Major-General in Gilbert and Sullivan's *Pirates of Penzance*. He was a delightful companion and like Bacon became a lifelong friend. He introduced me to Martha Graham, who was instructor for dance and body movement. Hanson brought in Rouben Mamoulian, who was establishing a School of Drama. He was a tall, scholarly-looking, nearsighted gentleman with thick glasses. These he counterbalanced by carrying a cane and wearing spats. Like most nearsighted people, he had a glance that seemed both sexy and hypnotic. He used his mesmeric look to good advantage at all times. Eric Clarke, director of the Eastman Theatre, joined Hanson for a conference. Clarke was six feet six, a polite, suave, businesslike Englishman. The opera department cooperated closely with the Eastman Theatre, and Clarke was soon one of my friends.

I WAS PLAYING piano in my studio one day when I was disturbed by a commotion and a voice shouting, "Gumpany meeting! Gumpany meeting!" Then there were loud poundings on studio doors.

In the corridor I saw singers emerging from studios yelling, "It's Val Rosing!"

A stocky figure stumbled toward the rehearsal room. He grabbed me. "Welcome, *Babushka*. . . . Gumpany meeting. All classes cancel."

There was a stampede to the rehearsal room.

Rosing concentrated. He closed his eyes. Everyone was quiet for several minutes.

"Haff discover new reproach to opera. . . . Is interrresting for opera make rhythmic movement from body to horchestra." He ate a prune, threw the pit across the room, ran over and picked it up, and snapped it toward the wastebasket, which he missed. "Now, please . . . heavrybody relax." We were all more at ease. "Like so," he said, pushing aside several people and spreading himself on the floor.

Everybody stretched out on the floor. After a few minutes a deep baritone voice was heard. "What do we do now?"

Rosing rolled over. "Relax. . . . Think of love."

There was quite a bit of heaving in the room.

"Not so rough," Rosing said. "Think of pink circle inside a skull, turning left to right. Now green circle other side, turning right to left. When I say hopp, change circles." A few singers were rolling and some were twitching. "Now . . . of love, again."

Two minutes later: *"Hopp, hopp.* Let's sing. *Ma, ma, ma, ma, ma, ma, ma, ma; mo, mo, mo, mo, mo, mo, mo, mo,"* he vocalized.

Everybody joined in, relaxed. The sound was magnificent.

Rosing looked pleased. "Method from Moscow Art Theatre." He hit a windowpane with a prune pit and left.

EUGENE GOOSSENS was the key artistic personality on the Rochester scene. As music director of the Rochester Symphony Orchestra, music director of the Rochester American Opera Company, and instructor of conducting at the Eastman School, his artistic influence permeated Rochester's artistic life. He guest-conducted in London, Paris, Boston, New York, and Hollywood. He arrived late in the season and left early. He was thirty-three years old and had already won an international reputation as an avant-garde composer and brilliant conductor of opera and symphony. He was famous as an interpreter of Stravinsky's music, as music director with Diaghilev in London, and as Sir Thomas Beecham's associate in the British National Opera Company. He made an immediate and strong impression on me. He was tall, willowy, and distinguished-looking. He wore a camel's hair coat and a black felt hat, the brim slightly bent down to cover his right eye. With his cane, spats, and custom-made shoes, he was the picture of a perfect gentleman, Mr. Elegant 1925.

GEORGE EASTMAN was duke of the "Duchy of Rochester" and the munificent donor of the Eastman Theatre and the Eastman School of Music. His mother, born a Kilbourn, loved music, particularly organ music. Kilbourn Hall was a memorial to her; it was ideal for chamber music and chamber opera. Eastman's private organist, Harold Gleason, played for him daily in his mansion at breakfast and in the evening. Mr. Eastman's aim was to provide the best in music for his beloved Rochester. He combined all theatrical resources in the large Eastman Theatre so that silent movies, symphony concerts, and operas could be played there. Kilbourn Hall, the great Sibley Library, and one unit of practice rooms and studios made up another complex. Public events were free of charge, or for minimal admission. Mr. Eastman also had a private string quartet, led by Gustav Tinlot. Stage presentations at the theater were lavish and included elaborate ballets, once the second act of *Boris Godunov*, and often single acts of musical comedies. Everything, including the silent movies, had a musical accompaniment played by a symphony orchestra of eighty-five. His hope was to lead the public to the niceties of the higher musical art with this entertaining but educational program.

THE MOST INTERESTING singers were George Houston, a handsome bass-baritone who had once assisted his blind evangelist father by singing during the collection, and who, after Rochester, went to Broadway and Hollywood where he organized his own opera company; Mary Silveira, an unusual lyric soprano who looked like Jenny Lind; Helen Oelheim, a healthy young woman who later sang at the Metropolitan Opera for many years; Ethel Codd, a nineteen-year-old Canadian who could sing just about anything; and her sister, Margaret Codd, who later sang in the Goldovsky Opera Institute and married the director, Boris Goldovsky. Coaching began at 10:00 A.M., and we usually rehearsed until 2:00 A.M., with time out for lunch and dinner.

Goossens's musical direction was impeccable. We were about to launch the Rochester American Opera Company with a performance of *Madame Butterfly*. At the same time we were preparing *The Marriage of Figaro*, *Cavalleria rusticana*, and *Pagliacci*. Goossens was a very good pianist. He knew the operas from memory but always used a score. His rehearsal routine was to call a complete cast, staff, and understudy reading. With Balaban at the piano, Goossens set an entire opera at the first reading, establishing the tempi, indicating the *rallentandi, accelerandi,* holds, cuts, and word changes. He demonstrated the diction he preferred, emphasized inflections, pointed out the dangerous spots in the ensemble, and explained how to overcome them.

Goossens was a flexible but secure conductor and the singers were always given their cues by a nod, a glance, or a lip signal. He was not a soul-searching German *Kapellmeister*, a dramatic

Italian *maestro,* or an overrefined French *chef d'orchestre.* His readings were sane, clear, lively, full of good contrast, and a little bit cool because he held the orchestra down so that the words could be understood, an essential requisite for doing opera in English for an English-speaking audience. His overall accomplishment as music director of the opera company was to weld a group of gifted but green singers, dancers, coaches, conductors, and orchestra musicians into a professional opera company in less than a year.

VLADIMIR ROSING used a different rehearsal technique. He muttered and mumbled about concentration and art and sometimes expounded on his long experience with the Moscow Art Theatre. But at heart he was a gypsy. He arrived late and left late and wore people out in rehearsals. He explained things in Russianized English. To demonstrate dramatic points he acted out scenes— not very convincingly, for he was nearsighted and occasionally tripped over his feet. He illustrated passages with his fine tenor voice, often in the wrong rhythm. His English was unique; he insisted on pronouncing *gnawing* with a hard *g.* His strength was that he had developed what he called rhythmic movement, a synchronization of the music and movement. When he had set a scene it worked rather well and resembled a half-human puppet show. Problems arose when, at a dramatic rehearsal, Rosing got the accompanist to slow the tempi to fit his concept of body rhythm. When at a later rehearsal the work was restored to the proper speed by the conductor in charge, the flailing, singing actors looked like animated manikins until movement and music were synchronized again in the proper tempo. Our problem was that Rosing had genius.

MARTHA GRAHAM, her assistant, Esther Gustafson, and their brilliant accompanist, Constance Finckel, occasionally attended opera rehearsals. Martha Graham's artistic ideals were fresh and quite different from those of the other directors at Rochester. She made suggestions about the visual aspect and movement in various works, and although she was just beginning to launch her own solo career she was extremely cooperative and helpful. In the Fern Restaurant after rehearsals, she and I had long discussions about the various arts. As with Edith McCormick, I had a real rapport with Martha and was very fond of her. She was warm, friendly, and stimulating. One reason that we got on so well was because of my friendship with Louis Horst, her musical mentor and adviser for her dances and constant companion for many years. Horst had been a pit musician and vaudeville piano leader. When he learned about my musical background, he immediately accepted me as an old pro.

Martha and I didn't discuss technical details of music or dance. It was the expressive content of the works that was at the core of our conversations. When she spoke, she gestured; she tried to speak from the depths of her personality, from her subconscious and her unconscious. It was always a vivid experience to be with her on these occasions. Music for her was related to movement and her subconscious gropings and often unclear initial yearnings led her to create art works with music and movement from her inner experiences.

For many years Horst was closely wound up in her career. He helped her to form her fantasies and thoughts and to shape them in movement; he selected music, composed for her, and rehearsed her dances. Horst considered himself an "accompaniment composer."

Martha's genius, combined with Horst's experience in the theater and his solid musical training, constituted a considerable artistic force. During the time they were at Rochester they gave much of their thought and energy to developing her dances and her first trio of dancers for a debut at the 48th Street Theatre in New York on April 19, 1926, and for another concert on May 27, 1926, in Kilbourn Hall. Her programs seemed very daring in some ways and her concepts of movement seemed at that time more lyrical than what I remembered of the dances of Mary Wigman, Clotilde von Derp, and Alexander Sacharof in Zurich. Martha's integration of music and movement was superior and was readily projected.

※※

WHEN I HAD been in the opera department for two months, Rosing decided to take the company on a short tour through western

Canada. Goossens was guest-conducting, and as someone was needed to fill the vacancies, Hanson appointed me executive director of the opera department. My job was to coordinate the activities of this large and complicated department. I accepted the job not realizing how trying it would be. The singers, all on scholarship, performed in the Eastman Theatre stage presentations, for which they rehearsed every day. They also sang roles in the operas and were in the choruses. The entire group of directors, conductors, stage managers, singers, and orchestra consisted of about one hundred and fifty people. It took three hours to prepare and post the call sheet every evening so that the next morning from nine o'clock on it could be followed precisely.

Thanks to Goossens, my life in Rochester got off to a good start. He invited me to share a studio with him and recommended my *Symphonic Poem* (now First Symphonic Fantasia) to Howard Hanson for performance at the second American Composers Concert.

HOWARD HANSON had accepted his position at Eastman immediately after completing a three-year fellowship at the American Academy in Rome. In Rome he had conducted and composed a number of his symphonic poems and his *Nordic* Symphony. In Rochester he proved to be a strong executive and completely devoted to the welfare of the school and to the development of American composers. He was also among the first to establish high standards for music in primary and secondary schools.

Hanson played his own compositions in Rochester and established himself as a talented composer, at his best in a romantic idiom. I was most impressed by his choral work, *Lament of Beowulf*, which has stood up well through the years.

His most significant contribution to American music was the inauguration of the American Composers Concerts at Eastman. His philosophy about American compositions was clear and sensible: they could neither be judged nor could they develop unless they were heard regularly and repeatedly. Hanson's feelings about American music have had a strong influence on the growth of American music in the last half-century.

Hanson programmed my First Symphonic Fantasia for the second concert in the composers series, November 25, 1925.

Hanson was a heavyhanded conductor who liked broad tempi. He was very competent, however, and a brilliant score reader. He presented hundreds of performances of American compositions in the next decades. I remember hearing Aaron Copland's *Music for the Theater*, which impressed me with its interesting rhythms, and Douglas Moore's *The Pageant of P. T. Barnum*. Quincy Porter's *Ukrainian* Suite was expertly written and was a precursor of his many masterly string quartets.

Of the performance of my piece Stewart Sabin wrote in the *Democrat Chronicle:* "There is real stuff in it. . . . A dignified musical expression . . . bits of music that set one thinking." Another music critic, formerly a sportswriter on the *Rochester Journal*, wrote: "Here's a well made bit of music; Mr. Luening was given quite a reception on its conclusion."

ROUBEN MAMOULIAN invited me to write the music for *Sister Beatrice*, a play in three acts by Maurice Maeterlinck. The work was announced as follows: "The Eastman School of the Dance and Dramatic Action Presents Rhythmic Drama to Music: A New Form of Theatrical Art Conceived and Developed by Rouben Mamoulian Presented Through the Medium of *Sister Beatrice*, a Play in Three Acts by Maurice Maeterlinck." The cast included Martha Atwell as Sister Beatrice and the Martha Graham dancers Betty MacDonald, Evelyn Sabin, and Thelma Biracree. The music was for organ, chorus, and contralto solo.

Mamoulian further defined the production as a synthesis of drama and dance:

> . . . true Theatrical Action completed by the sound of the human voice and music. It is based on the belief that the art of the theatre has for its medium the expressive, rhythmic, plastic movement of the actors, coordinated into one creative design by the stage director, with the spoken word, the art of the painter and the music constituting supplementary elements rather than actual necessities.
>
> The production of *Sister Beatrice* is a demonstration of the new form. Dramatic Action, esthetically expressing human emotion and thought on stage and combining the Dramatic and Dance forms of movement, is the supreme element. The Music completes the action and is being used throughout the whole play, not as an

incidental accompaniment but as an integral part of the performance on stage. The Spoken Word is treated not as a main element in the drama but as additional to Theatrical action. Scenery, Costumes, and Lights are used in the same way as Music and Word, supplementing theatrical movement and joining with it to form an artistic unit.

The movement of the actors, besides combining the drama and dance qualities, is stylized in order to convey the impression of the period. Old prints and paintings of the Fourteenth Century were studied for that purpose. Some new methods of staging and lights are introduced in the production.

The musical score was especially composed by Otto Luening to fit the action of the drama. It is written for organ and is suggestive throughout of the early Gregorian music, the period of the play being Fourteenth Century. A special new translation of the play was made by Paul Horgan. It is in rhythmic prose, preserving the color and character of the original French. The costumes and scenery were designed by Norman Edwards and kept in the style of the time.

Demonstrating a new theatrical form, the production of *Sister Beatrice* remains at the same time close to the true nature of theatre art, which is actual expression of human emotions and ideas on the stage.

Mamoulian molded the whole production with a psychic force that seemed to sculpt the performance. I attended all rehearsals. When the spirit moved me I improvised suitable continuous music. I observed the cast and Mamoulian as they responded to my improvisation. When they seemed to accept it as part of their dramatic experience I wrote it into the score. The final organist's score had very precise word cues and tempo marks that coordinated the music with the stage action. There was a song for the Virgin to sing on stage and an "Ave Maris Stella" that the opera chorus sang very beautifully. Horgan's words were poetic and I enjoyed the whole experience enormously.

The work was performed January 15 and 16, 1926, in Kilbourn Hall. Reviews were mixed. The *Times Union* announced it as a "most effective new art form. Very interesting," and called my music "dignified and beautiful." The local Hearst paper couldn't see it as a new form of theatrical art, but the critic wrote

that "the work of Otto Luening seemed a first-rate composition."
In retrospect, I think Mamoulian had an original concept.

WE PRESENTED *Madame Butterfly* as a trial balloon for the new
company on December 2, 3, 4, and 5, 1925. Of the excellent cast
Sherman, Hedley, and Oelheim were outstanding and later made
reputations in New York. Martha Graham and Mr. Cheba supervised the Japanese costumes and movement. The sets by Norman
Edwards were beautiful and convincing. Goossens made the orchestra sound lush, and the show was a hit. Rosing was given
major credit for making it all work.

Our Easter Operatic Festival in Kilbourn Hall began on
April 15, 1926. The cast of *The Marriage of Figaro* was as good as
that of any first-rate provincial opera company in Germany.
George Houston, John Moncreiff, Brownie Peebles, and Philip
Reep showed exceptional talent that was later recognized in New
York. *Cavalleria rusticana* and *Pagliacci* were the second offerings
of the company. Ethel Codd, Mary Bell, and Helen Golden attracted attention. The opera festival was a great success with
Rochester society and the press. In a repeat performance of *Madame Butterfly* Goossens's and Rosing's ideas projected and were
acclaimed by everyone. Lawrence Langner, a director of the New
York Theatre Guild since 1919, attended the performance and
booked the company for a week of guest performances for the
coming season at the Guild Theatre in New York. In the twenties
an invitation from the Theatre Guild was the highest recognition
we could hope for, so the future looked rosy.

To prepare the company for New York, Rosing and Goossens
arranged guest appearances at the Chautauqua, New York, opera
festival (July 8–13, 1926), followed by a week of concerts and two
weeks of opera at Conneaut Lake in Pennsylvania. In Rochester
Goossens had given me my big chance as a conductor by assign-
ing me two performances of *The Pirates of Penzance* with a half-
hour rehearsal to practice cues.

I became nervous during the rehearsal when I heard somebody behind my back beating time with his foot. I yelled, "Will
the idiot who is beating time please stop!"

It was Goossens.

After the rehearsal he called to me, "Splendid, dear boy, and I do admire your spirit."

As a result of this baptism by fire, he appointed me associate conductor of the tour and charged me with the job of breaking in the new chorus for our repertory of *Martha, The Pirates of Penzance, H.M.S. Pinafore, Cavalleria rusticana, Pagliacci,* and *The Marriage of Figaro.*

Few of our people knew those choruses, so I condensed rehearsals into three hours on the day before and the day of each performance, and was able to pound the music into the choristers' memories. But *Pagliacci* was very difficult, and in one of the performances I made a personal stage appearance with the chorus, disguised as a crippled old man. With a condensed score under my coat, I conducted the chorus with my back to the audience. It worked rather well, and as a reward, I was assigned to conduct one performance of each opera without rehearsal. In the *Pinafore* matinee I also had trouble. A vaguely familiar-looking wild man suddenly appeared on stage with the chorus. Eventually I recognized Rosing, who was pepping up the chorus by pushing them around. He was acting. He was so successful that the chorus forgot to sing. I repeated two entire sections before they regained consciousness and joined in with the orchestra.

In spite of problems, the tour went well and was invaluable experience for the company and for me in particular. I was now a seasoned opera conductor.

DURING THIS TIME, I had been very much attracted to Ethel Codd, one of the sopranos. She was a brilliant talent with great musical gifts, and quite convincing as an actress. I fought with her until we were engaged. We broke it off, turned it on, and then off. Following a particularly tough day of rehearsal, we had a big row and called everything off for good. I decided to end it all, so I took the train to Niagara Falls, where I planned to jump. I booked a hotel room and had a couple or six bourbons while contemplating this leap into infinity. After two or four beer chasers I was pretty drunk. I passed out in bed and woke up after twelve hours, not in the falls but still in bed, with a nosebleed and a terrible hangover. I took the train back to Rochester and walked to my room. After resting, I began feeling better, so I went to the living room, turned on the gas fireplace, and stuck my head in it. It was okay for a while, but then I didn't like the sweet smell, so I turned it off just as Ethel arrived. I had ashes on my forehead and must have looked terrible. It was a touching reunion with all sorts of explanations. We decided to get married at the end of the season.

THE COMPANY MOVED into the Woodward Hotel on 55th Street in New York and rehearsed day and night for a week of guest performances at the Theatre Guild theater starting April 5, 1927. We opened with *The Abduction from the Seraglio.* New York high society attended. The audience was enthusiastic and the press unanimous in its praise of the company as a whole and of the production. Ethel was singled out as Constanze. *Madame Butterfly* was praised for the innovative stage sets; Goossens's conducting and the acting of the singers were praised, though the latter's vocal powers were criticized. But the Theatre Guild was sufficiently enthusiastic to plan a return engagement. Rosing expanded his public relations by traveling and awakening interest in the company in other cities. While he pursued his idea of a tour he also hoped to perfect the performances in Rochester.

The most brilliant Rochester operatic event was the performance of *Carmen* in 1928, with Mary Garden in the title role. In preparation Goossens took the staff and singers through the opera once, then put Balaban and me in charge of preparing the production while he guest-conducted in New York City and Boston. He returned for the first orchestra stage rehearsal. Balaban and I had done quite a job of preparation, and Goossens and Mary Garden were able to run through the work with almost no stops, building it to a really sparkling performance.

≫≪

DURING 1927 administrative problems arose. The opera department was reorganized, Rosing left for New York to build an opera company, the drama department was eliminated, and Rouben Mamoulian left to produce Gershwin's *Porgy and Bess.* Rosing sometimes asked me to audition singers for him and his new company.

One day, in New Year's Town Hall, a chap named Thomas Dewey auditioned for the role of Valentine in *Faust*. He was about twenty-five years old and sang well, but Rosing disliked his stage appearance and thought he would look funny as Valentine.

I was detailed to accomplish a tactful brushoff.

Dewey explained that he sang in churches and synagogues but wanted to be a lieder and opera singer. As career insurance he was also studying at Columbia Law School. His wife was a musical-comedy singer.

I ventured to suggest that although he was a very good singer, the difficulties in an operatic career were great and the opportunities limited, so unless he was prepared to invest a lot of money it might be better for him to pursue his law career and sing as an avocation.

I saw Thomas Dewey again when he was running for President of the United States in 1948. We were both members of Phi Mu Alpha, an honorary music fraternity that had arranged a reunion and a campaign rally in a New York hotel.

Governor Dewey was punctual and dapper and greeted everybody very pleasantly. When we shook hands he smiled and asked, "How have you been getting along?"

I was astonished at his politician's memory and mumbled, "Up and down."

By then he and the other fraternity brothers had gathered around the piano and begun singing all the old fraternity favorites. Dewey's voice was lusty and pleasant and he sang in tune. He was obviously still a talented and enthusiastic singer.

During the campaign I noticed that his speeches were delivered with impeccable diction and with a round and resounding voice. I missed that vocal quality in Truman, Nixon, and Agnew, and I have been told that they studied only instruments in their youth. Perhaps all candidates should take voice lessons. A well-spoken speech, like a well-sung opera, would at least be pleasant to listen to, even when handicapped by a frothy or foggy text.

MOST OF THE coaches and talented young fellows on the faculty attended Goossens's conducting class. He gave us baton drill by writing complicated sequences of measures on the blackboard, such as ¾, ⅜, 2/2, 4/16, ⅝, 7/4, 7/16. We conducted patterns like this for hours on end in tempi ranging from *largo* to *prestissimo*. There were always two and sometimes four people at the grand piano playing the standard and modern symphonic repertory from score. One of us would conduct. Some didn't coordinate very well; others were overzealous and pushed their hand into a player's face for a *pianissimo*, or threw a menacing glance at the lower player of the four- or eight-handed team to get the authentic dramatic accent as played by trombone and tuba in the original. Goossens would occasionally retreat behind his handkerchief and indulge in some discreet, well-bred, and silent English laughs.

We plowed through scores up to Mahler and Stravinsky and then graduated to conducting the student orchestra. This we did at sight, for Goossens didn't like us to study scores in advance. I conducted the *Meistersinger* Overture, which I knew quite well from playing it many times in Zurich, and I really tore into it.

Goossens lost his poise. "I admire your spirit, dear boy," he said, shaking his head.

I asked him why he never let us study the scores we were conducting.

"Dear boy, for the first ten years of your conducting career you will be asked to substitute on a moment's notice, and you will either sight-read or be a failure."

In my subsequent career I did much last-minute conducting where I had to sight-read for student orchestras with an inadequate number of rehearsals. I don't remember ever having sufficient rehearsal time for any of the performances I conducted. Thanks to Goossens, I became a fluent sight reader and could conduct under almost any conditions without ever getting into technical baton difficulties.

ETHEL HAD PLAYED an important part in the development of the opera company. As Santuzza in *Cavalleria*, Constanze in *Seraglio*, the Countess in *Figaro*, and with roles in *Pirates of Penzance* and *Pinafore*, she had made a fine reputation, but she was gradually weaning herself from the opera company. Even before the Theatre Guild appearances Ethel had sung a Berckman song, *Spring in the Orchard*, with the Russian String Quartet on a League of Composers concert, January 12, 1926, in New York.

Then Goossens engaged her to sing Wagner's "Love Death" from *Tristan,* "Elsa's Dream" from *Lohengrin,* and an aria from *Tannhäuser* with the Rochester Philharmonic, which she performed with distinction. She sang beautifully my *Three Songs for Soprano and Small Orchestra* on the Music Teachers National Association program on December 30, 1926, with Howard Hanson conducting. On Christmas 1927 she performed the soprano part in Handel's *Messiah* with outstanding success.

We married after the Theatre Guild appearances in April 1927. On our honeymoon in Alaska we collected two of her brothers, who had been pioneers and roustabouts. Ethel discovered that they had voices, and she made plans for them to come to Rochester. For a while they and Ethel's talented sister Margaret boarded with us, and they did become singers: Arthur taught voice in Los Angeles, Frank (stage-named Larry Burke) worked in the movies; the role of the Street Singer in *The Informer* brought him fame for a while.

Goossens commissioned me to write *Serenade for Three Horns and Strings* for the Rochester Philharmonic. *Serenade* was premiered January 12, 1928, and it turned out to be a very romantic and easily accessible piece, tonal, melodious, and a bit jazzy. It was a strong audience success, but the Eastman School composers had a hard time placing it. They agreed that as a satire it was first-rate but as a straight piece it was no good. They then asked me to explain and analyze it, but I said that was their job. Goossens liked it and wrote an article saying that he detected the signs of a new romantic movement in contemporary music.

Hanson had me work out plans for the next semester for the opera department. The thought of taking part in Hanson's administrative scene-shifting was as distasteful as that of building yet another opera company in New York City. Ethel, too, wanted to try her wings in Europe. I think Hanson really liked me, and he respected my musical talents, so he kept on dangling various opportunities before me. He selected my *Serenade* for the American Composers Concert on March 20, 1928. The audience was to vote for one work to be published in the Eastman School series. After enthusiastic applause the audience selected the *Serenade,* far and away their favorite. Hanson and two judges conferred backstage. He then addressed the audience, telling them, "We don't know whether to be proud or ashamed of your choice." He explained that it was easy to write a piece like mine, which had lyric charm but was in no way profound. He went on to say that it was much easier to write a serenade than a more extended piece. He then announced that the jury had decided to ignore the audience vote and give the publication prize to *The Happy Hypocrite*, a ballet by Herbert Elwell. This didn't make me very happy, and the orchestra players and audience were puzzled by this strange "audience vote" that had been vetoed.

A week later, I told Hanson that Ethel and I planned to go to Europe for a year and wanted a leave of absence, as I would probably apply for a Guggenheim Fellowship. As far as I know, Hanson played nothing of mine for years, but eventually he did perform my *Suite for String Orchestra*. In 1945, Jacques Gordon played my Third String Quartet at Eastman. Larry Weld, in the Albany *Times-Union*, noted that the subject of the second movement consisted of twelve tones, so he deduced that this piece was extremely difficult and in the twelve-tone system (to which it was, in fact, in no way related). He wrote that the quartet was

. . . wholly abstract and beyond comprehension. It affronted the ear with harsh harmonic structures and was devoid of coherent melody. Before one can begin to appraise this kind of work he must first accept, if he can, the ultra-modernist school's arbitrary concepts of harmony, melody, and form. Until their formulas and purpose are shared by wider audiences and until there are a number of their works to establish any criteria we can only conclude that this type of work's appeal is solely cerebral and not sensual. We must add that generally this type does not provoke any symphathetic vibrations in our cerebral cells.

Another reviewer said: "The Luening opus proved a complete enigma. Its austerity and acidity were entirely unrelieved; its harmonies wholly ungrateful. The final sharp dissonant chord left the audience in complete wonderment in what, if anything, had been accomplished. If anything this is cerebral writing."

This put me way in advance of the avant-garde of that time. When the work was recorded in 1975, the reviewer in *Musical Quarterly* wrote that "the triad is frequently a clear point of reference and the piece has a lucid, classical clarity. There is diatonic lyricism and tonal order throughout. The use of tonality is personal, distinctive, convincing, and consistent." *New Records* commented that "the two string quartets are beautiful pieces. . . . I cannot imagine any chamber music fan, even of the old school, not reveling in the sounds." I never understood how my Third String Quartet could seem as problematical as they thought it was at the Eastman School in 1945.

With all of his unique notions of a director's duties, Hanson did a great deal for American music at a time when it was needed. He played everybody's compositions; his readings attracted attention, and works were sometimes published and often recorded by him. I believe he is at present underrated, for he is a fine musician and was a force in educational circles throughout the United States. He is a composer of talent and real craftsmanship.

IN JUNE 1928, Ethel and I took our savings and left for a year's stay in Cologne where Philipp Jarnach was now an important faculty member at the conservatory. We hoped to get Ethel into a German opera house and to find some conducting or teaching for me. After all, I was known in Zurich and Berlin, and was by now fed up with pioneering in the wastelands of the United States. Europe was waiting for us!

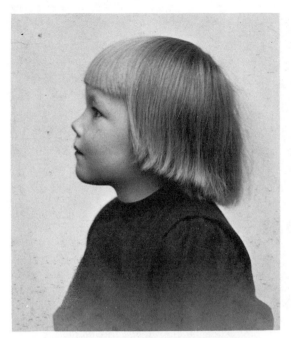

Myself, aged four, Wauwatosa, Wisconsin.

My parents, Eugene and Emma Luening, rehearsing at their apartment in Munich, 1916.

Here I am as Tony Lumpkin in James Joyce's English Players' production of *She Stoops to Conquer*, Pfauen Theater, Zurich, 1918.

At the Yaddo Music Festival, Saratoga Springs, New York, 1937. From the left are: Elizabeth Ames (director of Yaddo), Ralph Kirkpatrick, myself, Richard Donovan, and Quincy Porter. *(Courtesy Nation-Wide News Service)*

Rehearsing with Ethel Codd Luening at Sunnyside, our home in Bennington, Vermont, 1937.

Rehearsing the cast for the world premiere of Gertrude Stein and Virgil Thomson's *The Mother of Us All* at Brander Matthews Theater, Columbia University, 1947. (*Courtesy Warman/Columbia University*)

Discussing the score of my opera, *Evangeline*, with Jack Beeson (assistant conductor) and Nona Schurman (choreographer) at Brander Matthews, 1948. (*Courtesy Warman/Columbia University*)

With my wife, Catherine, at our wedding, Elba, Alabama, September 5, 1959.

At the International Composers Conference, Toronto, Canada, 1960. Left to right are: Joseph Tal, Hugh le Caine, Edgar Varèse, myself, Vladimir Ussachevsky, and Luciano Berio. *(Courtesy Peter Smith)*

With Vladimir Ussachevsky in McMillin Studio, Columbia-Princeton Electronic Music Center, New York, 1961. (*Courtesy Columbia University*)

Congratulating Roger Sessions after the performance of his *Divertimento* at Alice Tully Hall, New York, 1977. (*Courtesy Whitestone Photo*)

Examining the score of *Concerted Piece* with Leonard Bernstein in his New York studio, 1961.

Studying a score at home, New York, 1978. *(Courtesy Chou Wen-chung)*

Chapter 13

Interlude: Cologne
1928-1929

WE TRAVELED TO COLOGNE ON THE *Europa*, a fine, big ship. We ate too much and tried to work it off by running around the deck. This in turn worked up our appetites, so we kept on eating too much and arrived in Bremen fat and happy. In Cologne we found a furnished apartment on the Rhine. The rent was low but as part of the arrangement we promised to listen to our landlady, a broken-down soprano, sing "Ich küsse ihre Hand, Madam" and the very, very slow Brahms song *Ich sass zu deinen Füssen*. This part of the agreement was not a bargain.

Jarnach was now well established in a lovely garden apartment. After spending an evening discussing various brands of cigarettes and the literary output of James Fenimore Cooper, Jarnach heard Ethel sing. He predicted immediately that she would have no trouble getting on the German stage and he promised to introduce us to the right people.

Ethel took diction lessons with a German elocutionist named Liane Benner. This lady's method was so secure that she could even teach a dog how to bark in High German. Every vowel and consonant was put into properly phony phonetic paragraphs to provide practice. For letter *d* she used this: *"Dante dankte Daphne da drüben; dunkel dachte die dünstere Dorf Dame."* Madame Benner gave Ethel phonetic drill three or four hours a week and taught her impeccable German.

Jarnach arranged the promised audition within a month. While waiting I composed steadily. My style had moved in new directions. I had reexamined the overtone row and combined the sonority forms from it in a way that I called, for no good reason, "acoustic harmony." I have developed this considerably since then, but it began in Cologne. I composed songs for soprano to poems by Blake and Whitman.

Armed with these and some Mozart, including the Queen of the Night arias from *Die Zauberflöte*, we visited Jarnach and met Dr. Heinrich Jalowetz, Schoenberg's first student, who was then first conductor at the Cologne Opera; Eduard Erdmann, pianist and composer and head of the piano master class at the Hochschule für Musik; and the latter's wife and his cousin.

When Ethel had sung, Jalowetz and Jarnach spoke well of my songs and were enthusiastic about Ethel's Mozart. Erdmann, his wife, and his cousin didn't move a muscle, raise a hand, or say a word.

Jalowetz tried to break the ice by asking him to play.

Erdmann sneered, "I never perform in a private house."

I now understand Erdmann's reaction to my music much better than I did then. In his piano concerto of that period, a work on the long and loud side, he used every trick of the 1928 contemporary composer. His playing was of the monumental school. In my songs I had reduced my vocabulary to free-floating triadic combinations and a lyric and subdued melodic line that grew out of Blake's and Whitman's poems. One of Blake's lines, "To see a world in a grain of sand," was typical of the imagery of the poems. I doubt if Erdmann believed that a grain of sand should be allowed to confront a mountain like himself. He must have thought that I was either incredibly stupid or regressing musically and artistically into a never-never land.

As we left the party Jarnach turned toward me and asked, "Whatever became of that red-headed Irish writer who used to live in Zurich? He had talent."

I told him about Joyce's fame in the United States.

He growled, "A real artist. He wrote slowly."

Ethel kept on working at her German and we worked on German lieder and opera repertory. I finished quite a bit of piano music, including a *Dance Sonata for Piano* and my Third String Quartet. In these works I moved away from the Jarnach-Busoni influence, so when I showed Jarnach the compositions he was rather surprised. He spoke fairly well of the invention in my quartet but thought it was not convincing formally. It was indeed different and quite personal. The first movement was somewhat conventional; the second (there were only two) was a set of variations on a twelve-tone theme, but the variations themselves were not twelve-tone. The third quartet has had a strange history. It was premiered at Yaddo September 19, 1937, and then performed about once every ten years, always with a mixed reception. The Sinnhoffer Quartet performed it in Munich in 1971 and recorded it in 1972. Since then it has been heard quite regularly over the radio and has been performed as well, most recently by the Lydian Quartet in Carnegie Recital Hall in New York City.

Ethel sang for Walter Braunfels, director of the Hochschule, and for Hermann Abendroth, conductor of the Cologne Symphony Orchestra. Both gentlemen were enthusiastic and said that there were few singers in Germany who could sing Mozart with such style and flourish. In spite of the predictions of the musical authorities nothing developed. My own efforts to embark on a conducting career in Germany made little impression. Jarnach said that there were one hundred applicants for every opening. I felt rather silly. He then suggested I might want to write articles for some of the smaller magazines but explained that they didn't pay much. In the most tactful and roundabout way he asked me about my Rochester salary. When I mentioned $5,000 his jaw dropped and he lost his poise. "It will please you to know that is more than the salary of the director of the Hochschule," he murmured. I thought I detected a look of pity as he spoke—pity for my having given up a magnificent salary in order to make good in Germany. But he suggested that we attend the Contemporary Music Festival in Baden-Baden July 13–15.

We first enjoyed a brief vacation in the Black Forest. I was reminded of the peasants in Egern, for the flocks of flies around the peasant house we lived in showed us that our room was right above the pigsty. We took long walks in the woods and ate heavy meals consisting of pork, potatoes, and dark beer—which soon blotted out our Rochester memories.

BADEN-BADEN was a typical European spa in a beautiful setting, and we lived luxuriously in a fine hotel. It seemed that all the avant-garde composers in Europe were attending the festival.

Goossens arrived in a white suit with a pink carnation in the lapel, a panama hat, and a bamboo cane. "Dear boy, fancy seeing you here, and you, Ethel dahling. . . . For the baths or the music?"

"Music."

"Too bad. I wish you luck. . . . Lots of fog around here. Cheerio. We must have champagne later."

We went to a rehearsal of a new Jarnach organ piece. A lively, bumpy fellow who looked a little like a military J. S. Bach (without the wig) was arranging *Kinderfabrik*, a piece for mechanical organ and film by Ernst Toch. He was having trouble synchronizing the picture and the sound. He lost his temper and began hollering, making a great hullabaloo. A large Bavarian lady, a composer's wife, lost *her* temper and yelled, "What kind of a pigsty is this? Take that unadulterated crap out of here. You're using up all the rehearsal time and now it's Jarnach's turn. If you don't get out I'll throw you out!"

The man backed off, calmed down, and then finally made way for Jarnach.

"And who is that?" I inquired.

Jarnach looked a little annoyed. "That's Paul Hindemith, one of the directors of the festival. He's a bit of a thug, but he's not without talent. He writes a lot of music and much of it is bad, but some of it is very good."

Hindemith passed him on his way out.

"Hello, Paul," said Jarnach. "Very interesting piece by Toch. . . . I'm so sorry it wasn't properly prepared. By the way, do you have any of that Turkish tobacco that you found in Ankara on your tour?"

"No, but here's a Lucky Strike if you need a smoke. Are you on today's program?"

"Yes, a new organ work."

"Is that the one you sketched ten years ago in Zurich?"

"It's different now. I understand that you have written three quartets and a viola sonata since last April."

"I never remember these things. I must leave now."

There was silence while the organist prepared the registration for Jarnach's piece. Jarnach looked sardonic.

"Now you see, my dear Luening, how the European composers embrace and cooperate when they have a festival."

He capped his remark with a soft, friendly, ghostlike chuckle that modulated into a kind of disappearing echo. Then the organ-ist began rehearsing.

Jarnach's *Romanzero for Organ* was poetic, somewhat "white," and beautifully crafted. It seemed out of place in these avant-garde surroundings, but Jarnach had a unique reputation for being a great modern master of form. He was pleased with the performance, and with the organist we discussed the new *Roman-zero*, Jarnach's string quartet, and the problem of form in contem-porary works. Jarnach suggested that Busoni's opera *Doktor Faust* succeeded in welding libretto and music into a convincing form, or gestalt, as he called it.

We walked to an elegant restaurant. All the composers in at-tendance had decided to dine in this hotel, a sure sign that the food was superior.

Alois Haba, the great quarter-tone advocate, walked by our table and greeted Jarnach with a half-smile.

Jarnach was effusive in returning the greeting and then re-marked to me, *sotto voce*, "A terrible fellow. Very boring. Every time you ask him about a composition, new or old, a theatrical production, new or old, he always says, 'It's so boring, it's so bor-ing,' and proves himself to be the greatest bore of them all."

There was practically no conversation among the many well-known composers, who gave their undivided attention to the ex-cellent food and drink.

Jarnach remarked: "A love feast."

Fortified by cognacs, everybody went to the evening con-cert. Ernst Pepping's *Canonic Chorales* for organ played by the composer opened the program. They were in a newly discovered linear style. "To hell with the sound" seemed to be Pepping's motto, and he succeeded admirably in carrying out his ideal. After the second canon the audience began talking; after six canons Goossens and some of his friends walked out for refresh-ments. The conversation in the audience was so resonant that the last two canons were inaudible.

Pepping finished his group with a linear whimper; not one person applauded. Poor Pepping slid off the organ bench and sneaked out of the hall. But I learned later that he revised his style and made quite a reputation by using colorful modality in his church music.

The canons were followed by an opera, *In zehn Minuten*, by

Walter von Gronestay, a twenty-two-year-old Schoenberg student. The title suggested that we were about to hear a ten-minute opera, but the piece lasted a full hour. I had to agree with Alois Haba's all-purpose opinion—"It's so boring." But strangely enough, this impression has been with me for almost half a century, so how boring was it?

Hindemith and Toch's stunt with the mechanical organ and film seemed to be a misguided attempt, more energetic than artistic and slightly wacky and wobbly, but Jarnach told me that both composers were doing interesting experiments in Berlin by superimposing and mixing phonograph records; they were also working with electric and mechanical instruments. Their experiments had first been heard at the Donaueschingen Festival in 1926. It is obvious now that they were precursors of the *musique concrète* and the electronic music developments that took place in the late forties and early fifties.

Of the remaining works performed, *Wandlungen*, a cantata with text by Hölderlin and music by Josef Mathias Hauer, was impressive. Hauer had a reputation as the originator of one method of composing with twelve-tones. I was very much moved by his cantata, with its wonderful word settings, interesting melodic and harmonic turns, and fine vocal writing, which, taken together, awakened a strong emotional reaction in the audience. Hermann Scherchen, one of the sponsors of my First String Quartet's performance in Berlin, conducted the cantata magnificently. Scherchen's great contributions as a champion of contemporary music continued well into the sixties.

The festival was exhausting and only mildly enlightening. We found the state of contemporary music in Germany puzzling, so we were glad to return to our work in Cologne.

※

ETHEL'S SINGING began to attract attention in Cologne and we were engaged to do a benefit concert at the Wolkenberg Hall. One reviewer wrote: "She masters coloratura singing; relaxed and without tension, her singing fulfilled one's highest expectations. . . . One could lose oneself in her bell-like, pure pitch that always had a delicate, heartfelt charm. For the last group, her husband Otto Luening showed himself to be a remarkable flutist."

We were next engaged to do two programs for the Cologne Literary Musical Society. Ethel sang songs and arias by Bach, Handel, Mozart, Beethoven, Loewe, and Strauss, and a song of mine, at the Wolkenberg Hall. The review read: "Mozart and Handel were sung charmingly with elegant coloratura technique and warmhearted feeling by a promising American soprano who combines good diction with a spiritually profound interpretation." Artistically, Ethel was firmly established in Cologne.

While waiting for the offers that never came from the German opera houses, our social life began to develop in its own strange way. Jarnach introduced us to Herr von Harnack, the son of the famous nineteenth-century theologian Adolph von Harnack. The younger von Harnack was vice-president of the provincial Diet of the Rhine Province. He was a socialist, quite liberal, and an ardent amateur flutist. We met to play flute duets in the evenings in our apartments. After a tasty supper, the table was pushed back, and von Harnack produced a pile of flute duets by Haydn, Mozart, Kuhlau, Telemann, and Quantz; and "modern" works by Berbiguier and others. We played without stopping until midnight. Von Harnack was a delightful person, popular, well regarded in political circles, and quite a good flutist. We became good friends. Jarnach wrote me about his later career, but the Second World War blotted out all news until I read in the *New York Times* that von Harnack had participated in the plot against Hitler. The Gestapo arrested him and my father's ex-student and my friend Count Werner von der Schulenburg. Both were sentenced to death by hanging.

Walter Braunfels, the director of the Hochschule für Musik, also took us in hand. He was a good, conservative composer, and I had played his *Variations on a Fantastic Theme by Hector Berlioz* with the Zurich Tonhalle Orchestra in 1918. When we met, I played the opening of his work for him on the piano and he was impressed.

After introducing us to the finest restaurants in Cologne, Braunfels invited us to attend a Carnival ball. It was a real shindig. Everybody we knew was there and so were crowds of other Cologne artists. All were very high on Rhine wine and were dancing wildly.

The band blared loud and hearty and the men in our party,
led by Braunfels, grabbed the nearest women and stomped
around the dance floor in a kind of Rhenish one-step that I had
never seen before, nor have I since. The noise grew, and everybody got quite wild; it was Carnival, supposedly a catharsis before
Ash Wednesday ushered in repentance. Eventually, the floor was
so packed that the "dancing" couples just stood in one spot holding on to each other while stomping and drooling. In the intermissions the exhausted dancers headed for the nearest Rhine-
wine table to tank up for the next romp.

At eleven o'clock there were riffs, ruffles, and fanfares from
the band and in came Conrad Adenauer, the very popular Lord
Mayor of Cologne. He was an imposing figure, yet very much a
man of the people. He announced that he did not wish to inter-
rupt the flow of conviviality with a long speech. He lifted his glass
and drank a toast to the Rhine, to Rhine wine, and to the Carnival, and led the prancing throng back to the dance arena.

During the next intermission, Herr Adenauer came to our
table. As Braunfels introduced Ethel and me, Adenauer gave us
a friendly handshake. "*Amerikaner sind Sie? Prosit.*" We clinked
glasses. "Do you like our Rhine wine?"

"It's wonderful."

He smiled and strode off.

THE NAZIS later discovered that Braunfels was partly Jewish,
and he was dismissed as director of the Hochschule in 1933. He
tried to defend himself because he had fought at the front in
World War I and had been decorated numerous times, but Goeb-
bels was not impressed and had his music boycotted. After the
war he was reinstated as president of the Cologne Hochschule.
During his exile and boycott he kept right on composing numerous and substantial works. Conrad Adenauer, a Catholic, was
also dismissed as mayor in 1933. Subsequently he was jailed twice
by the Nazis. His great personal renaissance, which led him to be
chancellor of the German Federal Republic and a world figure of
great significance, is a matter of history.

I was introduced to the Nazi philosophy by our greengrocer,
whose store was across the street from our apartment. He and his

wife worked from 6:00 A.M. until midnight to make a bare living. We shopped there daily and he liked to talk with me. He described the economic difficulties in Germany but insisted that they would soon improve. He explained the program of a new party called the National Socialist German Workers party, Nazis for short. First, they would bring order to Germany and wrest economic control from foreigners and Jews. They embraced an optimistic philosophy with the motto *"Kraft durch Freude"*— "Strength Through Joy." He explained that their athletic clubs would soon be training paramilitary units; the shipbuilders in Hamburg and Bremen would develop minisubmarines and pocket battleships; the Luftwaffe, better and cheaper airplanes; and at the same time heavy industry would be developed from the light industry that was permitted by the Allies. Once Germany had regained her strength the Nazis would win back the territory lost in the two wars. The greengrocer's blueprint proved to be prophetic. I was disturbed that some of the people in the Literary Music Society and Frau Benner, the diction teacher, were much too enthusiastic about this oncoming party triumph. The existing government was socialist; the members, like von Harnack and Adenauer, were liberal and fair-minded men. They were tolerant—perhaps too tolerant for their own good—but I couldn't bring myself to believe at the time that my greengrocer's Nazis would really prevail.

I HAD APPLIED for a Guggenheim Fellowship. My supporting material included my First String Quartet, a rather craggy work, and *The Soundless Song*, an experimental score. I had a few letters of support from my friends. My only important endorser was Jarnach. Henry Moe, the secretary of the Guggenheim Foundation, acknowledged receipt of my application. Then there was a long silence, but we waited, and our funds shrank all too rapidly. A cablegram arrived: APPLICATION DENIED. HENRY ALLEN MOE. This meant immediate packing and booking passage if we were to have even one hundred dollars left on arrival in New York. Our goodbyes were fast but hearty; everybody said it was too bad; given more time, Ethel Codd Luening would have been engaged by a German opera house. Nobody said much about my own possible contributions to the German musical scene, and my outlook was more sober than it had been. I was anxious to get back to America, where I was sure great opportunities were now awaiting me.

Chapter 14

Interlude: Barnstorming in New York

1929-1930

WE ARRIVED IN NEW YORK IN the middle of April 1929. By then I knew that my request for leave of absence from the Eastman School had been tactfully turned into a severance by Howard Hanson. My first move was to pay a call on the Guggenheim Foundation. I asked Henry Allen Moe why the foundation had kept me dangling in Cologne until the very last minute and explained that we had used up all our money there and were now stranded in New York. Dr. Moe didn't bat an eye. "You were in the running until the very last minute, and your fate was decided by the flip of a coin. Put your application in again, and we'll see what happens." After a few pleasantries I parted from Dr. Moe. He later became a lifelong friend.

Ethel was in fine voice and was more immediately "marketable" than I. We had a hundred dollars in our pockets, so action was essential. She auditioned for the Judson Radio Corporation. The Columbia Broadcasting System was just starting, and William S. Paley's career was beginning to blossom. Ethel was booked on many commercial hours. She was highly regarded— she was a quick study and a first-rate musician. She became leading soprano with CBS at an annual salary of $5,000.

The main CBS conductor was Howard Barlow, a very nice man, an early-music major at Columbia University whose charm unfortunately did not reach to the tip of his baton. His performances were somewhat wooden and stodgy, but he was routined, and that was enough. Eugene Ormandy did opera hours on which

Ethel sang. He had been a violinist in the Capitol Theatre orchestra and came from Hungary. It didn't take a prophet to predict a brilliant career for him; his orchestral sound was transparent, his tempi very spirited, and the balances excellent. He looked thin and hungry. The other conductor was André Kostelanetz, who handled the light opera programs with finesse and style.

The conductors, Arthur Judson, and even Paley liked to play bridge, and Ethel and I were both invited to join them. But we didn't play; nor did we buy any stock in Columbia Broadcasting. It has dawned upon me recently that this was probably a mistake.

Ethel auditioned for the National Music League and they booked her—at first with their own accompanist. In May, however, the Yiddish Cooperative Heim Gesellschaft engaged me as accompanist for Ethel and for a Polish violin virtuoso, Erno Neufeld.

Neufeld was a gimlet-eyed and by no means dreamy virtuoso. For him an accompanist was a shadow man whose job it was to rapidly absorb lightning flashes from the head of the virtuoso. We rehearsed *Frasquita* by Lehár-Kreisler. Fortunately, I remembered the Lehár style from conducting in Zurich—but Kreisler . . . ! Neufeld played a *rubato* on every note; on half-notes he sometimes had two *rubati*.

Once, after I had chased him around as he flitted from phrase to phrase, he said, "Very good for opening, but now I will play it free and with *rubato*. Make subjective connection and accompany with your feelings."

"What about the notes?"

"Naturally," he said, not appreciating my wit.

We skated around *Frasquita* for fifteen minutes.

"You have talent for music, but lack certain experience. We will now play *Zéphir*, by Hubay."

No matter how the tempo was marked, Neufeld played fast. If the composer wanted an even, slow passage, Neufeld would hold the first note too long and then play the others fast. He had a lovely tone. I finally realized that I was accompanying a Hungarian gypsy. I forgot everything I knew and just let the gypsy in me loose.

Neufeld's piercing glance relaxed into a grin. "You play with me some more—I make a real good musician out of you. Now we play *Faust* Fantasy, by Wieniawski."

Here Neufeld, no longer constrained by my lack of subjective response, really let himself go. I lost him after the first half-page but I caught him on page two; we were together for about a page and then he began sprinting and I got winded. Pretending to find a misprint, I quit and rested for a while. Soon we were back at it and plowed through the fantasy. Neufeld said I could do it beautifully, but I must take it home and practice until it was perfect.

At the door of the studio he looked at me approvingly. "You have Hungarian or gypsy background? Or Jewish maybe?"

I said no, but I considered the question a compliment. I practiced the *Faust* Fantasy for hours. I haven't heard it since, but I know it was very difficult for me then. My method was to first practice it slow, with the right tempi, then slow with the wrong tempi. Then fast with the right tempi and fast with the wrong tempi; and then to top it off by playing the piece as fast and as soft as possible from beginning to end.

At our next rehearsal, he tore into the fantasy with even more abandon than he had shown the last time, and his tempi were all different, very subjective. I had become a good musical cowboy and this bronco couldn't throw me. When we finished, Neufeld, removing the sweat from his brow with a blotter, said, "You are very virtuoso accompanist. Will you come with me on tour? I will guarantee fifty dollars a week for two months, all expenses."

I said I would think it over.

I did. I stayed home.

THERE WEREN'T any openings for conductors. Looking for some free publicity, I wrote a letter to the *Musical Courier*, suggesting a series of solo concerts by orchestra-less conductors, which I thought would represent an immense saving. I still think it's a good idea. In the real concert world Ethel and I were soon booked on the Barbizon Plaza intimate recital series with Salvi, the harpist. For Ethel's last group she did *Frühlingstimmen* by Johann Strauss. Following the coaching by Neufeld, I gave a real

Viennese gypsy twist to the accompaniment, while Ethel did her usual magnificent singing. The house went wild.

Ethel was getting a bit nervous. She was doing most of the work. There wasn't much for me, and I was getting discouraged. I composed songs that Ethel sang, some piano pieces, and a *Fantasia for Organ,* which was performed and recorded forty years later, and *Fantasia Brevis for Clarinet and Piano,* which was played a few times in the next decade.

We lived in a one-room studio apartment, vintage about 1910. It seemed as though the studio was at one and the same time bedroom, bathroom, kitchen, vestibule, and music room, although it probably wasn't that bad. But the piano was a poor-sounding upright. Here on 91st Street, I waited for what Broadway called "the breaks."

✎

ONE DAY the phone rang.

"Here is Kiesewetter. Would you be free to conduct an opera hour on station WOR a week from Monday?" I pointed out that I had a very heavy schedule, but I might be able to work it in if the singers were good enough. "We use only singers from the American Opera Company, vocally coached by me. Come to my studio in an hour and we'll fix the program."

I made rapid telephone inquiries and learned that Kiesewetter was a prominent and excellent vocal coach.

At his studio he greeted me effusively, and suddenly from behind the sofa Mary Silveira, Brownie Peebles, and Lucian Ruttman—all from the old Rochester Opera Company—appeared, yelling, "Surprise!"

Kiesewetter took out his pencil, "Now let's make the program. It will be an hour's radio program on WOR. What would you like as an opener?"

I suggested the Overture to *The Marriage of Figaro.*

"Excellent," said Kiesewetter.

Silveira piped up, "Could I do 'Voi che sapete' from *Figaro*?"

"Sure, that will be lovely." Kiesewetter jotted it down. "But then what?"

"We need some dance music. I'll conduct Mottl's arrangement of the ballet suite from Gluck's *Iphigenia in Aulis.*"

Peebles moved in. "But I have nothing to sing."

"How about a duet with Mary?"

I thought fast. "I have it. Lady Harriet and Nancy's duet from Flotow's *Martha.*"

By this time the tenor was definitely grouchy. "Do I just turn pages on this program?"

"For you I have something special," said Kiesewetter, scratching his head with his pencil. "Flower Song from *Carmen.*" Ruttman beamed. "And it must be followed by something splendid. The Habañera, sung by Peebles, and Silveira doing Micaela's aria."

"And how do you plan to end the program, Maestro?"

"After Bizet, let's have some Rimsky-Korsakov. I'll do a suite from *Le Coq d'or.*"

"Bravo," said Kiesewetter, and he produced a chop-suey stick. "This is the rehearsal stick of Anton Seidl. He gave it to me and I'm giving it to you for good luck. Now let's rehearse."

I went to the piano and tore into the operas, and the singers sang their hearts out. It was a lovely rehearsal.

THE CONCERT took place on the following Monday. The orchestra, hardbitten Local 802 boys, were managed and generally kept in line by their regular conductor, George Shackley.

Shackley looked like an ex-pugilist who had gone into management. He greeted me with the tired, hardened pessimism of a Broadway regular. "Nice to see ya. I hope you know what you're getting into."

He introduced me to the boys, known as the Bamberger Little Symphony. The lads looked dubious, the way orchestra players generally look when confronted with a new conductor. Fortunately, I not only knew the programmed works backwards, but also forwards.

I slammed into rehearsal, bawled the guys out after the first measure for being too slow, snapped into a tempo that really made them exercise their fingers, shouted out a few wrong notes on the way, and after we finished the overture, commented that if things didn't go better from now on, we would need overtime. This shook up Shackley, but the boys played better.

The broadcast was a fantastic success. There was fan mail from all over the place. The radio column in the *World-Telegram* reported that it was the best program given on WOR in the last two years. Shackley called me the morning after the review. "We want you to do a series of opera, light opera, and symphony programs over WOR. The boys like you."

I began doing two shows a week. We did a lot of old light-opera favorites. For the symphony program I did Weber's *Frei-schütz* Overture, short works by Grétry and Beethoven, the *Nut-cracker* Suite by Tchaikovsky, Schubert's *Unfinished* Symphony, three pieces by MacDowell, and the *Children's Corner* Suite by Debussy—the last in a very fine arrangement by a French orchestrator. I closed with the *Marche hongroise* by Berlioz.

The response was good, and Shackley soon called me from his office. "We want you as regular conductor at WOR. Three programs a week, $5,000 a year guarantee. Any commercial programs are paid extra. Come around next Monday at six o'clock."

I arrived on the minute. Shackley wasn't there.

The doorman said to come back on Wednesday. I returned on Wednesday, but the door was locked. A sign on the office door read: BACK ON THURSDAY. On Thursday, no Shackley, but a note saying they had made other arrangements.

I met the drummer on Broadway. He said, "What the hell happened to you? We've been waiting for you to come back."

"I don't know. Do you?"

"No. Everything went very well. The men liked you and Shackley liked you. Crazy world. Don't take any wooden nickels. See you around."

Then Kiesewetter called. "McKosker, who owns the station, is a great friend of Philip James and gave him the job. The broadcasts were a great success; don't worry, you'll find something else. That's life on Broadway."

James was a good conductor and stayed at WOR for seven years, followed by Alfred Wallenstein, who did outstanding symphony and opera programs on WOR for many years. I guess Kiesewetter and I laid the foundation for something good. James and Wallenstein later became two of my best friends.

THE MAJOR EVENT of that year was when the Pro Musica selected my ten songs for soprano to be done at Carnegie Recital Hall on a program that included *Suite for Piano* by Ruth Crawford, *Pentagram Suite for Two Pianos* by Dane Rudhyar, *Study in Sonority for Ten Violins* by Riegger, and a string quartet by Adolph Weiss. It was a musicians' program and a musicians' audience, and my songs were well received. They were later performed a number of times, and four of them were published.

For a time, I functioned as corresponding secretary for the Pro Musica Society. It sounded and seemed like a great honor, but I was actually the booking agent in a concert bureau. Pro Musica had some dozen chapters around the country. It brought distinguished European musicians to this country by guaranteeing them a series of engagements at small fees, paid by the various chapters. Ten engagements at $300 each was sufficient inducement to bring Schoenberg, Ravel, Prokofiev, Tansman, Bartók, and others to the United States. I booked the tours for Prokofiev and Tansman.

Prokofiev's Town Hall recital was a great success, and I had a fine time talking with him. He was an enormous, husky, blond, blue-eyed, outgoing Russian, and that's how his music sounded: very healthy. He treated me like a long-lost brother, and made detailed promises about how we would get together on his way back from his tour, but I never saw him again.

ETHEL HAD to do a lot of rehearsing, but I had much time on my hands. My sister Helene and I and sometimes Ethel and her sister, Margaret, attended most of the concerts of the New York Philharmonic Society during the 1929–1930 season.

A power struggle was going on between the two first-rate conductors, who were of different schools. Mengelberg carried on the German tradition as I knew it from Strauss and Walter. Toscanini's career began in the opera house. His programs in the late twenties were somewhat limited in scope. In 1920, when I was in Zurich, Toscanini was known primarily as a very fine opera conductor at La Scala in Milan.

Neither of the conductors presented a repertory as catholic as the one the Tonhalle Orchestra played in Zurich from 1917 to 1920. As program-builders neither Toscanini nor Mengelberg could compare with Leopold Stokowski in Philadelphia, Frederick Stock in Chicago, or Koussevitsky in Boston. Stock had been representing all schools of contemporary music, including choral composers and American composers, for many years—a tradition established by Theodore Thomas in the nineteenth century. Stokowski did daring programs of works by Schoenberg, Berg, Varèse, and Ruggles long before these were fashionable. Stock, like Stokowski, would reprimand his audience if they were not attentive during the performance of a new work. Both conductors would sometimes repeat a work. Koussevitsky was a good friend of American composers and introduced many American works in Boston.

Eventually, the Philharmonic battle of orchestral styles reached the point where Mengelberg stated in an interview and before the orchestra that Toscanini had ruined the tone of the orchestra. Toscanini by then had won such an army of admirers and Mengelberg's objections seemed so prejudiced that the latter lost control over the orchestra and eventually his position as codirector.

❧❦

THOUGH I WAS not particularly inspired by the repertory of the Philharmonic, I was fascinated by the personality and development of Maestro Toscanini, the master conductor. He was a combination of Zeus, Verdi, my father, and an organ grinder. He looked like Mr. Italian Music Man. Legends had preceded him, many of them true. Some said he was so nearsighted that he couldn't use scores and had to memorize them. His assistant, Hans Lange, told me that the maestro learned a score by holding it two inches from his eyes and reading it through once, slowly and carefully. He slept about four hours a night. In the sleepless hours he studied scores. He told Lange that he was not interested in learning the contemporary music of the twenties. He had paid his debt, he maintained, by championing contemporary music when he was a young man; he mentioned his premieres of Puccini and his early performances of Stravinsky, Strauss, Elgar, and others. After hearing a work by Carl Ruggles he remarked that the hall should be fumigated.

On the podium his control was completely aural. He could hear almost anything that went on in the orchestra. His beats ranged from the stumpy to great dramatic circles that had an enormous swing to them. His movements were always meaningful to the players. He was obsessed with conveying the composer's message and impressing the orchestra with it. His dancelike sense of rhythm gave elasticity to even his heavier interpretations.

His hands were extremely flexible and very expressive. He sometimes used them as though he were playing on an instrument. A birdlike flutter of his left hand could be so delicate and expressive that the orchestra simply *had* to play *pianissimo*. On the whole, I think his spectacular effects were less the result of a virtuoso baton technique than of rigorous training of the orchestra. Even though he occasionally called the orchestra players cabbages, pigs, and idiots, they admired him and outdid themselves to meet his demands. He sang, bellowed, cursed, cajoled, and lost his temper, but he made the orchestra play.

The first concert I heard included an overture by Rossini (*L'Italiana in Algeri*) and *Il carnevale di Venezia* by Tomasini. These works, far removed from what I had learned to expect on symphony programs, were played with such brilliance and fire that it opened my ears to the possibilities of this kind of music on a symphony program, however strange it seemed. Brahms's Third Symphony was another revelation. From the third measure on, the counterrhythms were played with a precision new to my experience. He conducted the melodic lines with a very expressive lyric sweep. The total sound was one of a forward movement that I had not heard from German conductors. The typical Brahmsian harmonic figurations in the symphony were at times lyric and at times brilliant, but always very precise. The second movement was given a songlike reading that made the movement seem like a kind of symphonic aria. The Allegretto had a rather spooky, almost scherzolike quality; the last movement great breadth and vigor, again with special attention given to the counterrhythms and accents. Toscanini's tempi were faster than those usually heard. It didn't sound like the Brahms performances I had heard in Germany or played in myself. It was an exciting experience. His projection of the form of the work was lucid.

The heroism and passion in Wagner inspired him. He projected the Rhine Journey and Siegfried's Funeral March from *Götterdämmerung* so vividly that the entire drama of Wagner's scenes enchanted the audience. He read the scores meticulously but got the orchestra to play them with broad strokes, dramatic contrast, and with tempi that illuminated the real message of Wagner's music dramas.

After this concert, I fell completely under Toscanini's spell. I first heard him do Beethoven's *Eroica*, Seventh, and Second Symphonies, the *Leonore* Overture no. 3, and the *Coriolan* Overture. His tempi were very fast, but the structure was never muddled. The Beethoven of the Second, Fourth, Sixth, and Eighth Symphonies is more lyric and at times pastoral, but even these works were given a lyric-dramatic interpretation and never sounded pedantic or pallid.

Toscanini's performance of the *Coriolan* Overture was the most vivid of any I have ever experienced. He made the full drama come alive in Carnegie Hall. The power was projected by having the harmonies played at a very high dynamic level whenever a *forte* or *fortissimo* was called for, but within this amplitude rhythms and counterrhythms were all very carefully articulated. By contrast, the beautiful second subject was virtually sung by the performers. The singing quality in Beethoven's works was probably influenced by the coaching Beethoven did in opera houses and by his work with Salieri in vocal composition. This singing style was sympathetic to Toscanini.

Another great musical experience was Toscanini's performance of Haydn's symphonies in G Major (BH 13) and E-flat Major (BH 3). The German "Papa Haydn" tradition, complete with wig and ruffles, was thoroughly routed by Toscanini. I believe he had only recently discovered these works, and in his conducting of them he revealed Haydn's incredible sense and mastery of sound and orchestral colors. He brought out Haydn's genius for spare contrapuntal passages, and that he was indeed a precursor of Beethoven with much of the latter's power and perhaps an even greater differentiation of style from work to work. At these performances I learned that Haydn belongs to the small circle of composers who have penetrated the innermost secrets of music. Toscanini opened my ears to the superior, healthy, invigorating, old-new qualities of this grand composer.

His Mozart repertory for the season included the G Minor Symphony, the *Jupiter* Symphony, and the *Zauberflöte* Overture. He emphasized the Italian operatic influence in Mozart, something that I felt was missing in interpretations of some German conductors. Toscanini's tempi were very fast even in the slow movements, but the overall singing line was never lost. In the last movement of the *Jupiter* the interpretive qualities that I have described resulted in an extremely clear presentation of this fugal and highly contrapuntal work. For the first time I heard every single part all the way through the movement.

In program music like Respighi's *I Pini di Roma*, Strauss's symphonic poems, and Ravel's *Boléro* he made the descriptive program vivid but projected the structure simultaneously so that it enhanced the dramatic elements of the story. His performance of Berlioz's *Roméo et Juliette* was dramatic, but I found that it lacked the poetry that was in the Berlioz score. Some years later, I heard a performance by Alfred Wallenstein that was much more poetic. Wallenstein projected Shakespeare's thought more convincingly than Toscanini or any other conductor I have heard conduct this tonal drama.

I heard many performances by Toscanini, but gradually I slipped away from his spell. I had second thoughts about some of his contributions. That the maestro tuned up a generation of precision conductors can't be denied; but he was so autocratic and intolerant of any real rivals, many of whom he called clowns and cabbageheads, that he was at times hard to take. His extremely rapid pacing and occasional overdelineation of the musical content in scores gave to some works a heaviness and a power that they did not need. This applied mostly to his readings of Schubert, Schumann, some Mozart, some Brahms, and others. He did little for new music and he rarely played Americans. Until his retirement, his influence was very powerful, and many New York music lovers rated him as "the best conductor in the world." His interpretations, his tempi, his dynamics were the only models. This I found oppressive.

In spite of, or because of, his genius and quirks he was a

great freedom fighter. He refused to cooperate with the Fascists and had nothing to do with Mussolini, who put him under surveillance. He despised the Nazis and Hitler and would not conduct in Germany during that regime.

In his own way, too, he was also a supportive colleague. When eight years later Hans Lange and I gave the Philharmonic Symphony Chamber Orchestra concerts of neglected old and new works, he sent us his blessings for the concerts. A strange and wonderful man and one of the great ones.

BETWEEN THE eventful afternoons spent in the gallery of Carnegie Hall, I continued to look for a job. The best I could do was play my *Coal Scuttle Blues* at the New Year's Eve show at the Palace Theatre, dressed as a farmer. I was not reengaged.

One day, I chanced on Vladimir Rosing at the Hotel Woodward. We embraced. "How good to see you, Val!" I said.

"Feeling good," Rosing said, reaching into his pocket for a prune, his favorite health food. "Are you free?"

"Very much so," I admitted.

"For you I have a job. I am producing operetta. Beautiful masterpiece. *Three Little Girls* for J. J. Shubert, with cast from American Opera Company. I need music director. See Ma Simmons . . ."

Following Rosing's advice, I went to Ma Simmons's office for an interview. It was fairly warm but he wore a heavy coat with a fur collar. Simmons was known as the ex-accompanist of the great diva Nellie Melba. He was a superior musician and he now auditioned and hired singers and conductors for the Shubert theater chain.

Rosing had given me a big sendoff. Ma Simmons, suave and pleasant, said, "You have just returned from Cologne. How is Szenkar doing at the opera?"

I reported that he was doing very well.

"But his tempi are always a bit too slow," Simmons persisted.

"Which ones?" I asked.

"I see you have had a great deal of musical experience. Rosing wants you as music director." He took out a pack of Tareyton cigarettes. "Will you have one of these or do you prefer Turkish tobacco?"

I said I had found a special Persian blend in Cologne.

"Dear, dear. I forgot to get Persian cigarettes today, but may I offer you a liqueur? Cognac? Crème de menthe? Crème de cacao? Crème de chocolat? Or would you like to mix some of these?"

I declined.

"Rosing sings Moussorgsky songs beautifully." He sighed. "I suppose we have to talk about the material things. We can offer you two hundred a week."

I looked pained, got up, and took my hat. "I never discuss any salary under three hundred a week."

Taken aback but impressed, he hesitated a moment, and then said with a rather oily inflection, "I think we can meet that."

I was told later that I was the highest-paid conductor on Broadway at that time.

≥≤

I WENT to the Shubert Theatre to pick up the score and meet the cast. The principals were my old friends from the American Opera Company: Natalie Hall, Bettina Hall, Charles Hedley, and others. The twenty-four voices chosen for the chorus included many more from the American Opera Company. The show was a Viennese operetta with a libretto by H. Feiner and Hardt-Warden and music by Walter Kollo. The fine set of characters included such splendid names as Baron von Rankenau, Beate-Marie, Baron von Biebitz, Count von Rimbow, and other luminaries like Mrs. Munke, Otto Kunz (played by Harry Puck), von Hoffenstein, chamberlain to His Highness Prince Hochberg, Charlotte, forelady in a doll shop, and Little Hans.

The first scene was in the court theater in Vienna in 1846. There were seventeen different scenes, built on a new revolving stage. The production was very special and elaborate. The music had the lilt of a typical Viennese operetta in the tradition of those I had played and conducted in Zurich.

I heard bustling and mumbling as the door to the auditorium opened, and Ma Simmons deferentially guided a rather corpulent, cigar-smoking gent to the center aisle. With his hat on the back of his head, which was drawn into his coat, the newcomer resembled a turtle in its shell.

Ma Simmons called me over. "J. J., I want you to meet your music director, Otto Luening, just back from Europe. This is Mr. Shubert."

J. J. bit off a piece of his cigar and spit it out, looked me over, and said not a word as he headed for the middle of the theater and sat down. There were no scores. I asked Ma Simmons for some.

"You'll have to ask Mr. Shubert about that," he said.

I did, and J. J. growled, "Why don't they learn it by ear like everybody else on Broadway?"

I told him I had to have a score.

He called the house manager. "Why the hell haven't you given the leader here a score?"

The manager paled. "I have one here and I've had the text extracted for the singers."

"Well, give it to Mr. Blooming."

"The name is Luening."

"Okay, Mr. Booming, you can start with the rehearsal now."

"Thanks, Mr. Shaughbort."

J. J. looked to right and left and spit on the floor. "Well, what are we waiting for?"

Ma Simmons came over to me. "You mustn't be surprised, Mr. Luening. J. J. Shubert is in charge of the production and has to superintend all the shows that go on in the Shubert theaters. He is often a bit testy because he has three or four shows in rehearsal and an opening night or two to watch. There's a lot of money invested. Mr. Lee Shubert is the intellectual. He takes care of all the leases in the Shubert theaters and has his office upstairs, but he never comes out except to eat and sleep."

Rehearsals went on for six weeks. On March 22, J. J. appeared and bellowed, "Dress rehearsal tomorrow beginning at one at the Broad Street Theatre, Newark, New Jersey."

The next morning, on my way to the rehearsal, I discovered a letter in my mailbox from the Guggenheim Foundation, which said, "I have the honor to inform you that you have been awarded a Fellowship for the year 1930–31 to compose an opera, *Evange-*

line. The stipend will be $2,500." It was signed: "Henry Allen Moe, Secretary." With this in my pocket, I felt completely fortified and quite capable of facing anything, including J. J. Shubert.

I reached the theater an hour ahead of time, to find enormous confusion. Trucks with the scenery were arriving; the revolving stage was being unloaded; stagehands were fixing props; the cast was looking for their costumes and trying them on, yelling because they didn't fit, were torn, or had been lost; and the electricians had forgotten to connect the lights in the pit.

J. J. came forward and bellowed, "Get the rehearsal going. We're wasting money."

The people on stage tripped over each other as they found their places for the opening. The curtain was down and I played the overture. The curtain didn't rise, so I played it again.

J. J., not the most musical man in the world, came charging up to the stand. "Didn't you play that before?"

"Yah."

"Ya going to keep on playing it all night?"

"Until they get the curtain up."

"Oh, that." And off he went.

The show began. Everybody was so preoccupied with costumes and stage action that they forgot most of the music, and every number had to be repeated to get it straight. In one of the pauses J. J. bellowed, "Get more *pizzicato* out of the clarinets!"

"They can't play *pizzicato.*"

"What am I paying for? And get more horns in this number."

"There aren't any horns here."

"How do you know?"

"Because I'm a musician and, incidentally, you're not, and I wish you'd keep out of my business."

J. J. was thunderstruck. So were the cast and the orchestra. The concertmaster said, "Hold your temper." Hedley, the leading man, came over and whispered, "Have you gone nuts? He won't take that from you."

I whispered back, "I don't give a damn. I've just got a Guggenheim Fellowship for a year to compose my opera."

"What a break," said Hedley, and he passed the news on to the singers while the scenery was being repaired.

We opened the next night. The house was packed. The show went fairly well with the orchestra, but the revolving stage got stuck, so that scene changes didn't happen and actors sometimes had to sneak on from the wings. Sometimes the scene would change at the wrong spot and the actors would find themselves in a doll shop instead of a garden. But the singers were adroit and the chorus sang very well.

In the intermission Ma Simmons came around. "Some things are going very well; others, not so well," he said with artistic understanding.

"I'm so glad you came, Mr. Simmons," I said. "I'm leaving the show."

"What, what?" he said, losing his cool.

"Yes, I have just gotten a Guggenheim Fellowship for a year to write an opera."

Simmons recovered his poise. "The creative world may suit your temperament better. Not as glamorous, of course, as the theater, but rewarding, so I was always told by my friend L. Campbell-Tipton. You know him, of course."

"No, what did he do?"

"He was a very famous composer. Such is the fate of creators. . . . Soon forgotten. You won't leave at once, will you? We need to break in another man."

"The fellowship was announced in the *New York Times* this morning, and I want to get to work immediately."

"We'll have a man in tomorrow night to watch the show while you conduct, and he can take over the day after."

The orchestra had eavesdropped on this conversation. The trombone player sidled over. "Do you think the Guggenheim might have an opening for me? I'd like to get into high school applied music teaching. I don't like this racket."

My replacement arrived the next night and watched the show attentively. As I said goodbye to the cast and the orchestra, J. J. came stamping into the tuning room. "I hear ya got a big break as a writer." He looked sad. "Too bad. I kinda liked rassling with you about the music. Good luck."

I put my chopstick baton in my pocket and made the long trip home. Another facet of my career had ended.

Chapter 15

How to Make an American Opera
1930-1932

VLADIMIR ROSING HAD ASKED ME IF I would compose an opera for
the American Opera Company for the 1931 season. I found this
an excellent suggestion because of my operatic apprenticeship in
Zurich, Chicago, and with the company at the Eastman School.

Most previous American operas had failed because of bad
libretti, and singing foreign operas in English had been only partially successful because of poor translations. I decided that for
my own opera I needed a foolproof story. I looked for one that
was well known to every American schoolchild, that would make
it possible for me to use folk music, that could be done effectively
with a medium-sized orchestra, and that posed a minimum of
stage problems.

When I came upon *Evangeline*, I knew I had found my story.
Longfellow's dactylic hexameters, however, were not suitable for
my purposes, so I wrote my own libretto.

Longfellow's narrative poem was based on the expulsion
of the Acadians from Nova Scotia by the English. It describes
events that actually took place in Nova Scotia, Louisiana, and
Philadelphia. My story required ten scenes. These scenes were to
contrast strongly musically and visually. The music was planned
to avoid the Wagnerian through-composed style and leitmotiv
routine. The stage scenes were planned to project the story in its
most simple outlines.

The story is about rural, religious, hard-working peasants
who were forcibly displaced and deported. Their farms were lev-
eled because of governmental conflicts between England and
France, the decisions having been made thousands of miles from

Nova Scotia. The libretto describes the fate of the individuals affected by these decisions. It centers around Evangeline and Gabriel, who vow eternal love for each other on the evening before their wedding day and the day of deportation. The ensuing scenes show their search for each other after they are deported and separated, a search that eventually becomes an obsession tinged with fantasy. In the last scene, many years later, they finally meet, just before he dies.

I found that original documents, folk songs, dances, and other music existed in various libraries and depositories. I decided to let these sources help tell the story. It would be a kind of documentary opera. In the first two acts I used translations of the texts of the Canticles that the Acadians sang at the deportation and the Catholic "Ave Maris Stella" in Latin.

In the romantic scenes, the language is colorful and ecstatic, making the final vow of eternal love in Act I convincing enough to bind Evangeline and Gabriel together spiritually.

After the deportation, the group of Acadians around Evangeline and another group around Gabriel penetrate deeper and deeper into the romantic scenery of the Bayou Teche in Louisiana. In their obsession the protagonists' language becomes moonstruck and erotic, as they begin to despair of ever consummating a physical reunion. I planned more and more dreamlike stage pictures, up to the very last scene in a Quaker almshouse in Philadelphia. This realistic stage picture of a hospital room was to be lightened only by the sound of the offstage singing of "Oh Rose So Softly Blooming" in the Swedish church next to the hospital. The meeting of the two protagonists was expressed completely in pantomime.

Formally, the work was like a suite and avoided symphonic developments. There were numerous set pieces. Melodic recitatives, less musically defined than the set pieces, were used to bring these into focus and to accelerate the story. I conceived the work as a singers' opera, with the orchestra supporting and underlying but never overwhelming the voices. Full orchestral color was reserved for the choral sections and interludes. The solo passages were supported by a chamber orchestra, and the sound became almost like chamber music at times.

In contrast to most classical and nineteenth-century orchestral practice, the strings were not the orchestra's main body. I often used winds, percussion, or harp to provide the main color. Even when the strings did become the main body, there was a great deal of punctuating by the other sections. I planned very careful use of registers so that the instruments would be out of the singers' and each other's way. It was to be orchestration by resonance rather than orchestration by doubling. Each instrument and section was meant to have its own identity. My admiration for Mozart's *Figaro* made me want clarity in the sound, and Verdi's *Falstaff* inspired me to make plain, direct orchestral statements.

I did not want a fast operatic pace but rather wished to create a sense of animation and forward movement even in the short phrases and sections by having contrasts in the orchestral sound patterns. On the surface, this might seem somewhat like some of Debussy's instrumental practices. The difference was that I wanted small sections to blossom into much larger ones that were often apparently conventional melodic and rhythmic statements, individual because they were colored by Acadian folk tunes.

I had very definite ideas about how to stage *Evangeline*. I remembered how Martha Graham had coached the opera singers at Eastman in movement on the stage. Rosing himself was preoccupied with this and he called it rhythmic movement; the movement was either closely allied with the musical score or in countermovement to it. Both of these great artists were definitive and continuing influences on what I thought was needed to loosen up stilted operatic acting. Because of the historical quality of my opera, the directness of the characters, and the authenticity of the dramatic conflicts, I wanted the singing actors' movements to be nonoperatic and nontheatrical, but expressive and dignified projections of their emotional tensions.

Since I had already spent eight years in Europe, I asked the Guggenheim Foundation to bend their rules a little bit and allow me, while composing *Evangeline*, to retrace the wanderings of the Acadians in Nova Scotia and Louisiana. The foundation granted my request and I became the first Fellow to do his creative work on this continent.

≥⁄≤

GRAND PRÉ, Nova Scotia, was my first stop. The scenery and climate were as I had imagined them. The tides, coming from the
Bay of Fundy, were spectacular. A boat docked at high tide would
seem to be stuck fast in a muddy village street at low tide. Cape
Blomidon was beautiful and the little replica of an Acadian room
at the memorial site seemed authentic. The only problem was
that there were no Acadian descendants. They had not returned
after the deportation but had settled elsewhere in Nova Scotia
and various parts of the United States.

But there was something strange and invigorating about living right on the spot where the events of the opera-to-be had
taken place. Ethel and I walked around the village and looked at
the Memorial Church, then went up into the woods and along the
Gaspereau River, sometimes for ten miles, retracing the steps of
the Acadians and imagining how things looked before the modern
world had intruded. The still visible traces of salt marshes, the
purple hills, and the ridges of black, rich soil must have drawn
the early settlers to this spot and tempted them to fish, hunt, and
attempt to develop farms against all odds. There were still a
number of fine orchards to be seen. Beautiful French willows
made the landscape of meadow, marsh, forest, green slopes, orchards, and mountains soft, often hazy. But when the tides
came in, sometimes at an elevation of twenty-seven feet, it all
seemed rather formidable, and was especially breathtaking when
the northern lights flashed white, green, yellow, and pink over
the whole horizon.

Our living quarters were in Wolfville. The University of Aca-
dia loaned me a piano and we rented a small house next to a
cheerful brook, surrounded by wildflowers and completely furnished, with an old kitchen range and accessories.

I composed three pages every day and Ethel sang them. I
had such a clear picture of what I wanted that I hardly ever used
the piano. The opera progressed steadily until one morning on
my way down to the piano, the entire living room ceiling fell
down. I took it as an omen to move on. Our landlady tried to hold
us to our lease, ceiling or no.

As a very clever diplomatic gesture, Ethel and I decided to

take the landlady's grown son, Carl, out for a picnic and some rowing on a nearby lake. Carl began bracing himself with Canadian Club at 8:30 in the morning and when we had rowed to the center of the lake at 12:30, he decided that he wanted to take a swim. He was so tight that he could hardly stand. We tried to restrain him, but in he jumped and stayed under much too long. Finally the top of his head appeared, and we maneuvered the boat into position. Just as he was about to sink forever into the slime of Nova Scotia, we hauled him into the boat by some great feat of strength. His mother released us from our contract and even baked us a cake.

Before we left Wolfville, a great Acadian reunion took place, with delegations from other parts of Nova Scotia, Maine, and Louisiana. Singing, dancing, and general festivities brought life to the Memorial Church. An Acadian historian, Leander d'Entrement, a baron who alleged that he was a direct descendant of the Bourbons and who looked the part, suggested that we visit Digby and the Pubnicos.

A letter came from Rosing urging me to work faster. He was raising a huge guarantee fund for his next season and *Evangeline* was to be the novelty. My former patroness, Mrs. Edith Rockefeller McCormick, pledged $60,000 for the Chicago season, and Speaker of the House Nicholas Longworth was honorary president of the opera company.

We traveled—courtesy of the Canadian National Railroad—to the Pubnicos, where, we learned, Acadians still worked as farmers and lobster fishermen. The Pubnicos were tiny settlements about fifty miles south of Yarmouth, and were known quite plainly as Pubnico, East Pubnico, West Pubnico, Center East Pubnico, and Center West Pubnico. They were populated for the most part by four families—the D'Entrements, Amiraults, Le Blancs, and Landrys. The place in Center East Pubnico where we stayed was appropriately called the Evangeline Inn. It was run by the Amirault daughters. The baron's home, with a monument to the D'Entrements in the yard (raised by public subscription), was next to the inn.

The food was strange but good. Acadian rappi pie, a kind of a rabbit's soup with dumplings, was excellent. We were served coots every now and then—a duck that tasted like fish, probably from paddling around in salt water. Blueberry bogs covered the slopes and we had berries three times a day. The real treat was when some of our friends who were lobster fishermen brought in their catch several times a week. We were also served Acadian chicken stew with dumplings. The desserts often consisted of some very good wild berries that I had never tasted before.

Our room was tiny, but the inn furnished a good upright piano that had landed there somehow. There was no electric light, and we found the kerosene lamplight much softer. Toilet facilities were primitive, and out of doors.

Soon real Acadian descendants began arriving one by one, then two by two, and finally in droves, when they heard that a man was writing an opera about them. They all spoke eighteenth-century French, slightly tarnished, of course, because they had been exposed to mixtures of Indian, English, and Latin that had colored some of their phrases. Some of the women still had authentic costumes, and there was a living handicrafts tradition. We were able to take pictures and talk to many old people, listen to songs in the particular versions of this district, and to pass some time each evening listening to the stories they had heard from their grandparents. In their homes we still saw beautiful spinning wheels and old tools in their sheds. We bought some of their blankets and shawls to take back to New York and perhaps use in the opera.

Room and board cost us three dollars a day. The people were devout, straightforward, hardworking, and very pleasant to be with. Their tragic history had become for them a living memory, and they had a dignified image of themselves. I soon belonged, because I was writing their history.

Slowly it dawned on me that the Acadians were a civilization within a civilization. Physically, they resembled peasants and fishermen from Normandy and Brittany, but from years long past. Some looked like retainers from Louis XIV's court, some like characters out of Balzac's novels. They were small, dark, and volatile. Their songs were poetic and poignant, the French originals having been altered by church and Indian musical influences.

Every Saturday evening, people would come from miles around by horse and buggy, on horseback, by jalopy, or by boat, and I would play for them what I had written during the week. They remembered many of the song and dance tunes that I had incorporated into my score, and the event was more like a church service than an audition. Ethel sang everything beautifully, and I did what I could at the small piano. I had been sufficiently influenced by the Acadian songs and dances, the landscape, and the people, to produce a contemporary work that was completely convincing to these simple farmers and fishermen whose ancesters came to life in it. The experience was unique and I have had nothing like it happen to me since.

It took me about six months to finish the libretto and compose the first two acts in a short score. These acts and the last scene contained much choral singing, sometimes in eight parts, so I envisioned a choral group of at least forty voices. The opera was originally conceived for a medium-sized stage, so I wrote for an orchestra of about fifty that could be expanded or reduced by adjusting the number of strings.

Rosing was terribly anxious to hear the work and begged me to come to New York immediately. We left hurriedly, and when we arrived we had an audition for him and George Houston, the leading baritone.

Thomas Whitney Surette and Henry Allen Moe of the Guggenheim heard the first two acts and were enthusiastic about them, but two months later the splendid American Opera Company folded, a victim of the Depression. The canceled production did not inspire me to finish the work. Only a long rest and much self-discipline got me started on Act III.

☄

I HAD LEARNED in Nova Scotia that villages in Louisiana, like St. Martinsville, New Iberia, and Lafayette, were originally settled by the deported Acadians, where they are now known as "Cajuns." I went to St. Martinsville for several months to work on Act III.

The bard of the Evangeline story in that village was André Olivier. He ran the general store and had established a little museum with Evangeline memorabilia. He knew every episode of the Louisiana version of that saga and a few that never happened. In his version, Evangeline went mad under an oak tree that still stood right in front of his store. He said that on moonlit nights she could be seen wandering about looking for Gabriel. He hinted, but as a good Catholic could not openly confess, that he was the reincarnation of Gabriel.

The Cajuns in St. Martinsville were just as friendly as the Acadians in the Pubnicos had been, but they were much more prosperous. The village looked like a stage set. Between the drugstore, the Catholic church surrounded by palmetto trees, the red-brick schoolhouse, and the general store, there was a delightful little opera house. Here, from 1791 until the Civil War and even later, companies from New Orleans performed French operas in an attempt to keep the French tradition alive in America.

There were also some magnificent plantation manor houses. In the moonlight the Spanish moss covering the large oak trees looked like huge spiderwebs. Willows dipped down to the Bayou Teche. It was a strange new world for me. Handicrafts were not in evidence and I found no folk songs. A partial Americanization process was already taking place, but it hadn't got very far. Many blacks lived in the neighborhood, and I often heard magnificent singing coming from the outskirts of the village.

I lived in a tiny cold room in a boarding house, without a piano. A black woman appeared every morning at seven, lit a small fire, and fixed a pot of bitter brew called Creole coffee, which I was supposed to drink for my health, a harrowing experience for anyone coming out of a dead sleep. The food was so terrible that within three weeks I had lost both my appetite and most of my hair.

Miss Bernard, the public health nurse, was my guide and took me with her into the backwoods by car and on foot on her health rounds. Here, one saw an unbelievably primitive way of living. In one family there were eight children, all sick. The mother was bedridden, probably with tuberculosis; the father had syphilis. He kept the family alive by catching catfish.

One day Wade Martin, the sheriff (who later became governor), took Miss Bernard and me far down the Bayou Teche in his launch. Civilization slowly disappeared. This Louisiana no-man's-land worked on my imagination, and I was able to envision Act III; I heard music in my mind clearly enough to finish a few scenes.

I was introduced to and made an honorary member of the Poor Boys Club. This group centered in the parish and consisted of a Catholic priest or two and a number of Cajun descendants of my opera characters. At our Sunday evening parties, we played cards and cooked wonderful bouillabaisse. Then, before the fireplace, we would drink bourbon and they would tell fantastic tales about the backwoods.

With all the storytelling, discomfort, unreality, and beauty in St. Martinsville, I felt a somber reminder of what was going on in the rest of the country every night at ten-thirty when the Southern Pacific express train stopped at New Iberia. I would watch it pull in and marvel that in only a few minutes, hundreds of men, sometimes as many as four hundred, would emerge from the rods and the insides of boxcars for a breather in the railroad yard. They were Depression hoboes who rode the rails from coast to coast looking for work. Sometimes one or two of them would find something to do, but more often they were driven off the railroad yards by railroad police and out of the small towns by the sheriff, or put in jail for a while and run out later.

ETHEL HAD been on a concert tour in the Northwest and on the Pacific Coast. She stopped off at St. Martinsville for a few days and we then returned to Wisconsin for a rest.

A letter from the Canadian Pacific Railway came, offering Ethel, a native Canadian, a number of radio engagements in Toronto. They also wanted her to sing at Banff and Lake Louise in the Canadian Rockies. J. Murray Gibbon, the publicity director, later became interested in *Evangeline* because of the Nova Scotia scenes. The Canadian railroads were colonizers and really went all out for anything that called attention to their beautiful country, so Mr. Gibbon offered me a cabin near a camp on Castle Mountain in the Canadian Rockies and promised that the Canadian Pacific Railway would haul up a piano from Calgary if I would accompany one concert at Lake Louise. Ethel could join me on the mountain when she was not singing. This sounded idyllic, and after I got used to it, it was just that.

The exposure to Canadian outdoor life had a strange effect on my composing. As I became physically stronger and more active, I began eating enormous portions of food and drinking cases of

Bass ale. My composing began to dry up. The three pages a day I wrote when I was with my Acadian friends had now simmered down to one. Sometimes I wrote nothing for several days. The worst thing about it was that I began having secret doubts about the value of anything as esoteric as an opera. Everybody on Castle Mountain got along perfectly well without any music at all, and nobody was in the least interested in hearing me play either piano or flute. I offered them baroque and classical music and even suggested some folk songs, but the guests merely looked surprised. Of course, when we went to the hotels in Banff and Lake Louise for concerts, or when Ethel sang with the Heather Light Opera Company, we were back in a civilization where music belonged.

When I was on Castle Mountain, the grandeur of the scenery and the proximity of birds, animals, rivers, creeks, insects, and trees made me feel very much as I often had as a boy on the farm in Wauwatosa. Music in Canada seemed identified with the sound of wind in trees, birdsongs, thunderstorms, and waterfalls. Oddly enough, the opening up of this new sound horizon stayed with me for almost twenty years. Then, with the advent of *musique concrète*, tape music, and electronic sound manipulation, it became possible to make the sounds of nature part of the musical vocabulary. It was Messiaen, possibly the greatest influence on the artistic careers of composers who matured after 1950, who said that birdsong was a genuine source for music.

After two months of this Rocky Mountain interlude, Ethel and I rode in our Canadian Pacific Railway drawing room to Vancouver and then took a boat to Victoria, where we gave a very successful concert.

ETHEL LEFT for a concert tour down the Pacific Coast and I rented a marvelous if primitive cottage about thirty miles outside of Victoria in Deep Cove and stayed there all winter. It was a lonesome place. There were no neighbors and I had to walk a couple of miles for supplies. I set up a card table near the kitchen range. There I composed for about three hours a day, using the piano sparingly because of the cold. At night I would put heated rocks in my bed to get the dampness out and warm the sheets. I split logs for firewood and did my own housework and cooking. This meant that I lived mostly on *pot au feu* that I left to simmer on the back of the stove and warmed up for three or four days in succession. This fine food made me physically stronger than I had ever been.

After a rather steep and rocky climb down a bluff, some steps led to a beautiful beach where there were hundreds of screaming seagulls. It was a wild and lonesome beauty that I responded to. I had time to meditate about the relationship to nature of human and particularly cultural activities in our own or any other time. In the United States we were trying to harness nature or to supplant it with little consideration for the consequences. Exploiting nature for material comforts, we had not been alert to the artist's world. In Canada, with its thinner population, nature was an elemental force not to be denied. It was a strengthening experience for me to live in this environment. Taking care of myself even in a modest way helped me to regain an independence that had been mine in my youth. But I was terribly lonesome and had to once again find the artistic part of my own nature.

I felt again, as I did in the Canadian Rockies, that going through the headache of writing and later producing an opera was a strange way for a man on this continent to spend part of his life. I think these experiences prepared me in such a way that I had a real feeling and understanding for the youth subculture that began emerging in the sixties. The young generation then was making a valiant attempt to shed the things that they considered "irrelevant"—a word that I began to dislike enormously, but understood very well. But I was confined by my cultural inheritance and there was then no shortcut open for me to escape my destiny, nor is there now.

I learned to simulate the seagulls' call and they would fly around in enormous flocks squawking back at me. But with all my musings and conversations with them, I couldn't produce more than a page of piano score per day, and some days wrote even less.

I was happy when Ethel returned from her tour. The islanders had learned that we were around and requested a concert. The community center and concert hall was in the middle of some woods. A piano came from Victoria and the event was advertised in various island newspapers. An audience from nowhere and everywhere filled the house. We performed old and new music, including an aria from *Evangeline* and works by Wallingford Riegger and Henry Cowell. The admission charge was one dollar and we cleared about a hundred and fifty dollars, enough to pay the rent and pot au feu expenses for three months!

I finally finished the last scene of the opera, and we returned to New York with six hundred pages of short score and scenic and orchestral sketches in a briefcase that never left my hands.

The Guggenheim people, Henry Allen Moe and Thomas Whitney Surette, heard the finished work and were most encouraging, but the Depression was in full swing. The general mood in New York was ominous and rather frightening, and it didn't take me long to realize that the chances for a production were mighty slim. We had returned to civilization.

⋙⋘

SOME PEOPLE in New York seemed to think that the opera was pretty hot property and tried to produce it. One manager offered to book *Evangeline* on tour if he were advanced $250 and if we could get ready in two weeks. In the second paragraph of his letter he said that actually he needed to try it out first in Nova Scotia, thus upping the advance to $500. In the third paragraph of his letter, he had us booked in Nova Scotia, New Brunswick, Bar Harbor, Boston, Newport, other Atlantic Coast cities, and in towns in the Berkshires and the Adirondacks. At the end of the letter he thought he would need an additional $500 advance for bad-weather insurance, which made a grand total of $1,250.

A week later, he sent another letter asking for $2,750. Leopold Stokowski was interested in the opera but could not do it that year. I corresponded with the Canadian Pacific Railway's publicity agent about sponsoring a festival performance in Grand Pré with special trains and other splashy promotion. The agent later wrote that the railway had so few passengers that they were canceling trains. Even the Metropolitan Opera was mildly interested, but, like Stokowski, suggested the following year. The

Dominion Atlantic Railway in Halifax thought the opera would attract Acadian descendants from Louisiana, New England, Quebec, and New Brunswick, but they wanted to produce with only three people—Ethel as Evangeline, a tenor as Gabriel, and myself as pianist and narrator. We eventually gave up for a while.

Chapter 16

Frontier Music:
A University in Arizona
1932–1934

LIFE IN NEW YORK WAS UNBEARABLE, and we were on our way to financial disaster. I tried borrowing money from George Houston, but he wrote that he was stranded in St. Louis and couldn't pay his hotel bill. He then asked *me* for a loan, for he could not afford regular meals. Eugene Goossens was guest-conducting the NBC Orchestra and I approached him at a rehearsal. After a handshake he explained how busy he was and moved at a fast pace toward the exit. I trotted after him but he disappeared.

American composers, all of whom were in a rather weak position professionally, were at that time under attack. An interview with Arthur Judson, the manager of the New York Philharmonic and Columbia Artists Bureau, in *Musical Courier* was headlined: "Half-Baked United States Composers Menace Music; Orchestra Patronage Killed by High-Pressure of Some Americans, Asserts Manager; Upholds Eager Search of Toscanini and Stokowski for Scores." Stokowski did search, but Toscanini did little for American music.

I had only one encouraging letter—from Filomusi in Brussels. It was addressed to Sir Otto Luening, asking to see my *Trio for Violin, Cello and Piano.*

Ethel's sister Margaret lived with us, and from a meager scholarship she paid her part of the rent. I arranged trios for two sopranos and flute and we auditioned at NBC where Vice-President Lord gave us an A-1 rating. We asked why he didn't engage us, and he answered mournfully that even if we were the greatest artists in the world there were no jobs.

The streets were full of panhandlers and apple and match vendors. At Times Square it was not unusual to be stopped three or four times in five minutes by beggars who wanted a dime for a cup of coffee. The frightening Bonus March on Washington was underway, in which twenty thousand veterans of World War I organized and marched to support Senator Patman's bill for a bonus. Their camps in Washington were primitive and the city feared an epidemic. When the Senate defeated the bill, the veterans refused to return to their homes. President Hoover ordered Douglas MacArthur to use the U.S. Army to evict them, forcibly if necessary. MacArthur set the camps on fire and the army drove the veterans from the city. This tragedy excited the public and there was talk of a revolution.

I composed very little in that year. *The Dawn*, a song for soprano and piano for which I wrote the text, is rather revealing:

> *Oh the dawn is rising,*
> *Waking in my heart*
> *Though love and I did part*
> *Long ago—La, la, la, la, la.*
> *Oh the dawn is breaking*
> *Carried on the song of a lark.*
> *Oh the light is rising high*
> *Warming my heart*
> *Though love and I did part*
> *Long ago—La, la, la, la, la.*
> *Oh the dawn is breaking*
> *Carried by the song in my heart.*

This was dedicated to Ethel, who sang it beautifully; in the middle of a miserable period it feebly expressed my hopes for a better time.

On a lovely day in midtown Manhattan, I reached into my pocket for food money and subway fare and found my last dime. As I looked at it I remembered that for three years I had been offered an assistant professorship at the University of Arizona in Tucson. I didn't even know where Tucson was and called it

"Tuckson" and of course had turned down this insignificant offer, but as I contemplated the dime, the job seemed very good indeed. I phoned a collect wire to my Aunt Gretchen in Milwaukee: TEMPORARILY EMBARRASSED FINANCIALLY STOP GOLDEN OPPORTUNITY IN THE WEST TO REACH EVEN HIGHER PLATEAU OF MY ART STOP NEED TO BORROW $500 IMMEDIATELY TO TIDE ME OVER STOP LOVE AND KISSES STOP. I walked to our room on 91st Street. Bless Aunt Gretchen's memory, the money came next day. I had had enough of New York and decided to accept the offer from Arizona. I explained to Ethel that I hoped we would never again live through a time when she had no heart for singing and I couldn't compose. The Arizona job would help me to pay debts, meet current expenses, help support my parents and Ethel's foster mother (this was before social security), and pursue production possibilities for *Evangeline*. From Tucson Ethel could arrange tours in California, the Northwest, and Canada, until life became more stable in the East. Ethel was shocked at the thought of leaving the city of her greatest success. She sobbed uncontrollably. She looked terrible hurt. She sat silent for a moment, then wiped away her tears and announced to me in her melodious and lovely voice, "I'll put away my hopes and store them in the closet of my memories."

ETHEL PACKED our meager belongings, mostly scores, manuscripts, and books, and my flute, while I went to Philadelphia for an interview with President Homer Leroy Shantz of the University of Arizona. He offered me an appointment as assistant professor at a salary of $3,350.

My face must have fallen.

"Something wrong?"

"Can't you sweeten it up a bit, President Shantz?"

He did some mental arithmetic and then purred, "Let's make it thutty-five hundred."

I wrote my acceptance to the dean of the School of Music. On the Fourth of July, I had a letter from him explaining that $3,325 would be their top offer and that President Shantz reserved the right to reduce the salary at any time during the year.

We sent our trunks by slow freight and took a bus to St. Louis. There we changed to a parlor car of the Southern Pacific

Railroad, so as to arrive in Tucson in style. There was nobody at the station; the temperature was 110°, and nobody cared about style or anything else. We booked into the Santa Rita Hotel, a famous building that burned to the ground in the forties. It may have been imitation architecture, but to us it looked like a genuine late-eighteenth-century Spanish inn. Our room was large and hot, with an airplane propeller fan on the ceiling. A bellboy arrived with a huge bucket of ice. We collapsed on our beds and waited for evening to cool us off.

The desk clerk told us that the population of Tucson was about fourty-four thousand, half of it Mexican and Indian. The state had been admitted to the Union twenty years before. The university was a land-grant college, founded in 1891. We went for our walk. We were on the frontier!

The stark and beautiful mountains were like an opera set and seemed unreal. The palmettos, cacti, orange and peach trees, and oleander bushes exuded a sweet perfume that hung over the city. Many of the men walking around town wore cowboy outfits with high-heeled boots. The women wore light print dresses and sometimes Indian shawls or scarves. Most of the houses in the poorer sections of town were adobe. In the more affluent Mexican sections the houses were Spanish in architecture with balconies and beautiful yards where exotic trees, plants, and fruit grew in profusion, helped by private irrigation systems.

⊰⊱

I CALLED ON President Shantz next morning to pay my respects and find living quarters. He phoned a Mr. Haley, who offered to rent us an adobe house on the outskirts of the desert. We were shocked at the thought but found the house had a fair-sized living room, a bedroom, a studio, a kitchen, a bath, and a garden with oleander bushes, peach and apricot trees, and a hedge that looked like imitation fir trees.

"Fifty dollars a month unfurnished. You can buy your furniture and a grand piano at Steinfeldt's on the installment plan."

I hesitated. Mr. Haley asked me if I were a choral conductor. I said I could conduct anything.

Haley looked pleased. "I head the music committee of the

Second Methodist Church. We need a choral director. The job pays forty-eight dollars a month. Are you interested?"

"Could you round that out to fifty dollars? It will save book-keeping."

"You're hired."

I made one condition. "As soon as any member of the chorus begins telling me how to conduct, I will resign."

That was fine with Haley, and he was pleased that his rent was secure. I was pleased that I could pay it and this is how I began my career as a Methodist church choir leader and professor in Tucson.

I called on the dean. Walking through the campus I noticed rows of palm trees, cacti, scraggly grass, and sandy soil. The university architecture was eclectic; there were some attractive buildings from the nineties and some modern ones made of high-school red brick, not very attractive or useful but in 1932 "modern." The music building was old and its rows of studios, offices, and practice rooms generated a tremendous din and a lot of hot air from 8:00 A.M. to 11:00 P.M. There was no soundproofing or air conditioning. The dean's office was a model for any musicologist. Upon entering one saw a bookshelf with *Grove's Dictionary of Music and Musicians*, Will Durant's *History of Civilization*, the Bible, Percey Goetchius's *Harmony and Counterpoint*, *How to Orchestrate for the Movies* by Dr. William Axt, and the *Readers' Digest Greatest Quotations from the Greatest Literature, The Heart of an Anthology*. The dean told me he had been a captain in the Air Force. The strong lenses in his spectacles gave his blue eyes a gimletlike glint.

As we conferred, he furrowed his brow as though in deep thought but showed his humanity by releasing a chuckle about every half-minute. "Let's get down to business. I want you to reorganize the entire theory and composition department. How will you begin?"

"I'll examine all of the students in the School of Music."

"But many of them have passed their courses."

"We will call it an orientation examination."

"Good, good, good. I want you to come to the Rotary Club for lunch."

At the Rotary a rousing version of some of the finest Rotary songs soared to the rafters with the dean leading, his loud tenor voice slightly off-key. After we had wolfed our shrimp cocktails with tomato sauce and chicken with peas and mashed potatoes, the chairman announced, "During dessert, Professor Jones of the university will give us his famous lecture on snakes."

The professor carried a burlap bag to the platform. "Snakes like the desert (and I don't mean dessert, yuk, yuk) because it's warm. They are particularly fond of the Tucson desert because when it's too warm they can escape to the mountains, hide under ledges, or even lean against a sagebrush." He polished his glasses.

The dean whispered, "Just wait."

Professor Jones cleared his throat. "Snakes, like people, enjoy mating, but their litters are larger. It is said that a human being renews his skin once every seven years, but the rattler's skin falls off every year. At that time he is blind. Don't irritate him or bump into him intentionally or unintentionally or he will strike back. At other times he will probably not bother you unless you step on him. As an example . . ."

He opened the bag, sized up the situation, took careful aim, poked his arm in with a rapid motion much like snake striking, and pulled out a four-foot rattler. It was at that precise moment that I could not swallow a sour apple in my apple pie.

"This snake is only four feet long; some are eight feet, but rattlers aren't the worst ones. It's the coral snake that bears watching." He peered into the bag and it moved a little. He jerked his head back, then with a deft motion pulled out a little coral snake. "Very deadly. The only good thing about him is that his mouth is so small he can't sink his fangs. Of course, children and old people with loose skin had better watch out."

He produced other samples including a five-foot-long pilot rattler: "Nonpoisonous, perfectly harmless, catches flies and mosquitos, a nice housepet." He gave a short academic laugh, put the snakes back, tied up his sack, looked at his watch, and left, amid rapturous applause.

Next day, I began examinations. After reading them, I came to the sad conclusion that with the exception of three students everybody would have to review the elements of music. Most could not notate even simple music. The majority had good ears but they were untrained and most of them knew little about the standard music literature.

Now that I was a professor, I felt impelled to find interesting and useful textbooks for the students and make course outlines that would fit their situation and give them a broader cultural background. For ear training, sight singing, and harmony I used the George Wedge books that were standard texts at the Juilliard School in New York. This American pedant, cataloguer, and theorist never let the art of music interfere with his theories. His textbooks taught students how to meet state requirements for public school teaching. Everything else about his theories students would have to modify later. But the Wedge books were quite useful in establishing a basis for simple improvisation and keyboard harmony. I selected textbooks by authors from different countries so that students would get some idea of other musical cultures. For counterpoint I used Salomon Jadassohn's text. This nineteenth-century theorist, who also composed, had at one time been a piano student of Franz Liszt and had taught my father and influenced Busoni, who had recommended Jadassohn's texts. *Musical Forms* by Ernst Pauer (1826–1905) was a remarkable little volume packed with important information. This Austrian performer-composer-musicologist had studied piano with Mozart's son, Wolfgang Amadeus, and studied theory with Simon Sechter, with whom Franz Schubert had planned to study and who became the teacher of Anton Bruckner. Pauer, after a brilliant career as composer and performer, settled in London as lecturer, musicologist, editor, and critic. Definitions in his book were concise, informative, and attractively written and gave insight into the classical and romantic repertory. For music history I chose *A History of Music* by Paul Landormy, a Parisian who had studied philosophy, was trained as a singer, and became a composer, a music historian, and a critic; he organized a series of lectures on music with Romain Rolland and also founded and directed an acoustic laboratory in Paris. Hugo Riemann's *History of Music in Examples* was a fine collection of illustrations of baroque and Renaissance music that I played for the students.

MY OLD FRIEND Rollin Pease, from Chicago, professor of voice, one day offered to take Ethel and me on a drive in the desert. The idea was exciting.

His battered Ford went over the washboard roads at break-neck speed. "Better fast . . . you just skim over the top," he yelled as we hit a rock and almost ran into a giant cactus.

We crossed sand-filled gulleys, which he referred to as dry rivers, and he stepped on the gas. The wheels spun in the sand. The car crawled out, speeded ahead, hit another "dry river," and puffed to the other side.

"What's a dry river?"

"A river that has no water in it."

"Never any water?"

"Plenty of water in the spring when it comes down from the mountains." He came to a sudden stop. There was a foot-long lizard crossing the road. "Gila monster . . . not poisonous but so filthy that if he bites you you get an infection."

"What's the difference?"

"That's an academic question." He polished his thick-lensed glasses. "Don't see so good, so I drive with my brakes. Hang on tight." He pulled out a peanut bar which he passed around while he drove with one hand. Then, "Been in the academic racket long?"

"I was at Eastman at the University of Rochester for three years. . . . Let's see . . . oh, yes, did I say the University of Rochester?"

"Yes, you did say University of Rochester. . . . Mind if I give you a piece of advice?"

"Not at all."

"As soon as you get a university job, look for another one."

"Always?"

"Yep. Let's go," and he backed into and around cacti as he maneuvered for the return journey. Down went his foot on the accelerator. My teeth clattered as he hit rocks. "Dry river," he said.

PRESIDENT AND Mrs. Shantz held a reception at their home for the new faculty to meet the old faculty, the townspeople, the deans, two state senators, and the governor.

When it was my turn to be introduced to the governor, President Shantz modulated his voice to a soft but mellow, even buttery, purr. "Governor Hunt, I would like to present our new assistant professor of music. You pronounce his name as though it were spelled L-o-o-n-i-n-g. He is a splendid conductor, a brilliant musical theoretician, plays the organ, and is a fine flutist."

The governor said, "What? What was that you said?"

President Shantz again recited my credentials: ". . . and he also is a very fine flutist."

"Well," said the governor, "if he's such a helluva flutist, what's he doing in Arizona?"

⊱⊰

WE COULDN'T afford a car, so I walked the half-mile stretch to the university several times a day. Desert life was so strange that it was like a dream. Some cacti were fifty or sixty feet high—fantastic forms, like the Krazy Kat cartoons by John T. McCutcheon in the *Chicago Tribune*. Lively, friendly lizards ran around, and scorpions worked in the desert and sometimes turned up in the cuffs of my trousers.

The professors at the University of Arizona were underpaid, but they were devoted to teaching. As half the copper in the United States was produced in Arizona, the university's Department of Mines was important. The engineering faculty and students were a self-contained group—tough and efficient, and in direct contact with the great mining interests that paid most of the taxes in Arizona and were the main patrons of the university.

Professor Carpenter had charge of the Observatory, and let me peer through the enormous telescope. Stars in the clear southern air seemed to hang mysteriously low in the sky. Along with the poems of Stefan George and novels of Jules Verne, this stargazing influenced my composing and opened my imagination to a world of incredible new vistas and possibilities. I composed three short piano pieces, one called *Stars*, which Madame Eleanor Altman played at the university. Years later I composed two electronic works (for flute and tape music), *Fantasy in Space* and *Moonflight*, both slightly moonstruck.

Dr. Cummings and Professor Douglas of the Department of Archeology told us about the prehistoric origins of the Indians and showed us the Painted Desert with its many-colored layers of sediment that looked like huge colored sandboxes or crumpled crayon collections. They also showed us ancient Indian ruins, elaborate cliff dwellings, and the remains of pit dwellings. Professor Douglas pinpointed archeological dates by counting rings on tree stumps. The strange landscape, the interesting faculty—quite different from my Eastern friends—and the Indian sagas influenced my imaginative world more than music did. My composing dried up for a while.

Madame Altman, a student of Sigismond Stojowski and of Paderewski, was a first-rate teacher and a first-rate concert pianist who had come to Arizona for her health. Her recitals were built around the great nineteenth-century piano literature by Liszt, Chopin, Brahms, and Schubert; and included Beethoven, Bach, Busoni, and some Szymanowski. Her students revered her for her devotion to art, culture, and education as a part of daily life.

In the Tucson primary and secondary schools, Mr. Schultz taught his students vocal and instrumental music. One of them, Robert McBride, played clarinet brilliantly, later oboe and English horn, all instruments of the saxophone family, flute, French horn, trombone, and double bass. He was a fine pianist, a good organist, and an accomplished singer. I immediately appointed him my assistant.

My friend Rollin Pease had sung oratorios and song recitals in the Midwest for decades. I liked best the group of American songs that was inevitably last in his recitals. These ranged from *Do Not Go, My Love* by Hageman to *On the Road to Mandalay* by Oley Speaks, *Danny Deever* by Walter Damrosch, *Aurora Borealis* by Henry Hadley, and *By the Waters of Minnetonka* by Thurlow Lieurance. Professor Pease could create a glee club in half a semester, make a bus tour of Arizona for two weeks, bring everyone home safe and sound along with $500 in admissions money for the scholarship fund, and sing the *Messiah* the next night. A strong man, his family were ardent churchgoers. Whatever happened, they believed, had been ordained by fate, God, nature, or the Methodist Church. No matter how bad things were, no one in the Pease family ever complained.

In addition to McBride, I engaged Henry Johnson as an assistant. At his high school in Tombstone, Arizona, he had been given a fine all-around musical education. He was a very good violinist and violist, moved around on the French horn, trumpet, clarinet, bassoon, and a few other instruments. He was an excellent singer and won the Atwater Kent West Coast radio contest in 1933.

MOST OF THE students were musically inclined, intellectually curious, and enthusiastic. Some came from small Mormon settlements; some had German, Irish, or Italian ancestors who had come to Arizona as pioneers or for their health. A few students showed discernible strains of Spanish, Mexican, and Indian heritage. I soon discovered that Arizonians had a background of their own, a civilization that had grown from the frontier background, and I tried to get my students to affirm and develop it.

In early March 1933 we presented a student recital of original compositions performed, coached, and conducted by students. I helped only when absolutely necessary. The program included *Catullus 101* for chorus and string quartet by Betty Bandel; settings of Housman and Shelley by David Murdock; *Serenade and Sad Lullaby* for string quartet and *Breakdown Scherzo* for piano, both by Merle Kartchner; *Introspection and Study* for oboe and piano by Robert McBride; and shorter piano pieces. The hall was full and the entire program was a success. The students were so encouraged that they composed and prepared another program in three weeks. The packed house was again enthusiastic, and until I left Tucson there were programs of original student works about every six weeks, for large and enthusiastic audiences.

My teaching method was to confer with the students and find their strong points, then to get them interested in the art of music and the repertory. I then explained the necessity of steady practice to become competent and fluent in any field. The results were remarkable! Robert McBride, for example, was soon writing orchestra pieces that were later played by the Boston Symphony and recorded by RCA Victor. He subsequently had a brilliant career as a composer in the fields of both commercial and concert music. Henry Johnson became a first-rate conductor, music director of the Tucson Symphony Orchestra, conductor of the Providence, Rhode Island, Symphony, the Buffalo Symphony, and the Albany Concert Orchestra in WPA days, and led an army band in the Second World War. He returned to the university at Tucson as professor and brilliant conductor of the university orchestra.

Betty Bandel not only composed and played trumpet but was a serious student of English literature. While professor of English literature at the University of Vermont, she did interesting research on early American fuguing tunes. Merle Kartchner was the daughter of a Mormon cowboy and country fiddler from Snowflake, Arizona. She played hundreds of piano pieces, mostly folksongs, by ear. Her improvisations were exceptional. I encouraged her to accept her background and work with the music that grew out of it. She composed with skill and taste and soon earned a local reputation. Her methods for teaching elements of music to children were later widely used in the West.

Ted De Grazia was perhaps the most interesting of my students. He was a music major, but his real love was painting. I bought his first two *Imaginary Portraits* for three dollars and gave him my Swiss mountain boots. After managing a movie theater and trying various other enterprises he became a well-known professional painter and arts craftsman. His reproductions for UNICEF cards, his designs for prints, and his original paintings found a market. With the help of Indians, he built a mission in the mountains and an arts and crafts center. (In 1977, I read that to keep his wife from paying an exorbitant inheritance tax De Grazia had burned a million dollars' worth of his paintings.)

David Murdock was my first composition major and a very talented pianist. He was in Africa in World War II and wrote one of the World War II army songs, "Stella, the Belle of Fedela," that was sung by all of the ranks in North Africa and Italy. He had just been promoted to second lieutenant when he was killed, age twenty-seven.

⧓

MY DUTIES at the First Methodist Episcopal Church gave me new musical experiences and some new friends. The composers whose works had inspired the congregation in the past were Bendels-Stanley, J. Barnby, George Waring, Stebbins, Ryley, Faderlein, Voris, and others now forgotten. I strengthened this repertory by introducing Bruno Huhn, Tchaikovsky, Negro spirituals, and M. Enrico Bossi. The success of these daring composers gave me courage to move further afield by doing sacred works by Dudley Buck, Anton Rubinstein, Wagner, Donizetti, Harry Rowe Shelley, and Gounod.

In time, the congregation became so entranced with my conducting in a flowing robe that they insisted I conduct *them* when they sang hymns. For the congregation of some six hundred I whooped up the tempi a bit and the hymn singing became very spirited. The pastor, Dr. Montague, stopped me after a hymn. "I can't keep up with you around the curves," he panted. The good doctor got even with me in his sermons by describing in detail some of the personal habits of the Devil. He often wound up his descriptions with, "Sometimes I think I see him around me," and extended his arm, a finger pointed in my direction. I thought this was not sporting of him, because I couldn't respond except by speeding up the next hymn even more.

I finally taught the choir a program of Schubert, Beethoven, Haydn, Mozart, and Bruckner. The wife of the choir representative said I should stop performing all that modern stuff and do some old favorites by Barnby, Bendels-Stanley, Stebbins, and Ryley. I resigned immediately. My student Henry Johnson became my successor and brought the choir to new heights. My last service was attended by the bishop himself, and it was a gala affair.

To CELEBRATE his appointment, Henry Johnson drove us into the mountains to cool off after the service. From a clearing we saw below us what seemed to be a canyon with tents and people next to a stream bed, a thin thread of water flowing through it.

"What is this?" I asked.

"That's White River Canyon, and those are placer miners."

"Natives?"

"On the contrary. These are doctors, lawyers, businessmen, and their wives and families. They've all been washed up by the Depression and displaced. Some are hoboes. All of them mine fifty cents' or a dollar's worth of gold a day—enough to buy flour, bacon, dried beef, potatoes, and other staples. They grow a few vegetables, pick the edible cactus berries, and hunt rabbits and occasionally deer, I believe."

"Do they come to town?"

"Just to cash in. They have actually given up and are waiting for the world to stop spinning so that they can get on again."

I found it rather melancholy. It reminded me of the hoboes I had seen in Louisiana and brought home the fact that a depression not only depresses, but displaces and uproots people. I began to wonder if the heat and the strange surroundings would eventually get to Ethel and me, and whether we too might just dig for gold and forget about our previous life.

By the time we drove home, a rare desert storm had begun to swirl, and we locked ourselves in our house and forgot about all our troubles. There were ominous rumblings. Huge frightening bolts of lightning flashed over the purple and pink and blue sky, with the moon showing from time to time. The wind was very strong, and a heavy rainfall came with a downpour of huge drops. Whirlpools of sand came in through our windows and screen door, and got into our hair, our eyes, and the milk we were drinking. Our electricity failed. We used flashlights and saw centipedes crawling up our walls. We got one with a flyswatter. The house was stifling and scary, but everything stopped as quickly as it had begun; the moon came out and the usual inertia seemed to settle over the desert. We forgot all of our problems for a while, but we soon knew definitely that we would have to take some firm steps if we ever wanted to leave. The next day was hotter than ever. I think the desert frightened Ethel because it was so implacable.

≫≪

ETHEL HAD no teaching duties, so she set up an office in the house and, with her manager Ramona Little in Los Angeles, booked tours. She began studying Sophie in *Der Rosenkavalier* and Eva in *Die Meistersinger* in German, Gilda in *Rigoletto* in Italian, and Marguerite in Gounod's *Faust* in French. I coached all of these, for we were determined that she would go on with her career. She also practiced piano diligently and learned the accompaniments for the voice and flute numbers that we performed. We received a letter from the Columbia Broadcasting System in New York offering Ethel a job as soprano, and a letter from a choral society in White Plains, offering me a job as conductor. It was all too late and too little. We lacked money to go East and realized we would have to work our way back. It was cheery news when the American Opera Company in Chicago engaged us, for fifty dollars, to do excerpts from *Evangeline* on December 29, as a memorial to Edith Rockefeller McCormick, who had died that year. We had to bum a ride but the affair went well. Frederick Stock and his wife came, and Mrs. Freer, the president, awarded me the David Bispham Medal for American opera. One reviewer wrote: "His opera is a highly beautiful and significant piece of work." We tried to book other dates in Chicago but our joint fee of forty-five dollars was too high.

The National Federation of Music Clubs wanted to sponsor a production of *Evangeline* at the World's Fair in Chicago. They would do it in Soldier's Field on a huge scale. Frederick Stock backed this idea, but it collapsed. However, the Enchanted Island Children's Theater at the World's Fair wanted to engage us to do sixteen shows a day—admission ten cents. I asked for expenses, but learned that the Enchanted Island Theater had gone under.

A letter from my father, disapproving strongly of all outside concerts, accused me of undermining my job. I explained that the only way to solidify my job was to take Rollin Pease's advice and look for another one. But in Tucson we also learned to our dismay that the state warrants with which we had been paid were no longer being honored by the banks. We had almost no cash and there was nothing in our checking or savings accounts.

Ernst Bacon had arranged a concert at the Pacific Musical Society for January 12, 1933, in San Francisco. We made a little money and Ethel sang the Queen of the Night aria, some of *Rosenkavalier,* and an aria from Charpentier's *Louise* for Alfred Hertz and Molinari (who were most complimentary and made promises, though nothing developed). Ethel's brother, Frank, and his wife, Simone, were stranded in San Francisco, victims of the Depression. They had been living in a cellar; their clothes were shabby and they were undernourished. Luck changed when Frank appeared on the "Shell Hour" with Captain Dobie, was an instant hit, had four hundred fan letters in a few days, was billed as a star, and from then on was paid the princely sum of one

body, some country, or some army general, and they all laughed, a little too heartily, I thought.

Ethel and I were left out of the conversation. But while dessert was being served, Frau Major Solf asked rather fiercely, "And how do you like Germany now?"

I explained that we hadn't seen much of it. Then we escaped. I bought Hitler's *Mein Kampf* and some other National Socialist literature and spent the evening doing my homework.

When we met Dr. Reger the next morning, I had a vague idea how the political winds were blowing. Herr Langeheine told us about tickets.

"You can hear operas by Mozart and Wagner. Wagner is, of course, much better, but you can get tickets for either or both composers. Libretti and piano scores are at Otto Hallbreiter. Any questions?" We asked about box-office procedures. "Go to the Staatsoper at nine this evening and get a number. When it is called, report, and get your ticket order. Have your money and your passport in hand. They won't change more than five marks. Ask for a receipt, and leave your name and address. More questions?"

Silence. Langeheine clicked his heels, raised his hand, barked *"Heil Hitler!"* and did an about-face and left. Dr. Reger lingered.

"Are you related to Max Reger, the composer?" I asked.

"He was my uncle."

"I heard him play and conduct; I know his music well and have played some of it."

His melancholy face lit up. "He was and is Germany's finest composer. May I invite you for coffee?"

"Delighted."

Ethel went to the pension to vocalize. The students took off to practice the Nazis' Strength Through Joy—or Joy Through Strength? We arranged opera study for the morning and attendance at all evening performances.

Dr. Reger took me to the Regina Palast Café, where we had coffee and cognac. He asked me if I had been exposed to National Socialism. I told him about Frau Major Solf and that I had read *Mein Kampf* and other Nazi literature.

"Well . . . may I tell you what the end result of your research will be? You will discover that we are going to be embroiled in another war. It will be terrible. Europe will be destroyed and Germany will be in the middle of it all."

I was surprised to hear this said, in view of the prosperity on the streets and in shop windows. "Can't something be done to put on the brakes?"

"No, this is our destiny, and nothing can be done about it."

"But your partner Langeheine and Frau Major Solf tell me that the National Socialists will soon control everything everywhere, and life will be beautifully regulated."

"*Ach,* these two-hundred-percent Nazis. What do they know about life and death? I am talking about destiny, not about the party or Hitler. They, too, are subject to larger forces that cannot be controlled. I will do what I can to help you while you are here, because you know my uncle's music and you are a composer. I have direct access to the Berlin Nazi headquarters and will get you special permissions. Would you and your students like to visit a labor camp?"

I accepted the invitation.

FOR OUR morning opera studies we looked at scores and libretti, and I played excerpts at the piano. The students were excited because each performance was a "first" for them. The Wagner performances in the Prinzregenten Theater included *Der Fliegende Holländer, Tannhäuser, Lohengrin, Tristan und Isolde, Die Meistersinger,* and *Die Walküre.* Karl Boehm was chief conductor, very solid in those days, but less artistic than he became later. The Mozart performances took place in the Residenz Theater and were in the best Munich tradition. After my nineteen-year absence from Munich, my reactions to some of the performances startled me.

The Venusberg ladies in the *Tannhäuser* ballet were of heroic build. The stage was small, and they made seductive movements to lure Tannhäuser from the straight-and-narrow path, but they sometimes grazed each other as they bumped and ground their way through the dance. I was reminded of the waitresses at the Hofbräuhaus who balanced six steins without spilling a drop as they walked through the crowds. And our hero

Tannhäuser was a throaty, slow-moving, rotund, German tenor whose name escapes me. Just why Venus and the girls could be so excited by this dope was hard to understand—as the students pointed out. I explained that Wagner's work was symbolic and nothing was to be taken literally.

But *Tristan* was another blooper; Petzold, the tenor, was a very good musician without much voice, so he became a "psychological" actor, undoubtedly inspiring the stage director, who—like Karajan at a much later date—decided to light the opera in various shades of black. With a sunken orchestra pit, the results sounded as though the singers were cheering each other up by singing in the dark. Petzold's voice had a. slight bathroom echo, and I had to produce a hell of a lot of symbols to explain things satisfactorily for the students.

Die Meistersinger (a rather long national anthem) had been adopted by Hitler. The cast, orchestra, and conductor made this work into a virtuoso declaration of independence for Germany, for all time. The performance was first-rate. The chorus sang ecstatically, as if they were at a victory rally in wartime, and the audience was absolutely hypnotized. At the end, the audience, fortified by ample food and drink at the intermission, rose to the occasion with applause so enthusiastic and long that there were twenty-two curtain calls.

The Mozart repertory included *Die Zauberflöte*, *Die Gärtnerinn aus Liebe* (*La finta giardiniera*), and *Don Giovanni*. With the exception of *Die Zauberflöte*, with its complicated Masonic symbolism, the libretti were direct and did not have to be explained to the students.

DR. REGER took us to the labor camp near Dachau. It was like the Civilian Conservation Corps in the Great Depression, except that the Nazis wore brown uniforms and acted like soldiers. We next visited the Braune Haus, an overpowering building flying many Nazi flags. The rushing brown-shirters and SS men with their stuffed brown suitcases made every move look like important business. Dr. Reger asked what else we would like to see, and I suggested the Dachau concentration camp. "That will be difficult to arrange," he said. "I must get permission from Berlin. Only a few reporters are allowed to visit, and it will take at least

ten days for an answer. Can you wait that long?" I suggested that
he try.

ETHEL AND I noticed that wherever we went we met someone
from Frau Major Solf's pension. Even at the zoo, two of our pension mates kept an eye on us from bicycles. This endless shadow-
ing began to make us very nervous. In a café a man opened a
conversation in much-too-perfect pseudo-Oxford English and
asked what we thought of the Nazis. I gave relevant answers and
countered with naive and embarrassing questions: was Alfred
Rosenberg, who was trying to purify the German race, perhaps
himself Jewish? The conversation rapidly shifted to artistic matters, but we soon left the café.

We took the students to Tegernsee and Egern where I had
attended the peasant school. We walked from the railroad station
to the inn on Neureuth mountain. During our midday meal I
asked, in my rusty Bavarian dialect, a peasant who was enjoying
his beer and claimed to be from Egern if he had gone to school
there and if he remembered a fellow who was called "Amerika
Sepperl."

"You mean Der Otti?" he said.

I told him I was Otti. There was a lot of Bavarian cussing and
clinking of beer mugs. He wanted to talk to me, without the
students. He told me the Nazis were terrible, that the peasants
hated that kind of regimentation and regularly sabotaged crops or
slowed up trains and damaged tracks. I asked if it worked.

He said, "Until we get caught; then we are shipped off to
Dachau. But there are a whole lot up here in the mountains who
are just as independent as they ever were."

These Bavarian peasants and many people in Munich were
devout Catholics. Cardinal Faulhaber consistently took a strong
stand against the Nazi excesses, though some Catholics joined the
party. In Egern I was told that my former violin teacher and her
brother had moved to Munich. It was rumored that his job was to
sterilize the people who were unfit to perpetuate the pure Nazi
race.

IN MUNICH, I visited my old tutor, Dr. Loewe, who still lived at
35 Tengstrasse. As he received me, he put his hand to his lips,

signaled for me to lower my voice, and led me onto the balcony.

"I think we can speak safely here, if we don't raise our voices," he whispered. He was still teaching, though he said that it was difficult because everyone was constantly being watched—in school, in the district, on the block—and that there was a Nazi watching the house at that very moment. His apartment was bugged. He whispered, "But if you are very careful, you can in school still express your ideals so that the right people understand them, and the others are not too antagonistic."

I asked about Frau Loewe.

"It was too much for her . . . eventually she gave up her resistance and died."

As I left, he looked old and sad. After World War II, I tried to find him again but uncovered no trace of him. He was a great and brave teacher and I cherish his memory.

My other teacher and friend, Philipp Jarnach, lived in Polling, near Munich. After meeting us at the station he suggested a walk through the fields. He stopped in the center of some pastureland.

"Now we can talk, but look around! We're not near a tree, are we?"

He told me teaching at the conservatory in Cologne was difficult, but not impossible. A Nazi student had confronted him in class with, "You always talk about Mozart, but Max Reger was *ein grösserer* composer, and he's German, not Austrian." Jarnach answered, "Quite possibly true, depending on what you mean when you say great." The fellow looked puzzled, but backed off.

I invited Jarnach to come to the United States and stay with us at Bennington until he found a position. He explained that his wife and son were German citizens and it would be too much of an adjustment to move to the United States. I ventured to say that I thought he would have to do some adjusting here in Europe. He looked at me thoughtfully for several minutes, then said, "Well, let's walk."

When I saw him after World War II he told me that after Cologne had been bombed five hundred times, he too was drafted to dig trenches to hold back the American army. As he took out his first shovelful of dirt he remembered what I had said nine years before about the adjustment he would have to make in

Europe. As he told about this his laugh suggested his sweet-sour memory of what might have been. He did not visit America until twenty-five years later.

WHEN WE were about to leave for a ten-day stay in Salzburg, Frau Major Solf bade us farewell: "Goodbye, Herr Professor, and the next time you visit you will see what the Nazi party has done for Germany and for the world. I hope you have a good trip. *Heil Hitler!*"

When we met Dr. Reger at the station, he told us that Berlin had denied our request to visit Dachau. Then he asked me if we had any cash. I explained that we had about ten thousand marks for expenses in Salzburg.

"It is against the law to take more than ten marks per person out of Germany," he said solemnly.

"Thanks for telling me. We will peel off what we may take and deposit the rest in the Deutsche Bank."

"It is against the law for foreigners to open bank accounts in Germany."

"Very fine regulations, for everyone except foreigners who bring in money. Now what?"

Dr. Reger looked sad and shrugged. "It will be a terrible war and Europe will be destroyed."

"Dr. Reger, I will give you our ten thousand marks and collect the cash when we return. You are the official Nazi liaison officer for the DAAS for our group. We will hold you personally responsible."

He winced, then mumbled that he would do it. Jane went to the ladies' room to unpin the ten thousand marks to leave with him. The station dispatcher hollered, *"Einsteingen!"*—"All aboard!" The students galloped onto the train, and we were on our way to Salzburg.

LIFE IN Salzburg was more relaxed. Dr. Schunter was now preoccupied with a group stranded in warring Spain, but he wired us board, room, and ticket money promptly. We saw *Jedermann*, by Hugo von Hofmannsthal, in a simple production with local talent; it was quite moving. The other memorable event was Gluck's *Orfeo und Euridice* at the Festspielhaus. The Vienna Philharmonic and the chorus of the Vienna State Opera under Bruno Walter performed the music with a marvelous orchestral and vocal tone; the ballet from the Staatsoper was beautifully trained. Orpheus was sung by Kirstin Thorborg and Eurydice by Jarmila Novatná, who sang and acted convincingly. Walter paced the opera perfectly, something that is essential in Gluck's works, for when the tempi are too fast the music seems unemotional and when they are too slow the music is dull and monotonous. Walter's balances and pacing created an unforgettable performance.

When we returned to Munich, Dr. Reger was at the station. He proudly handed me our 10,000 marks. Within the week the members of the group dispersed, most of them leaving for individual vacation trips in Europe. Ethel and I headed for Bremerhaven and the S.S. *Europa*.

On board ship, Ethel and I tried to quiet our somewhat jangled nerves. I was shakier than Ethel, because I had remembered the old Germany. On August 20 a cablegram from Mother announced the death of my brother Hans. He was the first one in our close family to die, and it was a terrible shock for me. I was surprised, because I thought I was sophisticated and above emotional reaction to the inevitable. Fortunately, we went immediately from New York to Bennington and were very busy with concerts—which cushioned the shock. Ethel and I decided that we would never again lead a student tour in Europe; it was too nerve-wracking for people who want to sing and compose music.

≈≈

THE STUDENT ensembles eventually developed into an exceptionally fine college community orchestra. In addition to the music faculty the orchestra members included faculty from other divisions. From the social science division Thomas Brockway and Lucian Hanks played clarinet, George Lundberg played violin, and David Truman played flute. From the science division Paul Garrett played violin and Dr. Chassell played flute. In the first years the orchestra had sixteen to twenty players.

Beginning in 1936, we did joint concerts with the students that included works composed on campus, a tradition that has continued at Bennington. The music faculty taught with zeal. Mariana Lowell's method was to get students to play pieces straight through without stopping, in spite of mistakes. I stressed intonation. When the students listened to each other play, they also heard the composition. I conducted in different tempi to get them to follow. Ear-training classes improved listening and soon the students were able to project the gestalt of the work they performed. My class, History and Analysis of Music (nicknamed by the students the "Mystery and Paralysis of Music"), introduced them to the orchestral and operatic literature through recordings. Students wrote a report or analysis every week, and I discussed works in class. It was a class in concentration, ear training, and memory training. I compiled a long reading and listening list, to widen the horizons of the class sessions.

The women were possibly faster and more adroit in theoretical studies than the men I had taught. The women, however, would not start composing until I explained to them that literate musicians should be able to write music as well as read it, and that I did not expect masterpieces that would put Beethoven's Ninth and Mahler or Bruckner symphonies in the shade. Writing dance scores and reading wonderful poets like Emily Dickinson, Edna St. Vincent Millay, and Emily Brontë eventually got them started. I mentioned Francesca Caccini, whose music we performed, and the contemporary English composer Rebecca Clarke, and suggested that they look ·at reproductions of Georgia O'Keeffe's paintings. This, too, seemed to do the trick. They started composing short pieces and could hear that they were quite original. The entire Bennington faculty supported us in these beginnings. The Bauhaus slogan "Less is more" also helped. I showed them jewelry and miniatures and played Renaissance music, all small or short works, but beautifully crafted. I was myself recovering from the notion that only the German tradition and the second Viennese school had produced good music. I discovered Henry Purcell, Vivaldi, and Gustav Holst—who all taught in girls' schools and whose superb music-making became a model for me.

❧❦

In 1937, Henry Johnson joined the faculty. He played violin, viola, horn, and trumpet, sang baritone, and was a fine conductor. We performed a Couperin ritournelle for soprano, two flutes, and three violins, and a Stamitz sonata for flute, violin, cello, and piano, because of the excellent string writing. The next student-faculty concert included *Le Printemps* by Darius Milhaud. One of my students asked what Milhaud meant by subconscious composing. And I explained . . . the stream of consciousness at work! After performing *Il canto della lontananza* by Malipiero, for violin and piano, we had to describe what it meant to be an "original" composer. Cecilia Drinker invited the orchestra for a music day at the home of her parents, Henry and Sophie Drinker, in Philadelphia. She played Mozart's *Andante for Flute and Orchestra* very beautifully. The orchestra played the free counterpoint of the Purcell fantasias with real conviction, and remarkably well in tune. At Bennington Jane Hutchins, a student assistant on our recent German excursion, conducted a Handel concerto bravely and Haydn's Symphony no. 49, *La passione,* expressively. I had the chorus sing Francesco Gasparini's Mass in G and an impromptu by Sibelius—the first for its fine vocal counterpoint, the second for its somewhat oily Nordic quality.

Carlos Buhler, a former Busoni student, practically dared me to play the *Undine* Sonata by Carl Reinecke, a very beautiful romantic composition for flute and piano, the remarkable B Minor Trio Sonata by Bach, sonatinas for flute and piano by Darius Milhaud and Philipp Jarnach, and the *Albumblatt* for flute and piano by Busoni. Buhler was a brilliant but erratic player; at concerts he was inspirational and took off on his own. I had to be prepared for anything but I kept in touch, and we occasionally gave brilliant performances of the Milhaud, the Jarnach, the Reinecke, and the Busoni. I don't think Bach would have cared much for the way we played his sonata. McBride gave a fine performance of Mozart's Oboe Quartet in F Major, and then of his own *Wise Apple Five,* a jazzy piece for clarinet and string quartet. Mariana Lowell, Margaret Auë, Henry Johnson, and I performed Mozart's Flute Quartet in D Major with a real sense for Mozart's operatic tempi, influenced by my memories of Richard Strauss and Eugene Goossens. The high spot of my chamber music playing was when Lowell, Johnson, and I played Reger's Serenade in

G Major, Op. 141A, for flute, violin, and viola. (Reger was not very well known in America, and I had always liked him best for his chamber music and thought it should be played.) I loved this trio in G major because, through free chromatic treatment, he obtained exceptionally rich sounds from his small combination. It was both interesting to play and good to listen to. George Finckel, a masterly Bennington cellist, gave a performance of my *Variations on Bach's Chorale Prelude Liebster "Jesu wir sind hier" for Cello and Piano* and of my *Aria for Cello and Piano*. Finckel's virtues were a rich cello tone, technical precision, and a real penetration of the expressive content—qualities needed to project those works, and the works made a strong impression. With Buhler, we repeatedly performed Goossens's *Trio for Flute, Cello and Piano* with a rubato so free that the musical strand played by the individual instruments almost broke, but didn't.

Ethel and I introduced my *Suite for Soprano and Flute*. Everyone wanted to know the language she was singing in. It was a vocalise, sung on syllables—very hard to explain in those days. Ethel also sang six songs by Charles Ives, and there was much interest in them.

Julian De Gray was our most formidable faculty member. He spoke a dozen languages, all with a slight accent. He knew the great piano literature from memory and astonished the community by giving profound performances of all the Beethoven piano sonatas in nine Sunday recitals.

Ethel and Kit Osgood presented *An American Potpourri,* with students doing most of the singing. It included Nova Scotia folk songs, anonymous sixteenth-century music, New England music of the seventeenth century, Billings's fuguing tunes, eighteenth-century and Moravian music, early hymns, ballads and Civil War songs, ballad-opera arias, white spirituals, Negro spirituals, and minstrel songs. As a finale, the entire company sang "Listen to the Mocking Bird."

We performed many of our works in Bennington churches. When the college wanted to cancel the candlelight services during World War II, Reverend Booth protested, because our concerts were some of the best morale builders in the community. At one concert, as a tribute to him, the chorus sang Debussy's *Blessed Damozelle* and the orchestra played Bach's *Brandenburg* Concerto no. 5.

Gregory Tucker wrote incidental music for Sophocles' *Electra*, and I wrote a score for Lorca's *Blood Wedding* (*Bodas de Sangre*), both performed by the drama and music departments.

Thomas Whitney Surette sent a letter saying he thought the faculty and students had created something very fine and unusual, unique among American colleges, and that it might well serve them as a model. He approved of my teaching method.

But the honeymoon didn't last forever. I had a letter from Father: "I told Aunt Gretchen about your triumphs. '*Es wird schon schief gehen*' ['It will go crooked'] was her comment. Your brother Fred asked me if I couldn't get you to stop wasting your time with music that nobody knows and no one likes. I should influence you to write a piece like 'Alexander's Ragtime Band' or 'After the Ball Is Over.' I wrote him I didn't think you would care to do that; of course, Johann Strauss was a very fine musician. Does this suggest anything to you?"

Student activities in general had progressed so far that I and William Schuman at Sarah Lawrence planned a meeting of students to organize the Intercollegiate Music Guild of America, to take the lead in arranging intercollegiate musical events, just like debating teams and basketball and football leagues. Bennington, Bard, Vassar, Westminister Choir College, Sarah Lawrence, Columbia, Barnard, and Princeton sent representatives, and Walter Piston and Roy Harris joined our advisory board. The guild developed festivals and symposiums, and it continued to function for a number of years, to the point that it became quite common to have student-initiated arts festivals at many colleges. Although the guild was stopped by the war, I like to think that its pioneer activities stimulated the formation of Composers Symposia and the American Society of University Composers, several decades later.

In June 1939 the drama, dance, and music departments did Molière's *Intellectual Ladies* (*Les Précieuses ridicules*) in translation by Wallace Fowlie, directed by Francis Fergusson, settings by Arch Lauterer, ballet interludes choreographed and directed by Martha Hill and danced to music by Lully; musical director, Otto Luening. The character Dottore in the ballet was danced by Carol Channing. After the show there was a party, and she did impersonations of the faculty and I of the students. She won the contest.

Chapter 18

The WPA and
a Chamber Orchestra
1934-1975

DURING OUR YEARS AT BENNINGTON, Ethel and I were frequently off campus. In Washington, in 1942, at the Starlit Concerts given by the Library of Congress, with Ralph Kirkpatrick and Lois Wann, I played the Bach E-flat Major Sonata for flute and piano and the Trio Sonata in E-flat Major for flute and oboe by Handel. In preparation, Kirkpatrick drilled us less than usual. When I mentioned this, he said he now liked to rehearse "subconsciously." Soon after this program Ethel and I were both on the WNYC American Music Festival radio broadcast in New York. We were very much impressed by the other artists in the festival: Glenn Miller, Jimmy Dorsey, Red Allen, Eddie Allen, Eddie Condon, Henry Brant, Virgil Thomson, Willie Kapell, and Morton Gould.

Ethel and I heard the Vermont State Symphony, the first state symphony orchestra in the country, perform Brahms's Second Symphony in Burlington, under the baton of Alan Carter. He rehearsed the separate units in various towns and villages and then brought them all together for one mammoth rehearsal and concert on the same day, in the town that had booked them. Carter chose me for the board.

The Depression had put most of the musicians in Vermont out of work. College faculties expressed their indignation by attending meetings and writing articles. As early as April 1934, while I was still in Arizona, *Musical Courier* printed an interview in which I suggested that because of the chaotic conditions in the

world of art and education, and in music in particular, "an immediate conference of representatives from all musical organizations
in the United States should be called." Representatives from
schools, foundations, churches, unions, management, and radio
stations should meet. I suggested also that a general plan—to improve permanently the existing conditions—be presented in
Washington, with recommendations that the musical profession
be included in the public works and other relief programs that
were getting underway, and that we should aim for the creation of
a new cabinet post, a secretary of the fine arts. I suggested that
state, county, and municipal orchestras and opera companies be
organized and supported by public funds, along with a national
conservatory, and that composers should be commissioned to
write works. I made the further rather radical suggestion that if
we couldn't take care of the existing performers and teachers, we
had better cut back on educating and graduating from our music
schools more performers and teachers and instead develop intelligent listeners. From Bennington I wired President Franklin D.
Roosevelt a condensed version of my interview, emphasizing the
need for a federal music project and a relief program under the
Works Projects Administration for the thousands of unemployed
musicians. Various government departments expressed some interest in some of these ideas and indicated that the program
would soon be functioning. In 1935, under Harry Hopkins, the
Federal Arts Project, Theatre Project, Writers Project, and Music
Project were launched and continued until 1939, when they
began to taper off.

꙰꙰

THE WPA FOCUSED national attention on the arts on a broad scale
and as a part of our national life. During the WPA era, the Arts
Project resulted in thousands of paintings, drawings, sculptures,
and murals. The Writers Project sponsored state, regional, and
municipal guidebooks and other reference documents. The
Theatre Project introduced and supported playwrights, actors,
directors, and composers who later played an important part in
the American cultural world. The Music Project gave approximately four thousand performances each month from the standard

repertory. It provided employment for copyists, solo and orchestral performers, and conductors, and presented a large number of American compositions. Concerts were free and reached a wide national audience.

Paul Pelton, associate conductor of the Vermont State Symphony, was appointed the director of the Vermont WPA project and ran it in the New England town-meeting tradition. He invited me to be on the state advisory committee. Local advisory committees were set up in seventeen towns and villages. In Wilder, two housewives, the overseer of the poor, a teacher, and a bookkeeper made up the committee. In Grand Isle, the town clerk, the librarian, six farmers' wives (who were all former music teachers or students), the county superintendent of schools, and a merchant's wife ran the project.

Isabel Emory, a student of George Lundberg at Bennington, compiled a questionnaire that was sent to the fifty-eight towns and villages. They answered that they needed programs of music instruction in their schools, and so the WPA set up vocal sight-reading classes, instrumental instruction, folk music groups, workshops for theory and orchestration, music appreciation classes for adults, and organized performing groups. Many classes and rehearsals were held in private homes in the rural districts and we were informed that this helped the communities overcome rivalries, antagonisms, and confrontations.

The WPA regional bureaucracy was sometimes comical and at other times exasperating. All project workers had to be approved by the Bureau on Intake and Verification. This bureau knew nothing about music and scheduled strange happenings, like opera performances without orchestra and singers. In the orchestra project workers got a fixed hourly rate for a twenty-five-hour maximum work week and had to punch time clocks. On a given rehearsal day twenty saxophones, two violins, six horns, three flutes, a bass, and three percussion players might show up. Just as the conductor lined up his mixed personnel and was about to begin, workers who had put in their twenty-five hours would punch the clock and leave on the dot. Good project directors learned how to handle practically any combination.

Even so, the effect of the WPA program was good. One fan letter to Pelton stated:

The influence of the Vermont State Music Project, brief as its existence has been, will be felt for years. It is not overstating the case
to say that works done so far will remain in the memory of a majority as long as they live. People, both children and adults, who
could not read music, now read, write and sing music. Instrument
players who were beginners are now in the intermediate stage.
. . . Choral singing has been revived. . . . There has been engen-
dered among the people of this state an enthusiasm and liking for
music which is very definitely a living thing and which is increasing month by month.

The Vermont Civilian Conservation Corps, too, gave classes in elementary theory, piano, woodwinds, brass, and choral and community singing, all of which were well attended.

This experience had a strong influence on me because it was
similar to the early activities of the New England composers, such
as William Billings, and the Vermont composers Hezekiah Moors,
Jeremiah Ingalls, and Justin Morgan. It reinforced a certain
homespun—perhaps corny—quality in my musical nature.

Franz Lorenz, a former cellist with Stokowski and Toscanini,
visited me at the college and suggested establishing a symphony
orchestra in Bennington with himself as director. I explained that
the Vermont State Symphony was barely surviving, that there
were few musicians around, that the winters in Bennington were
very cold and would keep people away, and that there was no
suitable hall. We finally decided to organize the Bennington
County Musical Society for children.

With the help of Dr. Elizabeth McCullough, the college
physician, and Jean Brockway and others, Mr. Lorenz was soon
teaching most of the town's musical children between the ages of
six and eighteen. When they could hold their instruments he
would seat them in his chamber orchestra, and, against the rules
of educational psychology, he would conduct them as if they were
the New York Philharmonic or the Philadelphia Symphony Orchestra, alternately bellowing and smiling at them. With infinite
patience he taught them to put their fingers down on the right
part of the string. He pushed their bows around until they could
do it on their own. During the intermissions he would tell them
stories about his boyhood in Hungary. They loved it.

On May 31, 1937, the Children's Orchestra gave a concert in

the First Methodist Church in Bennington for one hundred people. It was such a success that the orchestra toured neighboring villages, charged a dollar admission, and in Orleans took in $350 that was used to buy instruments for the orchestra. Their June schedule shows best how the orchestra served the community. On June 3 they played in Pownal, on June 4 at the Craftsbury graduation, and on June 7 at the Pownal Church. By this time, Carl Ruggles was guest violist and soon I played the Bach B Minor Suite for flute and strings at Williams College. John Mc-Cullough arranged a benefit in the Yellow Barn in Old Bennington. As guest conductor I did the *Toy* Symphony of Haydn (or Leopold Mozart) with the president of Bennington College and resident trustees playing the toy instruments while the children played the regular ones. The kids were particularly pleased when a trustee came in too soon with the cuckoo or missed the nightingale call by a few beats. We raised $800 for the orchestra.

The Bennington County Musical Society demonstrated almost better than any other group that a musical climate in which music lovers of all kinds could develop was feasible, desirable, and useful. Among the many distinguished young musicians of today whose careers began with this group are Joan Brockway, Michael and Chris Finckel, and Robert and Alison Nowak.

Governor George Aiken was an enthusiastic member of the Children's Orchestra advisory committee. He introduced several concerts, suggesting to the audiences that communities should see that the artistic talents of their children were developed as a counterfoil to juvenile delinquency. For a while the state appropriated matching funds. In 1939, as federal support tapered off, Governor Aiken supported a plan to ask each town for three dollars monthly towards each WPA worker's pay. In Bennington our job was to raise $720 in a hurry. I wrote Governor Aiken requesting more time before the state stopped its support. He answered that he would appropriate $600 from a special fund. To show his appreciation Lorenz had the orchestra play the string version of Carl Ruggles's *Angels* in one concert and then, before an audience of three hundred people at Bennington College, performed Robert Volkman's difficult *Serenade*. He had me conduct my *Suite for Strings*, which the orchestra played with spirit and a fine tone.

In 1937, I applied to the Carnegie Foundation for a grant for a state circulating music library. The foundation asked for a large committee to run the library. Paul Pelton and I enlisted Governor Aiken and Francis Bailey, the state commissioner of education, to serve on the committee, with Pelton as chairman. We asked for scores, recordings, and books about music, especially American music, which would be distributed by book wagons provided by the Vermont State Library Commission. In March 1939 the Carnegie Foundation granted us $2,000 for a circulating library to be used for rural music in Vermont. In 1940 we circulated thirty-five hundred items in the month of July alone, so we asked for a supplemental grant, which we were denied. The WPA ran the library until 1942. Then the Vermont Council on Adult Education took it over and Governor Aiken approved an annual appropriation. As late as 1975 the library was still functioning.

I WAS GETTING more and more restless at Bennington, for I had the feeling that the faculty and administration believed, as often happens in country colleges, that they had my number and knew just what I would do, how I would play, and what I would be composing for the next twenty years. I didn't know this myself. When the war stopped artistic efforts, the college ran a farm and grew its own food (at, I suspect, a much greater expense than the prices at the grocery).

DURING THE WPA days, I had engaged the Albany Concert Orchestra for a very low fee to play on campus and conducted Weber's *Euryanthe* Overture, Mozart's Symphony in G Minor, my *Suite for String Orchestra*, and Berlioz's Rákóczi March from *La Damnation de Faust*. The Rákóczi March shook Bennington to its very foundations. The orchestra played with us again for our commencements, and I conducted the Purcell *Five-Part Fantasia for Strings* and Mozart's *Jupiter* Symphony, and Barbara Coffin sang Mozart arias. Henry Johnson followed with the *Rococo Variations*, for cello and orchestra, and the Piano Concerto in G Major by Tchaikovsky with Margaret Auë and Gregory Tucker as soloists. Students played along at this concert. From then on the Bennington orchestra performed longer works. Reinforced by Fellows and students like Carol Haynes, Chandler Cowles, Mimi Wallner,

Marianne Wilson, Diana Marvin, and Alice Rowley, the student conductors, arrangers, and composers played an increasingly important role.

Following our sabbatical in 1939, I received a phone call from Minneapolis: "Professor Luening, you are being seriously considered as chairman of the University of Minnesota music department. Are you interested?"

I inquired about my duties, which sounded as if they would be largely administrative, so I said that I must think about the offer. A few days later, I had a call from the University of Minnesota's president urging me to take the position. I explained that I had been a good musical citizen and pulled my weight, but that I had fears about the size of the job in Minnesota.

"In Minnesota you won't be a musical citizen, you will be a musical statesman!" he said.

"That's what I am afraid of, Mr. President. I don't think I'm your man."

"What did you say?" He sounded incredulous.

"I am afraid that I can't accept your kind offer."

"Well," he said, "when you come to your senses, call me."

❧❦

IN 1935, CARL Miller, music director of the New York City Federal Music Project, had written me that my *Serenade for Three Horns and Strings* had been performed numerous times before enthusiastic audiences. Subsequently, Franco Autori (later associate conductor of the New York Philharmonic) wanted more of my works to perform with the Bronx Symphony Orchestra and the Greenwich Symphonietta. Such neighborhood concerts interested me greatly, because they were reaching new audiences and government-supported music and art was one of my fondest hopes. Autori performed my First Symphonic Fantasia with the Brooklyn Symphony Orchestra at the Brooklyn Museum, the American Museum of Natural History, and McMillin Theatre at Columbia University; soon after there followed four performances by the Buffalo Philharmonic and the Providence Symphony. The WPA even paid me fifty dollars as rental and royalty fee for a week of performances.

A well-known composer friend wrote me that he had heard Autori's performance. "How you have grown in your mastery of the medium since that early work of yours I heard in Rochester in 1926," his letter said. It was the same piece he had heard in 1926. I have never fully recovered from this experience. If professionals cannot tell after an interval of a few years whether they are hearing the same piece or a new one, how can we expect critics and untrained listeners to follow carefully composed music in detail after one hearing? Composers must probably be satisfied with an impressionistic response, or address themselves only to select and small groups of professionals, or simplify their music, and be very, very patient. After this unsettling experience, my *Serenade for Three Horns and Strings* was performed a number of times in the Bronx Community Building and in the American Museum of Natural History. I did not hear any of these performances, but I was encouraged when my compositions stood the test of repeated performances before a wide variety of audiences, under various conductors, and by different orchestras.

In June 1935, Gerald McGarrahan invited me to conduct a concert of the Greenwich Symphonietta at the Brooklyn Museum. For the first half of the program I chose Mozart's overture to *The Marriage of Figaro*, the Queen of the Night aria from *The Magic Flute*, which Ethel sang, and his Symphony in C Major, the *Jupiter*, no. 41. I knew the works from memory and had a simple but effective conducting technique whereby I gave preparatory beats for tricky entrances with a flick of the wrist. The best New York WPA orchestras were excellent and included some of the city's finest players as guest or regular members. The Mozart works were a rousing success; there were cheers from the large audience and a salute from the orchestra. The second half of the program included the first performance of the impressionistic *Lady Who Sings* by Evelyn Berckman and Mouton's arrangement of Debussy's *Children's Corner Suite*, and ended with a splashy performance of the overture to *Russlan and Ludmilla* by Glinka. I immediately had other invitations to conduct, and for a while I flirted with the idea of pursuing a conductor's career.

I conducted similar concerts in surprisingly good halls, like the Bronx Community Building, Washington Irving High School, and the American Museum of Natural History. Chalmers Clifton, the general director of the project, invited me to conduct two chamber orchestra concerts in the Federal Music Project Theatre of Music in 1937. I prepared them with only six hours of rehearsal time. At the first one Ethel sang a concert aria of Mozart's and I included the *Jupiter* Symphony and the Berckman piece. As novelties I included the jazzy *Workout* by Robert McBride and my own *Prelude to a Hymn Tune by William Billings*. The American works were so well received that Clifton asked me to do an all-American concert.

The best WPA symphony orchestra by then was so good that Sir Thomas Beecham performed two lesser-known Haydn symphonies with such style and vitality that the event was the talk of the town for a time. In June 1937, I gave a program at Washington Irving High School with the same orchestra: Beethoven's Fifth Symphony; Grieg's Piano Concerto in A Minor; Delibes' "Bell Song" from *Lakmé,* sung by Ethel; my horn serenade; and Wagner's *Meistersinger* Overture. By then my reactions were fast enough so that as I heard mistakes I shouted them to the orchestra while we continued playing, correcting them while we paused before repeating the section. Thanks to Goossens's early training, I never made mistakes with the beat. I didn't waste the orchestra's time and they didn't waste mine.

In 1938, Clifton invited me to conduct the best WPA symphony orchestras in New York and Boston. This all went to my head. I caught myself saying to a player, "Mitch, I haven't seen you since you played the solo in Mozart so beautifully in the Bronx." Just like Artur Nikisch! But WPA funds were being cut back. These concerts were postponed several times and finally canceled, and that sobering experience was the end of my conducting career with the WPA.

Also in 1938, the New York Federal Music Project took over the Composers' Forum Laboratory. This group introduced composers who were relatively new to the New York audience. The WPA cooperated with well-known music schools in and out of New York and asked me to arrange a forum for the Bennington composition students, and the program was broadcast over radio station WNYC. Then William Schuman and I arranged a joint program of compositions and performances by Bennington and Sarah Lawrence students.

The forum also programmed several of my shorter works as well as some works by Ruth Crawford and Hans Eisler. In April, my Third String Quartet was given a fine performance before a small audience. At another forum Ethel sang a group of my minute songs and my *Suite for Soprano and Flute*, which attracted attention because of the clear lines and brilliant vocal passages. During that time I was perfecting my music in short forms and music for small combinations. The *Suite* survived and was later recorded.

Ashley Pettis, director of the forum, wrote me that he was impressed by the fine talent shown in the Bennington student program. Six months later another letter came asking me to wire President Roosevelt and urge him to rescind the order to reduce WPA personnel. But as we approached the war years the project slowly tapered off. The WPA era was over in 1943. However, I believe that the programs in music and theater continued to affect our national life. They were perhaps indirectly responsible for many community activities thought worthy of support in the 1965 bill for the National Endowment for the Arts and the National Endowment for the Humanities.

❧❦

SOON AFTER we arrived in Bennington, Ethel and I had begun to build a personal artistic base in New York and elsewhere. We took a studio apartment at 39 West 67th Street and commuted back and forth, spending three or four days in each place. In 1935 Aaron Copland asked us and Robert McBride to perform Copland's *As It Fell upon a Day* at the New School for Social Research in New York. This imaginative work uses the individual lyric characteristics of voice, flute, and clarinet to their best advantage, and for me it is one of Copland's best pieces. This was an important concert, for Copland was the power behind the League of Composers and the New School for Social Research was the show window for the avant-garde. We attracted the attention of the sophisticated New York entrepreneurs of contemporary music.

The Music Guild invited us to broadcast three of my songs and *The Quiet Pool* by Evelyn Berckman. Of my *Here the Frailest*

Leaves of Me, the *Musical Courier* wrote: "It is music of exceptional merit." These introductions brought us many small engagements, and in 1936 the League of Composers sponsored us at the French Institute. We performed my *Mañana,* arranged for voice and piano, and *Dr. Johnson's Tour of the Hebrides* for voice and flute, composed for us by Berckman. At the New School I arranged a program with Marc Blitzstein and Aaron Copland. Ethel sang songs by Ernst Bacon and Berckman, and we did a *Vocalise for Voice and Flute* by Henry Cowell. I played my *Concertino for Flute and Chamber Orchestra* (but with piano instead) and Gregory Tucker played my *Dance Sonata for Piano.* Copland played his *Passacaglia for Piano* with a strong touch and a nononsense interpretation. Bacon's early songs had a Viennese flavor but were also influenced by American folk music. My *Concertino* had a linear, sometimes polytonal, and neoclassical style that puzzled the audience, as did much of my 1920s music for many years. In the *Dance Sonata* I used what I called "acoustic harmonies": freewheeling segments of the overtone row, with jazzy rhythms. The work made an impression. Ethel and I did recordings of songs of mine and she sang Copland's *Vocalise,* with him at the piano.

We thought we needed to do some barnstorming to toughen up, so we asked Bennington for a leave of absence for April 1937 to tour Western Canada. We went to Saskatoon and Prince Albert, Saskatchewan; Victoria, British Columbia; and Dauphin, Manitoba. In addition to our usual program of old and new music, Ethel sang the Jewel Scene from Gounod's *Faust* in costume and with action. We hauled a spinning wheel and costumes across the continent, and it was worth it, for Ethel was a fine actress. She was given an ovation in Saskatoon, the town where she had begun her career, singing Mabel in *The Pirates of Penzance.*

When we came home we did a number of broadcasts on the NBC Music Guild Hour in New York. From Handel's cantata *Pensieri notturni di Filli* we did the lively "Nel dolce dell' oblio." Ethel did two cantatas by Buxtehude, *O fröhliche Stunden* and *Singet dem Herrn*—so beautifully that Musicraft recorded them together with the Handel, and the exceptional quality of these recordings was mentioned in reference books for many years.

We kept on doing contemporary music, and Henry Cowell

arranged a concert at the New School where the net proceeds were divided 70–30 between the artists and the school. The concert was a great artistic success. Our seventy percent amounted to $13.07.

We booked Town Hall for our New York debut recital on March 22, 1937. The program included the aria "Ich bin in mir vergnügt," with flute, from the cantata *Von der Vergnügsamkeit* by Bach; the Sonata in A Minor for flute and figured bass by Handel; a concert scene and aria, "Ma che vi fece, o stella!" by Mozart; my *Lyric Song for Voice and Flute;* a rhythmically strong *Music for Voice and Flute* by Wallingford Riegger; *Vocalise* for voice, flute, and piano by Cowell (with Far Eastern overtones); "Rory More's Cascade" from *Dr. Johnson's Tour of the Hebrides* by Berckman; *Nonsense Syllables*, for voice and flute, by Robert McBride; and "Queenie's Song," arranged for us with flute from *The Second Hurricane* by Aaron Copland.

Ralph Kirkpatrick and I made a new edition of the Handel sonata especially for this concert. For days we tested every possible trill and tried different phrasings, dynamic ranges, tone colors, and pacings. Kirkpatrick made a realization of the figured bass. A week before the concert, he wrote from London praising our painstaking editing, but explaining that he had since learned that a good Handel performance meant throwing all inhibitions to the wind, tearing loose and playing with abandon, and taking an uninhibited approach more that of an Italian tenor than a musicologist. Possibly even the free improvisational style of our jazz players would work. I survived this test by the skin of my teeth and gave a fairly good performance.

The large audience included musicians active in New York contemporary music circles: Varèse, Riegger, Carlos Salzedo, Copland, Adolph Weiss, Marc Blitzstein, Carl Ruggles, Quincy Porter, and Evelyn Berckman. We were warmly applauded. Henrietta Weber reported in the *New York Evening Journal* that we were "two real people . . . music makers with a true musical background . . . clear soprano voice with a practically flawless technique. A composer and musician of many fine qualities . . . entertaining and convincing argument in favor of our modern musical thought . . . . a salvo for their taste and progressiveness as well as their performance."

In 1937 the Metropolitan Opera Guild invited me to give a lecture on Mozart's operas. I used for my lecture musical examples from *Figaro*, which Ethel sang stylishly, accompanied by the Phil-Sym String Quartet with Willard Rhodes at the piano. The program was repeated and broadcast over NBC's national "blue" network.

IN 1934, ARTUR Schnabel had raised, with a benefit concert, more than a thousand dollars for the Bennington College scholarship fund. After the Schnabel concert, in the rain in front of Carnegie Hall, John McCullough, then a student at Yale and the son of Bennington trustees Mr. and Mrs. Hall Park McCullough, spoke with me about another benefit. He mentioned that Toscanini had been asked to conduct a benefit for Bennington with a chamber orchestra, but that he declined because of heavy commitments and bursitis. Toscanini recommended his associate Hans Lange. I thought that we ought to arrange a series of concerts with well-balanced programs of baroque, classical, and contemporary compositions for chamber orchestra that would project the Bennington Idea. I discussed the plan with Dr. Leigh and the music faculty and everyone was enthusiastic, so we went to work.

Hans Lange, too, was enthusiastic and cooperative, and so was Bruno Zirato, the manager of the chamber orchestra. We decided to present the New York Philharmonic Symphony Chamber Orchestra in a series of five concerts at Town Hall. The orchestra would consist of first-desk men from the New York Philharmonic Symphony Orchestra. Mrs. Richard Dana, Mrs. Percy Jackson, Mrs. Hall Park McCullough, Mrs. Theodore Steinway, and Mrs. Clarence Woolley were the guiding lights on the New York committee throughout the series. To coordinate the series was quite a job for me, as I did much of the organization from Bennington by phone, and I had to deal with Arthur Judson's office, Bruno Zirato, Dr. Carlton Sprague Smith of the New York Public Library, and various people in Bennington. This administrative work served as a unique introduction to New York City concert life. I was also the unofficial associate conductor to Lange and helped him with his programs.

Toscanini was interested in the programs and made the wise suggestions that we use one combination of instruments for each concert and that the soloists be members of the orchestra. As soon as I started work on the project, I received good, bad, and harebrained suggestions about programming from practically everybody in New York, or so it seemed. I suggested to Lange that we should do programs that were varied, and that they should not be done in chronological order. The New York committee insisted upon chronological programs, but otherwise they left us to do our own program-making and enthusiastically approved a contemporary music program. Lange and I proposed that the program notes should be written so that they would be intelligible to an unsophisticated audience; we offered to make musical analyses for the program annotator.

The subscription sales were slow and the New York committee asked all of us in Bennington to sell tickets. The publicity agent talked me into researching articles about chamber orchestras and ghostwriting an article for the newspapers. The musicians were extremely cooperative. Ralph Kirkpatrick accepted a solo engagement for the colossal fee of fifty dollars. Orchestral soloists cost us twenty dollars apiece.

The first concert took place on November 11, 1935, and included music of the sixteenth, seventeenth, and eighteenth centuries, such as *Seven Teares* by John Dowland; a concerto for oboe and strings by Handel; a concerto for string orchestra by Jean-Baptiste Lully; four fantasias for strings by Henry Purcell; a concerto for harpsichord by Giuseppe Sammartini; and Symphony no. 2 for Strings and Cembalo by C. P. E. Bach. *Time* magazine said this concert "aroused more real enthusiasm than any other musical event in the current Manhattan scene. . . . The evening sensation was a set of fantasias by Henry Purcell . . . so vital and direct, so tender, so craftily sure, that the audience behaved as though it had just heard the percussive *Boléro* or driving *Pacific 231*. The final Fantasia had to be repeated." In the *New York Times*, Olin Downes said that "it was by far the most interesting feature of a season that has started in a dull and mediocre manner. The course that has been pursued in arranging them is entirely worthy of the reputation of the College."

The next four concerts were devoted to seventeenth- and eighteenth-century music (J. S. Bach, Stamitz, Gossec, Piccini, and Leopold Mozart), the music of the classical period (including works by Henri Joseph Riegel, Boccherini, and Haydn), romanticism in music (with works by Anthony Holborne, Johann Rosenmüller, Carl Maria von Weber, Walter Helfer, and Daniel Gregory Mason), and modern chamber orchestra music (with works by Dante Fiorillo, Carl Ruggles, Gustav Holst, David Diamond, Darius Milhaud, and Paul Hindemith).

The ticket sales for the second concert were slow, but Hall Park McCullough said that the college couldn't buy publicity of this kind for fifty thousand dollars. Those of us who believed we were projecting the Bennington Idea felt heartened. The second and third concerts attracted a great deal of attention and very good critical comment, but for the last two, some of the reviewers were beginning to focus their enthusiasm on the soloists, sometimes forgetting the compositions. The contemporary concert had a mixed reception.

We ended the season with a deficit of $224.90. When the management raised the orchestra's fee to $1,000 per concert and included fees for conductor, contractor, manager, and publicity agent, I was shocked. After our brilliant first year we were expected to continue to dig out unknown hits, but only those that would pay off. While planning for the next season, the committee began searching for sure-fire programs. Everyone was suggesting slogans that would sell the series. My favorites were "Five Enjoyable Monday Evenings" and "Five Monday Evenings Without Gloom." When we announced for the next season discoveries of works by Nicola Porpora, Orlando Gibbons, and early American music, the *Times* wrote: "A refreshing departure from the oft-repeated platitudes of the average program." The committee wanted me to conduct two programs and Lange three. I was flattered but failed to see why he shouldn't conduct them all, so I declined the invitation.

Lange was suddenly appointed the associate conductor of the Chicago Symphony Orchestra and was late with program suggestions. My job as a coordinator became a headache when Lange suddenly wired me to conduct the rehearsal for Karl Ditters von Dittersdorf's *Combattimento del umane passioni*, the A Minor Violin Concerto by Bach, Cassation in D Major by Mozart, *Portrait of a Lady* by Deems Taylor, and *Workout* by Robert McBride. This change of pace brought me out of the doldrums. I just about memorized the scores after twelve hours of study. The rehearsal went very well. In the Taylor the orchestra asked for a 5/8 section to be taken in 2 and I danced my way through 2 plus 3, 3 plus 2 beats and single beats, in fine style. Zirato wrote me: "The orchestra personnel of the Philharmonic Symphony Chamber Orchestra and Mr. Van Praag, one of our founders, have reported to me the outstanding success that you had in a rehearsal of the second concert of the Bennington College Series. I understand you had your rehearsal on the most difficult numbers on the program: the *Workout* by McBride, and the Taylor *Portrait of a Lady*. Please accept my most sincere congratulations." He then said I was the logical man to take Lange's place when he went to Chicago permanently. He even suggested that I might join the orchestra as a founder.

Suspecting that Zirato was as much interested in my fundraising genius as in my musical gifts, I set some pretty strong conditions, including one that gave me complete control of the orchestra and guest conductors. He backed off on that, suggesting John Barbirolli as guest and Lange as permanent conductor. I couldn't see the sense of that and suggested going on as we were. The Association of American Colleges wanted to book the orchestra on tour.

I had a letter from Father: "Glad to hear of your success. Don't be fooled by applause. It soon fades away. Everything is cause and effect: What goes up must come down. Love."

The New York committee was overworked and we had to pull things together before making plans for the next season. Lewis Jones and others at Bennington became interested in organizing what we called the Bennington Guild. Like the Theatre Guild in New York, members would purchase season tickets. The guild would sponsor activities that projected the Bennington Idea. But the project was premature and didn't win support.

The first three programs of the 1936–1937 series were very well received, particularly a sonata by Rosenmüller; the *Ukrainian* Suite, for strings, by Quincy Porter; and Ernest Bloch's *Concerto Grosso*. McBride's *Workout* was a sensational success and had to be repeated. Then Lange wired me from Chicago to conduct the fourth concert: a sonata for strings by Giovanni Pergolesi; a *canzone* by Giovanni Gabrieli; *The Village Festival* by Stephen Foster; *Songs of Three Queens* by Lazare Saminsky; *Concerto for Clarinet* by Busoni; *Prelude and Three Small Fugues* by Paul Nordoff; and my *Prelude to a Hymn Tune by William Billings.* The audience's response was enthusiastic. The press coverage was extensive, with headlines and double headlines in eight New York newspapers and national magazines. Busoni's *Concerto* was described as an "important number." Some reviewers liked my *Prelude,* others my exacting and precise conducting and my talent and authority as a conductor.

Ticket sales dropped off precipitously in the second half of the season and Ethel and I had to send out five hundred personal letters to keep things moving. Zirato sent us a congratulatory letter once sales had improved, but we didn't think we could possibly carry on the necessary public relations, conduct, sing, coordinate the series, and at the same time do our own work.

But the tempo accelerated and by the end of the season there was a profit of $12.12. The committee was delighted and suggested dropping Lange and turning the concerts over to me for a third season. Zirato had booked some engagements in Virginia, and at Swarthmore and Columbia University, with me at the helm, but everybody was tired of selling tickets. In May, Zirato suggested canceling the series if subscription sales did not improve. I sold half of the boxes, but I told Zirato that he and the committee would have to sell the rest or I would turn into a professional fund raiser and no longer be a musician.

On October 7, 1937, Zirato wrote that the committee had decided to cancel the concerts, describing himself as "heartbroken." I was touched, drank a solitary toast to him and the committee, and answered, "Probably the work done has had quite an artistic effect. . . . I have often noticed that things materialize later than one hopes." To Mrs. Steinway I wrote: "Perhaps the right people will yet find each other and the idea that was put forth in the last two years will again come to life in some form or other. What was of real value was not lost and can't be lost." The Bennington students shed a few tears. No one else really cared when the series died.

In 1975, Howard Shanet wrote about the series in *Philharmonic: A History of New York's Orchestras:* "Another school of musicians, reacting against the master conductor syndrome, began to show an interest in chamber orchestras of moderate proportions as an antidote to the grandiosity of the master conductors. . . . The [Bennington] programs were given . . . with an attempt at authenticity that the big Philharmonic had seldom approached. . . . While the Chamber Orchestra lasted, it opened the minds of many New Yorkers to a musical literature and an aesthetic viewpoint that the parent orchestra had not been able to present under the rule of the master conductor."

Chapter 19

Lange Festivals, Southern Barnstorming
1934 - 1952

As Toscanini's associate conductor, Hans Lange directed the Philharmonic Symphony subscription concerts for several weeks every season during the maestro's absence. He held his own against the star glamour of Toscanini by introducing a great deal of new music, particularly works by English composers. I remember his superb performances of Vaughan Williams's somber F Minor Symphony and his *London* Symphony.

Lange asked me to compose a chorale prelude for the chamber orchestra series. I discovered William Billings's *Hymn to Music* and made a set of variations from it. First performed on the Bennington series and then at the Yaddo Festival and on radio, and later recorded by Dean Dixon and the Vienna Symphony and published by C. F. Peters, it is still in the repertory. Lange asked me to recommend short American works for his Philharmonic subscription concerts. I suggested Robert McBride's *Prelude to a Tragedy*, which Lange performed with great success. I also recommended Carl Ruggles's *Men and Mountains* for both the chamber orchestra and the subscription concerts, and it aroused much attention. He followed this with a performance of works by Bernard Rogers and William Grant Still. Lange then asked me to compose two "symphonic interludes" for the subscription concerts. The first was three and a half minutes long and the second seven minutes.

The *Two Symphonic Interludes* premiered on April 11 and 12, 1936, and were broadcast over the CBS national hookup. The performances were very good. The audiences, unaccustomed to hearing many American or even contemporary works, were surprisingly receptive and called me on stage a number of times while bravos echoed through Carnegie Hall. There were many favorable notices in a dozen newspapers and magazines. The consensus was that I had something to say and knew how to say it, that I orchestrated with great competence, that my sense of form was strong, that I was individual in an authentically creative capacity, and that my music was "dignified." The radio audience sent me a batch of fan letters. The *Interludes* were soon published.

Within a year, the Civic Orchestra in Chicago played them under Lange, as did the Chicago Symphony under the direction of Frederick Stock. The Chicago audience and some of the critics called the works radical if not futuristic, but Eugene Stinson in the *Chicago Daily News* considered them powerful and the best at which modernism aims. Stock also performed the *Interludes* with the Chicago Symphony in my hometown Milwaukee. The music critic Hans F. Emmerling (the name of my boyhood dentist) drilled me by calling them noisy and ultramodern and labeling them "strong medicine." The audience was lukewarm. My brother Fred was so upset that he wrote my father urging him to make me stop disgracing the family. He said the title of one of my pieces should be "The Last Agonies of a Frying Egg." Father and Fred wrote back and forth and to me. The *Two Symphonic Interludes* were a major family scandal for many years.

I decided to promote the *Interludes* personally and sent scores to twenty conductors. Stokowski read them through with the Philadelphia Orchestra and I believe he performed them once; Ormandy and Sevitsky read them; Klemperer was interested, but I didn't follow through; Vladimir Golschmann performed them with the St. Louis Symphony in February 1939, and there was a review by Harry Burke in the *St. Louis Globe-Democrat* with a detailed analysis and a fine description of the expressive content of both *Interludes*. I believed that the works made a strong impression because the first one used an orchestral palette based on free linear counterpoint, and the second one used carefully balanced "acoustic" harmonies that I had been developing since 1928. Both were somewhat new but aurally comprehensible. The Vienna Symphony Orchestra, Dean Dixon conducting, recorded them in the 1950s and they have since occasionally been played live and over the radio.

≫≪

IN 1934, BENNINGTON needed a summer activity in keeping with its ideals—and to keep its employees busy. Martha Hill proposed the Bennington School of the Dance. The six-week program attracted the best modern dancers. Martha Graham, Doris Humphrey, and Charles Weidman each came for a week of workshops and performances. A large enrollment of dance teachers who were not particularly interested in performance made the classes somewhat hybrid. In 1934, Graham, Humphrey, and Weidman gave solo recitals, and Hanya Holm gave a demonstration that netted $373. The first year was profitable.

For the next four years, the School of the Dance expanded, giving as many as nine performances annually. Besides being a training center for teachers, the school became a unique theater enterprise and an incubator for the New York dance scene. Louis Horst, senior music director, and Norman Lloyd, who had been a dance pianist and later became educational director of the Juilliard School and director of the arts program for the Rockefeller Foundation, introduced the dancers to many of the best contemporary composers, who composed music for them. In 1935, I saw Martha Graham dance in *Panorama*—music by Norman Lloyd, stage set by Arch Lauterer, with mobiles by Alexander Calder. In 1936, Humphrey-Weidman presented *New Dance*, with a score by Wallingford Riegger. The music was sufficiently strong to be recorded as a suite and was a good example of Riegger's fine formal sense.

Doris Humphrey was impressive during the rehearsals because of her businesslike direction. Charles Weidman showed his virtuosity and occasionally his Chaplinesque humor. The other composers who wrote for festival events were Henry Cowell and Lehman Engel. A Bennington student, Esther Williamson, wrote much music for the younger dancers. In 1937, Hanya Holm did an abstract piece called *Trend*, and there was an opening dance by Martha Graham with music by Norman Lloyd and a stage set by Arch Lauterer. The dancing made less of an impression on me than the music of Varèse that was used. An early recording of his *Ionisation* and the New Music Quarterly Recording of *Octandre* was played on a fine Paneyko machine. I was astonished by the *Ionisation* performance because, besides its percussive novelites, the piece had an organic form, a characteristic of all of Varèse's work.

In 1938 the dancers were involved in music and stories that had grown out of the American folk background. Martha Graham did *American Document*, based on a minstrel show. The music by Ray Green was very effective, with the individual pieces separated by spoken lines. Graham wrote some of the words herself.

Erick Hawkins made his debut as Martha's partner. The combination of speech, music, movement, and some remarkable scenic touches by Arch Lauterer made the work a real contribution to the American theater. Another work with an American background was *Frontier*, with music by Horst and setting by Noguchi. Its sparse, effective movements and a lean score made the dance seem very symbolic. It gave me ideas about using uncomplicated sounds as symbols.

In 1939 the School of the Dance was expanded to become a Summer School of the Arts for dance, music, theater design, and drama. The faculty members were paid $1,000 for eight weeks of teaching. A festival was scheduled for a full week in August 1940. Hill, Lauterer, Fergusson, and I were in charge, along with the coordinator of the project, Mary Jo Shelley.

For the contemporary music program I chose a quartet movement by Quincy Porter; *Dryades et Pan* for violin and piano by Karol Szymanowski; and songs by Charles Ives, Ernst Bacon, Theodore Chanler, Marc Blitzstein, and Paul Bowles. We also performed Samuel Barber's moving *Dover Beach*. Works by composers-in-residence included a *Suite for Piano and Flute* by Lionel Nowak (whose great reputation as composer-pianist for the Humphrey-Weidman dancers was equaled by his gift as a composer of chamber music), three of my *Eight Inventions for Piano*, Robert McBride's *Wise Apple Five*, and my *Evening Song* and *Morning Song* for voice and flute. The Bacon songs were done with sensitivity by Ruth Ives, who was one of the best singers of contemporary songs. Ethel's performance of *Jimmy's Got a Goil* (text by e e cummings) and *Letter to Freddie* (text by Gertrude Stein) gave her a chance to show her talent as a comedienne.

Ralph Kirkpatrick programmed a Rosenmüller sonata and two psalms by J. J. C. de Mondonville. Ethel and her students performed excerpts from *The Fairy Queen* by Henry Purcell, which was later repeated in a workshop production with costumes and orchestra.

Francis Fergusson wrote a melodramatic farce called *The King and the Duke,* based on *Huckleberry Finn.* Gregory Tucker composed the music and conducted. The ensemble included Roger Goeb, who was on the composing staff and played cornet, and Norman Lloyd, who played both snare and bass drums, sometimes simultaneously. The musicians were set up in an L shape backstage, and we used a second conductor to relay the beat to the players in front. Fergusson later told me that the work had been published and often performed.

With Louis Horst as composer and music director, Martha Graham's group premiered *El Penitente.* Erick Hawkins played the Penitent and Merce Cunningham the Christ figure. At the last minute Horst asked McBride and me to play the score in the performance, with him at the piano. It was another Martha Graham success. Horst's score was economical and direct, a model of its kind.

During the 1940 season, Graham's company also performed *Every Soul Is a Circus,* with music by Paul Nordoff, and with Erick Hawkins as the Ringmaster, Merce Cunningham as the Acrobat, and Jean Erdman as a Spectator. This performance showed me how satire, ridiculous situations, and silly stage behavior could entertain while still carrying a message. *Letter to the World* was another premiere, with music by Hunter Johnson. It was a haunting experience that projected the world of Emily Dickinson so vividly that I reread her poems and set ten of them to music.

For the 1941 festival I changed the music programming. Ralph Kirkpatrick played two solo harpsichord recitals of seventeenth- and eighteenth-century music. I invited Henry Cowell to direct a concert of contemporary music with Lionel Nowak, Ruth Ives, Ethel, and myself as performers. Cowell selected the *Divertimento* for flute and piano by Richard Franko Goldman, later director of the Peabody Conservatory; a sonata by Walter Piston for flute and piano; *Music for Flute and Percussion* by Lou Harrison with Cowell and Frank Wigglesworth playing percussion to my fluting; a group of songs, one by John Becker, a radical composer from the Midwest; and Cowell's early works for prepared piano. The program went smoothly and was very well received.

With endless energy and finesse, the theater and music departments booked themselves into the General Stark Movie Theatre. While the actors did vaudeville scenes for a whole month, the two departments scheduled performances of *The School for Wives* by Molière with ballet music by Lully, and *The Impresario* by Mozart for August 3 and 4. Francis Fergusson made a fine translation of *The Impresario* and staged both works. Billy Park painted stage sets. Newell Jenkins, a fellow who later made an international reputation for his performances and recordings of seventeenth- and eighteenth-century music, was rehearsal pianist, and I was music director. The orchestra consisted of teaching fellows and members of the Vermont State Symphony and guests from the neighborhood. I rehearsed them in small groups and sometimes individually. The League of Composers Wind Quintet from Tanglewood, friends of mine, were passing through town and offered to play the performance without rehearsal and without fee. The quintet included flutist Van Vactor; Adolph Weiss, bassoon; Alvin Etler, oboe; John Barrows, horn; and Robert McBride, clarinet. Since they were first-chair members in leading symphony orchestras, I was delighted to have them. Ethel and her sister, Margaret Codd; Ruth Ives; and Richard Chamberlain were the soloists in *The Impresario*.

In the 1941 festival, the concerts were enjoyed by a small audience. The Humphrey-Weidman *Decade*, with its brilliant diversity, attracted much attention, and Martha's whimsical *Punch and Judy*, with McBride's colorful score, was an immediate success. It reminded me of European puppet shows. I felt this theatrical approach had considerable possibilities and recalled Busoni's *Arlecchino*. The surprise of the festival was the performance of Mozart's *Impresario*. The reviewer from *Variety*, who took time out on his way to Canada to attend the performance, wrote: "[*The Impresario* was] presented in English for the first time in this country . . . a performance that was probably equal to anything the Metropolitan might have done, staged simply, set costing

$12, three vocalists all showing pains-taking care and preparation, delightful acting ability and thoroughly adequate voices. . . . Otto Luening presided over the festivities with brilliance and precision."

The comptroller of the college informed us at the opening of the 1941 summer sessions that the 1940 festival had just about broken even. At the final 1941 accounting all sorts of hidden expenses emerged. When the comptroller added the depreciation of the plant and wear and tear on the lawns during our use of the campus, we blanched. In view of these things, the college decided to cancel further plans for the School of the Arts, and to use the campus for more realistic purposes in the summer. As a token of appreciation, the college continued to invite Martha Graham and Louis Horst to prepare her New York performances in Bennington.

ALAN CARTER and I succeeded in getting a state committee to meet with Governor Wills in the beautiful State Capitol Building in Montpelier to create a Vermont Festival of the Arts to take place in Middlebury, July 24–26, 1941, preceding the Bennington Festival. Governor Wills agreed to be honorary chairman.

The festival, sometimes called the Green Mountain Festival, took place as scheduled. The program included performances by the Humphrey-Weidman company with music by Lionel Nowak and Lehman Engel; Martha Graham's *Every Soul Is a Circus* with the original cast; and the Bennington County Children's Orchestra with myself as soloist in the Bach B Minor Suite. Two concerts by the Vermont State Symphony Orchestra, Alan Carter conducting, included Haydn's *Military* Symphony, Beethoven's Overture to *Egmont*, Tchaikovsky's Symphony No. 6 (*Pathétique*) and his G Major Piano Concerto with José Iturbi as soloist. As a dress rehearsal for the Bennington Festival, we did *The School for Wives* and *The Impresario*, conducted by myself. Helen Harkness Flanders gave a program of American folk songs and ballads with bagpipes. There were also lectures: "New Frontiers in American Culture" by Louis Untermeyer; "The Dance" by John Martin; and "Contemporary Music" by Virgil Thomson.

Thomson spoke positively about what had been accomplished in Vermont, was delighted with *The Impresario,* and wondered if the singers were from the Metropolitan. All in all, the festival was a backbreaking task, but it worked. Carter and I thought that we had built the base for an annual cooperative festival for the state of Vermont. In the long run our guess was right, but there were still many obstacles to overcome.

⤬

IN 1936, QUINCY Porter asked me to submit works for the third Yaddo Festival. I suggested that Ethel and I perform Dante Fiorillo's songs and that the committee consider neglected older works for their programs. I had a letter from the director, Elizabeth Ames, appointing me to the festival committee, which included Porter, John Duke, Richard Donovan, and Ralph Kirkpatrick as consultant for old music.

I went to Yaddo in June for the committee meeting.

After I had worked the heavy iron knocker on the door for some time, I was admitted to the mansion. There was a fountain in the front hall and dazzling collection of bric-a-brac, and a small Russian sleigh. Quincy Porter took me on a quick tour, on which I saw a handsome dining room, a concert hall, and beautiful sleeping rooms. The romanesque bathtubs were so big as to be suitable for group bathing. As an aside of historical interest, I was told that Edgar Allan Poe wrote "The Raven" at Yaddo, when it was still a farm, and frightened the farm boys as he wandered about declaiming, "Nevermore!" Katrina Trask established Yaddo in 1899. Its quiet, esoteric life is threatened only during the racing season, when horseflies and bugle calls from the track briefly disturb those who are in retreat.

At the committee meeting we formulated our aims and purposes and issued a press release that introduced the Yaddo Music Group: a group of musicians—both composers and interpretative artists—invited to be in residence from August 24 to September 16. The aim was to make possible an intimate and informal relationship between composers and performers during the preparation of works. Most of the time would be devoted to contemporary music, but there would be some performances of music of the past. Another aim was to eliminate as much as possible the aspects of competition and professionalism and to make music for its own sake.

We recruited an orchestra of twenty-two. We read through sixty compositions informally and performed twenty-seven of them on our final programs. These included Wallingford Riegger's *Dance Suite* and Dante Fiorillo's controversial *Songs*. Roger Sessions' *Piano Sonata* struck me as being an extension of the aesthetic of the second Viennese school; Walter Piston's *Piano Trio* was the best of America's academic composing; McBride's *Workout* for oboe and piano was a work that merged jazz with other musical elements into a new form; Quincy Porter's Fifth String Quartet showed his mastery of this medium. My *Fantasia Brevis* for clarinet and piano interested the composers because of my use of what I called "acoustic harmony."

Ralph Kirkpatrick discovered a remarkable sonata for strings by Johannes Rosenmüller. I played Vivaldi's lively flute concerto *The Goldfinch* with Ralph. Ethel sang recitatives and arias from operas and cantatas by Rameau, Scarlatti, and Lully; Handel's expressive and brilliant *Il Penseroso* (with flute and strings) was the high point of her offerings. None of us was accustomed to such carefully rehearsed performances of both old and new music on the same program.

The small invited audience was enthusiastic. The New York press gave the Yaddo Festival much space. The *Times* staff correspondent, Howard Taubman, attended rehearsals and performances and spoke with the composers. He wrote a detailed, understanding, and positive review, which ended by saying that the festival was "a forum of composers of varying tendencies and that is achievement enough because contemporary music, whether we like it or not, represents our time, and its direction should be of as much concern as trends in other pursuits." Porter suggested making study recordings of all performances to be sold to educational institutions at cost. For this noble enterprise everyone contributed their services. Forty-nine recordings made available some new American music for study purposes.

In 1937 we read through 125 works and performed 37. The orchestra gave a fine reading of my *Prelude to a Hymn Tune by William Billings,* under my direction. Gerschefski's *Classic*

Overture seemed mighty witty to me, but there were no other orchestral discoveries that year. We did play Haydn's symphony *Le Matin*, and Ethel sang Mozart and Bach arias. David Diamond wrote and Ethel and I performed *The Mad Maid's Song* for flute and voice. Ethel also sang two songs by Evelyn Berckman, who in later years won fame as an author of mystery stories. My Third String Quartet was beautifully performed by the Walden Quartet from Cleveland.

For the 1938 festival, Ralph Kirkpatrick suggested that all the old music should be given on one program. I didn't like the idea too much and wrote to Porter that we needed to break down the artificial differences between old, classical, romantic, contemporary, Communist, Fascist, New England, and Parisian music, as far as the actual experience of hearing music is concerned.

In 1938 thirty-nine compositions were performed and broadcast by WNYC radio in New York. We also made fifty-four recordings. Gail Kubik and the brilliant pianist Gunnar Johansen joined the group. Ethel, Johansen, and I played Cowell's *Vocalise*. Johansen and Hildegarde Donaldson performed David Diamond's *Sonatina for Violin and Piano*, which I liked for its clean, neoclassical style. Johansen played his own *Praeludium, Invention, Chorale and Toccata* for piano.

Kirkpatrick performed *Leçons de Ténèbres* by Couperin, and the Walden Quartet performed William Schuman's Second Quartet—a work so original that I engaged them to play it at Bennington. Howard Taubman of the *New York Times* was especially impressed by Paul Creston's *Choric Dances* and found Ross Lee Finney's *Sonata for Violin and Piano* "interesting." I discovered Theodore Chanler's *Epitaphs*, for voice and piano.

AFTER THE strenuous activities we sometimes relaxed by playing chamber music late at night. One night, at 2:00 A.M., Ralph and I played Bach's B Minor Trio Sonata for flute and piano. I think it was one of the best performances I have ever heard. On these occasions the group would urge me to do impersonations of everyone in and out of sight. I am afraid my sketch of Koussevitzky didn't get me any performances with the Boston Symphony Orchestra. But a staff correspondent of the Associated Press came by and later ended his dispatch by describing me as "not only a serious composer but one of the shrewdest musical parodists alive." This went all over the country and I won an instant reputation as a great wit. People began laughing even when I was serious and would let out guffaws after just looking at me. The power of the press! My recorded impersonations helped to sell the festival records. The Yaddo collection was often used in classes at Bennington, at Converse College, and later at Harvard and other institutions.

In 1940, Lois Wann (oboe), John Kirkpatrick (piano), and Lionel Nowak (piano) joined the group. The latter had the reputation of being the best sight reader in the business. He read piles of piano music without blinking, reading sometimes from almost illegible manuscripts. At the festival *Four Preludes and Fugues* by Roy Harris and *Five Songs* by Ives, sung by Ethel with Nowak at the piano, were given convincing readings. McBride and Nowak played Cowell's Chorale and Ostinato no. 1 and no. 2 for Oboe and Piano. I was impressed with David Diamond's conducting of his own tightly knit *Concerto for Chamber Orchestra*.

Dante Fiorillo had shown me several duets for woodwinds by Alan Hovhaness. Those with flute I played through, and the others I read from the score. We selected his *Prelude and Fugue for Oboe and Bassoon* for the concert—a piece that was a simple and direct musical statement, and an early premiere of a now famous composer.

I returned to Yaddo in 1951 and 1952, the year of the ninth and final festival, which was called Twenty-Five Years of American Music. Yaddo was important to me in a number of ways, not the least of which was that it gave me my first opportunity to study and play a large number of American compositions and perform and conduct many of my own. It was also at Yaddo that I met the poet May Swenson, whose *Tiger's Ghost* I set to music, and Joseph Machlis, a young musicologist who restored my flagging sense of humor.

※

IN OUR MANY discussions about education, Dr. Leigh often mentioned the General Education Board (GEB), which John D. Rockefeller founded in 1902 to reform and improve secondary and higher education. By 1960, the GEB had spent $324,194,920.83—one third of which went to Negro schools and a million dollars of which went to the American Academy in Rome for the study of ancient culture. In 1917 the GEB recommended reforms that prompted the secretary of the American Academy of Arts and Letters to issue a sternly critical statement: ". . . The defects, narrowness, and lack of vision of the program constitute nothing less than a challenge to every man of liberal culture. . . . The new system is frankly utilitarianism to the verge of materialism." In the thirties the GEB gave half a million dollars each to Bennington, Sarah Lawrence, Stephens College, and the University of Minnesota in support of John Dewey's philosophy of progressive education.

In the thirties and forties, many college presidents and foundation executives either discovered the existence of the arts or believed that they should be doing something about them. Most of these administrators needed consultants or guides for their new adventures in the arts. In 1937 the Association of American Colleges (AAC) launched the Concert Project with a grant from the Carnegie Foundation. Eric Clarke, a knowledgeable amateur English musician and the brother of the well-known composer Rebecca Clarke, was the director of the project. He had been director of the Eastman Theater, and later became the administrative director of the Metropolitan Opera in New York. The aims of the Concert Project (which later became the Arts and Humanities Project) were to stimulate interest in music and the arts as integral parts of higher education. To this end it prepared programs of particular interest for individual colleges and provided these at cost to the members of the AAC. Experimental in character, the project's various offerings had features that were not available to these colleges through ordinary channels.

Clarke combed colleges to find people who could express themselves in unusual ways and who could serve as peripatetic professors to spread the verities of the arts. Clarke's ideal professor was expected to maintain a high standard of performance in his field and to be a person who viewed his field as a part of liberal culture—one who was interested not only in those people who studied his subject, but in the many more people who did not. Clarke believed that Bennington was one of the best places to recruit such professors. His first choice was Julian DeGray, who performed a large piano concert repertory, knew twelve languages, and had taken the humanities program at Columbia. Clarke then invited Ethel and me to tour the Midwest for two weeks. We were given an honorarium of sixty dollars per visit, and expenses. Our itinerary included Stephens College for Women in Columbus, Missouri; Principia College in Elsah, Illinois; Rockford College for Women in Rockford, Illinois; and Knox College in Galesburg, Illinois.

Before we left on the tour we went to Wisconsin for Christmas. When I told Father about the plan, he said, "An excellent opportunity. You can try out your joint programs together. You, Otto, like to lecture and have not had much formal education in America. You must use your head. For the first half-hour, just ask questions. You will then be able to make helpful suggestions and deliver a good lecture."

Our train schedule was tight. We traveled between 7:00 A.M. and 1:00 A.M. the next morning, often arriving at inconvenient hours, without time to unpack or eat. During the two weeks, we gave four formal concerts and four informal ones, chosen from the repertory we had tried out many times. In addition to our concerts, I gave lectures on a wide variety of subjects, a task that while diverting was also exhausting.

At Principia, a Christian Science college, our concerts were a great success—but not, according to the dean, as good as those in the regular artists' series. I reminded him that the fee for each of us was around twelve dollars per day. After I gave my lecture, "The Creative Impulse as an Essential in Life," he complained that I talked too much about craft and too little about faith. But when he read that the St. Louis Symphony was playing my *Two Symphonic Interludes,* he arranged interviews on radio and with students about "how to do it. . . ."

At Stephens, Maud Adams, the famous Peter Pan, headed the drama department. Because I had seen her in that play in Milwaukee when I was eight she opened all doors for me. The music and humanities departments at Stephens were first-rate, but they were overshadowed by Miss Adams, whose students all wanted to play Peter Pan when they grew up. . . .

At Knox College, I addressed the entire student body at

8:00 A.M. President Carter Davidson introduced me: "Mr. Luening teaches at Bennington College, which has the highest tuition of any college in the country. The college does a great deal in the field of the arts. If you would pay us the highest tuition in the country, *we* would do great things in the arts. Now Mr. Luening will talk to you about art."

The Illinois farm boys were scuffling their feet and coughing. I was only half awake, but I had a brilliant idea. I pointed to a big fellow in the front row and said, "I see you wear a green necktie."

He looked nervous. I pointed to a fellow behind him. "And you, a red sweater."

They both looked nervous.

"He likes green, you like red. That represents different artistic tastes."

I slowly got around to blue and brown jeans, wide and narrow tuxedo pants, blonds and brunettes, blue eyes and brown eyes. The coughing had stopped. This was barnstorming of a high order. Ethel sang songs from Carl Sandburg's *Songbag*. He was born in Galesburg and I talked about him. The boys cheered. I described a hornpipe and played a Handel jig and explained that modern composers also write compositions based on dance music: "Listen to this. It's called 'In the Groove.' Had Handel written it he probably would have called it 'In a Lovely Myrtle Grove,' but Robert McBride likes Benny Goodman. Do you fellows know Goodman?"

All hands were raised.

After we played, a stupendous ovation with foot-shuffling and dog barks greeted us. I was trembling from lack of breath. President Davidson walked over. "I didn't think you would make it; I was testing you." He congratulated Ethel. "They don't like to talk about Art. They like to play and sing. Come to the house for dinner."

At the president's house some faculty members congratulated us for talking about art without being physically assaulted. We had a quiet meal talking about art. After dinner, Ethel saw some ballads lying on the piano and asked who sang. The president said he did. She asked him to sing and he chose "The Gravedigger's Song."

He had an excellent bass voice and with a little encouragement sang nine more solos. He produced a volume of male quartets. Two members of the music faculty, the president, and I joined forces and sang for an hour. He was excellent and finally explained that he had been a member of the Harvard Glee Club. Palestrina and Bach were next. We finished singing them at ten-thirty, but he thought they were a little highbrow, so he dug out a couple of volumes of college songs. By eleven-thirty three of us were still going strong, but the voice teacher was hoarse. The president insisted upon another half-hour of songs. We wound up with "Good Night, Ladies." He was a fine sight reader and we had a great time. We asked him if he ever sang with the students but he shook his head. "It is bad for discipline." He became president of Union College in the 1940s and had a brilliant academic career. Knox College had quite a musical atmosphere, but was a bit rough around the edges. . . .

At Western Reserve University in Cleveland, the high-powered music faculty did not need helpful advice but good concerts instead. We did some unusually interesting Bach and Mozart. I spoke before a small audience about the influence of composers on their composing students. We played works by Busoni, Jarnach, Luening, and McBride. It served as a nice study of craftsmanship as it is handed over from teacher to students, but the faculty really wanted me to do impersonations, and I obliged for an hour and a half. . . .

We returned to Bennington exhausted. Our honorarium for the tour was $216. Eric Clarke wrote that everyone liked our visit, and he wanted to know if we would like to make a longer tour in the South during our 1939–1940 sabbatical. It was an opportunity for Ethel to sing often in concert and at my lectures. It was also a great opportunity for me to find out what was going on in colleges and universities. I had never experienced a class reunion, fraternity life, or a commencement. We agreed to go on the tour for slightly more than three months starting in February 1940. We were both anxious to see if we could make a living by free-lancing, so we took off an extra semester without pay.

WE VISITED twenty-one colleges and universities in South Carolina, North Carolina, Alabama, Georgia, Florida, Mississippi, Arkansas, and Tennessee. Mr. Clarke explained that southern colleges lagged behind the educational standards of the rest of the country and were still recovering from near-bankruptcy caused by the Depression. In addition to our concerts and classes, he hoped that we would "join in." "Sing along," he said as he hoisted his six-foot-four frame onto his desk and sang in a fine tenor Brahms's *Were I a Pretty Little Bird*. We applauded. He hoped that we would support the faculties and students as they tried to reorient themselves and save their schools. It sounded somewhat more like a rescue operation than injecting cultural vitamin shots.

It was impossible to make a train schedule that would work. So we packed our traveling library, clothes, and flute into the trunk and back seat of our 1930 Auburn convertible and drove in a frightful blizzard from New York toward Winthrop College in Rock Hill, South Carolina. We arrived and just had time to unpack when the president phoned to tell us that we were scheduled to rehearse in the Arts Center in a half hour.

We were astonished to find ourselves in a first-rate modern theater, seating about two thousand. The president explained, "If you put up a building, it will eventually be used for what it was intended. This is one way to get things going." An enthusiastic audience of seventeen hundred attended our concert. Miss Turner from the English department arranged a program of folk music. We used songs from Nova Scotia that I had heard when I was composing *Evangeline*, and I showed the students how the songs had influenced the opera. We had a follow-up program in which Ethel sang New England folk songs and some from the Hebrides. Then Miss Turner and Ethel illustrated how composers used poems by Shakespeare, Goethe, Whitman, and the Elizabethans. I helped at the piano. Cooperation was excellent and our discussions were fruitful. Winthrop planned to examine their regional music. The visit was deceptively easy and pleasant.

FOR MORE more than three months I drove our Auburn—with only one train interlude. The schedule was tight, roads were not well marked, gas stations were few and far between, and backroad shortcuts were hazardous. There were some roads that consisted of planks laid across a base of small rocks and covered with

fine gravel that washed away when it rained. On a warm day the
air was sweetly perfumed by the foliage; sometimes we heard
nightingales and mourning doves. . . .

Limestone College for Women in Gaffney, South Carolina,
wanted us to show how one went about teaching non-music students appreciation of music. Limestone had no budget for music.
There were no scores and books and very few recordings. I later
told Eric Clarke about the college's needs, and eventually a gift
from the Carnegie Collection arrived.

Ethel and I went to a combined American literature and general music class and talked with the students about regional
music. The students sang songs they knew. I played a fuguing
tune by William Billings, one of America's first composers who,
I told them, armed only with a pitchpipe and his genius, wrote
original music for New Englanders to sing. I also played a tune by
Conrad Beissel, a self-taught German genius who joined the
Seventh Day Baptists (Dunkers) and founded the Ephrata Cloister in Pennsylvania before the Moravians arrived. (He was the
basis for one of the characters in Thomas Mann's *Doktor Faustus*.)
We had a few Moravian compositions with us and the students
were interested to learn that Benjamin Franklin had printed
Beissel's hymn collections. A girl volunteered to sing some Kentucky mountain songs.

The students knew many folk songs from memory, so we
were able to make an easy transition to American poets like Whitman, Longfellow, Emerson, and Thoreau, who had influenced
and were still influencing American vocal composers, including
Charles Ives. They were extremely interested and rather excited
when Ethel sang McBride's *Nonsense Syllables* with flute accompaniment, which reminded them of speaking in tongues, an experience they had had at revival meetings. . . .

Converse College in Spartanburg, South Carolina, was a
famous women's liberal arts college that had relatively strong financial support. Its academic standards were high, its auditorium
was excellent, and it was the leading music school in the South. It
supported an annual, nationally known music festival that imported its main events. Ernst Bacon was dean of the School of
Music. An advocate of musical Home Rule for our country, he
was making Converse into an important regional center. He

wrote to us that he needed help to bring about a cultural turnaround at this old and established college. For our public concert we performed some lesser-known Bach, Mozart, Schubert, and contemporary Americans, including some of Bacon's songs. On the next afternoon we gave "A Panorama of American Music," starting with Billings and stressing indigenous developments, with many illustrations. We discussed in detail the possibilities inherent in the region around Converse and made suggestions about how to develop the music life. A program of chamber music with the Converse faculty included a quartet, *Tocanta*, that Cowell wrote for Analee Camp, Ernst Bacon, and the Luenings. Bacon insisted on a program of musical satires. He found them an effective way to bring ideas to the attention of the American public in a way that they could understand. My "musicological lecture"—"The History of the Violin Bow from Horse to Hindemith," which gave plenty of background material about horses, eventually arrived at the wood in the bow, and left out music altogether—was a success. The program was a real demonstration of style differences, all of which I improvised, vocally and on the piano. . . .

Paine College in Augusta was originally a black Methodist coeducational liberal arts college—biracial in its leadership, mostly black in enrollment. Its aim was to develop mutual understanding and esteem between blacks and whites, but in 1940 visiting a Negro college in Atlanta was risky, and we were labeled "nigger-lovers" by the town for living on campus. Professor Fax of the music department arranged for the entire faculty and staff to meet with us collectively and privately. They wanted guidance and suggestions about how to broaden and strengthen their curriculum.

At our first meeting we discussed post-Depression poverty, the neglect of building and maintenance programs, and details of the curriculum. Ethel and I were now educational, artistic, and cultural consultants. Two librarians complained that they had no money for books. I told the president that as a seventh-grade dropout much of my education had been acquired at libraries; I suggested that even a small investment and a drive for book gifts would bring substantial rewards. A discussion with Miss Clark of Home Economics and with Mrs. Ross, the dietitian, was off our usual track. I suggested that George Washington Carver's idea of concentrating and developing what was right around him— peanuts, yams, soybeans and cotton—was one way to handle a slim budget. The home economics lady wanted to know how to make simple homes attractive. She showed us some hooked rugs, pottery, carvings, woven baskets, and needlework with individual designs. She said the students were good at handicrafts, but she didn't believe their works were useful. We suggested that these artifacts could be used as attractive decorations in simple homes.

Mr. Brown from History and Mrs. Steeley from Sociology wondered if they should first teach local history and then go back to Negro history in America and Africa. I thought it was a fine idea, and Ethel suggested that they keep in touch with the students who had painted most of the originals hanging on the walls and start an art department.

The group had a simple dignity that was beautiful. Before and after each discussion they bowed their heads in silent prayer. Reverend Paul from Religious Education and doctors Cutler and Chandler from Science explained that they all worked for the moral and cultural development of the students. We spoke about Protestant, Catholic, and Jewish religious music by classical composers. They did not know much about it. In the distance, we heard students singing hymns expressively. We urged the faculty to develop their own religious music at Paine.

We left exhausted but exhilarated. A letter from President Peters reached us en route, thanking us and praising Ethel's singing. . . .

The Georgia State College for Women in Milledgeville was a businesslike teachers' training institute. At a faculty meeting we attended we heard discreet complaints about workloads and teaching methods. Some of the faculty remembered their youthful ideals and Ethel got them to sing folk songs and spirituals. Later we were ushered to a glee club meeting, where I was supposed to talk on "The Value of Music in Leisure Time." Instead, I asked the hundred women in the auditorium to sing some of their favorite songs. They whooped and yelled. The librarian got out the choral numbers they were studying, and I conducted. Ethel then coached some of the very good singers. One of them asked to sing a blues number and I called on the others to harmonize.

We continued for two hours, and at the end I remarked that they had demonstrated the title of my lecture.

The following day, I gave my then-famous lecture called "Music in Everyday Life." The auditorium was full of southern beauties, half of whom looked bored. Some were writing letters home and others were knitting.

"I see that a lot of you are not interested in music. We'll see about that."

The knitting stopped.

"I have no objections if you write home while I am giving this talk. My lecture will be a background for your writing. We have background music for practically everything. Music to listen to while we do something else, for instance; music to listen to while taking a bath or while stealing hubcaps. Some people like to listen to music while they are listening to music. I am going to make a record that you could listen to for the background information while I am giving the lecture."

The students shrieked with delight; my wit had slain them. I talked about foot-tapping, movie music, folk music, and hymns, and how many great composers had incorporated these things into their own works. Ethel sang beautifully. The women thought us a great team. . . .

I had heard from Francis Fergusson at Bennington about the strong literary tradition at Vanderbilt, of which Allen Tate, Robert Penn Warren, John Crowe Ransom, Andrew Lytle, Donald Davidson, and Cleanth Brooks had been or were a part. Our schedule at Vanderbilt was a clear indication that this institution already had a cultural tradition and a valuable one. They wanted a lecture on old and new American music, with recordings, followed by discussions with both students and individual faculty members. I was able to use the Yaddo and New Music Quarterly recordings, and the discussions were lively. Before our concert Donald Davidson had us meet his writing group, with whom we discussed musical settings of poems by Emily Dickinson, e e cummings, Gertrude Stein, and Whitman, by the composers Ernst Bacon, Marc Blitzstein, Ives, and Paul Bowles (who later also won fame as a writer). This led to a special session by George Pullen Jackson and a double quartet of his Old Harp Singers, who sang a number of white spirituals for us. They then gave a stirring reading of American choral music, both old and new, that we had brought with us. Jackson had revived the wonderful white gospel songs from the Sacred Heart and the Southern Harmony collections. Their performances were very moving, and it was our earliest experience with the roots of what has since become known as a type of gospel music. By the time we gave our concert everybody was geared to it. Our last group included some folk songs, and with the help of the Old Harp Singers I got the entire audience of about eight hundred to sing along. . . .

At Georgia State Women's College in Valdosta (now coeducational) the president, Dr. Frank Reade, complained bitterly about financial difficulties. He said the only course for the college was to become part of the state university system, a trend we heard about elsewhere. He tried to compensate for faculty shortages by using recordings and the college radio station for educational purposes. At a conference with a group of faculty members, we suggested that recordings could be used in music, literature, and language classes for study purposes. Carefully planned education programs for the college radio station also seemed a natural way to strengthen the college's position in the local community. . . .

Ouachita College, a Baptist College in Arkadelphia, Arkansas, was located near a diamond mine. One could pay for the right to dig for diamonds and we tried to arrange this, but the Ouachita authorities thought we were being paid to do other things. At chapel the first-rate college choir sang for us, and then I spoke for an hour about the relationship and influence of dance on concert music. My lecture was a complete disaster. Nobody even looked pleased. I asked what I had done wrong, and they explained that dancing was not permitted at that Baptist institution. In a meeting, the music, speech and drama, and English department faculties, some students, and the president, got down to business: "How do you streamline the music curriculum while upholding Baptist traditions?" The faculty really opened up with their problems. We suggested that with such an excellent choir director and such good voices, church music could be developed and strengthened. The suggestion was greeted with discreet cheers. . . .

Mississippi State College arranged a conference with two professors of physics, four of English, two of history, a mathematics professor, the bandleader, and the dean of the school of education to cross-question us for several hours about how these different subjects were taught at Bennington, and we discussed late into the night Bennington's education policies. There were many class visits, and then I conducted a huge band in a rehearsal of Hanson's *Nordic* Symphony. They were remarkably good. Everyone was also very much interested in the contemporary music we had brought with us. It was a good mixture of practical music and aesthetic interest. . . .

The Alabama College for Women in Montevallo had a very good general faculty with many graduates from the best Eastern universities. Professor LeBaron from Harvard ran the well-organized music department. He did not seem to like the idea of visitors from a new and experimental college coming in to look over his department. He asked me to lecture about American folk music. In the evening we again performed and discussed American music, old and new. Later, we met with drama, dance, history of civilization, and American history classes and ended with a bull session to show them just how music fits with everything.

WE LEFT our car in Wilton, Alabama, and traveled to Jackson, Tennessee, by train. We set out at 11:30 A.M. The parlor car on the Missouri-Ohio was of nineteenth-century vintage. A wood-burning, iron-bellied stove was stoked by the brakeman. The swivel seats were covered with well-worn plush. The cars were segregated and there were many more blacks than whites riding. We arrived at Maplesville, Alabama, where we made another connection for Jackson and arrived at eight-forty-five in the evening. No dinner was served, but we did have coffee and donuts.

Lane College in Jackson was a coed, black, Methodist Episcopal college. In spite of General Education Board grants, it was having serious financial difficulties. As at Paine, the president scheduled a meeting with the entire faculty and staff, twenty-one in all. The participation of chemistry and biology professors, the secretaries, the matrons, the athletic coach, and the business manager made it a novel experience. We spent an afternoon discussing the Bennington educational innovations. The Lane staff was a devoted and dedicated group of people with high ideals, who were determined to succeed in spite of their poverty. I learned later that the parents of Alex Haley, the author of *Roots*, had been connected with the college some years before our visit.

As at Paine, I lectured about accepting and developing regional and racial backgrounds and building the library, art department, and vocal music. Their singers had beautiful voices and the glee clubs were outstanding.

On route I had a telegram from Frederick D. Keppel, president of the Carnegie Foundation, inviting me to take part in a symposium entitled "Characteristics of American Culture and Its Place in General Culture" at the General Meeting of the American Philosophical Society in Philadelphia. I left Ethel behind and went to the symposium. Though it was a great rush, I was terribly impressed with the fast company I was keeping. Among the distinguished speakers were Lewis Mumford, Archibald MacLeish, and Professor Dayton C. Miller, the foremost authority on acoustics, who delivered a paper called "The Pipes of Pan, Old and New."

My paper was called "Music." I gave a panoramic view of the American musical scene beginning with music in the colonial period, and used records to accent certain points. I said that I thought American musicians were no longer second-class citizens, that American popular music had made its influence felt in the world, that American-trained singers and instrumentalists were developing their own style, that our school system was developing literate musicians and sensitive audiences, that American folk songs had been discovered by a larger public, and that American composers, as a group, had arrived. I also mentioned the emergence of electrical instruments.

I joined Ethel at Coker College in Hartsville, South Carolina. We were asked to introduce the student body as a whole to wider musical experiences than they had had. Ethel and I talked about the relation of music to society and about music as therapy, and Ethel showed how different languages affected songs and opera. The president later wrote us to say that because we had introduced them to folk music they had been inspired to get Sandburg to start a festival featuring folk music and spirituals. He also said that we had bucked up the music department.

WHAT I LEARNED at these colleges can't be measured. I hope that Ethel and I brought something to them. I know that by the

seventies all of these colleges had expanded greatly. Some became a part of state university systems, some became universities, faculty and students tripled in numbers, folk and choral
music flourished, and many building programs were underway.
These colleges were living symbols of a Southern renaissance. I
like to believe that the Carnegie Foundation's Art and Humanities Project for the AAC had something to do with this.

It was nice to learn years later that all of these institutions recovered and made valuable educational contributions to their
various regions. We knew that after the Depression dedicated
faculties subsidized students by working overtime for long hours
and low pay. Students and their families, too, made heavy sacri-
fices, but everybody believed in the value and necessity of education.

Chapter 20

The Business of Music
1936 to Present

ON JUNE 4, 1936, I RECEIVED A LETTER from Henry Cowell in
care of the sheriff at Redwood City, California, in which he said
that he was being held on a homosexual charge. Cowell asked that
his friends not believe the Hearst newspaper reports, but only
the court record. In October 1936 he was sentenced to San Quentin for a term of one to fourteen years.

Some of Cowell's friends felt compelled to sustain his reputation as a composer and to keep New Music Editions (NME) and
New Music Quarterly Recordings (NMQR) going. Cowell had
contributed and collected substantial sums to start these ventures
devoted to the publication and recording of experimental, or, as
he called it, "ultramodern" music.

Dr. Leigh and the Bennington College Cooperative Store
were interested in the two projects, so I wrote to Cowell offering
to take over NME and NMQR until he was released. His answer
came with stickered instructions from the California State Prison
System about how to correspond with prisoners. Cowell said that
Gerald Strang would run NME in Los Angeles, where it was established. He asked me and Wallingford Riegger to carry on
NMQR. NMQR was in bad shape, as arrangements that had been
made for Columbia Records to take it over had fallen through.

By November of 1936, I had organized a board of directors
consisting of Riegger, Harrison Kerr, and Edwin Gerschefski in
New York; Gerald Strang in Los Angeles; Cowell; and Gladys
Stevens and myself in Bennington. I was chairman and coordinator. All committee members, wives, and friends pitched in to
make things work. The Bennington Coop acted as distributor on

commission. Performers too volunteered their services. Recordings and pressings were made in New York.

Communication with Cowell was complicated. My main correspondents in the West were his mother, Olive Cowell, in San Francisco, and Strang; some of Cowell's friends in the East were Riegger, Percy Grainger, Ethel, and I.

Cowell's accommodation to life in San Quentin was remarkable. He first worked as spooler in the jute mill. The prison psychiatrist and Dr. Schuder of the education department soon had Cowell conducting music classes, and the bandleader used him as an arranger. Later, Cowell rehearsed the band every day, composed a symphony for it, and organized a string orchestra.

Ethel became his liaison in the East for ordering and receiving pieces to be performed. His *Two Chorales and Ostinato* were played at Yaddo and in New York, and were recorded. Ethel requested that he compose a vocalise for voice, flute, and piano for the Yaddo Festival. She needed to have the approval of the warden and his secretary, who then stamped the copy and sent it to her. It was performed at Yaddo, at Bennington, and in New York. Henry sent long and detailed directions for performance. He composed *Song of Life* and *Chorus for Contraltos,* both of which were performed at Bennington and elsewhere, and *Tocanta* for soprano, flute, cello and piano, which we did at Bennington and at Converse College.

As absentee committee member for NME and NMQR, he wrote detailed opinions about everything, ranging from the selection of compositions and artists to public relations, complimentary copies, advertising, and pricing. He even arranged that the NMQR releases be acquired by the San Quentin education department and added to the prison library.

Cowell's projects were important to us because, although there had been some attempts to record, and Cos Cob Press and Arrow Press had published some contemporary scores, most of the work remained to be done. When launched, NMQR had three hundred subscribers. In two years this had shrunk to fifty, even though the early list of recordings was quite distinguished: Ruth Crawford's *Andante for String Quartet* with the New World String Quartet; the Finale from Wallingford Riegger's *Trio for Flute, Harp and Violoncello* with Georges Barrère, Carlos Salzedo, and Horace Britt; Charles Ives's *Barn Dance* and *In the Night* and Carl Ruggles's *Lilacs and Toys*, performed by the Pan American Orchestra, Nicolas Slonimsky, conductor, and soprano Judith Litante; Cowell's *Suite for Woodwinds* and Nicolas Berezowsky's *Suite for Woodwind Quintet*, performed by the Barrère Ensemble of Woodwinds; George Antheil's Sonata no. 2 for Piano, with Lydia Hoffman; Ives's *General William Booth Enters into Heaven*, performed by Radiana Pazmor, soprano, and Genevieve Pitot, piano; Walter Piston's *Three Pieces for Flute, Clarinet and Bassoon* with the Barrère Ensemble; Richard Donovan's *Two Songs with String Quartet* and his *Suite for Piano;* Aaron Copland's *Vocalise* with Ethel singing and the composer at the piano; my songs *Only Themselves, A Farm Picture, Here the Frailest Leaves of Me,* and *Hast Never Come to Thee an Hour,* with Ethel singing and myself playing flute in one and piano in three; Elie Siegmeister's *The Strange Funeral in Braddock;* and music by the Cuban composers Amadeo Roldán, José Ardevol, and Alejandro García Caturla.

We had a mailing campaign. The main job was to raise money, build up the subscription list, and fill orders promptly. There was not much artistic activity—mostly business. We anticipated an annual deficit of two hundred dollars.

Because of an illness, Charles Ives declined my invitation to be a member of the board, although he did contribute one hundred dollars every month, a much-needed subsidy. In the thirties, Ives was known as a composer to only a small group of admirers. His second career was life insurance. He became the head of the largest insurance company in the country, and he amassed what was then a fortune. He subsidized the printing, recording, and distribution of his own works, and he was a generous supporter of a number of contemporary music ventures.

In 1938, I wrote to Ives again and received a letter from his son-in-law saying that Ives would continue to send fifty to one hundred dollars per month for NME and NMQR. He also offered to subsidize one of his own works and a work by a younger composer.

Drawing on his business experience, Ives discussed a plan with Riegger and Lehman Engel to establish a partial merger and closer cooperation between NME, NMQR, and Arrow Press.

Riegger and Copland were lukewarm about the idea. Copland suggested I make the decision. After numerous conferences and letters, I thought I discovered a rivalry between Copland, Cowell, and Varèse about leadership in aesthetic matters, so I concentrated on cooperation in practical matters of mutual benefit—though I, like everybody else, was not able to free myself of "enlightened" self-interest.

By 1939 THE need for all nonprofit groups to cooperate in their distribution was evident to everyone. Riegger suggested a motto: "The more irons we have in the fire, the fewer headaches in the future." I invited William Schuman, the twenty-nine-year-old composer who was making waves in New York music waters, to join the NMQR board. He was too busy to join the board, but his administrative genius became apparent when he tried to get Columbia Records to take over NMQR and to get us three hundred ten-dollar subscriptions. Columbia had already turned us down, so Bill suggested a merger that included the American Composers Alliance. We weren't ready for this either, but Bill persisted and eventually merged just about everything in town when he became president of Lincoln Center in 1962. NMQR rewarded Schuman for his interest and ideas by recording his *Quartet for Four Bassoons*. Our more prosaic job was to keep NMQR afloat. After limited promotion we had good reviews in Cleveland and Chicago. Even the conservative *Boston Transcript* gave Ives a rave review, and *Time* magazine wrote: "It has taken a generation for concertgoers to realize that . . . Ives is no crackpot, but one of the most authentic . . . contemporary U.S. composers." Heartened by this sensational response, the board members sent out hundreds of personal cards; single sales picked up, but no one wanted to subscribe to records they hadn't heard.

In 1938 we released Edgar Varèse's *Octandre* for flute, oboe, clarinet, bassoon, trumpet, horn, trombone, and string bass, conducted by Nicolas Slonimsky (Varèse's first instrumental work on discs, after *Ionisation* for percussion), and six songs by Ives, sung by the baritone Mordecai Bauman. These were followed by recordings of works by Paul Bowles, Quincy Porter, Mary Howe, David Diamond, Ernst Bacon, and myself. This was a fine list of new names but the record-buying public didn't agree. Business went from bad to worse. The Cooperative Store notified us it would terminate our agreement in October 1939. Our losses had been two hundred dollars annually, but we still had $637.25 in cash, just about enough to pay our bills.

NMQR moved to Gerschefski's basement apartment in New York, until, helped by the tireless efforts of Miss Sidney Robertson (whom he later married) and other friends, Cowell was paroled and returned to New York. The company was renamed New Music Recordings, and distribution was handled by the American Music Center until NMR folded in 1948.

But the idea we were projecting took hold in the thirties and forties, and there were numerous attempts by Columbia, Westminster, Mercury, Capitol, and the Eastman School to bring out contemporary American music. Most of them were short-lived.

In 1949 the Alice M. Ditson Fund at Columbia University granted $5,000 to the American Musical Associates to establish the American Recording Society (ARS), an outgrowth of the Children's Record Guild that had been launched by the Greystone Press, a publishing firm. Horace Grenell, Douglas Moore, Quincy Porter, and I were the officers of Musical Associates, with Henry Allen Moe as legal adviser. Grenell was the director-producer, and his job was to develop a mail-order subscription record club using all of the resources of book-club publicity to launch the project.

By February 20, 1953, ARS had recorded fifty-six compositions by fifty American composers and, in addition, minstrel songs of the nineteenth century, Back Bay psalmody, and Catholic mission music. Conductors and instrumental and vocal soloists included fine American artists such as Dean Dixon, Beveridge Webster, Bernard Greenhouse, Bethany Beardslee, and the Berkshire, Walden, and New Music quartets. Two hundred thousand dollars was spent in advertising for subscribers.

The circulation from September 1951 to April 1954 ranged from 4,000 to 29,000 per record. The subscribers list reached 50,000. The average sale was 5,300. ARS proved that there was a market for recordings by American composers, and the upshot was that Mercury, the Eastman School, the Concert Hall Society, and Decca entered the field with more vigor, and Columbia moved its chamber-music project off the shelves.

In November 1952, Greystone Press notified Grenell that they had enough names and records available in the Children's Record Guild and Young Peoples Records to maintain its large subscription list. They turned to standard works and so ARS was phased out. Musical Associates earned royalties in the amount of $5,000.

In early September 1954, Oliver Daniel, coordinating manager of the American Composers Alliance and the greatest promoter of American composers I have ever known, had dinner with me at the Gold Rail restaurant near Columbia University. He had been recording works by ACA composers. We decided that with the American Musical Associates' $5,000 and a further subsidy of $10,000 from ACA, we could launch a new company devoted to the recording of American compositions. Composers Recordings was incorporated on September 30, 1954, by Oliver Daniel, Douglas Moore, and myself. The first board of directors, two-thirds American Composers Alliance and one-third American Musical Associates, included Avery Claflin, Quincy Porter, Douglas Moore, Oliver Daniel, William Bergsma, Henry Cowell, Robert Ward, Horace Grenell, Alfredo Antonini, and Otto Luening.

Avery Claflin was the first president of Composers Recordings, Inc. (CRI). He had had a fine career as a composer, but like Charles Ives, thought better of it, and became president of the French American Banking Corporation in New York. His setting of *Lament for April 15* with text from Tax Form 1040 was one of our best sellers. When he retired from the bank, he was just the man we needed to keep an eye on the bottom line. Subsequent presidents were David Hall, Chou Wen-chung, Jack Beeson, F. Blair Weille, and myself. Carter Harman became executive vice-president and producer in 1967. The board has included a number of the most prominent names in American music as members. Among those who were active through many years were Roger Goeb and Oliver Daniel (for a while both indispensable), Vladimir Ussachevsky, Hugo Weisgall, Richard Donovan, Charles Dodge, John Lessard, William Mayer, Frank Wigglesworth, Charles Wuorinen, Hale Smith, Raoul Pleskow, Carl Sigmon, Joan Tower, Pril Smiley, Nicolas Roussakis, Robert Miller, Robert Ward, Mark Brunswick, and Eugene Bruck.

I was president from 1968 until 1970. I suggested that we needed legal and business minds on our board of directors, and Robert Miller, a lawyer, and my nephew David Luening, an executive at IBM, were elected. In April 1975, I was reelected with Jack Beeson as copresident. Our job was to convert CRI to tax-exempt status. In October, Beeson, Miller, and I visited the New York IRS office for this purpose but were turned down. We appealed to the Washington IRS office. We put all the facts on the table and made an impassioned plea for American composers. Our application was considered carefully and at length, and we were granted tax-exempt status effective January 1, 1977. Blair Weille, the new president, and William Mayer, the new chairman, aided by Verna Fine Gordon, are developing mail order merchandising.

CRI, having begun with very little capital, could record only compositions that were subsidized. Subsidy came from individuals and over the years from a number of universities, orchestras, and foundations. CRI is now a multiple-purpose organization with an archive of twentieth-century music. The policy is to keep recordings in press. The catalogue in 1980 listed 900 compositions by 460 composers on 300 records. The company records mostly works by living composers and does not duplicate records available on other labels. It does reissue, whenever possible, records deleted by other companies and recordings of historical interest. Twenty-four CRI composers are Pulitzer Prize winners.

꙾

IN THE THIRTIES a main problem confronting American composers was the lack of a central reference library and distribution facility. No one knew how to get hold of American music. The WPA material was hard to find, and publishers rarely looked beyond their own limited lists.

Quincy Porter, Henry Moe, and I had discussed this problem in Bennington in the fall of 1938 and in January 1939. Moe, Thomas Whitney Surette, Porter, and I met in New York to found the Council for the Advancement and Diffusion of American Music. Moe offered his services as legal adviser and drew up a statement of aims and purposes to facilitate fund raising. The council's purposes were the advancement and diffusion of knowledge, understanding, and appreciation of music, particularly music by American composers. The council proposed to establish a center for the distribution of published and recorded American music of a "serious" nature and to make available at a convenient location in New York City all existing publications and recordings of this music insofar as its facilities would permit. The council believed after three years the center would be a self-supporting enterprise. I was delegated to sound out various composers and organizations and spoke with Aaron Copland, Mary Howe, Harrison Kerr, William Schuman, and the New Music Quarterly Recording Committee, all of whom were enthusiastic about the American Music Center.

Various organizations then elected members to represent them on the council: Copland represented Arrow Press and ACA; Howard Hanson, Eastman School Publications and Recordings; Marion Bauer, Society for the Publication of American Music; Quincy Porter, Yaddo and New England Conservatory Recordings; and myself, New Music Publications and New Music Quarterly Recordings.

In March 1939 we met at Copland's 63rd Street studio to incorporate the American Music Center (AMC) as a nonprofit educational corporation. The charter members were Marion Bauer, Copland, Hanson, Porter, and myself. Porter and I were appointed fund raisers. Our budget was set at $2,695 for the first year. In August the Weyman Trust in Boston granted us $2,500, renewable in 1940. The center was opened in November 1939 at 37 West 42nd Street in New York City.

A press release announcing the center as a nonprofit dealer for American music from all publishers at list price appeared in New York, Boston, Pittsburgh, Chicago, Cleveland, and Los Angeles. Some newspapers ran Sunday articles.

For the next twenty years I served as chairman of various AMC boards that included many of our prominent American composers. I was often in the office in New York and the rest of the time I supervised the center by mail, telephone, and telegram from wherever my travels took me. Harrison Kerr as secretary was the first indispensable man; Ray Green, the second. Both were overworked and underpaid, but devoted to the cause of American music.

In 1941 we sent scores worth several thousand dollars to eight foreign countries, fifteen symphony orchestras, CBS, NBC, fifty-three universities and colleges, and forty libraries in the United States.

Our activities attracted the attention of Nelson Rockefeller. In the early forties he wrote us from the Washington office of the Coordinator of Inter-American Affairs, asking us to administer a commissioning project for Latin American composers, to assemble music for deposit in Latin America and to arrange for an exchange of music by North, Central, and South American composers. Henry Cowell, then working in the New York coordinator's office, and Charles Seeger of the Pan American Union, developed these projects with the help of the AMC.

With the endorsement of Frederick Keppel, the Carnegie Foundation gave us a grant to carry on our work and said we were an operating agency that deserved support. For the first twenty years of AMC our projects rapidly folded, and it looked many times as though we would have to close shop. Something always happened to save us at the last minute.

Mrs. Ann M. Gannett and the National Federation of Music Clubs were our major supporters for several years. Then, Broadcast Music Incorporated (BMI) and the American Society of Composers, Authors and Publishers (ASCAP) took over.

At the annual federation meeting in Detroit in 1941, John Paine, secretary of ASCAP, Merritt Tompkins, president of BMI, and Roy Harris and I as composer representatives presented a cooperative plan that ensured ongoing financial support for the AMC. Paine, a splendid gentleman, had worked hard for years to develop this idea. The federation members were enthusiastically in favor of our plan. Immediately after the meeting, Paine had a fatal heart attack; it was a great blow for American music, and we had to do everything over again. We did organize an ASCAP and ACA reading committee to find suitable scores for Artur Rodzinsky, conductor of the New York Philharmonic. We also began an ASCAP-ACA survey and catalogue of available works by American composers.

During and after World War II, the federal government saw the value of music as a cultural weapon. From 1945 to 1949 the AMC acted as operating agent for the Department of State (music division and Division of Cultural Cooperation), the Library of Congress, and the Pan-American Union (music division), all in Washington, D.C.; and for the Office of War Information Overseas Broadcast (music division) and the Office of the Coordinator of Inter-American Affairs in New York. In 1946 the State Department corresponded with Kerr about establishing libraries of American music in Europe. This and the deposits in Latin America led to the establishment of music libraries under the United States Information Agency throughout the world. The center helped to move over one hundred thousand scores of American music from publishers' shelves into these libraries.

In the 1940s, Harrison Kerr was made Chief of Music, Arts, and Exhibits in the Department of the Army, Civil Affairs Division, and Ray Green came to the AMC as executive secretary in December 1948. Together with Carlos Moseley, Kerr developed the first Visiting Artists program with Germany, financed by the Rockefeller Foundation and the Oberlaender Trust. The first artists were Tom Scott (folk singer), Patricia Travers (violinist), Ralph Kirkpatrick (harpsichordist), the Yale Glee Club, the Walden String Quartet, and Mack Harell, baritone.

Together with Ray Green and Ernst Bacon, I worked on an elaborate proposal to commission, perform, and record American compositions under a grant from the Ford Foundation. This involved six symphony orchestras, those of Boston, San Francisco, Minneapolis, Knoxville, Oklahoma City, and Washington, D.C., and Composers Recordings, Inc. Boston dropped out and Rochester was added. Green and Edward D'Arms, who was with the Ford Foundation, worked out the details of the application to present to the board. The Martha Baird Rockefeller Foundation gave us a grant while we were waiting for the decision from Ford. The board of AMC was on vacation, and Green and I had to drive around New England to get approval for the application from the board members.

The 1957 fall board meeting of AMC was poorly attended, and those present commiserated because finances were so bad that the center couldn't possibly survive. But Green and I insisted that we wait for the decision from Ford. Two weeks later, D'Arms called me saying that he had tried to get in touch with the AMC office but that there was nobody there. (The secretary had taken a day off because there was no business.) D'Arms wanted to tell me that the Ford Foundation had granted us $210,000 for the commissioning project. When this was announced on the front page of the *New York Times* it made a significant impression. The attendance at the next board meeting was one hundred percent.

Following this project, Quincy Porter was elected chairman for a year, then Mel Powell was elected president, Lester Trimble, secretary, and Dai Keong-Lee, treasurer. They developed a plan for a broad membership organization. Subsequent presidents were Hugo Weisgall, Ezra Laderman, Leo Kraft, and Charles Dodge, who, with the help of professional executive secretaries Toni Greenberg and Margaret Jory, have led the center in new directions. In 1963 the American Music Center was declared by the National Music Council to be the official United States information center for music.

≫≪

I RECEIVED a letter while in Bennington inviting me to "attend a dinner to mark the foundation of the American Grand Rights Association, Inc. on Thursday May 14, 1936, at Hotel Madison, 15 East 58th Street, New York." About forty prominent American composers attended the dinner. Virgil Thomson was there, and I thought he was the wittiest man I had ever met.

Cocktails were jumbo-sized. We were served several excellent wines and the best Hennessey, with coffee, and cigars that seemed a foot long. A gentleman introduced a corporation lawyer unknown to most of us. He made a stirring speech about not being able to live by bread alone or not being able to live by spirit alone, I'm not sure which, and after resounding applause, the charter of the new association was passed around and we were told to sign on the dotted line, which we did.

Following the dinner, Evelyn Berckman, Roger Sessions, Edgar Varèse, and I met in a bar and discussed the curious proceedings of the evening. My colleagues said they would study this strange association, and Evelyn would write to me at Bennington. While waiting for news I heard rumors that the Grand Rights Association had stockholders, and that American composers were being used as a front so that the association could collect performance fees for European composers like Puccini, Strauss, and Mascagni. It was all very vague. Two weeks later I was invited to attend a meeting of composers to discuss the new association and make further plans. The invitation was signed by Sessions, Aaron Copland, Thomson, and Varèse, a tough group to hoodwink. The upshot was that most of the concert and opera composers decided that the Grand Rights Association was of no value. It was subsequently dissolved in Albany. It accomplished one important thing, in that American "serious" composers became aware of the business of music.

At a meeting on December 19, 1937, a proclamation was drawn up and published in the January–February 1938 issue of *Modern Music*. Entitled "The Composers Organize," it said: "The American composer of serious music is about to proclaim a new principle for his work as a creative artist. He intends to campaign for the right to make a living by composing. Up to now it has been taken for granted that he shall write sonatas and symphonies on the side, while the real business of supporting himself and his family occupies most of his time." Other objectives were to collect royalties and performance fees for composers, to promote the performance of American music and the commissioning of new works, and to make the American Composers Alliance the official voice of the American composer, which is so seldom heard. The proclamation was signed by virtually every prominent American composer of "serious" music. About two-thirds of these composers actively engaged for decades in what was probably one of the first "rights" movements in this country.

The ramifications of the "business of music" were much wider and more complex than we had at first imagined. In February 1938, ACA held a meeting and issued a further statement of its aims and guiding principles. These centered around the economic rights of composers of serious music: We called for just compensation for their works, in the form of royalties and minimum fees, and the fostering of international exchange; we urged institutions supported in part by public patronage or public funds to allocate a portion of their budget for the commissioning of works by American composers of serious music; and we emphasized the necessity of developing a standard contract, establishing minimum rates in motion pictures, dance, theater, radio, and similar fields, and protecting the artistic and legal rights of the serious composer.

The *ACA Bulletin* of 1938 printed a summary of our aims: "The composer plays a very minor role in the musical counsels of the nation. WE WISH TO CHANGE THAT! The composer comes last instead of first in the musical scheme of things. WE WISH TO CHANGE THAT! The cultural future of music in America depends on the development and encouragement of a sound native music. WE WISH TO FURTHER THAT!" There was much haggling about calling ourselves serious composers or composers of serious music. Is a scherzo serious? Is *The Barber of Seville* serious? We finally called it "standard music" and later on "concert and opera music," leaving movie and dance music to settle into their proper places later.

The first ACA board had Copland as president, Goddard Lieberson as vice-president, Henry Gerstle as treasurer, and Harrison Kerr as secretary. David Rubin and Roger Goeb followed as managers and Oliver Daniel as coordinating manager.

The American Society of Composers, Authors and Publishers—founded by Victor Herbert—had been until 1938 the main organization to collect performance fees and royalties. It was beginning to have problems with the antitrust division of the Department of Justice. The founding of Broadcast Music Incorporated was a countermove on the part of broadcasters to license radio rights.

ACA was wooed by everybody. Sidney Kaye, general counsel of BMI and a famous copyright lawyer, told me that our music was not popular with broadcasters, but that we had prestige value. With a majority of lyric writers, pop composers, and publisher members, ASCAP did not seem particularly interested in a separate group of "serious" composers, but they hinted that our most prominent members might be desirable members of the serious-composer minority at ASCAP. We haggled for three years, because none of us knew the counterpoint of the music business, although some of us were trying hard to learn.

I SOON LEARNED that the place of the American composer of serious music in the business world was not very secure. Pop music brought immediate and large financial returns. Our kind of music was a long-term investment. Walter Hinrichsen, the president of my publisher, C. F. Peters, told me that it sometimes takes ten to twenty years of promotion to find out if a work is commercially successful. But classical music is a magnificent long-term investment; Beethoven, Schubert, and others became multimillion-dollar concerns—in due time. In some cases it takes fifty years to achieve significant commercial returns.

The people I had to negotiate with did understand that we had high prestige value, partially because of the works we had written and also because of our institutional connections. In negotiations I explained that everybody knows what research and development means in industry. I took the position, and still do, that contemporary composers are the research and development group in music. We discover and test new sounds, new musical forms, and new ways of using instruments. When we are successful our findings filter through into the pop field, the movies, and television, where the substantial and immediate monetary awards are to be had. I also argued that just as we know the meaning of soil erosion in agriculture and that soil has to be renewed from time to time or it becomes depleted, so, too, must music—indeed all the arts—be renewed to keep it from stagnating. Too much repetition eventually produces ennui, and pieces of music, literature, or painting can wear out from overfamiliarity. This analogy, too, seemed to work—and still does.

The bickering and arguing at our committee meetings was endless, but eventually BMI offered ACA $10,000 for our radio rights. We might have become a composers' club with an annual dinner meeting or have had our best members join ASCAP, but we could no longer explore possibilities. We had no money, so we voted to sign the BMI contract. Copland resigned as president, and I was elected, with Elliott Carter as treasurer and Kerr continuing as secretary. Henry Brant, John Cage, Robert Ward, and

Frank Wigglesworth became new members of the board. We now became composer-businessmen dealing with lawyers—Ray Burdick for ACA and Robert Burton for BMI. I was reelected president in 1948 and served until October of 1951. After working out a licensing point system and deducting our operating expenses from the BMI payment in 1947, $3,976.70 was left for composers, the average royalty per member, $91.47. In 1948 the average dropped to $63.72, and for 1949 it was down to $31.31. Financially, my term as president was a joke. We needed a much better contract for 1950 or we would have only $1,825 to distribute to the members, everything else going into overhead.

In 1947, Carl Haverlin was elected president of BMI. He not only liked and believed in good music, but he had a historical point of view. He knew the difference between long-term projects and speculation with short-term results. He understood that time was needed to launch and to make accessible and popular certain kinds of music, and he gave us all the support that he could get from his board of directors throughout the years of his office.

ACA has been consistently run by a rotating board of directors who were often prominent composers, including Richard Donovan, Robert Ward, Quincy Porter, Henry Cowell, Ben Weber, Charles Dodge, Nicolas Roussakis, and Vladimir Ussachevsky as presidents.

In spite of our own pitiful financial arrangements in those early days, we became aware that there were big spoils to be had in the world of music when a number of enormous antitrust suits were filed by the Justice Department. Committees of the Senate and the House, including the then-Interstate Commerce Committee, were investigating BMI and ASCAP. The Federal Communications Commission entered the fray. The question of payola came up. There was a real struggle between ASCAP and BMI.

The actions finally culminated in 1958 in a $150-million antitrust suit filed by Arthur Schwartz and others including Menotti, Virgil Thomson, and Douglas Moore. They sued BMI, RCA, NBC, CBS, MBS, and ABC. Eventually the judge threw the suit out, but some consent decrees, both for ASCAP and BMI, were eventually hammered out and entered. I was impressed. Music was being taken seriously by law enforcement agencies, big-money interests, and educators. Concert composers would surely have a place until they got lost in the shuffle. A letter came from Father: "I hope you don't believe what you read in the papers." I wondered how Busoni would have reacted to all this.

In these hearings Carl Haverlin made noble statements about music in general and BMI in particular. Right through the fifties and later, Haverlin and the subsequent presidents —Burton, Sour, and Edward Cramer—were consistent in their support of good concert music. Eventually BMI took over the collection activities from ACA and paid composers advance guarantees directly for radio rights. They gave sufficient support to enable ACA to launch several programs. Roger Goeb developed the Composers Facsimile Editions and we had a library to make composers' works available. We engaged Oliver Daniel as coordinating manager. He suggested we send tapes and recordings to educational broadcasting stations, support local festivals in the Midwest and Far West, form a joint ACA-ASCAP committee to screen works for conductors, begin cooperating in making records with RCA, the Rachmaninoff Society, Remington, and later CRI, and promote works on the radio. We finally straightened out our contract forms and could get our works published.

Under Daniel's guidance, ACA sponsored concerts at the Metropolitan Museum and the Museum of Modern Art. In the next years ACA made contributions in support of some fifty concerts of new music that were given from coast to coast and in Berlin, Germany, and Belgium. ACA also contributed to the Fishcreek Festival in Wisconsin and the Group for Contemporary Music in New York.

In 1978 the American Composers Orchestra performed at the Kennedy Center in Washington, D.C. Francis Thorne is currently the executive director and Nicolas Roussakis is president of ACA.

There have been major changes in the American musical scene in the past twenty-five years. Pop music and country music now dominate the money market in a big way. The *ACA Bulletin* is now called *Many Worlds of Music,* and concert music has consequently been given much smaller space. Composers' guarantees have been continued by BMI, but nobody seems to understand how to handle concert music that has not yet reached the mass market.

One argument that I used and still use with varying degrees of success is that different types of music, like different cars, have different values and uses. A Plymouth and a Porsche are not in the same price range; neither should a pop song of thirty-two measures be in the same price range as a half-hour symphony or an opera. The expenses in preparing the material for performance of the latter two and the time spent in composition are not comparable to those of the pop song.

Perhaps the capital investment by the composer of concert and operatic music can be covered only by substantial endowments and commissions, with the fervent hope that the eventual cultural enrichment of the nation will be worth the investment. The arts and artistic talent are, after all, a national resource that has to be nurtured, cultivated, supported, and preserved.

ᗝᖘ

IN 1943, I HAD a letter from Mrs. Ann M. Gannett, president of the National Federation of Music Clubs, outlining plans for giving support to creative musicians and for commissioning composers. She wrote that the federation needed a broad-minded professional musician as chairman of its American Composition Committee. I had been strongly recommended and Mrs. Gannett offered to appoint me and promised all possible support. The federation had a half-million members in its hundreds of clubs and an American Music chairman in every state. I envisioned the federation as a force for making American music known, so I accepted the invitation. In my imagination I could hear the ladies singing our songs and applauding our symphonies. It was my first chance to organize a national committee and I thought big. Mary Howe, Marion Bauer, Arthur Shepherd, Douglas Moore, Henry Allen Moe, Eric Clarke, and Quincy Porter were recruited. I wanted a composer-member from every state.

I arranged lists and reviews of American compositions to be printed in the *Music Clubs Magazine*. These eventually included 150 works that were relatively unknown at the time, like the

Third Symphony of Wallingford Riegger, the Third Symphony of
Walter Piston, the Fourth Symphony of William Schuman, the
Fourth Symphony of David Diamond, the *Viola Concerto* of
Quincy Porter, *The Seine at Night* by Virgil Thomson, *Hymn and
Fuguing Tune* by Henry Cowell, and *Ford's Theatre Suite* by
Ernst Bacon. Fifty chamber music works were also reviewed. The
board was impressed and voted that all members of the clubs
assess themselves five cents annually to support American composition. Envelopes containing such sums as 95¢ and $2.35 came
from places as far away as Fargo, North Dakota, and Kennebunk-
port, Maine. The *Washington Times-Herald* said that this program was the greatest service the federation had done for the nation's music.

From 1943 to 1948 the federation concentrated on being an
information service for American music. Operated through the
American Music Center, it supplied information to the clubs and
to the public at large. The federation compiled biographical data,
sent out compositions for examination, and suggested procedures
for state music contests. In cooperation with the orchestra committee, the federation sent clubs lists of recommended American
works for large and chamber orchestras, lists of recordings, and
lists of specific instrumental works (i.e., for violin, for piano, etc.)
for program use.

My work with the federation was heady on-the-job training
in the methods of American public relations. But in 1948 I resigned. The federation had fiscal problems, and I was heavily
obligated elsewhere. When I neglected composing for too long, I
lost vital energy. I could replenish myself only by writing music
and practicing flute or piano.

⊰⊱

AS A RESULT of my activities in the business of music, I won a
reputation with foundations for "knowing the field." In 1933,
Henry Allen Moe recommended me to the Oberlaender Trust as
musical consultant, and I served until 1950. The trust cooperated
with the State and War departments, the High Commission for
Germany, and German émigré committees to bring about cultural
exchange between the two countries. Among the people we

brought over from Germany were Paul Hindemith and Dr. Leo Schrade, who taught seminars at Yale University; Dr. Heinrich Jalowetz (Arnold Schoenberg's first student), who taught at Black Mountain College; and Philipp Jarnach. The trust also funded the Drinker project to resurrect the music of the Ephrata Cloister in Pennsylvania.

Until 1940, I helped Moe and Thomas Whitney Surette select music fellows for the Guggenheim Foundation by reading the applicants' scores and playing them at the piano. (Records and tapes were not widely used at that time.) I later served on the foundation's Educational Advisory Board from 1961 until my retirement in 1970.

In 1944, I was appointed to the advisory committee of the Alice M. Ditson Foundation at Columbia University, and I still serve on it.

IN 1946, DR. Robert D. Leigh asked me to be consultant for "The Public Library Inquiry," conducted by the Social Science Research Council for the American Library Association on a grant from the Carnegie Foundation under Leigh's direction. The study was to be "an appraisal in sociological, cultural, and human terms . . . of the extent to which the libraries are achieving their objectives, and of the library's potential and actual contribution to American society." The subjects included mass communications (radio and television), adult education, recreation, and freedom of the press. I saw the study as an opportunity to continue my education; it was related to music; and I needed the money. Dr. Leigh showed me how to compile questionnaires, conduct interviews, and research library deposits. I visited fifteen libraries, sent out sixty questionnaires, and held 150 interviews. My report, *Music Materials and the Public Library*, was a summary of music activity in the United States from the earliest crude church choirs to the latest symphonic and juke-box records. I recommended regional depositories, expansion of interlibrary loan, and the establishment of record libraries—of which there were few at that time.

In Louisville, I discussed with Mayor Charles Farnsley a plan for commissioning the recording, performance, and distribution of works by contemporary (mostly American) composers. The circulation would be to schools, libraries, and radio stations. Our conversations led Mayor Farnsley to visit the Rockefeller Foundation. A grant of $400,000 was made by the foundation to the Louisville Orchestra. This was a major breakthrough for contemporary and community music.

IN 1948 A FOUNDATION asked me to make a confidential impressionistic study of organizations that were influential in the development of contemporary music in the United States. I studied eighty-one organizations, including some little-known ones such as the Hymn Society of America, Associated Glee Clubs, National Association for Harpists, National Dance League, U.S. Army and Navy Bandsmen's Association, and the National Folk Festival. I recommended that fifteen institutions or areas of activity be given support, and a number of these recommendations were followed.

IN 1956, COMMUNITY Research Associates engaged me as staff member for Culture and Leisure Time Resources for their Morningside Heights–Manhattanville study. In broad terms, we were to assist the institutional and citizen leadership of this area to develop a program for making it a more physically attractive, socially helpful, economically prosperous, and culturally satisfying neighborhood in which to live and work. David Rockefeller financed the study and was chairman. The committee included the presidents of the great institutions in the neighborhood, including some trustees of Columbia University, St. Luke's Hospital, and the Cathedral of St. John the Divine, and the presidents of the Manhattanville community centers. The large research staff included experts in fields ranging from street planning and urban renewal to psychiatric social services and the New York City Board of Education. It was again a great opportunity for continuing my education in social studies and getting to know my neighborhood. I visited twenty-two institutions and interviewed forty individuals, including some Harlem residents and board of education supervisors. My report suggested establishing a Bureau of Community Activities, with a coordinator for public events and a weekly calendar. The other staff members made detailed recommendations for neighborhood changes, but it took ten years for some of them to become effective.

IN MARCH 1960, Community Research Associates appointed me Consultant for Education, Culture, and the Arts to advise a bank in a New England town how to spend the income from one of their trust funds. Bankers had always told me all about music, and this job seemed like a grand opportunity for me to tell them how to spend money. The experience gave me an insight into a thriving New England town and the conflicting interests of the many institutions that rely on the private sector for support.

MANY OF my previous experiences in field studies were coordinated when, in 1963, Frederick H. Burkhardt, president of the American Council of Learned Societies, invited me and Lionel Nowak to discuss music education in primary and secondary schools. He initiated the Yale Seminar for Music Education, under the chairmanship of Professor Claude F. Palisca. The committee consisted of conductors, music educators, jazz players, music critics, singers, university professors, composers—and bureaucrats from Washington, D.C.

Our report, published by Yale in 1963, was distributed by the Department of Health, Education and Welfare. We recommended that past values in music education be kept alive, but with innovations that called for substantial reforms. The report was widely discussed and generated mixed reactions, but eventually it had an effect on primary and secondary music education. From that year on, various government agencies and corporations began emerging as increasingly influential patrons of the arts.

Chapter 21

Columbia University
1943 to Present

MOST OF THE PROJECTS THAT Ethel and I were engaged in at Bennington were discontinued when World War II began; other projects lost funding and tapered off by 1942. It seemed to me that our friends and colleagues thought our activities and opinions were predictable. Even Ethel and I were beginning to be bored. One December evening in 1943, I received a phone call from Douglas Moore at Columbia.

The connection was bad, and I could not hear him clearly. He said—I thought—"Would you like to be chairman of the Barnard music department? You are just the man we need."

I asked him to repeat his offer, which he did. I said, "I guess I'm interested. What's this all about?"

"I'll write you," he said. "Goodbye."

Moore's letter said that I was being considered as chairman, his former post, and also as music director of Opera Projects at Brander Matthews Hall, I would have an assistant conductor and I would be associate professor, with a full teaching load that would eventually include a graduate seminar in music composition. The salary was $5,000—$500 less than at Bennington.

Ever since the Depression, I had held a strong opinion about jobs. Unless a new position offered something positive in experience or money, I saw no reason to leave the old one unless conditions were so horrible that I just had to escape. I still feel somewhat the same about changing jobs, so I viewed the offer with some skepticism.

I had met Douglas Moore at an American Composers Concert in Rochester. His *Pageant of P. T. Barnum* for orchestra had startled me because of its strong American background and strange orchestration. In the late thirties Ethel and I performed excerpts from my *Evangeline* for his opera class at Columbia, and he liked it. It was the beginning of a long and fruitful friendship.

Moore was distinguished-looking and solidly built, with a fine head of hair and friendly, alert, twinkly, expressive, keen brown eyes. He was a chain smoker and walked with just a hint of a nautical roll. He had studied with Horatio Parker at Yale and had fallen in love with 1890s musical comedies and nineteenth-century ballads, which were important influences on his compositional style. Later he studied with Vincent d'Indy and Nadia Boulanger in Paris and with Ernest Bloch in Cleveland. He was executive officer of the Columbia music department. At meetings in New York I had gotten to know him as a friendly and cooperative colleague.

His compositions fell into two categories: some were in an unpretentious and authentic American style; some orchestral and chamber works showed a French influence in the harmonic treatment. As first I missed smoothness in his orchestral writing, but later found that it had character. His vocal writing was fluent and his prosody excellent, and his tunes had an American feeling about them.

I was anxious to hear more about Barnard, but there was no news from Moore. Ethel and I went to New York, anyway, on January 2, 1944, to spend the winter period.

A week later Harry Partch arrived. After corresponding with me for ten years, he appeared at our New York studio door, saying, "I'm Harry Partch. It's been so nice this way; let's never become friends."

He had hitchhiked and ridden rods from the West Coast. He had just picked up his instruments from where he had stored them; at the moment, they were sitting in a borrowed car. He wanted us to store them in our studio for an indeterminate time— which we did. We had Moore over to meet Partch. He came, and Partch sang and played. Moore was tremendously impressed, arranged an audition with the League of Composers committee, and we hauled the instruments to the American Music Center. Partch sang excerpts from his *U.S. Highball, A Musical Account of Slim's Transcontinental Hobo Trip*, with his own text. *U.S.*

Highball is the story of five hoboes—including the protagonist, Slim, who describes a trip on a freight train from Carmel, California, to Chicago. Partch's text has an intensity, an eccentric sense of humor and drama, even a hallucinatory quality. At one point in the text, an old man who lived in a piano crate says to a younger hobo, "It is tough riding the drags on a night like this. I know. I was a bum myself."

There were astonished inquiries: "But is it music?" We had all been exposed to the New York line about creativity, but here was a man who built his instruments and invented new ones, wrote his texts, played his accompaniments, sang his works, hitchhiked across the continent, and got his friends to transport his instruments from city to city and from concert to concert. All of this was done on a hundred dollars a month and in a forty-three-tone-to-the-octave scale instead of the usual twelve. The league committee was bowled over and immediately arranged his debut at Carnegie Recital Hall for April 22, 1944.

The event was a shock for the reviewers. In addition to *U.S. Highball*, Partch performed *Barstow, Eight Inscriptions on a California Highway Railing; San Francisco, a Setting of the Cries of Two Newsboys*; and *Y. D. [Yankee Doodle] Fantasy*, which was dedicated to Ethel, who sang it with astonishing virtuosity and with marvelous control of the pitch. Henry Brant joined her with virtuoso playing on a ten-cent-store tin flute. It was hard for the press to realize that Partch had been a hobo for almost eight years, had ridden the rails, lived in "jungles," worked in wheatfields, and done odd jobs, as he went from library to library, from coast to coast, to do his research in acoustics. The refined scale with forty-three steps for his instrumental works was devised primarily so that the inflections of his speech-music, as he called it, could be properly supported by his instruments. His work and his demonstrations had made clear to me certain things about Greek and Oriental music that I had only surmised. Against our Western harmonic, orchestral, and contrapuntal overloading, Partch's music showed ways of refining the melodic line itself.

Moore arranged for an article to be written about Partch in *The New Yorker*, hoping it would help to focus attention on Partch—and it did. By this time, public relations for American composers had become a matter of great concern for all of us. Art for art's sake was temporarily moribund, and the business of music was our new field of action. Partch repeated the League of Composers performance at Brander Matthews at Columbia, and it was again a shocking success—just what I needed to be involved with as an introduction to my scholarly academic role at Barnard!

BENNINGTON ENGAGED Partch for a fifty-dollar fee that spring for a concert. He hitchhiked to Vermont. His concert was brilliant and enthusiastically received. I had supported his application for the Guggenheim Fellowship that he got in 1943. Some months later, he returned to Bennington to discuss his instruments and make alterations on them, and to write music for Ethel. From that time on, he kept in touch with me with vivid letters and messages through intermediaries as he hitchhiked back and forth across the continent. He sold his records by mail order, and I was his agent. He sent me manuscripts for comments and in 1949 asked me to write a foreword for his *Genesis of a Music,* published by the University of Wisconsin Press.

In 1959, Columbia, in cooperation with the Juilliard School, and with a grant of ten thousand dollars from the Ditson Fund, brought the University of Illinois production of his *The Bewitched—A Dance Satire* to New York, and it was a brilliant success. Partch continued his work in California and made more recordings. CRI now has in its catalogue *The Bewitched, In Petaluma, Music Magazine,* and *Cloud Chamber Music.* Partch died of a heart attack on September 5, 1974.

⊱⊰

IN LATE January, Douglas Moore invited me for an interview in his Columbia office. Accustomed to the Jennings mansion at Bennington, I wasn't impressed by his tiny room or the other cramped offices, each shared by two instructors, or the unattractive classrooms and the shabby second-hand furniture.

Moore told me Columbia was planning an Arts Center or a School of the Arts.

"How long have you been planning?" I asked.

Moore cleared his throat twice. "Since Edward MacDowell came to Columbia in 1896."

He went on about the department's hopes and plans for the

future. I asked about my future chances. After a carefully timed pause he made a salary offer of $5,000. I explained I needed $500 more.

Professor Moore's face fell. "You wouldn't want the whole deal to fall through for a measly five hundred dollars, would you?" he asked.

"Well, perhaps," I said.

What an administrator, I thought, but that $500 would put me into a higher salary bracket and affect my future eligibility for promotions, pensions, and other fringe benefits. I was by no means so tired of Bennington that I simply could not stand working there, so I stood firm. Professor Moore's lips tightened and he excused himself to phone Dean Gildersleeve.

After an interval, he returned, saying that Dean Gildersleeve would like to have a luncheon conference with us in two days. He described her as a real bluestocking, a Barnard graduate, a very good administrator, a great lady, and a fine scholar. He invited me for cocktails at his apartment on Riverside Drive.

As we left he reminded me of the first secretary of the embassy in Paris about to take off for a tennis match with a Herr Klugensberger, a banker from Switzerland. I trotted alongside him across Broadway and down the Drive to his apartment. When he got going he rolled along like a sailor.

The Moores' beautiful living room overlooked the Hudson. A freighter passed in the twilight. Moore fixed drinks and we clinked glasses.

"The beginning of a beautiful friendship," he announced, and his lips twitched slightly. I couldn't tell whether he had leered or smiled at me.

We shook hands. He gave a short, resonant guffaw, caught himself, and remarked that he loved the sea, the Hudson, and the ships that were passing. He remarked that he had been executive officer of a destroyer in World War I.

"Was that why you were appointed executive officer of the music department?" I asked.

He examined me carefully to see if my remark was malicious in intent, and saw that it wasn't. "Well, hurrumpf, that might have been the reason. It has certainly helped. I had quite a musical reputation in the Navy for my destroyer songs."

"Destroyer songs? A new art form, no doubt."

"Very American. We've got to get away from that Schubert–
Schumann–Hugo Wolf lieder-cycle mania, and make some of our
own songs. Would you like to hear one?"

"Sure," I said, settling myself with my drink, as he settled
himself at the Mason & Hamlin. "The first one is 'Wilhelmine
Klotz.' I think you'll like the German background," and he tore
into a raucous waltz song about the various exploits of a dainty
German girl named Wilhelmine Klotz who weighed three
hundred pounds. He was only a fair pianist, and had a composer's
voice, but he sang with convincing dramatic inflections and obviously enjoyed what he was doing.

I forgot all about Barnard's reputation for scholarship and
asked him to sing another one. He obliged with a song about life
on a destroyer, very risqué for those years, with plenty of
"damns," "hells," and "bastards," and ending with a climactic
"son of a bitch." This was drama and comedy in the raw, and I felt
that Professor Moore and I were really going to get along just
fine. I asked him whether he had ever done any tap dancing. He
said he'd given it up because of a back strain but still liked to
shuffle a bit. I joined him in a few steps.

The door opened and in came a very beautiful lady accompanied by two attractive young girls.

"My wife, Emily. My daughters, Sarah and Mary."

I gave Sarah a private salute. She was a student at Bennington.

Mrs. Moore said, "Both Douglass and Sarah have told me so
much about you and all the fine work you've done at Eastman and
Bennington."

Mary asked whether I was planning to hear *Tristan* at the
Met. Mrs. Moore then asked about my life in Switzerland after
World War I and mentioned Moore's contact with Boulanger in
Paris. The ladies were curious about my composing. Not a word
was said about Barnard.

We talked about American poets and authors and musical
comedies. American art of all kinds seemed to be very important
in this household. James Joyce, Debussy, and French and Italian
opera were respected, but American art was home base. Although
my own background was different, I shared this feeling. We
agreed that an American art was possible to achieve. I had long

felt that imitation of the nineteenth-century European giants was a fruitless task. Moore and I were compatible. After a while we confessed our love and admiration for the music of Johann Sebastian Bach and this seemed to put a seal on all of our aspirations. It was the first of many extremely warm social and artistic gatherings at the Moores' Riverside Drive apartment and at their house in Cutchogue, Long Island.

"Be prompt day after tomorrow," Moore said as I left.

I ARRIVED at the Barnard Deanery at twenty-five minutes past twelve noon. Moore was waiting. At twelve twenty-nine and a half, the door opened silently and in glided an impressive lady who greeted Moore with just the right degree of cordiality and administrative reserve. At exactly twelve-thirty the clock chimed eight times, and I was introduced. We went through the small talk and then the sherry-and-crackers ritual with style and academic abandon.

A quick glance around revealed that the Deanery was furnished in 1910 eclectic style, probably with gifts from trustees. There was a reproduction of *Whistler's Mother* and some 1890s bric-a-brac on a table. Dean Gildersleeve, at first rather shy, soon relaxed and spoke of the weather. I felt at home and reasonably safe in my formal blue suit, white shirt, blue tie with diagonal white stripes, and well-shined shoes.

"How long have you been at Bennington?"

"Ten years."

"You have accomplished much. Do you think you could do as well here?"

"That depends on student and faculty cooperation."

"We haven't done much in the arts." She looked sad, then brightened. "Of course, we have the Greek games."

Moore broke in to say, "I'll tell Mr. Luening about the games later."

The dean went on. "Our English department is very fine; they believe all students are illiterate until they graduate." She then asked how music related to other subjects.

I explained. "Songs, operas, and oratorios use words—Goethe, Schiller, Heine, Pushkin, and the Elizabethans wrote the words for thousands of these. Professor Moore has set Stephen Vincent Benét. I have composed Blake and Whitman songs . . ."

"I didn't know musicians were that literary!"

"Some prefer the physics of sound—you know—acoustics. A fundamental tone has a certain number of vibrations and upper partials." The Riverside Church tower clock obliged by striking sixteen bells before one. "If you listen carefully, Dean Gildersleeve, when the clock strikes one you will hear the big boom and several higher sounds all at once."

The clock boomed one. She listened attentively. "Gracious— I hear them—and to think that until now I've missed all the overtones!"

"Only consciously, Dean Gildersleeve—subconsciously you heard them."

"I hope so—Shall we have lunch?"

The luncheon talk reminded me of Sunday dinner at Aunt Gretchen's in Milwaukee. No ideas intruded on our gustatory enjoyment. After a cheerful discussion about the annual rainfall in New Hampshire and Vermont, Moore and I took our leave. Dean Gildersleeve gave me a knowing look and a special hand pressure somewhat like the secret grip of my Boy Scout troop in Madison.

"She likes you," said Moore.

"And I like her—she's great."

Moore mumbled, "Very scholarly. . . . Would you like to be guest conductor for the premiere of Bernard Wagenaar's opera, *Pieces of Eight,* in May? Have Bennington give you a three-month leave."

I agreed to try for it.

"Let's visit Dr. Milton Smith, the director of Brander Matthews Theatre," Moore said. "We cooperate with him and the Columbia Theatre Associates."

BRANDER MATTHEWS was a tiny, attractive theater, seating about two hundred. At a rolltop desk piled high with manuscripts, clippings, cigarette butts, costumes, and letters sat Dr. Milton Smith. "My arthritis is killing me," he groaned and cracked his neck.

"Sorry Milton," Moore said. "Meet Otto Luening, guest conductor of our coming *Pieces of Eight* opera premiere."

"Another one of those lousy operettas. *Paul Bunyan* was a flop, but Benjamin Britten and W. H. Auden had talent. *A Tree on the Plains* by Ernst Bacon and Paul Horgan was a near miss, and now Wagenaar! The only good 'operetter' was the *Burglar's Opera* by Munday and Eager. All about the Macy's store." Chuckling, he recited the synopsis, which sounded mighty corny to me. As he steered us onto the stage, Dr. Smith impressed me as a mixture of country editor, country storekeeper, and country doctor.

The stage was large and the shop was roomy, but the sunken orchestra pit was two feet too narrow for comfort. The conductor would have to conduct the orchestra with one hand and the singers with the other; possible, of course, but difficult.

"Why don't you use a piano and keep those impertinent orchestra musicians out of the theater?" Smith growled. "They are always too loud."

"We must be going," said Moore nervously.

I shook hands with Smith, who sneered, "It's not too late to quit."

On our way across campus I asked Moore if Dr. Smith was always in such a good mood.

"He pretends to hate music but he runs a tight ship, is a good carpenter, and has his crew build houses, outdoor scenes, and interiors by the dozen. His wife, Helen Claire, is a fine professional actress, and sometimes she and Broadway actors like Alfred Drake do leads here, for the fun of it."

That afternoon, I met Lewis Jones, the Bennington president, at a cocktail party and told him I was thinking of going to Barnard. "That skunk; that cheapskate!" he roared.

"Who?"

"The Barnard trustee I dined with three weeks ago. I bragged about you and our music department. Now he steals you."

"All for the best, I hope."

"So do I. Well, good luck."

"Wait a minute; I haven't accepted formally."

"You will. Columbia, Juilliard, New York—too much glamour."

In ten days, I showed Wagenaar's score to the conductor,

Professor Dittler, and to my assistant. In two hours Dittler returned the music and stated that his orchestra could not play it if they practiced a hundred years. My assistant announced the workshop had almost no men, but he phoned around to arrange auditions. I mentioned the orchestra problem to Moore.

"You'll have to get on the phone and find your own group."

"Does the job pay anything?"

"It's a great opportunity for the singers—show window, press reviews—they are glad to volunteer. The orchestra is made up of students—we allow ten dollars for meals and taxis."

Pieces of Eight, a Riverside Drive–Long Island version of Gilbert and Sullivan, was not an opera but a comic operetta. Bernard Wagenaar was an experienced European composer living in the United States. His music was moderately difficult, his vocal writing singable, and his melodies and harmonies agreeable. The libretto, by Edward Eager, an experienced Broadway wordsmith, was about eighteenth-century pirates, New England spinsters, and Captain Kidd. It was dominated by low comic rhyming and by references to the visceral organs. At times the jokes became scatological. It was too late for me to suggest changes so I recruited my forces by telephone, and began rehearsing.

The singers, all then unknown, included Patricia Neway, who later made a career at City Center and internationally in Menotti's *Consul* and his other works. From then on, I picked a few winners for each of my productions. Wagenaar played rehearsals to keep his opus from falling apart, and I did all the coaching.

During our long stage rehearsals, Milton Smith and Eager would whinny their approval after each witty line. I didn't, because I had nothing to whinny about: I had only four two-hour orchestra rehearsals. I memorized the score and nursed the players along, scene by scene, at a slow tempo. Attendance was irregular because of examinations. One singer was in service at the Brooklyn Navy Yard and was often called up for duty. There were no male understudies because of the war. I had to put it together like a jigsaw puzzle.

The dress rehearsal went well—and when it was over, Smith hollered, "Now that I have seen it, I know it will be a flop—the timing is off."

On opening night the theater was packed with singers, conductors, stage directors, students, and the press. As I entered the pit, Dr. Smith whispered, "You've got a turkey on your hands. Good luck."

The performance was rewarded by enthusiastic applause. Some reviewers reported a flop or at best a near-miss because of the libretto, but fortunately they praised my musical direction and my "conviction, understanding, verve, and animation," and the beautiful playing of the orchestra. Moore said I was a "howling success" and Wagenaar said I had done one swell job. I was lucky. My professional reputation was saved by the skin of my teeth and Barnard formalized my appointment.

Now I was an associate professor at Barnard College, Columbia University in the city of New York. We returned to Bennington to pack and found a card from Edgar Varèse: "Glad to have you with us. Cordially, Varèse."

After winding up business in Bennington, we visited Carl Ruggles at the Arlington Inn on our drive to New York. On the third day, he bellowed, "Are you staying in Vermont or going to New York? If you are going, tell Varèse I'm composing a piece that will blow the goddamn audience right out of their seats . . . and pants, too."

He roared, we howled, Mrs. Ruggles said, "Now, Carl," and we went on our way at last.

❧❦

I FOUND AN apartment at 119th Street and Claremont Avenue. F. Scott Fitzgerald had once lived in the neighborhood and Ferruccio Busoni had had an apartment at 116th and Riverside in 1914. Riverside Park and the Hudson River were magnificent; Douglas Moore lived around the corner and my Barnard office was a short walk away.

Ethel's studio on 67th Street had a telephone, and she was hoping daily to hear favorable news about her audition at the Metropolitan Opera. The new apartment had no phone because of the war. It was roomy and quiet so I could work.

Two days later, I visited Barnard. Professor Cady, who shared my office, showed me around. We entered a large, beautifully furnished room, with a Steinway concert grand at one end, a collection of baroque and Renaissance instruments in locked cases around the walls, and attractive oil paintings and Gobelins on the walls. There was a striking portrait of Dean Gildersleeve.

"A perfect room for chamber music," I said. "What happens here?"

"This is the College Parlor. The music club meets here, the faculty has teas, and there are large faculty meetings."

"No concerts?"

"Mr. Swan of Buildings and Grounds wants to preserve the valuable equipment."

"By not using it?"

"Why don't you visit him in his downstairs office?"

Mr. Swan's secretary said that he could give me an appointment in ten days. I called him on the public phone in the lobby.

"Come right in," said Mr. Swan, and to the astonishment of his secretary I walked into his office.

"I'm the new music chairman, and I would like to know how many pianos Barnard owns."

Mr. Swan fished out a chart marked PIANO MAP. "Twenty-four," he said.

"Where are they? I have seen only two."

He pointed to the map of Barnard buildings, which bore twenty-four crosses.

"Are they being used?" I asked.

"Don't know," he said, lighting his pipe. "They are all gifts and we just store them."

"Can I look?"

"Sure," he said, and he handed me the map.

The next hour was spent finding the pianos. They were in coal bins, in dormitories, in storerooms, in the gymnasium, under the elevator shaft, and behind the boiler room. Six seemed usable, eighteen were covered with dust and had broken keyboards and split sounding boards. Mice had enjoyed chewing up the felt hammers of three. I suggested repairing some of the pianos and discarding the others.

I WALKED through the campus to have lunch with Moore. The Faculty Club, our luncheon rendezvous, was post–World War I modern. It looked as though the furnishings and the library itself were mostly gifts, a very mixed selection of not-too-attractive armchairs, sofas, and old books.

The dining room was soon crowded with energetic faculty members. The food was academic—not very tasty, but nourishing. The fragments of conversation that floated around the hall were on a high plane: "But the tse-tse fly . . ." "More eliptic, differential operators on manifolds . . ." "MIT is ahead in principles of statistical inference . . ." "But ancient Near Eastern tests will be very practical in the future . . ."

Moore looked disinterested as I told him about my Barnard visit. "Yes, yes, but it is only the branch store; here is something more interesting. President Butler appointed me to the Alice M. Ditson Fund committee a few years ago, and I am nominating you. Now let's visit the Columbia music department."

I had seen McMillin Theatre previously. In the elevator of the Journalism Building, Moore introduced me to Dean Ackerman, then whispered on our way out, "Dean Ackerman is with the School of Journalism. He is a famous World War I correspondent. He lets us have rooms on the sixth floor."

We went into the office area. He showed me my studio, room 604, with a grand piano and shelves for scores and books. Classrooms were drab and made Bennington seem luxurious by comparison.

Moore sent the secretary in the main office to round up the faculty. Everyone was very friendly. After introductions were over, the professors pulled out their watches, mumbled about other appointments and disappeared either into their offices or into the elevator.

"Here's your schedule," Moore said. "I put you down for an evening class in General Studies, Music I. It will pay three hundred dollars extra for the semester." Moore looked at his watch and rushed for the elevator.

I went upstairs to examine the music library. It was a small but very good collection of books and scores, without much contemporary music and with a rather small record library, not as good as the one at Bennington. I went home to think.

AT THE beginning, the Columbia music department seemed strange. Professor Lang was building a musicology empire. Professors Willard Rhodes and William Mitchell were my friends. The practicing musicians on the faculty seemed restricted by their surroundings. The music scholars discussed unknown music authoritatively and they were impressive with their course outlines, schedules, textbooks, and esoteric tidbits. I once lost control and said that musicology was "words without song." My remark was not appreciated but was widely quoted.

Moore arranged a party to introduce Ethel and me to the music faculty. Ethel performed her favorite arias, and I accompanied. Our colleagues were enchanted. Then Moore, a rather mischievous executive officer, suggested that I do musical impersonations like those he had seen at Yaddo. I demurred, but he insisted. I did takeoffs of a French tenor singing Fauré, a German baritone singing a Strauss song, the famous German musicologist Dr. Hasenschweiss lecturing about and performing a fugue for the Apfelorgel (an unknown baroque instrument), some contemporary songs and poems, and Hindemith explaining how music flowed in currents and undercurrents.

My indiscretions were received with guffaws, cackles, and cheers. Apparently everyone at the Columbia music department had been waiting a long time for just such an evening. My slightly barbed lampoons seemed to be what was needed to loosen things up and at the same time establish my position at Columbia. The piano and vocal improvisations were accepted as my musical credentials, my improvised lectures as my scholarly credentials. Professor Lang was overheard saying, "That man could be dangerous."

ETHEL TOOK part in the November 26, 1944, program and reception at the Dalcroze Auditorium given by the International Society for Contemporary Music in honor of Schoenberg's seventieth birthday. She sang beautifully five songs from Opus 6, Opus 14, and Opus 16. I was immensely taken with *Der Wanderer* from Opus 6 because of the moving postromantic, poetic quality about it. Edward Steuermann, a piano pupil of Busoni's and a composition student of Schoenberg's, gave a masterly performance of *Five Piano Pieces*, Opus 23, Schoenberg's first serial music.

I was busy preparing the December production of *The Jealous Husband* by Pergolesi, a work I found charming. A string orchestra and harpsichord gave harmonic and rhythmic support, and the vocal writing was superb. The score was well received by the audience and press. I discovered the splendid French-Canadian tenor Léopold Simoneau. He wanted to learn English diction, so I coached him. He believed that English was a ridiculous language and insisted on pronouncing the *g* in *gnaw* and *thought*. His acting was quite good. A few years later the Metropolitan Opera engaged him to do Mozart.

A day after the Pergolesi dress rehearsal, I was having a cup of coffee in Chock Full O' Nuts. A young man sitting next to me asked whether I had conducted the opera. He went into a complimentary discourse about the virtues of opera in general, Pergolesi in particular, and my conducting.

"Are you related to the Schoenberg singer, Ethel Luening?" he asked.

I explained, and he was most generous in his praise of her singing.

"I am Jack Beeson, just in from the Eastman School . . . staying in town."

He knew Moore, and I suggested that he get in touch with the theater and the music departments. He immediately volunteered to help around the theater while he was getting his bearings in New York.

≫≪

AT OUR INITIAL Ditson Committee meeting, Moore and I proposed that we schedule the first Annual Festival of Contemporary American Music at Columbia University for May 1945, devoted to the performance of significant chamber and orchestral compositions by contemporary American composers, and an opera premiere. We would begin by commissioning American composers for orchestral and chamber music works, and a librettist and composer to do an opera. The programs would be selected by a committee consisting of the advisory committee of the Alice M. Ditson Fund, Pulitzer Prize winners in New York, and the Department of Music of Columbia University.

The first Columbia Festival began with an orchestral concert by the NBC Symphony Orchestra conducted by Dr. Howard Hanson, who won the 1945 Ditson Award for an American conductor. The University of the Air of the National Broadcasting Company, station WEAF, broadcast the orchestra concert nationally. Two chamber music concerts were broadcast over station WNYC.

The orchestral program included *Rounds for Strings* by David Diamond, in which he used canonic and fugal devices with an expressive lyric adagio between two fast movements. The piece is today a part of the permanent repertory. Hanson's Symphony no. 4, a Pulitzer Prize winner, with movement titles Kyrie, Requiescat, Dies Irae, and Lux Aeterna, was received respectfully. Sigmund Rascher played Henry Brant's *Concerto for Saxophone and Orchestra,* a piece I liked because of the masterly way Brant handled the orchestral balances, and because of Rascher's brilliant performance. Walter Piston's Symphony no. 2, a Ditson Fund commission, had flowing themes developed canonically, a slow movement with a quiet lyric development of a motive from the beginning, and a vigorous rhythmic, marchlike finale. Piston's symphony, academic writing in the very best sense of the word, was widely praised.

Recruiting orchestra and cast for the festival opera and arranging for regular attendance was difficult during World War II. I was feeling the pressure, when, one day, Dean Gildersleeve asked me to come to her office.

"Professor Luening, I have five hundred dollars in my discretionary fund that I want to place at your disposal. Use it as you please. I think you are overworked. Hire a secretary, take a vacation, or get some help with the operas you are conducting."

I was speechless. "Can you afford it?"

"Contingency."

She held out her hand. I took it between mine. She looked straight at me. She reminded me of my sister, Helene.

I used $250 to pay debts and engaged Jack Beeson to be my opera assistant—the beginning of our long professional association and friendship. When I told the Columbia faculty about my windfall, they went into shock.

The festival opera was Normand Lockwood's *The Scarecrow.* The libretto by Dolly Lockwood was an adaptation from Percy MacKaye's play of the same name based on Hawthorne's story "Feathertop," about witchcraft in a small town in Massachusetts

Bay Colony in the seventeenth century—a fable dealing with humanization through the love of a magically vitalized scarecrow for a lovely but spell-cursed girl. It reminded me of certain E. T. A. Hoffmann tales.

I was happy when Lockwood told me that I was carrying the torch and keeping the flame burning for American opera, that I responded to what composers were driving at, and that I understood their music. A distinguished audience came to the opening, including many conductors, stage directors, and singers. The audience reception was cordial.

The general reaction was that Lockwood's first operatic venture showed technical mastery, dramatic feeling, and sensitivity for the text that underlined the drama—and that he wrote beautiful melodies. The staging, which projected the fantastic, eerie quality of the work, was a credit to Milton Smith. *The New Yorker* spoke of the work as having "clarity, movement, and sense." My conducting was described as being "highly commendable," "expert," "effective," and "competent." The now defunct *New York Sun* wrote that it was "prophetic and encouraging to promote the performance of a work based on an American scene, historic event, and folklore." This success made my Columbia teaching job much easier. I was told confidentially that public recognition when positive had a real place in the academic environment. I kept this in mind during my entire academic career.

I was appointed music director of Brander Matthews Theatre in 1944. A year later Assistant Professor Willard Rhodes was appointed music director of the Opera Workshop. Former assistant conductor with the American Opera Company and with the Cincinnati Zoo Opera, he was an excellent musician.

The overall direction of opera productions was in the hands of Milton Smith and myself, as director of Opera Projects for Columbia University. The main productions were under the auspices of the Columbia Theatre Associates and the music department, with grants from the Ditson Fund.

Smith ran Brander Matthews like a provincial German repertory theater, with a training school for theater and the opera workshop. The theater school taught everything that was needed to put on a show: building scenery, acting, making costumes, stage designing, running the box office, painting posters, and tending to publicity. The opera department did not provide voice lessons, but concentrated on stage action, body movement, and the production of scenes and entire operas—some with piano accompaniment and some completely mounted with costumes, scenery, and orchestra.

My job as music director was somewhat like being General-musikdirektor in a small Swiss or German city. I saw it as a great opportunity to develop an apprentice system for the musical theater. Dr. Smith consulted with me quite regularly about all musical matters that took place in the theater. I cooperated with Willard Rhodes and the Opera Workshop and gave the workshop singers first consideration for the larger productions in Brander Matthews Theatre. I tried to lend support to good projects when the workshop ran into problems with money or personnel.

AT THE 1945 Ditson Fund meeting, I proposed that we commission an opera from Gian Carlo Menotti. I knew that he had a good sense of the theater and had had some success with his operas. The committee agreed, so Douglas Moore arranged a conference with him.

Menotti arrived at Moore's apartment at precisely five o'clock. I liked him immediately. Moore offered drinks but Menotti, looking very businesslike, declined. He was handsome and wore his clothes with casual elegance. I thought he resembled an Italian marchese and was a bit like a Latin movie star, or perhaps like a very rich member of the jet set who was interested in the arts. His face had the mobile expression of an intellectual, sophisticated young Italian. His eyes were expressive. When Douglas and I tried to be humorous, he sometimes looked very sad and troubled, but when we were serious, he often laughed. He apparently enjoyed taking the other side of the subject.

When we offered him a commission, Menotti said that he was fed up with composing operas and wanted simply to compose instrumental music. His reason was that stage directors never carried out his intentions.

We assured him that *we* would.

"Could I produce and direct my own opera?" he asked.

"Yes, certainly, that would be marvelous."

"Could I also conduct it?"

"I'm the music director, but if you want to conduct, go ahead and I will help in every way. I don't recommend it, though. It's too dangerous"—and I explained the Brander Matthews pit problem to him.

After our discussion, he relaxed with a vermouth and said he was interested and would get in touch with us. A week later he accepted the commission, and decided on Oliver Smith as stage designer, himself as stage director, and myself as conductor.

Meanwhile, Paisiello's *Barber of Seville*, translated by Phyllis Mead, was scheduled for February 13, 1946. This opera, first performed in 1782, had remained a popular favorite in Europe until 1816. It had last been performed in the United States in French in New Orleans in 1810. The work, based on Beaumarchais' *Barbier de Seville*, was charming; the music was somewhat Mozartian, but without Mozart's sophisticated counterpoint and orchestration. As far as we knew, our production was the first twentieth-century public revival of this piece. Milton Smith's crew built a two-story house as a set. He trained the cast to climb ladders, run over roofs, jump out of windows, and leap from turrets, all with fascinating lighting effects. In fact, the lively acting style did not help the musical ensemble one bit. We provided musical color by having a harpsichord and a mandolin join the string orchestra.

The music delighted the audience and critics. The *Herald Tribune* found the performance sufficiently lively to "demonstrate that a cultural institution like Columbia University can take a very real part in the active, producing art world [and] be a stimulus to that world by raising the intellectually low level on which that world habitually operates." WNYC broadcast the dress rehearsal.

In January 1946, Menotti had finished his opera, *The Medium*. Moore, Milton Smith, and I met him in Moore's apartment. Menotti outlined the story of his phony fortune-teller who is finally tripped up by her own deceptions, and proceeded to play and sing it for us. We were immediately taken by the validity of his dramatic conception and by the original theatrical and musical qualities of his score.

Milton Smith was relieved that Menotti was staging the work. He predicted a near-flop: "It's great, but the second act is exactly like the first, and you can't do that in the theater. You've got a half-turkey on your hands, Otto." Moore and I didn't agree.

Menotti, Beeson, and I put out a dragnet around town and we heard about one hundred and twenty singers in February. Menotti was friendly, tactful, and meticulously fair in the auditions. He spent weeks looking for the perfect face, the perfect type, the perfect voice for the lead. One afternoon, a woman with an imposing figure and an expressive face came for an audition. Her voice was as thrilling as her appearance. Clara Mae Turner was also a fine musician and looked just right for the role of the Medium. Menotti was ecstatic. She soon knew her part musically, so we began stage rehearsals.

From the first rehearsal on, Menotti proved to be an extremely adroit, skillful, and original stage director. He was kind and fair to the artists and always gave the understudies enough rehearsal time. He was almost psychic in his reactions. He often wandered around the theater with his back turned to the stage and would suddenly about-face with "You were too far stage left" or "This scene must be more realistic." It was as though he was trying to get the mental image he had of his opera into focus. This image was what he projected to the people on the stage. He was unlike Vladimir Rossing, who had to push the singers around to get his productions into shape. Menotti was more like a bard, composer, or playwright who wanted the performance to fit an inner image.

On sizing up the Brander Matthews pit, Menotti had wisely held his orchestra down to twelve players plus piano four hands. I picked an excellent group of Columbia and a few Juilliard players. Besides the dress rehearsal, I had six two-hour orchestra rehearsals. Menotti was behind schedule with his orchestral score and was entangled with other performances that had developed for him. In the initial rehearsal, the orchestra was still reading the first act while he passed out parts for the second. I kept right on and suddenly found myself conducting a section for which Menotti had not yet notated the score. Fortunately I knew it by memory from the piano score. There I was, conducting the orchestration that had not yet been notated!

Menotti wanted to achieve a powerful musical-theatrical unity. *The Medium*'s story—of a fortune teller who makes money as a spiritualistic phony and who, one evening, thinks she feels a cold hand at her throat and is made to wonder whether her fraudulent séances are not perhaps real—was masterful in its conception. As a librettist, Menotti created situations and incidents that led to credible climaxes. Individual sections of the opera were carefully conceived; they were musically complete in themselves and colorful in orchestration. The melodic invention was clean and transparent.

As stage director, Menotti brought out every event on the stage with dramatic clarity and precision. I think I matched him musically. He insisted from the first rehearsal that the total theatrical effect be the main drive of the piece. When it was a matter of theatrical effect versus musical precision, he would tell me to forget the musical precision. But we rehearsed so carefully that in the performances, it was a pleasure to control the whole operation from the pit.

By now, Brander Matthews had made a reputation as a tryout theater. Many prominent conductors, stage directors, singers, and actors came to openings and even to dress rehearsals. For the premiere Serge Koussevitsky, Dimitri Mitropoulos, Alfred Wallenstein, and Artur Rodzinski sat in the second row.

The performance was remarkably smooth; not one slip. The singers, who were beautifully costumed, acted with animation. The performance was described as *"grand guignol"* in style. The work was an immediate hit. There were favorable reviews in the national press, and plans were made to perform the work on Broadway. Clara Mae Turner was engaged by the Metropolitan Opera and began a distinguished career. Later, *The Medium* moved to the New York City Center where, with Thomas Schippers conducting, it had a successful run. The entire cast was used in a movie that brought international fame to the work. It became part of the permanent repertory and was recorded, and Menotti's publisher reports that it now has had around four hundred performances annually. Menotti considers it his most personal work, important in the development of his style; he feels this work and *The Consul* are his best. Some composers thought the work gave the right direction to American chamber opera.

THE DITSON committee wanted to commission Copland to write an opera, but he was busy. I suggested Virgil Thomson and Gertrude Stein. They accepted. (It turned out to be Stein's last important work, finished in February 1946.) Virgil immediately got busy and by Christmas 1946 he presented us with *The Mother of Us All.*

Like most composers, Thomson is not a brilliant pianist, nor is his voice attractive; however, his prosody and diction are impeccable, and his dramatic presentation not to be forgotten. Milton Smith, Douglas, and I cheered when Virgil finished playing and singing the opera, but Milton bowed out, alleging that he couldn't understand what Gertrude Stein was driving at. She had indeed fashioned a wacky, fanciful presentation of Susan B. Anthony's fight for women's suffrage and the unveiling of her statue in the Congressional Hall of Fame. A row of historical figures appeared in the opera, dreamy and somewhat posterlike. It was a patriotic, witty, and thoughtful libretto.

The auditions for *The Mother of Us All* took place in January in Virgil's apartment in the Chelsea Hotel and at Columbia. We heard about two hundred singers. Ten were from the opera workshop. The others were guests from around town. The opera called for a cast of thirty-one and Virgil wanted them all to sing well and look nice. When Dorothy Dow appeared for an audition, Virgil thought her ideal for the role of Susan B. Anthony.

I knew some of Thomson's music, and like many of his colleagues had not made up my mind whether Virgil was always pure of heart or sometimes, as a composer, somewhat underdeveloped technically. After reading the score of *The Mother of Us All,* I knew he was pure of heart. His apparent urban primitivism was due to his refusal to write music that he could not hear. When he was setting words, as in this work, his prosody was elegant and eloquent. His orchestration never overpowered the vocal line. Like hymns, folk songs, and American ballads, his tunes were easy to sing and hear, and his choral writing had a nice lilt and spirited rhythms. On some of his fanfarelike passages he would spend an hour arranging the alternation of tonic and dominant, so that they would be just right. With the perfection of their relationship he reestablished them in their rightful place in twentieth-century music.

Virgil assembled a large staff. Maurice Grosser made a scenario of the opera. John Taras, a ballet dancer and dance director, staged the work, devising subtle patterns of movement for the singers. Milton Smith's crew built the scenery and did the lighting. Jack Beeson and I kept Thomson out of the way until the singers were note-perfect.

I taught the cast the tempi Thomson gave me, but at the first ensemble rehearsal something went wrong and Virgil got quite fussy and nervous. I couldn't tell how fast he wanted one section to be. He began barking at the singers. When this reached a climax, one of the cast said, "Mr. Thomson, if you keep carrying on like this we won't be able to sing at all. I can't perform under these conditions." I took Virgil out of the rehearsal room and told him that he should control himself; the young singers were doing their best and did not respond well to temperamental outbursts. Virgil looked downcast. We returned and he apologized to the cast. "Have I been naughty? I'm sorry. I'll behave myself."

Thomson's method of getting excellent diction from the singers was to wander through the theater and scream, "Out, out, out!" An unconventional method, but it seemed to work.

The augmented student orchestra was very good. Virgil invited everyone in town, including Olin Downes, the music critic of the *New York Times,* to come to the dress rehearsal.

During the rehearsal, I was working on balances with the orchestra, when Virgil came running down to the pit, shouting, "Louder, louder, out, out!" Virgil tore down a canvas curtain in front of the pit.

Of course this made both the orchestra players and the singers nervous. I told the orchestra to calm down and to play everything *fortissimo*.

Thomson came back to the podium again and said to me through the din of the orchestra, "I think it's a bit too heavy, Puss." From then on everything went beautifully.

The house was packed on opening night. The performance was smooth until the final scene, when the trombonist bobbled a note in a solo. There was a shout from the back of the hall: ". . . the bastard!" It was Virgil providing some last-minute critical comment.

As usual Brander Matthews was full of famous conductors and stage directors, including Mitropoulos, Ormandy, Eugene Goossens, Alfred Wallenstein, Koussevitsky, Alexander Smallens,

Leon Barzin, and Frank St. Leger, as well as Edward Johnson, the director of the Metropolitan Opera. Goossens was particularly impressed with the performance and with my conducting.

As Goossens's assistant in Rochester I had spent many hours learning how to balance a baton in my palm, but at Brander Matthews I conducted without a baton.

"Damned good thing you're not using a baton," Goossens said. "You'd get all tangled up in such cramped quarters. Bravo, my boy, bravo."

Koussevitsky gave me a friendly handshake and whispered, "Good job." Mitropoulos said, "First-rate performance. Of course, it's not a very difficult score." Ormandy made a point of saying that he didn't know how I did it. Wallenstein was surprised at the quality of the student orchestra.

In our program notes, we described The Mother of Us All as a political fantasy about nineteenth-century America. Some reviewers, however, felt that the opera presented a serious story about Susan B. Anthony and her fight for women's suffrage. The reviewers spoke of Thomson's uncanny talent for setting English words, his limpid and transparent score, and his delicate ear. They liked his melodies, his use of common chords as support material, his adroit but offhand modulations, his deft use of the small group of instruments. Thomson's imagination, directness, and simplicity set off the intricate words. It was warm, affectionate, melodic music, with folksy and modal tunes and hymns full of touching moments.

Just before I entered the pit for the second performance, Virgil pulled me aside. "The pacing was too slow last night. Take twenty minutes off the playing time."

The performance was smooth—exactly twenty minutes shorter than opening night. Virgil was impressed by the faster pacing and mentioned the incident in his autobiography.

The Music Critics Circle voted The Mother of Us All a special award. The Koussevitsky Foundation offered Thomson a commission for another opera. Soon after its premiere at Brander Matthews, the opera was performed at Western Reserve in Cleveland and at Harvard. Since then, it has had more than a thousand performances, mostly with college and community companies.

In May 1947, at the Columbia Festival, the NBC orchestra conducted by Alfred Wallenstein made a hit with Douglas Moore's Symphony no. 2 in A. Wallenstein also conducted Ross Lee Finney's *Variations, Fugue and Rondo,* for orchestra, Finney's salute to American primitive William Billings.

At the chamber music concert at Columbia, Adolph Weiss was praised for his expressive twelve-tone *Septet* and Roger Goeb for his straightforward and accessible *Prairie Songs.*

≥≤

At the 1948 meeting of the Ditson committee, I was startled when Henry Moe, our senior member, proposed that we produce *Evangeline* at Brander Matthews. I refashioned the score to fit the limitations of the Brander Matthews theater and got Nona Schurman, a choreographer, to direct. The premiere was on May 5 and the production ran through May 12. The program read:

Evangeline
An Opera in Three Acts

Text and Music by Otto Luening
Stage Direction by Nona Schurman
Sets and Costumes by Karl Bruder
Lighting by Gretchen Burkhalter
Stage Manager, Ruth Dodge

Because of the rhythms, the opera was more difficult to sing than I had imagined, but eventually everybody, including the forty-voice chorus and the twenty-five-piece orchestra, did a more than creditable job. Jack Beeson, who organized and coached the production, was invaluable. The chorus and the orchestra were made up of students from Columbia and a few from Juilliard, as well as some friendly secretaries and faculty wives. (Among the hundred and fifty singers we auditioned was James McCracken, now an internationally known dramatic tenor, who was then studying with Everett Anderson.) The chorus was actually outstanding, and the cast was uniformly good. Everett Anderson was brilliant as Benedict (he later conducted and directed his own operatic productions in Oregon and Florida) and Teresa Stich-

Randall gave a stirring performance as Evangeline. This was Stich-Randall's first major role and it helped to launch her career, which eventually took her to leading European opera houses and the Metropolitan.

On opening night, the principals and the chorus were applauded after each scene and I was called out repeatedly at the end. Some of New York's most meticulous professionals, including Carlos Salzedo, Riegger, and Cowell, were enthusiastic about the production and came backstage afterwards. Both Peter Mennin, now president of the Juilliard School of Music, and Robert Ward gave us compliments. Dr. Ernst Lert, stage director at La Scala and the Metropolitan Opera, was also enthusiastic. He called *Evangeline* a *Liederspiel*—a song play. (He also suggested that I rewrite one scene, which I found impossible to do.)

The national and international press covered the production and the reviews were mixed. Then Virgil Thompson wrote an article in the Sunday *Herald Tribune* in which he called *Evangeline* "a work of far deeper expressive intensity than this listener had imagined." Thompson, too, called it a *Liederspiel* and noted that it was united in form like a musical suite. He continued: "Nothing could be more deceptive than the taste and skill of this composer. . . . My last visit settled the matter for me. Otto Luening is really an original composer and his textures are both highly personal and expressive. They grow on one, acquire interest and meaning: they are thought through in every way, they are a master's work."

L'Evangeline—the Moncton, New Brunswick, French-language newspaper—sent a correspondent to a rehearsal, who wrote a detailed account of the production for the Acadians in Canada and elsewhere. He said: "Today we are assisting at the birth of a work which is able to portray as well or better than a poem our story, our sufferings, our people, for the music is not limited by the restrictions which language imposes. . . . In offering to Otto Luening our gratitude we are expressing the wish that this first presentation of his work has a real success presaging the glory that consecrates worldwide fame."

I felt *Evangeline*'s fame was late in arriving, but was glad when people began to hear the music. Millions in Eastern

Europe were able to hear the Moon Scene suite from *Evangeline*, conducted by Emerson Buckley and featuring an aria sung by Teresa Stich-Randall, when WQXR made a tape for Voice of America. Ernst Bacon and Ruth Ives produced the opera with two pianos at Syracuse University, and the students thought it was "undeniably expressive and powerful."

In 1955 the Acadians in St. Martinsville, Louisiana, invited me to present scenes from the opera at the bicentennial celebration of their deportation—the *"dérangement,"* as they called it. Columbia agreed to send me, so in October I found myself in St. Martinsville with André Olivier and the Poor Boys Club. There they all were: the descendants of my operatic characters. They wore costumes, danced in the streets, sang folk songs, and made wonderful Acadian food (in fact, the Poor Boys Club cooked up a special recipe for me). In the Evangeline Museum a few score pages, slightly chewed by mice, were on exhibit. For four days there were pageants, arts and crafts exhibitions, performances of French plays, and endless parades. People canoed on the Bayou Teche and church bells rang constantly. Visitors came from an Indian reservation, from Lutcher, Lafayette, Natchitoches, and New Orleans to see stomp dances performed by Indian friends of the Acadians. Polka contests were also featured. Pete Seeger played his harmonica and his banjo, and students from the School of the Deaf in Baton Rouge square-danced.

My "Scenes from *Evangeline*" followed the Pontifical Mass on Sunday, October 30. It took place in the high school. I used tapes of the Columbia production as I narrated the story and played the piano. The audience was absolutely silent; their concentration seemed complete. After I played the hymn "Oh Rose So Softly Blooming," everyone sat quietly for some ten minutes, contemplating, I supposed, the history of their people. It was an unusual and moving experience. I returned to New York feeling that I, too, had become one of the characters in my opera.

I was reminded of my feelings in St. Martinsville when, years later, in 1971, I presented scenes from *Evangeline* in Grand Isle, Maine, at the invitation of a Mr. Michaud of the Historical Society. About fifty people, including Father Parent, assembled to hear excerpts from the opera in that beautiful place. Father

Parent told me afterwards that the program was more like a religious service than anything he had ever attended outside of church.

In 1974, I revised the last scene of *Evangeline* and wrote fairly detailed notes on the production, including lines from Longfellow's *Evangeline,* which can be read between scenes. C. F. Peters published these and the piano score.

≫≪

BRANDER MATTHEWS in 1949 presented A *Drumlin Legend,* a music play in three acts with music by Ernst Bacon and text by Helena Carus. I conducted. Perhaps the most notable debut was that of Charles Wuorinen as a member of a chorus of school children. (It was during an intermission at the dress rehearsal that he asked me if he could show me his Fugue in D Major, so beginning a long friendship and professional relationship.)

The opera was not especially well received. It was an allegory about the wood sprites of the Catskill Mountains and seemed somewhat far-fetched to our audience after the realism of *The Medium* and the Stein-Thomson glamour of *The Mother of Us All.* However, reviewers praised the artful simplicity and charm of Bacon's music.

THE 1949 FESTIVAL concerts were extremely interesting, with chamber music by David Diamond, Colin McPhee, Charles Ives, Carl Ruggles, and Edgar Varèse. Stravinsky's Mass, six Palestinian songs by Wolpe, and four sonatas by John Cage were also performed. On the CBS Symphony program two commissioned works—Randall Thompson's A Minor Symphony, no. 3, and Hindemith's *Concerto for Flute, Oboe, Clarinet, Harp and Orchestra*—were given their first performances.

The 1950 Columbia Festival presented the *Dickinson Songs* of Aaron Copland; Ben Weber's *Canticle of Canticles* for voice, wind quintet and string trio, with Bethany Beardslee singing the soprano solo; and a *Divertimento* by Andrew Imbrie. We also did a concert of American folk music with the Old Harp Singers of Eastern Tennessee, under the direction of Sidney Cowell, and the CBS orchestra program included Carter's *Holiday Overture,*

William Bergsma's First Symphony, and Cowell's Fifth Symphony—all important firsts for New York City.

FROM 1941 TO 1958, forty-one operas and plays, either premieres or classical revivals, were produced in Brander Matthews Theatre. Besides the ones mentioned earlier, the opera premieres included *Paul Bunyan*, by W. H. Auden and Benjamin Britten, conducted by Hugh Ross, a work that is now being revived; *A Tree on the Plains*, by Paul Horgan and Ernst Bacon, conducted by Nicholas Goldschmidt; and *Acres of Sky* by Zoë Schiller and Arthur Kreutz. I conducted the last one.

Willard Rhodes conducted *Sir John in Love* by Vaughan Williams, *Giants in the Earth* by Arnold Sundgaard and Douglas Moore, and *Hello Out There* by William Saroyan and Jack Beeson. Emerson Buckley conducted *The Boor* by John Olan and Dominick Argento and *Gallantry* by Moore.

Plays with music included *Iphigenia in Tauris* and *Euripides*, translated by Witter Bynner, with choral settings by Claude Latham; *Poor Eddie*, a dance drama with songs, book by Dooley, music by Albert Rivett, choreographed by Doris Humphrey, and starring Charles Weidman; and *The Dream*, a multimedia show by Reich and Sergievsky.

There was a special performance of Stravinsky's *Histoire du soldat*, produced by the International Society for Contemporary Music and Columbia Theatre Associates, and conducted by Mitropoulos.

In 1959 the theater was razed and the Columbia Law School was built on the site. Columbia has been unsure about what to do with the arts program ever since Mozart's librettist, Lorenzo Da Ponte, arrived in New York in 1805 and won $500 in a lottery, which he spent buying Italian books for the Columbia library. A worm-eaten volume of Boccaccio with a broken binding was the only Italian book there, and Da Ponte was rewarded for his gift by being made honorary professor, an appointment that did not include stipend or students. Da Ponte solved his academic problems by opening up a vegetable and fruit market, a speakeasy in Elizabeth, New Jersey, and a bookshop, and by giving private lessons. Ever since Edward MacDowell tried to establish a School of the Arts at Columbia early in the century, there have been many discussions and proposals. In 1965, Jacques Barzun and Davidson Taylor finally got such a school underway. After twenty-two years of discussions, a Columbia University Music Press was also established. Schuyler Chapin is now dean, and Chou Wen-chung, a former composition student of mine, associate dean, of the School of the Arts.

≫≪

DURING THE YEARS that we produced opera at Columbia, I saw a great deal of Varèse. He was a remarkably friendly and supportive colleague. He attended not only opera performances, but rehearsals too. When things were rough at rehearsal and I was fully occupied with trying to whip my pickup orchestra into shape, Varèse would sit in the first row, hanging over the railing, waiting to cheer me on at intermission. "Don't worry about the oboist, Luening. He's sharpening his reed. He'll be in tune by the time you start again." He was very enthusiastic about Dorothy Dow and Teresa Stich-Randall. Along with other radical composers such as Salzedo, Riegger, and Cowell, Varèse was a strong supporter of *Evangeline*. Fifteen years after its performance, he astonished me by talking about it in detail and even quoting sections from the libretto and singing musical phrases.

Varèse, Riegger, and I tried to establish a café life for musicians in New York. We first met at the Blue Ribbon Restaurant, but when a waiter told Carl Ruggles, who was a guest, that he thought Mozart was a greater composer than Beethoven, Ruggles raised hell and said we would have to go to another place. Varèse arranged for us to meet at Monte's, an Italian restaurant in Greenwich Village. We met there for almost a year, but when word got around that Monte's was an artists' café and busloads of tourists stopped in for espresso, we couldn't get a seat.

Varèse's favorite composer was Heinrich Schütz. Monteverdi ran a close second. He admired Schütz for the powerful, expressive effects the composer achieved with the utmost economy of means, and Monteverdi for his daring exploration of new harmonic possibilities. He also admired Obrecht because of his contrapuntal mastery and harmonic clarity. He often spoke of Richard Wagner's expressive dramatic power and of Berlioz's use of timbre as part of his structure. Varèse referred to his own work as "organized sound." He liked to talk of Beethoven's Ninth Symphony because in it Beethoven had combined vocal and instrumental forces and words.

We often talked about the different effects of dissonance on resonance in voices and in instruments. Varèse thought that ferocious dissonances in vocal writing often sound out of tune and suggested that the rhythm of the prosody and even counter-rhythms in melodic passages were the elements that brought vocal music alive. His interest in vocal music stemmed from his study with Vincent d'Indy and Albert Roussel at the Schola Cantorum in Paris, where Gregorian chant and early polyphonic choral compositions were emphasized. During his years in Paris, Varèse founded the Choeur de l'Université Populaire and the concerts of Le Château du Peuple. In 1907, when he was in Berlin, he organized the Symphonischer Chor to perform the older polyphonic music. Varèse, a protégé of Debussy, also spoke often of the older musician's use of new sounds. Varèse told me that his music was not understood by Debussy, but that Debussy had told him he had the right to be original if he expressed himself clearly.

In Berlin, Richard Strauss became one of Varèse's patrons. Later, Varèse met Busoni, whose book *Sketch of a New Esthetic of Music* made a profound impression on him. They became friends and Busoni sponsored him. One of the reasons for my friendship with Varèse was my own association with Busoni. Busoni had opened up a new world of sound for both of us.

Varèse's studies in Paris centered on mathematics and science, but his cultural interests were broad and he conversed easily about a vast number of matters that affected contemporary life. He did not believe in antiquarianism, and conducted old music with passion and dedication. For the contemporary music world, he did much to support what he considered authentic modern trends.

In February of 1942, I received an announcement from the Greater New York Chorus, of which Varèse was the musical director. He had formed a composers' committee, which included Bartók, Schoenberg, Villa-Lobos, Riegger, Ruggles, Fiorillo, and Harrison Kerr, and he wanted me to join. Varèse saw the new chorus as experimental and democratic, a real force in music; he was planning to include folk music and contemporary compositions.

He asked me to make an arrangement of the folk song "Wayfaring Stranger" for the chorus. I did not hear from him again until 1943, when he sent me a George Pullen Jackson notation of "Wayfaring Stranger" and some notes about possible rhythmic construction and use of soloists. He wanted me to finish the arrangement for a concert of international folk songs, an old interest of his that had been reawakened by the Pan American Union concerts. I was so busy that I couldn't finish the arrangement, but Varèse sent me an invitation for the concert. His sponsors included Mayor LaGuardia of New York, the Countess of Gosford, Prince and Princess zu Löwenstein, Count and Countess de Saint-Exupéry, Madame Elsa Schiaparelli, and Miss Anne Morgan. The chorus was named the Greater New York Chorus and was organized to raise funds for the children of war-torn France. He took the chorus into different New York neighborhoods where, in addition to international folk songs, it sang early motets.

Varèse later reorganized the chorus and did two concerts in collaboration with the New Music Society at the New School for Social Research. Frank Wigglesworth and I helped him recruit a group of twenty-two voices for these concerts. The first concert, March 30, 1947, and called "Modern Music of the Sixteenth and Seventeenth Centuries," included works by de Grigny, Couperin, Monteverdi, and Schütz. A second concert, held on April 20, 1947, was called "New Music of Today" and included works for chorus by the American pioneers James Lyon, Justin Morgan, and William Billings; premieres of my *Alleluia* and of Ruggles's *Organum* in a two-piano arrangement; song arrangements by Lubin, Cage, Apostel, Schoeck, Webern, Berg, Mahler, Bartók, and Hovhaness; and premieres of Varèse's *Etude for Chorus, Percussion and Piano* and of Frank Wigglesworth's *Choral Study* for chorus, two pianos, and solo voices. Virgil Thomson wrote a review in the *Herald Tribune* saying that the concert represented what is really new in music. Varèse repeated my *Alleluia* again over WNYC. This piece was published in the Westminster Choir College Series and is still performed. I used my annual royalties to take Varèse for dinner at Monte's. "The Alleluia dinner," he called it.

IN 1948, I recommended Varèse to teach a course on twentieth-century music during Columbia's summer session. He agreed. I was among a small number of composers he discussed in detail. He wanted me to write a presentation for him in which I would try to define my musical credo—my aesthetic and technical aims in music. He also wanted a score, a record, and an analysis of a work of mine.

I found it rather difficult to formulate my ideas for him, but I wrote that the contemporary composer needs to have a thorough knowledge of acoustics and theoretical systems. In addition to the usual practical and theoretical studies in harmony, counterpoint, and form, I said the composer should pay some attention to dynamics and phrasing, as I thought those things had been neglected, and I advised study of canonical techniques. I stated that composers should recognize that there are two great divisions in composition: vocal and instrumental music. Composers of vocal music should take advantage of poetry, drama, folk songs, and other literary sources. Besides studying the technical and expressive possibilities of all existing instruments, composers should try to imagine other possibilities. I thought they should make stylistic studies of works in various periods, be fluent in reading scores, and have the ability to hear any kind of music. I differentiated between self-expressive, mechanical, or self-therapeutic music, and those compositions that had artistic validity. I suggested that composers should have a natural contact with musical material, whether as performers, singers, or conductors. Composers should select what to them are the most meaningful materials from the world of tone and fashion them into new forms and tonal relationships that are inherent in the nature of the material. Contrasting elements should be balanced in a work and should highlight the central idea. Scores should be lucid and free of extraneous material. I said further that I thought the melodic-rhythmic element in its broadest meaning best represented the composer's personality; that it doesn't matter what systems a composer uses, but he should think and feel music and cultivate a balance of emotions, with thought that is charged with feeling. (Varèse had spoken once about the logic of the emotions and the passion of thought.) If this thinking-feeling process is itself dynamic, then form will never become formula and the composer will never imitate even his own works. As in science, pure music and applied music should go hand-in-hand. Though pure music is probably for the few, and folk music and popular music for the many, I hoped that the various types of music would have the power to animate or quiet the intelligence and to awaken or soothe the emotions, so helping man to understand his nature and being and perhaps helping him to gain a semblance of balance.

Varèse also took over my graduate seminar for composers for a semester.

When a teacher assigns his students to a colleague temporarily, it often creates problems. But Varèse worked with all of my students with equal attention—and gave many of them new perspectives. One student, not especially talented, had a composing block, but Varèse with great patience helped him to overcome it.

Varèse was not only a superb musician, composer, and teacher, but a close friend. He and his lovely and gifted wife Louise gave wonderful parties at their house on Sullivan Street in Greenwich Village, where Varèse showed off his cooking skills.

After he became famous, everyone claimed Varèse. He was called a futurist, a dadaist, and a cubist composer, none of which, he said, was accurate. He was a rugged individualist who, while he supported the aesthetic aims of different groups, remained ideologically independent. He died in New York on November 6, 1965.

⧓

ONE OF MY jobs at Columbia was to teach and develop a master of arts seminar for musical composition, under the Faculty of Philosophy. After some conversations with possible degree candidates, I saw that their backgrounds were so diverse and sometimes so deficient in certain areas that I admitted them only after a personal interview. Academic records were a poor description of a candidate's abilities and deficiencies. I developed a system of individual musical diagnoses and prescription. I gave personalized aptitude tests, from which I drew musical and psychological portraits—a slightly offbeat system, but it seemed to work.

I quickly realized that there were not enough courses in any university to supply each one of the candidates with what is needed to survive and be reasonably contented in the academic world or in the professional world of music. Remembering my own experiences, I tried from the outset to develop in all my students the habit of self-study. In the seminar, when I detected weaknesses I would suggest whatever studies were necessary for the candidate to overcome them. I also suggested that the great musical resources of New York City should be used by the student and that he or she should, in some way, become an active participant in the musical life of New York.

The seminar met for several hours weekly, and when necessary I held private conferences. It was a kind of apprentice system, for I was more interested in establishing myself as an older professional and more experienced colleague than as a maestro or a professor who knew all the answers. Candidates brought works in progress almost every week. I read everything through at the piano. I felt my job was first to understand what the composer was trying to express. If, after my best efforts, a passage or a section was unclear to me, we would try to determine why. Sometimes the student was at fault, and the piece needed reworking; sometimes it was my fault, and I needed to study and play the piece again.

I would often suggest procedures that would strengthen each student's musical background. These included analyzing obscure works from the sixteenth or seventeenth centuries, reading through nineteenth-century German song literature, studying Berlioz scores, examining Rimsky-Korsakov's *Foundations of Orchestration*, examining compositions of Weber, scanning a score of Harry Partch or Joseph Matthias Hauer, and reading Busoni's *Sketch of a New Esthetic of Music*. I also made such mundane suggestions as the need for composers to practice piano, to join a chorus, or to attend rehearsals of the student orchestra. I avoided analyzing most contemporary music and never played my own, for I wanted my students to select their own influences and make up their own minds. After all, they would be stuck with themselves, and not with me, for the rest of their lives.

There were required classes for all composers in the fields of theory and music history. They needed this background if they planned to teach, and for a number of years the musicologists— and particularly William J. Mitchell, the theory professor—were quite cooperative in developing the program. We often suggested specific contemporary and older works for study outside the class. I was just as interested in my students' works as I was in my own, and in their successes and failures as well.

All in all, it was a strong enough approach in music training that many of my students were active in New York music life while still in school. The graduates branched out into many music fields and a number of them later became or remained my friends and co-workers, and in some instances took over jobs that I had started. I believe I avoided the usual teacher–student fixation without losing sight of what I thought was necessary to teach and to learn. I think I learned at least as much from my students as they did from me, perhaps more.

Some careers of graduates have been interesting and parallel to mine. Robert Kurka graduated in 1948. His well-formed thesis composition, *Concerto for Violin and Chamber Orchestra*, was not premiered until 1978. His opera *Good Soldier Schweik* has been in the world repertory for some time. He died at the age of thirty-five. Peter Davis reviews for the *New York Times*. Marvin Levy's opera *Mourning Becomes Electra* was performed by the Metropolitan Opera in New York. William Hellerman is president of the Composers' Forum. William Kraft became assistant conductor of the Los Angles Philharmonic and is a prominent West Coast composer. After my retirement Roy Travis, Ezra Laderman, and Karl Korte each invited me to conduct their classes during their sabbatical leaves. John Corigliano, whose works attracted much attention when they were performed by the New York Philharmonic, was a very lively undergraduate. So was Eric Salzman, who has written extensively about contemporary music. I often worked together with former students; my compositions were both rejected and accepted by them, and some students even wrote letters of recommendation for me.

※※

In 1945, Alan Carter announced the formation of the first Middlebury Composers Conference and Chamber Music Center. As with Yaddo and Bennington, the idea was to bring together composers and expert chamber-music players. It was also hoped that the conference would create amateurs' interest in contemporary music. Richard Donovan and I made up the composing staff. The chamber players were Edward Ideler and Virginia de Blasiis, violins; Alan Carter, viola; George Finckel, cello; and Raoul Spivak, from Argentina, piano. Alfred Frankenstein, a music critic, was also invited. In one of his reports he wrote that the composers greatly benefited from having chamber ensembles and audiences on which to try out their works, and that Donovan and I, by taking into account the individual composers' tastes and potential, helped them to formulate their own ideas. Composers were able to test directly the practicability of their works. As it happened, in that particular year composers avoided both atonality and the twelve-tone technique.

Alexander Broude, Rockwell Kent, Pete Seeger, and Frankenstein gave lectures on, respectively, publishing, the current state of the arts, folk music, and music criticism. The staff pay was one hundred dollars, plus room and board, but often we returned our fees to pay for the scholarships for participants. For a number of years there was an unwritten rule that scholarship recipients, once they were financially stable, would reimburse the conference so that others would benefit. Unfortunately, that practice did not last.

In the next few years the composing staff included Halsey Stevens, Roger Goeb, Theodore Strongin, Esther Williamson, Lionel Nowak, Normand Lockwood, Ingolf Dahl, Frank Wigglesworth, Edgar Varèse, and Charles Wuorinen. Since then the participant-composers have included some of the best young talents in the country. Besides readings and performances, tapes were made. Invaluable for audition purposes, the tapes gave many composers their first chance to present music for fellowship applications.

The Middlebury conference also became a place where musicians who passed through town could drop by and play. Among them were Siegfried Rascher, Michael Rabin, Orrea Pernel, Claude Frank, and Nathan Milstein. One morning Milstein arrived and at a moment's notice we gave Bach's G Major *Brandenburg* Concerto for flute and violin, with Edmund Haines at the piano, a very spirited reading.

In 1951 the conference moved from Middlebury to Bennington. At present the conference is divided into two camps: one at Bennington (with Lionel Nowak as chairman), which is primarily for amateur players and composers who write for amateurs, and the other at Johnson College (with Davidovsky and Gui-Gui as directors), for professional players and composers. There is also a six-week composers' workshop at Bennington College.

At Middlebury financing was a problem. For many years we had been, in effect, a cooperative. The staff divided up the balance of the income from tuition after paying all the bills. The shares ranged from twenty-five to ninety dollars. We were regularly bailed out by the Alice M. Ditson Fund, the Rockefeller Foundation, and by contributions from former participants. At Bennington we were assisted by BMI, ASCAP, and the Record and Transcription Fund, and though we had annual deficits of a hundred dollars, we were far more stable. In 1961, I resigned from the board of directors, though I continue to serve as an adviser and sometimes as a member of the faculty.

Besides the invaluable music contacts and the fund-raising experience that the conference gave me, I composed a number of works for particular performers. These were my sonatas for bassoon, trombone, bass, and violin, all with piano; *Three Nocturnes for Oboe and Piano; Legend for Oboe and Strings; Trio for Flute, Violin and Piano;* First Suite for Flute Alone; and various cello works including my *Suite for Cello and Piano.* The works for bassoon, trombone, and bass and the *Trio* were all influenced to an extent by the many baroque works that were played at the conference. My sequence of movements was often slow-fast-slow-fast, but the dancelike fast movements were not imitative of old dance forms. In these works I set the piano part so that it never masked the solo instruments. The slow movements had a clear expressivity, while the fast ones were rollicking, sometimes even raucous. These sonatas are played quite regularly now. In the *Trio* the spacing was such that the instruments did not mask each other, and the rhythms, although simple, often used misplaced accents that gave the piece a contemporary sound. The pieces for oboe were very much influenced by Robert Bloom's superlative oboe playing. I got to know every note on his instrument, and with this in my aural memory I developed romantic possibilities for the instrument that had previously escaped me. My Third Sonata for

Violin and Piano took me eight years to complete because it was "simple." Maurice Wilk played it in Australia and in Europe with Paul Jacobs at the piano until Wilk's untimely death in 1950. George Finckel also had a strong influence on my string composing; I wrote many cello works for him and got to know all the possibilities of that fine instrument. My *Suite for Cello and Piano*, although moderate in length, has a spaciousness about it that comes from keeping cello and piano out of each other's way. It has atonal and polytonal sections, some of which are based on acoustic harmonies, while others use a retrograde technique. (I had discovered that a good melodic line can work both forward and backward—not a new discovery, as Bach and others proved.) In the last movement of the *Suite*, unusual scale formations and rhythms combine to create an Oriental effect.

Many works by other composer-participants went through this process of practical testing with performers. This arrangement makes the Bennington-Middlebury conference one of the best places in the country for young composers (and sometimes old ones) to get their bearings.

≽≼

MAX POLLIKOFF participated in the Bennington conference for many years. In 1956 he established a contemporary chamber music series at the Young Men's Hebrew Association in New York City. From 1956 to 1974 (when support was withdrawn from the series), over two hundred composers had works performed. Among those composers were such well-known names as Elliott Carter, Chou Wen-chung, John Cage, Vladimir Ussachevsky, and Leonard Bernstein. In addition to Americans, Pollikoff introduced a number of foreign composers, such as Giacinto Scelsi of Italy, José Siqueira of Brazil, Niels Viggo Bentzon of Denmark, Victor Legley of Belgium, and Saburo Takata of Japan. Pollikoff was the main fund raiser for the series, as well as being artistic director.

Pollikoff had a strong influence on me as a composer, and I wrote three solo violin sonatas for him, which he played often. He recorded the third. Many of the works I composed at Bennington were performed on his series. I played in the performance of my *Trio for Flute, Violin and Piano* and my *Trio for Flute, Violin and*

Soprano. My *Duo for Violin and Viola* made a strong impression on some avant-garde composers. They wanted to know what my system was. I gave a mysterious answer then, and I must confess now that I didn't have a system. Julius Baker played my *Song, Poem and Dance for Flute and Strings,* a work that was well received—though certain critics were wary of the last movement, which was quite jazzy.

≥≤

IN 1946, WHILE I was preparing *The Medium* and trying to meet heavy medical expenses, a communication arrived from the National Institute of Arts and Letters. I thought it was an appeal for funds and didn't open it for several days. It was a letter from Van Wyck Brooks, saying that I had been selected for an award of $1,000 from the National Institute. The citation said that I was admired for my activities on behalf of others and that my accomplishments as a composer were underestimated. Though I knew of Brooks, I knew nothing about the institute, so I did some research.

The institute was founded in 1898 as an offspring of the American Social Sciences Association. It was incorporated by an act of Congress that was signed by President Taft in 1913. In 1940 the American Academy of Arts and Letters was founded as an inner body of the institute. In 1923 a joint headquarters was established at 633 West 155th Street in New York City in a new building donated by Archer Milton Huntington, who also created endowments for the institute. (On December 30, 1976, the two institutions were amalgamated as the American Academy and Institute of Arts and Letters.)

The goal of the organization is to foster, assist, and sustain an interest in literature, music, and the fine arts in our society. It singles out and encourages individual artists and their works by giving awards and prizes; it gives exhibits of art and manuscripts, sponsors readings and performances, and purchases works of art from members, supervising their distribution to museums.

Election to the institute has for many years been considered the highest form of artistic recognition in this country. Nominees in each category are voted on by the entire membership. There are no dues or initiation fees, and an eleven-member board of directors governs the affairs of both institutions. Nominations for any awards or for music scholarships are accepted only from the members. All officers and committee members work without remuneration.

In 1946 the recipients of awards included Kenneth Burke, Malcolm Cowley, Marianne Moore, and Jack Levine. I was delighted to be in such company, until I saw that the music recipients—Norman Dello Joio, Robert Palmer, Peter Mennin, and Robert Ward—were fifteen to twenty years younger than I. My student Robert McBride had been given an award four years before. I realized that I was a late bloomer and had no reason to feel cocky about the award.

The presentation of the awards at the annual May meeting took place in the beautiful auditorium of the National Institute. Senator J. William Fulbright delivered the Blashfield Address. The Overture from my *Suite for String Orchestra* was played, and I felt that I had been properly introduced to the fraternity of American artists. I went back to work the next day and had no contact with the institute until 1952, when I was elected to the membership.

The election was a great experience for me, as I was in the company of such distinguished people as Henry Steele Commager, Eudora Welty, Tennessee Williams, and Jacques Barzun. When I attended my first committee meeting, I was no longer in awe for being honored. For the first time in my life I was among fellow artists to whom I did not have to explain my art and its function or validity, or to justify it in any way.

Since then, the gatherings at the Academy Institute, ably arranged by Felicia Geffen and Margaret Mills, have been very important to me.

Chapter 22

Compositions and Composing
1918 - 1976

BEFORE COMING TO NEW YORK CITY, I had lost few members of my immediate family. (My Aunt Josephine and cousin Wolfgang, who lived in Hamburg, Germany, had been trapped in Hitler's cauldron during World War II and had both committed suicide in Berlin.)

A month after Ethel and I arrived in New York, my father—who was ninety-three—died in Oconomowoc, Wisconsin. He had written poetry, composed, and taught until he was eighty-nine. Then he had two strokes that interfered with his speech and movement.

When I last saw him he stumbled into the room and greeted me with "I'm only half a man now," then ordered the housekeeper to bring champagne.

His hands shook as he poured our drinks. He chain-smoked cigarettes.

I remonstrated; I thought he would have another stroke.

"You are trying to tell me, an old wreck of ninety-one, what is good for me. Let me tell you that if anybody can get any kind of pleasure out of life without hurting someone else, and he doesn't do it, he's a damn fool. Your health!" He raised a shaking glass.

In spite of his age, his death came as a shock. He had been a focal point all my life, even if for many years it had not been clear whether he was a very self-centered man or a wise and good father. The latter feeling won out, as I began to understand his brilliance and genius and to realize that many disappointments had made him reflective and somewhat sad, but never resigned to his fate.

My brothers and I buried him in Milwaukee's Forest Home Cemetery in a plot with his ancestors, surrounded by the trees he loved. We played one of his favorite recordings, the Allegretto from Beethoven's Seventh Symphony. Following the funeral, about twenty-five of us went to Aunt Gretchen's house, where nostalgic talk carried us back to the old songs. We gathered around the piano and sang German, French, and English songs, finishing with American popular songs. Our voices rang through the house on the lake bluff and for an hour we felt like a family. From that day on we met after funerals and sang the old songs; but the chorus grew weaker each time.

My sister died of cancer in 1947. She was a beautiful and gifted woman, but her life was sad and unfulfilled. When an offer of a teaching appointment that she had waited for for years arrived by mail, she was in a coma and died a week later. She had once sung small roles at Covent Garden.

When my mother died in 1950, there was no singing. She had been bedridden for ten years, crippled by arthritis and always in pain. She had been mentally alert, cheerful, and never complained, and her remarkable spirit (she remained without fear of anything or anybody) kept the family in touch with her and each other until her death at the age of ninety. My father was the center of her life, and she asked for nothing better.

Another relative had a nervous breakdown. . . .

These experiences with death and illness crowded my life so that I simply saw everything that came my way as a responsibility that had to be met. With no health insurance or social security benefits to aid Mother or Father, and theirs and my own savings badly depleted by the Depression (mine were in a sorry state when my father died), my brothers and I had to meet these financial responsibilities.

Expenses for all of these emergencies ran for me to more than twelve hundred dollars per month for a while, a staggering amount for a professor to raise in those years, so I taught evening classes, coached singers and composers privately, was music consultant, and lectured. My schedule was filled from 9:00 A.M. to 2:00 A.M. I had no time to feel like a martyr or a hero or an art-for-art's-sake composer. The jobs simply had to be done as they accumulated.

DURING MY years at Barnard and Columbia, I became increasingly active on and off campus. In spite of my financial obligations, my desire to help create a climate in which music, the other arts, and the humanities could flourish remained strong. I loved to cooperate with people and found almost everyone interesting. I enjoyed tackling almost any project that came along, and I learned much on each job. For diversion I read many works on normal and abnormal psychology, studied psychiatry, and had no trouble in relating to all kinds of people. Had I been born a woman I am afraid I would have been permanently pregnant—people could talk me into anything in those days.

Although I sketched and composed a fair amount during most of these years, I neglected promoting my compositions. It took me decades to admit that unlike in Europe, where introductions from prominent colleagues were sufficient to launch one, in the United States some degree of self-promotion was needed to make a career. Being a good musical citizen and writing good works was not enough. My reputation as a composer fluctuated unduly, because I rarely followed up my occasional successes until years later.

When Ethel and I came to New York in 1935 for the two-month Bennington nonresident term, my works were beginning to be performed. A group of songs, sung by Ethel, and five of my *Eight Preludes for Piano*, played by Lydia Hoffman Behrendt, were on the February 13 League of Composers program at the New York Public Library. The performances were excellent. The program included Sessions's *Three Piano Pieces*. He seemed to be moving toward Schoenberg and the second Viennese school. I was moving away from Schoenberg, although my *Soundless Song* from 1924 used a primitive kind of twelve-tone manipulation in the accompaniment around a diatonic melody set to my own esoteric words. My 1938 Dickinson song, *If I Can Keep One Heart from Breaking*, is like a hymn, quite diatonic, but I thought of the harmonic and melodic materials in a personal way and heard them clearly with my inner ear. *Only Themselves* (from 1936) is a two-line Whitman aphorism set in the piano accompaniment with crashing dissonant chords and a throbbing rhythm. The vocal line is strong and declamatory.

The first prelude is a study in major thirds. The second is in free dissonance with tone clusters. The third prelude was based on major seconds and perfect fifths used atonally. It expands from two-part writing to seven- and back to three-. The fourth prelude is an invention in two sections with eight three-part chords as interludes. It has a tone center, but the upper melodic line moves atonally and with rubato throughout and is imitated freely by the second part. Number five is an atonal joke around a Swiss dance—the harmonies in and out of focus. The last three of my set of eight piano preludes are built on the tone A and its upper partials. The upper partials are a precise number of vibrations apart. Each such interval has its own partials. From this vast field of sonorous relationships I selected groups that were most suitable for the mood of each prelude. To make these sonority forms effective the registers of the piano, the rhythms, and the dynamics are integrated with the melodic lines to produce a convincing overall form. The sixth and seventh preludes are crashingly loud; the eighth is *mezzo-forte* and *mezzo-piano* with a buildup only in the last third of the piece. These works were thirty seconds to two minutes long. They were a revolt against what seemed to me to be the overblown rhetoric of Mahler, Bruckner, Wagner, and, yes, my heroes, Richard Strauss and Schoenberg. Leopold Stokowski described this style of mine, when he conducted my *Pilgrim's Hymn* with the New York Philharmonic, as consisting of elements that resembled slogans, aphorisms, or Indian mantras.

After the League of Composers concert, Varèse told me that he found my crashing Whitman song remarkable and the last two preludes fine sound pieces. The audience was cordial and the other composers quite interested by my departure from prevalent fashions among the modernists: imitation Stravinsky and extensions of Schoenberg serialism. But there were also the iconoclasts: Varèse, Riegger, Salzedo, Weiss, Cowell, Rudhyar, Brant, Chavez, Ives, Ornstein, Antheil, Crawford, Donovan, Fine, Ruggles, Piston, and others. These composers received limited attention from the League of Composers, so they did their own promoting. G. Schirmer's published three of my Whitman and Blake songs, and Elliott Carter wrote a sensitive, complimentary review that won many new friends for me.

In early May, 1938, the University Women's Chorus performed my *Sun of the Sleepless*. This short poem and another

Byron text, *If That High World,* were set in 1927 and were the first works that I composed after vowing that I would never write another note that I couldn't imagine with my inner ear. Musically, they represented for me a great clarification and simplification. Both were published and are performed from time to time.

These performances indicated to me that while many of my colleagues were moving toward a greater complexity, I was seeking clarity and simplicity. The Schoenberg followers were interested in me. Adolph Weiss congratulated Ethel and me in Bennington in 1941 for the splendid New Music Quarterly Recording of my *Suite for Soprano and Flute.* "Ethel's singing is perfect," he said, "and even Schoenberg really liked your music, and said that you are a very skillful composer."

As Schoenberg didn't like much contemporary music, and urged his students to be composers first, not theorists, Weiss's report surprised and pleased me, because my four-movement *Suite* was very simple and direct—and not at all Schoenbergian, as the term is understood. One movement is for solo voice, one for solo flute, and two are duets. The work was composed under control of my inner ear and was more a subconscious than conscious expression. Thirty years later I used the first movement in a ballet for Doris Humphrey and José Limón and made an electronic adaptation of the same movement; it was called *In the Beginning.* I used the same material in the first movement of *A Wisconsin Symphony,* composed in 1975. Schoenberg's influence on me in Munich was strong, but my music subsequently went through many transformations.

In my five-minute chorus *Alleluia,* dedicated to Varèse, I wanted to achieve a compressed expressivity of the kind that exists in much Renaissance music. My materials came from the first five partials of the harmonic series, but I used them freely, with C as a tonal center. The directness of the piece was influenced somewhat by Billings. Virgil Thomson said that it was gracious, sonorous, and eloquent. When Varèse repeated it on WNYC, someone from Westminster Choir College heard it and published it. Choral directors performed it, observing that it had a new sound. It is probably the most popular of my compositions; it has sold thousands of copies.

❧❦

I SPENT THE summer of 1945 teaching in New York and Vermont and shaping up my Third Sonata for Violin and Piano. I also worked on my *Suite for String Trio*. This satirical piece with take-offs on an ancient dance, a modern dance, and a fugue, lay dormant for thirty years. I retitled and rearranged it in a short suite as *Four Cartoons for Woodwind Trio*. These and a 1918 *Prelude* and *Fugue* (both) *for Flute, Clarinet and Bassoon* were recorded by the Bennington Woodwind Trio for Golden Crest Recordings, and published in 1976. I had learned by that time not to worry too much about whether a work was old or had just been composed. Old or new, I wanted my works to be well written and formally balanced no matter what style I evolved.

Lionel Nowak gave a concert at Greenwich House that included my *Two Piano Inventions*. This event took place in the middle of my family tragedies, and inspired me to compose again.

WNYC programmed "The Music of Otto Luening" on February 15, 1946, as part of the Seventh Annual Washington's Birthday Festival of American Music. Gregory Tucker, the brilliant Bennington pianist, gave the U.S. premiere of my *Dance Sonata for Piano*, composed in 1929. Based on what I call acoustic harmony, it uses only the ten upper partials in various arrangements as free-moving basic harmonies, over which melodic-rhythmic lines sound. The movements—slow, fast, slow, fast—resemble baroque sonatas in form, but the melodic treatment in the slow movement has an indigenous flavor, and the fast ones are a jazzy march and a one-step. George Finckel, the Bennington cellist, played my *Variations on Bach's Chorale Prelude "Liebster Jesu wir sind hier,"* which I composed for him, one of my numerous compositions written for particular performers. This work was a slight token of my undying love and admiration for Bach, particularly for his chorale preludes. Bach often made several settings of the texts and melodies of hymns by Luther and others, each one of which was complete in itself. The various chorale preludes he composed to them were really tone poems. Bach taught me that if a musical idea is strong enough, it can be varied and paraphrased many times, gaining new expressivity without losing its character.

A month later, *Coal Scuttle Blues* (first composed in 1922) was premiered in Times Hall. This was my first joint composition, a genre that I have often had to explain. My piece was quite a novelty. At the Eastman School I played the piece hundreds of times. Ernst Bacon made a concert paraphrase for solo piano in 1928. I made suggestions and revisions of his arrangement, he made others of mine, and finally the piece was published. I was still not satisfied and made further revisions that Bacon thought were incomplete, so he began working on an enormous virtuoso two-piano version. He sent this to me for further suggestions, which I made and he accepted, and the two-piano version was published in 1945. Bacon predicted a brilliant future for this jazzy tour de force. The audience was delighted, and Virgil Thomson commented on its subdued sound and its interest in melodic, rhythmic, and prosodic design rather than oratory. It was so subdued that it never reached the larger public.

Lazare Saminsky took a great liking to my setting of Byron's *Sun of the Sleepless*. Saminsky, a pupil of Rimsky-Korsakov, acted, talked, functioned, and looked like an orthodox rabbi. He had great connections in Europe and South America. For many years he performed my music at the annual Temple Emmanu-El Festivals in New York. He liked my fresh sonorities and transparent style and my curiously naive but radical vagaries.

René LeRoy, the great flute virtuoso, played my *Monologue for Flute Alone* at a New Music Society concert at the New School in New York. This piece, which became the first movement of my First Suite for Flute Alone, was a twelve-tone piece (though none of the twelve-tone advocates seemed to notice it, which pleased me very much). LeRoy recorded part of the suite and played it again at Barnard College, but I had to wait for twenty years to have it published. It is now a part of the flutist's repertory.

A song of mine was done at the University of Oregon's spring festival and my *Prelude* and *Pilgrim's Hymn* (both) *for Chamber Orchestra* were played at the University of Washington's music festival and by the New Haven Symphony. University festivals and regional music programs began to include my music, events that were important to me.

In *Music Journal* of November 1947, I published an article called "Composers and the Public." My thesis was that in spite of the great musical activity in the United States, few performers, managers, and patrons really took the time to study the repertory. I suggested that the tax-paying American composer be represented on every program given by tax-free American institutions. I hoped that schools and colleges would also take up the cause of the American composer. I am not sure that the article did much good, for thirty years later I gave a lecture for the Music Educator's National Conference titled "Lack of Communication in a World of Communications," in which I said that the problems of limited representation and lack of communication have remained for the American composer, although the production of practically everything has increased.

ONE DAY, I was called out of class at Columbia by a wide-eyed secretary, who announced that the New York Philharmonic was on the line. Leopold Stokowski wanted to play a work of mine with the orchestra. He suggested my *Two Symphonic Interludes* but asked me if I would like him to do something else. I said I would send him my Second Symphonic Fantasia and the *Prelude* and *Pilgrim's Hymn.* He was wonderful to work with and phoned me again to say that he would either do the fantasia three times, but not on the national broadcast, or the *Pilgrim's Hymn* once on the broadcast. I chose the latter. There were short, typed notes from him asking for performance suggestions.

I phoned the Philharmonic office to see if I could attend a rehearsal. "Mr. Stokowski permits nobody to attend his rehearsals," said the secretary.

I called backstage and asked for the orchestra manager, whom I knew slightly. He said, "Stokowski never lets anybody come to his rehearsals, but you *have* conducted the orchestra, so—here he comes; I'll ask him right now."

I heard him put the question and then Stokowski's voice. "Luening wants to come? Certainly, any time, for any rehearsal."

The next day, I went to Carnegie Hall. I was the only person in the hall, and Stokowski gave me a private concert.

At the first rehearsal he played, besides the *Pilgrim's Hymn,* Debussy's *Prélude à "L'Après-midi d'un faune,"* Griffes' *The Pleasure Dome of Kubla Khan,* and Cowell's *American Piper.* At the second rehearsal, he played Khachaturian's Symphony no. 2.

In rehearsal the *Pilgrim's Hymn* sounded beautiful. Unfortunately, the performance was a bit shaky; but Stokowski with great skill covered up a wrong entrance by the flute. A few years later, he gave a fine performance of my Second Symphonic Fantasia with the New York Philharmonic.

⤳⤆

BUT MY extracompositorial activities were not conducive to producing any new works. A few other Blake and Shelley songs were performed in Germany, in San Francisco, and, with the cooperation of the musicians' union, in Town Hall and Carnegie Hall in New York City. Some of the reviews read: ". . . powerfully conceived," ". . . songs which are that rarity, settings that really enhance the poems" ". . . elegant of line, poised of harmony . . . it is . . . gentle, sophisticated, moving song." Much later, *Love's Secret* and *Divine Image*, both for soprano and piano, were recorded by Mildred Miller of the Metropolitan Opera for Desto. The composition of My Third Symphonic Fantasia was begun, but I lost the score. John Wummer, the first flutist of the New York Philharmonic, played my First Short Sonata for Flute and Piano at the National Association of Conductors and Composers.

My *Trio for Flute, Violin and Piano* was first performed at Bennington, a tribute to the Handel sonatas I had played often and liked so well. Dedicated to Douglas and Emily Moore, it is moderately difficult and meant to be accessible to average performers. When it was first performed in Pollikoff's "Music in Our Time" series in New York on April 14, 1956, *Saturday Review* wrote: "Otto Luening's fine Trio for Flute, Violin and Piano . . . employs the traditional elements of music (tonality, counterpoint, melody) in a conservative, modern idiom. The appeal of this music lies in its freshness and in its natural vitality. Based clearly on baroque form it is chamber music in the best sense of the word." Some years later Pollikoff, Charles Wuorinen, and I played the piece a number of times in New York and on tour, but it was not published until 1971.

All of these performances made me ponder the direction my musical life was taking. I remembered the example of Theodore Thomas, who popularized symphony orchestras in America and who told my father that we need music directors—not stars—in this country. In spite of his contacts with Ignaz Moscheles, Salomon Jadassohn, and Richard Wagner, my father considered himself not a master or a star, but a loyal and good servant of music. Busoni considered it his duty to support the new and to help his students. Andreae was an advocate of apprenticeship. "You must win your spurs in America," he said. Schoenberg once wrote that when you are faced with a difficult problem you should remember that God gave you strength to solve it.

These thoughts gave me strength, of course, but there was a period in my life when I had a composing block. I went to unburden myself to my friend Martha Graham. We had coffee and she told me about her own experience with "blocks." "Every morning," she said, "you must first spend time on your own creative work. Later in the day you can do other things. I have been teaching long hours for many years and that is what I must do."

Her wise advice has helped me ever since.

Chapter 23

Scherzo and Adagio: Gambling and Divorce
1912 - 1973

IT TOOK YEARS FOR ME TO ADMIT that part of my nature believed in and relied on chance, Lady Luck, the subconscious, or God to help me out of trouble when the going was rough. Even as a child of five, the oppressiveness of Father's dominating personality, four older brothers, a sister, and a busy mother seemed too much to bear. So I made up a prayer to get me out of trouble without benefit of church. It went like this: "I pray to Thee, O God on high." This was enough to rescue me for many years. It sometimes works now.

When my parents took me to Munich in 1912, the world of chance became literal. Father began playing the Bavarian State Lottery. I heard him muttering to Mother that you never know what you might win and asking if she would like a nice villa on Tegernsee. He did win, once: a free ticket!

At the time his income was low, Father stayed home and played cards. He taught Mother and me the German game Sechs und Sechzig. Every evening, after I had practiced, when I wasn't at the opera or attending a concert, we would sit down in the kitchen—Father armed with three bottles of beer and I with a cup of chocolate—and play cards, sometimes for three hours. I gradually realized that it wasn't only how you played the game, but that there was an element of chance in how the cards you were dealt fell. I learned to weigh my chances and became a pretty good card player before I was fifteen.

When I came to Chicago in the twenties, my brother Eugene

had weekly poker parties at his apartment and I learned this exciting game. At the Stratford Theatre our intermissions became poker sessions. Our first winnings and losses were moderate, but my gambling fever rose when the game was changed to Red Dog—with much higher stakes. When several members lost their monthly salaries in an evening, wives complained and the management put an end to gambling in the theater. I don't remember gambling again until I joined the Bennington College faculty in 1934.

To get away from the rather rarefied intellectual atmosphere at Bennington—and the bitter cold on wintry nights—a few faculty members formed a poker club. I was asked to join. Sitting around a warm fireplace or stove, fortified by bourbon and good food, we played poker right on through the night. The stakes were low and losses were held to eight dollars. The poker activity at Bennington continued with greater regularity and higher stakes as the years went on, but my appointment as professor at Columbia diverted me from the poker studies I had begun at Bennington, although I occasionally reappeared as an inept guest.

It was during the music festivals at the Yaddo artist colony in Saratoga Springs that I realized that the East also had trotting races. I had seen and admired the great trotter Dan Patch as he raced at the state fair in Milwaukee when I was about eight. I looked over the horses at Saratoga with interest, but I was performing and composing and was much too involved with the chances and risks involved in music-making to be diverted by the horses.

In 1951, I was invited to stay at Yaddo for several months to compose my *Louisville Concerto,* commissioned by the Louisville Orchestra. While I worked evenings in my beautiful tower studio, I could hear from the track the distant bugle of the starter and sometimes (or did I imagine this?) the trotting of the horses as they made their way around the oval. As my piece progressed, I remembered that Louisville too had a great horse tradition. To my astonishment, I discovered that the second theme of the first movement was decidedly horsey in character, with an underlying trotting rhythm and an occasional neigh of despair from the losers.

I was well into my composition when I felt the need for some relaxation. An Armenian writer guest suggested a visit to the track. I was impressed with my partner's professional approach. In Armenia he had grown up with horses.

He observed, "To hell with the *Racing Form* or the *Morning Telegraph*. I size up horses by looking at them."

We watched the horses make their trial run and he predicted solemnly, "That black one with the silver streak in her mane is by far the best. I'm betting two dollars on her."

I liked the looks of a very lively little brown mare. She seemed to me to have the light feet of a ballet dancer, so I decided to put my two dollars on her, fifty cents on each foot.

We first placed our bets, then looked at the odds. The Armenian's horse was paying four to one; mine, sixty to one, but it was too late to do anything but root and hope.

The bugle sounded its clarion call. The horses charged from the starting pen, and then, wonder of wonders, my brown horse forged ahead by three lengths, increased the lead to sixth lengths, held it, and made the rest of the field look like stray horses. This, I learned, was called a towline.

I got $120 for my two dollars. This most unfortunate happening made me think that I really knew how to pick winning racehorses, so I immediately made a few more bets and lost. But my friend warned me never to wear out my luck, so we left early. On subsequent visits to the track I lost about half my winnings before I transfered my nightly activities back to piano and score desk.

I RETURNED to Yaddo in the mid-fifties to put the finishing touches to my *Kentucky Concerto*, then titled *Louisville Concerto*. The first version had heavy rhythms to describe the flat races. I decided woodblock taps were ideal for the trotters and much more attractive, so I made this important change. Another guest, also a professor, was writing a book about horses. Because of his enthusiasm, at Yaddo the painters began painting horses and the poets writing poems about horses, and I had a hard time not falling into the rather horsey rhythms of the *William Tell* Overture in my own composition. Fortunately, the professor's relationship to horses was both so artistic and so theoretical that there was no need to go to the track for either inspiration or action. We simply discussed artistry on the track, the theory of betting, the beauty of horses, and the social position of jockeys. This helped to conserve our rather slim financial resources for a while.

But even the most virtuous actions come to an end.

One day the professor, looking disturbed, came to me and said, "I have suddenly been called back to New York. I must leave day after tomorrow."

"I'll miss you and our talk about horses," I replied.

"I appreciate your sentiment, but I don't know how I'll ever make it to the city."

"What's the trouble?"

"I lack ten bucks. Have you any suggestions?"

His request disturbed me, because a check I was expecting had not arrived, and I had just about three dollars in cash. "I'm sorry, but I'm broke," I said. "What do we do now?"

The professor was a man of few words. "How much have you got?"

"Three dollars."

"Added to four of my own that makes seven. Deducting one dollar for taxi, it would allow us two bets at the track plus admission. There is nothing else to do."

He phoned for a cab, we arrived in style, and the professor flourished his way through the admissions gate. Without consulting program, tote sheet, or newspaper, he went right up to the two-dollar window and placed a bet on number four to win. I put one on number six to place. We lit up his last two cigarettes and strolled nonchalantly to the track. The bugle blew and the horses paraded, but we didn't look. The gate rose, the race started, and with our backs turned to the track we discussed the history of some great former champion horses. After the race and a breathless wait, the payoffs were flashed on the board: the winner, number four, paid forty-two dollars; number six placed and paid eighteen dollars. "Strike while the iron is hot," said the professor as we ran to collect.

The second race had several dark horses and the professor said the only way to handle the whole thing would be to put eight numbers in his hat and draw. He drew number two and I number four. He bet ten dollars to win, and I put in two dollars to place.

At the payoff the professor picked up $125, and I lost my two. He gave me sixty dollars and said, "This is your commission for splitting the taxi bill."

For the rest of the afternoon we simply could not lose. We now had so many one- and two-dollar bills stuffed in our pockets that we were afraid we'd be robbed. We took a limousine back to Yaddo. In the entrance hall the other guests had assembled for tea. The professor sat down on a cushion, took out his wad of bills—thick enough to choke a cow—and threw it in the air! I followed suit.

Our friends were astonished, and so were we as we picked up the money and counted it. Our initial four-dollar investment had brought us a return of around three hundred and fifty dollars, nothing spectacular but enough to get the professor home safely in a parlor car and enough to provide me with bourbon money for the next month or so.

This experience had a very bad effect on me. When I returned to New York I was sure that my real field of mastery was in the area of psychic betting. I had a long discussion with D. K. Lee, a student in my seminar (who composed the music for *Teahouse of the August Moon*, and other works), about the validity of hunches, or the "hunch with a Ph.D.," known as intuition. He thought my position was very interesting and suggested that we test it at the Yonkers track. Our first six trips were inconclusive. We came home at one in the morning with tired legs and backs, our stomachs jumping from beer and hot dogs. We won some and we lost some, but never more than sixteen dollars plus expenses on one trip. But we thought that now we had reached solid ground in the gambling arena. We decided that having broken even on conservative bets we would each invest seventy-five dollars in our future.

We had our usual ups and downs for the first several races. I was thirty dollars and D.K. about forty dollars ahead when the last race was announced. D.K. put substantial bets on the various horses he was inspired to select. I waited hopefully for the spirit to move me. It did. At about one minute before the window closed I galloped to the window and put all my money except two dollars, the fare home, on number five to place. The bell rang, the gates opened, the race was run, and my horse came in seventh! D.K.'s bets were closer; his horses came in fourth, fifth, and sixth.

We landed at the Gold Rail on Broadway for a sandwich and coffee but found to our dismay that between us we only had one dime left. We signed our checks and slouched home. This rather sobering experience closed the Yonkers chapter and ended my serious scientific work at the track.

For a few years I felt no need for gambling, but I became increasingly aware that my affair with Lady Luck had not yet ended. My marriage was becoming increasingly negative. Being catapulted to the role of an avant-gardist in the area of electronic music was, of course, rewarding in some ways, but in other ways very taxing. I was a university professor, subject to the academic restraints and the boredom and frustration of committee meetings; there was also the exciting but demanding relationship with my students. I enjoyed sharing thoughts and time with them, but it exhausted me. Gradually, although it wasn't at all clear to me, I was heading for a major change in my life. I slowly realized that my relationship with Ethel had been a gamble I had lost.

✄✄

MY MARRIAGE with Ethel ended in 1959. The experience was very depressing and sobering, and dampened the excitement of my work at Columbia. The exasperating thing about the whole business was that it took me an inordinately long time to understand the reasons for my broken marriage. A decision to seek a divorce brought me no satisfaction, and I was slow to act.

For the first fifteen years, our marriage had been reasonably successful. Ethel was a goodhearted person, beautiful, friendly, affectionate, and appreciative. She had many talents in addition to her exceptional musical ones, and a touch of genius. She was a lively and interesting companion and was well liked by my friends.

Certain things, however, were a pall under which she had struggled since childhood. Both of her parents had died when she was ten, and she and her sister were brought up by a very strict aunt in Leavenworth, Washington. Her two brothers were adopted by an uncle in Manitoba, Canada. Ethel took a job with the John Deere Plow Company when she was sixteen and soon became assistant town clerk in Humboldt, Saskatchewan. Her handsome father, Alfred, and her beautiful mother, Winifred, had been excellent semiprofessional singers who sang in concerts and oratorios in Western Canada. They died in their mid-thirties. At the age of sixteen, Ethel became the surrogate mother of the family and carried out her duties with devotion. She was first a church singer in Western Canada. Then she joined a traveling light opera company that played in Vancouver, where she auditioned for Vladimir Rosing, director of the Rochester American Opera Company. He discovered in her one of the most promising talents of her generation and offered her a scholarship in the opera department of the Eastman School of Music, which she accepted.

We married in 1927, when she was twenty-two and I was twenty-seven. Ethel had taken on the job of launching her talented brothers, Frank and Arthur, and her sister, Margaret. The strain of watching her sister and brothers go through the ordeals necessary to arrive at their goals was trying for Ethel, and I lacked constructive ideas. We were engrossed and submerged in our own careers, and our marriage had been preceded by a stormy and unsettling courtship.

By 1928, after Ethel had indicated it often, I realized that she really had one overwhelming ambition, and that was to be a star in the Metropolitan Opera. And her objective was clearly defined for the next sixteen years. In 1944, just before I came to Columbia University as a professor, Ethel had a number of auditions at the Metropolitan for Edward Johnson, Edmund Ziegler, and Frank St. Leger. She coached with St. Leger and soon was auditioning for Bruno Walter. He became more and more interested in her brilliant performances of lyric-dramatic coloratura parts and finally asked her to brush up the Queen of the Night arias from *Die Zauberflöte* for him. Walter decided that she was just right for the part, and her manager, Mr. Stein, was all set to draw up a contract for her Metropolitan debut.

Then there was a delay, followed by a further delay. The Met management explained that Mr. Walter was out of town. The next news was that he had postponed his final decision until a later, indefinite time. There was no word, either positive or negative, from anyone at the Met or from her manager in the next months. It was rumored that Walter had left. She cultivated other interests. When we moved to New York in 1944, I found an apartment on Claremont Avenue, but she wanted to stay in our studio on 67th Street. She is still there.

After a few years of withdrawal from the musical scene, she did begin singing again, and spent a few weeks at the Bennington Composers Conference, where she sang a song of mine and gave a magnificent first performance of a song by Louis Calabro.

In the years that followed, she discovered she had a talent for painting. She made hundreds of drawings and oil paintings that were quite remarkably good. She also taught herself to play violin, viola, and guitar, and led a quiet life. Eventually she sold some pictures, began playing chamber music, and busied herself with church work and a sorority she had joined in her youth.

Separated since 1944, we tried to patch things up for fifteen years without success. I was told by a doctor and some other friends that our fifteen years of waiting was an error in patience. I began to think that perhaps a divorce would help us get back on our feet, but I secretly doubted if it would help me to find the personal contentment, security, or happiness that had so far completely escaped me. Everything had gone on too long, and although as a musician I looked forward to further professional stimulation, the idea of picking up a personal life after this sad experience with Ethel seemed impossible.

No ONE IN my family had ever been divorced, and when I announced my intent eyebrows were raised. Everything became quite unpleasant. Fred decided that perhaps it was my fault; Bob thought Ethel was taking me for a ride. Nobody believed that we had tried valiantly to stress the positive things in our relationship, and that it just hadn't worked. Neither one of us could reform or adjust, because we didn't really know what we were supposed to reform or adjust to.

I consulted the cheery dean of the law school at New York University, who knew how to take divorces in his stride. First he arranged a separation agreement. In it I agreed to help Ethel until I retired. After thirty-two years of marriage the scene was a bit theatrical, but we signed and that was that. The dean then engaged a lawyer for me in Reno and told me that the whole business would probably cost two thousand dollars. Money was scarce, so the very thought of such a vast sum was sobering. The dean sobered me up further by asking me to pay his fifty-dollar fee on the spot.

I took a plane for Reno the next day, carrying with me my flute, manuscript paper, notepaper, unfinished compositions, riding togs, and some heavy reading. I was going to make use of my six weeks in Reno by improving my mind and by dipping into the Bhagavad Gita and into my spirit too. Ethel found a lawyer in New York to represent her interests. We were now in the business of getting a divorce.

When I landed in Reno, I went directly to the Mapes Hotel. After discreet inquiries I found that both the hotel and the gambling rooms were occupied twenty-four hours a day by folks waiting to get a divorce. Everybody was very nice but rather reserved. There was a certain genteel atmosphere about the place that I had never experienced before.

The next day, I saw my lawyer. Everybody in his office was efficient, friendly, and sympathetic. I understood why when I learned that the senior partner was himself getting a divorce. The firm had arranged for me to stay at a boarding house run by a couple that married each other after their two previous divorces. I needed a secretary. A most sympathetic lady who had only three more weeks to go before her knot would be untied applied and helped me.

At the boarding house I was permitted to sleep but was warned not to make any noise. This seemed unfair, because I had already been disturbed by people snoring at all hours. At breakfast I was told that all the boarders were either "taking the cure," as they called the process of getting a divorce, or were dealers in the gambling houses. Everybody needed his or her rest; music was definitely not part of it, so I became mute.

I embraced the higher life by concentrating on the spiritual planes and composing, but there was something eminently seductive and hypnotic about the twenty-four-hour-long string of snores that I was exposed to. There were not only solo snores, but duets—some high, some low. There were fast snorers, slow snorers, loud and soft snorers. The sounds were all so related to two-part counterpoint, cantus firmus, and percussive invention that composing was simply impossible. I couldn't even read. Everyone talked only about divorce and gambling. I tried walking, but the sun was too hot in the daytime. At night the streetlights were dim, my glasses needed refitting, and my night vision was poor.

I developed nervous symptoms. My left eyelid twitched. I had a toothache. I went to a dentist. He took one look at the tooth from the outside and said, "That tooth has to be pulled." I said, "Not by you," paid him ten dollars and left. After this experience I figured that I would have to do something or I would be off my rocker before my divorce suit would go to court, so I blundered into the library at the University of Nevada, Reno, for a little peace and quiet.

Apparently all my favorite books were in circulation. On the music shelf I found only one title, *How to Love Any Kind of Music,* and it scared me off. I stumbled into a corner where there was a neat shelf marked GAMBLING. Why not make a scholarly study of gambling while in one of the great gambling centers of the world? Field work in the many splendid gambling houses that were open day and night would be quite easy. I had almost six weeks to go, and by then I should be an expert gambler. My secret passion for this vice came from a primitive and compelling attraction I had never understood. Here and now was my chance to learn, so I first tackled books on the theory of gambling.

It didn't take me long to ascertain that gambling—like sex and alcohol—has been with us for a long time. That it is an ancient art, or perhaps a science, became clear to me. Early friezes and decorations I found in a gamblers' art book included pictures of familiar-looking squares made of bone with spots on them. Could these be ancient dice? Some decorations included squares and rectangles that resembled modern playing cards. Illustrations from a later period showed wall decorations with men tossing coins. In China, the I Ching, or Book of Changes, used for purposes of divination, included as part of the ritual the tossing of coins for heads or tails. Could this have been gambling? One author wrote that the Chinese seem to be among the most experienced and sophisticated bettors in the world, something worth knowing.

I also reread *The Gambler* by Dostoevski. This portrait seemed to me to be a brilliant description of a nineteenth-century gambler and his entourage around the roulette table in a European casino.

The most impressive description of twentieth-century gambling was in Dr. Edward Bergler's book *The Psychology of Gambling*. Dr. Bergler, an eminent psychiatrist and psychoanalyst, states categorically that because of house percentages and other odds it is impossible to win in the long run. He alleges that gamblers play because they want to lose. He states that they are also all slightly megalomaniacal, that a deep background of superstition influences them, and that most gamblers secretly believe in magic. Their problem is that at the same time another part of them doesn't really believe in any of these aids for winning, so they go back to the gaming tables to lose some more. Gambling, he writes, does not cause neurosis but is a result of a neurosis.

At this point in Dr. Bergler's book, I was quite shaken up, because it was an accurate description of myself. With all of the regularities of professional life, I had always secretly believed that hunches, good omens, intuition, playing cards, and other divining media could carry me over life's rough spots. Horse races were often spiritually uplifting—until I counted my money. Bergler states at the end of his book that while the prognosis for curing a gambler is excellent, it is still a gamble, for a gambler shows up for treatment only when he or she is losing. As soon as gamblers are back in the chips they feel better, stop treatment, and gamble heavily so that they can lose some more. Was I a chronic loser?

I turned to science for enlightenment and looked into the laws of probability, sometimes called the "science of chance." To grasp their provisions, even when they are presented at great length and in detail, is not for mathematical nitwits like myself, and a condensation is the best I can offer to the reader. Apparently, it is probable that anything or nothing has happened, is happening, won't happen, or will happen to somebody someplace at some time. This means that it doesn't really make much difference what one does, because in the overall picture everything is already either balanced off nicely or off-balance. The problem of probability can be solved by being in the right or wrong place at the right or wrong time. For instance, in gambling, when you

do or do not select a number in roulette it may come up or not,
but you have to see to it that you're present or not when it happens or not in order to collect or not. Of course, somebody always
collects or not, but it may be you or not, unless you're there or
not, or have somebody working for you—or not.

AS I PURSUED my studies, I realized what a circuitous route my
life had taken until Reno. Which of my lives was real: my straightforward professional life, or my secret life, in which I tried to figure the odds and win? Or did I really want to lose? I was no
longer sure of anything. I had to admit that those who had best
figured the odds were clearly the gambling clubs and the income
tax bureau, with a fixed percentage per game coming to the house
or state. They can't really lose with that procedure and there is
nothing neurotic about it, but is it right? I was puzzled.

But I had enough of the history and development of the ancient and ignoble activity of gambling. I now wanted to get into
the action itself, so I moved out of the library.

Reno is known as "the biggest little gambling capital of the
world." All the gambling clubs are run very smoothly on a
twenty-four-hour basis, so that if anybody has a hunch at any time
of the day or night, he or she can follow it up immediately by galloping to a gaming table. If it doesn't work at one club, there are
plenty of others. In the fifties the clubs served excellent meals
and drinks, very inexpensive and sometimes even on the house,
though eating was never supposed to interfere with gambling.

A young male employee at one of the clubs told me that he
wanted to get out of the business because he was beginning to
believe that all human beings are slightly cracked, although
harmless most of the time. Some of the employees just loved
watching the gambling show as it twirled around them like a
roulette wheel, but one fellow said he was damn tired of repeating the same motions fourteen hours a day. While making change
he muttered to me, "I don't see that I'm any different from the
slot machines." There were philosopher-employees who said it
was all a part of human nature and that the odds were that you
would run into the same hooey no matter what you did, so your
choice made no difference as long as you could pay the bills.

At the roulette tables I found women croupiers who were so

detached that they seemed inhuman. One spiritual type told me, just as I was about to drop my last dollar, that she believed honesty was the best policy and that if people aren't really on the up-and-up they may not be caught, but their evil deeds will haunt them until they repent. She looked at me so soulfully that I had to slink shamefully away from her table and go to the slot machines in another club. But my favorite girls and the most colorful of the lot were the Fatima types, symbols of Oriental curiosity.

The musical background in most clubs often consisted of one of Borodin's Polovtsian Dances from *Prince Igor*, a gypsylike tune that blared out over loudspeakers for hours on end. The mysterious Fatimas worked so fast while I was listening to the music that they looked as though they had three arms. While watching that third arm I lost many a bet.

The staffs in the houses wore a variety of costumes that can best be described as slightly modified Western. They varied from sheriff regalia to cowboy and cowgirl motifs. This gave a pleasant out-of-doors touch to the clubs, and when the personnel went out on the streets it gave a nice indoor touch to the out-of-doors. The ladies sometimes wore a modified nurse's costume, which seemed to lend comfort when the money was going in the wrong direction.

The owner of one of the clubs looked like Buffalo Bill. To prepare me for the kill he lectured me about various aspects of gambling. He said that through the ages stakes had varied enormously. Straws, pebbles, bullets, coins, property, and wives had all been used. The latter were often wagered as double or nothing. He explained carefully, as he rattled his silver dollars, that in a democratic society we use mostly money, and there was absolutely no truth to the rumors that wives, other female relatives, or girl friends were ever thrown into the pot for a wager.

The methods that are used in gambling houses are endless. They include, in roulette and other games, theories of numbers that come from ancient China, the Sumerians, and particularly from Pythagoras. They lead the ambitious player into arithmetic, geometry, calculus, and other studies that are so complicated and time-consuming that they will often keep the player away from the gaming table.

One favorite theory is to number the alphabet as follows: A = 1, B = 2 C = 3, D = 4, E = 5, F = 6, etc. Instead of playing abstract and cold things like numbers, the player bets meaningful names of people, places, and events. For instance, Babe = 2, 1, 2, 5. These numbers can be bet in that order, or one could take the first pair, 21, or the second pair, 25. But these two cannot be added and used in roulette because there is no 46 on the board. When all the first four numbers are added they equal 10, a fine round number; there have been many winners on 10. Of course, the player must not forget that Babe or no Babe he must be there when his number comes up and forget his theories, or according to the laws of probability someone else is likely to walk off with his winnings—or perhaps even pick up Babe.

During my field work, I learned that many people believed that their telephone numbers, their birthdates, or their street numbers had some special charm. Social security numbers were also very popular. Everybody in the gambling houses kept going at top speed trying out systems except one young lady who, like myself, was doing some research. She saw me watching other players, sidled up to me, introduced herself as an ex-Barnard student, and then asked, "Could you tell me, sir, why people do this?"

❧❧

MY THEORETICAL studies of gambling and the field work took almost two weeks. During this time I did very little betting, but I had made up my mind that, now that any constructive thought about my former life with Ethel was impossible, and I was unable to compose, play, or listen to any of my kind of music, I would see if I could earn a living as a gambler for the next four weeks.

My first step was to establish regular office hours. I arrived at the gambling house by 11:00 A.M. and stayed until 3:00 or 4:00 A.M. daily. I arranged with the Mapes Hotel not to cash more than one hundred dollars worth of checks each week, thus putting a stop to any disastrous losses.

I began my gambling by trying, with moderate luck, various slot machines. I found it paid off to look rather disgusted most of the time. This unsettled the staff and sometimes induced the management to inspect the machines, buy a drink, and hand out a dollar to replenish the machine. At one club I began with the dollar slot machine. After the manager saw me lose ten cart-wheels he dropped fifteen silver dollars into my winner's bin, and I started playing again with enthusiasm. I was pushed into further action whenever I would hit a jackpot of either ten or fifteen dollars. These fell with an enormous, orgasmic racket. I soon lost everything and moved on.

I found it good to saunter out with dignity, preferably wear-ing or carrying a black Western sombrero. Once I put this hat on while still in the club, and I was offered credit privileges.

I soon gravitated toward the roulette tables, and found my-self drawn to those with the most artistic croupiers. Some of them were most graceful when they used the lariat style as they threw the roulette ball. This free, sweeping motion made it look as though they were about to lasso all the numbers, with the possi-ble exception of the zero. Some of the ladies threw with such style that I was literally paralyzed and thought for a moment that I was watching a rodeo. A few losses brought me back in a hurry to the business at hand.

Another favorite method of throwing was called "scrubbing the numbers." The croupiers would swing the ball around with a scrubbing motion as though they were trying to eradicate the memories of past losses and to clean the number for the next crowd. This was done with such vim and vigor that on occasion I would give the croupier a dollar only because he was working so hard. An opposite method was the relaxed twirl. Here, a croupier tries to find out just how slowly she can make the ball and wheel turn without having them both stop.

Now that I was a regular gambler, I could observe the other patrons, who were almost without exception nice, solid-looking, conservative, steady, rather dull and square-looking middle-class Americans. There was nothing flashy about them, nothing desper-ate, and they didn't seem to be having much fun. Most of them, like myself, gambled hard for long hours for low pay.

A few elderly ladies arrived weekly from San Francisco. When they had lost a bundle, the house would pay their return fare. The next week they would return. The very wealthy customers had private gambling rooms, and my lawyer advised me to keep away from them and only play right out on the floor.

Roulette became my steady game, and I worked out a method that kept me in business. I watched the table and carefully noted every number that won. I put down five or six chips on the numbers that had not turned up for a long time. I was a silly method, all wrong, but it worked for a while. One of my numbers would come in for an overall win of possibly twenty-six chips. I would put half my winnings on the other numbers that hadn't yet shown. If I lost I would cut the play down to one chip. In a couple of days I ran my winnings up to a couple hundred dollars. I then ran them down with equal skill to five dollars and sometimes even less. Then, fortified by a meal and a couple of drinks, I got back in action again and recovered my lost fortune. A day's work meant sixteen to seventeen hours on the floor with very little time out for meals.

Eventually the business became monotonous and physically painful. I developed leg cramps and backaches from standing around the table for hours in a state of muscular and nervous tension. Semihypnotized by the twirl of the wheel and the jumping of the ball, my eyes would get tired, but like everybody else in the place I felt that there was an important job here that had to be done, and so I kept right on working through the monotony. The up-and-down curves of winning and losing exhausted me psychically, but a strange inner voice told me to keep right on and that I would win eventually. As I began reaching the end of my great gambling study, I hit rock bottom. By eight o'clock one evening I had lost a hundred dollars—my entire fortune. Digging through my pockets, I found only a few nickels, dimes, and pennies. I moved to the slot machine, lost the dimes first, then the nickels, and was left with four cents. The proprietor directed me to a penny slot machine emporium across the street, so with dignity I moved in to recoup my fortune.

My first cent brought me two plums and a lemon—a blank. My second cent brought me two lemons and a plum—another blank. By then I was in a high state of tension, all keyed up, and quivering inside. I felt like the string on a bow about ready to shoot an arrow into the air. I couldn't bear to watch the slot machine. With my back turned I heard the welcome jingle of a jackpot. I had hit three bars, and won a dollar. I changed the dollar into dimes and nickels and crossed the street and worked the senior slot machines with nickels, dimes, quarters, and then dollars, until I had won my way back to the roulette table. By four in the morning I had recouped seventy-five of my hundred dollars.

I played daily for another week, and it was the same monotonous grind. I experienced the same ups and downs, the same physical and psychic strains, with about the same overall financial results as before. When I quit, I found my noble experiment had earned me about fifty dollars a week, clear profit.

My time sheet showed that I spent at least a hundred and five hours a week in the gambling palaces. My rate of profit came to less than fifty cents an hour. Splendid pay when there is nothing else to do, but I decided that teaching at a university, although risky and often lacking some of the finer tensions that gambling offered, paid better even when salaries were at their lowest.

After six weeks, I had exhausted Reno's possibilities and Reno had exhausted me, so I flew back to Columbia University, adjusted and chastened. A colleague greeted me with typical academic humor. "Nice to see you back, gamboling on the green." Very funny!

Fourteen years later I opened an Off-Track Betting telephone account for $100. In a year I made four bets and lost only forty-four dollars. Can it be that gambling no longer has the charm to soothe this savage breast?

Chapter 24

Electronic Music
1906 to Present

IN 1906 MY FATHER READ AN ARTICLE in *McClure's* magazine about Dr. Thaddeus Cahill's Dynamophone—"an extraordinary electrical invention for producing scientifically perfect music." Father, a traditionalist who nevertheless liked to speculate and make predictions about the future, thought Dr. Cahill's machine augured a fantastic new world of music. My brothers bought Columbia and Edison talking machines with disc records. We stuffed the lily-shaped horns of the machines with pillows or paper or played the records without horns to see what would happen. On his vacations, my brother Dix, then a student at MIT, got magnificent results by cranking the machine slowly to make the pitch waver. But these novelties soon wore off and I heard no more about electronic music until I arrived in Zurich in 1917.

In Zurich, I read Busoni's *Sketch of a New Esthetic of Music,* in which he alluded to Cahill's machine and predicted that electronic sound production pointed the way toward the music of the future. When I returned to Chicago in the early twenties I discussed at length with my brother Dix—by then a practicing engineer—how to untemper or retune a piano. Nothing came of this and I began instead an extensive study of acoustics.

In 1923 my father wrote to Thomas Edison, suggesting that he invent an instrument that could do for sound what the microscope did for the eye—a machine that would enable one to hear the grass grow. Edison replied that this would be very difficult because there was at that time no standard of measurement for the tremolo in the human voice and little was known about vibrato.

Dayton Miller's *Science of Musical Sound*, published in 1916 and revised in 1922, brought me to the world of Helmholtz, the nineteenth-century physicist, and to the more recent theories of sound production. Both Miller and Helmholtz defined sound, the ear, noise and tone, pitch, intensity and loudness, tone quality, and many other aspects, and restated the traditional premise that sounds have fundamentals and overtones in ratios of 2:1, 3:2, 4:3, 5:4, etc. Each fundamental and overtone has its own frequency—the number of complete vibrations to and fro per second. This led me in my compositions to emphasize certain segments and combinations from the overtone row, using these as norms. I reasoned that because they existed in nature, they would be audible—if within the thresholds of hearing.

In the early thirties, when I reviewed Harry Partch's *Monophony* and read Henry Cowell's *New Musical Resources*, I was reinforced in my conclusions. At Bennington, with the assistance of the scientists Paul Garrett and Ed Jordan, I examined sound, using methods like the spectrum charts for the study of light sources. When Hindemith came to Bennington I discussed my findings with him; he was interested, but there remained many unanswered questions. In the mid-thirties I asked Henry Allen Moe of the Guggenheim Foundation for an introduction to Dr. Dayton Miller, who was a professor at the Case Institute in Cleveland.

Dr. Miller invited me to visit his laboratory and was remarkably friendly and cooperative with a greenhorn. He cheerfully showed me slides and his instruments and played many sounds, but then explained that his main interest was currently ether drift. His description of his experiments in that field was over my head in every way, and I was at once astonished, dismayed, and disappointed. Then he began discussing flutes. It took me fifteen minutes to discover he knew everything there was to know about this instrument. When I told him that I played a handmade Tillmetz flute he literally jumped for joy and took me into a special room where hundreds of flutes were on display. This was the most important flute collection in the world. It is now housed at the Smithsonian Institution.

In his acoustics studies Miller had compared and tested timbral differences in flutes by producing sounds from grenadill, cocoanut wood, bamboo, clay, silver, platinum, gold, bronze, glass, and tin flutes. My favorite was a Chinese pigeon flute made of lightweight clay, open at one end, with three holes in it, and shaped like a sweet potato. When tied to a pigeon's leg, wind action caused a *whoo-whoo* sound as the bird flew.

My speculations about sound production had until then been exciting to me, but I needed reassurance and had many questions ready. They must have seemed elementary, but Dr. Miller drew them out of me: Does each overtone have its own set of overtones? His answer was yes. Are there undertones? This was still speculation. Can different overtones be emphasized? That is the reason the timbres of a flute and a clarinet are different from each other and from other instrumental sounds. The human ear has an upper and lower threshold of hearing; does this mean that the lowest note on the piano produces large numbers of overtones that are in the range of our hearing, but that the same pitch in the top octave produces overtones above the upper threshold of our hearing? If so, do musical sounds affect us differently in different ranges? Certainly. Do the number of vibrations have anything to do with rhythm? Yes; a low tone on the piano sets up a rich complex of overtones that takes time to be perceived and savored; a very high tone has overtones that are beyond our upper threshold of hearing and they will die out unless the fundamental is struck again or they are sustained. How are scales derived from the overtone row? The whole- and half-tone scales as we know them probably came from hand positions on a string or a tube.

In the thirties I had little opportunity to work directly with electronic sound-producing instruments of the kind I felt were essential to finding new sound limits in music. In 1947, Harry Partch's far-reaching theoretical researches in the world of sound stimulated me to write in a foreword to his book *Genesis of a Music:* "If, in the future, these ideas are used in conjunction with electronic and other scientific developments in sound, one may expect a strange and beautiful music to result."

AFTER WORLD WAR II, rumors reached musical circles in the United States that new kinds of sound production were being tried in Paris. Vladimir Ussachevsky gave the first public demonstration of "tape music experiments" (as we called them) at his

Composers Forum on May 9, 1952, in McMillin Theatre at Columbia University.

Ussachevsky joined the Columbia University music department as an instructor in 1947, after military service. He was born in Manchuria in 1911 and came to the United States when he was twenty. He studied at Pomona College and later with Bernard Rogers and Howard Hanson at the Eastman School of Music, where he earned a Ph.D. in composition. He audited my Columbia composition seminar as a first step toward reentering the composing world after his extended military interlude. He impressed everyone with his sensitive settings of Rilke poems, a poem for flute and orchestra, a cantata, and a piano concerto, and with his great ability as a contrapuntist and choral composer.

By 1951, recording equipment at Columbia included an Ampex 400 tape recorder (7½ and 15 ips), a borrowed Magnachord from Harvey's Radio Shop, a Western Electric 639 microphone, and a boxlike device rigged up by the young engineer Peter Mauzey to create feedback for reverberation. Ussachevsky experimented with this primitive equipment, and between the fall of 1951 and March 1952 accumulated enough material to present his work at his Composers Forum in May.

Of this forum, Henry Cowell wrote in *Musical Quarterly* of October 1952: "Ussachevsky is now in the process of incorporating some of these sounds into a composition. The pitfalls are many. We wish him well."

I was directing the composers' program at the Bennington Composers and Chamber Music Conference in August 1952, and I persuaded Ussachevsky to transport the laboratory from New York to Bennington where we could, individually and together, investigate the possibilities of the strange new medium. We set up a small, primitive studio in a corner of the rebuilt Carriage Barn, which was used as a concert hall by Bennington College. Violin and clarinet interested us, but we decided to concentrate on our own instruments—flute and piano. We were both fluent improvisers and both of us sang, after a fashion. Many of these early experiments were improvised and immediately discarded. We had to invent several kinds of rudimentary musical shorthand, which were later much expanded, to notate the experiments we wished to preserve. We soon saw that the possibilities were endless, and we felt the need to limit ourselves to specific objectives. We had a choice of working with natural and "nonmusical" sounds like subway noise and sneezes and coughs, or widening the sound spectrum of existing instruments and bringing out new resonances from the existing world of instruments and voices. We chose the latter. We did not yet use oscillators. Soon I was impelled to try my first tiny compositions, using the flute as a sound source.

We used two basic manipulations. Simple as feedback and speed variation in a two-to-one ratio may seem now, their use for artistic purposes was at that time a revelation for both of us. Speed variation simply means playing a tape at a speed other than that of the original recording. The pitch and the quality of the sound are affected. The greater the transposition, the more noticeable are the changes in timbre, but the ratio of the overtone series remains unaffected. In other words, a flute sound can be transposed an octave or even more below the natural flute range or an octave or more above its natural range. A tuba timbre can be made to sound in the normal range of a violin. A violin timbre can be made to sound in the range of a contra bass.

Feedback is the automatic, controllable repetition of a sound or sounds being recorded on magnetic tape. On a professional tape recorder, the tape passes by a race head, then a record head, and then a playback head. Sound is heard a fraction of a second after it has been recorded through the playback head. If the output of the playback head is shuttled back to a record head, everything that is being recorded will be repeated immediately. The length of the sound pattern is dependent on the rate of repetition, so an overlapping of the original and the repetition takes place. With each repetition the quality of recording deteriorates.

Musically, even these simple explorations showed that the flute, transposed an octave below its normal range, did not sound like a bass flute, because without the problem of breath control and with electronic amplification much longer phrases could be produced than would have been possible with a regular bass flute. The same could be said about a violin transposed two octaves below its range. The musical values would be quite different from that of a cello or contra bass.

Ussachevsky and I both felt that with these new resources at our command the next problem was to complete small compositions. We chose to fashion compositions based on musical values rather than to explore the shock value of the new medium. We had learned from our research that amplified sound could damage hearing and could even kill. We were interested in controlling this powerful new medium.

For a composers' party at Bennington we were asked to prepare several short compositions. Our "works"— *City Nocturne*, *Country Nocturne*, and *Insect Nocturne*—were all based on flute sounds. After we played them, the other composers, astonished by our discoveries in the world of sound, countered with much applause and some grumbling. Lionel Nowak and Roger Goeb were fully aware that we were working with very primitive means but were generous and almost solemn as they congratulated us. Other composers came around and said, in effect, "This is it"—"it" meaning the music of the future. Ussachevsky and I were rather surprised at such a response. We had performed the compositions as entertainment for the party and had not expected a profound reaction.

The news soon reached New York, and Oliver Daniel asked us to produce a group of short works for the Leopold Stokowski concert at the Museum of Modern Art in New York under the auspices of the American Composers Alliance and Broadcast Music, Inc. We had only our shaky traveling laboratory to work in, and neither Ussachevsky nor I was very enthusiastic about the concert. But Daniel was persistent, and eventually we did transport our equipment in Ussachevsky's car to Henry Cowell's cottage in Shady, New York. We borrowed another portable tape recorder, carpets to deaden the sound, and an oversized wooden speaker, and went to work.

With my flute as sound source, I developed three short compositions. *Fantasy in Space* was a short piece in which the flute was used as a virtuoso instrument. The piece was designed to communicate with audiences conditioned to impressionistic, virtuoso, and tonal music in its broadest sense. In addition to the procedures already described, I used acoustic relationships that produced interesting "sonority forms," as I called them. E minor, A minor, and C-sharp minor triads in varied combinations brought out overtones and created resultant tones that gave the recorded flute a rich sound. After taping the first sound series, I listened to these on earphones, and, while hearing these, taped a second sound series over the first. I repeated the process until I had the equivalent of a flute quartet, all played by myself. This method was later named sound-on-sound. The separate sound series we called components. At the end of the composition I included a folklike melody, modal in character and played straight, to bring the listener back to a familiar musical experience.

In *Low Speed*, I made some simple sketches on which I based my improvisations. I transposed the first component an octave below normal flute range. The second component was a perfect fifth above the first; the third component a perfect fifth above the second; and the fourth component a perfect fifth above the third. This emphasis on the second overtone has long been used for fugal answers, a perfect fifth above the tonic. In *Low Speed* the overtones of D and A combined and sounded resultant tones, which added a new character to the natural flute tone. A tonal center was established by causing one easily recognized tone to vibrate with ever-increasing intensity. The resultant tones, not actually played on the flute, eventually produced a kind of unearthly and ghostlike counterpoint. The overall effect was that of a solemn, perhaps sacred, composition with some Oriental allusions.

Invention in Twelve Tones was based on a twelve-tone row with three variations. These developed into a triple canon and were combined with another triple canon moving twice as fast. This was combined with yet another. I again used headphones and controlled the sound and rhythms of my playing so that the end result was freer and more elastic than in much twelve-tone music. Peter Mauzey had a very helpful feedback device that could be easily plugged in. The flute sounds were to my ears new and mysterious, and had a certain cushioned quality. Ussachevsky had already used the piano as a sound source in somewhat the same way and had transformed familiar sounds into others, like deep-toned gongs and bells, organlike clusters, and a gamelan orchestra.

In Cowell's cottage we learned a great deal about getting maximum results with minimum equipment. By experimenting with the hanging of carpets and drapes we were able to make tapes with enough quality to last a quarter of a century. Even our large wooden speaker was extremely useful for certain kinds of recordings. In any event, we learned how to manage it and our not-too-carefully-balanced tape recorders.

After two weeks, we moved the peripatetic laboratory to the Ussachevsky living room in New York, where Betty Ussachevsky responded to further developments with endless patience and interest. Arturo Toscanini's sound engineer, David Sarser, invited us to try out our experiments in the basement sound studio in the maestro's Riverdale home. We sometimes worked there from midnight until three in the morning. My *Invention* was mixed on the fine collection of tape recorders at Union Theological Seminary. This gave much-needed ecclesiastical support to our venture.

Important pop musicians asked to hear a preview of our work and wanted to know whether we could make a tape music arrangement of popular old tunes. We explained that this was possible, but we wanted to avoid too-early commercialization and allow time for testing and improving the new materials.

≈≈

THE FIRST public concert of tape recorder music in the United States took place at the Museum of Modern Art on October 28, 1952. The program began with several pieces for traditional instruments, including the first performance of Elliott Carter's *Eight Etudes and a Fantasy for Woodwind Quartet;* Lou Harrison's *Suite for Violin, Piano and Small Orchestra;* and *Symphony on Poems of William Blake* by Ben Weber. Ussachevsky's *Sonic Contours* and my *Low Speed, Invention,* and *Fantasy in Space* were second on the program. Stokowski, who had reviewed Cahill's Dynamophone demonstration in 1906, made the following announcement:

> I am often asked: What is tape music, and how is it made? Tape music is music that is composed directly with sound instead of first being written on paper and later made to sound. Just as the painter paints his picture directly with colors, so the musician composes his music directly with tone. In classical orchestral music many instruments play different groups of notes which sound

together. In tape music several or even many tapes are superimposed; the tapes sound together the groups of tones that are recorded on them. So, essentially, it is a new way of doing what has been done for centuries by old methods.

Assisted by Mauzey, Ussachevsky and I performed the strenuous job of hauling and setting up the equipment. Ussachevsky ran the Ampex during the concert.

The reception of the electronic works was sensational. Part of the audience thought we had invented music, the rest that we had ruined it. Jay Harrison wrote in the *New York Herald Tribune:* "It has been a long time in coming, but music and the machine are now wed. . . . The result is as nothing encountered before. It is the music of fevered dreams, of sensations called back from a dim past. It is the sound of echo. . . . It is vapourous, tantalizing, cushioned. It is in the room and yet not part of it. It is something entirely new. And genesis cannot be defined."

Nat Hentoff wrote in *Down Beat* that he liked my *Fantasy in Space. Time* magazine said: "The twentieth-century instrument is the record machine—a phonograph or tape recorder."

I had been accustomed to a fair amount of publicity, but it had been rather personal. Now we seemed to be quite impersonal objects in the full glare of the American publicity and public-relations machine. *Billboard* spoke of "weird effects." Peggy Glanville Hicks in *Vogue* wrote a provocative article describing "tape music," as it was then called:

There is a quality of premonition, a vertigo that precipitates in the mind a view of a future in space. Occasionally it evokes a primeval world, predating human occupation. . . . It seeps in at a subconscious level, suggesting and underlining moods and the free association activity of the unfocused brain. It propounds a world of the mind dehumanized, outside individual entity and scope, universal, interplanetary; an outer space where being develops a supreme indifference to personal incarnation and its specific viewpoints warmed by blood. . . . One cannot but feel that [electronic music] has put in its appearance quite punctually and for some important role in the scheme of things to come.

In a subsequent issue, *Vogue* published a list of twenty-eight "system changers," and Luening and Ussachevsky were among them. This impressed us both very much until we read the list. Some of the others were Laverne, who used glass walls for dividing rooms; Lily of France, who reduced weight with a girdle; jet-powered helicopters; the UNIVAC; and the Necchi, a simplified sewing machine with automatically adjusting attachments.

Of the student papers, the Columbia *Spectator* spoke of "deep-throated rumbles and high crystal bell tones that echo and spin . . . science fiction music," and the Barnard *Bulletin* noted that "the music completely fills the room with throbbings." These reviews resulted in better class attendance. We were no longer professors but avant-garde space cadets.

AFTER THE initial excitement, there were other reactions that helped me to keep my balance. Most musicians of my age were somewhat suspicious and disapproved of my participation in such a risky adventure. Some thought I should know better, others that I was just fooling around. A few thought it important that the medium be investigated but safer for them if Ussachevsky and I took the risks while they waited to see how it would all turn out. Then there were the professional avant-gardists who thought we had invented music only for that week. Now *they* would move into the fray and show how to do it perfectly. Another group of young (and a few not-so-young) musicians saw the medium as a new sound source that had to be mastered, if only as part of their technical background. Varèse was almost the only composer who worked consistently, first in his own studio, then in ours, and then in Paris. At the beginning there were few others who experimented or produced compositions. Ours being an electronic age, scientists, engineers, and technologists were the ones who got on the bandwagon and cheered. For them we were definitely on the right wavelength. Ussachevsky and I appreciated our new friends and tried to explain to our musical colleagues that they had better learn what the new medium was about or the engineers would indeed take over. In those years nobody paid much attention, but we were able to set up some training courses a few years later and in general managed to keep our own sense of proportion.

THE MUSEUM of Modern Art program was broadcast over many radio stations in New York and elsewhere, and Ussachevsky, Mauzey, and I gave a live interview-demonstration on Dave Garroway's news and talk program, *Today*, on NBC television. We transported the heavy equipment through the rather gloomy streets of New York to the RCA studio for a 5:00 A.M. rehearsal. A member of Local 802 demanded my union card. I told him I was no longer a member, but if any union flutist could play this program I would be glad to have him take over. The union delegate left. Eight businesslike union engineers then tried to connect Mauzey's little box but could not make it work. Five minutes before the telecast Mauzey was allowed to connect his own machine.

Garroway gave a flowery introduction about the mysteries of electronic music. Fatigue made Vladimir and me look somewhat starstruck and geniuslike. The camera focused on us as I improvised sequences on the flute. At the controls of the tape recorder Ussachevsky made simple electronic transformations for the viewers. We were tense and preoccupied and hoping that nothing would go wrong. During this improvisation I looked up for a moment and was startled to see a mounted policeman, a man on a motorcycle, and a number of pedestrians staring at me, some with noses pressed against a plate glass window. The studio was on the ground floor of the RCA exhibition hall on 49th Street, and the telecast was in public view! The program was seen in forty cities.

The next day we were truly famous. We were the subjects of an endless number of interviews, newspaper articles, and letters and calls from friends, enemies, and relatives—which have continued with varying degrees of intensity until now.

In April 1953, Radiodiffusion Française in Paris included our "tape music" in their "First Decade of International Experimental Music." For a concert on June 12 in Paris, under the same auspices, Broadcast Music Incorporated sent Ussachevsky to represent our work. In spite of different aesthetic ideas, our works were being received with interest and respect and heard by important Europeans.

OLIVER DANIEL suggested that Stokowski commission us to do a short piece for Daniel's CBS program, *Twentieth Century Con-*

cert Hall. We decided on *Incantation*, which was made entirely in the peripatetic laboratory housed in the Ussachevsky living room. For sound materials we used flute, alto recorder, voice, bell sonorities, a plate, and a piano. We produced all sounds ourselves and did the taping. After the CBS broadcast our few available works were in demand as background music for radio and television shows.

Audiences liked the bright and lively "orchestration" and new musical ideas without always knowing what they were. When the pieces were programmed as tape or electronic music, there was controversy about their validity, originality, and inhuman and human qualities, mostly by people who knew little about what was going on.

David Broekman repeated the Stokowski program in 1953 on the "Music in the Making" series at Cooper Union under the partial patronage of the Music Performance Trust Fund and the American Federation of Musicians Local 802. We took an important step in establishing good relations with these organizations. The office of the president of the musicians' union, James Petrillo, called me to say that Petrillo had read that we had a composing machine. I explained that the machine could not compose music, but that it reproduced sounds and needed a musically literate operator who could press buttons at the right time. This pacified him, and he assured me that James Caesar Petrillo's American Federation of Musicians would never try to stop technological progress. But David Broekman announced at the concert that electronic music probably meant the end of live music, and this sent shivers down the backs of the timid.

An irate, umbrella-waving lady accosted me after the program. She wanted to know why I did it.

I said, "I'm a musician and it's a musician's job to study sounds, even if they are new. What's wrong with it?"

Her face turned purple. Swinging the umbrella dangerously she shrieked, "Wrong with it? I get absolutely no emotional reaction from this experience!"

Then two fellows steered Ussachevsky and me to a corner and asked in confidential undertones whether we were Rosicrucians. We told them we were not, but they smiled knowingly as they left, obviously recognizing us as Cloud Nine people.

Other radio performances in 1953 and 1954 included one on WNYC with David Randolph and one on WNYC's American Music Festival, as well as an interview-demonstration with Bill Leonard and me on the CBS Radio program *This Is New York.*

Concert performances were programmed at the Arts Festival at the University of Illinois, Urbana, and at an arts festival in Boston. CBS television's *Studio One* used our background tape music for "Crime at Blossoms" with Patricia Collinge. The news reached academic circles and our works were performed next at Juilliard, Barnard, Sarah Lawrence, Duke University, Eastman, Reed College, University of Oregon, and Capetown University.

We were anxious to go forward with our work, and Ussachevsky and Mauzey spent much time bolstering up our shaky equipment. I took to the lecture circuit. The New York City Department of Education and the Music Educators National Conference in Washington, D.C., asked me to address them. I made the statement that I believed electronic music was here to stay and must be studied. In 1954 the Acoustical Society of America asked me to give a demonstration, "American Tape Music, Past, Present, Future," under the general heading of "Some Aspects of Musical Acoustics." Cyril Harris was chairman and our supporter. Some years later he tore out the insides of Philharmonic (now Avery Fisher) Hall in New York City and put them in again to correct the acoustics. He was also responsible for the fine acoustics at the Metropolitan Opera House and in Minneapolis's Orchestra Hall.

On May 2, 1953, the New Research Foundation of the New York Academy of Sciences invited us to give a lecture-demonstration. *The New Yorker* said that for twenty minutes "we listened now reverently, now calmly, now passionately to a variety of compositions for piano and flute, ranging from the soporific to the exasperating," and Dr. Oncley said that they were "a sequence of musical stimuli of no associative value to condition the emotional responses." Artists at the Edward MacDowell Colony heard a demonstration with interest and there was lively talk about technology and the arts. My program for the National Institute of Arts and Letters in 1954 was greeted with good-natured applause punctuated by discreet chuckles. But the poets Marianne Moore,

Leonie Adams, and Louise Bogan congratulated us for finding "a new resonance."

THE LOUISVILLE Orchestra had commissioned me in 1953 to compose a piece for their 1954 season. A faculty grant from Barnard College was to help with copying expenses, always a major burden. I invited Ussachevsky and he consented to producing a joint composition combining the new sounds with those of a symphony orchestra. *Rhapsodic Variations for Tape Recorder and Orchestra* seemed an apt title. The synchronization of the tape sounds with symphony orchestra presented us with new problems and demanded invention of a notation that the conductor could follow.

Balancing tape-recorded sounds with the live sounds of a symphony orchestra took careful ear training. We weaned ourselves away from an orchestral style that was too reminiscent of romantic, baroque, or classical music. We were extending sounds of instruments but not imitating their past use. I notated percussion sounds and rhythms that William Kraft put on tape. Ussachevsky created free-floating clusters from piano sounds for the last movement and composed a particularly effective section for transposed timpani, and a brilliant cadenza. I furnished basic orchestral material and flute variations. The piece was to be about twenty minutes in length, and we hoped that because of its inherent musical qualities it would hold the audience's attention instead of driving them from the hall because of its shock value.

DURING THIS period Ussachevsky and I had the sole responsibility of developing our work. We decided that in the United States it would be wise to be supported by universities and with foundation grants. On campuses one could consult—in addition to music professors—scientists, engineers, psychologists, literary people, performers, and composers, and, in most colleges, theater groups. We needed such connections in order to explore the new medium intelligently and to make it available to the public.

For several years, I had been discussing various other musical projects with Edward D'Arms and John Marshall of the Rockefeller Foundation. As our project took form they became interested in it. The foundation gave Barnard College a grant to purchase an Ampex tape recorder. As our plans developed our budget grew, and we had to cover various expenses from personal funds. Our experimental program was tolerated by most of the members of the Columbia music department and supported by some of the university administration, notably Jacques Barzun and President Grayson Kirk, but it was not part of the university curriculum. As is usual in such research we developed it and composed our works while carrying full teaching loads at the university.

In general Ussachevsky and I worked quite independently. Our collaborations took the form of criticisms and suggestions offered to each other at frequent stages along the road. Sometimes we exchanged or borrowed material from one another. We respected each other's ideas. At first I worked directly with the machines and did some recording, but I decided that after age fifty it was possible to acquire only the skill needed to handle machines but not the necessary speed. Later, I used technical assistants.

THE ELECTRONIC sound possibilities had a strong influence on my thinking and feeling. Imaginative and emotional worlds I had dreamed about opened up for me. My ear became so acute that all music took on a new meaning. Some old and new music seemed more beautiful than ever before, and when I composed for conventional instruments the music seemed more free and fresh.

The Copyright Office in the United States demanded musical notation to file copyrights of electronic works. Often we only approximated very complicated sound patterns by notation, and we could only hope that conductors would listen to the tape part for orientation.

The score of *Rhapsodic Variations* was tried out at the Bennington Composers Conference in 1953, and there was little reaction. It was programmed on March 20, 1954, by the Louisville Orchestra, Robert Whitney conducting. Mr. Whitney was just a bit annoyed when he discovered he would have to follow the tape recorder. "If I could only look it in the eye," he sighed. It is believed this was the first performance anywhere of tape-recorder music with symphony orchestra. The composition, well received by the audience, was acclaimed as a pathbreaking work by some critics and described as the beginning of the end of instrumental music by others.

The first recording of our tape music was released by Gene Bruck on the Innovations label in the same year. Alfred Frankenstein wrote: "The composers have entered this vast new realm in a sense of high adventure, but also with a sense of responsibility." A recording of *Rhapsodic Variations* was released a year later and other critics described it as a serious and fascinating listening experience.

Alfred Wallenstein, conductor of the Los Angeles Philharmonic, was the next one to commission us. He requested an orchestral paraphrase of our two early pieces, *Fantasy in Space* and *Sonic Contours*. The new piece was titled *A Poem in Cycles and Bells for Tape Recorder and Orchestra*. The problem was to arrange, synchronize, and balance original tape music with a symphony orchestra. Wallenstein played it several times in Los Angeles in 1954. The work was later recorded and played widely by orchestras and over radio.

TRUSTEES OF the Rockefeller Foundation, Henry Allen Moe, and Wallace K. Harrison, one of the architects of Rockefeller Center, became interested in our work and suggested that we might find monetary support for it. Millicent McIntosh, president of Barnard, attended one of our demonstrations and applied for funds to support our work.

In June 1955, Barnard College received a grant of $9,995 from the Rockefeller Foundation for Ussachevsky and me to do creative research in electronic music in Europe and America. I made appointments by letter and overseas telephone with the Groupe de Recherches Musicales de l'Office de Radiodiffusion-Télévision Française, in Paris and the Nordwestdeutscher Rundfunk in Cologne. Varèse, Riegger, and Pierre Boulez (who had been invited to give his Composers Forum at Columbia University) suggested that we write Hermann Scherchen for an invitation to the forthcoming International Congress for Electronic Music at his estate in Gravesano, Switzerland. Responses were speedy and cordial. Dr. Trautweim, who had helped Hindemith develop his system of composition in the twenties, cabled WEL-

COME from Düsseldorf. We were sent long lists of people to visit, among whom were few musicians. I realized that I would have to do background reading to communicate. I began with Norbert Wiener's *Human Use of Human Beings* and Claude Shannon and Warren Weaver's *Mathematical Theory of Communication* and found them rather rough going for a beginner.

⤝⤞

REPRESENTATIVES of the Recherches Musicales, with Bernard Blin at the head, met us at Paris's Orly airport. He and his companions rolled out the red carpet and treated us like conquering heroes. We had just settled in our hotel when they drove us to their laboratory to observe their work.

There was a great spirit of camaraderie and cooperation and little competition in those pioneer days. The archivist, Suzanne Lafont, showed us the files of seven years of experimental work. We were offered microfilms for our own reference library. M. Blin even showed us their intermural file, which contained plans for future experiments. They added to our long list of people to visit or write, articles to consult, and microfilms and tapes to acquire.

The prevailing spirit was to mop up the rubble left over from World War II and to build a New World. It need not be brave—only new. Some wanted to fly over the rubble, others to destroy it with a well-directed assault of sound and light vibrations. The slogan seemed to be "God is dead . . . long live x/y!" The processes were vibrational; the Past, Present, and Future of Hardware was the technological field of study. Everyone was active, serious, and good-natured, but not particularly witty or humorous. Even jokes had to be carefully analyzed and prepared before being cracked.

Dr. Abraham Moles, research fellow of the Centre National de la Recherche Scientifique, was an exception. He was a small man and he traveled between vibrations and hardware with the skill and beauty of a dragonfly. He introduced us to the psychiatrists Dr. Robert Française and Dr. Verdeau and his wife (who, herself, was a medical doctor and psychologist). They were conducting experiments at the Centre de Sainte Anne Psychiatrique with the physical and emotional reactions of people to sound and light. They invited us to join them as observers in the "Madhouse of Paris," as they called it.

ONE AFTERNOON, we drove by cab far out into the country and through a grove in a park with the atmosphere of Debussy's *Pelléas et Mélisande* to an enormous, fortresslike building that seemed hundreds of years old. The driver shrugged his shoulders as he pocketed his fare, mumbled *"Voilà,"* and drove off. I felt as though we had landed in an old French horror movie.

As we entered the building the musty ordor of generations of sick people and a smell of formaldehyde hung in the air. A white-robed attendant ushered us into a small whitewashed room with one small window and a hard-backed white chair. Dr. Française invited Ussachevsky to take part in an experiment. Ussachevsky agreed and was escorted into an adjoining room. I wanted to join the party but was told to wait in the room. After sitting for half an hour on a hard white chair I thought perhaps I had been forgotten, and this frightened me. I could almost hear the attendant say, "So, you say you are an American who composes electronic music—have you ever received radio messages directly, or heard voices?" but Dr. Française eventually beckoned me to the adjoining room, where I felt more at ease.

A young fellow who looked like a peasant was trussed up in what resembled a barber's chair. He was apparently in a catatonic state. An intern was shining a bright light into the man's eyes to get a reaction, but he remained rigid. I was taken to the next room for the Ussachevsky experiment. My friend sat on a chair, "wired" for sound. Head, chest, legs, and solar plexus were nicely padded. He looked interested but hot and uncomfortable.

Dr. Française exuded the friendly authority and endless patience that were the professional trademarks of the practicing psychologist-psychiatrist. He told me he was a composer and psychologist doing research with Mrs. Verdeau in aesthetics and in the psychology of music. He proclaimed, "You do electronic music, but I am used to deviants. They are all the same."

How French! I thought.

Ussachevsky stirred uneasily but the doctor went on explaining the experiment. An electroencephalograph measured brain waves, heartbeat, respiration, and emotional reactions. Dr. Française explained that the latter center in the feet and legs, and that there is a measurable emotional response to changes of volume. There is no difference in the physiological reactions to dissonant and consonant chords. The untrained listener finds loud dissonances incoherent and confusing but not disagreeable. Music has an emotional effect on female schizophrenic patients, who react to it sometimes even when in a catatonic state. There were no studies about attention span but the researchers had learned that too much repetition creates boredom and that the social milieu has something to do with reactions. I was tempted to comment that Berlioz, Bach, and even Beethoven, deprived of these insights, could only try their best, but I was discreet.

For the Ussachevsky experiment the music was Bach's G Minor Organ Fugue. Dr. Française pointed to the electroencephalograph and explained that some people talk great musical responses but don't show reactions at all. Others react too violently. That was good to know. Ussachevsky knew and liked every note of the fugue, so the graph recorded a bulge before the entrance of each theme, countertheme, inversion, and interesting modulation. His extremely acute ear also responded to pops, other surface noise, and slips by the organist. This astonished Dr. Française and Dr. Verdeau, who had difficulty interpreting his graphs.

Suddenly, ghastly shrieks and the noise of breaking glass and falling objects came from the room next to us. The researchers abandoned Ussachevsky and galloped to the scene of the commotion.

Ussachevsky, still immobile, yelled to me over the recording of the Bach, "I think the catatonic chap has had a reaction."

After fifteen minutes the doctors returned, out of breath but looking pleased, and calm. "Just a little adjustment; a successful experiment," they reassured us. They unharnessed Ussachevsky.

After complimenting him on his reactions, Dr. Verdeau offered to drive us back to Paris. Just to be on the safe side, on our way out we waved to the catatonic. He looked disgusted.

At the hotel we were still somewhat shaken and we ordered double cognacs.

Dr. Verdeau looked pleased as he sipped absinthe and invited us back. "That catatonic case is interesting; perhaps we can try the Bach on him next. You could help us interpret the graph."

We assured him that we had learned much about the power of light and sound and regretted that because of our imminent departure we could not accept.

"Too bad," he said. "You could be good researchers!"

WE SPENT the afternoon and evening with Pierre Schaeffer of the Groupe de Recherches Musicales and the Groupe de Musique Concrète/Club d'Essai—a well-known engineer who had announced the liberation of Paris over the radio in the Second World War. He had given a Concert of Noises (or Concert des Bruits) over French radio in 1948, using a series of montages on phonograph records. He invented the name *"musique concrète"* because the basic material is not abstract and is organized experimentally—unlike regular music, written in visual symbols, which become sound when they are played. He and Pierre Henry had composed an opera, *Orphée,* that caused an international scandal when it was performed at the Donaueschingen Festival in Germany in 1953. Professor Adorno, the leading music aesthete in Frankfurt, wrote that the opera was "a frightful machine that keeps on running without mercy."

Schaeffer was developing a new aesthetic, but it was the aesthetic of an engineer. In certain ways it advocated destroying the Western tradition of orchestration, but he did suggest to us a new way of composing, and of using language and responding to sound through an experimental approach. He admitted that technically the Italian futurist Russolo had been his precursor. He explained and demonstrated his machines, the morphophone and phonogene. The latter was a tape recorder with twelve different speeds connected with the twelve intervals of the chromatic scale, controlled by a keyboard and enabling transpositions over two octaves. The morphophone controlled different timbres and an artificial echo. It could make violin tones sound like percussion instruments and piano chords sound like an organ. Schaeffer spoke of the need for training courses for the oncoming generations. In his program note to one of the earlier concerts, he wrote, "It takes just one more step to conclude that the world is absurd, full of unbearable contradictions"; but he went on to say that he had the duty to lead possible successors to his intellectually honest work, to the extent to which he helped discover a new way to create sound, and the means—as yet approximate—to give it form. He suggested that photography upset painting and that recording would upset music, and he spoke of a new art of sound. Messiaen, Pierre Boulez, Jolivet, Phillipot, Barraud, and a few others were the musicians who tried using the new medium, but except for Boulez, most of them soon lost interest.

THE NEXT morning, we again met Dr. Moles—the small, wiry man with a large, wiry brain. He roamed over the whole musical aesthetic horizon with us in his conversation, told us about his book, which explained the laws of melody and harmony via information theory, and told us that his approach to music was psychological and sociological in addition to being semantic and aesthetic. He was applying information theory to the aesthetics of perception in the fields of music, noise, and speech. He took us to the film department where we saw a film by Fulchignoni about a little town in Colombia that educated people entirely by radio. The music combined conventional music with concrete sounds. Then we saw a film about Leonardo da Vinci, with verse choruses and old music combined with concrete sounds by Pierre Henry and Schaeffer. Schaeffer scheduled a studio and a technician for me, and in three hours I produced very good basic sounds for part of my Humphrey-Limón ballet.

Maurice Martenot, the inventor of the Ondes Martenot, invited us to visit his studio. Of the many electric and electronic instruments developed in the late nineteenth and early twentieth centuries, this was one of the few survivors. Mr. Martenot was a pleasant, cultured composer-inventor. His instrument was a useful, practical melodic instrument that sounded somewhat like a violin, although it was played with a keyboard. Two hundred eighty composers had written for the instrument at that time. Since then many more, including many of the most prominent European composers, have used it.

WE SPENT the following evening with M. Blin and a young poet and producer at the Club d'Essai. Blin explained that the Club had three branches: research, education, and performance. He took us to a television seminar that was training television programmers and producers. The faculty members came from the Sorbonne and from professional scientific schools. We saw experimental photographic shots of the Paris harbor that used very fine color and were exceptionally clear and beautifully composed. The gentlemen explained their language study. In the diction class they differentiated between oratorical, dramatic, grammatical, flat, emotional, bilingual, and trilingual exercises, and practiced greater and lesser inflections. Some scripts were specially devised for demonstrating effective use of language over radio and television. Other scripts were used for poetry readings by actors or poets. They were attempting to develop a nonrhetorical style of reading, which allowed the poem's imagery to play on the listener's imagination. They studied speech counterpoint. This reminded me of the demonstration by Henri Barzun at the Dada performances in Zurich. Blin stated that speed spacing and pitch spacing in recitation were not yet developed.

Music was to them an associative experience tied to films. A psychologically effective sound track of concrete sounds would strengthen speech images. They sometimes used primitive and derivative materials. Their budget was small for such grandiose ideas, and they needed more musicians on their staff. The relationships between the visual and the aural, whether language, concrete, or instrumental, and between movement, music and speech, costume, and stage design, were very much in my mind, because I was working on the ballet for José Limón and Doris Humphrey, but I had to supply the musical information myself. The Club d'Essai did have good speech musicians and acousticians on the staff, but they were still dealing with distortions of familiar material. I had to do my own musical thinking.

M. Blin was vitally interested in communications. He asked about Lazarsfield opinion polls, the speech laboratories at MIT, and the speech laboratory of Miss Bailey and Mrs. Pleasants at Barnard College. In his group the poets Jean Tardieu and Paul Claudel and some actors and psychologists were working on the differentiation of mood with tapes that expressed humor or patriotism through a speech chorus: it was improvised stream-of-consciousness, lyrics that seemed to flow from the subconscious onto the tape and then were shaped by splicing the tape and rearranging the segments.

⋈

I SOON noticed that in engineers' jargon Ussachevsky and I, with relatively modest input, were getting a great deal of feedback. The world we were discovering was in many ways strange and new to me. Musically, of course, I was quite well prepared for it. In the fields of psychology and psychiatry my lectures with Dr. Bleuler in Zurich and attendant readings had given me a head start. In the visual and theater arts my experiences with the Sezession in Munich and the Dada group in Zurich gave me a vivid introduction to the avant-garde. But now I was confronted with technology, physics, communications, and mathematics, areas in which my experience was extremely limited. I had never taken a science or mathematics course. I had taught myself elementary algebra and had waded through the Einstein-Infeld book on quantum theory and books by Wiener, Weaver, and Shannon.

The list of people and institutions we were to interview or visit included Dr. Winckel of the Technical High School in Berlin, Professor Souriau, a lecturer on aesthetics at the Sorbonne, a professor of psychology at the University of Strasbourg, the director of the Danish State Radio in Copenhagen, the director of the Institute of Physics at Göttingen, the Technical Radio Institute in Nuremberg, and the Society of Tonagraphy and the Phonetic Institute in Hamburg. We were also to meet a half-dozen manufacturers of tape recorders and study acoustics, information theory, music sociology, and other topics.

So far, I had gotten along pretty well with our new friends. Even the most hidebound specialist, when asked what the human use of his exploration would be, liked to expound his philosophy and to give an impassioned statement about what he believed in. The people we met were convinced that we needed to rebuild our world, and that they and we were destined to make significant contributions.

WE VISITED Hermann Scherchen, who was in Paris rehearsing for a concert. He remembered the premiere of my First String Quar-

tet in 1924 in Berlin at the Melos Society, of which he was a
founder. Scherchen's brilliant career covered all phases of music:
composing, conducting, publishing, research, and performance.
He was an extremely gifted and powerful champion of contemporary music. He was self-taught. From 1911 on, he had conducted
numerous premieres of now-famous pieces, including Schoenberg's *Pierrot lunaire* and his *Chamber Symphony,* Opus 9. He
lived in Switzerland, where he kept the best German music alive.
He had invited us to attend the International Congress for Electronic Music to be held on his estate in Gravesano, Switzerland.
European leaders in all fields touching on electronic music—
including composers, technicians, engineers, psychologists, and
critics—would be guests. The staff of Radiodiffusion gave us a
rousing sendoff, and the next day we left for Cologne with our
briefcases full of letters of introduction and notes about new discoveries.

I WAS SHOCKED to find that Cologne was still a rubble heap. After
more than five hundred air raids in World War II, whole sections
of the city had been destroyed. Some had been rebuilt, but the
appearance of the city was so changed I could hardly get my bearings.

Dr. Herbert Eimert was director of the Cologne Electronic
Studio at the Nordwestdeutscher Rundfunk. He was a German
composer and critic who knew Jarnach and Busoni, so I was per-
sona grata. He offered to play for us works that had been performed on an electronic music program in Cologne. Dr. Eimert
had been experimenting with electronic music since 1951. His assistants were Karlheinz Stockhausen and an engineer, Herr
Vogel. I had prepared myself by reading *Die Reihe (The Row),*
the Bible of the Cologne group, published by the Northwest German Radio. Stockhausen was only twenty-seven at the time and
belonged to the group of young German composers who emerged
after World War II and discovered Schoenberg, Webern, Berg,
Busoni, Bartók, Varèse, Ruggles, Cowell, and other composers
who had been boycotted by the Nazis. In Cologne Eimert led the
group to post-Webern serialism and in electronic music to sine
waves in which the overtones are suppressed. The total control
and purification of sound at the Cologne studio set it apart from
musique concrète. Although both Eimert and Stockhausen had

worked in Paris, Eimert, together with Dr. Meyer-Eppler and Robert Beyer, made the first sound models. Dr. Eimert was happy with the "neutral but rather strong" directness of the sound and its rigid and inflexible electronic quality, particularly suitable to satisfy the German yearning for *das Ding an sich* ("the thing in itself"). After these original experiments a group of composers at the Cologne studio began producing compositions.

Stockhausen was the most talented. Tall and handsome, he impressed me as being a cross between Siegfried and a space cadet. He played his piece, *Studie no. 1,* a well-knit composition, post-Webern in its orientation but thoughtful and poetic. The other composers seemed more fanatically involved than artistically productive. I rather liked a piece with bell sounds by Eimert and one by the Swede Bengt Hambraeus. I asked Stockhausen if I could observe him working over materials in the studio. He answered that any fool could do electronic music, one needs only to know the permutations and logarithms. Properly chastened, I asked him about his previous training, and he said, "Oh, that's all a thing of the past," and I realized that God was indeed dead.

I needed more electronic components for my ballet. Dr. Eimert assigned an engineer technician to be my assistant. To show me the equipment he played background music he had invented and in a few hours we had constructed components for my ballet that sounded so ominous that the people in the adjoining studio had to stop working. I selected these sounds by ear; my assistant was surprised at the very fine differentiations. The Cologne composers all made strange graphs and notations that they handed to him to be transformed into sound. There was no uniform notation, and he said he had learned how to guess his way through these homemade hieroglyphics. At dinner my assistant complained that for electronic music an engineer is essential but unrecognized. He said that although Stockhausen worked with logarithms and permutations, he came to the studio at night and adjusted sounds by ear. My assistant at Cologne was the first engineer I knew who had artistic aspirations. Now there are hundreds of them.

DR. MEYER-EPPLER was head of the Phonetics Institute at the University of Bonn. He knew Varèse and Schaeffer and had taught most of the people who worked in the Cologne studio, particularly the engineer Enkel, Dr. Eimert, and Stockhausen. He was an amateur musician and had made two reels of experiments. He told me I could use them in my ballet if I liked, but they were not suitable. He gave us a long list of books to read and bookstores to visit, and reported that the Russian Institute of Electronic Music had closed in 1954 because it brought no human satisfaction. He had brought about cooperation between the University of Bonn and the radio station in Cologne. He was the main source of information in Germany about electronic music. He advised us to publish our work methods and requested our tapes for his library. He believed that Cologne and *musique concrète* would find a common aesthetic ground later; we became good friends and I saw him several times in Europe and the United States.

Dr. Meyer-Eppler was the best type of postwar German scientist and was interested in reestablishing international relations. He was helpful and interested in my work and reinforced many of my ideas.

It was difficult to realize that our pioneer work was being received with such interest and cordiality. Europeans have always had great respect for research, science, and the arts. Worldly success was pleasant for them, but it was not essential to prove one's worth. Worldly success was ephemeral; knowledge and insight were eternal values, so they said.

WE VISITED Dr. Friedrich Trautwein at Düsseldorf. He had done extensive acoustical research with Paul Hindemith after the First World War that became the basis for the composer's theoretical system, *The Craft of Musical Composition*. Dr. Trautwein had developed the Trautonium. His student Oscar Sala invented a Mixtur-Trautonium. A demonstration showed that both were exceptional electronic performing instruments. Trautwein, an engineer but also a musicologist and an organist, built his electronic instruments using a low-frequency generator. They were modeled after instruments built by Helberger, Lertes, and Mager. Sala's Mixtur-Trautonium was accepted as a musically valid instrument by the composers Paul Hindemith, Harold Genzmer, Richard Strauss, Werner Egk, Hans Werner Henze, Carl Orff, and Paul Dessau, who lived in East Germany. It was used widely for movie music. The instrument demanded a new kind of virtuosity that Sala himself mastered, but he had few student-apprentices.

IN HAMBURG we visited my old friend and professor, Philipp Jarnach. After an interval of nineteen years he seemed to pick up the threads of our friendship with no difficulty and to accept the electronic music development as a perfectly natural evolution. He made me feel that I had now completed a large circle that had begun in Zurich in 1917.

Because of family circumstances, Jarnach stayed in Cologne through the war, even though he had opportunities to come to the United States. He had survived the air raids on Cologne and kept his counterpoint classes at the conservatory going. When the English moved in they made him conductor of the Bonn Symphony Orchestra. Later he became director of the State Conservatory of Music in Hamburg, where his influence as a teacher was felt by a new generation. He helped to restore German music to its former place of honor.

WE FLEW to Lugano to attend Scherchen's International Congress, held under UNESCO auspices. Scherchen invited us for all of his sessions, and although we lived in a hotel in Lugano we took our meals at his estate in Gravesano. His studio was on a beautiful hillside surrounded by vineyards. An orchestra of thirty-five players with whom he was making recordings and conducting acoustic experiments lived in the village. Many of the guests to the congress lived on his estate. Everybody appeared for meals at the rustic and colorful dining hall. Pasta, prepared with a special sauce, was brought out in huge tubs. Then green salad and bowls of fresh-picked fruit and flagons of red wine stamped from grapes on the estate were served.

Delegates were present from Switzerland, Germany, England, France, Italy, Austria, Sweden, Denmark, and Holland. Ussachevsky and I represented the United States, together with a Dr. March, whom I did not know. There were only a few composers among the representatives and guests: the Cologne group, a Mr. Johanssen from Finland, Pierre Schaeffer from Paris, Marc Wilkinson, a former Columbia student, and Yannis Xenakis from Greece.

The scientists included the heads of the Paris and Cologne

studios, chief engineers from the BBC, the heads of the Swiss telephone and telegraph company and of the Italian radio chain, the inventor of the German tape recorder, and other radio people. There were also psychologists and aestheticians like Dr. Moles and some experts in the field of entertainment music.

Every morning before the sessions Scherchen led the visiting engineers and technical experts in a twenty-minute swim around his pool, which was about twenty-five feet square. After breakfast the sessions began. On the first morning Scherchen made me chairman of the first lecture and discussion session. There was simultaneous translation into German, French, and English. Dr. Moles translated my shaky French.

After a two-hour luncheon and a nap, I introduced Schaeffer, who talked about the effect of electro-acoustical technology on music. A demonstration of electronic wind and string instruments followed.

At supper I met my friend Ray Travis, then a conducting student of Scherchen's.

He told me how Scherchen taught: "He tells me to memorize Mahler's Second Symphony. After a couple of weeks he takes me up on the hill. 'Now we will see if you know the score. What is the second clarinet playing in measure two-forty-seven? . . . Sing the violin melody that begins at measure three hundred. . . . What are the chords in measures four-forty through four-forty-five?' He's tough."

Travis became a first-rate conductor in Europe with an enviable reputation.

After the second-day swim around the pool, Scherchen discussed soundproofing with all the distinguished leading European engineers. He said their theories about studios were wrong, and that he had found a solution of his own. The ladies on his estate had been up all night stuffing egg crates with cotton and paper and sewing covers for them.

For rehearsal the egg crates were hung around the studio and Scherchen announced, "Gentlemen, I think your findings were too theoretical. The egg crates will improve things."

The orchestra played a Bach *Brandenburg* concerto and the scientists agreed that the acoustics were perfect, but they wondered why Scherchen had gone to the trouble and expense of inviting them as consultants just to prove that he knew the right answer. He was a fanatic, but first-rate.

Meyer-Eppler spoke about perspectives for future cooperation between musical, electro-acoustic, and communications research. After the usual lunch and nap there was a demonstration of entertainment music with much discussion. The experts had analyzed it and knew how to produce it. "Narcotic music," as they called it, is used for broadcast and television. The harmony and counterpoint are rather obvious and there is a pseudocontent; the orchestration is acoustically anonymous and full-sounding, loud with few pauses; it is rarely transparent and plastic; ostinati are used a lot and themes resemble one another and have no profile; the sound is monotonous, often technically deformed (too much "high-fidelity"); the slogan for the composer is "Don't be creative," and the audience too is deformed or misinformed. The experts recommended that musicians oppose this and take a stand against commercial pressures. They described some eight-hour television tapes with frequencies and dynamics so neutralized that the content was musically nil and didn't interfere with anything on the screen. Such background music is nonsemantic and nonaesthetic; written titles are the important artistic animators.

By the time we left Gravesano, we had a list of almost three hundred people and institutions we had either met, visited, or were planning to meet or visit. The direction of all these new friends was definitely toward the future. Only Scherchen himself, Philipp Jarnach, and to a lesser extent Herbert Eimert had a real relationship to the musical world I had grown up in. I hated to leave Scherchen.

WITH AN introduction from Leopold Stokowski, we visited Dr. H. J. von Braunmühl, the director of Baden-Baden Radio. He perfected the tape recorder in Germany during World War II. Von Braunmühl lived in England after the war and worked for British Acoustic Films. He was consultant for Ampex, which had taken over recording patents from Germany after World War II. His technical director, Dr. Heck, explained in detail his Klangumwandler, a frequency changer that promised to produce a great number of timbre variations without losing much quality or a sense of pitch. A few years later Ussachevsky was invited to work on new experiments in a specially-built studio in Baden-Baden.

In Milan, Luciano Berio, who had seen the possibilities of electronic music when he heard our 1952 New York concert, had set up the Studio di Fonologia Musicale, together with Bruno Maderna, a distinguished composer, conductor, and a student of Scherchen's. They had already produced an electronic score for a film and several other interesting experiments. We were invited to work in the studio. With the help of a technician I was able to produce new components for my ballet. Seventeen years later Berio and Maderna were world-famous. In New York they conducted and performed with the New York Philharmonic, the City Opera, and the Juilliard School. Maderna's early death in 1973 was a great loss to the musical world. Berio joined Boulez on the Direction Committee of the Institut de Recherche et Coordination Acoustique/Musique (IRCAM) of the Centre Georges Pompidou in Paris in 1977.

In Rome, electronic music was mostly used in television on sound tracks for horror pictures and science fiction and special-events films. At the American Academy in Rome Ussachevsky and I prepared our composition, *A Poem in Cycles and Bells*, for recording in Copenhagen. We desperately needed the three days to get back to music again and to make score and parts foolproof. On our way to Copenhagen we visited the Albiswerke in Zurich, where we found a very flexible and useful sound filter that we later purchased for our Columbia studio.

In Copenhagen, the third team of the Royal Danish Radio Orchestra was engaged to tape our *Poem in Cycles and Bells*. A small subsidy from the American Composers Alliance gave us little rehearsal time. I had worked out precise conducting techniques, but there were language difficulties. I spoke no Danish and little French; the orchestra did not like to hear German and knew little English. My Italian was operatically expressive but fractured. I had to resort to grunts, groans, and pantomime to communicate with the orchestra. I wore an earphone on one ear to hear the tape part and listened to the orchestra with the other ear. Ussachevsky supervised the recording in the control booth, but there was only a one-way wire and I had to shout and signal to communicate with him. After forty-five frantic minutes of explaining I realized that with my funny linguistic sounds, one phone over my ear, and strange electronic sounds coming from a tape, the orchestra probably thought we had dropped in from Mars.

Then I had a stroke of genius. Removing the earphone, I said in a meaningful voice, "Please play this work just like you play Sibelius."

There was a ripple through the orchestra as they passed the word along, "Sibelius, Sibelius, Sibelius." The orchestra literally rocked with joy and played brilliantly for the rest of the rehearsal, which we miraculously compressed into an hour and a half.

I HADN'T seen Munich since 1936, so this was a great homecoming for me. But the city had been badly damaged. The few hotels were all occupied. A pension in the outskirts thought it could accommodate us. Ussachevsky was finally provided with an oversized bed too long for anyone else, but there was nothing for me. I grumbled something about this being a hell of a homecoming after twenty years. A staff conference solved the problem by having a bed made up for me in a bathtub. I did not mean to be ungrateful, but this drove me right from the pension to the Hofbräuhaus. I was happy to notice that in spite of the destruction, the spirit of beer-drinking had not changed in Munich.

Our most interesting experience there was a meeting with composer Karl Amadeus Hartmann, who had studied at the Munich Royal Academy of Music and later with Scherchen and Anton Webern. His great contribution was the organization of the Musica Viva society, which played the most interesting new music under internationally known conductors and soloists. He had kept this music alive during the Nazi regime. He was interested in electronic music but said that the audience for contemporary music was about a tenth of one percent of the total audience. He had to make tapes of his concerts and broadcast them to reach a larger audience, but the audience was one hundred percent against it, and he felt that it would take twenty-five years before electronic music would be accepted in Germany.

Carl Orff, who had been a fellow student of mine, was interested in Sala's Mixtur-Trautonium and used it for plays. He was also interested in electronic music although his later stage works were monodic like those of Harry Partch.

WE FLEW to London and went to the BBC to discuss with Dr. Alexander the establishment of an electronic studio in London. The English were in a planning stage. In 1972 there was more action in this field at the BBC, and some private electronic music studios in England had made real contributions.

We flew to New York from London, dizzy and exhausted from the incredible impressions of the musical world to come and of a new Europe completely different from the one I had known as a young student. It took years to assimilate everything we had experienced. We made many lasting friends with whom we have remained in touch. We were now ready to discover electronic America.

※※

IN EUROPE we were known as artists, scholars, and inventors. When we returned to New York we were also widely known—but in another sense. One interviewer wrote: "[This is] the strangest music this side of paranoia. It sounds like putting your socks on under your skin." A well-known socialite wanted to know if we were having a lot of fun with our toy. For several years we were of great interest to reporters and interviewers. *High Fidelity* magazine, *Arts Digest, Harper's, Horizon, The Reporter, Saturday Review of Literature, Aufbau,* and *Il Messagero* in Rome, and later *Esquire, Playboy,* and many others sought us out. There were also radio and television appearances on *Studio I, Today,* on the "Wide, Wide World" series, and on shows on smaller stations. These "public relations" hardly created a permanent home for our work, so we tried to find out what was happening in the field of electronic music in the United States and Canada.

In this formative stage there was little communication among the small groups of dedicated workers in the field. The Theremin, named after its inventor, had indeed been properly demonstrated and a number of compositions had been written for it, but it was not a permanent conquest. Theremin and Henry Cowell built the Rhythmicon, which could play metrical combinations of unlimited complexity using a photoelectric cell. It was demonstrated at the New School for Social Research but did not make its way. Chavez and Varèse had written about possibilities of electronic music in the twenties and thirties, and Henry Brant had experimented with directional sound in the United States before similar music was produced in Europe. The most distinguished physicist we met was Hugh LeCaine of the National Research Council in Ottawa. This first-rate scientist was a fine organist with an excellent ear. He invented a touch-sensitive polyphonic keyboard called the Sonde that produced two hundred sine waves, and the LeCaine multitrack tape recorder for the University of Toronto. A pioneer in designing electronic music instruments, he made early designs of voltage-control circuitry. As a composer he produced in 1955 attractive variations on the sound of a dripping drop of water, called *Dripsody*. The National Research Council also supported the very early experiments of Norman MacLaren, who drew sound on film. At the University of Illinois, Professor L. A. Hiller, Jr., and his research associate, L. M. Isaacson, began in September 1955 to write the first computer program for producing music. It resulted in the *Illiac Suite for String Quartet* that was published by New Music Editions in 1957.

We visited the Bell Telephone Laboratories and learned that in 1948, Homer W. Dudley had demonstrated the Vocoder for Dr. Meyer-Eppler at Bonn University. The Vocoder was a compound device consisting of an analyzer and an artificial talker. It was used for Meyer-Eppler's first experiments in electronic music.

Dr. Harvey Fletcher had for decades been doing important acoustical research at Bell and had tried to establish an Institute of Music at Columbia University for examining sonic phenomena. Nothing came of it so he built a laboratory at Brigham Young University in Provo, Utah, and continued his distinguished work there. At the Bell Telephone Labs we met a research group that under the direction of Dr. Goodman began programming musical compositions on the IBM 705 computer in 1955. We heard a fifteen-second sequence that sounded like squawks to us, but the engineers were elated, and they were right—it was the beginning of an astonishing development that led to computer music.

It seemed that in the United States most basic research in

acoustics was carried on in the Defense Department and was top secret. This was also true of most of the basic research at universities, where it could only be carried out under government contracts. With a few notable exceptions, our large corporations wanted their research programs to be commercially feasible within six months. One of the notable exceptions was the RCA Sarnoff Laboratories, where Dr. Harry Olson and Herbert Belar built the first comprehensive electronic music system designed to produce any sound, the Mark II Electronic Music Synthesizer. This was a misnomer because it couldn't synthesize music, but it could synthesize sound.

The commercial studio of Louis and Beebe Baron produced electronic sound scores for films such as *Atlantis, Jazz of Lights,* and *Forbidden Planet.* They did not call their products music. They used electronic generators as their sole sound source. John Cage and his friends often worked in the Baron studio. The Cage group also made highly fragmentary tape compositions for multiple-speaker projections.

Edgar Varèse had a primitive studio in Greenwich Village where he produced his *Déserts,* with his technical assistant, Ann McMillan. He completed it at the Musique Concrète and Marconi studios in Paris. In *Déserts,* Varèse used electronic sound contrasting with live instruments, somewhat like a concerto grosso. At Bennington College, Lionel Nowak and Lou Calabro were experimenting, as were some Eastman School students and a group at radio station KPFA in Berkeley, California.

In June 1956 we attended the Second International Acoustic Congress in Cambridge, Massachusetts, where we saw Meyer-Eppler demonstrate excerpts from Stockhausen's *Gesang der Jünglinge* and met a young man named Enrico Ferretti who was beginning to synthesize compositions at MIT. Most of the papers presented were too technical for me, but a member of the Russian delegation, the distinguished physicist Nikolay Andreyev invited us to demonstrate our work at their hotel. The visit was a bit frightening, for the hotel was under heavy security. One young Russian scientist told me that while physics was his official life, he was a poet in his private life and wrote anything that pleased him. When we inquired about Theremin there was a long silence. Many years later on a trip to Russia, Ussachevsky—who speaks fluent Russian—learned that Theremin was no longer working with the physics of sound. He was with the Soviet defense department.

THE PUBLICITY we received no doubt had much to do with the fact that some of my older music was also being performed. The young pianist Don Shapiro did some piano preludes and harpsichord variations in Israel. A ballet, *Of Identity,* for which we had composed electronic music, was performed at the Brooklyn Academy of Music, and then the American Mime Theater took it on tour. My *Alleluia,* written for Varèse, was broadcast on the Church of the Air over CBS radio. My Second Sonata for Violin and Piano (1922) surfaced at the New School for Social Research. This piece was described as having an "airy, almost Franckian lyricism." Actually, the one-movement piece grew out of the first three chords into a chain of phrases that moved from turbulent to quiet moods. *Rhapsodic Variations* was recorded by the Louisville Symphony, Robert Whitney conducting, and was broadcast over many stations here and in Italy and Switzerland. Among my other triumphs was *The Tiger's Ghost,* a two-and-a-half-minute mixed chorus with text by May Swenson, which was sung on a world tour by Leonard de Paur's Infantry Chorus.

DAVID BROEKMAN and Dean Johnson E. Fairchild, of Cooper Union, founded the "Music in the Making" series at Cooper Union, and Broekman conducted the first concert in 1952; he had been a music editor, composer, and conductor in Hollywood, and music director at CBS. In New York he was music director for the television series "Wide, Wide World" and other TV spectaculars. He was a tall, well-built Dutchman with gray hair and penetrating blue eyes. As a conductor he had the aura of a board chairman of an international cartel.

In order to make the concerts work, Broekman had to arrange matters between Local 802 of the American Federation of Musicians and its officials James C. Petrillo and Al Knopf, the Music Performance Trust Fund, and the Cooper Union Forum in New York. The Performance Trust Fund served as trustee of a self-imposed tax arrangement between recording companies and the American Federation of Musicians. The fund collected a "royalty" of one cent to two and a half cents on each record, the income of which was spent on free concerts given by unemployed musicians, who were to be paid for their services. Samuel R. Rosenbaum of Philadelphia was the sole trustee of the fund from 1948 until 1970, and during this time he allotted approximately $100 million for free concerts. Most of this money went to bands and orchestras that reached a large audience. Music in the Making also received some funds. The concerts were aired on WNYC, and Local 802 permitted Cooper Union to make tapes that were kept in an archive at Columbia University.

Broekman was assisted by an informal program committee consisting of Wallingford Riegger, Henry Cowell, and myself. The primary aim of the concerts was to perform contemporary American orchestral music. Broekman used a group of about fifty musicians from Toscanini's defunct NBC Symphony of the Air. He also added players from the New York Philharmonic Symphony and from the CBS orchestra.

At one of the first concerts a corps of press representatives attended. Broekman thought it a golden opportunity to tell the press just why he thought music critics were valueless or even detrimental to the arts. His speech was broadcast over WNYC, and it took quite a bit of coaxing from others to get the critics to review subsequent concerts.

The atmosphere at Cooper Union was informal. Some of the audience came in to keep warm or to sleep. One evening Francis Perkins, the critic for the *Herald Tribune,* arrived early and read a paper while waiting for Broekman's downbeat. An overly efficient usher moved in on him. "We don't want any bums at these concerts. Pick up your bag and beat it, and don't come back." Perkins, a gentleman, a Democrat, and a fine reviewer, complained to Broekman—who personally ushered him to an aisle seat in the third row.

On one of the forums, *Marginal Intersection No. 1,* by Morton Feldman, provided a sample of "register" music. The musicians were given indications as to whether they were to play in the high, medium, or low register of their instruments; within that register they could play any note they liked. This was the first time an orchestral work by Feldman had been performed. It was beautiful, exciting, and hypnotic. A member of the audience insisted on having the piece repeated. The naughty orchestra players stuck to the indicated registers but selected as notes within the registers their favorite solos from classical and romantic music. A great time was had by all.

When Broekman performed my *Kentucky Concerto*, for orchestra, it was a great success with the audience. At the panel discussion, which took place after every forum, one of the panel members thought that the piece was too popular and that it really should be called *Saturday Night at the Firehouse*. A young woman in the audience came to my defense. "I think what has been insinuated about Mr. Luening's piece is all wrong," she said. "When I arrived here I felt somewhat depressed, and his *Kentucky Concerto* gave me unadulterated pleasure from the first note to the last. I feel as if I could fly." She flapped her elbows a bit. The audience cheered, and I blushed. I have not forgotten that perceptive young woman.

Broekman was very friendly about playing my music. He did my *Pilgrim's Hymn* on his opening concert, October 12, 1952, together with works by Roger Goeb and John Cage. In all he performed nine of my works, the most important of which was the premiere of the Second Symphonic Fantasia on October 18, 1957. This piece puzzled some people because of its rather continuous melodic invention. The overall form balanced many instrumental contrasts, but this was not always perceived. I also used certain materials that, because of their forthrightness (or, as some said, their vulgarity), shocked people.

In the first five seasons, 163 contemporary compositions, most of them world premieres, were played. Among the composers, some of whom had been waiting twenty years to have their works presented—and who now have sizable reputations—were John Cage, Arthur Berger, Feldman, Alan Hovhaness, Elliott Carter, Frank Wigglesworth, Roger Sessions, Henry Brant, Ulysses Kay, and Gunther Schuller. Schuller's *Symphony for Brass and Percussion* and Third Stream Music represented new concepts. Brant's *Rural Antiphony* was directional music that antedated Stockhausen and other European composers by a number of years. The programs also included *Symphonia* by Ezra

Laderman; *Somewhat Pop Music* by John Lewis, Teddy Charles, George Russell, Bill Russo, and John LaPorta; and works by Messiaen and Boulez.

For the March 6, 1955, concert Broekman invited me to conduct the *Symphony for Strings* of Persichetti; the Fifth Piano Concerto of Hovhaness, with Maro Ajemian as soloist; *Trio-Concerto* by Robert Nagel; and *Labyrinth* by Henry Brant. It was the best professional orchestra I had ever conducted, but it was so exhausting that I had to tell Broekman that I couldn't conduct again while I was working on electronic music at Columbia.

Broekman died of a heart attack in 1958. He was a valuable man in the contemporary music scene. I replaced him as music director and Howard Shanet was appointed conductor. Charles Wuorinen joined the selection committee. Among the many new composers whose works we performed were Ruth Anderson, Esther Williamson Ballou, Genevieve Chinn, Julia Perry, Leni Alexander, and Mishika Toyama.

Howard Shanet later developed the International Festival of Contemporary Music, which included works from composers in England, Czechoslovakia, Norway, Mexico, Uruguay, Finland, and Canada. Each season the compositions became more difficult to perform within our budgeted rehearsal time, but the concerts attracted much attention from the press and were considered an integral part of New York's concert life for ten years.

≽≼

USSACHEVSKY AND I were not diverted for long from our main task of advancing electronic music. At Columbia, Douglas Moore gave us permission to deal directly, in matters of funding, with President Kirk and Jacques Barzun, who was soon to become provost of the university. Most of the members of the music department thought that electronic music was a harmless hobby. As we did not let our "hobby" interfere with our teaching duties, and as it cost the department no money, there was no reason for departmental opposition. I urged Moore and Dr. Paul Henry Lang to keep in touch with future developments, for I believed that it was something the musical world would have to cope with.

Moore was interested in our work, but Lang neither listened, watched, nor visited our laboratory. He seemed to hope that electronic music would just fizzle out.

I LEARNED to communicate with scientists and engineers by observing and working with them and by reading many articles. The best engineers were artistic and were concerned with the human aspects of what we were all doing. Of course there were morons among the technicians, such as the engineer who told me at 3:00 A.M. on Riverside Drive that he would, "by God, perfect controls on all audio equipment so that when I notice the conductor letting the violas drag I can speed them up myself." This was the first time I heard of someone conducting the conductor. In the future the objective may well be to interpret the prototype out of existence.

Psychologically, I had to do some balancing, probing, and adjusting. Some admirers of my new work had catapulted me into the avant-garde, while forgetting the early part of my career entirely. New friends knew only of my later work. Circumstances seemed to be carrying my present self away from my past self. This cultural schizophrenia was uncomfortable and was as unacceptable to me then as it is now. I had always considered the old and the new to be interrelated. Busoni had stated this succinctly in his *Sketch of a New Aesthetic of Music:* "In the new and the old there is good and bad, what is genuine and what is counterfeit. Nothing can be absolutely modern. Things have simply originated at an earlier or later date and have bloomed longer or withered sooner. There was always the avant-garde and always the old."

The University of California Press asked me to write an essay, "New Sound Techniques in Music," for their book *Art and Artist*, which included essays by Henry Moore, Jean Renoir, and Jean-Paul Sartre. It gave me a chance to straighten out the early history of electronic music and make our work known in new and respectable circles. I tried to relate the experimental developments of the twentieth century with those of the past. I also found it rewarding to search for aesthetic values in the new world of sound. After discovering that with electronic sound almost anything was possible, it was necessary to meditate about how much of it it was possible to perceive, and by what means it could bring human satisfaction along with the novelty of the shock.

Humanists, musicologists, some critics, musicians, and sometimes diehard laypeople liked to ask, even before things were really under way: "But is it music?" . . . "But is it really great music?" . . . "But will it displace music?" Some hated electronic music without ever having heard any. Others proclaimed that it was a great medium, but that we must wait for great composers who knew how to use it before we could develop it.

Some reviewers said that the new sounds were not like the music of the past. This remark is still heard nowadays. The obvious answer then and now is, "Why should it be?" The fear that electronic music threatens old music and live music is groundless as long as people keep on playing and singing and are willing to pay for their symphony orchestras, opera companies, and chamber music.

In 1956, Doris Humphrey commissioned me to compose, for the Juilliard School's Fiftieth Anniversary, *Theatre Piece No. 2 (Concerto for Light, Movement, Sound and Voice)* for the José Limón Dance Company. The Ussachevsky living room was overloaded with the traveling laboratory, so we moved it to a room in my apartment at 405 West 118th Street. My assistant Chou Wen-chung helped me work on my ballet at odd hours of the day and night. Doris Humphrey outlined her story line and made a time schedule for the separate sections. She then made a detailed measure or beat chart for the entire half-hour ballet, indicating to me just what the dancers should be doing rhythmically. She made only one error in the entire score. In two measures she beat quarters instead of eighths. At the rehearsal the dancers were left with their feet in the air waiting for music, but they got them down. She also talked me into writing the spoken text for two 1930 satires: a love scene from a movie and a German poem for a contemporary twelve-tone song.

The rehearsals at Juilliard were difficult. The musical director told me that it was too late to use strings for my performance. I thought it would be effective to use only a brass ensemble, percussion, narrator, recorded voice on tape, piano, and myself as conductor, so I did.

The dance company was first-rate and Doris was a fine director. At an open rehearsal, just as the conductor left his stand after the previous piece, the tape recorder emitted an enormous honk. In the intermission the maestro alleged that I had done it on purpose, which I denied, but things went from bad to worse. The pit caught on fire and rehearsals were postponed for a week. Fortunately there was no personal or musical damage, and we actually had more time to synchronize everything further in a rehearsal room.

On opening night Ussachevsky operated the tape recorder. He looked a bit constrained, pale, and worried. I had given the downbeat, so I could only continue and hope that he was well. The performance was smooth and the audience cordial. Later I asked Ussachevsky whether he had been ill during the performance, and he said, "Yes, indeed. There was a loose connection. Had I moved one inch to the left some frightfully loud noises would have brought your premiere to an unhappy end." We shook hands and congratulated ourselves for having pulled the show through.

Walter Terry wrote of the show in the *Herald Tribune:* "The Otto Luening score provides a tonally fascinating and dramatically pertinent basis for the choreography. . . . The initial section suggests pre-human action, growth and metamorphoses through patterns as eerie and as hypnotically remorseless as the accompanying music . . . has enormous incantational power."

OUR NEXT major joint assignment came in the same year as *Theatre Piece No. 2.* Orson Welles neeeded an abstract sound score for his production of *King Lear* at the New York City Center. Marc Blitzstein, who introduced us to Welles, wrote the regular score. Ours underlined a number of Lear's psychological states, provided storm music and horse sounds, and otherwise toned up the show.

We badly needed a studio. Because of the late-night noise in my apartment, the neighbors, suspecting subversive activities, complained to my landlord. This was fortunate, for I rented from

Columbia University. I reported to President Kirk that unless we could have space on campus our work would be practically halted, or we would be in real trouble with my neighbors and my land-lord—Columbia University! The president looked shocked, and soon found a suitable and charming dwelling—which looked like a house by Charles Addams—on the site of the former Blooming-dale Insane Asylum, now the site of Ferris Booth Hall, the Co-lumbia College student center.

Welles came to hear our works. Being a man of considerable physical size and a personage of importance, it took him a bit of time to settle himself on our shaky chairs. Then he commanded, "Proceed!" and we played tapes for him. After five minutes he announced, "This is the greatest thing that has happened for the theater since the invention of incandescent lights!"

Welles wanted forty-four cues, and after we produced one he would listen with his uncannily keen ears, then comment on and name the sound: "We'll call this one Tinkerbell, baby." Or: "Oooh . . . there's a nice low sound . . . that's Fat Mama." Once he said: "That's not the sound you played for me yesterday, lads. The other one had more blue in it." And he was right.

Imagination and long, rough hours were needed for the job. Welles's demands were high and our equipment was still limited. Ussachevsky once worked for thirty-five hours without stopping. I once lasted as long as twenty-two hours with a two-hour break for a nap, and then went another twenty hours. We kept ourselves going with chocolate egg malted milk. Chou Wen-chung, Stanley Tonkel, and a technician from City Center alternated during the twenty-four-hour shifts to help us keep things in order. The job was so hectic that at one point I spent most of the night simply keeping things labeled and catalogued. Cues were getting lost, and we were so tired we began to do things twice. We had gotten hold of some oscillators and made some pure electronic sounds, but mostly we modified instruments and voice. We produced whatever was missing on the spot.

One morning at three-thirty Tonkel arrived and found Us-sachevsky and myself before a microphone with our heads in two cartons, tapping out a *William Tell* Overture tattoo with our fingers. With great professional reserve he asked no questions. Eventually we explained that we had discovered the best sound for galloping horses' hooves ever to be heard on screen, radio, or in the theater. We tapped our hollow cheeks and recorded this. He wished us luck.

When we finished the cues we hauled everything down to City Center in Ussachevsky's car. Welles was directing, as well as playing the role of Lear. He had devised an impressive stage set, with eerie lighting rather on the dark side. The actors were under his complete control. His phenomenal memory and booming voice made his directions easy to follow.

We synchronized our abstract sound score between 1:00 A.M. and 4:00 A.M. On the first try everything seemed to fall apart, because the electricians' union would not allow Ussachevsky to operate the tape recorder. He relayed his suggestions to the union sound man, who couldn't read music.

Things were messed up and the show slowed down, causing Welles to say, "When I last heard these sounds, they were absolutely wonderful. Now they are ruining the production."

I echoed back, "Patience, Maestro, patience," and explained matters to him.

Finally it all fell in place. At one of the dress rehearsals Welles arrived in an ambulance with his right leg in a cast. The night before he had tripped on the darkened stage and broken his ankle. Two days later he tripped again and broke his other ankle. Nevertheless he arrived promptly each day in an ambulance, on a stretcher, smoking a big cigar. This great trouper conducted the final rehearsals and played the three-week run in a wheelchair. On opening night I couldn't take it any more, so I had dinner in the Carnegie Tavern and missed Act I. From then on I saw every performance. I still think it was the greatest Lear performance I have ever seen or will ever see. The press predicted great possibilities for electronic sound in the theater.

⤝⤞

BY THE MID-fifties, RCA had demonstrated the Olson Belar Sound Synthesizer, and Dr. Olson, one of the inventors, had published his book *Musical Engineering*. Some of his statements suggested that music was still in its infancy. This riled music traditionalists. It did not help matters when RCA released a demonstration record on which existing instruments were imitated and the pop tune "Nola" was synthesized to sound like conventional instruments. RCA hoped to use the synthesizer to produce pop music and to reproduce great voices of the past, perhaps Caruso's. Eventually they realized that getting satisfactory results from this machine needed carefully trained musicians.

Ussachevsky was anxious to work with the synthesizer and possibly to get the future loan of it for our budding laboratory. At the suggestion of Dean Davidson Taylor and with an introduction from President Kirk of Columbia University I wrote to several RCA executives. Professor Milton Babbitt of Princeton University, who had been working theoretically with electronic sound since the late thirties, was also interested in the synthesizer. Believing there is strength in numbers the three of us joined forces and were granted an interview with Dr. Elmer W. Engstrom, executive vice-president of RCA, who gave us permission to work on the synthesizer at the Sarnoff Laboratories. This interview was my first with a top executive of a major corporation, and it made me nervous as a cat. I estimated that the company time used in our conference with Dr. Engstrom must have been worth at least fifteen dollars a minute, or twenty-three cents a second. The more nervous I got the slower I talked, and the more patient and quiet Dr. Engstrom seemed to be. He granted our request gracefully, quietly, and with corporate authority. As I left I was shaking.

Columbia and Princeton paid our expenses for this preliminary research. I was about to leave for the American Academy in Rome as composer-in-residence, so my colleagues suggested I be the first to get materials from the machine. I produced some sounds with the help of Mr. Belar, one of the inventors. I saved them for years and later I developed and modified them and used them in my *Synthesis for Orchestra and Electronic Sound.*

In July 1957, Ussachevsky and I compiled a report of 155 pages for the Rockefeller Foundation based on experiences gained from our travel grant. There was an introduction of one brief paragraph, then a three-page summary with conclusions. This was followed by a historical outline, including a quotation from *New Atlantis* by Sir Francis Bacon (1627) and a report on our European and United States trip. We then made specific recommendations for an electronic music center to be established in this country. For our report, we engaged Dr. Moles and Dr. Meyer-Eppler as consultants for the histories of electronic music in Paris and Germany.

Ussachevsky and I listed sixteen of our individual and collective compositions. These had already been given about seventy-five performances. Our four recorded works were among the earliest discs anywhere. As the law did not permit copyright of sounds by depositing tapes, a practice that was prevalent in various European countries, all electronic works were written in musical notation in order to be registered. This meant inventing a notation for almost every work.

The Luening-Ussachevsky Report to the Rockefeller Foundation was favorably received by the foundation officers and presented to the trustees. Babbitt, Ussachevsky, and I discussed the presentation of our ideas with Clarence Fahs of the foundation. We suggested an inter-university center, but Mr. Fahs thought that as the three of us were able to cooperate we should limit ourselves to a joint Columbia-Princeton project. He suggested that Professor Roger Sessions of Princeton join with the three of us. Mr. Fahs then requested tapes of our work to play at the next trustee meeting. I learned later that the strange sounds caused great consternation and that our application was almost rejected, but Henry Allen Moe and Wallace K. Harrison spoke up so strongly in our favor that we were voted a grant of $175,000 for both universities for a period of five years.

Columbia University agreed to provide space, technical assistance, materials, and electronic equipment, and to invite other composers to work in the studio without charge. With our engineer, Peter Mauzey, we planned a control console and nineteen speaker outlets for public concerts in McMillin Theatre. For the first year, we had to rent the RCA synthesizer, but later RCA gave us the machine on indefinite loan.

The Committee of Direction of the Columbia-Princeton Electronic Music Center consisted of professors Luening and Ussachevsky from Columbia and professors Babbitt and Sessions from Princeton, with Professor Ussachevsky as chairman. The grant to carry out these objectives actually amounted to $17,500 annually for each university—not a vast sum for a new program but a windfall that enabled us to establish a center that would be taken over by the two universities after five years.

The composers we invited to work in the center were an international group who had enjoyed exceptionally broad musical training and experiences under Rockefeller, Guggenheim, or other fellowships. The first one was Mishiko Toyama from Japan, then Bulent Arel from Turkey, Mario Davidovsky from Argentina, Halim El Dabh from Egypt, and Charles Wuorinen from the United States.

Miss Toyama was so anxious to be accepted that she sat in front of my office until I engaged her to copy my music and teach my future wife, Catherine, piano, and introduced her to Ussachevsky to arrange studio time. Many more composers than we could accommodate wanted to work in the studio.

As soon as possible we invited distinguished composers from this country and abroad to work in the Electronic Music Center, or EMC. Varèse revised the electronic part of *Déserts* at the center with the assistance of Arel and Max Matthews. We were host to Luigi Dallapiccola, Toshiro Mayuzumi, Dmitri Shostakovich, Igor Stravinsky, Luciano Berio, and almost a hundred other composers. Composers who worked in the studio later included William Overton Smith, Mel Powell, István Anhalt, Charles Whittenberg, Malcolm Goldstein, Alwin Nikolais, Walter Carlos, Ross Lee Finney, Ilhan Mimaroglu, Jon Appleton, Jacob Druckman, Emmanuel Ghent, Harvey Sollberger, and Charles Dodge.

LEONARD BERNSTEIN and the New York Philharmonic commissioned Ussachevsky and me to compose our *Concerted Piece for Tape Recorder and Orchestra*. It was performed on a Young People's Concert and televised on March 10, 1960, followed by four regular performances in Carnegie Hall and a CBS network broadcast.

After the many performances there was of course much fan mail and the usual interviews and press articles. Bernstein had such standing with other conductors that in the next years there were numerous performances of the *Concerted Piece* and a recording by the brilliant young conductor José Serebrier. We were enough of a success with the Philharmonic audience that in the following decade a number of new electronic pieces were listened to attentively but not always enthusiastically received.

The ultimate accolade came from my brother Fred in one of his "Dear Skeezicks" letters. He and his wife Myrtle had seen the Bernstein concert on television.

Most interested in hearing one of your recent compositions and seeing your presence on the screen. Nice work, boy, nice work. . . . I'm old. Music still must include melody. I cannot understand beatniks or modern paintings, Dali or Picasso or their ilk. However, I tried hard to imagine myself in a spaceship hearing the music of the revolving stars or the clatter of meteorites against the ship's shell or the explosion of the sun or maybe Mars or Venus or some other planet. . . . Obviously only a few talented composers can get onto a Bernstein program. . . . I remember melodies that bring me back to my childhood, to experiences in my youth, and memories of the trees and woods and nature's own murmurs and silences. . . . I'm living in the past. You are searching for the sounds of the future and putting them in your compositions. . . . We were especially interested in shots of the audience during the Bernstein concert and in the ways the kids' eyes sparkled and their smiles broadened when your composition was played. They seemed to understand. . . . Congratulations on the recent venture. Good luck in the future and whether I understand it or not it is rather evident that melody is on the way out and the tones of the future are to be our music as time goes on.

THE COLUMBIA-Princeton Electronic Music Center gave its two initial concerts on May 9 and 10, 1961, before invited audiences consisting of distinguished people in the art world. Jacques Barzun gave a brief introduction to the concerts. The pieces played were *Electronic Study No. 1* (Davidovsky), *Leiyla and the Poet* (El Dabh), *Creation and Prologue* (Ussachevsky), *Composition for Synthesizer* (Babbitt), *Stereo Electronic Music No. 1* (Arel), *Gargoyles for Violin Solo and Synthesized Sound* (Luening; Max Pollikoff, violin), and *Symphonia Sacra* (Wuorinen; the Harrt Chamber Players, Bert Turetsky, director). Technical assistance was provided by Malcolm Goldstein, Edward Schneider, and Peter Smith; Richard Greenfield did the lighting.

Some reviewers said the concert was of historic significance.

In the *New York Times* Harold Schonberg wrote a thoughtful review in which he quite accurately described the medium and the intents of the composers, predicting that other composers would follow along the lines of my *Gargoyles*, with live instruments and symphony orchestras with tape. He wrote that it was the start of a revolution. Schonberg followed with an article in the Sunday *Times* in which he went into the technical aspects of electronic music in detail. He mentioned the endless musical possibilities and regretted that the medium had not been available to Charles Ives.

But Dr. Paul Henry Lang, the Columbia musicologist and a reviewer for the *New York Herald Tribune*, wanted to save the art of music and wrote an article attacking new music. He wrote that the Columbia-Princeton concert was an interesting affair that might have far-reaching consequences. Then he misquoted Jacques Barzun's introductory remarks, which, as his assistant had covered the concert, Lang had apparently not heard. Now Dr. Lang emerged as the defender of the faith and developed a poor man's instant aesthetic in his Sunday *Herald Tribune* articles. He attacked electronic music composers and total serialism, asserted the twelve-tone school was okay but questioned whether electronic music had any place in the continuation of an organic musical culture. He then produced Sauveur from the seventeenth century, reminding us that this founder of modern physical acoustics was deaf. He did not mention Beethoven. At the same time Dr. Lang continued by asserting that sound in itself was not the only important thing in music. He then attacked Columbia, Princeton, and the humanities division of the Rockefeller Foundation. In his zeal he accused the universities of teaching the composition of electronic music in the schools of liberal arts and implied that students might be earning counterfeit degrees. As both universities were not yet offering courses in electronic music but only invited qualified students to work in the center on a postgraduate level, the article caused a furor.

Jacques Barzun summed the matter up in a brief letter published in the *Herald Tribune* on May 28. He explained that what he had told the Columbia audience was that if they were to understand what they were about to hear they must lend their minds to it. To do it they must assume—not believe or conclude, but assume—that previous means of musical expression were exhausted. "It is because audiences and critics approach the new in the self-indulgent mood of a political crowd at a rally, hostile or infatuated, that the history of artistic change is such a sorry spectacle of fighting in the dark," he wrote.

Dr. Lang was a practical man and soon recovered from his terrible vision of the musical apocalypse with himself in the middle of it, so he ended the newspaper battle with one more article, "Electronic Game: Its Ground Rules." Admitting that electronic music would figure in the news more and more, he made an attempt to clarify the rules. He put the American exponents right back where we were: conventionally trained musicians, some of us of a rather conservative bent, experimenting with new tonal resources. This he considered a harmless pastime, although the one legitimate facet of electronic music. He predicted that in the hands of "truly creative" artists these resources would prove useful! He then demolished the European electronic music composers. He outdid himself in praise of the singer and performer as a foil for electronic musicians, science, and technology. Alas, he forgot to mention the entire art and craft of instrument building, the development of the organ—that queen of instruments, now run electrically—and the influence of such developments on composers and on the history of music. But Dr. Lang meant well.

≫≪

BETWEEN 1961 AND 1968 the most important event was the acceptance of the electronic medium by primary and secondary schools and by popular composers. Joseph Machlis asked me to make recordings of electronic music to coordinate with and illustrate his high school and college music-history textbooks. In 1968 the International Electronic Music Catalog, compiled by the Groupe de Recherches Musicales de l'Office de Radiodiffusion-Télévision Française and the Independent Electronic Music Center, Inc., in the United States, and distributed by the Massachusetts Institute of Technology, listed 5,140 new compositions. Thousands more have been produced in the last decade. Five hundred thirty-six studios in thirty-nine countries were listed in the catalog, and one can assume that since then the number has doubled. In 1968 one estimate counted 550 studios in the United States alone, exclusive of private or commercial ones, and this number has since doubled.

Synthesizers are smaller and less expensive and a number of them are portable. Some of them are suitable for home studios. This mushrooming of the new means of sound production is not an unmixed blessing, for some works produced in primary and secondary school classrooms seem to represent an easy way out of budget difficulties and often do not establish a solid base for music training or artistic expression. Some of the so-called electronic music used in film, television, and theater we discarded twenty years ago. Galloping novelty was taking place in many fields and dissemination was so rapid that the matter of quality was in many instances not even considered.

A former Columbia graduate student, Walter Carlos, became a virtuoso on the Moog Synthesizer and his *Switched-On Bach,* an arrangement of various of Bach's works for electronic sounds, was the best-selling record of its kind. Edward Cramer, in the January 1979 issue of *Billboard,* wrote: "Pop music owes a debt to Varèse, Luening, and Babbitt." Salvatore Martirano, at the University of Illinois, invented another type of electronic performing instrument and there are many others. Pril Smiley has produced many sound scores for theater and television, and Alice Shields, a fine singer and composition student of mine, has composed electronic operas.

The pop field has by now discovered electronic playing and electronically controlled instruments, and electric pianos and organs abound. Jimmy Guiffre and Oliver Nelson are among those who have used various attachments with saxophones, flutes, clarinets, and other instruments. With a tool as flexible as the tape recorder, various styles of music, like blues, jazz, rock, Indian ragas, and serial music can be mixed and treated electronically. Many avant-gardists, in their rush for novelty, have combined the new sounds with lights, words, movements, audience participation, and electronically produced paintings and drawings, with occasional excursions into the world of incense and perfumes, a poor man's Scriabinesque "total experience."

Just how sound travels in outer space, or what happens to it, is not completely known, but there has been much research in the field of sounds produced by animals. Recorded whale sounds were used by composer Alan Hovhaness in a symphony.

The explorations seem to be never-ending. The pioneer computer works by Lejaren Hiller, Leonard Isaacson, and Hugh Le-Caine have been followed by developments at the Bell Telephone Laboratories and at Princeton by Max Mathews, John Pierce, James Tenney, Charles Dodge, and Ussachevsky. Some of these computer works are already on discs. Most of the composers involved predict that the computer attached directly to the synthesizer will introduce us to an entirely different kind of musical world.

The details of the growth and spread of the medium are astonishing. Three recent Pulitzer Prizes in music were awarded for works that used electronic sound—to Leon Kirchner, Charles Wuorinen, and Mario Davidovsky.

As people love to say, "This is all old stuff"—and perhaps it is. Orcus Research in Kansas City published a book in 1971 called *Bio Music*, by Manfred Eaton. The term, as used by Orcus Research, "described a class of electronic systems that used biological potentials in feed-back loops to induce powerful, predictable, repeatable, psychological states which can be elegantly controlled in real time. The types of states which can be programmed are as powerful as the chemical drug states, and the hallucinogenic powers of electronic sensory feedback systems can be controlled and guided with a precision utterly impossible with chemical methods."

Many of the present experiments are still inconclusive, but this all sounds like an exciting new world to come. I have always believed that if we develop a sense of responsibility and if we have a deep desire to bring human satisfaction to individuals, our vision will be penetrating enough to add our new findings to the greatness of the past. Only then can we move forward into a future that will hold beautiful new experiences that are as yet undreamed of.

Chapter 25

Elba, Rome, Tunisia
1954 - 1971

IN THE LATE 1950s, as my professional reputation grew, my connections with my family in Wisconsin and elsewhere became more tenuous. Aunt Tillie and Aunt Claire, both at eighty-eight, and Aunt Gretchen, at ninety-five, died in Milwaukee in the late fifties. Aunt Claire, however, saw her lifelong dream of a Civic Symphony Orchestra in Milwaukee materialize. Aunt Gretchen, who with her limited income had always bailed out family members in financial straits, gave her home and property to the county as a historical site. Like my brother Fred, Aunt Tillie's children Claire and Edgar stayed in Milwaukee. My other brothers, cousins, nephews, and nieces had moved west, south, and east. Wisconsin was becoming a memory.

In 1954, I met Catherine Johnson Brunson, a beautiful lady from Alabama. She had studied music and had earned an M.A. at Columbia in musicology. In 1949 she had heard Stokowski conduct my *Pilgrim's Hymn for Chamber Orchestra*. At Columbia she was assistant to Ruth Ihrig, the remarkable executive secretary of the music department. The department activities had expanded so that the workload was heavy, but Ruth and her staff managed to keep everything going and everybody happy.

I asked Catherine to assist me in bringing order to my correspondence and music manuscripts. This she did while teaching at the Packer Collegiate Institute in Brooklyn. There, in addition to the usual music classroom activities, she was rehearsal and performance pianist for the annual production of Gilbert and Sullivan adaptations. She was then a good pianist and able to handle any ordinary school and teaching duties, but she had never put on school shows. For a while I tried to impress her with my expertise in this field, but she was soon able to manage by herself.

Catherine thought I should meet her family. I liked the idea of returning to the South, which I had last visited on the college tour in 1937. We flew to Dothan, Alabama, and Catherine drove the one hour to Elba. The semitropical foliage, the red clay, and the quiet green forests awakened in me memories of a romantic South.

The Brunson home was called The Hill. It was surrounded by spacious lawns and woods. Mockingbirds led a chorus of birds each morning. The house was a union of old and new lines and designs, a "lived-in" house of simple beauty and dignity. Catherine's father, John Franklin Brunson, was known to everyone as Mr. John. Like many in my own family, he was a self-made man. He had taught school, played saxophone, and sung in church. He then worked in insurance and banking in Elba and other towns in southern Alabama. He founded the Elba Insurance Agency in 1928 and the Elba Merchants Exchange (now the Elba Exchange Bank) in 1931. Both are still operating. His wife, known as Mrs. Ola, had interests in the local school, local politics, and the local literary club.

Mr. John and Catherine's brother-in-law asked me about my Wisconsin family. I remarked that I had looked into my family tree and found that I was the sap. No one laughed, and my own chuckle turned into a gurgle and then a cough. I remembered not to mention that my grandfather, Colonel Jacobs, had been through the South with his regiment, the 26th Wisconsin Volunteers, in the Civil War.

I then heard about the Brunson pioneers. The first ones came with the Puritan clergyman Thomas Hooker from England to Massachusetts in 1633, and went from there to Connecticut, South Carolina, and Alabama. Joshua Brunson married Sylvia Pinckney of the Charleston family of American patriots and statesmen. Charles Pinckney (1757–1824) and Charles Cotesworth Pinckney (1746–1825) were delegates to the Constitutional Convention in 1787 and signed the Constitution. Charles Cotesworth Pinckney was the Federalist presidential candidate in 1804 and 1808. Thomas Pinckney (1750–1828) was governor of South Carolina and aided in the ratification of the Constitution. Mrs.

Ola's relatives—the Duncans, the McDuffies, including George (1790–1851), a governor of South Carolina and a U.S. senator, and the Wade Hamptons—all had owned plantations, farms, and businesses in the South and have been active in state and local politics and community development up to the present time.

I ventured the opinion that the Wisconsin settlers were also pioneers, though they had arrived two hundred years later and came from France, England, Germany, Norway, Sweden, and Poland.

"Foreigners," somebody said.

I said, "Like General Eisenhower, President Roosevelt, and Admiral Zumwalt. . . ."

I was worried that my religious background would not be acceptable to the Brunsons, since many of my Wisconsin ancestors were anticlerical, but when Mr. John invited me to the Coffee County Livestock Auction I felt that I had been accepted by the family.

Catherine and I returned to New York and for the next two years considered marriage. I thought that marriage would be too risky for her, as I had to help Ethel financially, and I pointed out that composing operas and concert music was more an addiction than a paying profession. In the United States such people are considered freaks, at least until they have achieved financial success. Catherine thought otherwise.

CATHERINE AND I were married at The Hill on September 5, 1959. My nephew Eugene, a Unitarian minister, performed the service. Other than Eugene, his family, and his brother Bill, none of the Luenings were present. It was just as well, for a Luening family gathering in praise of Wine, Women, and Song might have been too resonant for Alabama.

Mrs. Ola made the house beautiful. Catherine's sisters, their husbands and children, and a few other guests attended. We had champagne, and for the wedding music Catherine chose my Dickinson song *If I Can Keep One Heart from Breaking* as entrance music, my *Prelude to a Hymn Tune by William Billings* as exit music, and my *Kentucky Rondo* (for orchestra) for the post-ceremony festivities. She also used Virgil Thomson's *Louisiana Story* to give the southern touch.

On holidays, I was treated to marvelous demonstrations of

southern culinary art. Heartwarming presents would arrive, beautifully packaged and with cheerful messages from this gracious family.

Catherine and I hoped that our marriage would develop and that we would help each other to grow as people, artists, and teachers. Her charm and talents as a hostess and her real concern for others has won her many friends here and in Europe. She was appointed to the faculty of the Spence School in New York in 1963 and has taught general music, singing, Orff instruments, recorder, and piano. She has directed the Christmas shows, which have included her adaptations of Menotti's *Amahl and the Night Visitors,* Humperdinck's *Hansel and Gretel,* Victor Herbert's *Babes in Toyland,* and Dickens's *Christmas Carol,* with music by Bryceson Treharne.

Catherine's activities at Spence got me interested in writing music for children. I made twelve recorded lessons for Silver Burdett's "Making Music Your Own" for the first six grades, useful for classroom teachers with limited musical resources. I had hundreds of fan letters from children. I also made a filmstrip, "Famous Musicians at Work." I got more letters and this encouraged me to write easy recorder duets and piano ensembles. Later, Ruth McGregor commissioned me to write three ensembles for the Greenwood Music Camp. These works are possibly among my most significant compositions.

We returned to Alabama the year after our wedding and spent time on the beach near Panama City, Florida. Moonlight walks on the snow-white sand, swimming in the warm Gulf, driving up and down the coast, stopping at fisheries for lobster and beer in the daytime—all these things put me into a relaxed mood for composing, and I sketched my *Gargoyles for Violin Solo and Synthesized Sound,* which was later realized in the Columbia-Princeton Electronic Music Center, just in time for the 1961 program.

≫≪

IN 1921, I HAD applied for a fellowship at the American Academy in Rome. I was rejected because, I heard later, I was "too radical."

The academy was founded in March 1894 by the architects

and artists who planned the 1893 World's Fair in Chicago and who launched the "city beautiful" movement. Among those architects were Charles McKim, William Mead, and Stanford White, whose design for the Rome academy was in part a reaction against the influence of the French beaux arts school on American art and architecture. The academy had the support of wealthy patrons of culture and it was chartered by Congress in 1905. The fellowships were for bachelors—"to develop their powers and complete their training under the most favorable conditions . . ."

Music fellowships were first offered in 1921. Between that time and World War II, when the academy was temporarily closed, the composers who studied at Rome included such stalwarts as Leo Sowerby, Randall Thompson, Roger Sessions, Samuel Barber, Howard Hanson, Vittorio Giannini, and others, who, as a group, served to counterbalance the influence of American composers attracted to Paris to study with the charismatic Nadia Boulanger.

The academy reopened in 1946, with Laurance Roberts as director, assisted by his wife Isabel; the secretary was Princess Margherita Rospigliosi. Roberts made the American Academy the major artistic and cultural center in Rome, frequented largely by Roman high society and distinguished foreigners.

From 1947 on, I served on the Rome music jury until I was elected trustee in 1950. I acted as chairman of the music jury every three years until 1971, when I retired.

There were some disagreements among the trustees and members of the juries about the choice of applicants, many of whom were far more radical than the pre–World War II fellows. A large number of competent twelve-tone, serial, electronic, and aleatoric composers were applying. As a rule, I looked for the best candidate in each style, and then compared those candidates to determine which one of them was the most inventive and musical. This method worked for a while, but there were strong differences of opinion among the members of the jury.

Remembering my own youthful activities in Europe, I recommended that the Rome fellows get into the flow of Roman musical life. Nicolas Nabokov had arranged with the Italian radio station RAI to have an annual orchestral concert with music by the fellows. The academy paid the conductor and soloists and RAI furnished the hall and orchestra and made tapes for broadcast. This gave young composers a unique opportunity to have their works played and recorded. In spite of some difficulties, the tradition persists today.

IN 1958, I WAS invited to be composer-in-residence. I was lodged in a small, handsome apartment with an excellent cook and housekeeper named Assunta. As composer-in-residence, I had an opportunity to serve as a kind of musical ambassador from America to Italy. As a protégé of Busoni and a pioneer in electronic music, which made me a member of the avant-garde, I felt I had solid credentials.

Princess Rospigliosi arranged for me to meet with Mario Labroca, the director of RAI. Labroca's *String Trio* had been played at the Venice Festival in the twenties, and he had been director at La Scala and was a distinguished critic and musicologist. He was pleased when I mentioned his activities to him, and he offered the American Academy the use of the RAI String Quartet and Severino Gazzelloni, the famous flutist, as chamber music soloists; Ferruccio Scaglia, his best conductor; and the RAI Orchestra for the orchestra concert. I suggested we include on the program a young Italian composer named Castaldi, and Labroca added DuBois from the French Academy in Rome to make the program international. Labroca then scheduled the Stanley Hollingsworth *Stabat Mater* for Turin and promised to perform a work by Salvatore Martirano on the Rome radio. He asked me to compose a work for Gazzelloni.

When I rehearsed my composition, called *Song, Poem and Dance for Flute and String Quartets,* the playing of the quartet was heavy and dull and certain jazzy passages sounded square and corny. I exhorted the players in English, German, and Italian, without getting any reaction. Finally I lost my temper and danced around the room, shouting, "*E Rossini in Chicago, è Rossini in Chicago!*" They were astonished and joined in the shouting, and we danced around the room and sang. Then they played beautifully. This episode taught me a lot about rehearsing; only the results count.

The chamber music program at the Villa Aurelia included

compositions by Harada, William O. Smith, Hollingsworth, and myself. The fashionable audience loved it. Hollingsworth and Harado had works on the orchestra concert, a candlelight affair in the villa's gardens. The wind blew the sheet music around so the ensemble was not exactly precise, but it was a romantic evening. The American Academy's relationship with RAI seemed firm, and I promised Maestro Labroca to arrange exchange performances in the United States.

I gave a dinner for some of the leading young men on the Roman musical scene. Domenico Guaccero and Paul Ketoff were trying to establish electronic music in Rome. Ketoff was perfecting his Synket—a synthesizer with keyboard. I recommended his installing one at the academy. Bill Smith, John Eaton, and later Martirano became much interested in electronic music and helped me with two programs I gave at the embassy theater that were well attended by an international audience.

After one of the programs, Signora Panni invited me to a party at her lovely villa. I withdrew to the bar because of the noise. Another loner was having a scotch.

When I introduced myself, he bowed stiffly and said, "Shostakovich."

We discovered that Copland and Wallingford Riegger were our mutual friends. He said he would soon be visiting the United States. I invited him to take over my Composers Seminar at Columbia for a session.

"If I can get permission," he said sadly.

The Soviet ambassador to Italy was at the party and I suggested that we immediately try to get his endorsement. The ambassador looked like a tough American ward politician. I was introduced and wasted no words.

"Your Excellency, I'm inviting Maestro Shostakovich to visit my seminar at Columbia University in New York. Will you please get him permission?"

His Excellency looked quizzical and was silent for a time. Then he said, "You are here, Maestro Shostakovich is here, and I am here at Signora Panni's party. There is no reason why something similar cannot happen in New York."

I bowed. Shostakovich flashed a quick smile. Signora Panni sighed.

As he shook my hand, he gave me a longer smile. "It can happen." (In 1959, Shostakovich and a delegation of Soviet composers arrived at Columbia. They visited my seminar, my opera class, and the Electronic Music Center. BMI gave them a party. There were many toasts and the vodka was strong. Just as he was about to introduce our distinguished guests, the State Department toastmaster passed out cold, and Ussachevsky and Nicolas Slonimsky had to take over. Soon everyone was shouting, and it must have been a great party, because for many years Soviet visitors kept coming to Columbia.)

Luciano Berio invited me to attend the ISCM Festival in Naples, which was directed by Pierre Boulez. Berio, Boulez, and Bruno Maderna took me along to all their favorite eating places— because, I imagined, I had known James Joyce and Busoni. I don't recall them asking me for my opinion of either political or musical matters.

The eight programs at Naples showed me clearly just what the European avant-garde was doing. In addition to the modern classics—Webern, Schoenberg and Stravinsky—I heard uneven piano music by Stockhausen and Boulez's *Piano Sonata,* which seemed conservative. But I liked Berio and Maderna and found the electronic music from Milan and Cologne interesting. This was all serious business and after the last concert some members of the audience got into an argument with some performers about the value of Webern as a composer. The shouting became so loud that the disputants were ushered out of the hall into the alley next to the conservatory. There was near-physical violence and the finale consisted of Gazzelloni and a friend chasing the anti-Webernites down the alley. All for contemporary music.

It was evident, though, that the European radio stations were really doing a job to make contemporary music known. Only about a hundred people came to the concerts, but RAI, like other European stations, had an ongoing commissioning program for composers. The tapes were given repeated performances over various stations, and commissions were sometimes quite substantial.

The cultural officer at the American embassy thought my programs at their theater were the most novel and fascinating they had had for years and Laurance Roberts was pleased that I had gotten RAI to cooperate. I took compositions by Domenico Guachero and the remarkable Count Giacinto Scelsi to New York and got them performed by Nicolas Roussakis at Barnard College and at Max Pollikoff's series.

AFTER LEAVING the American Academy in 1958, I kept in touch and arranged to start a record collection there. John Eaton and Bill Smith wrote me that they were earning a living with their pop music, but that RAI was being reorganized and that there wouldn't be any more concerts. When Roberts resigned, Richard Kimball became the director in 1959. He urged me to come to Rome and reestablish relations with RAI.

In 1960, I went over for a few weeks. I learned that no one knew anything about Giulio Razzi, who had replaced Labroca at RAI. Perhaps RAI was offended that the academy was not aware of Razzi's background. He was a nephew of Puccini, a former conductor at La Scala where he was Toscanini's assistant, and a composer of opera. Margherita Rospigliosi arranged for Kimball, Robert Moevs (the composer-in-residence), and myself to have an interview with Razzi. When I asked Maestro Razzi about his operas and his regime at La Scala, he was pleased; he served us tea with arak and then told us that we could have an orchestra of one hundred players, and that Scaglia would conduct our academy concert. Razzi became a good friend and visited the academy several times. At the suggestion of Hubert Doris, my former composition student and later chairman of the music department at Barnard, I paid a call on Alba Buitoni, who ran a splendid concert series in Perugia. She had studied with Edwin Fischer and was a patron of music. I suggested exchange concerts, and after she came to the Villa Aurelia for a dinner conference the series got under way.

The Ditson Fund provided money for the American Academy to buy a tape recorder and to build a small tape studio, for which Ketoff later built a Synket. George Wilson arranged an electronic music concert in Rome, and I recommended *Fontana Mix* by John Cage and works by Bill Smith. I also tried to arrange an ISCM Rome-America Exchange Concert in New York. In a year Richard Kimball had persuaded the American Italy Society to contribute toward the Music in the Making series and I got the

Record and Transcription Fund to pitch in. I put Mr. Siegel of WNYC in touch with Razzi, and WNYC broadcast academy tapes in April 1961. Carl Haverlin and BMI contributed to the concert, as did Frank Wigglesworth and Jack Beeson.

I was succumbing to my affliction of trying to pull everyone together, so I communicated with the United States Information Service, the Italian Ministry of Education, the Ministry of Cultural Affairs, and the Ministry of Telecommunication and Finance. Maestro Razzi offered to let academy students work in the Milan electronic laboratory, and we arranged an electronic concert for the 1961 Spoleto Festival, which was quite successful.

In October 1961 the Cooper Union Exchange Concert finally took place, with myself as director. Sophie and Harvey Sollberger opened the concert with a flute duet by Petrassi. Joseph Eger played a horn sonata by Paul Nelson, and Max Pollikoff played a sonatina by Guaccero. Eaton's *John Donne Cycle* and works by Aldo Clementi and George Wilson completed the program. It was remarkable that the American Academy in Rome, the American Italy Society, the American Music Center, Cooper Union, and the Recording Industries Music Performance Trust Fund cooperated.

The electronic studio in Rome was being developed under Ketoff's direction. The Perugia exchange concerts continued, and Kimball talked about the possibility of exchange concerts with the Florence Conservatory. There was an electronic festival in Rome, with television coverage, and Smith reported that my *Gargoyles for Violin Solo and Synthesized Sound* was very well received. By 1962, the music program at the American Academy in Rome was booming.

※※

IN JANUARY 1963, I was invited by Anis Fuleihan to attend as an observer a conference on Mediterranean music in the cultural center of Hammamet in Tunisia. I was not sure why I was invited, but my students, who were by that time getting used to me, thought it was exotic, and my stock went up immediately.

The trip from Rome to Tunisia was beautiful. A crescent moon seemed to cut into the sky. At the Tunis airport I hassled with customs agents in bad French; then, as some villainous-looking taxi drivers tried to grab my luggage, I was rescued by the cultural attaché from the American embassy and loaded on a bus for Hammamet. The bus was full of delegates from all over Europe and the Middle East. I did not know anybody and was silent. I looked at the landscape, with the moon shining down upon it, and the strange architecture. It was somewhat disquieting because we were stopped every few miles by roadblocks manned by soldiers who, with guns and flashlights, examined the bus. I was carrying my flute case, which looked as if it contained a sawed-off gun, and I felt a little shaky. A sergeant who spoke English told me that there had been an assassination attempt on President Habib Bourguiba the day before. It seemed as though I were in a Foreign Legion movie.

The next morning in my room in Hammamet I was awakened by strange calls. The Arab morning prayer! I looked out and saw the Mediterranean, beautiful and blue, but an early meeting of delegates spoiled the view. The French and Arab press and the Tunisian radio were conducting interviews.

Most delegates were rather anti-American. I was supposed to give a demonstration, but the other delegates took up so much time that until the Greek delegate, Mr. Papaioannou, insisted on acting as my interpreter I was afraid I wouldn't be heard. My program was received with astonishment, and I later had to repeat it for the Voice of America and the French radio station in Tunis. There was some argument about the origins of electronic music. I made a strong case for Busoni as a precursor.

I overcame my doubts about the usefulness of the Tunisian conference when Dr. Hourani, our host, arranged a concert in the hall of the fabulous dreamlike Arabian Nights "Cultural Center" in Hammamet. A Spanish soprano and I were the stars. She sang beautifully, and when she had finished I lost my head and gave her a resounding kiss. This seemed to be against Middle Eastern traditions. The audience gasped and her accompanist gave me a murderous look. I learned later that he was having an affair with her. But when I took out my wooden flute and, accompanied by Papaioannou, played Mozart's *Andante* and a Handel sonata, I redeemed myself. Huge, handsome black African retainers brought in big bowls of figs, oranges, and dates from the garden, and everybody, including the soprano's accompanist, was happy.

Next day, President Bourguiba invited the delegates to his palace for tea. On our way Anis Fuleihan ran through a red light, and the police told us that they were going to lock us up. Jail is no joke for foreigners in Tunis. Once you are in, it is very hard to get out. Fuleihan argued with the officer in Arabic, but it didn't do any good. Finally he told the officer that we were on our way to have tea with the president. This statement had the effect of making us look more suspicious, but the officer finally agreed to escort us to the palace. If we were not admitted, we would be jailed.

The sentry admitted us to the palace grounds, which again reminded me of Hollywood's Foreign Legion pictures and Hollywood sets. President Bourguiba was cordiality personified. We were served exotic fruit juices from enormous tankards and choice fruit from big bowls. After handshakes and photographs we went on our way.

Mr. Papaioannou invited me to give a lecture at the Athens Technological Institute, which was connected with the Doxiades Institute for Environmental Planning that allegedly planned the capital of Pakistan. I was impressed and immediately accepted the invitation.

I took my wife. Catherine flew with me from New York to Athens. We were startled to find a world so removed from the Europe we were accustomed to. We took a trip to see the Delphic Oracle. From a balcony at the hotel that faced a beautiful valley with natural acoustics, I played the flute solo from Gluck's *Orfeo und Euridice*. The sound seemed to echo for miles, and a number of Greek workmen stopped their jobs to look for Orpheus. We visited an amphitheater with such perfect acoustics that one could hear, in the last row, a pin dropped on the stage. In Athens we managed to get an apartment with a lovely view of the Acropolis.

The lecture-concert was in the garden of the institute. A full moon lit up the Acropolis. I presented a program of works we had produced in America, and everyone was attentive and seemed to enjoy it. Two cats who were roaming the garden not only enjoyed the concert, but joined in, at first meowing softly, then howling loudly in a duet that persisted through the postconcert question period.

A man in the audience asked me how I made electronic music. I explained it to him, but five minutes later he asked me again. I explained.

Three minutes later he was on his feet again, so I said, "I will now tell you how to make an imaginary electronic composition using the cats as a sound source. I am taking the big cat's meow and transposing it down four octaves; imagine the sound of an enormous cat. Now I will take the meow of the little cat. Using primitive speed-up, I transpose the meow up several octaves. Imagine a bunch of little-cat sounds, over the bass of the big-cat sounds. If I add normal cat sounds to these, either individually—in duet, or in a nicely timed combination with high and low sounds—we have a catatonic composition. However, there is no tonality, only a tonic—a *cat*atonic."

My questioner bowed. "Now I understand perfectly one aspect of electronic music."

This event was described in the Athens press.

IN FEBRUARY 1965, I was again invited by the academy in Rome to be composer-in-residence. I worked during this time with John Eaton and helped to bring about cooperation between the United States Information Service, the Academia Philharmonia, the ISCM, RAI, and the American Academy. We arranged a series of six concerts; all of the above groups shared expenses. This was unheard-of in Italy. Eaton and I were even invited by the avant-garde group Nuova Consonanza to perform in some of their programs. Catherine helped with the planning, and gave a glamorous reception for the musicians.

At the end of the 1965 season, John Eaton played his first composition for the Synket at Villa Aurelia. I was in the ensemble. Jack Beeson took over as composer-in-residence in the fall.

During Beeson's term I had a letter from him in which he said that the RAI administration had been shaken up and the exchange concerts halted. Various strikes had made it difficult to put on concerts. Musical factions were warring and it seemed that there was a conservative reaction against contemporary music in all Europe. Since that time Richard Trythall has settled in at the academy as a working musician and once again has established a liaison between the academy and Roman musical life, with the help of Frank Wigglesworth who was composer-in-residence at the time Trythall came to the academy.

Chapter 26

Coda
1965 to Present

I WAS SCHEDULED FOR RETIREMENT from Barnard College in 1965, and was unsettled by the remarks of well-wishers: "It won't be long now. . . . Are you moving to Florida?" . . . "Do you still compose?" Once, an overly solicitous friend, seeing me waiting to cross a street, asked me how I felt and then hoisted me over the curb.

Much of the world I knew in America and Europe was being transformed. During the mid-sixties, before the student unrest, I could feel a slow ferment growing among the students. One of my students, Faye Silverman, representative of the Barnard Students for a Democratic Society and a talented composer, told me that morale was low. The students were out of touch with the administration. One of their petitions had been tabled for eight months. The junior faculty members were restless, too. It was more difficult for me to undertake academic and aesthetic activities, but I hung on. A pleasant side of the retirement minuet was that some of us academicians were singled out for good-conduct medals and honors. Some of these honors were personal and unusual enough for me to mention here.

In 1965, the Columbia Faculty of Philosophy appointed me professor for a year. I was then discreetly examined for signs of senility, and my contract was renewed until 1968. I was appointed chairman of the music department in Columbia's School of the Arts in 1966 and was reappointed until 1970. Then I became Professor Emeritus. (Like statutory rape, this "honor" depends entirely on age.) I was made an honorary member of the Columbia chapter of Phi Beta Kappa. The joint chapters of Phi

Beta Kappa asked me to be a Visiting Scholar in 1966, and for the next three years I lectured and performed at thirty-three colleges and universities as far west as Wyoming and as far south as Florida. At the end of these tours I understood student unrest.

The Juilliard School appointed me to teach composition in 1971–1973. Bennington College appointed me as a Hadley Fellow for a semester in 1975. I got to know the freshman class, though it took me half a semester to get them to talk. Faculty and students played a program of my works, and I am still on the staff of the Bennington Summer Composition Workshop. I now visit universities only as a composer-in-residence or visiting composer. I get along well with the present generation of students; they seem to like to discuss many of their problems with me. After participating in seminars at the University of Mexico I was commissioned to write *Two Mexican Serenades* for the university ensemble. In 1978–1979, I visited Peabody Conservatory, the University of South Carolina, and the University of Wisconsin (Parkside), where I gave a concert of my own works, ten miles from where my great-grandfather built his log cabin in 1839.

≫≪

ALTHOUGH PREDICTABLE, student unrest at Columbia was a great shock for me. The history of those events is beyond the scope of these memoirs, but I must report some of them that made a deep impression on me.

On April 4, 1968, I was teaching my chamber music class when the blare of a bullhorn interrupted us. We heard that Martin Luther King had been assassinated. The class, the best one I ever taught, was paralyzed for at least ten minutes. I tried to get back to the Schubert quartet we were listening to, but no one wanted to listen. One student said that paying attention to a Schubert quartet was self-indulgent and pointless in a brutal society that condoned the war in Vietnam and whose leaders were being assassinated. I tried to reach the students but their will to concentrate had been broken. That class was the end of an era for me.

When I returned to Columbia from a Phi Beta Kappa visit on April 23, 1968, I learned that students were occupying Hamilton

Hall and the president's office, and that there were police on campus. I was fatigued from my tour and Catherine thought I should stay home, but I had a strong conviction that I should be on campus. I sloshed through mud and rain to Hamilton Hall. Some of my black students were standing guard behind barricades; Dean Coleman was being held hostage. I asked to go in to hear grievances from the students. I was told that once admitted I would have to stay there. This made no sense to me, so I went to Seth Low Library, which is the administration building. A line of police security guards and deans stood in the corridors. The scene made me feel angry, and I told the police lieutenant in charge that I wanted to speak to the students. After conferring with the deans, he waved me up the stairs.

A group of students were sprawled in front of Dr. Kirk's office, surrounded by canned foods, crates of oranges, gallons of milk, sleeping bags, and blankets. The group gathered around me, and I said that at some point communications on campus would have to be reestablished, that I had been talking things over with students for almost half a century and did not plan to stop now. I made a deal. If they would explain their point of view to me, I would do impersonations for them in the Rotunda if they could wheel out the piano. I was getting hoarse, so someone gave me an orange, and they then told me their grievances. Mark Rudd appeared from the inner office to say that they should not speak to faculty members; they might be influenced.

The students ignored him. They said they had lost faith in the administration and trusted only very few of the senior faculty members, among them professors Lionel Trilling, Carl Hovde, Jack Beeson, Eric Bentley, and Walter Metzger. Real communications on campus were almost nonexistent. I fell quite naturally into the role of mediator, and offered to help. The students pushed the piano into the Rotunda and sat around it, and I did a Chinese opera for them, a French tenor song recital, the Ride of the Valkyries, and a story about a beautiful garden at Columbia with flowers—"whether they live or die is up to you and the administration." The Rotunda was surrounded by police, university security guards, and university officers. The students applauded vigorously. After I finally lost my voice, there was nothing left to do but to go home.

At 2:30 A.M. I phoned Provost David Truman, an old friend, and suggested that he should personally visit Dr. Kirk's office to discuss the issues with the students. He was most grateful but sounded somewhat doubtful, so I called again at three-thirty. He thanked me profusely, but nothing happened.

My musical episode with the students was reported on the front page of the *New York Times* and in the international press. I was a campus hero for a couple of weeks. At my Phi Beta Kappa lectures I was known as a hero from the battlefield at Columbia. The Columbia students asked me to wander around campus to calm everybody. Sometimes I talked at the sundial, and a few times I used a bullhorn and advised the students to finish their courses and help the professors keep the academic records straight, because they would be needed in the future. My advice was not very exciting or fashionable. Other buildings were occupied. I went to Fayerweather Hall. It was barricaded with planks and chains, and a guard tried to keep me out, but I insisted and the student committee delegated two black women to inform me about Harlem and the Morningside Heights community problems. After an hour I left. The next day the students yelled down from the president's office that I couldn't talk to them anymore.

Soon a number of faculty members volunteered to stand between the radical SDS and the conservative students (athletes, mainly, and my student Neil Levin), the security guards, and police, to prevent violence. Jack Beeson, Joel Newman, Harvey Sollberger, Charles Wuorinen, Ernest Sanders, and I were among those who mediated at Low Library.

When the mood grew more intense, I just wandered through the crowd, which had by then the peculiar restlessness and nervous movement of a mob, and tried to be a calming influence.

Within a few days, a number of faculty and student committees were formed. Most committee members did not do thorough homework, so the meetings were often too long, too slow, and quite inconclusive. Soon all the committees were paralyzed. The activists seemed to lose sight of the issues and the trustees were simply too slow and heavyhanded to be of any help. On April 30, I came to the campus at 12:30 A.M. There was an ominous quiet, but the police details seemed to be moving off campus. In Philosophy Hall, Charles Wuorinen and I discussed the clear and present dangers with a black man—I believe, a Mr. Luther—who phoned the mayor's office to request mediation. I went home reassured; but at 2:30 WKCR was broadcasting the details of a police bust.

Before it was all over, there were: a student strike, a change in the administration, and police occupation of the campus. A police lieutenant told me, "We know these are students and not criminals," but another policeman told me that if these were his children he would kill them. Hundreds of students were arrested and there were many injuries.

I held my classes in my apartment and all my students eventually passed their examinations. The student unrest wounded Columbia and other universities and they are only now recovering. I believed then, as I do now, that many of the students' complaints were justified. However, the methods used to resolve them, by both students and administration, seemed clumsy and archaic and reminded me of the Zurich general strike of 1918.

≫≪

ON FEBRUARY 16, 1970, there was a call from Bucksport, Maine, informing me that my brother Robert had died of a heart attack. Twenty years before, Bob and his wife, Virginia, had built a charming house on Jacob Bucks Pond—"to get away from it all." They were happy there until Virginia died of cancer, following a year of treatment. Bob then went to England and considered going to Australia, but would not come to New York. He hated cities.

I went with my nephews Bill and David to make funeral arrangements. The road to the house was covered with two feet of snow, so we walked in, crossing the frozen pond. Bob's body was already at the undertaker's. Virginia's ashes were still in a cardboard box in a closet.

I carried Virginia's ashes over the pond to the undertaker's car on the upper road. When I got in he said, "Take Virginia on your lap—it's easier." The will directed that no religious services were to be held. The cemetery was an old one in the country. Virginia's father was buried there. The ground was too hard to dig a grave, so Bob was cremated and both his and Virginia's ashes were kept in urns for a burial in July.

The burial took place on a cool, drizzly day. It was decided that I would give the graveside eulogy and play on the flute Bob's favorite music: the Mozart *Andante* and the solo from Gluck's *Orfeo und Euridice*. Catherine, Ethel, the widow of my brother Hans, and my niece Lejo were other family members who attended, along with a man from the local gas station and a friend, Miss Jones. My eulogy was a sketch of two rugged individuals who had lived in their own way and never complained. When the ashes were put in the ground and the grave was covered, the sound of the flute rose toward the climax in the *Orfeo* solo. The drizzle stopped, the sky cleared, and as the sun came out a large flock of birds sang with the flute melody. Bob and Virginia would have liked that.

※※

THESE EVENTS had a definite effect on my composing—an effect that I can't yet fully assess. Depleted of much energy, I concentrated on composing shorter chamber music. I also did an electronic flute-and-tape-music piece called *Moonflight*, which was sent to the crew of Apollo II at NASA. A nice letter from Neil Armstrong said that in their last two flights around the moon the astronauts heard eerie music, but they assumed it came from the lunar module transmitter when it separated from the command module, a rather disappointing assumption.

Because I had worked in electronic music I had a reputation among the younger generation as a radical, even avant-garde composer. But my conservative background puzzled them as much as the electronic music puzzled my more conventional colleagues. The new generation seemed particularly interested in the works I had written in the twenties. Ned Rorem sent me a fan letter when the Sinnhoffer Quartet recorded and performed my Second and Third String Quartets, written in that period. Wuorinen, Sollberger, and the Group for Contemporary Music consistently introduced my early chamber music. The brilliant organ virtuoso Fred Tulan discovered my *Chorale Fantasy for*

Organ and performed it many times in the United States, in Notre Dame in Paris, and in Westminster Abbey. José Serebrier performed my orchestra music. Gunther Schuller discovered my *Music for Orchestra* and conducted it with the American Composers Orchestra in Alice Tully Hall in May 1978.

ACA presented me with their Laurel Leaf Award for fostering and encouraging American music and the American Music Center presented me with their Letter of Commendation. The Thorne Music Foundation gave me an award and the Guggenheim Foundation awarded me a third fellowship in 1975 to revise *Evangeline*. In 1963, Walter Hinrichsen of C. F. Peters began to publish my works. Later, Highgate Press and Joshua Corporation brought out more works, mostly chamber music.

In 1965, Catherine and I were in Europe for my birthday. Fellows at the American Academy in Rome (some on Fulbright fellowships) wrote variations on a theme of mine for flute solo and Severino Gazzelloni played them brilliantly at the academy. A message came from Radio Zurich, saying that they wanted to broadcast the Rondo from my *Kentucky Concerto* and tape two interviews with me to be used as intermission talks for the Tonhalle Orchestra, in which I had played as a teenager.

From Zurich, Catherine and I went on to Munich, and while we were at the Bayerischer Hof a messenger arrived from the Rathaus with a gold-embossed letter tied with a blue ribbon. It read:

Dear Professor,

On the occasion of your 65th birthday, the Capital City of Munich is planning to have a reception and luncheon on Wednesday, April 28, 1965 at 1:00 P.M. . . . in the Rathaus. I would be pleased if you could accept this invitation to attend.

With the expression of my highest esteem,

Dr. Vogel, Mayor

I liked that because I remembered being an enemy alien in Munich in 1917. At the luncheon a group of musical dignitaries that included my student Alfred Goodman had come, and we had a fine time. The mayor invited us to the old town hall for the birthday party of Carl Orff, who had been a year ahead of me at the Munich academy. The moon was shining brightly, and Orff and I went onto the roof, where he described in detail how he had composed his opera *Der Mond*.

At the luncheon at the Rathaus, Karl Höller, the director of the Hochschule für Musik—the same Munich Royal Academy that had expelled me in 1917—announced that he had arranged a performance of my *Flute Trio* at a student concert at the Hochschule, and invited me to address the faculty. I did, and, when I spoke of the good old days, they all laughed until their necks cracked and bellies shook. I shifted to impersonations and sang a song from "the good ole days," in Bavarian dialect: *"Und der Ochs hat gelacht, und die Kuh hat gelacht . . ."* ("And the ox laughed, and the cow laughed"). This was such an instantaneous and profound hit that I thought they would offer me a professorship. Instead, Dr. Goslich said that the Bavarian Radio wanted to do two programs of my works, each of these called "Portrait of a Composer." They were broadcast a number of times. It seemed to me that I was getting quite a bit of recognition for having won the musical endurance contest; but, after all, I had been at it professionally since 1915! Still, I was surprised to receive an envelope from the Wisconsin Assembly with a resolution commending "Otto Luening, a native of Milwaukee and former Madison resident, for his contributions to 'the best in our arts which continue apace through the years of our eventful era.' " It was a long text and it began making me feel that I had better get back to Wisconsin.

Catherine and I returned to New York from Munich. ACA, the Music Center, the Ditson Fund, and a few other people arranged a birthday party at Columbia and rounded up many of my former students. They looked hale and hearty, and I told them that apparently my survival techniques had worked for them and to keep right on. Things were reasonably quiet for a while but 1970 brought another round of celebrations, with birthday broadcasts by WNYC, WBAI, the Albany radio station, and the Munich radio. Then ACA and Composers Recordings Incorporated got to work with C. F. Peters and BMI and proceeded to round up all my students, friends, and colleagues for a real bash. I had a letter from Philipp Jarnach: "Have a good time. When they give you a party on your 70th, it generally means they have paid their dues and you won't see another celebration, so think of me as you drink a glass of champagne."

In 1975, I was really astounded when I heard that a lot of other things were being planned. At a concert of Hear America First, Ursula Oppens premiered my *Sonata for Piano in Memoriam Ferruccio Busoni*. Raymond Erickson of the *Times* wrote that it was a first-rate work. At the concert Oliver Daniel presented me with a silver tray, a gift from my students. There was also a citation from Hunter College High School, which said, among other nice things, that I had shown leadership in developing music materials for elementary schools.

C. F. Peters, Evelyn Hinrichsen, BMI, ACA, and Charles Wuorinen gave me another party, with champagne and delicious food, at Charlie's house on West End Avenue in recognition of my efforts on behalf of American composers.

The recognition of my music by my native state actually began in 1964 when students at the University of Wisconsin asked me to give two lectures on electronic music. BMI commissioned my *Synthesis for Orchestra and Electronic Sound*, which was played by the Milwaukee Symphony, with Harry John Brown conducting, in the Pabst Theater in October 1965. I had heard my father conduct there when I was five years old. The Madison Symphony Orchestra then played the *Concerted Piece for Tape Recorder and Orchestra* I had done with Ussachevsky, and shortly after I was invited to the state capital to address the legislature. I thanked the legislators for their resolution on my behalf and remarked that it seemed to imply: *Come home, all is forgiven and forgotten*. I was also asked to address the Wisconsin Senate. As I was ushered in to the Senate chambers by the lieutenant governor, he said, as we approached some steps, "Careful, Senator."

In 1975 the Milwaukee Symphony commissioned me to compose a work for them. I got a grant from the National Endowment for the Arts to write my *Wisconsin Symphony* for the Bicentennial Celebration.

The *Wisconsin Symphony* was performed three times in Milwaukee in January 1976 and once at Ripon College. Kenneth

Schermerhorn conducted the Milwaukee Symphony, the orchestra my father had attempted to found and dreamed of conducting in the nineteenth century. When Catherine and I heard my work given such a fine reading, I was moved to tears. The large, enthusiastic audience gave me a rousing welcome. A few old friends, including the family doctor, John Wilkinson, and his wife, came to a beautiful party that the directors of the symphony had arranged. A week later, a local radio station broadcast my music for twenty-four hours. The Wisconsin State Legislature handed me a second resolution expressing thanks for my symphony. Cedarburg, where my grandfather had settled in 1840, asked me to be a Bicentennial speaker, and Catherine and I went there for a week. I saw where my great-grandfather Neukirch had settled in 1839.

The Wisconsin Youth Orchestra, based in Madison, programmed my *Wisconsin Suite* at the Kennedy Center in Washington for my birthday on June 15, 1976. Merle Montgomery had arranged the Bicentennial series, of which this was a part, with the National Music Council, the National Federation of Music Clubs, and Exxon as sponsors. The performance was brilliant and the conductor, James Latimer, called me to the podium. He announced that on nomination of the Youth Orchestra the Madison Board of Education had awarded me an honorary high school diploma. Exxon gave a marvelous party with two quarters of roast beef and an enormous birthday cake that was consumed by the orchestra and their families in *tempo prestissimo.* The score and stage designs of my opera, *Evangeline,* were on exhibit in an upper hall.

In 1977 the Youth Orchestra invited me to conduct rehearsals of Beethoven symphonies in Madison. Some of the members were from my alma mater, the Randall School. The first orchestra, consisting of one hundred high-school students from all over the state, played like professionals. The second orchestra, also of one hundred players, was almost as good, and the Junior String Ensemble players, ages nine to twelve, couldn't have been more attentive. At the end of the rehearsal, Mr. Latimer waved me to the podium and presented me with a plaque: A WISCONSIN YOUTH ORCHESTRA GUEST CONDUCTOR. A representative from the mayor's office read a proclamation recognizing my work and declared May 28 and 29 "Otto Luening Weekend in the City of Madison." A representative of the governor also read a long and effusive resolution that made it "Otto Luening Weekend for the State of Wisconsin." Professor Garth presented me with a medallion of the Wisconsin Academy of Sciences, Arts and Letters. On the next day Catherine and I went to the convocation of the University of Wisconsin at Randall Field. There I was awarded an honorary doctorate in fine arts, which I considered a tribute to my family, particularly to my father, who was appointed director of the university's School of Music in 1909.

In 1979 the University of Wisconsin at Parkside commissioned me to compose and conduct *Potawatomi Legends for Chamber Orchestra* for its tenth anniversary. The premiere is scheduled to be near the port where my great-grandfather Neukirch debarked in 1839; the Potawatomi tribe still camped near his log cabin at that time.

Recently I was reminded of my debut in America, in 1920, as a piccolo player in an American Federation of Musicians band in Chicago's Grant Park: In 1979, Stephen Ovitsky, music director of the park, informed me that when Pope John Paul II held mass in the park for one million people my *Entrance and Exit Music* (for trumpets, trombones, and cymbals) was played as fifteen cardinals entered the park and took their places.

WITH NO MORE parties in sight, I have begun to play flute again—in Carnegie Hall, at the Maison Française at New York University, and at the University of South Carolina. (I conducted the Sage Symphony and the Vermont Symphony in that state).

Government and business corporations have now discovered the arts. Most musicians seem too famous, too busy, too tired, or too discouraged to attend to their business as much as they did formerly. A new partnership of the arts with business and politics has developed and may be necessary and desirable for a while. But artists will have to study politics and business; politicians must study artists and corporations; and business people will have to learn about the world of art and politics.

As Busoni told us in 1918: "One must practice!"

A Selected List of Compositions*

Key to the music publishers: ACA (American Composers Alliance, 170 West 74th Street, New York, N.Y. 10023); AMP (Associated Music Publishers, 866 Third Avenue, New York, N.Y. 10022); ASUC (American Society of University Composers, c/o Joseph Boonin, Inc., P.O. Box 2124, South Hackensack, N.J. 07606); BH (Boosey and Hawkes, 30 West 57th Street, New York, N.Y. 10019); BM (Belwin Mills, 25 Deshon Drive, Melville, N.Y. 11747); BP (Bradley Publications, 43 West 61st Street, New York, N.Y. 10023); CFPC (C. F. Peters Corporation, 373 Park Avenue South, New York, N.Y. 10016); EBMMC (Edward B. Marks Music Corporation, 1790 Broadway, New York, N.Y. 10019); HP (Highgate Press, Galaxy Music Corporation, 2121 Broadway, New York, N.Y. 10023); JC (Joshua Corporation, c/o General Music Publishing Co., Inc., 145 Palisade Street, Dobbs Ferry, N.Y. 10522); JP (Juilliard Publications, Lincoln Center Plaza, New York, N.Y. 10023); MMC (Merion Music Corporation, c/o Theodore Presser, Inc., Bryn Mawr, Pa. 19010); NVMP (New Valley Music Press, Smith College, Northampton, Mass. 01060); PD (Pietro Deiro, 133 Seventh Avenue South, New York, N.Y. 10014); RRTC (rights reverted to composer Otto Luening); TPI (Theodore Presser, Inc., Bryn Mawr, Pa. 19010); WLPI (World Library Publications, Inc., 2145 Central Parkway, Cincinnati, Ohio 45214).

1917
First Sonata for Violin and Piano (ASUC)

---

* Most of the compositions included in the following Selected List have been mentioned and/or described in the text and will be cited in the Index.

1918
Sextet (flute, clarinet, horn, violin, viola, violoncello; HP)
Variations on *Christus der ist mein Leben* for Four Horns (HP)

1919
First String Quartet (1919–1920; HP)
Sonatina for Flute and Piano (NVMP)

1921
Music for Piano—A Contrapuntal Study (HP)
Trio for Violin, Cello and Piano (HP)

1922
Three Songs for Soprano and Piano or Small Orchestra (HP)
Chorale Fantasy for Organ (WLPI)
Second Sonata for Violin and Piano (HP)

1923
The Soundless Song (soprano, flute, clarinet, 2 violins, viola, cello, dancers, and light; songs also for soprano and piano; text and music; HP)
Second String Quartet (CFPC)
Concertino for Flute and Chamber Orchestra (CFPC)
Music for Orchestra (HP)

1924
Trio for Flute, Violin and Soprano (HP)
First Sonata for Cello Solo (HP)
First Symphonic Fantasia (ACA)

1927
Gliding O'er All (song* for soprano and piano; RRTC)
If That High World (chorus; CFPC)
Sun of the Sleepless (women's chorus; RRTC)
Serenade for Three Horns and String Orchestra (HP)

1928
Young Love (song; HP)
Auguries of Innocence (song; HP)
Infant Joy (song; HP)
To Morning (song; HP)

* All of my songs were written for soprano and piano.

Locations and Times (song; HP)
Visored (song; HP)
Wake the Serpent Not (song; HP)
A Roman's Chamber (song; HP)
The Birth of Pleasure (song; HP)
Third String Quartet (CFPC)
Six Short and Easy Piano Pieces (BP)

1929
For Like a Chariot's Wheel (song; HP)
I Faint, I Perish (song; HP)
A Farm Picture (song; AMP)
Goodnight (song; HP)
Here the Frailest Leaves of Me (song; AMP)
Dance Sonata for Piano (HP)
Coal Scuttle Blues (two pianos; AMP)
Fantasia for Organ (CFPC)
Fantasia Brevis for Flute and Piano (TPI, Presser-NME)

1930
Short Fantasy for Violin and Horn (HP)
Evangeline (opera libretto, piano score, stage directions;
    1930–1932, 1947; CFPC)

1932
The Dawn (song; HP)
When in the Languor of Evening (soprano solo, chorus, in-
    struments; ACA)
Five Intermezzi for Piano (1932–1936; HP)

1933
Mañana (violin and piano; HP)

1935
Two Symphonic Interludes (CFPC)
Six Piano Preludes (1935–1951; HP)

1936
At the Last (song; HP)
Swing, Swing and Swoon (song; HP)
Forever Lost (song; HP)
Only Themselves (song; TPI, Presser–New Music Edition)

Hast Never Come to Thee (song; HP)
Suite for Soprano and Flute (1936–1937; HP)
Andante for Piano (HP)
Eight Preludes for Piano (TPI, Presser–New Music Edition)
Fantasia Brevis for Violin, Viola and Cello (HP)
Fantasia Brevis for Clarinet and Piano (TPI, Presser–New Music Edition)

1937
At Christmastime (song; HP)
Noon Silence (song; HP)
Venilia (song; HP)
Suite for String Orchestra (BH)
First Short Sonata for Flute and Piano (or Harpsichord) (HP)
Prelude to a Hymn Tune by William Billings (orchestra; CFPC)

1938
Two Piano Inventions (TPI, Presser-Mercury)
Eight Inventions for Piano (JC)
Short Fantasy for Violin and Piano (HP)
Fuguing Tune for Woodwind Quintet (flute, oboe, clarinet, bassoon, horn; AMP)

1939
Second Symphonic Fantasia (1939–1949; ACA)

1940
First Short Sonata for Piano (HP)
The Bass with the Delicate Air (flute, oboe, clarinet, bassoon; HP)
Variations for Harpsichord or Piano (BP)

1942
Dickinson Song Cycle (1942–1951; HP)
Fantasia for Harpsichord or Piano (BP)
Variations on Bach's Chorale Prelude *Liebster Jesu wir sind hier* for Cello and Piano (JC)
Aria for Cello and Piano (1942–1943; HP)

1943
Third Sonata for Violin and Piano (NVMP)

1944
Alleluia (chorus; TPI, Presser-Merion)

1946
Ten Pieces for Five Fingers for Piano (BP)
Suite for Cello and Piano (HP)
Pilgrim's Hymn for Chamber Orchestra (TPI)

1947
First Suite for Flute Solo (HP)
Prelude for Chamber Orchestra (HP)

1949
Love's Secret (song; EBMMC)
Divine Image (song; EBMMC)

1951
She Walks in Beauty (song; HP)
The Harp the Monarch Minstrel Swept (song; HP)
The Tiger's Ghost (chorus; HP)
Three Noctures for Oboe and Piano (JC)
Kentucky Concerto (orchestra; HP)
Kentucky Rondo (orchestra; HP)

1952
Legend for Oboe and Strings (HP)
Trio for Flute, Violin and Piano (HP)
Sonata for Bassoon and Piano (HP)
Fantasy in Space (flute and tape music; HP)
Low Speed (flute and tape music; HP)
Invention in Twelve Tones (flute and tape music; HP)

1953
Second Suite for Flute Solo (BM)
Suite for Bass and Piano (HP)
Sonata for Trombone and Piano (HP)

1954
Rhapsodic Variations for Tape Recorder and Orchestra (in collaboration with Vladimir Ussachevsky; CFPC)
A Poem in Cycles and Bells for Tape Recorder and Orchestra (in collaboration with Vladimir Ussachevsky; CFPC)

1955

Wisconsin Suite (Childhood Tunes Remembered) for Orchestra (JC)

Incantation (tape music; in collaboration with Vladimir Ussachevsky; HP)

1956

Theatre Piece No. 2 (RRTC)

1957

Serenade for Flute and Strings (HP)

Gay Picture (piano; MMC)

1958

Second Short Sonata for Piano (HP)

Sonata for Viola Solo (HP)

Sonata for Bass Solo (HP)

(Second) Sonata Composed in Two Dayturnes for Cello Solo (NVMP)

First Sonata for Violin Solo (CFPC)

Song, Poem and Dance for Flute and Strings (HP)

Lyric Scene for Flute and Strings (CFPC)

Third Short Sonata for Piano (JC)

1960

Three Fantasias for Solo Guitar (HP)

Gargoyles for Violin Solo and Synthesized Sound (CFPC)

1961

Third Suite for Flute Solo (JC)

Fantasia for String Quartet and Orchestra (CFPC)

1962

Trio for Flute, Cello and Piano (CFPC)

Sonority Canon for Two to Thirty-Seven Flutes (HP)

Three Duets for Two Flutes (NVMP)

Synthesis for Orchestra and Electronic Sound (CFPC)

1963

Elegy for Violin (CFPC)

Fourth Suite for Flute Solo (JC)

Duo for Violin and Viola (JC)

March for High and Low Instruments (any combination; JP)

Suite for High and Low Instruments (HP)

1964
Lines from a Song for Occupations (chorus; CFPC)
Entrance and Exit Music (trumpets, trombones, cymbal; CFPC)
Concerted Piece for Tape Recorder and Orchestra (in collaboration with Vladimir Ussachevsky; CFPC)

1965
Fanfare for a Festive Occasion (brass and percussion; CFPC)

1966
Third Short Sonata for Flute and Piano (NVMP)
Fantasia for Cello Solo (NVMP)
Broekman Fantasia for String Orchestra (HP)
Trio for Three Flutists (HP)
Third Sonata for Violin and Piano (NVMP)

1967
Fourth Short Sonata for Piano (HP)
Bells of Bellagio (piano four or six hands; CFPC)
Rondo for Accordion (PD)
Fourteen Easy Duets for Recorders (CFPC)

1968
Meditation for Violin Solo (CFPC)
Second Sonata for Violin Solo (CFPC)

1969
Fifth Suite for Flute Solo (JC)
Trio for Trumpet, Horn and Trombone (CFPC)
Moonflight (flute; tape music; HP)

1970
Third Sonata for Violin Solo (CFPC)
Psalm 146 (chorus; CFPC)
Introduction and Allegro for Trumpet and Piano (CFPC)

1971
Eight Tone Poems for Two Violas (JC)
Second Short Sonata for Flute and Piano (NVMP)
Chorale Fantasy and Fugue for Organ (WLPI)

1973

Sonority Forms (orchestra; ACA)

Electronic Doubles of Chorale Fantasy and Fugue (WLPI)

Six Proverbs (soprano and piano; HP)

1974

Elegy for the Lonesome Ones (two clarinets and strings; ACA)

Prelude for Flute, Clarinet and Bassoon (HP)

Fugue for Flute, Clarinet and Bassoon (HP)

Short Suite (Four Cartoons) for Flute, Clarinet and Bassoon (HP)

Mexican Serenades (winds, percussion, contra bass; HP)

1975

A Wisconsin Symphony (orchestra; ACA)

Third Symphonic Interlude (orchestra; JC)

1976

Suite for Two Flutes and Piano with Cello Ad Lib. (JC)

Canons for Two Violins and Flute (ACA)

1979

Canons for Two Flutes (ACA)

Short Sonatas for Piano nos. 5, 6, 7 (ACA)

Short Symphony (ACA)

Fantasias on Indian Motives for Flute Solo (ACA)

1980

Potawatomi Legends for Chamber Orchestra (ACA)

Discography*

Columbia Records
Gargoyles for Violin and Synthetic Sound (Max Pollikoff, violin; ML 5966, MS 6566)

Composers Recordings Inc.
A Poem in Cycles and Bells for Tape Recorder and Orchestra* (Otto Luening, Royal Danish Radio Orchestra; CRI 112)
Concerted Piece for Tape Recorder and Orchestra* (José Serebrier, Oslo Philharmonic Orchestra; CRI 227)
Fantasia for Organ (Ralph Kneeream; CRI 219)
Kentucky Rondo (F. Charles Adler, Vienna Symphony Orchestra; CRI 103)
Suite from *King Lear* for Tape Recorder* (CRI 112)
Symphonic Fantasia I (F. Charles Adler, Vienna Symphony Orchestra; CRI 103)
Synthesis for Orchestra and Electronic Sound (David Van Vactor, Hessian Radio Symphony; CRI 219)
In the Beginning (electronic sound; CRI 268)
Trio for Flute, Cello and Piano (Harvey Sollberger, Fred Sherry, Charles Wuorinen; CRI 303)
Sonata for Violin Solo no. 3 (Max Pollikoff; CRI 303)
Second String Quartet (Sinnhoffer Quartet; CRI 303)
Third String Quartet (Sinnhoffer Quartet; CRI 303)
Fugue and Chorale Fantasy with Electronic Doubles for Organ and Tape (Alec Wyton; CRI 334)

* Compositions done with fellow-composer Vladimir Ussachevsky.

Piano Sonata In Memoriam Ferruccio Busoni (Ursula Oppens; CRI 334)

Third, Fourth, Fifth Suites for Flute Solo (Harvey Sollberger; CRI 400)

Desto

Divine Image (Mildred Miller, mezzo; Edwin Biltcliffe, piano; DST 6411-12)

Fantasy In Space (electronic sound; DC 6466)

Incantation for Tape Recorder* (DC 6466)

Invention (Otto Luening, flute; tape recorder; DC 6466)

Love's Secret (Mildred Miller, mezzo; Edwin Biltcliffe, piano; DST 6411-12)

Low Speed (Otto Luening, flute; tape recorder; DC 6466)

Legend for Oboe and Strings (Erik Larsen, oboe; José Serebrier, Oslo Philharmonic Orchestra; DC 6466)

Lyric Scene for Flute and Strings (Per Oien, flute; José Serebrier, Oslo Philharmonic Orchestra; DC 6466)

Moonflight (Otto Luening, flute; tape recorder; DC 6466)

Prelude to a Hymn Tune (Dean Dixon, Vienna Symphony Orchestra; DST 6429)

Two Symphonic Interludes (Dean Dixon, Vienna Symphony Orchestra; DST 6429)

Golden Crest Recordings (220 Broadway, Huntington Station, NYC)

Short Suite for Woodwind Trio (Sue Ann Kahn, flute; Gunnar Schonbeck, clarinet; Maurice Pachman, bassoon; CRS 4140)

Prelude and Fugue for Flute, Clarinet, and Bassoon (Sue Ann Kahn, Gunnar Schonbeck, Maurice Pachman; CRS 4140)

Louisville Recordings

Rhapsodic Variations for Tape Recorder and Orchestra* (Robert Whitney, Louisville Orchestra; LOU 545-5)

Silver Burdett

12 Recorded Lessons for the First Six Grades (Making Music Your Own)

A Selected List of Writings

"Die Musikpflege in den Vereinigten Staaten" ("The Cultivation of Music in the United States"). *Melos: Zeitschrift für Musik*, Vol. 10 (October 1929).

"Music." *Proceedings of the American Philosophical Society*, Vol. 83, No. 4 (September 1940).

"Douglas Moore." *Modern Music*, Vol. 20, No. 4 (May–June 1943).

Foreword to Partch, Harry, *Genesis of a Music*. Madison: University of Wisconsin Press, 1949.

Music Materials and the Public Library: A Report to the Director of the Public Library Inquiry. New York: Social Science Research Council, 1949.

"New Sound Techniques in Music." *Art and Artist*. Berkeley and Los Angeles: University of California Press, 1956.

"Karlheinz Stockhausen." *Juilliard Review*, Vol. 6 (Winter 1958–59).

"Wallingford Riegger, 1885–1960." *New York Times*, April 9, 1961.

"Some Random Remarks About Electronic Music." *Journal of Music Theory*, Vol. 8 (Spring 1964).

"Experimentelle Musik in den Vereinigten Staaten." *Neue Züricher Zeitung*, April 30, 1967.

Contributions on Karlheinz Stockhausen and Arnold Schoenberg in Kraemer, Uwe, ed., *Komponisten über Komponisten*. Wilhelmshaven: Heinrichshofens Verlag, 1972.

"An Unfinished History of Electronic Music." *Music Educators Journal*, Vol. 55, No. 3 (November 1968). Reprinted in part in

Russcol, Herbert, *The Liberation of Sound: An Introduction to Electronic Music.* Englewood Cliffs, N.J.: Prentice-Hall, 1972.

"Elektronische Musik" in Blaukopf, Kurt, *50 Jahre im Hörfunk: Beiträge und Berichte (50 Years of Broadcast Music: Contributions and Reports).* Vienna and Munich: Jugend und Volk, 1973.

"Monos, Hombres y Máquinas" ("Monkeys, Men, and Machines"). *Talea* (National University of Mexico), No. 1 (September–December 1975).

"Origins," in Appleton, Jon H., ed., *The Development and Practice of Electronic Music.* Englewood Cliffs, N.J.: Prentice-Hall, 1975.

Electronic Tape Music, 1952: The First Compositions (with Vladimir Ussachevsky). New York: Highgate Press, 1977.

Index

Illustrations follow page 280.